World Economic and Financial Surveys

GW01006270

WORLD ECONOMIC OUTLOOK
April 2005

Globalization and External Imbalances

International Monetary Fund

©2005 International Monetary Fund

Production: IMF Multimedia Services Division
Cover and Design: Luisa Menjivar-Macdonald
Figures: Theodore F. Peters, Jr.
Typesetting: Choon Lee

World economic outlook (International Monetary Fund)
    World economic outlook: a survey by the staff of the International
Monetary Fund.—1980– —Washington, D.C.: The Fund, 1980–

    v.; 28 cm.—(1981–84: Occasional paper/International Monetary
Fund ISSN 0251-6365)
    Annual.
    Has occasional updates, 1984–
    ISSN 0258-7440 = World economic and financial surveys
    ISSN 0256-6877 = World economic outlook (Washington)
    1. Economic history—1971– —Periodicals.   I. International
Monetary Fund.   II. Series: Occasional paper (International
Monetary Fund)

HC10.W7979   84-640155

                                   338.5'443'09048—dc19
                                        AACR 2 MARC-S

Library of Congress   8507

    Published biannually.
ISBN 1-58906-429-1

                    Price: US$49.00
        (US$46.00 to full-time faculty members and
            students at universities and colleges)

                  Please send orders to:
       International Monetary Fund, Publication Services
       700 19th Street, N.W., Washington, D.C. 20431, U.S.A.
          Tel.: (202) 623-7430   Telefax: (202) 623-7201
                E-mail: publications@imf.org
                Internet: http://www.imf.org

recycled paper

CONTENTS

Tables

Figures

ASSUMPTIONS AND CONVENTIONS

A number of assumptions have been adopted for the projections presented in the *World Economic Outlook*. It has been assumed that real effective exchange rates will remain constant at their average levels during January 31–February 28, 2005, except for the currencies participating in the European exchange rate mechanism II (ERM II), which are assumed to remain constant in nominal terms relative to the euro; that established policies of national authorities will be maintained (for specific assumptions about fiscal and monetary policies in industrial countries, see Box A1); that the average price of oil will be $46.50 a barrel in 2005 and $43.75 a barrel in 2006, and remain unchanged in real terms over the medium term; that the six-month London interbank offered rate (LIBOR) on U.S. dollar deposits will average 3.3 percent in 2005 and 4.1 percent in 2006; that the three-month euro deposit rate will average 2.3 percent in 2005 and 2.9 percent in 2006; and that the six-month Japanese yen deposit rate will yield an average of 0.1 percent in 2005 and of 0.4 percent in 2006. These are, of course, working hypotheses rather than forecasts, and the uncertainties surrounding them add to the margin of error that would in any event be involved in the projections. The estimates and projections are based on statistical information available through end-March 2005.

The following conventions have been used throughout the *World Economic Outlook:*

...   to indicate that data are not available or not applicable;

—   to indicate that the figure is zero or negligible;

–   between years or months (for example, 2003–2004 or January–June) to indicate the years or months covered, including the beginning and ending years or months;

/   between years or months (for example, 2003/04) to indicate a fiscal or financial year.

"Billion" means a thousand million; "trillion" means a thousand billion.

"Basis points" refer to hundredths of 1 percentage point (for example, 25 basis points are equivalent to ¼ of 1 percent point).

In figures and tables, shaded areas indicate IMF staff projections.

Minor discrepancies between sums of constituent figures and totals shown are due to rounding.

As used in this report, the term "country" does not in all cases refer to a territorial entity that is a state as understood by international law and practice. As used here, the term also covers some territorial entities that are not states but for which statistical data are maintained on a separate and independent basis.

FURTHER INFORMATION AND DATA

This report on the *World Economic Outlook* is available in full on the IMF's Internet site, www.imf.org. Accompanying it on the website is a larger compilation of data from the WEO database than in the report itself, consisting of files containing the series most frequently requested by readers. These files may be downloaded for use in a variety of software packages.

Inquiries about the content of the *World Economic Outlook* and the WEO database should be sent by mail, electronic mail, or telefax (telephone inquiries cannot be accepted) to:

World Economic Studies Division
Research Department
International Monetary Fund
700 19th Street, N.W.
Washington, D.C. 20431, U.S.A.
E-mail: weo@imf.org   Telefax: (202) 623-6343

PREFACE

The analysis and projections contained in the *World Economic Outlook* are integral elements of the IMF's surveillance of economic developments and policies in its member countries, of developments in international financial markets, and of the global economic system. The survey of prospects and policies is the product of a comprehensive interdepartmental review of world economic developments, which draws primarily on information the IMF staff gathers through its consultations with member countries. These consultations are carried out in particular by the IMF's area departments together with the Policy Development and Review Department, the International Capital Markets Department, the Monetary and Financial Systems Department, and the Fiscal Affairs Department.

The analysis in this report has been coordinated in the Research Department under the general direction of Raghuram Rajan, Economic Counsellor and Director of Research. The project has been directed by David Robinson, Deputy Director of the Research Department, together with Tim Callen, Division Chief, Research Department.

Primary contributors to this report also include Nicoletta Batini, Roberto Cardarelli, Dalia Hakura, Thomas Helbling, Subir Lall, Sam Ouliaris, Martin Sommer, S. Hossein Samiei, Nikola Spatafora, and Marco Terrones. Paul Atang, Angela Cabugao, Nathalie Carcenac, Stephanie Denis, Toh Kuan, Yutong Li, and Paul Nicholson provided research assistance. Mahnaz Hemmati, Laurent Meister, Casper Meyer, and Ercument Tulun managed the database and the computer systems. Sylvia Brescia, Celia Burns, and Seetha Milton were responsible for word processing. Other contributors include Reena Aggarwal, Maud Bökkerink, Michael Bordo, Hamid Davoodi, Aasim Husain, Dermot Gately, Jean-Jacques Hallaert, Panagiotis T. Konstantinou, Ayhan Kose, Philip Lane, Douglas Laxton, Chee Sung Lee, Gian Maria Milesi-Ferretti, Prachi Mishra, Dirk Muir, Christopher Otrok, Jens Reinke, Andrea Richter Hume, Calvin Schnure, Irina Tytell, and Linda Tesar. Marina Primorac of the External Relations Department edited the manuscript and coordinated the production of the publication.

The analysis has benefited from comments and suggestions by staff from other IMF departments, as well as by Executive Directors following their discussion of the report on March 21 and 23, 2005. However, both projections and policy considerations are those of the IMF staff and should not be attributed to Executive Directors or to their national authorities.

FOREWORD

The *World Economic Outlook* is a cooperative effort. The core staff members, who tirelessly put together the *World Economic Outlook,* are few, but by drawing on staff elsewhere they access the vast fount of knowledge embedded in the IMF. I thank David Robinson, Tim Callen, members of the World Economic Studies Division, and all the IMF staff from other divisions and departments who worked together to bring this *World Economic Outlook* to you.

The world economy enjoyed one of its strongest years of growth last year. The robust growth is expected to continue this year, albeit at a more moderate pace. One of the most heartening aspects of the growth has been the performance of the poorest countries, including those in sub-Saharan Africa.

As encouraging as the higher growth rate is the finding in the first essay of Chapter II that the volatility of economic growth has decreased in most developing countries over the past three decades. The fact that volatility remains higher than in industrial countries, however, suggests that there is still room for improvement. The essay finds that output volatility in developing countries is driven by country-specific factors rather than regional or global factors—particularly in sub-Saharan African countries. Greater expenditure restraint during cyclical upturns, more developed financial sectors, and structural reforms that diversify the production base will reduce volatility further and enhance growth performance.

One recent development that serves to dampen volatility in developing countries is the growth in remittances described in the second essay in Chapter II. For many countries, remittances have been a large and growing source of foreign exchange that has proven to be more stable and less procyclical than other external sources of finance. Remittances can also aid macroeconomic stability, mitigate adverse shocks, and reduce poverty. Given these benefits, the essay emphasizes the need to encourage additional remittances, for example by reducing the cost of sending remittances as well as impediments to their flow. Any regulation prompted by concerns about the risk of terrorism or money laundering will have to be carefully thought out, so that these flows can be better monitored without causing them to dry up or go further underground.

Let me turn now to a more worrying aspect of global growth—the continuing divergent patterns of growth. Both the euro area and Japan are growing more slowly than the other major regions of the world. This has not helped global current account imbalances, which are continuing to widen.

The current account imbalances probably have their roots in two investment booms and busts. In east Asia, excessive investment growth in the early 1990s collapsed after the Asian crisis in 1997–98. Savings, on the other hand, did not, leaving east Asian economies with an excess of savings over investment—a current account surplus, which had to be invested elsewhere. In the United States, the last years of the twentieth century were ones of rapid productivity growth and increasing investment. Capital was drawn in from abroad, bidding up asset prices in both the stock market and housing market. U.S. households, feeling wealthier, reduced savings further, continuing a decade-long trend of falling household savings. Thus the counterpart of Asian current account surpluses was increased U.S. investment and lower savings—a U.S. current account deficit.

The bursting of the IT bubble led to a significant fall in U.S. investment. Ordinarily, this should have led to a narrowing of the U.S. current account deficit. It did not because the United States adopted expansionary fiscal policies, in part to stimulate the economy. Moreover, the Federal Reserve also followed extremely accommodative monetary policies, so that even though the stock market lay moribund, housing prices (and real estate investment) continued increasing. With public savings falling steeply and household savings continuing their decline, the fall in investment was met by an even greater fall in savings, and the U.S. current account widened steadily.

What about other areas of the world? Partly as a response to the investment excesses during Japan's bubble years in the late 1980s, and partly because Japan was in transition to a slower-growth aging economy, investment fell significantly in Japan over the 1990s. Savings also fell in tandem (in no small measure as a result of public dissaving as efforts to stimulate the economy continued). Thus Japan's current account surplus stayed fairly constant as a share of GDP despite the fall in investment. In China, the infrastructure needs of an economy experiencing explosive growth prompted immense investment, especially in the past few years. However, both the demographic transition and the transition from an uncompetitive protected socialist economy to a competitive market economy with few safety nets have given citizens the incentive to save more, so savings have more than kept pace. Thus, China's current account surplus remained fairly constant until recently, though with the recent slowdown in investment, it has started increasing considerably. Finally, large euro area countries like France and Germany also experienced a slowdown in investment after the IT crash. But the differing response of savings (falling in France; rising in Germany partly because housing prices have not been buoyant, partly because labor market reforms and pension reforms may have increased anxieties and thus the propensity to save) account for why Germany's current account surplus has grown substantially while France's has not.

The net effect of the worldwide fall in investment (e.g., in China) and the different response of savings has been large and growing current account deficits in the United States, and large surpluses in emerging Asia and Japan, as well as in individual countries in the euro area. Recently, surpluses have also emerged in the Commonwealth of Independent States and the Middle East on the backs of rising commodities prices.

As Chapter III in this *World Economic Outlook* suggests, the expansion of cross-border financial flows have allowed real imbalances like the ones I have just described to be financed more easily. Yet it is hard to think that this situation where young, relatively poor countries of the world save more than they invest while the rich aging countries of the world do not is a long-run sustainable equilibrium. At this stage of world demographic evolution, as Chapter III in the last *World Economic Outlook* suggested, the reverse flow seems more appropriate. Apart from the small but costly risk of an abrupt unwinding of the large and growing current account imbalances, the inconsistency of current account imbalances with plausible long-run equilibria makes it necessary to shrink the imbalances.

Before describing policies, let me turn to another concern. I started this introduction noting the strong growth in the global economy. Clearly, strong growth always carries with it the risk of hitting supply constraints. Rising spot oil prices and futures prices have put us on notice. Chapter IV of the *World Economic Outlook* indeed notes that the oil market will remain vulnerable to shocks in the medium run, given that supply and demand will remain roughly in balance, allowing limited prospects for building spare capacity. Particularly noteworthy is that transport demand is likely to take off in a number of emerging markets including China, where per capita income is reaching the level where car demand explodes. Higher oil prices, and the greater likelihood they will persist, now suggest the risks to the WEO growth projections should be weighted to the downside.

Both the large current account imbalances and the limited spare capacity in oil are risks that are typically in the background, but come to the forefront every so often with foreign exchange or oil price movements. Even though exchange or price volatility grabs the attention of politicians for a while, the policies needed to tackle the underlying problems require not just expenditure of political capital, but also sustained political effort over a much longer period. Clearly, the danger is that the consequences have to become far more obvious and painful before the necessary will is found to act.

What policies are necessary? Start with current account imbalances. In the United States, corporate investment is recovering as the excesses of the past are worked off, so it is imperative that savings increase. A credible program for medium-term fiscal consolidation is of the essence. The worldwide increase in real long-term interest rates as investment increases and as the extremely lax monetary conditions—which seem to be holding down long-term rates—tighten will also help. Not only will higher rates directly increase incentives to save, but they may also slow the growth rate of asset prices such as those of housing, leading to greater indirect incentives to save. Since these effects are likely to be larger in the United States, they will help narrow imbalances.

In emerging markets (apart from China), by contrast, the onus will be on increasing both the quantity and quality of investment. Key to this will have to be improvements in the investment climate, coupled with financial sector reform that allows resources to be allocated better. And in countries like Germany and Japan, structural reforms to labor, product, and financial markets can increase the efficiency of investment and growth potential. As the growth rate of these countries increases, their domestic demand can help make up for the necessary slowing in the growth of domestic demand in the United States, as they did so effectively the last time the U.S. current account deficit narrowed, in the late 1980s.

Exchange rates will play their part in guiding adjustment. Thus far, however, the depreciation of the dollar since end-2001 has had little effect on the current account imbalances. In part, this may be because a variety of changes documented in Chapter III have made trade less responsive to changes in exchange rates. Another explanation is that much of the depreciation of the dollar has taken place against economies that have been cyclically weak. In particular, depreciation against the fast-growing economies of emerging Asia has been limited. Since the reserve buildup by some of these economies is creating difficulties in monetary management, and since the distortions needed to maintain relatively fixed exchange rates in the face of appreciation pressures are coming in the way of financial sector development, the benefits of fixity are rapidly waning and the costs mounting. More exchange flexibility will be in everyone's interest.

One cannot ignore the fact that a number of emerging markets started building reserves to buffer themselves against the shocks emanating from international financial markets. While financial sector development will make their economies more resilient to shocks, we also need to ask whether international financial arrangements to borrow offer adequate comfort to emerging economies. A common pool of reserves is less costly than individual buffers, so part of the reform agenda has to be to find ways to enhance confidence in existing common pools like the International Monetary Fund.

On the oil front, Chapter IV offers a number of policy prescriptions that might help reduce volatility in oil markets. These include measures to make the oil market work better, reduce obstacles to investment, increase buffers, and improve conservation. As with the current account imbalances, multilateral cooperation can be very helpful in furthering some of these measures.

Despite the near certainty of rising interest rates, and the possibility of significantly higher oil prices, world economic conditions are still favorable. This is an ideal time to undertake the reforms that are needed to bolster medium-term prospects. As I have argued, there seems little sense of urgency in political circles, in part because the consequences of the imbalances have not been painful as yet, and in part because many of the reforms will bear fruit only in the medium term, while in the short term some of them may be painful. Politics is about the short term, however, so the timing of pain and gain in such reforms is exactly the opposite to that typically preferred by politicians. Every once in a while, however, true leaders emerge who rise above ordinary politics and focus beyond the here and now. It is on them that we must rest our hopes for reform.

Raghuram Rajan
Economic Counsellor and Director, Research Department

ECONOMIC PROSPECTS AND POLICY ISSUES

The global economic expansion has remained broadly on track, evolving largely as expected when the last *World Economic Outlook* was published in September 2004. After averaging about 6 percent in late 2003 and early 2004, global growth moderated, accompanied by a significant slowdown in industrial production and global trade, reflecting both a return to a more sustainable pace of expansion and the adverse impact of higher oil prices (Figures 1.1 and 1.2 and Table 1.1). Most recent data suggest that this slowdown has begun to bottom out, and forward-looking indicators appear consistent with solid expansion in 2005, although rising oil prices are an increasing risk. Despite the appalling human cost and physical destruction of the December 2004 tsunami and the substantial budget and balance of payments implications for some affected countries (Box 1.1, "The Indian Ocean Tsunami: Impact on South Asian Economies"), the impact on growth is expected to be modest.

This overall picture, however, hides growing divergences across regions. In particular:

- *The expansion has become less balanced.* Growth has been stronger than expected in the United States, where the "soft spot" proved more moderate than previously thought; in China, where activity remains buoyant despite tightening measures; and in most emerging market and developing countries. In contrast, growth in Europe and Japan has been disappointing, reflecting—to different extents—faltering exports and weak final domestic demand (and, in Japan, revisions to the national accounts methodology).
- *Global current account imbalances have widened.* The U.S. current account deficit is estimated at a record 5.7 percent of GDP in 2004, with the effects of the depreciation of the U.S. dollar to date offset by continued strong domestic demand relative to its trading partners and

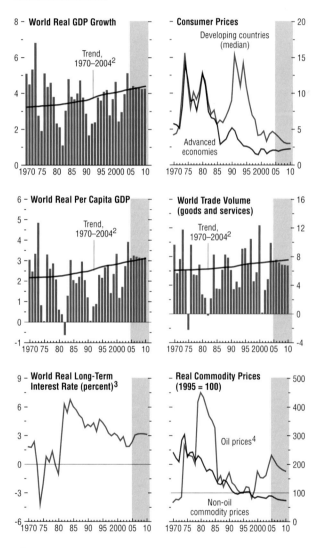

Figure 1.1. Global Indicators[1]
(Annual percent change unless otherwise noted)

Global growth is expected to moderate in 2005, but stay above trend, while inflation remains subdued.

[1]Shaded areas indicate IMF staff projections. Aggregates are computed on the basis of purchasing-power-parity (PPP) weights unless otherwise noted.
[2]Average growth rates for individual countries, aggregated using PPP weights; the aggregates shift over time in favor of faster growing countries, giving the line an upward trend.
[3]GDP-weighted average of the 10-year (or nearest maturity) government bond yields less inflation rates for the United States, Japan, Germany, France, Italy, the United Kingdom, and Canada. Excluding Italy prior to 1972.
[4]Simple average of spot prices of U.K. Brent, Dubai Fateh, and West Texas Intermediate crude oil.

Figure 1.2. Current and Forward-Looking Indicators
(Percent change from previous quarter at annual rate unless otherwise noted)

Industrial production and trade growth slowed during 2004, but business and consumer confidence remain generally solid.

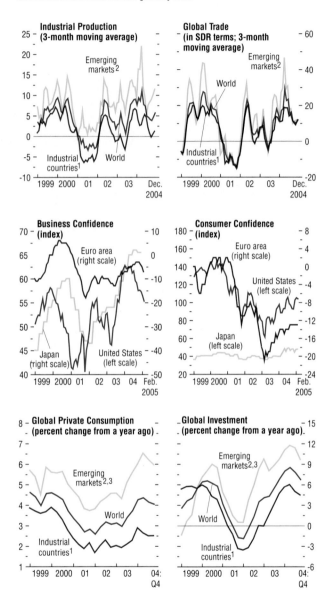

Sources: Business confidence for the United States, the Institute for Supply Management; for the euro area, the European Commission; and for Japan, Bank of Japan. Consumer confidence for the United States, the Conference Board; for the euro area, the European Commission; and for Japan, Cabinet Office. All others, Haver Analytics.

[1]Australia, Canada, Denmark, euro area, Japan, New Zealand, Norway, Sweden, Switzerland, the United Kingdom, and the United States.

[2]Argentina, Brazil, Bulgaria, Chile, China, Colombia, Czech Republic, Estonia, Hong Kong SAR, Hungary, India, Indonesia, Israel, Korea, Latvia, Lithuania, Malaysia, Mexico, Pakistan, Peru, the Philippines, Poland, Romania, Russia, Singapore, Slovak Republic, Slovenia, South Africa, Taiwan Province of China, Thailand, Turkey, Ukraine, and Venezuela.

[3]Data for China, India, Pakistan, and Russia are interpolated.

higher oil prices. This is matched by current account surpluses in emerging Asia, Japan, the oil-producing countries in the Middle East and the Commonwealth of Independent States (CIS), and—to a much lesser extent—the euro area. In emerging Asia and the oil-producing countries, external reserves have also continued to rise sharply, with a significant portion believed to be held in U.S. dollars.

- *Partly reflecting these developments, the U.S. dollar has depreciated further,* matched by appreciations of industrial and emerging market currencies, including several in emerging Asia (Figure 1.3). Since early September, the U.S. dollar has fallen some 6 percent in trade-weighted terms—mostly in late 2004, with major currencies remaining relatively range bound so far in 2005—and by a cumulative 17 percentage points from its February 2002 peak. To date, adjustment has been orderly, and—with options market data suggesting that implied volatility remains moderate—markets appear sanguine that this will continue to be the case.

Despite moderating global growth, oil prices have remained high and volatile. After rising sharply through mid-October, oil prices subsequently fell back sharply, but have recently rebounded to new nominal highs, driven by continued strong demand, uncertainties about Organization of the Petroleum Exporting Countries (OPEC) production plans, and falling non-OPEC supply, all exacerbated by a very low level of excess capacity (Appendix 1.1, "Recent Developments in Commodity Markets"). As of early April the spot oil price stood at $52.96 a barrel;[1] futures markets project prices to average about $54 a barrel in the remainder of 2005, falling back somewhat in 2006 and beyond. With excess capacity expected to remain low—and mainly in the form of heavy crude, for which refining capacity is limited—oil prices are likely

[1]The oil price used in the *World Economic Outlook* is the simple average of the spot prices of U.K. Brent, Dubai, and West Texas Intermediate crudes (respectively, $53.46 a barrel, $49.56 a barrel, and $55.85 a barrel on April 6, 2005).

Table 1.1. Overview of the *World Economic Outlook* Projections
(Annual percent change unless otherwise noted)

	2003	2004	Current Projections		Difference from September 2004 Projections	
			2005	2006	2004	2005
World output	**4.0**	**5.1**	**4.3**	**4.4**	**0.2**	**—**
Advanced economies	2.0	3.4	2.6	3.0	−0.2	−0.3
United States	3.0	4.4	3.6	3.6	0.1	0.1
Euro area	0.5	2.0	1.6	2.3	−0.2	−0.6
Germany	−0.1	1.7	0.8	1.9	−0.4	−1.0
France	0.5	2.3	2.0	2.2	−0.3	−0.3
Italy	0.3	1.2	1.2	2.0	−0.2	−0.7
Spain	2.5	2.7	2.8	3.0	0.1	−0.2
Japan	1.4	2.6	0.8	1.9	−1.8	−1.5
United Kingdom	2.2	3.1	2.6	2.6	−0.3	0.2
Canada	2.0	2.8	2.8	3.0	−0.1	−0.4
Other advanced economies	2.5	4.4	3.4	3.9	0.1	−0.1
Newly industrialized Asian economies	3.1	5.5	4.0	4.8	0.1	−0.1
Other emerging market and developing countries	6.4	7.2	6.3	6.0	0.6	0.4
Africa	4.6	5.1	5.0	5.4	0.6	−0.5
Sub-Sahara	4.2	5.1	5.2	5.6	0.6	−0.6
Central and eastern Europe	4.6	6.1	4.5	4.5	0.6	−0.3
Commonwealth of Independent States	7.9	8.2	6.5	6.0	0.1	—
Russia	7.3	7.1	6.0	5.5	−0.2	−0.6
Excluding Russia	9.1	10.5	7.7	7.0	0.8	1.2
Developing Asia	8.1	8.2	7.4	7.1	0.6	0.6
China	9.3	9.5	8.5	8.0	0.5	1.0
India	7.5	7.3	6.7	6.4	1.0	—
ASEAN-4[1]	5.4	5.8	5.4	5.8	0.4	—
Middle East	5.8	5.5	5.0	4.9	0.5	0.3
Western Hemisphere	2.2	5.7	4.1	3.7	1.1	0.5
Brazil	0.5	5.2	3.7	3.5	1.2	0.2
Mexico	1.6	4.4	3.7	3.3	0.3	0.5
Memorandum						
European Union	1.2	2.5	2.1	2.5	−0.1	−0.4
World growth based on market exchange rates	2.7	4.0	3.2	3.4	−0.4	−0.3
World trade volume (goods and services)	**4.9**	**9.9**	**7.4**	**7.6**	**1.0**	**0.1**
Imports						
Advanced economies	3.6	8.5	6.5	6.3	0.8	0.9
Other emerging market and developing countries	8.9	15.5	12.0	11.0	2.7	—
Exports						
Advanced economies	2.8	8.1	5.9	6.8	—	−0.4
Other emerging market and developing countries	10.7	13.8	9.9	9.7	3.0	−0.4
Commodity prices (U.S. dollars)						
Oil[2]	15.8	30.7	23.2	−5.9	1.8	23.2
Nonfuel (average based on world commodity export weights)	7.1	18.8	3.8	−5.1	2.0	7.8
Consumer prices						
Advanced economies	1.8	2.0	2.0	1.9	−0.1	−0.1
Other emerging market and developing countries	6.0	5.7	5.5	4.6	−0.2	0.1
London interbank offered rate (percent)[3]						
On U.S. dollar deposits	1.2	1.8	3.3	4.1	0.2	—
On euro deposits	2.3	2.1	2.3	2.9	—	−0.5
On Japanese yen deposits	0.1	0.1	0.1	0.4	—	−0.2

Note: Real effective exchange rates are assumed to remain constant at the levels prevailing during January 31–February 28, 2005. See Statistical Appendix for details and groups and methodologies.

[1]Includes Indonesia, Malaysia, the Philippines, and Thailand.

[2]Simple average of spot prices of U.K. Brent, Dubai, and West Texas Intermediate crude oil. The average price of oil in U.S. dollars a barrel was $37.76 in 2004; the assumed price is $46.50 in 2005, and $43.75 in 2006.

[3]Six-month rate for the United States and Japan. Three-month rate for the euro.

Figure 1.3. Global Exchange Rate Developments

The U.S. dollar has depreciated since September 2004, accompanied by moderate appreciation of most industrial and emerging market currencies.

Percent Change from February 2002 to March 24, 2005

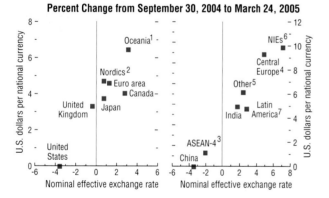

Percent Change from September 30, 2004 to March 24, 2005

Sources: Bloomberg Financial Markets, LP; and IMF staff calculations.
[1] Australia and New Zealand.
[2] Denmark, Norway, and Sweden.
[3] Indonesia, Malaysia, the Philippines, and Thailand.
[4] Czech Republic, Hungary, and Poland.
[5] Russia, South Africa, and Turkey.
[6] Hong Kong SAR, Korea, Singapore, and Taiwan Province of China.
[7] Argentina, Brazil, Chile, Colombia, Mexico, Peru, and Venezuela.

to remain volatile, with options market data suggesting some upside risk. In contrast, prices of nonfuel commodities have leveled off since mid-2004, with rising beverage and metals prices offset by falling prices of some food and agricultural raw materials, most notably cotton. The semiconductor market has also weakened markedly, owing to large inventories and substantial excess capacity; while forward indicators are mixed, most analysts project a significant slowdown in semiconductor sales in 2005.

Inflation and inflationary pressures remain relatively subdued, with few signs to date of significant second-round effects from higher oil prices (Figure 1.4). With monetary tightening cycles under way in most cyclically advanced countries, and inflationary expectations generally well grounded, inflation is expected to remain moderate in the near future. However, inflationary pressures will gradually increase as the expansion proceeds, and two potential upside risks bear close monitoring. First—consistent with the strong pickup in corporate profits—unit labor costs in most industrial countries have fallen significantly. While this may partly reflect structural factors—such as rising competition from emerging markets in Asia and Europe—there is potential for a significant rebound as labor market conditions tighten, especially if labor productivity growth were to weaken. Second, monetary policy in a number of emerging markets—notably in Asia and the CIS—is increasingly complicated by strong external inflows. While the impact on domestic liquidity can be temporarily offset through sterilization, in the absence of greater upward exchange rate flexibility, inflationary pressures will eventually rise.

The recovery has continued to be supported by favorable financial market conditions, with policy rates in most countries still close to zero in real terms, although there has been some tightening in conditions recently as U.S. long-term interest rates have risen and corporate and emerging market spreads have widened (Figures 1.5 and 1.6). Nevertheless, equity markets across the globe remain robust; long-run interest rates still appear well below equilibrium levels; and spreads are close to historical lows; private capital inflows to emerging markets have also been strong (Table 1.2). These developments partly reflect improved fundamentals, including well-grounded inflationary expectations, strengthening corporate balance sheets, and reduced external vulnerabilities in emerging markets. However, the highly accommodative monetary conditions across the globe, accompanied by a continuing search for yield, and—in the case of low long-run interest rates—an ample supply of investable funds have also played an important role (see Box 1.2, "What Are the Risks from Low U.S. Long-Term Interest Rates?"). Correspondingly, as stressed in the IMF's April 2005 *Global Financial Stability Report*, financial conditions could tighten markedly, particularly in the event of unexpected shocks.

Looking forward, global GDP growth is projected to moderate to 4.3 percent in 2005, 0.8 percentage point slower than in 2004, and to remain at about that level during 2006. Underlying this, the slowdown during 2004 is expected to bottom out in early 2005, with global growth increasing marginally thereafter, aided by a gradual recovery in the euro area and Japan, as well as strengthening activity in much of emerging Asia (Figure 1.7). The expansion will continue to be underpinned by accommodative macroeconomic policies, albeit to a lesser extent than in 2004 (Figure 1.8); improving corporate balance sheets; supportive financial market conditions; a gradual rise in employment; and continued strong growth in China. Looking across the major countries and regions:

• Among *industrial countries*, the U.S. economy has continued to grow at or above trend, driven by strong domestic demand. With most forward-looking indicators remaining solid, the expansion is set to continue in 2005, although—with household savings close to zero—a retrenchment in private consumption remains a risk, particularly if house price increases were to slow. In contrast, growth in most other industrial countries has fallen short of expectations. In the euro area, GDP growth slowed markedly in the second half of

Figure 1.4. Global Inflation
(Annualized percent change of three-month moving average over previous three-month average)

Headline inflation has fallen back following the mid-2004 spike owing to higher oil prices; so far, there is little sign of substantial second-round effects on core inflation.

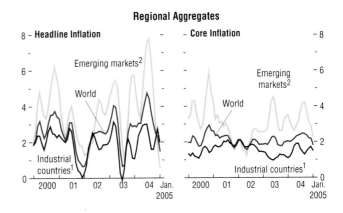

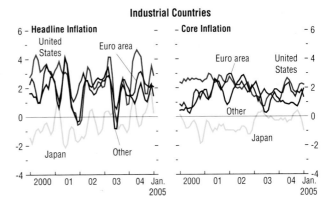

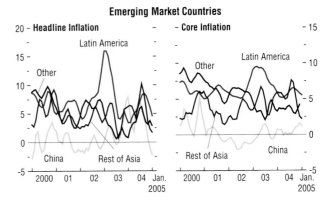

Sources: Haver Analytics; and IMF staff calculations.
[1]Canada, Denmark, euro area, Japan, Norway, Sweden, United Kingdom, and United States.
[2]Brazil, Chile, China, India, Indonesia, Hungary, Korea, Mexico, Poland, South Africa, and Taiwan Province of China.

Figure 1.5. Developments in Mature Financial Markets

Financial market conditions remain unusually benign, with long-term interest rates and spreads at exceptionally low levels.

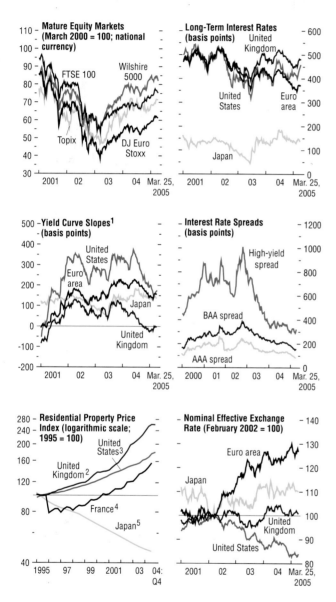

Sources: Bloomberg Financial Markets, LP; Office of Federal Housing Enterprise Oversight; Japan Real Estate Institute; Halifax; National Institute for Statistics and Economic Studies; and IMF staff calculations.
[1]Ten-year government bond minus three-month treasury bill rate.
[2]Halifax housing index as measured by the value of all houses.
[3]House price index as measured by the value of single-family homes in the United States as a whole, in various regions of the country, and in the individual states and the District of Columbia.
[4]Housing price index: all homes.
[5]Urban land price index: average of all categories in six large city areas.

2004, as the contribution of net exports turned sharply negative. While some tentative signs of renewed growth are emerging, confidence indicators have generally eased and the upturn in 2005 is expected to be significantly weaker than earlier thought. Growth in Japan has stalled since the second quarter of 2004, as exports, investment, and consumption faltered; however, recent data generally suggest activity is picking up, and strong corporate profits and solid consumer and business confidence should support a renewed expansion during 2005, albeit at a weaker pace. In both the euro area and Japan, further sharp currency appreciation is an important risk.

- In *emerging markets*, GDP growth in 2004 exceeded expectations in almost all regions, and continued—albeit generally slower—growth is projected during 2005, consistent with global developments. In emerging Asia, China's economic momentum remains very strong, notwithstanding tightening measures by the authorities, and investment remains unsustainably high; growth in India also remains quite robust. While strong growth in these countries will support activity elsewhere in the region, much continues to depend on extraregional developments—particularly the extent of the correction in the information technology (IT) markets, which has contributed to a marked slowdown in growth in some Asian countries during 2004. Activity in Latin America has continued to exceed expectations, aided by high commodity prices, improving external confidence, progress with structural reforms, and in some cases a continued rebound from earlier crisis-induced slowdowns. Fiscal management has been less procyclical than in past upswings, and most countries in the region have taken advantage of favorable financial market conditions to improve debt structure and prefinance 2005 obligations, although high levels of public debt and financial dollarization remain key sources of vulnerability. In the Middle East, GDP growth is projected to slow moderately as oil output plateaus owing to limited excess capacity. The prospect of continued high oil prices offers an important opportunity to address fiscal weaknesses and accelerate the reforms needed to reduce unemployment in the face of rapidly growing labor forces. In Turkey, the economy continues to grow strongly and the inflation target has been met, but high public debt and the large current account deficit underscore the need for continued fiscal prudence and reform. Growth in transition economies remains strong, aided by buoyant commodity prices, although the recent deterioration in the investment climate in Russia is a concern. European Union (EU) accession countries continue to grow solidly, with the key vulnerabilities being large fiscal and external deficits, particularly in Hungary.

• Among the *poorest countries*, GDP growth in sub-Saharan Africa rose to 5.1 percent in 2004, underpinned by generally prudent macro-economic policies; buoyant commodity prices, although some countries have been hit hard by falling cotton prices; improved weather conditions, notably in Ethiopia; and debt relief under the Heavily Indebted Poor Countries (HIPC) initiative. In 2005, GDP growth is projected to remain robust, underpinned primarily by continued strong growth in oil-producing countries as new capacity comes on stream; however, much depends on improved political stability—the recent peace agreement in Sudan is a welcome step—and favorable weather conditions.[2] The ending of world textile trade quotas will also pose a major challenge for many poor countries in Africa, south Asia, and Central America (see Box 1.3, "The Ending of Global Textile Trade Quotas").

The balance of risks to the short-term outlook is tilted to the downside. On the one hand, the cyclical rebound could continue to be stronger than expected, especially given improving corporate and household balance sheets

[2]Since 1990, sub-Saharan African GDP growth in the current year has been overestimated by an average of 0.7 percentage point in spring *World Economic Outlooks*, in part because such expectations were not in fact fulfilled.

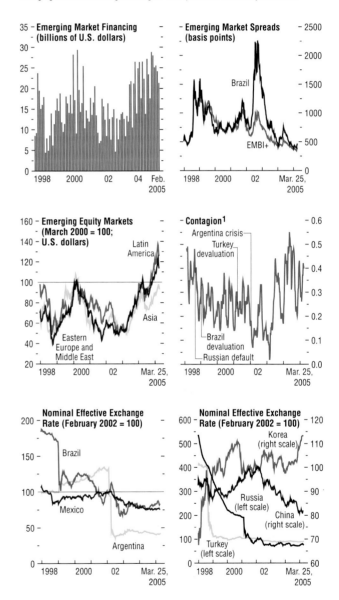

Figure 1.6. **Emerging Market Financial Conditions**

Emerging market borrowing has surged, with spreads at historically low levels.

Sources: Bloomberg Financial Markets, LP; Capital Data; and IMF staff calculations.
[1]Average of 30-day rolling cross-correlation of emerging debt market spreads.

Table 1.2. Emerging Market and Developing Countries: Net Capital Flows[1]
(Billions of U.S. dollars)

	1997	1998	1999	2000	2001	2002	2003	2004	2005	2006
Total										
Private capital flows, net[2]	198.4	84.8	89.1	60.8	60.9	75.8	149.5	196.6	175.1	193.9
Private direct investment, net	147.2	159.8	173.3	174.3	184.7	144.4	151.9	186.4	217.4	222.3
Private portfolio flows, net	60.4	42.5	69.1	20.5	−86.9	−90.0	−9.9	28.8	2.3	16.0
Other private capital flows, net	−9.2	−117.6	−153.3	−134.0	−36.9	21.4	7.5	−18.6	−44.6	−44.4
Official flows, net	27.7	53.5	18.2	−42.7	1.8	8.5	−58.1	−58.0	−65.0	−55.3
Change in reserves[3]	−105.2	−37.4	−93.5	−121.9	−115.1	−194.4	−369.3	−518.9	−523.4	−515.7
Memorandum										
Current account[4]	−83.5	−51.9	38.9	126.6	89.4	142.5	233.8	336.3	395.4	345.8
Africa										
Private capital flows, net[2]	14.3	10.8	11.5	−1.7	7.6	6.9	12.3	11.4	15.6	13.5
Private direct investment, net	7.9	6.6	9.0	8.0	23.0	14.8	14.6	15.4	16.7	16.6
Private portfolio flows, net	7.4	4.3	9.1	−1.8	−7.7	−0.9	0.4	3.9	2.7	3.1
Other private capital flows, net	−1.1	−0.1	−6.6	−7.9	−7.7	−7.0	−2.8	−8.0	−3.8	−6.2
Official flows, net	−4.5	2.9	1.1	−0.2	−2.6	3.8	2.8	−0.5	−1.4	0.7
Change in reserves[3]	−11.3	1.7	−2.8	−12.8	−11.9	−8.1	−19.2	−33.1	−34.3	−32.1
Central and eastern Europe										
Private capital flows, net[2]	20.2	27.2	36.7	39.1	12.2	55.3	52.0	60.6	65.8	57.7
Private direct investment, net	11.6	19.2	22.6	23.9	24.2	25.1	15.1	22.1	29.5	29.0
Private portfolio flows, net	5.4	−1.4	5.7	3.1	0.5	1.4	7.1	24.9	22.4	19.1
Other private capital flows, net	3.2	9.4	8.4	12.2	−12.4	28.7	29.8	13.6	13.9	9.6
Official flows, net	−3.3	0.3	−2.6	1.5	5.5	−7.6	−5.5	−6.9	−5.0	−3.3
Change in reserves[3]	−10.7	−9.5	−11.3	−2.9	7.4	−10.5	−11.4	−12.9	−6.9	−5.1
Commonwealth of Independent States[5]										
Private capital flows, net[2]	19.9	6.7	−6.4	−13.0	−1.8	−9.5	16.4	2.9	−6.4	2.7
Private direct investment,net	5.9	5.3	4.2	2.4	4.6	3.9	5.3	7.7	8.6	9.4
Private portfolio flows, net	17.6	7.7	−3.1	−6.1	−9.2	−8.2	−4.8	−1.1	−10.8	−2.8
Other private capital flows, net	−3.7	−6.3	−7.5	−9.4	2.8	−5.3	15.9	−3.7	−4.3	−3.9
Official flows, net	8.6	10.0	0.1	−4.3	−4.5	−1.7	−5.2	−1.0	−5.4	−1.7
Change in reserves[3]	−4.3	7.5	−2.7	−17.2	−11.3	−11.8	−33.8	−55.5	−69.8	−70.7
Emerging Asia[6]										
Private capital flows, net[2,7]	36.5	−49.9	11.8	−2.0	10.7	23.9	56.1	130.1	108.9	115.0
Private direct investment, net	55.7	56.6	67.1	67.1	54.8	52.5	70.6	87.0	104.3	105.8
Private portfolio flows, net	6.8	8.7	55.8	20.0	−57.6	−62.0	2.5	25.8	11.2	9.1
Other private capital flows, net[7]	−26.0	−115.2	−111.1	−89.2	13.5	33.3	−17.0	17.3	−6.6	0.2
Official flows, net	22.7	15.4	−0.2	1.0	−6.6	−0.2	−14.4	7.0	16.7	17.2
Change in reserves[3]	−36.0	−52.9	−87.5	−61.2	−89.6	−158.4	−235.7	−344.3	−310.0	−315.5

(Figure 1.9); growth could also prove stronger than expected in China in 2005 (although, as discussed below, at the risk of a sharper slowdown later on). On the downside—apart from geopolitical concerns, which remain significant if unquantifiable—the key risks include the following:

• *Financial market conditions could tighten significantly.* A sharp increase in U.S. long-run interest rates—which have risen by some 50 basis points since early February—would adversely affect domestic demand, especially if driven by a rise in inflationary expectations or weaker foreign demand for U.S. securities

(Box 1.2); prompt significant financial market deleveraging and downward adjustments in prices of riskier assets, underscoring the need for vigilance by both supervisors and regulators; and lead to a significant deterioration in emerging market financing conditions. If higher U.S. rates led to higher long-run interest rates elsewhere, they would also raise the risk of a synchronized decline in housing markets, which is of particular concern where housing prices are already elevated and household balance sheets are most exposed to rising rates. In addition, as discussed below, with the U.S. current account deficit remain-

Table 1.2 *(concluded)*

	1997	1998	1999	2000	2001	2002	2003	2004	2005	2006
Middle East[8]										
Private capital flows, net[2]	7.9	19.1	–3.1	–2.2	4.5	–4.0	–2.4	–21.0	–31.2	–25.1
Private direct investment, net	8.3	10.1	4.5	3.5	6.8	4.2	11.6	8.8	9.5	11.2
Private portfolio flows, net	–6.8	–2.3	0.7	3.9	–2.9	–4.9	–5.1	–10.5	–15.0	–12.3
Other private capital flows, net	6.4	11.3	–8.3	–9.6	0.5	–3.3	–9.0	–19.3	–25.7	–24.0
Official flows, net	–1.1	7.9	14.3	–33.3	–16.4	–5.5	–44.6	–49.2	–61.6	–57.6
Change in reserves[3]	–16.6	8.9	–1.0	–29.5	–11.3	–3.5	–33.4	–51.2	–81.2	–79.1
Western Hemisphere										
Private capital flows, net[2]	99.6	70.8	38.7	40.5	27.8	3.3	15.2	12.7	22.4	30.3
Private direct investment, net	57.7	62.0	65.9	69.3	71.3	43.8	34.7	45.4	48.7	50.4
Private portfolio flows, net	29.9	25.5	1.0	1.3	–10.0	–15.5	–10.1	–14.2	–8.2	–0.1
Other private capital flows, net	12.0	–16.7	–28.2	–30.1	–33.6	–25.0	–9.5	–18.5	–18.1	–20.0
Official flows, net	5.4	16.9	5.5	–7.4	26.4	19.8	8.7	–7.3	–8.3	–10.5
Change in reserves[3]	–26.4	7.0	11.8	1.6	1.6	–2.3	–35.8	–21.9	–21.3	–13.2
Memorandum										
Fuel exporters										
Private capital flows, net[2]	25.3	17.7	–21.2	–51.8	–13.7	–24.9	4.5	–25.8	–53.6	–41.7
Nonfuel exporters										
Private capital flows, net[2]	173.1	67.0	110.3	112.6	74.7	100.7	144.9	222.4	228.7	235.6

[1]Net capital flows comprise net direct investment, net portfolio investment, and other long- and short-term net investment flows, including official and private borrowing. In this table, Hong Kong SAR, Israel, Korea, Singapore, and Taiwan Province of China are included.

[2]Because of data limitations, "other private capital flows, net" may include some official flows.

[3]A minus sign indicates an increase.

[4]The sum of the current account balance, net private capital flows, net official flows, and the change in reserves equals, with the opposite sign, the sum of the capital account and errors and omissions. For regional current account balances, see Table 25 of the Statistical Appendix.

[5]Historical data have been revised, reflecting cumulative data revisions for Russia and the resolution of a number of data interpretation issues.

[6]Consists of developing Asia and the newly industrialized Asian economies.

[7]Excluding the effects of the recapitalization of two large commercial banks in China with foreign reserves of the Bank of China ($45 billion), net private capital flows to emerging Asia in 2003 were $101.1 billion while other private capital flows net to the region amounted to $28.0 billion.

[8]Includes Israel.

ing at record levels, further—and possibly disorderly—depreciation of the U.S. dollar cannot be ruled out.

- *As the* World Economic Outlook *went to press, oil prices had risen nearly $6 a barrel above the* World Economic Outlook *baseline for 2005; the market remains highly vulnerable to shocks, with significant upside risk over the longer term* (see Chapter IV, "Will the Oil Market Remain Tight?"). In the past, a permanent $5 a barrel increase in oil prices has been expected to lower global GDP growth by up to 0.3 percentage point; in practice, the impact over the last year has been less than feared, partly because higher prices have in part been a consequence of strong global growth, and partly reflecting the greater credibility of monetary policies (so that interest rates have not had to be raised to ward off second-round inflationary effects). The impact of further

sharp increases, however, could be more marked, especially if they were to adversely affect confidence or inflationary expectations; there would also be a greater danger of negative supply-side effects over the longer run. Higher oil prices also pose particular risks for cyclically less advanced industrial countries, some heavily indebted emerging markets, and many poor countries.

- *The global expansion is becoming increasingly unbalanced.* Global growth remains unduly dependent on the United States and China; growth in the euro area and Japan—together accounting for nearly one-fourth of global output—has once again been disappointing. If this situation persists, it will widen global imbalances; it would also raise the risks of a more significant slowdown later on, especially if growth in the United States and China were to weaken simultaneously.

Figure 1.7. Global Outlook
(Real GDP; percent change from four quarters earlier)

After some slowdown during 2004, global growth is expected to stabilize at slightly above trend levels in 2005 and beyond.

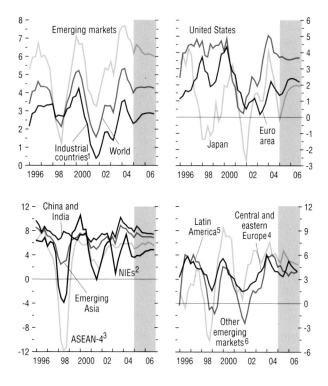

Sources: Haver Analytics; and IMF staff estimates.
[1]Australia, Canada, Denmark, euro area, Japan, New Zealand, Norway, Sweden, Switzerland, the United Kingdom, and the United States.
[2]Hong Kong SAR, Korea, Singapore, and Taiwan Province of China.
[3]Indonesia, Malaysia, the Philippines, and Thailand.
[4]Czech Republic, Estonia, Hungary, Latvia, and Poland.
[5]Argentina, Brazil, Chile, Colombia, Mexico, Peru, and Venezuela.
[6]Israel, Russia, South Africa, and Turkey.

In some respects, industrial and developing countries are better placed to manage these risks than they were in the past. Macroeconomic policy frameworks, particularly on the monetary side, have improved; economies have generally become more flexible, albeit to differing extents; financial institutions are more resilient to shocks, as past *Global Financial Stability Reports* have emphasized; and external vulnerabilities in emerging markets have been reduced significantly. That said, the scope for short-term policy maneuver in response to the unexpected is limited, and a combination of shocks—such as lower global growth, higher interest rates, and rising oil prices—could create significant difficulties for many emerging market and developing countries. Moreover, three overarching global vulnerabilities remain, which—while essentially medium-term in nature—are increasingly affecting the short-term outlook.

• *Global imbalances have deepened,* and WEO projections suggest little improvement in the foreseeable future. The U.S. external deficit has so far been financed relatively easily, aided by continued financial globalization. However, the demand for U.S. assets is not unlimited and, as recent market reaction to the possibility of central bank reserve diversification underscores, a continuing sharp rise in U.S. net external liabilities will carry increasing risks (see Chapter III, "Globalization and External Imbalances"). As a matter of arithmetic, a reduction in global imbalances will require domestic demand to grow more slowly than GDP in the United States, and to grow faster than GDP in surplus countries. This will likely need to be accompanied by a further depreciation of the U.S. dollar over the medium term, and by appreciations elsewhere—including in a number of countries in emerging Asia. The broad strategy to address imbalances—medium-term fiscal consolidation in the United States; steps toward greater exchange rate flexibility, supported by continued financial sector reform in emerging Asia; and continued structural reforms to remove supply constraints, enhance investment efficiency, and boost growth in Europe and Japan—is generally agreed, but implementation has lagged (Box 1.4, "What Progress Has Been Made in Implementing Policies to Reduce Global Imbalances?"). As discussed in more detail below, the pace at which oil-producing countries utilize higher oil revenues will also play an important role.

- *Fiscal positions in many countries remain very difficult, posing a significant medium-term threat to macroeconomic stability.* In the largest industrial countries, fiscal deficits remain high—except in Canada—while projected improvements are generally unambitious, and in many cases not underpinned by credible measures (Table 1.3). In emerging markets, fiscal indicators have generally improved, notably in Latin America, but many countries have a long way to go to bring public debt ratios to sustainable levels (between 25 and 50 percent of GDP).[3] Despite some progress, notably in the euro area and Japan, most industrial and emerging market countries remain ill-prepared for coming pressures from aging populations, with health care systems in particular requiring greater attention.

- *Structural weaknesses constrain growth in key areas and increase vulnerability to shocks.* Challenges vary widely across regions, but include accelerating labor and product market reform in the euro area; addressing remaining corporate and financial sector weaknesses in Japan and much of emerging Asia; strengthening the investment climate in Latin America; improving banking supervision in central and eastern Europe; and developing the institutional infrastructure for non-oil sector development in the Middle East.

Beyond the potential risks to macroeconomic stability, these three vulnerabilities pose significant downside risks to global growth. As past *World Economic Outlooks* have noted, history sug-

[3]See "Public Debt in Emerging Markets: Is It Too High?" *World Economic Outlook*, September 2003, for a detailed discussion.

Figure 1.8. Fiscal and Monetary Policies in the Major Advanced Countries

Monetary policies are generally expected to tighten moderately in 2005, although fiscal policies are more mixed.

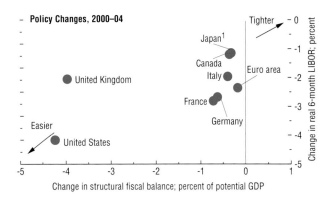

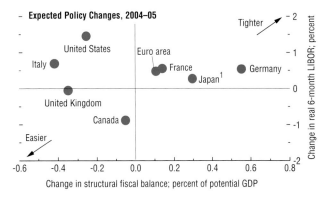

Source: IMF staff estimates.
[1]For Japan, excludes bank support.

Figure 1.9. Household and Corporate Balance Sheets

Corporate profits have grown strongly, aided by falling unit labor costs. Household savings diverge widely across regions, but in most cases have continued to decline, partly reflecting rising net wealth.

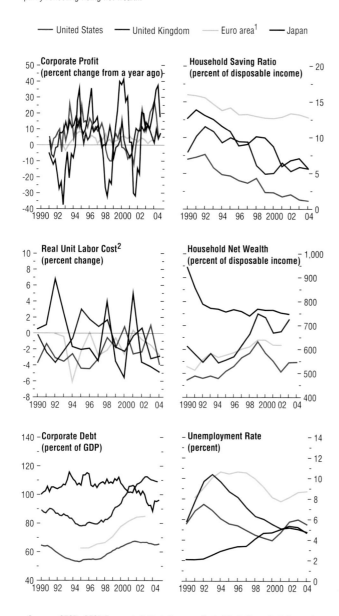

Sources: OECD, *OECD Economic Outlook;* European Central Bank; Haver Analytics; and IMF staff calculations.
[1] Excludes Luxembourg for the household saving ratio. For household net wealth, includes France, Germany, and Italy. For corporate debt, includes Austria, Belgium, Finland, France, Germany, Italy, the Netherlands, Portugal, and Spain.
[2] Unit wage cost for the United Kingdom.

gests that even an orderly adjustment in the U.S. current account imbalance is likely to be accompanied by slower U.S. growth. Given the constraints described above, this is unlikely to be offset by stronger activity elsewhere. Moreover, rising public debt—either implicit or explicit—will put upward pressure on long-run interest rates, as well as increasingly limiting the scope for policy adjustment in response to unexpected shocks. Finally, structural rigidities limit the ability to take full advantage of the opportunities from globalization—including the emergence of China—and technological change.

Against this background, the key policy priorities appear to be the following.

- *First, with policy interest rates generally well below neutral levels, most countries will eventually need to transition toward higher interest rates; however, given the divergences noted above, the appropriate timing and pace increasingly differ.* Among the largest countries, there is a strong case for monetary conditions to be tightened in China to prevent a resurgence of investment; in the United States, a measured pace of tightening remains appropriate for the time being. In contrast, in Japan the quantitative easing policy should remain in place until deflation is firmly beaten; in the euro area monetary policy should remain firmly on hold until a self-sustaining recovery is clearly established, and if present economic weakness persists and inflationary pressures remain subdued, the possibility of an interest rate cut cannot be ruled out. In the event of further dollar depreciation, monetary policy should be increasingly differentiated, with an increased bias toward tightening in the United States and toward easing in countries with appreciating currencies. In emerging markets, the appropriate response varies, but in many cases—notably in emerging Asia—greater flexibility in exchange rates will be necessary. In this connection, while exchange rate appreciation will worsen the current account, it also tends to reduce external debt ratios—owing to the valuation effects discussed in Chapter III—thus helping to improve sustainability.

Table 1.3. Major Advanced Economies: General Government Fiscal Balances and Debt[1]

(Percent of GDP)

	1989–98	1999	2000	2001	2002	2003	2004	2005	2006	2010
Major advanced economies										
Actual balance	−3.5	−1.2	−0.2	−1.8	−4.1	−4.6	−4.2	−4.2	−4.1	−3.0
Output gap[2]	−0.2	0.6	1.4	−0.1	−1.4	−2.0	−1.2	−1.3	−0.9	—
Structural balance	−3.4	−1.4	−1.3	−1.9	−3.6	−3.8	−3.7	−3.7	−3.7	−3.1
United States										
Actual balance	−3.4	0.6	1.3	−0.7	−4.0	−4.6	−4.3	−4.4	−4.2	−2.9
Output gap[2]	−0.8	1.9	2.2	−0.5	−2.0	−2.5	−1.6	−1.3	−1.0	—
Structural balance	−3.1	−0.1	0.5	−0.6	−3.3	−3.7	−3.7	−3.9	−3.9	−3.0
Net debt	54.1	44.6	39.3	38.3	40.9	43.6	45.2	47.0	48.7	51.0
Gross debt	69.5	62.8	57.1	56.6	58.6	60.5	61.0	61.9	62.7	62.3
Euro area										
Actual balance	. . .	−1.3	−1.0	−1.8	−2.4	−2.8	−2.7	−2.6	−2.6	−1.5
Output gap[2]	. . .	0.2	1.6	1.1	—	−1.3	−1.2	−1.5	−1.2	—
Structural balance	. . .	−1.5	−1.9	−2.5	−2.6	−2.4	−2.0	−1.9	−1.9	−1.4
Net debt	. . .	61.8	59.3	59.1	59.1	60.8	61.3	61.6	61.6	59.8
Gross debt	. . .	72.2	69.6	69.6	69.5	70.8	71.2	71.6	71.5	68.9
Germany[3]										
Actual balance	−2.5	−1.5	1.3	−2.8	−3.7	−3.8	−3.7	−3.5	−3.4	−2.0
Output gap[2]	1.1	0.2	1.6	1.1	−0.1	−1.5	−1.1	−1.6	−1.1	—
Structural balance[4]	−3.3	−1.9	−2.5	−3.9	−3.7	−3.5	−3.1	−2.5	−2.3	−1.6
Net debt	38.4	54.9	52.8	53.5	55.5	58.7	61.1	63.6	65.0	66.0
Gross debt	50.3	61.2	60.2	59.4	60.9	63.8	66.1	68.6	69.8	70.3
France										
Actual balance	−3.7	−1.8	−1.4	−1.4	−3.2	−4.2	−3.7	−3.1	−3.1	−1.0
Output gap[2]	−1.0	−0.6	1.2	1.0	—	−1.4	−1.3	−1.4	−1.1	—
Structural balance[4]	−2.9	−1.4	−2.0	−2.1	−3.2	−3.2	−2.7	−2.6	−2.3	−1.0
Net debt	37.7	48.8	47.5	48.2	49.1	53.9	55.4	56.1	56.5	53.3
Gross debt	46.9	58.5	57.1	56.8	58.7	63.6	65.0	65.7	66.2	63.0
Italy										
Actual balance	−8.4	−1.7	−0.6	−3.0	−2.6	−2.9	−3.0	−3.5	−4.3	−3.4
Output gap[2]	—	−0.5	0.7	0.9	—	−1.2	−1.7	−2.2	−1.9	—
Structural balance[4]	−8.2	−1.6	−2.3	−3.6	−3.5	−2.6	−2.6	−3.0	−3.5	−3.4
Net debt	106.6	109.2	105.6	105.5	103.1	103.1	102.6	102.2	102.4	105.7
Gross debt	112.7	115.5	111.2	110.7	108.0	106.3	105.8	105.4	105.5	108.9
Japan										
Actual balance	−1.9	−7.2	−7.5	−6.1	−7.9	−7.8	−7.1	−6.9	−6.5	−6.4
Excluding social security	−4.1	−8.2	−8.0	−6.2	−7.7	−7.9	−7.0	−6.7	−6.1	−5.7
Output gap[2]	0.9	−1.7	−0.4	−1.3	−2.6	−2.3	−0.9	−1.3	−0.5	—
Structural balance	−2.2	−6.5	−7.2	−5.5	−6.8	−6.8	−6.7	−6.4	−6.3	−6.4
Excluding social security	−4.3	−7.8	−7.9	−5.9	−7.1	−7.4	−6.8	−6.4	−6.0	−5.7
Net debt	23.3	53.8	59.3	64.6	71.6	76.0	82.0	88.9	94.3	111.2
Gross debt	85.6	131.0	139.2	148.9	158.5	164.7	169.4	176.0	180.0	187.5
United Kingdom										
Actual balance	−3.7	1.0	3.9	0.8	−1.7	−3.3	−3.0	−3.1	−2.9	−2.4
Output gap[2]	−0.2	−0.1	1.0	0.9	−0.2	−0.7	−0.2	—	—	—
Structural balance[4]	−3.6	0.9	1.3	0.2	−1.9	−3.0	−2.7	−3.0	−2.9	−2.5
Net debt	33.4	40.1	34.3	32.8	32.8	34.6	35.2	36.9	38.0	41.2
Gross debt	43.8	44.7	41.7	38.5	38.1	39.5	40.4	42.0	43.1	46.3
Canada										
Actual balance	−5.1	1.6	2.9	1.1	0.3	0.6	1.4	1.3	1.2	1.4
Output gap[2]	−0.3	0.7	2.1	0.4	0.7	−0.3	−0.4	−0.5	−0.3	0.1
Structural balance	−4.8	1.3	1.9	0.8	—	0.8	1.6	1.5	1.4	1.4
Net debt	78.9	75.4	65.3	59.5	56.5	51.9	47.6	43.9	40.6	28.3
Gross debt	110.5	111.6	101.5	99.1	95.4	90.9	84.3	78.7	73.8	55.6

Note: The methodology and specific assumptions for each country are discussed in Box A1 in the Statistical Appendix.

[1]Debt data refer to end of year. Debt data are not always comparable across countries. For example, the Canadian data include the unfunded component of government employee pension liabilities, which amounted to nearly 18 percent of GDP in 2001.

[2]Percent of potential GDP.

[3]Data before 1990 refer to west Germany. Beginning in 1995, the debt and debt-service obligations of the Treuhandanstalt (and of various other agencies) were taken over by general government. This debt is equivalent to 8 percent of GDP, and the associated debt service, ½ to 1 percent of GDP.

[4]Excludes one-off receipts from the sale of mobile telephone licenses (the equivalent of 2.5 percent of GDP in 2000 for Germany, 0.1 percent of GDP in 2001 and 2002 for France, 1.2 percent of GDP in 2000 for Italy, and 2.4 percent of GDP in 2000 for the United Kingdom). Also excludes one-off receipts from sizable asset transactions, in particular 0.5 percent of GDP for France in 2005.

Box 1.1. The Indian Ocean Tsunami: Impact on South Asian Economies

On December 26, 2004, a magnitude 9.0 earthquake occurred off the west coast of Sumatra, Indonesia, setting off a string of tidal waves in the Indian Ocean that caused a natural disaster of tragic proportions. The human toll has been devastating, with over 140,000 people estimated to have lost their lives and a further 150,000 missing. Over 1½ million were displaced from their homes by the disaster. The countries suffering the highest casualties were Indonesia (227,000) and Sri Lanka (37,000), with India (16,500) and Thailand (8,500) suffering major losses as well.[1] Deaths were also reported in Bangladesh, Malaysia, Maldives, and Myanmar, as well as in Seychelles, Kenya, Somalia, and Tanzania.

The human cost of this disaster is clearly beyond measurement. While it is still too early to know the precise economic costs, in some countries and areas they will be sizable. Because so many homes have been destroyed and livelihoods lost, the disaster will cause hardship for hundreds of thousands of individuals. Preliminary damage and needs assessments, undertaken by the World Bank and Asian Development Bank in conjunction with national authorities, have already been completed. Based on these preliminary assessments, damage is estimated at 4½ percent of GDP (2005, pre-tsunami) in Sri Lanka, 1½ percent of GDP in Indonesia, ⅓ percent of GDP in Thailand, and less than ¼ percent of GDP in India. The damage sustained by Maldives, estimated at about one-half of GDP, was far more significant in relative terms than that sustained by the larger countries, owing to extensive damage to infrastructure and tourism facilities.

Despite the considerable physical damage, which will take years to repair, in most cases the disaster is not expected to have a major impact on economic growth. Tourism was one of the hardest-hit sectors, especially in Maldives and

Thailand. However, it is expected to recover relatively quickly (with tourists diverting to unaffected areas, such as the western coast of Thailand and Bali), and certainly faster than when severe acute respiratory syndrome (SARS) hit the region in 2003. The other sector that sustained a serious blow was fishing; Sri Lanka is estimated to have lost nearly two-thirds of its fishing fleet. In this case, recovery could take much longer, as it will be difficult for surviving fishermen, many of whom are poor, to finance the acquisition of new boats and fishing gear. Agriculture has also been damaged in some small areas, with paddy production likely to suffer over the medium term from the salinity of the flood waters.

In the near term, the loss of housing and jobs in the most affected sectors and regions will inflict a considerable cost on countless individuals and families. All in all, however, because tourism and fishing account for a relatively small share of national economies, the direct impact of the disaster on total economic growth is likely to be marginal in most countries. And to the extent that reconstruction efforts are launched quickly, growth in the most severely affected countries is likely to meet, or may even exceed, pre-disaster projections. The exceptions to this are Sri Lanka, where growth this year could be reduced by ¾ percentage point, and Maldives, where severe damage to the tourism industry, which accounts for roughly one-third of GDP, could reduce growth by up to 5½ percentage points, to 1 percent. A more modest impact, on the order of ¼ percentage point, is forecast in Thailand. There may be some direct impact on inflation in the most heavily impacted countries as food and transportation prices rise, though this should generally be temporary and limited to the affected areas.

In the most seriously affected countries, public spending is expected to rise considerably to finance reconstruction. In Indonesia, such spending in 2005 is projected at ½ percent of GDP ($1.7 billion), and initial plans in Sri Lanka call for 2½ percent of GDP (about $½ billion) in reconstruction spending this year. In

Note: The author of this box is Andrea Richter Hume.
[1]Figures include the missing, most of whom are presumed dead.

The Indian Ocean Tsunami: Human and Economic Impact on Southern Asia

	Human Toll		Real GDP Growth in 2005[1] (projection, in percent)		Damages[2]		Aid Pledges[3] (US$ millions)
	Dead and missing	Displaced	Pre-tsunami	Post-tsunami	US$ millions	% of GDP	
India	16,389	646,967	6.8	6.8	2,000	0.2	0
Indonesia	>227,000	>425,000	5.5	5.25–5.5	4,500	1.6	3,955
Maldives	108	13,000	6.5	1.0	406	47.0	108
Sri Lanka	36,940	420,259	6.0	5.3	1,000	4.5	308
Thailand	8,438	. . .	5.9	5.6	500	0.3	0
Total	288,875	1,505,226	. . .	. . .	8,406	. . .	4,371

Source: United Nations and national official estimates, and IMF staff projections.
[1]IMF staff estimates.
[2]Based on preliminary damage and needs assessments undertaken by the World Bank and Asian Development Bank in conjunction with national authorities and other international agencies. Uses pre-tsunami forecasts for 2005 GDP.
[3]Represents actual commitments made to date.

Maldives, reconstruction spending during 2005 is expected to amount to 13 percent of GDP ($110 million).

Potentially sizable reconstruction expenditure may present a macroeconomic management challenge to the hardest-hit economies. To the extent that such spending generates demand for imports, the balance of payments will come under pressure, though significant financing should be provided by donors in the form of grants and other assistance (see below). In fact, large aid inflows could also put upward pressure on regional exchange rates, as evidenced already in Sri Lanka. To the extent that such spending falls on domestic products and services, however, it could stoke inflationary pressures, suggesting that monetary authorities will need to remain vigilant.

In most countries, financial assistance from the donor community is expected to play a major role in financing reconstruction. At the annual Indonesia donors' meeting held in mid-January, donors pledged nearly $4 billion to finance reconstruction spending in 2005–09, covering most of Indonesia's tsunami-related financing needs. Of this, roughly $1.7 billion was pledged for 2005. Maldives is expecting about $67 million in disbursements of new grants and concessional loans in 2005. However, substantial additional contributions are needed to close the financing gap. In the case of Sri Lanka, the government expects to receive about

$500 million in assistance during 2005. But with public reconstruction projects expected to cost $1½ billion over the next three years, Sri Lanka is seeking additional donor financing to limit the burden on the public purse.

The IMF has been actively engaged in assisting governments in the affected countries cope with the aftermath of the disaster. Assistance is being provided in several ways. On the technical front, the IMF has been supporting government efforts to assess the implications of the disaster for macroeconomic policy, including the likely impact on economic growth, fiscal policy, and the balance of payments. On the financial front, quick-disbursing funds are available under the IMF's emergency assistance for natural disasters policy, designed for cases in which a natural disaster has a large negative impact on the balance of payments. Normally, access of up to 25 percent of a member's quota in the IMF is granted, though access can be larger in exceptional cases. The IMF's Executive Board recently decided to set up an administered account to subsidize emergency assistance for natural disasters provided to its poorest member countries (i.e., those that are eligible for the IMF's Poverty Reduction and Growth Facility).

On March 4, the IMF's Executive Board approved emergency assistance of SDR 4.1 million (about $6.3 million, or 50 percent of quota) for Maldives, and SDR 103.35 million (about $157.5 million or 25 percent of quota) for Sri

Box 1.1 *(concluded)*

Lanka. The approved amounts became available immediately. The rate of charge on the assistance will be subsidized to 0.5 percent a year, subject to resource availability. Sri Lanka is also benefiting from the IMF's policy on repayments, which has allowed it to shift repayments to the more extended "obligations" basis following the disaster. In the case of Indonesia, because the disaster is expected to have only a minor impact on the balance of payments, no request for emergency IMF financing is expected.

The Paris Club of official creditors has offered a debt moratorium to the tsunami-affected countries. In mid-January, they offered a temporary moratorium on debt payments from the countries affected by the natural disaster, until further information from the damage and needs assessments became available. In early March, creditors agreed not to expect any debt repayment on eligible sovereign claims from the affected countries until December 31, 2005. (The moratorium would cover overseas development assistance as well as previously rescheduled commercial credits.) The deferred amounts would be repaid over five years (including one year of grace), and moratorium interest accrued in 2005 would be capitalized and paid with the deferred amounts. The moratorium interest rates would still need to be determined on a bilateral basis with each creditor.

A temporary moratorium on debt service to Paris Club creditors would bolster reserves and help finance reconstruction without requiring offsetting spending cuts or a diversion of domestic financial resources. A one-year moratorium would entail significant debt-service savings in 2005, amounting to $0.3 billion for Sri Lanka and $4½ billion for Indonesia. The Sri Lankan government has welcomed the offer, but has expressed its intention to continue to press for an extension of the moratorium for two more years. The Indonesian government has expressed strong interest in the offer as well. For Maldives, because debt owed to the Paris Club is very small, the debt relief offer is not much help.

India and Thailand, which have sizable foreign reserves, low external public debt, and ready market access, have declined the Paris Club's offer. Thailand has also turned down most other offers of aid, and is planning to self-finance its reconstruction needs. The government has already approved a relief package amounting to about 0.8 percent of GDP ($1½ billion). India has accepted reconstruction loans from the World Bank, the Asian Development Bank, and the United Nations amounting to roughly 0.15 percent of GDP, which will cover most of the estimated damage cost. The government has already released some additional budget spending in calamity relief for the most affected states this year, and next year's budget, announced at end-February, proposes an additional relief package for the Andaman and Nicobar islands.

- *Second, full advantage must be taken of the expansion to address the medium-term risks outlined above.* While this will in many cases require greater policy ambition, increased policy credibility will also be critical. Notably, prompt action—along the lines described above—is needed to assist adjustment in global imbalances. An orderly and gradual adjustment of global imbalances is most likely to be feasible if all countries are playing their part in

addressing what is fundamentally a multilateral problem, and if financial markets are convinced that strong and realistic medium-term policy frameworks are in place. If, in contrast, markets start to doubt the resolve of policymakers and simultaneously assess that the current account deficit will become unsustainable at some point, they are likely to sell dollar assets preemptively, substantially raising the risk of an abrupt dollar adjustment.[4]

[4]See Rajan (2004).

- *Third, from a multilateral perspective, successful and appropriately ambitious trade liberalization under the Doha Round remains critical to support medium-term global growth.* The priority now is to translate the mid-2004 framework agreements into a more specific policy package to be taken up at the December 2005 World Trade Organization (WTO) Ministerial Conference in Hong Kong SAR. While there has been considerable progress in agriculture, some key issues—including the transition period for eliminating export subsidies and the depth of cuts to domestic agricultural support—remain to be resolved. This in turn would facilitate more ambitious agreements in areas such as services, where progress has so far been slow.

Finally, most developing countries continue to face enormous challenges in meeting the Millennium Development Goals.[5] While India and China are likely to achieve the goal of halving poverty between 1990 and 2015, on current trends most sub-Saharan African countries will miss this target by wide margins; the outlook for achieving most other key Millennium Development Goals is even less promising. In this connection, even if the IMF staff's relatively upbeat growth forecasts are achieved, in most countries projected growth remains well short of what is required. With macroeconomic stability now broadly achieved, the key remains to press forward with the remaining policy and governance reforms required to improve the growth and investment environment (see the second essay in Chapter II, "Output Volatility in Emerging Market and Developing Countries"). As one element, it will be essential that the benefits of newfound oil resources—as well as other natural resources—be effectively utilized.

To be successful, such efforts must be supported by substantially higher assistance from the international community. To date, despite important progress, developed countries have yet to deliver on the commitments they made in 2002 at Monterrey, commitments that themselves fell well short of what is needed to meet the Millennium Development Goals. As the UN Millennium Project Report (UN Millennium Project, 2005) stresses, the year 2005 should inaugurate a decade of bold action. Two particular priorities are a substantial increase in official development assistance—still less than one-third of the UN target of 0.7 percent of GNP—targeted on those countries with strongest policies and most severe poverty; and a substantial improvement in market access for developing countries under the Doha Round. In this connection, with some three-fourths of the world's poor working in rural areas competing with industrial country farmers who earn one-third of their income from subsidies, an early reduction in agricultural trade barriers is especially important. But it is also worth recalling that developing countries would reap the largest gains from their own trade reforms, underscoring the need for all countries to take full advantage of the Doha Round to liberalize.

United States and Canada: More Ambitious Fiscal Consolidation Is Needed in the United States

In the United States, the slowdown in mid-2004 proved relatively mild. After slowing sharply in the second quarter, consumption growth picked up briskly, reflecting the ebbing impact of higher oil prices, rising equity and house prices, and higher spending on automobiles in response to manufacturers' incentives. Business investment—while still below historical norms at this stage of the cycle—also grew solidly, aided by buoyant corporate profitability, which has been underpinned by continuing strong—albeit slowing—productivity growth that has contained labor costs. While the current account deficit—discussed further below—continued to widen, real GDP growth for 2004 is

[5]See the April 2005 *Global Monitoring Report* for a full discussion.

Box 1.2. What Are the Risks from Low U.S. Long-Term Interest Rates?

This box examines the reasons for the low level of U.S. long-term interest rates, and assesses the risks to the global economy of an unexpected rise. Dipping below 4 percent in mid-February, nominal yields on 10-year U.S. government bonds have been close to long-term lows and were actually falling even as the Federal Reserve started to raise the federal funds rate (see the figure).[1] Nominal rates subsequently backed up to about 4½ percent in early April, but remained low by historical standards. While the low level of nominal rates partly reflects subdued inflation, a comparison of nominal and inflation-adjusted yields indicates that real returns are also abnormally depressed. This has helped support wealth and domestic spending, including by increasing borrowing in the relatively interest-sensitive mortgage market that has helped buoy house prices.[2]

Low nominal bond yields in part reflect easy monetary conditions and the gradual expected pace of tightening made possible by a high level of monetary credibility. In contrast to earlier episodes of monetary tightening, expectations of future inflation have remained well anchored even as markets project a slow withdrawal of monetary stimulus, partly reflecting a significant level of economic slack that has limited inflationary pressures. The more recent rise in long-term yields can largely be attributed to a partial reversal of these forces due to some increase in inflation concerns as well as expectations of a less gradual tightening. Markets expect the short-term federal funds rate to rise from 2¾ percent currently to some 4 percent by end-2005. As long-term rates reflect the expected future path of short-term rates (plus a liquidity premium) the slow pace of anticipated tightening helps keep long-term rates down—the yield curve

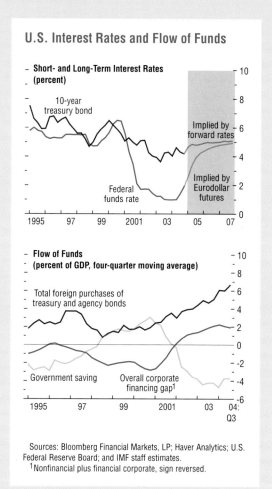

U.S. Interest Rates and Flow of Funds

Sources: Bloomberg Financial Markets, LP; Haver Analytics; U.S. Federal Reserve Board; and IMF staff estimates.
[1]Nonfinancial plus financial corporate, sign reversed.

Note: The author of this box is Calvin Schnure.
[1]Low rates are not simply a U.S. phenomenon, and indeed nominal yields in many industrialized countries are below those on U.S. treasuries.
[2]The outstanding stock of mortgages as a share of GDP is at a record high, having risen by an unprecedented 9 percentage points since 2001, to 61 percent.

implies that 10-year interest rates would rise by some 50 basis points over this period. However, this would still leave nominal and real rates well below historical averages, which Chairman Greenspan has described as "a conundrum."

Beyond the expected path of monetary policy—and the possibility that markets are simply mispricing—current yields could also reflect a range of factors, including economic fundamentals, structural considerations, and cyclical dynamics. Among these are the following.

• Economic fundamentals appear unlikely to help explain the remaining gap in long-term yields. The U.S. government is projected to continue to run a sizable fiscal deficit over the next few years, implying significant issuance of government bonds that will tend to raise real returns. Technological change associated with the information technology (IT) revolution also appears to have raised the trend growth of productivity and real GDP, increasing the rate of return on capital and hence real interest rates (see Laubach and Williams, 2001).

- Structural factors could be playing a role in depressing long-term yields. Greater risk aversion induced a flight to quality after the equity market decline in 2000, increasing demand for government bonds and moderating yields. In addition, regulatory changes such as those encouraging a closer match between the duration of assets and liabilities of pension funds may have also bolstered demand for long-term bonds (these issues are discussed in more detail in the IMF's April 2005 *Global Financial Stability Report*).

- Cyclical factors, in the form of an ample supply of loanable funds, are also likely to be depressing long-term real interest rates. Firms and foreign investors are providing record sums. With buoyant corporate profitability as yet not significantly offset by higher investment, the overall corporate financing gap of nonfinancial and financial businesses has improved by an unprecedented 5 percentage points of GDP since 2001 (see the figure). Over the same period, inflows of foreign capital have risen by a similar ratio, with about half of the increase coming from foreign official purchases of U.S. treasury and agency securities—largely reflecting reserve accumulation in emerging Asia—and the remainder from the private sector. The resulting increase in the supply of funds has more than offset the rapid rise in borrowing by the government over the same period, helping to put downward pressure on real rates.

Against this background, what might be the risks of an unexpected rise in U.S. long-term interest rates? The most benign scenario would be if long-term interest rates were driven upward by a reduction in net loanable funds owing to increased investment by domestic

firms. While the rise in rates could have adverse consequences for the domestic housing market and consumption, rising business investment would help offset the effects on aggregate demand. That said, higher U.S. bond yields would have negative spillovers to the rest of the world through borrowing costs, as long-term interest rates are highly correlated across countries and emerging market spreads generally rise in tandem with U.S. long-term rates.

A rise in interest rates unaccompanied by higher aggregate demand—for instance, driven by a weakening of corporate profits or a rise in inflationary pressures—would be a significantly greater concern. One worrisome scenario is that labor productivity growth slows more than currently expected, squeezing profit margins, lowering equity valuations, and driving up wage pressures as slack in labor markets is reduced. Again, the upward pressure on U.S. long-term interest rates would likely dampen demand for housing as well as consumer spending, but with no offset from stronger business investment. Lower domestic demand would also exacerbate international spillovers by reducing demand for foreign goods. More generally, the impact of slower productivity growth could have other negative consequences for growth and inflation in the United States and elsewhere.[3]

Finally, a reduction in the net supply of funds from the rest of the world could generate similar risks for the U.S. economy, but not necessarily for other countries. Such an outcome could reflect a reduced foreign private sector appetite for U.S. assets owing to concerns about the value of the dollar or a tapering of official inflows. The consequences elsewhere would depend upon the reasons for a slowing of funds to the United States. Assuming the slowing largely reflected more pessimistic perceptions of the U.S. economy, it could conceivably increase the funds available in other markets.

---

[3]Further increases in risk aversion in response to negative shocks in general could provide some offsetting downward pressure on U.S. bond yields through a "flight to quality."

Table 1.4. Advanced Economies: Real GDP, Consumer Prices, and Unemployment
(Annual percent change and percent of labor force)

	Real GDP				Consumer Prices				Unemployment			
	2003	2004	2005	2006	2003	2004	2005	2006	2003	2004	2005	2006
Advanced economies	**2.0**	**3.4**	**2.6**	**3.0**	**1.8**	**2.0**	**2.0**	**1.9**	**6.6**	**6.3**	**6.1**	**6.0**
United States	3.0	4.4	3.6	3.6	2.3	2.7	2.7	2.4	6.0	5.5	5.3	5.2
Euro area[1]	0.5	2.0	1.6	2.3	2.1	2.2	1.9	1.7	8.7	8.8	8.7	8.4
Germany	−0.1	1.7	0.8	1.9	1.0	1.8	1.5	1.2	9.6	9.2	9.4	9.2
France	0.5	2.3	2.0	2.2	2.2	2.3	2.0	1.9	9.5	9.7	9.5	8.9
Italy	0.3	1.2	1.2	2.0	2.8	2.3	1.8	1.8	8.7	8.3	8.0	7.6
Spain	2.5	2.7	2.8	3.0	3.1	3.1	3.1	2.7	11.3	10.8	10.3	9.9
Netherlands[2]	−0.9	1.3	1.5	2.2	2.2	1.4	1.4	1.1	3.8	4.6	5.3	5.0
Belgium	1.3	2.7	2.1	2.3	1.5	1.9	2.2	2.0	7.9	7.8	7.8	7.7
Austria	0.8	2.0	2.1	2.3	1.3	2.0	2.0	1.8	4.4	4.5	4.5	4.2
Finland	2.4	3.7	3.1	3.0	1.3	0.1	1.3	1.6	9.0	8.8	8.4	8.1
Greece	4.7	4.2	3.0	3.0	3.4	3.1	3.1	3.1	9.7	8.9	8.8	8.8
Portugal	−1.2	1.0	1.8	2.3	3.3	2.5	2.2	2.2	6.4	6.8	6.8	6.8
Ireland	3.7	5.1	4.8	4.6	4.0	2.3	2.1	2.0	4.6	4.5	4.1	4.0
Luxembourg	2.4	4.4	3.5	3.4	2.0	2.2	2.3	2.4	3.8	4.4	4.8	5.2
Japan	1.4	2.6	0.8	1.9	−0.2	—	−0.2	—	5.3	4.7	4.5	4.4
United Kingdom[1]	2.2	3.1	2.6	2.6	1.4	1.3	1.7	2.0	5.0	4.8	4.7	4.7
Canada	2.0	2.8	2.8	3.0	2.7	1.8	2.1	1.9	7.6	7.2	7.2	7.1
Korea	3.1	4.6	4.0	5.2	3.5	3.6	2.9	3.0	3.4	3.5	3.6	3.3
Australia	3.4	3.2	2.6	3.3	2.8	2.3	2.7	2.7	6.1	5.5	5.1	5.3
Taiwan Province of China	3.3	5.7	4.0	4.3	−0.3	1.6	1.6	1.5	5.0	4.6	4.3	4.2
Sweden	1.5	3.5	3.0	2.5	2.3	1.1	1.6	2.4	4.9	5.5	5.1	4.4
Switzerland	−0.4	1.7	1.2	2.0	0.6	0.8	1.2	1.0	3.4	3.5	3.7	3.5
Hong Kong SAR	3.2	8.1	4.0	4.0	−2.6	−0.4	1.0	1.1	7.9	6.8	5.7	4.9
Denmark	0.4	2.3	2.2	1.9	2.1	1.2	2.0	1.8	5.8	5.9	5.6	5.5
Norway	0.4	2.9	3.7	2.8	2.5	0.4	1.4	2.1	4.5	4.4	4.0	4.0
Israel	1.3	4.3	3.7	3.6	0.7	−0.4	1.0	2.0	10.8	10.4	9.8	9.5
Singapore	1.4	8.4	4.0	4.5	0.5	1.7	1.5	1.5	4.7	4.0	3.6	3.4
New Zealand[3]	3.4	5.0	2.8	2.6	1.8	2.3	3.0	2.7	4.6	3.9	3.8	4.2
Cyprus	1.9	3.7	3.8	4.0	4.1	2.3	2.5	2.5	3.5	3.4	3.2	3.0
Iceland	4.3	5.7	5.4	2.5	2.1	3.1	3.4	3.5	3.3	3.1	2.3	1.7
Memorandum												
Major advanced economies	2.0	3.3	2.5	2.9	1.7	2.0	1.9	1.8	6.7	6.3	6.2	6.0
Newly industrialized Asian economies	3.1	5.5	4.0	4.8	1.5	2.4	2.2	2.3	4.3	4.1	4.0	3.7

[1]Based on Eurostat's harmonized index of consumer prices.
[2]The consumer price forecast does not include any possible statistical effects from the planned reform of the health care system in 2006.
[3]Consumer prices excluding interest rate components.

estimated to have reached 4.4 percent, significantly above potential (Table 1.4).

With incoming data generally robust, and business and consumer confidence strong, the outlook for 2005 is encouraging. GDP growth is projected to average 3.6 percent, somewhat higher than expected in the September 2004 *World Economic Outlook,* with a moderation in private consumption growth—reflecting the gradual withdrawal of fiscal and monetary stimulus and some rebuilding of household savings—offset by continued strength in investment. The risks to the forecast appear broadly balanced,

with upside risks from the strength of corporate balance sheets, as well as rising housing and equity prices, offset by the possibility of a more pronounced rebound in household savings, higher long-run interest rates (see below), and continued oil price volatility.

The current account deficit has, however, continued to widen—to 5.7 percent of GDP for 2004 (Table 1.5)—despite the significant nominal effective depreciation of the dollar over the past three years. In part, this can be explained by faster growth in the United States relative to its advanced economy trading partners over the

Table 1.5. Selected Economies: Current Account Positions

(Percent of GDP)

	2003	2004	2005	2006
Advanced economies	**−0.8**	**−1.0**	**−1.1**	**−1.1**
United States	−4.8	−5.7	−5.8	−5.7
Euro area[1]	0.3	0.4	0.5	0.5
Germany	2.2	3.6	3.8	3.4
France	0.3	−0.3	−0.4	−0.1
Italy	−1.5	−1.5	−1.3	−0.9
Spain	−2.8	−5.0	−4.8	−5.4
Netherlands	2.9	3.4	4.2	4.5
Belgium	4.4	4.2	4.3	4.2
Austria	−0.9	−0.7	−1.0	−1.1
Finland	4.2	4.5	4.7	5.0
Greece	−6.2	−4.1	−3.5	−3.2
Portugal	−5.5	−7.9	−7.1	−6.9
Ireland	−1.4	−1.5	−1.7	−1.4
Luxembourg	9.4	7.1	9.2	10.1
Japan	3.2	3.7	3.3	3.5
United Kingdom	−1.7	−2.2	−2.3	−2.4
Canada	2.0	2.6	2.6	2.5
Korea	2.0	3.9	3.6	2.9
Australia	−5.9	−6.4	−5.6	−5.7
Taiwan Province of China	10.2	6.2	6.6	5.9
Sweden	7.6	8.1	6.1	7.0
Switzerland	13.2	12.0	11.1	11.3
Hong Kong SAR	10.3	9.6	9.4	9.3
Denmark	3.0	1.4	1.9	1.7
Norway	12.8	13.7	16.2	14.9
Israel	0.1	0.1	−0.2	—
Singapore	29.2	26.1	23.4	22.9
New Zealand	−4.2	−6.2	−6.4	−6.6
Cyprus	−3.4	−4.1	−3.4	−2.7
Iceland	−4.1	−5.2	−10.1	−11.8
Memorandum				
Major advanced economies	−1.6	−1.7	−1.9	−1.8
Euro area[2]	0.3	0.6	0.4	0.4
Newly industrialized Asian economies	7.4	7.1	6.8	6.2

[1]Calculated as the sum of the balances of individual euro area countries.

[2]Corrected for reporting discrepancies in intra-area transactions.

same period, and the lags with which exchange rate changes can be expected to feed through to net exports.[6] Indeed, little improvement is expected over the medium term, for a number of reasons: the growth differential in favor of the United States is expected to persist, offsetting some of the lagged effects of exchange rate movements; planned medium-term fiscal adjust-

ment is insufficiently ambitious in contributing to increased national savings; and private investment levels are expected to catch up with historical norms. In addition, the combination of higher U.S. interest rates and rising net foreign liabilities will lead to an inexorable rise in interest payments abroad.

The market's concerns about the medium-term sustainability of the current account deficit have been the main factor driving the weakening of the U.S. dollar, although financing of the deficit thus far has not been a problem. Portfolio investment into the United States by both private and official investors has remained resilient despite the dollar's weakening. Foreign investors maintained a steady demand for debt securities, including treasury, agency, and corporate bonds throughout 2004, and they also stepped up purchases of equities by the end of the year. Purchases of securities originating or routed through Europe dominated, supported by rising Japanese investor interest in high-grade bonds and a pickup in official purchases from Asia late in the year.

Inflationary pressures have remained generally modest owing to the continued presence of economic slack and benign labor market conditions (Figure 1.10). Core inflation indicators have edged up, but second-round effects of the increase in oil prices have been generally well contained. The latter is, in part, attributable to the clear communication strategy of the Federal Reserve, which also ensured an orderly market response once the tightening cycle got under way in June 2004. Looking ahead, however, policy rates still have significant room to rise from their current low real levels before monetary policy becomes more neutral. The Federal Reserve's policy of tightening at a measured pace therefore remains appropriate for the time being, conditional on signs of inflationary trends in incoming economic data releases. The main risks to inflation are from pressures in the labor

[6]Federal Reserve Chairman Greenspan recently (in remarks at the Advance Enterprise 2005 Conference, February 4, 2005) suggested that increased hedging and greater variability in profit margins of foreign exporters may have lengthened the lag with which exchange rates affect net exports.

Figure 1.10. United States: Selected Financial and Economic Indicators

Inflation and interest rates remain subdued, and domestic demand is robust.

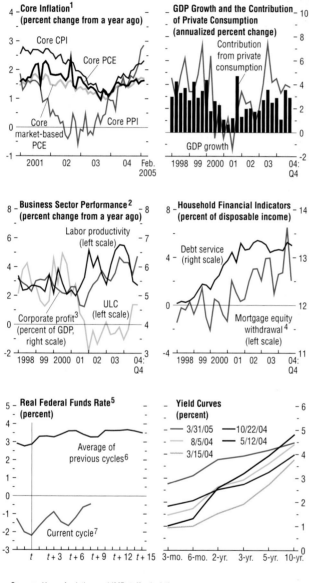

Sources: Haver Analytics; and IMF staff calculations.
[1] Excluding food and energy. PCE refers to personal consumption expenditure.
[2] Labor productivity and unit labor cost (ULC) in the nonfarm business sector. Corporate profit is after-tax profit without inventory valuation and capital consumption adjustments.
[3] After-tax corporate profit without inventory valuation and capital consumption adjustments.
[4] Defined as home mortgage borrowing less nominal residential investment.
[5] Federal funds rate minus year-over-year CPI inflation.
[6] Includes four tightening cycles, which began in March 1984, August 1987, April 1994, and July 1999 based on the Federal Reserve Board's discount window borrowing rate.
[7] Tightening began in June 2004 based on the Federal Reserve Board's discount window primary credit.

market, as slack diminishes and labor productivity slows, as well as from a further rise in oil prices.

A striking feature of the current conjuncture has been the persistently low level of long-term interest rates, although they have risen by some 60 basis points since early February (Box 1.2). From the beginning of the current U.S. monetary tightening cycle through early February, long-term interest rates actually declined as investor interest in fixed income securities persisted and inflationary expectations remained well anchored, leading to a substantial flattening of the yield curve. This, in turn, is likely to have moderated the impact on economic activity of the increase in policy interest rates. Adverse inflation surprises, a further weakening of the dollar and a sudden portfolio shift out of U.S. securities, a large-scale switch into equities from bonds, or increased long-term borrowing by the corporate sector all have the potential to lead to further upward pressures on long-term interest rates. Corporate balance sheets, after several years of restructuring, appear reasonably resilient to any abrupt long-term rate rises, but segments of the household sector, especially if faced with significantly slowing housing prices, may be forced to increase savings rapidly. The financial market impact of a sharp rise in interest rates is difficult to assess, but the long period of low interest rates and consequent risk taking may well have created pockets of exposure highly vulnerable to unexpected interest rate increases, and market intermediaries and regulators need to be vigilant to signs of emerging stresses.

The U.S. fiscal deficit (as a percentage of GDP) is now the largest among the major advanced economies, with the exception of Japan. Fiscal consolidation presents an important policy challenge going forward, both to ensure medium-term fiscal sustainability in the United States and to facilitate an orderly reduction in global current account imbalances. The U.S. administration's FY2006 budget proposal reiterates its commitment to halve the central government deficit by 2009, although a slight

Box 1.3. The Ending of Global Textile Trade Quotas

On January 1, 2005, quantitative restrictions that had been limiting trade in textiles and clothing for the past 40 years were eliminated. Up to the end of the Uruguay Round in 1994, trade in textiles and clothing was governed by over 1,300 bilateral quotas as part of the Multifiber Arrangement (MFA). In 1995, the MFA was replaced by the World Trade Organization (WTO) Agreement on Textiles and Clothing (ATC), which set a 10-year transitional period for the phasing out of the quotas. In practice, liberalization took place mostly at the beginning of 2005. Of the four WTO members that maintained import restrictions under the MFA, only Norway eliminated its quotas ahead of schedule.[1] In contrast, Canada, the European Economic Communities (EEC), and the United States backloaded liberalization. As a result, 83 percent of quotas covering about 80 percent of the value of imports under quotas during the ATC's reference period were left to be eliminated in 2005.

The quota expiry affects an important share of developing country exports. The United States and European Union alone accounted for more than half of the almost $400 billion in world imports of textiles and clothing in 2003, and developing countries for almost two-thirds of world exports. For about half a dozen countries textiles and clothing exports represent more than 50 percent of total exports. Unsurprisingly, therefore, during much of the 1990s, developing countries criticized the European Union and the United States for the slow pace of their liberalization.

Recently, however, there have been increasing concerns about the impact of liberalization. While developing countries overall are expected to benefit significantly in terms of exports and employment, the gains will be distributed unevenly. The quota system ended up protecting the export markets of the less competitive developing country exporters. Thus, some countries may face balance of payments pressures stemming from the liberalization as well as significant adjustment costs—the textiles and clothing industry often accounts for a disproportionate share of manufacturing employment and is geographically concentrated.

Experience from the elimination of earlier quotas, model simulations, and exporters' relative success in quota-free markets all indicate that only a handful of countries—in particular, China, India, and Pakistan—may end up reaping the benefits of liberalization. The phasing out of some textiles quotas in 2002 led to a sharp change in the structure of imports into the European Union and the United States. For these products, only China, Romania, and the Czech Republic were able to increase their exports to the European Union, while only China, Pakistan, and India increased their exports to the United States. Moreover, because of increased competition, the elimination of quota premia, and sluggish global demand, unit prices decreased substantially.

The table presents the results of an IMF staff simulation with the GTAP model of international trade. A flurry of other published simulations of the impact of the quota expiry virtually all come to similar conclusions.[2] The experience of traditionally quota-free countries also suggests that the liberalization might lead to a consolidation in the number of source countries and confirms the competitive strength of China, India, and Pakistan. China accounts for more than half of imports of clothing into South Africa, Australia, and Japan, which were quota-free markets. (Interestingly, China's share in Switzerland's imports of clothing did not increase and remained at the low level of about 10 percent.) China's potential exports attract

Note: The author of this box is Jean-Jacques Hallaert. Yongzheng Yang ran the GTAP simulation.
[1]In 1994, the MFA had 44 members, but only 6 participants (Canada, the EEC, the United States, Norway, Austria, and Finland) applied restraints under the Arrangement. Austria and Finland joined the EEC in 1995.

[2]For a review of quantitative studies, see OECD (2004).

Box 1.3 *(concluded)*

**Impact of Quota Elimination on Textiles and
Clothing Exports**

	Exports	
	Billions of 1997 U.S. dollars	Changes in percent
Developing countries	19.0	9.6
China	24.2	51.2
India	10.3	97.2
Rest of south Asia	1.5	12.1
Middle East and north Africa	−2.8	−29.9
Mexico	−3.3	−44.4
Central America and Caribbean	−4.3	−47.3
South America	−0.2	−7.0
Southern African Customs Union	−0.2	−21.3
Rest of sub-Saharan Africa	−0.4	−21.6

Source: IMF staff simulation with the Global Trade Analysis Project (GTAP) model.

Note: For a description of the GTAP modeling framework, see Hertel (1997). The model uses data for 1997. As a result, recent regional trade arrangements and preferential schemes such as the Everything but Arms (EBA) initiative and the African Growth and Opportunity Act (AGOA), which have an impact on textiles and clothing trade, are not taken into account.

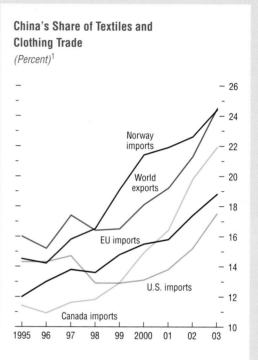

China's Share of Textiles and Clothing Trade
(Percent)[1]

Source: World Trade Organization.
[1]China's share of world exports of textiles and clothing; and China's share of imports of textiles and clothing by Canada, European Union, the United States, and Norway.

much attention because while China already accounts for a rapidly growing share of world textiles and clothing exports (see the figure), its market share is expected to increase still further in the period ahead. And indeed, dynamic growth in China's imports of textiles and clothing machinery suggests that production capacities are building up.

The prospects for rapid and substantial change in world markets have prompted protectionist action targeting mainly China. Calls by some developing countries at the WTO to extend the quota system for a number of additional years were unsuccessful. U.S. manufacturers have filed a flurry of petitions under the special textiles safeguards included in China's WTO accession protocol, which allows limiting temporarily the increase in imports of Chinese textiles and clothing products that cause "market disruption." In contrast, the European Commission has not yet taken recourse to safeguards, but has indicated that it would take action if Chinese imports were diverted to the EU market as a result of U.S. safeguards. The European Commission has also proposed to

exclude imports of Chinese textiles and clothing from its Generalized System of Preferences scheme (GSP). Finally, both the European Union and the United States have publicly called on the Chinese authorities to take steps to moderate China's exports of textiles and clothing. China announced recently that it would impose export taxes on 146 categories of textiles and clothing exports. (Turkey also imposed safeguards against Chinese exports. Argentina has established the legal framework for the use of safeguards against Chinese exports.)

Model simulations suggest that restraining Chinese exports may slow the speed of structural change in the textiles and clothing sector but would not eliminate it, in part because other competitive suppliers—for example, in south Asia—could be expected to take advantage of restrictions on China. Moreover, this process is likely to distort the world market—distortions that the ATC intended to eliminate. Because quotas limited exports from efficient producers, importers such as retailers maintained a diversified supplier network, which they intend to streamline substantially when the quotas are eliminated. But the protectionist activity appears to have sown uncertainty, prompting importers to maintain a more diversified sourcing structure than they otherwise might have. As a result, the adjustment shock on less competitive suppliers would be lessened, though one would expect this effect to gradually weaken over time.

How should countries respond to the competitive challenge? The appropriate response is specific to country circumstances. In some cases, countries may be able to specialize in particular market niches. A common theme must surely be to tackle avoidable export hurdles. This might include cutting red tape, ensuring that access to low-priced inputs is not encumbered by import barriers or financing restrictions, ensuring the most efficient transport logistics, and creating an environment that favors investment.

increase in the nominal deficit is projected this fiscal year, largely reflecting supplemental funding for Iraq and Afghanistan. Medium-term fiscal plans are, however, not ambitious enough, and there are substantial risks that even they will not be achieved. Current budgetary plans assume historically tight expenditure restraint—with an envisaged reduction in nondefense discretionary spending to its lowest share of GDP in over 40 years—and do not include additional funding for Iraq and Afghanistan or the costs of reforming the Alternative Minimum Tax and social security.

Looking ahead, fiscal policies should aim for structural balance, excluding Social Security, over the course of the economic cycle. This objective would require a reduction of the deficit by 1 percentage point of GDP each year through the rest of the decade. With limits to discretionary spending cuts, broadening the tax base—including by shifting toward a more consumption-based system—will need to play an important role toward more ambitious consolidation. The recent appointment of a bipartisan panel on tax reform could play a facilitating role in these endeavors, including by exploring the potential for measures such as reducing the wide array of tax write-offs. The recent emphasis on Social Security reform is also welcome, but personal retirement accounts will not be sufficient

to place the program on a financially sound footing to avoid widening fiscal deficits and rising debt in the coming decades, and will entail significant transition costs in the medium term. The priority needs to be on eliminating the funding deficits of the system by slowing benefit growth and/or increasing contributions. The much larger unfunded liabilities of the Medicare system also need attention, with the recent drug benefit plan exacerbating the system's enormous funding gap.

In Canada, growth recovered to 2.8 percent in 2004, aided by booming commodity prices. The economy is expected to maintain its momentum in 2005 underpinned by strong gains in employment and solid corporate earnings. With signs of shrinking economic slack, the Bank of Canada began to gradually withdraw stimulus in the fall, but has paused more recently in response to the currency's appreciation and little sign of inflation and wage pressures. A measured and patient pace of tightening remains appropriate in this context. Fiscal policy has contributed to maintaining the sound macroeconomic performance, with the general government running a significant surplus. In light of the implications of changing demographics, the government's ongoing plan to reduce debt ratios is appropriately ambitious, but priority also needs to

Box 1.4. What Progress Has Been Made in Implementing Policies to Reduce Global Imbalances?

Global imbalances have become more accentuated over the past year. In the United States, the current account deficit has widened to 5.7 percent of GDP, while the surplus in Japan has increased. Emerging Asia has continued to run a large current account surplus, and current account surpluses have increased in the Middle East and Russia as high oil prices have provided a significant boost to export revenues—in dollar terms, these surpluses are currently of a magnitude broadly similar to those in emerging Asia and Japan. As a result of these developments, the net external liabilities of the United States, equivalent to 25 percent of GDP and over 250 percent of exports at end-2003, have increased further, and the net external assets of emerging Asian countries, Japan, the Middle East, and Russia have risen.

Since one country's deficit is another country's surplus, policies to support an orderly resolution of global imbalances are a shared responsibility. In the Communiqué of the last meeting of the International Monetary and Financial Committee (IMFC) in October 2004, IMF Governors therefore underscored the importance of progress in several areas, including medium-term fiscal consolidation in the United States; steps toward greater exchange rate flexibility in emerging Asia, accompanied by continued financial sector reform, as appropriate; and continued structural reforms to boost growth in Europe and Japan. While there has been some progress toward implementing the strategy outlined above, it remains limited.

- In its recent budget, the U.S. administration reiterated its commitment to halve the central government fiscal deficit by 2009. The IMF staff continues to believe that this objective is insufficiently ambitious; moreover, there are substantial risks that it will not be achieved, since the projections exclude any additional funding for Afghanistan and Iraq; do not take into account the costs of reforming the

Note: The main authors of this box are Tim Callen and Gian Maria Milesi-Ferretti.

Global Current Account Imbalances

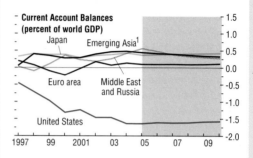

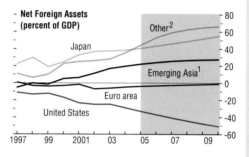

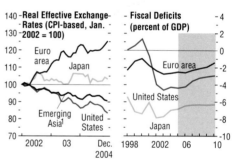

[1]Consists of China, Hong Kong SAR, India, Indonesia, Korea, Malaysia, the Philippines, Singapore, Taiwan Province of China, and Thailand.
[2]Consists of Egypt, Jordan, Kuwait, Oman, Russia, and Saudi Arabia.

Alternative Minimum Tax or of Social Security reform; and assume an unprecedented degree of expenditure restraint.

- There has been some progress in advancing structural reforms in Europe—including labor market reforms in Germany (Hartz IV) and France (allowing an enterprise to negotiate deviations from the 35-hour work week collectively with its labor force) and raising the effective retirement age in Italy—but, overall, the implementation and impact of the Lisbon strategy have been mixed at best, and reform fatigue has set in early. The European Commission has therefore recently proposed to prioritize the reform agenda, focusing more directly on measures to raise productivity and increase employment, although the recent rejection of the European Commission proposals to liberalize trade in services is a setback to reform efforts. In Japan, banks have continued to strengthen their balance sheets—nonperforming loans have declined further and capital positions have improved—and indicators of corporate financial health have improved. However, as discussed in the main text, significant problems remain, underscoring the need for further progress. Little has been done to tackle the inefficient nontraded goods sector.

- In emerging Asia, some currencies—including the Korean won, Thai baht, Taiwan dollar, and the Indian rupee—have exhibited somewhat greater flexibility against the U.S. dollar since mid-2004. Elsewhere, no concrete actions have been taken, although preparations for more flexible exchange rate management have continued—including through ongoing efforts to strengthen the banking system in China. In terms of financial sector reforms—which are key to sustaining stronger domestic demand in many of the NIEs and ASEAN-4—financial soundness indicators continue to improve,[1] but significant challenges remain, including further reducing high nonperforming loans and accelerating progress in debt restructuring in Taiwan Province of

China and Thailand and addressing the household debt delinquency problem in Korea.

In sum, despite some progress, a credible policy package to address the imbalances over the medium term does not yet appear to be in place. Indeed, the current *World Economic Outlook* projections—which are based on the assumption of constant real exchange rates—envisage little change in the current constellation of global imbalances over the medium term. Specifically, the U.S. current account deficit remains around 5.5 percent of GDP while the surplus in Japan increases to over 4 percent of GDP. Surpluses in emerging Asia, the Middle East, and Russia are projected to narrow, although this will importantly depend on reforms to boost domestic demand in emerging Asia and on the pace at which higher oil revenues are spent in the latter two. The lack of progress in reducing imbalances clearly raises risks in the future. An abrupt decline in investors' appetite for dollar-denominated liabilities—a low-probability but high-cost event—could engender a rapid dollar depreciation and a sharp increase in U.S. interest rates, with potentially serious adverse consequences for global growth and international financial markets.

Finally, it should be noted that the global current account discrepancy widens by 0.4 percentage point of world output during 2004–10, indicating growing multilateral inconsistency in the projections. While some rise in the discrepancy is normal in an environment of rising interest rates and slowing global trade growth,[2] this nonetheless represents an additional important uncertainty about the future behavior of global imbalances.

[1]See Chapter II of the April 2005 *Global Financial Stability Report* for a detailed discussion.

[2]See Appendix II, Chapter 1, of the October 2000 *World Economic Outlook* for a detailed discussion.

continue to be given to structural reforms aimed at boosting productivity growth and economic flexibility. Fundamental reforms to

increase the efficiency of health care systems are also needed to cope with emerging demographic pressures.

Western Europe: Renewed Concerns About the Strength of the Recovery

The modest recovery that had taken place in the euro area since mid-2003 lost momentum during the second half of 2004. Domestic demand has remained subdued against the backdrop of high and volatile oil prices and long-standing structural weaknesses, while slower global growth and the appreciation of the euro have undercut export growth, which was a key driver of the economy in the first half of 2004. Strong profit growth has yet to feed into a decisive upturn in investment spending as companies continue to focus on restructuring their balance sheets, while slow wage and employment growth and lagging confidence have held back consumption. As a result, area-wide GDP grew by just 0.2 percent (quarter-on-quarter) in both the third and fourth quarters of 2004. Activity contracted in Germany, Italy, the Netherlands, and Greece in the fourth quarter, but growth accelerated in France and Spain.

Economic indicators in early 2005 have been very mixed. While industrial production and retail sales in the euro area firmed in January, business and consumer confidence have generally been weak. Against this background, the 2005 growth forecast has been revised down to 1.6 percent (compared with 2.2 percent in the September 2004 *World Economic Outlook*). Underlying this projection is the assumption that growth will gradually pick up during the course of the year, although at a slower rate than previously expected. The favorable global environment is expected to underpin exports, investment should strengthen as corporate profits remain healthy, and a gradual improvement in the labor market is expected to support a pickup in consumer spending. The risks to this outlook, however, lie predominantly on the downside.

- Growth remains overly reliant on global developments, particularly in Germany, where external demand accounted for three-fourths of growth in 2004. German exports have grown strongly, boosted by the marked decline in unit labor costs and the favorable export structure—a high share of IT-related goods, a high proportion of exports going to China and the United States, and limited exposure to competition in third markets from emerging Asian countries (Figure 1.11). However, if large global current account imbalances put renewed upward pressure on the euro, or the downturn in the IT sector is more prolonged than expected, export growth will be affected.

- High and volatile oil prices, a drop in business confidence, an increase in household saving in the face of ongoing uncertainties about future pension and healthcare reforms, or a sharp drop in house prices in some countries— notably Ireland and Spain—could hold back domestic demand.

Headline inflation in the euro area continues to hover around 2 percent owing to the effects of oil price increases and hikes in indirect taxes and administered prices. Underlying price pressures, including wage and unit labor costs, however, are well contained—consumer price index (CPI) inflation excluding energy, food, alcohol, and tobacco was 1.4 percent in February 2005, compared with 2 percent in mid-2004— and headline inflation is expected to fall below 2 percent later this year as the impact of one-off factors wane. In these circumstances, monetary policy should remain firmly on hold until a self-sustaining recovery is clearly in place. Indeed, a further cut in interest rates cannot be ruled out if current economic weakness or a further appreciation of the euro were to result in lower-than-expected inflation.

Although fiscal deficits in the euro area are smaller than in the other major currency areas, public debt levels are high, and policy settings remain insufficient to deliver the budgetary adjustments required to cope with the fiscal pressures of population aging. The euro area–wide fiscal deficit is estimated at 2.7 percent of GDP in 2004, with deficits in France, Germany, and Greece all exceeding 3 percent of GDP. Budgets for 2005 envisage varying degrees of fiscal consolidation across the euro area. Although budgetary adjustments are projected in France and Germany, they rely on one-off measures, and questions remain whether the policies are in place to achieve and sustain the targets, while in Italy the budget deficit is projected to increase substantially. A faster-than-currently-planned pace of fiscal consolidation is needed in countries with weak budget positions, based on high-quality measures, allowing the automatic fiscal stabilizers to operate around the adjustment paths.

Reforms to the Stability and Growth Pact (SGP) have recently been agreed in Europe. The agreement provides governments with significant additional fiscal policy flexibility. It does not, however, strengthen enforcement mechanisms under the pact, which have proved ineffective in the past (France and Germany have been in breach of the deficit limit for three successive years and there has been fiscal misreporting by Greece), nor the incentives to adjust in good times—the Achilles' heel of euro area fiscal policies. A strong fiscal framework clearly remains an essential part of monetary union in Europe, and it is important that the implementation of the reformed SGP restore the credibility of the framework. In the final analysis, this credibility depends on fiscal policies at the national level, particularly in the larger countries. The reformed SGP's encouragement of better domestic governance arrangements is thus welcome. The establishment of national budgetary councils to publish independent assessments of budgetary policies and the long-term sustainability of public finances could be helpful in fostering transparency and greater public awareness and debate about appropriate fiscal policies.

Structural reforms need to be at the heart of Europe's efforts to improve its growth performance; higher potential growth, in turn, would help strengthen the medium-term fiscal position and facilitate the operation of the SGP. Labor utilization rates need to be raised in the face of stagnating working-age populations, while total factor productivity growth in the euro area has not matched the acceleration seen in recent years in the United States. But, as the High-Level Group headed by Mr. Wim Kok recently concluded, progress with implementing the structural reform agenda in Europe has at

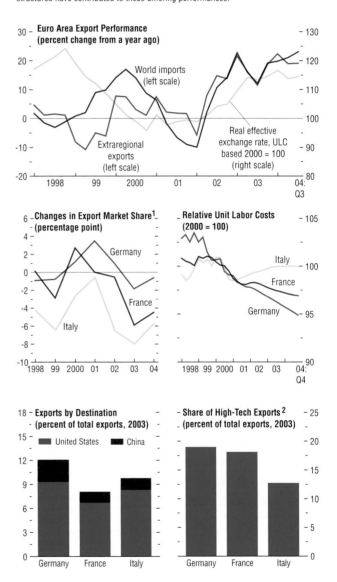

Figure 1.11. Western Europe: Export Performance in Germany, France, and Italy

Despite exchange rate appreciation, export performance in the euro area has been robust. It has, however, varied across countries, with Germany outperforming, and France and Italy underperforming. Trends in unit labor costs and export structures have contributed to these differing performances.

Sources: IMF, *Direction of Trade Statistics;* United Nations Commodity Trade database; and IMF staff calculations.
[1]Calculated as export volume growth minus partner countries import volume growth.
[2]Defined as exports of pharmaceutical products, office and data processing machines, telecommunications equipment, electrical equipment, and scientific instruments.

best been mixed over the past five years. On the positive side, in centrally led areas, such as the Financial Services Action Plan, important progress has been made, while reforms have also been initiated at the national level, including pension, health care, and labor market reforms in Germany (under Agenda 2010) and in France, and pension reforms—including raising the effective retirement age—in Italy. Nevertheless, these reforms need to be deepened and prioritized, with a greater focus placed on addressing current distortions in the labor market—particularly overly generous entitlement systems (reducing such entitlement benefits would also have fiscal savings), high tax wedges, and restrictive labor laws—and on promoting greater competition in product markets. In this regard, the recent rejection of the European Commission proposals to liberalize trade in services in Europe is a setback to reform efforts.

Economic performance in the United Kingdom remains robust. Having slowed gradually through the year, as higher mortgage rates and weaker house price appreciation dampened consumption, GDP growth is estimated at 3.1 percent in 2004 and is projected at 2.6 percent this year. Domestic demand remains the key driver of growth, underpinned by continued robust wage growth and strong corporate profitability. Relatively high consumer indebtedness and the possibility of a sharp drop in house prices do present risks to this outlook. With the economy operating at or near full capacity, the Bank of England has tightened monetary policy over the past year, and is well positioned to respond to unexpected developments in either direction. Fiscal policy has provided substantial stimulus in recent years, and steps are needed to accelerate the pace of fiscal consolidation—which is very modest in the recent budget—to meet the government's budgetary objectives over the course of the next economic cycle. A recent Interim Report by the Pensions Commission has questioned the adequacy of private saving for retirement, and it will be important to encourage higher saving to ensure

that pensioners do not fall back on the state in the future.

Elsewhere in Europe, growth in the Nordic countries accelerated in 2004, owing to exports (Sweden, Denmark), stronger investment (Sweden, Norway—the latter driven by the oil sector) and fiscal expansion (Norway and Sweden). In all three countries, monetary policy settings remain accommodative and will need to tighten as the recovery proceeds, while fiscal consolidation will be required to meet medium-term targets. In Switzerland, growth accelerated to 1.7 percent in 2004 as exports benefited from stronger global demand and expansionary fiscal and monetary policies boosted domestic demand. Monetary tightening has begun—although interest rates remain low—and measures will be needed to bring the fiscal position back to balance. Efforts to increase competition in domestic markets are needed to raise potential growth.

Japan: Will Growth Resume?

After growing strongly in the first quarter of 2004, the Japanese economy subsequently stalled, recording near-zero growth in the remainder of the year. Weaker global demand for IT products has undercut export and private sector investment growth, while consumption spending has declined. Real GDP is now estimated to have grown by 2.6 percent in 2004, some 1.8 percentage points lower than projected in the September 2004 *World Economic Outlook*, about 1 percent of which reflects methodological changes in the construction of the Japanese national accounts.

The stagnation of the economy during the last three quarters of 2004 has raised concerns about the short-term outlook. However, while there are downside risks, most notably from continued volatile oil prices and the possibility that a sharp appreciation of the yen could further undercut exports, there has been a noticeable improvement in economic fundamentals in recent years.

• The corporate sector is now stronger as profitability has increased (the ratio of current profits to sales stood at about 3.5 percent in

2004, the highest since the 1980s), leverage ratios have declined, and productivity gains have been made. Reflecting these improvements, corporate bankruptcies have fallen to their lowest level in a decade. Stronger corporate balance sheets and profits should support increased investment going forward.

- The banking sector has also strengthened its financial position. The major banks, in particular, have improved their capital base and reduced their nonperforming loans (which the government expects to fall to about 4 percent by March 2005), and this has resulted in credit rating upgrades. The banks' improved financial health has supported a more accommodative lending attitude, although outstanding credit continues to decline, albeit at a moderating pace.

- Japanese corporations have taken advantage of the changing structure of global production and significantly increased their exposure to the fast-growing Asian region. Reflecting these increased trade linkages and, more generally, an increased synchronization of Japan's business cycle with those of Asia (most notably China) and the United States since the late 1990s, net exports have been a key engine of growth in recent years (Figure 1.12). With activity in Asia and the United States expected to remain strong in the near term, this should support a resumption of export growth.

While recent indicators have been somewhat mixed, together with stronger fundamentals they broadly suggest that growth should regain some momentum during the course of this year, although this rebound will be tempered as firms run down their inventories (particularly in the IT sector). Consequently, the economy is expected to grow by 0.8 percent in 2005, accelerating to 1.9 percent in 2006.

While deflationary pressures have eased in recent years, with the year-on-year decline in the core CPI now close to zero, a further appreciation of the yen or a more prolonged economic slowdown could put downward pressures on prices. In these circumstances, the Bank of

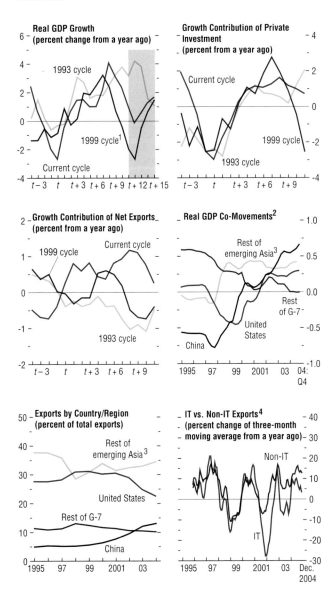

Figure 1.12. Japan: Where Is the Economy in the Current Expansion?

Net exports have been an engine of growth in the current expansion reflecting increased trade linkages and business cycle synchronization with Asia and the United States.

Sources: IMF, *Direction of Trade Statistics;* CEIC Data Company Limited; Haver Analytics; United Nations Commodity Trade database; and IMF staff estimates.
[1]Output growth during 1999 cycle peaked in 2000Q4.
[2]Ten-year rolling window of the year-over-year real GDP growth correlations.
[3]India, Indonesia, Hong Kong SAR, Korea, Malaysia, the Philippines, Singapore, Taiwan Province of China, and Thailand.
[4]IT defined as office machinery, automatic data processing machinery, telecommunication machinery, electronic integrated circuits, and scientific and optical instruments.

Japan should maintain a very accommodative monetary policy until deflation is decisively beaten. Consideration also needs to be given to the appropriate monetary framework for a post-deflation environment. In this regard, once deflationary pressures have receded, the announcement of an explicit medium-term inflation objective would be helpful to stabilize inflation expectations.

Against the background of high public debt and intensifying demographic pressures from population aging, fiscal consolidation is a priority. Notwithstanding the recently adopted tax measures, the structural fiscal deficit is projected to decline only slightly to 6.4 percent of GDP in 2005. Over the medium term, the government plans to achieve a primary surplus by the early 2010s. However, the measures to achieve this goal have yet to be specified and a sizable surplus may be needed to put the public finances on a sustainable path. To increase the credibility of its plans, the government should consider announcing specific measures to achieve them, including further cuts in public investment, a broadening of the tax base, and an increase in the consumption tax rate. The government also needs to push ahead with further social security reforms to rein in medical and long-term care expenditures.

To create the conditions for sustained growth over the medium term, Japan needs to accelerate its structural reform program.

- In the financial sector, bank profitability and capital bases need to be strengthened further so that these institutions are able to extend credit and support investment and growth. The government has recently announced a reform plan aimed at creating a more efficient and flexible financial system, including strengthening the regional banks. The government also plans to privatize Japan Post, and it will be important to ensure that a level playing field is created among the entities resulting from the breakup of Japan Post and their private sector competitors.
- In the corporate sector, despite recent welcome improvements, in some cases debt levels remain high and returns on assets low. The continued presence of unviable firms in a number of sectors negatively affects the profitability of healthier entities, implying that broader progress in corporate restructuring is needed.
- Other reform priorities are increasing competition in the sheltered sector of the economy (including deregulation in the retail sector and by facilitating market entry and exit), enhancing labor market flexibility (including by increasing pension portability), and public enterprise reform.

Emerging Asia and the Pacific: A Continuing Expansion, but External Surpluses Persist

GDP growth in emerging Asia picked up to 7.8 percent in 2004 (Table 1.6), 0.5 percent higher than projected last September, and the highest since the Asian crisis. This strong result, however, owed much to the buoyancy of activity in late 2003 and early 2004. Since that time—with the important exception of China—GDP growth in most countries has slowed noticeably, partly a return to more sustainable levels, but also reflecting the moderation of the global expansion, the correction in the semiconductor market, and higher oil prices (although the impact of the latter was muted because the region mainly imports heavy crudes whose price increased relatively less in 2004—Appendix 1.1). Headline and—to a lesser extent—core inflation rose, but as yet remain moderate. In some cases (notably India, Indonesia, Malaysia, and Thailand), this partly reflected substantial oil price subsidies, reflected in a commensurate deterioration in the fiscal position.

Recent developments have been dominated by the recent catastrophic tsunami, and the devastating losses of human life and property inflicted on Indonesia, Sri Lanka, India, Thailand, and several other countries in the region. As discussed in Box 1.1, reconstruction costs—and the impact on fiscal and external balances—in the affected countries will be

Table 1.6. Selected Asian Economies: Real GDP, Consumer Prices, and Current Account Balance
(Annual percent change unless otherwise noted)

	Real GDP				Consumer Prices[1]				Current Account Balance[2]			
	2003	2004	2005	2006	2003	2004	2005	2006	2003	2004	2005	2006
Emerging Asia[3]	**7.4**	**7.8**	**7.0**	**6.9**	**2.4**	**4.0**	**3.7**	**3.2**	**4.4**	**4.4**	**3.9**	**3.5**
China	9.3	9.5	8.5	8.0	1.2	3.9	3.0	2.5	3.2	4.2	4.2	4.0
South Asia[4]	**7.1**	**7.1**	**6.5**	**6.3**	**3.9**	**4.3**	**4.6**	**4.0**	**1.4**	**0.1**	**−0.7**	**−0.6**
India	7.5	7.3	6.7	6.4	3.8	3.8	4.0	3.6	1.2	0.3	−0.3	−0.3
Pakistan	5.6	6.5	6.7	6.3	2.9	6.7	7.9	6.5	4.1	0.3	−1.2	−0.8
Bangladesh	5.4	5.4	5.5	5.9	5.4	6.1	5.7	4.5	0.1	−1.2	−2.4	−2.5
ASEAN-4	**5.4**	**5.8**	**5.4**	**5.8**	**4.0**	**4.4**	**5.3**	**4.5**	**5.7**	**5.5**	**4.4**	**3.3**
Indonesia	4.9	5.1	5.5	6.0	6.8	6.1	7.0	6.5	3.0	2.8	2.2	0.9
Thailand	6.9	6.1	5.6	6.2	1.8	2.7	2.9	2.1	5.6	4.5	2.0	1.4
Philippines	4.7	6.1	4.7	4.5	3.0	5.5	6.8	4.9	4.3	4.6	2.6	2.0
Malaysia	5.3	7.1	6.0	6.2	1.1	1.4	2.5	2.5	12.9	13.3	13.6	12.2
Newly industrialized Asian economies	**3.1**	**5.5**	**4.0**	**4.8**	**1.5**	**2.4**	**2.2**	**2.3**	**7.4**	**7.1**	**6.8**	**6.2**
Korea	3.1	4.6	4.0	5.2	3.5	3.6	2.9	3.0	2.0	3.9	3.6	2.9
Taiwan Province of China	3.3	5.7	4.0	4.3	−0.3	1.6	1.6	1.5	10.2	6.2	6.6	5.9
Hong Kong SAR	3.2	8.1	4.0	4.0	−2.6	−0.4	1.0	1.1	10.3	9.6	9.4	9.3
Singapore	1.4	8.4	4.0	4.5	0.5	1.7	1.5	1.5	29.2	26.1	23.4	22.9

[1]In accordance with standard practice in the *World Economic Outlook*, movements in consumer prices are indicated as annual averages rather than as December/December changes during the year, as is the practice in some countries.
[2]Percent of GDP.
[3]Consists of developing Asia, the newly industrialized Asian economies, and Mongolia.
[4]Includes Bangladesh, India, Maldives, Nepal, Pakistan, and Sri Lanka.

substantial. However, in most cases—except Maldives and to a lesser extent Sri Lanka—the impact on GDP growth will be small, since the affected areas account for a small portion of output, and the adverse effects are largely offset by reconstruction activities. For 2005 as a whole, regional GDP growth is projected to slow to a still robust 7 percent, with a moderate slowdown in China, continued strong growth in India, and—in the NIEs and ASEAN-4—a gradual recovery from the slowdown in the second half of 2004, underpinned by strengthening domestic demand. Short-term risks are tilted somewhat to the downside. On the one hand, GDP growth in China could be stronger than expected, boosting activity—especially in the NIEs—in 2005, albeit at the risk of a more pronounced slowdown later on.[7] On the other hand, oil prices—including for heavy crudes—are presently significantly above the WEO baseline, and in some countries the eventual

pass-through of earlier increases will adversely affect demand. In addition, excess capacity in the IT sector could take longer than expected to work off, endangering the expected pickup in domestic demand, and external demand—particularly in Japan and Europe—could be weaker than expected. The Philippines and Indonesia are also relatively exposed to higher U.S. interest rates.

The tension between the objectives of maintaining low inflation and nominal exchange rate stability remains a key issue across the region. Given the strength of external positions, most countries are undertaking substantial sterilization, an activity that is generally costly and increasingly difficult to sustain over time (Figure 1.13). Looking forward, assuming constant real effective exchange rates, current account surpluses are generally expected to remain high (and given the rising global current account discrepancy—Box 1.4—risks are

[7]See "What Are the Risks of Slower Growth in China?" Box 1.2, *World Economic Outlook*, September 2004, for a detailed discussion.

Figure 1.13. Emerging Asia: Current Accounts, Savings, and Investment

High current account surpluses have been underpinned—to different extents—by strong productivity growth and savings, and relatively weak investment. Along with buoyant capital inflows, this has required substantial sterilization efforts across the region.

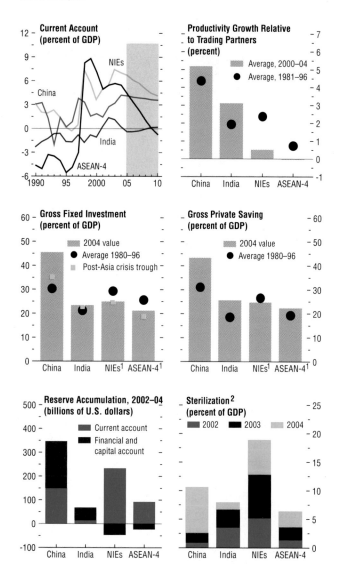

Sources: Bloomberg Financial Markets, LP; CEIC Data Company Limited; and IMF staff estimates.

[1]Weighted by PPP-GDP.

[2]Approximated as the increase in reserves minus the increase in base money.

on the upside); while individual country situations differ, regional currencies will likely need to appreciate significantly in real terms over the medium term. In these circumstances, barring unforeseen adverse developments, capital inflows may also remain buoyant. Against this background, greater exchange rate flexibility—both vis-à-vis the U.S. dollar and in trade-weighted terms—will be increasingly desirable from the perspective of short-run monetary management as well as consistent with medium-term fundamentals. While recent signs of greater exchange rate flexibility in a number of countries—notably Korea—are welcome, this now needs to be extended more broadly across the region.

Turning to individual countries, GDP growth in China—despite recent tightening measures—has remained very strong, with some slowdown in investment growth offset by a pickup in exports. While CPI inflation is still low, cost-push pressures—including wages and utility shortages, especially electricity—are becoming more widespread. Given the considerable economic momentum, further tightening of monetary conditions is likely to be required to prevent a resurgence of investment; with continued strong upward pressures on the renminbi from current and capital account inflows, this would be facilitated by greater exchange rate flexibility. The recent real effective depreciation of the renminbi and continued strong productivity growth relative to trading partners would help mitigate possible adverse effects on employment. On the fiscal side, the deficit in 2004 was considerably lower than budgeted primarily owing to surging revenues; maintaining a tight fiscal stance would help contain demand pressures, as well as help address medium-term expenditure pressures arising from potential bank restructuring and pension liabilities, and social and infrastructural needs. With investment in China extraordinarily high as a percentage of GDP, a key medium-term challenge is to improve the efficiency of investment, accompanied by a welfare-improving shift in the composition of demand toward consumption. In this connection, further progress with bank and public enterprise reforms remains critical; greater labor market flexibility—including easing restrictions on internal migration—would also help manage the challenges of a rapidly growing labor force.

In the NIEs and ASEAN-4 countries, with the expansion set to continue, monetary tightening cycles are generally under way, with the exception of Korea, where domestic demand continues to be held back by overindebtedness in the household and small and medium-sized enterprise sectors. While domestic demand growth has picked up, its level remains strikingly low, with investment ratios in many cases barely above post-Asian crisis lows. While this may be partially cyclical in nature, it also underscores the need for further improvement in the investment climate, including through addressing remaining financial and corporate sector weaknesses and, in some cases, measures to improve infrastructure. Fiscal positions have generally improved since the crisis, but public debt remains high, a particular risk in the Philippines, where progress in implementing the fiscal elements of the new administration's reform package is lagging. Public debt in Indonesia, while declining sharply recently, is also elevated; while tsunami-related expenditures will be largely financed by higher aid, progress in reducing fuel subsidies, attracting private investment in infrastructure, and improving tax administration is needed to maintain confidence that deficits and debt will remain sustainable over the medium term. More generally, pressures from aging populations require increasing attention, and in some countries—including Korea, where dependency ratios will rise especially sharply—further action is needed to head off future pension fund shortfalls.

GDP growth in India has slowed modestly, but is expected to remain robust, with the impact of uneven monsoons and higher oil prices being offset by buoyant industrial activity and strong investment. In response to a sharp rise in inflation in the second half of 2004, and easing liquidity conditions—in part reflecting buoyant

capital inflows—the Reserve Bank of India has appropriately raised interest rates and allowed somewhat more exchange rate flexibility. Inflation seems now to be moderating, but with short-run interest rates still very low in real terms and commercial credit growth exceeding 25 percent, the Reserve Bank of India will need to continue to monitor the situation closely. Since the general government deficit is still close to 10 percent of GDP, fiscal consolidation remains a key challenge, the more so given the ambitious social agenda set out in the new government's Common Minimum Program (which could ultimately raise expenditures by 10 percent of GDP). Beyond the medium-term risks to macro stability, and the constraints the deficit places on a pickup in investment, it may also constrain progress on structural reforms (notably in the financial sector). Recent fiscal responsibility legislation provides a good medium-term framework, but needs to be more fully implemented, with the proposed deficit reduction in the FY 2005/06 budget falling below the minimum annual adjustments the legislation requires. Further efforts to strengthen state government finances, which account for one-half of the overall deficit, are also essential. While the budget proposed only modest structural reforms, the strong economic environment provides an important opportunity to improve the business climate—a key step toward increasing private sector participation in infrastructure—including through addressing labor market rigidities; agricultural reform, which is critical for poverty reduction; further trade and capital liberalization; and strengthening the financial sector, which remains exposed to interest rate risk given its large holdings of government securities.

Elsewhere in south Asia, GDP growth has picked up markedly in Pakistan, while fiscal adjustment—supported by official inflows and debt relief—has led to a substantial improvement in public and external debt indicators. Further efforts to broaden the tax base and reduce evasion will be needed to maintain this improving debt trajectory while financing

Table 1.7. Selected Western Hemisphere Countries: Real GDP, Consumer Prices, and Current Account Balance
(Annual percent change unless otherwise noted)

	Real GDP				Consumer Prices[1]				Current Account Balance[2]			
	2003	2004	2005	2006	2003	2004	2005	2006	2003	2004	2005	2006
Western Hemisphere	**2.2**	**5.7**	**4.1**	**3.7**	**10.6**	**6.5**	**6.0**	**5.2**	**0.4**	**0.8**	**0.2**	**−0.5**
Mercosur[3]	**2.6**	**6.1**	**4.4**	**3.7**	**13.4**	**5.7**	**6.4**	**5.0**	**1.5**	**1.9**	**0.7**	**−0.3**
Argentina	8.8	9.0	6.0	3.6	13.4	4.4	7.7	6.7	5.8	2.0	−1.2	−2.9
Brazil	0.5	5.2	3.7	3.5	14.8	6.6	6.5	4.6	0.8	1.9	1.1	0.4
Chile	3.3	6.0	6.1	5.4	2.8	1.1	2.5	3.1	−1.6	1.5	0.9	−1.3
Uruguay	2.5	12.0	5.0	3.5	19.4	9.2	7.0	6.2	0.7	−0.3	−0.2	−0.6
Andean region	**1.4**	**7.3**	**4.2**	**4.0**	**10.5**	**8.3**	**6.9**	**7.9**	**3.5**	**4.4**	**3.7**	**2.6**
Colombia	4.0	4.0	4.0	4.0	7.1	5.9	5.2	4.8	−1.5	−1.1	−2.6	−2.6
Ecuador	2.7	6.6	3.9	3.7	7.9	2.7	2.0	2.0	−1.7	−0.5	0.8	1.2
Peru	3.8	5.1	4.5	4.5	2.3	3.7	2.1	2.4	−1.8	−0.1	0.5	0.2
Venezuela	−7.7	17.3	4.6	3.8	31.1	21.7	18.2	25.0	13.6	13.5	12.0	8.4
Mexico, Central America, and Caribbean	**1.9**	**4.0**	**3.6**	**3.5**	**6.0**	**7.1**	**5.1**	**4.1**	**−1.6**	**−1.6**	**−1.8**	**−2.0**
Mexico	1.6	4.4	3.7	3.3	4.5	4.7	4.6	3.7	−1.3	−1.3	−1.4	−1.6
Central America[4]	3.5	3.5	3.2	3.4	5.7	7.2	6.0	5.0	−5.1	−5.1	−4.4	−4.0
The Caribbean[5]	1.4	2.1	3.0	5.3	19.4	29.0	7.8	6.7	0.4	−0.6	−2.7	−2.5

[1]In accordance with standard practice in the *World Economic Outlook*, movements in consumer prices are indicated as annual averages rather than as December/December changes during the year, as is the practice in some countries.
[2]Percent of GDP.
[3]Includes Argentina, Brazil, Paraguay, and Uruguay, together with Bolivia and Chile (associate members of Mercosur).
[4]Includes Costa Rica, El Salvador, Guatemala, Honduras, Nicaragua, and Panama.
[5]Includes Antigua and Barbuda, The Bahamas, Barbados, Dominica, Dominican Republic, Grenada, Guyana, Haiti, Jamaica, St. Kitts and Nevis, St. Lucia, St. Vincent and the Grenadines, and Trinidad and Tobago.

future social and infrastructural expenditure needs. In Bangladesh, GDP growth also remains solid despite devastating flooding last year. With macroeconomic management generally prudent, the central task is to press ahead with the structural reform agenda—strengthened tax administration, rehabilitation and divestment of the Nationalized Commercial Banks, and restructuring of energy sector enterprises— a task complicated by recent political tensions. While Pakistan has made substantial progress in modernizing its textile industry, adjustment to the ending of world textile trade quotas will be a major challenge for Bangladesh, underscoring the need for early development and implementation of a restructuring plan for the industry.

In Australia and New Zealand, GDP growth in 2004 remained strong, although activity moderated in the second half of the year, reflecting slowing global growth and higher oil prices; past exchange rate appreciation; and some easing in buoyant housing markets. In Australia, supply-

side constraints, especially on exports, also contributed to slowing growth, while in New Zealand, lower net migration was a factor. The Reserve Bank of Australia (RBA) and Reserve Bank of New Zealand (RBNZ) each raised interest rates by 25 basis points in March 2005, the first such action from the RBA since late 2003, whereas the RBNZ had lifted rates by 150 basis points in 2004. With growth expected to slow in both countries in 2005, it is unclear if further monetary tightening will be necessary. Much will depend on labor market developments as unemployment is at historically low levels in both economies. Fiscal positions remain strong, characterized by budget surpluses and low and declining government debt, but both countries face significant pressures from aging populations, underscoring the need to press forward with reforms to increase labor participation; boost productivity, which despite recent progress is still well below U.S. levels; and keep health and pension spending on a sustainable path.

Latin America: Is Fiscal Policy on the Right Track at Last?

The strength of the recovery in Latin America has continued to exceed expectations, and regionwide growth in 2004, at 5.7 percent, was the highest since 1980 (Table 1.7). Growth was particularly strong in Argentina, Venezuela, and Uruguay—as these countries recovered from deep recessions—and in Brazil and Chile, which continue to benefit from sound macroeconomic policies and structural reforms. The favorable external environment continues to support economic activity, but it is now domestic demand that is leading growth, with private consumption and business investment growing briskly. Inflation, although remaining generally well contained, has picked up in a number of countries, while the current account recorded a surplus of 0.8 percent of GDP in 2004. In the Caribbean, growth in a number of countries was badly affected by the impact of hurricanes.

Looking forward, economic activity in the region appears to be easing to a more sustainable pace, and growth of 4.1 percent is projected for 2005. This outlook is not without risks, however, particularly if oil price volatility continues, interest rates in industrial countries rise more sharply than expected, spreads on emerging market debt continue to widen, or industrial country growth slows in a prolonged way. A further limited and orderly depreciation of the U.S. dollar is unlikely to have significant repercussions for Latin American economies as many regional currencies track movements in the dollar quite closely, although a disorderly depreciation could have a more serious impact if it resulted in turbulence in global financial markets and a deterioration in financing conditions for emerging markets.

It is encouraging that, in contrast to recoveries in the 1990s, many governments have taken advantage of the favorable economic conditions to strengthen their fiscal positions, prefinance their 2005 obligations, and improve their debt structures, although there are differences between fiscal developments in major oil-exporting and other countries in the region (Figure 1.14).

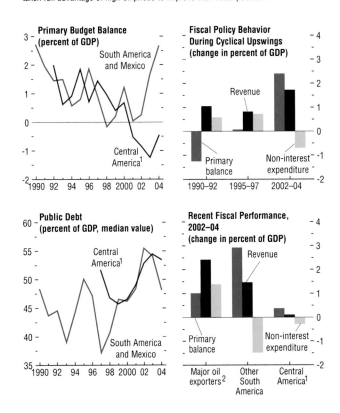

Figure 1.14. Latin America: Fiscal Performance Is Improving, but Public Debt Remains Too High
(Unweighted averages)

Fiscal performance in Latin America has been stronger during the current recovery than in cyclical upturns in the 1990s. Public debt, however, remains too high in many countries in the region. Further, oil-exporting countries have not taken full advantage of high oil prices to improve their fiscal position.

Source: IMF staff calculations.
[1] Consists of Costa Rica, El Salvador, Guatemala, Honduras, and Panama.
[2] Consists of Ecuador, Mexico, and Venezuela.

- In major oil-exporting countries—Ecuador, Mexico, and Venezuela—the increase in oil prices has resulted in significant revenue gains. Primary expenditures, however, have also risen substantially. Compared with 2002, the primary budget surplus in 2004 was only modestly better in Mexico—where there is a policy focus on raising public capital expenditure—and Ecuador, but rose more substantially in Venezuela.

- Other countries—with the exception of Argentina—have generally seen more limited revenue gains. Many of these countries have reduced primary expenditures (as a percent of GDP), and the average primary surplus has improved substantially since 2002. In Central America, primary expenditure restraint contributed to a small improvement in the primary surplus during 2002–04.

The improvement in budgetary outcomes is welcome, but public debt in Latin America, while declining, remains high and is a significant source of vulnerability (recent valuation gains from the appreciation of local currencies against the U.S. dollar have contributed to the reduction in debt, although it is unclear whether these gains will be sustained). Consequently, fiscal consolidation and more general measures to improve public debt sustainability—including structural reforms to boost growth—remain a priority, and the current favorable economic outlook provides an important opportunity to push ahead in these areas. It is particularly important that oil-exporting countries take full advantage of current high oil prices to strengthen their fiscal positions. A clear lesson from previous episodes of fiscal consolidation is that budget surpluses must be pursued in a sustainable manner, rather than based on unrealistic spending cuts or distortionary taxes that undermine efficiency and growth, and that ultimately have to be reversed. In this regard, strong institutions that support prudent fiscal policy are essential. In addition, fiscal reforms will need to focus on strengthening the tax base and increasing room in the budget for additional spending on infrastructure investment and the social safety net (although improv-

ing the effectiveness of the delivery of social services and ensuring that the social safety net is well targeted will be as critical to efforts to reduce poverty and inequality as additional spending).

Given the recent uptick in inflation, central banks in a number of countries—including Brazil, Mexico, and Peru—have appropriately tightened monetary policy, and have thereby enhanced the credibility of their relatively new inflation-targeting frameworks. Exchange rate flexibility has played a key role in supporting these frameworks, as well as in helping to improve external sector performance and increasing the region's resilience to shocks. While the inflation-targeting frameworks do not preclude intervention in the foreign exchange market—indeed, building reserves as market conditions permit remains a priority in Argentina and Brazil—such intervention needs to be consistent with achieving the inflation objective. With inflation now much more firmly under control, countries should be taking every opportunity to enhance incentives for local currency intermediation.

Turning to individual countries, the strong recovery in Argentina is continuing. The economy expanded by 9 percent last year, with business investment growing robustly. Inflation has picked up in recent months, but is expected to end the year within the central bank's target band. Fiscal performance exceeded expectations in 2004, with the primary budget surplus estimated to have reached 5.1 percent of GDP. If the recovery is to be sustained and unemployment reduced, continued prudent fiscal policies—which facilitate debt reduction, the phased elimination of distortive taxes, and increased social and infrastructure spending—the normalization of relations with private creditors and greater progress with structural reforms will be required. In Uruguay, the recovery is advancing ahead of expectations—with growth of 12 percent last year—and financial indicators have continued to improve, although public debt remains very high.

In Brazil, the government's adherence to sound macroeconomic policies and its pursuit of structural reforms are paying off. The economy—spurred by robust investment and strong exports—grew strongly in 2004, and is expected to expand by a further 3.7 percent this year. Inflation has picked up and the central bank has responded by raising interest rates on a number of occasions since September. Fiscal performance has exceeded expectations, with a primary surplus of 4.6 percent of GDP in 2004. It will be important to maintain a tight fiscal stance in 2005 and beyond to continue bringing down public debt, and fiscal adjustment will have to be supported by tax and pension reforms. The authorities have recently passed legislation for bankruptcy reform, judiciary reform, and public-private partnerships, and should continue to take advantage of the current favorable conditions to press ahead with their reform agenda.

The Chilean economy is expanding robustly, spurred by strong export growth—related to the favorable copper market—and private investment. Inflation has returned to the official target range (after falling below the target in early 2004) and the central bank has begun to tighten monetary policy. The government continues to adhere to the structural budget balance rule, and strong revenues underpinned an overall fiscal surplus of over 2 percent of GDP in 2004.

In the Andean region, the Venezuelan economy is expected to slow in 2005, although there are upside risks in the oil and non-oil sectors. It is important that the authorities take decisive measures to strengthen the fiscal position, reduce reliance on oil prices, and implement market-friendly reforms to maintain bouyant activity in the non-oil sector. In Colombia, growth remains robust, although the current account deficit is expected to widen, reflecting in part a decline in export volumes. In Peru, growth is also strong; and the central bank met its end-2004 inflation target. Exchange rates in both Colombia and Peru have appreciated against the U.S. dollar, and the central banks have stepped up purchases of foreign exchange to limit upward pressures on their currencies. (Colombia has also introduced restrictions on short-term capital inflows.) It is important, how-ever, that exchange rate management remain consistent with achieving stated inflation objectives. In Ecuador, growth has been boosted by a substantial increase in oil exports, providing the government with a favorable environment to press ahead with its reform agenda.

Mexico is experiencing a broad-based recovery, spurred by the upturn in the U.S. manufacturing sector and financial sector reforms that have boosted confidence and domestic demand. Consumer price inflation, however, has been above the Bank of Mexico's 2–4 percent target range, and monetary policy has been tightened over the past year. On the fiscal side, while the government's budget targets have been met, fiscal consolidation needs to be strengthened at a time of high oil prices and a recovery in growth. This will require expenditure restraint and tax reform to increase revenues from the non-oil sector. Further structural reforms beyond those in the financial sector are needed to boost medium-term growth, including reforms in the energy and telecommunications sectors to raise efficiency and promote investment, and labor market reforms to increase productivity and employment in the formal sector.

In Central America, growth has picked up and economic imbalances have been reduced, although volatile oil prices present a risk to the outlook. Ratification of the Central American Free Trade Agreement (CAFTA) would provide a much needed growth impulse, particularly against the background of the recent elimination of world textile trade quotas which will likely hurt the textile sectors in a number of countries in the region (Box 1.3). Accelerated structural reforms, supported by sound fiscal and monetary policies, will be needed to maximize the benefits of CAFTA and meet the competitive challenges in key export markets. In the Caribbean, a number of countries face significant difficulties in the aftermath of recent hurricanes. Volatile oil prices and high public debt levels present further challenges in the region, and efforts are particularly needed to strengthen budgets and improve public debt sustainability.

Table 1.8. Emerging Europe: Real GDP, Consumer Prices, and Current Account Balance
(Annual percent change unless otherwise noted)

	Real GDP				Consumer Prices[1]				Current Account Balance[2]			
	2003	2004	2005	2006	2003	2004	2005	2006	2003	2004	2005	2006
Emerging Europe	**4.6**	**6.2**	**4.5**	**4.5**	**9.5**	**6.7**	**5.4**	**4.1**	**−4.3**	**−4.9**	**−4.7**	**−4.3**
Turkey	5.9	8.0	5.0	5.0	25.3	10.6	9.0	6.1	−3.4	−5.2	−4.5	−3.7
Excluding Turkey	4.1	5.5	4.3	4.3	3.7	5.2	3.9	3.2	−4.7	−4.8	−4.8	−4.6
Baltics	**8.0**	**6.9**	**6.9**	**6.3**	**0.6**	**3.1**	**3.9**	**3.6**	**−8.8**	**−10.9**	**−10.3**	**−9.6**
Estonia	5.1	6.2	6.0	5.5	1.3	3.0	3.7	2.7	−13.2	−13.8	−11.0	−9.7
Latvia	7.5	8.0	7.3	6.2	2.9	6.3	5.7	5.3	−8.2	−12.3	−10.9	−9.8
Lithuania	9.7	6.6	7.0	6.8	−1.2	1.2	2.9	3.0	−7.0	−8.6	−9.5	−9.3
Central Europe	**3.6**	**4.8**	**3.8**	**3.9**	**2.2**	**4.2**	**3.1**	**2.7**	**−3.9**	**−3.8**	**−4.0**	**−4.0**
Czech Republic	3.7	4.0	4.0	3.9	0.1	2.8	2.5	2.7	−6.2	−5.2	−4.8	−4.4
Hungary	3.0	4.0	3.7	3.8	4.7	6.8	4.0	3.8	−9.0	−9.0	−8.6	−8.1
Poland	3.8	5.3	3.5	3.7	0.8	3.5	3.1	2.5	−1.9	−1.5	−2.1	−2.5
Slovak Republic	4.5	5.5	4.8	4.9	8.5	7.5	3.6	2.8	−0.9	−3.4	−6.0	−4.6
Slovenia	2.5	4.4	4.0	4.0	5.6	3.6	2.3	2.0	0.1	−0.6	−1.4	−2.2
Southern and south-eastern Europe	**4.6**	**7.2**	**5.3**	**5.0**	**10.7**	**9.5**	**6.6**	**4.8**	**−6.8**	**−7.2**	**−6.4**	**−5.8**
Bulgaria	4.3	5.7	5.5	5.5	2.3	6.1	4.0	3.5	−9.3	−7.4	−7.6	−6.9
Cyprus	1.9	3.7	3.8	4.0	4.1	2.3	2.5	2.5	−3.4	−4.1	−3.4	−2.7
Malta	−1.8	1.5	1.5	1.8	1.9	2.7	2.4	1.9	−5.8	−10.3	−4.0	−3.0
Romania	5.2	8.3	5.5	5.0	15.3	11.9	8.2	5.7	−6.8	−7.5	−6.9	−6.3

[1]In accordance with standard practice in the *World Economic Outlook*, movements in consumer prices are indicated as annual averages rather than as December/December changes during the year as is the practice in some countries.
[2]Percent of GDP.

Emerging Europe: Current Account Deficits Remain a Challenge

In 2004, emerging Europe enjoyed its strongest growth performance since the beginning of transition, as robust economic activity in central Europe and Turkey broadened the expansion that was led by the Baltic states and southern and southeastern Europe. The initial recovery, with rapid domestic credit growth financing a consumption boom in much of the region, has broadened to the export sector, even though exchange rates—despite some recent depreciation—have strengthened markedly since 2004. Current account deficits, however, have generally widened as strong domestic demand boosted imports while inflation rose in most countries in the region—with the notable exception of Turkey—in response to higher global oil prices, the effects of domestic credit growth, and one-off EU accession–related tax adjustments (Table 1.8).

Looking ahead, the pace of activity is expected to moderate in 2005 as the cycle matures in central Europe and the Baltic states, and Turkey's growth eases to a more sustainable pace. In turn, this is expected to lead to some narrowing of current account deficits and lower inflation across the region. The risks to the outlook appear tilted to the downside at this juncture. A prolonged slowdown in western Europe would likely hurt export growth, while a further sharp decline of the U.S. dollar against the euro also presents risks, as most regional exchange rates move with the euro. While the majority of regional exports are to western Europe, those economies with more significant non–euro area exports could see their current account positions deteriorate, while most countries will get little benefit from valuation effects on external debt as a relatively small proportion of liabilities are dollar denominated. The continued rise in oil prices presents a further risk to growth and current accounts. Finally, the rapid growth of credit presents a risk to banks in a number of countries, particularly if credit quality were to weaken in the face of an unexpected slowdown in growth or large exchange rate movements, and this poses a challenge for banking supervision.

Against this outlook, the region's high and widening current account deficits remain a key vulnerability. The underlying sources of these deficits, however, vary across countries (see Figure 1.15), suggesting differing policy priorities.

- In the Baltic countries and southern and southeastern Europe, investment rates have risen but saving has stagnated as a decline in private saving—due to strong credit growth that has financed increased consumption—has offset improving fiscal balances. Measures to contain current account deficits therefore will need to focus on restraining domestic credit growth and increasing private saving, while maintaining tight fiscal policies.
- In central Europe, while investment rates have declined, deteriorating fiscal balances have contributed to widening current account deficits in a number of countries. The key policy challenge is to foster the recent pickup in investment to underpin future growth prospects, while also reining in current account deficits. This will require ambitious fiscal consolidation to raise saving, while implementing reforms—including in the labor market and the state-owned sector—to improve the investment climate. Attracting more foreign direct investment will also help with the financing of the current account deficits.

Turning to developments in individual countries, Poland has enjoyed a strong recovery on the back of buoyant exports and large inventory accumulation. Inflation has risen owing to a number of one-off factors including accession-related tax increases, but wage pressures remain limited against the background of a still weak labor market. Growth is expected to moderate somewhat, with the strengthening of the zloty in 2004 slowing exports, while past interest rate increases are expected to ease inflationary pressures by moderating domestic demand. The implementation of the Hausner plan has been disappointing, and it will be important to press ahead both with the unfinished parts of the plan and with broader fiscal reforms.

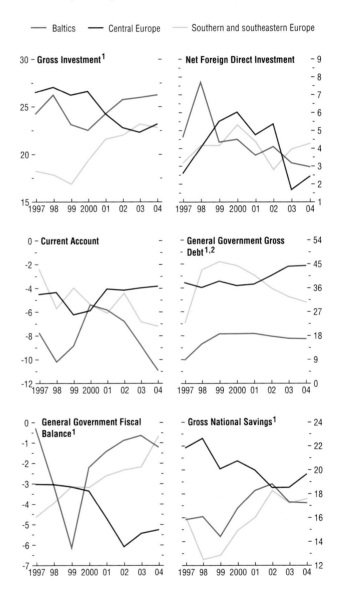

Figure 1.15. Emerging Europe: The Challenge of Current Account Deficits
(Percent of GDP)

National savings have stagnated, but investment has been higher.

[1]Weighted by PPP-GDP for the aggregates.
[2]For southern and southeastern Europe, net debt is used for Cyprus.

Economic activity in Hungary has continued to strengthen, with moderating consumption growth being offset by a rebound in investment and exports. Looking ahead, growth is expected to slow somewhat, while the recent strength of the forint and low wage pressures suggest moderate inflationary pressures. The twin fiscal and current account deficits remain the main risks to the outlook, given the sizable external financing requirements going forward and the sensitivity of capital inflows to changes in the market environment. The fiscal targets in the medium term envisage relatively unambitious consolidation, and stronger fiscal efforts centered on expenditure restraint are needed to maintain confidence, reduce the external deficit, and pave the way to ERM II accession.

In the Czech Republic, the recovery has continued at a relatively stable pace, led by rapidly rising exports and related investment. Strong domestic demand and increases in indirect taxes in the run-up to EU accession pushed inflation higher in 2004, although it remained well contained, and the monetary tightening cycle in place last year ended with a cut in interest rates in January 2005. Strong growth and higher VAT and nontax receipts helped revenues in 2004, although further fiscal adjustment is a key policy priority, with the authorities' three-year adjustment plan an important component of further consolidation. As in other countries, further structural and labor market reforms also need to be pursued. In the Slovak Republic, growth picked up in 2004 as domestic demand strengthened, headline inflation remained high largely owing to administered price and indirect tax increases, and the current account deficit widened. Growth is expected to ease somewhat this year, but fiscal consolidation should be accelerated given the back-loading under the government's current three-year fiscal framework and the risks to inflation.

In the Baltic countries, activity remains strong, supported by robust domestic demand and exports. Following accession to the European Union, monetary policies in all three economies are well anchored, with Estonia and Lithuania

joining the ERM II mechanism in end-June 2004, and Latvia pegging the lat to the euro at the beginning of 2005. Strong credit growth, fueled by foreign borrowing by banks, has contributed to high current account deficits, and these are expected to moderate only slightly this year as growth eases to more sustainable rates. Efforts to increase domestic savings will be key to reducing the vulnerabilities going forward, accompanied by strong supervision of the banking system. Slovenia entered the ERM II arrangement at end-June 2004, but reducing inflation to the Maastricht criterion level and maintaining competitiveness, including through labor market reforms and wage policies, present a continuing policy challenge.

Growth in Bulgaria and Romania continues to be strong, fueled by rapid credit growth. As a result, current account deficits remain high and underscore the need to maintain tight fiscal policies and contain wage and credit growth going forward. Structural reforms to improve the investment climate would help boost foreign direct investment. The National Bank of Romania has allowed greater exchange rate appreciation to achieve its inflation objectives, and progress in structural reforms and the fight against corruption need to be stepped up to allow smooth entry into the European Union in 2007. In Bulgaria, a 25 percent increase in the minimum wage and pressures for fiscal easing prior to the mid-2005 parliamentary elections have reduced the scope to contain the current account deficit.

In the Balkan countries, while growth has picked up in Bosnia and Herzegovina and in Serbia and Montenegro, current account deficits remain high, highlighting the need for structural reforms to boost export competitiveness. In Croatia, economic activity has slowed, in part owing to fiscal consolidation, inflation remains subdued, and the current account has narrowed somewhat. Looking ahead, tight fiscal and monetary policies will be needed to further reduce the current account deficit.

Strong macroeconomic policies and structural reforms, along with improved confidence,

Table 1.9. Commonwealth of Independent States: Real GDP, Consumer Prices, and Current Account Balance

(Annual percent change unless otherwise noted)

	Real GDP				Consumer Prices[1]				Current Account Balance[2]			
	2003	2004	2005	2006	2003	2004	2005	2006	2003	2004	2005	2006
Commonwealth of Independent States	**7.9**	**8.2**	**6.5**	**6.0**	**12.0**	**10.3**	**11.4**	**8.8**	**6.4**	**8.5**	**9.4**	**6.9**
Russia	7.3	7.1	6.0	5.5	13.7	10.9	11.8	9.7	8.2	10.2	11.4	8.7
Ukraine	9.6	12.1	7.0	4.0	5.2	9.0	12.5	5.9	5.8	11.0	7.2	2.5
Kazakhstan	9.3	9.4	8.0	7.7	6.4	6.9	7.3	6.5	−0.2	2.3	1.8	−0.8
Belarus	6.8	11.0	7.1	6.0	28.4	18.1	13.0	11.0	−2.9	−3.0	−3.4	−3.3
CIS-7	**7.2**	**8.4**	**9.5**	**14.2**	**8.6**	**7.9**	**8.9**	**7.3**	**−6.9**	**−9.4**	**−3.6**	**0.8**
Armenia	13.9	10.1	8.0	6.0	4.7	7.0	2.0	3.0	−6.8	−5.8	−5.5	−5.5
Azerbaijan	10.8	10.1	21.6	38.3	2.2	8.1	7.6	5.0	−28.3	−27.3	−7.8	6.0
Georgia	11.1	8.5	6.0	5.0	4.8	5.7	6.8	4.0	−7.2	−7.5	−8.1	−6.0
Kyrgyz Republic	6.9	6.0	5.0	5.9	3.1	4.1	4.0	3.7	−2.8	−3.0	−6.3	−4.6
Moldova	6.3	7.0	5.0	4.0	11.7	12.3	10.0	8.1	−7.3	−7.1	−6.1	−5.9
Tajikistan	10.2	10.6	8.0	7.0	16.4	7.1	5.7	5.5	−1.3	−3.9	−4.2	−4.2
Uzbekistan	1.5	7.1	3.5	2.5	14.8	8.8	14.1	13.0	8.9	0.8	4.5	3.9
Memorandum												
Net energy exporters[3]	7.6	7.4	6.4	6.4	12.8	10.4	11.3	9.4	7.1	9.0	10.3	7.9
Net energy importers[4]	9.2	11.5	7.0	4.5	8.8	10.1	11.7	6.5	2.1	5.5	3.1	0.4

[1]In accordance with standard practice in the *World Economic Outlook*, movements in consumer prices are indicated as annual averages rather than as December/December changes during the year as is the practice in some countries.
[2]Percent of GDP.
[3]Includes Azerbaijan, Kazakhstan, Russia, Turkmenistan, and Uzbekistan.
[4]Includes Armenia, Belarus, Georgia, Kyrgyz Republic, Moldova, Tajikistan, and Ukraine.

spurred robust growth in Turkey in 2004, while inflation fell to its lowest level in 30 years. The current account deficit widened, however, while its financing, albeit at short maturity, was supported by improving market sentiment and helped by the European Union's decision to begin accession negotiations with Turkey in October 2005. Looking ahead, growth is expected to ease to more sustainable rates, although the current account deficit may be adversely affected by the appreciation of the lira and strong domestic demand. Abrupt shifts in market sentiment pose a risk to the financing of the current account deficit, and policies should focus on reducing the deficit and maintaining market confidence—including on the fiscal side by ensuring that the target for the primary surplus is achieved, and exceeded if strong growth leads to significant revenue overperformance—and reducing public debt, which, despite recent gains, remains high. At the same time, sustaining the positive growth momentum will require persisting with structural reforms, including with

respect to taxes and expenditures; strengthening the legal and supervisory system for banks; state bank restructuring; and improving the investment climate to attract nondebt inflows.

Commonwealth of Independent States: Has Disinflation Bottomed Out?

Growth in the Commonwealth of Independent States remained very strong during 2004, underpinned by buoyant energy and metals prices and strong domestic demand, and reinforced by strong regional linkages that boosted exports from energy importers. Looking forward, while GDP growth is expected to moderate to more sustainable levels in 2005, the outlook remains generally favorable; external and commodity price developments are expected to be generally supportive of activity, although capacity constraints and inadequate investment are beginning to limit the benefits that some economies can reap (Table 1.9). A further rise in oil prices is the key upside risk to the outlook while, as discussed below, the signs of recent weakening growth and investment in Russia pose a potential downside risk, given its dominant role in the region.

Countries in the region have in general made impressive progress on disinflation in recent years with sound monetary and fiscal policies in the context of a commodity price boom (Figure 1.16). However, with concerns about capacity constraints against the background of strong growth, capital inflows, and many country authorities' efforts to slow currency appreciation, signs are emerging that the pace of disinflation may be slowing down significantly, presenting policymakers with a challenging environment. Sustaining disinflation will require prudent management of the revenue gains from oil and commodity exports under mounting pressures for domestic spending, and making the transition to more flexible exchange rates. More generally, monetary policy and banking supervision need to deal with the challenges of rapid money and credit growth in this environment.

Turning to developments in individual countries, GDP growth in Russia slowed in the second half of 2004, mainly owing to weakening oil production growth and a slowing of investment. While the underlying reasons for these developments are not fully clear, they include the fallout from the Yukos affair, which led to oil supply disruptions and reignited concerns about the protection of property rights and increased state intervention; slower credit growth in the aftermath of the mid-2004 banking sector turbulence; and slow progress with reforms. The forecast for 2005 assumes a gradual reversal in these developments, but much will depend on early measures to improve the investment climate, including limiting regulatory intervention and reinvigorating the reform effort. Despite the slowdown, inflationary pressures remain strong, with labor markets in high-growth regions particularly tight; with external reserves continuing to rise rapidly—the rising current account surplus has more than offset the capital account deterioration—greater upward exchange rate flexibility will be needed if the official inflation

Figure 1.16. CIS: Has Disinflation Lost Momentum?

The commodity boom has helped current account and fiscal balances, but inflationary pressures remain.

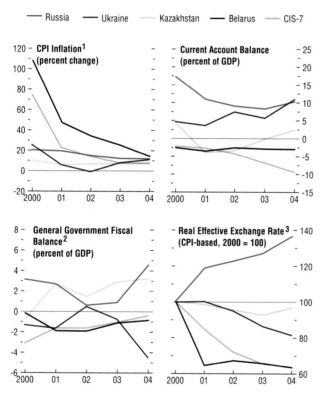

Sources: IMF, INSDATA; and IMF staff calculations.
[1] December-over-December percent change. For 2004, it is November-over-November percent change. CIS-7 is weighted by PPP-GDP, excluding Georgia owing to lack of data.
[2] CIS-7 is weighted by PPP-GDP.
[3] CIS-7 is weighted by PPP-GDP, excluding Georgia owing to lack of data.

target for 2005 is to be achieved. Additionally, it will be important to avoid any further discretionary relaxation of fiscal policy—in this connection, the authorities' intention to prepay Paris Club debt is welcome. That said, once inflationary pressures ease, more of the oil market–related revenues could be used to support a well-designed structural reform program.

In Ukraine, GDP growth soared to 12.1 percent in 2004, driven primarily by external factors—including booming metals prices, strong demand in China and Russia, and a highly competitive exchange rate. This was accompanied by a sharp increase in the current account surplus to 11 percent of GDP, and—with monetary policy primarily aimed at maintaining the nominal peg to the U.S. dollar—rising inflation. In 2005, GDP growth is projected to moderate, but—with the financial turbulence surrounding the December presidential elections likely to have only a temporary adverse effect—remain strong. With the key short-term challenge to reduce overheating pressures and bring inflation back to single digits, monetary policy will need to be tightened, aided by a more flexible exchange rate policy. With budgetary policies having been eased markedly in the run-up to the elections—including a sharp hike in pensions—this will need to be supported by substantial fiscal consolidation. Over the medium term, the key challenge remains to build the institutions necessary to support a market economy and—with private investment still very low—to improve the investment climate.

GDP growth in Kazakhstan remained rapid in 2004, underpinned by high global oil prices and an expanding oil sector, and the outlook for 2005 remains highly favorable. With demand pressures intensifying, and inflation currently above the authorities' band for the year, overheating has become a risk. While the budget should remain in surplus in 2005 and is not expected to impart further stimulus, continued large foreign inflows will keep pressure on monetary policy and increased upward exchange rate flexibility will be needed. With credit growth booming, heightened vigilance over

banks' portfolios is desirable, accompanied by increased efforts to strengthen bank supervision. Adjustment of banks' reserve requirements—particularly on foreign liabilities, which are rising rapidly—should help moderate credit growth and inflows of capital. While diversification beyond the oil sector is important to help achieve stable medium-term growth, the use of industrial policies that can lead to distortions and the misallocation of resources should be avoided.

The strong growth momentum in the largest countries of the region has provided support to the low-income CIS-7 economies, with the more advanced reformers once again on average faring better. Azerbaijan benefited from higher oil and gas prices and associated foreign direct investment, while higher metals prices benefited Tajikistan (aluminum), Armenia (copper), and the Kyrgyz Republic (gold). Uzbekistan's current account surplus shrank with the fall in cotton prices and energy sector–related imports. Given their relatively high debt burdens—except in Armenia—the CIS-7 economies remain vulnerable to changes in the external environment, while several countries will also find it very challenging to achieve their Millennium Development Goals. This underscores the need to pursue long-term fiscal and structural reforms and to improve the business environment, and the importance of strong and sustained support from the international community. Greater harmonization of trade rules with multilateral standards, liberalization of transit regimes within the CIS-7 and with neighboring countries, and the removal of nontariff barriers also need high priority to pave the way for growth going forward by realizing the gains from closer economic integration with larger economies and diversification of the export base.

Africa: Turning The Corner?

In sub-Saharan Africa, real GDP growth accelerated to 5.1 percent in 2004 (2.8 percent in per capita terms), the highest in almost a decade (Table 1.10). Growth has been underpinned by

Table 1.10. Selected African Countries: Real GDP, Consumer Prices, and Current Account Balance
(Annual percent change unless otherwise noted)

	Real GDP				Consumer Prices[1]				Current Account Balance[2]			
	2003	2004	2005	2006	2003	2004	2005	2006	2003	2004	2005	2006
Africa	**4.6**	**5.1**	**5.0**	**5.4**	**10.6**	**7.7**	**7.7**	**5.9**	**−0.3**	**0.2**	**0.8**	**0.5**
Maghreb	**6.1**	**4.9**	**4.2**	**4.7**	**2.2**	**3.1**	**2.9**	**2.8**	**7.2**	**6.8**	**7.7**	**7.3**
Algeria	6.9	5.3	4.6	4.7	2.6	3.6	3.5	3.5	13.3	13.3	15.4	14.7
Morocco	5.2	3.5	3.0	3.8	1.2	2.0	2.0	2.0	3.6	1.2	—	0.3
Tunisia	5.6	5.8	5.0	5.9	2.8	3.6	2.5	2.5	−2.9	−2.1	−2.5	−2.5
Sub-Sahara	**4.2**	**5.1**	**5.2**	**5.6**	**13.3**	**9.1**	**9.2**	**6.8**	**−2.7**	**−1.9**	**−1.3**	**−1.6**
Horn of Africa[3]	**1.9**	**9.1**	**7.2**	**6.9**	**10.6**	**8.6**	**6.6**	**6.1**	**−6.7**	**−6.7**	**−5.5**	**−6.2**
Ethiopia	−3.9	11.6	5.7	4.6	15.1	9.0	5.4	5.0	−2.7	−6.1	−8.1	−7.5
Sudan	6.0	7.3	8.3	8.6	7.7	8.4	7.5	7.0	−8.2	−6.8	−4.5	−5.5
Great Lakes[4]	**4.1**	**5.4**	**5.3**	**5.9**	**8.2**	**6.9**	**6.8**	**4.1**	**−2.4**	**−4.0**	**−5.4**	**−6.4**
Congo, Dem. Rep. of	5.7	6.8	7.0	7.0	12.8	3.9	12.7	5.2	−1.5	−2.5	−4.8	−6.7
Kenya	1.6	3.1	3.3	3.7	9.8	11.5	6.6	3.6	−0.2	−3.7	−4.9	−5.7
Tanzania	7.1	6.3	6.5	7.0	4.5	4.6	4.3	4.0	−2.4	−5.8	−5.4	−6.6
Uganda	4.7	5.9	5.2	6.4	5.1	5.9	3.5	3.5	−6.2	−1.9	−4.4	−6.0
Southern Africa[5]	**2.5**	**4.9**	**5.9**	**9.1**	**59.9**	**40.3**	**27.1**	**18.1**	**−4.0**	**−0.1**	**−1.5**	**−1.1**
Angola	3.4	11.2	13.8	24.5	98.3	43.6	20.1	11.7	−5.2	6.5	3.3	4.7
Zimbabwe	−10.0	−4.8	−1.6	—	431.7	282.4	187.2	103.7	−5.0	−5.3	−2.7	−3.7
West and central Africa[6]	**7.2**	**5.6**	**5.5**	**5.8**	**9.4**	**8.2**	**9.4**	**5.5**	**−3.6**	**−0.4**	**2.4**	**1.3**
Ghana	5.2	5.5	5.6	5.9	26.7	12.6	14.5	8.4	1.7	1.2	−1.3	−0.6
Nigeria	10.7	3.5	7.4	5.8	14.0	15.0	14.8	7.3	−3.7	2.8	7.8	5.1
CFA franc zone[7]	**5.4**	**7.6**	**4.0**	**4.2**	**1.3**	**0.7**	**2.8**	**2.9**	**−4.0**	**−2.6**	**−1.7**	**−1.5**
Cameroon	4.5	4.3	3.9	4.6	0.6	0.3	2.0	2.0	−2.4	−1.7	−0.6	−0.8
Côte d'Ivoire	−1.6	−0.9	−1.4	2.0	3.3	1.5	2.0	2.0	3.9	3.1	4.1	3.5
South Africa	**2.8**	**3.7**	**4.0**	**3.5**	**5.8**	**1.4**	**4.5**	**5.0**	**−0.9**	**−2.5**	**−3.0**	**−2.6**
Memorandum												
Oil importers	3.5	4.7	4.5	4.8	10.1	6.8	7.2	5.9	−1.8	−2.7	−3.1	−3.1
Oil exporters	8.3	6.2	6.4	7.1	12.4	10.6	9.0	5.8	3.9	7.7	10.2	9.0

[1]In accordance with standard practice in the *World Economic Outlook*, movements in consumer prices are indicated as annual averages rather than as December/December changes during the year, as is the practice in some countries.
[2]Percent of GDP.
[3]Includes Djibouti.
[4]Includes Burundi and Rwanda.
[5]Includes Botswana, Comoros, Lesotho, Madagascar, Malawi, Mauritius, Rep. of Mozambique, Namibia, Seychelles, Swaziland, and Zambia.
[6]Includes Cape Verde, The Gambia, Guinea, Mauritania, São Tomé and Príncipe, Sierra Leone, and CFA franc zone.
[7]Includes Benin, Burkina Faso, Central African Republic, Chad, Rep. of Congo, Equatorial Guinea, Gabon, Guinea-Bissau, Mali, Niger, Senegal, and Togo.

the strength of the global economy, including high oil and commodity prices, improved domestic macroeconomic policies and progress with structural reforms, and the ending of several protracted armed conflicts. Growth was particularly strong in countries where oil production increased sharply (notably Angola, Chad, and Equatorial Guinea) and where agriculture recovered after a drought (Ethiopia and Rwanda), but conflicts and political instability (Côte d'Ivoire) and poor governance (Zimbabwe) continued to affect some other countries. Despite the appreciation of currencies

pegged to the euro, high commodity prices underpinned an improvement in the region's current account balance. Inflation continued to decline, reaching single digits in 2004, the lowest rate for nearly three decades, although inflation in some countries—notably Zimbabwe— remained very high.

Looking forward, prospects generally remain favorable, with growth of 5.2 percent in 2005 and 5.6 percent in 2006 projected, aided by prudent macroeconomic policies, continuing structural reforms, and a supportive global economy. Oil-exporting countries are expected to enjoy the strongest growth—as production continues to expand—while growth in non-oil-producing countries is expected to be affected by the slowdown in non-oil commodity prices. In particular, Benin, Burkina Faso, and Mali will continue to be hurt by persistently low cotton prices. Seychelles and Somalia were hit by the recent tsunami. While the tsunami's impact on growth in the Seychelles is expected to be modest, the fiscal position and balance of payments will be adversely affected this year. For Somalia, insufficient information is available to make an assessment of the tsunami's impact on the macroeconomy. There are several important risks to this outlook, however, including a less benign global economy and a disorderly depreciation of the dollar. In particular, a sharp depreciation of the dollar is likely to weaken non-oil exports of the CFA franc zone countries given their peg to the euro and their increasing dependence on dollar-zone markets (United States and Asia). Moreover, higher oil prices would adversely affect growth and the balance of payments in non-oil-producing countries, particularly if non-fuel commodity prices weaken. A further important challenge for a number of countries in the region (notably Kenya, Lesotho, Madagascar, Malawi, Mauritius, South Africa, and Swaziland) will be adjusting to the elimination of world textile trade quotas, which will increase the competition they face in the United States and the European Union from low-cost Asian countries; as a result textile production, employment (primarily of women workers), and exports are likely to fall.[8]

The encouraging growth performance in recent years has renewed optimism that sub-Saharan Africa may be entering a period of strong and sustained economic expansion.

• Per capita income growth in sub-Saharan Africa has accelerated and become positive over the past five years—a significant improvement compared with the previous two decades

when sub-Saharan Africa recorded the worst growth performance among developing country regions.

• Per capita income volatility in sub-Saharan Africa has fallen over the past two decades, particularly among CFA franc zone countries (Figure 1.17). As discussed in Chapter II, however, sub-Saharan Africa remains the most volatile region of the world. In the absence of well-developed capital markets and insurance schemes—such as the social security systems prevalent in industrial countries—the effects of volatility in poor countries are substantial, as households and firms face large non-insurable employment, income, and investment risks (see Pallage and Robe, 2003).

What factors help explain this stronger growth and lower volatility? While growth and volatility are influenced by many factors, economic reforms—that result in scarce resources being used more efficiently and in improved incentives for investments in high-return activities—and strong macroeconomic policies have played an important role in improving the prospects for sustained growth and macroeconomic stability across the world (see Chapter II and Krueger, 2005). A large number of countries in sub-Saharan Africa have made progress in reforming their economies and strengthening macroeconomic policy implementation over the past decade, and an important part of the improvement in growth and reduction in volatility in the region can be attributed to these reform and stabilization efforts (see the IMF's forthcoming sub-Saharan Africa *Regional Economic Outlook*). One component of this has been the adoption of trade reforms that, by introducing more competition and mitigating the negative effects of volatility on economic growth, have helped improve the growth potential of countries in sub-Saharan Africa (Box 1.5, "How Does Macroeconomic Instability Stifle Sub-Saharan African Growth?"). Trade regimes

[8]This negative effect, however, will be mitigated by the existence of preferential trade agreements with the United States and the European Union and other trade actions affecting Chinese exports in this sector.

Figure 1.17. Sub-Saharan Africa: Output Growth and Volatility

Macroeconomic volatility has a significant adverse impact on growth. The reduction in volatility in sub-Saharan Africa is one of the factors that has helped improve growth in recent years.

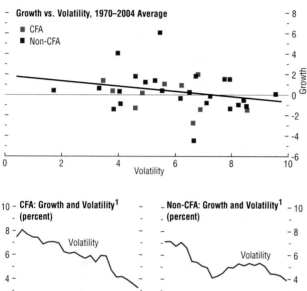

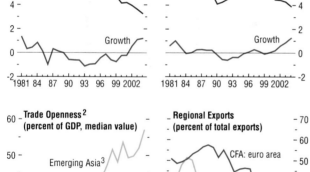

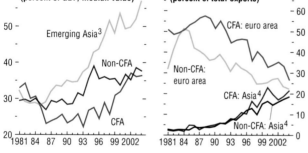

Sources: IMF, *Direction of Trade Statistics*; INS DATA; Penn World Table Version 6.1; and IMF staff calculations.
[1]Median per capita output growth and volatility (standard deviation) of growth rates calculated over a 10-year rolling window.
[2]Defined as the ratio of exports plus imports to GDP.
[3]Consists of China, Hong Kong SAR, India, Indonesia, Korea, Malaysia, the Philippines, Singapore, Taiwan Province of China, and Thailand.
[4]Excluding Japan.

in countries in sub-Saharan Africa, however, remain generally more restrictive than in the dynamic economies of emerging Asia.

Despite these encouraging developments, per capita income growth in most countries in sub-Saharan Africa is still unlikely to be sufficient to meet the Millennium Development Goals. Therefore, countries need to deepen their reform programs to further strengthen growth prospects, including by promoting private sector investment, developing infrastructure, and strengthening institutions (including better transparency, governance, and property rights). Progress under the New Partnership for Africa's Development—a multicountry initiative to make progress in these areas—has so far been slow and limited. In addition, further trade, financial sector, and public sector reforms remain key to enhancing growth prospects in the region. These reforms must be complemented by continued prudent macroeconomic policies, including better fiscal management of oil and commodity revenues. The implementation of an effective strategy to moderate the impact of the HIV/AIDS pandemic is also critical. The international community, in turn, must support these domestic reform efforts with increased aid, debt relief, and improved market access.

Turning to sub-Saharan Africa's largest economies, South Africa is experiencing stronger output growth and important gains in formal sector employment. The economy expanded by 3.7 percent in 2004, and growth is expected to reach 4 percent this year. Activity is being underpinned by buoyant domestic demand, which has been fueled by low interest rates, the wealth effects of booming asset prices—particularly housing prices—and, lately, more expansionary fiscal policy. As a result of strong domestic demand and continued appreciation of the rand, the current account deficit widened to 2.5 percent of GDP in 2004. Capital inflows, buoyed by high domestic returns, have helped the central bank to continue to strengthen its international reserves position. The inflation outlook looks broadly favorable, although monetary

Box 1.5. How Does Macroeconomic Instability Stifle Sub-Saharan African Growth?

Many countries in sub-Saharan Africa have undertaken important steps to generate a more stable macroeconomic environment in recent years. However, output volatility remains high, adversely affecting long-term growth, and more needs to be done to create an environment under which the strong and sustained growth needed to reduce poverty can be attained. Recent research shows that volatility has a particularly damaging effect on economic growth in low-income countries (Hnatkovska and Loayza, 2005). The countries in sub-Saharan Africa, in addition to being poor, share several other common features that further magnify the negative effects of volatility on growth. This box briefly reviews some of these features, which are associated with the dynamics of investment, the strength and composition of economic linkages with the global economy, the development level of the domestic financial sector, and the nature of macroeconomic policies.

Dynamics of Investment

Investment plays a critical role in transmitting the negative impact of volatility to growth in Africa (Kose, Prasad, and Terrones, 2005). While sub-Saharan Africa's low rate of investment has always been a major impediment to economic growth, the high volatility of investment in the region has been particularly damaging (see Fischer, Hernández-Catá, and Khan, 1998, and the October 1999 *World Economic Outlook*). The average growth rate of investment in sub-Saharan Africa has been the slowest of any region over the past three decades, while its volatility has been the highest (see the figure).

Why has the volatility of investment been so high in sub-Saharan Africa? The major culprit driving investment volatility in the region has been the high risk attached to the return on investment. The average risk on investment return is determined by several factors, including those affecting overall macroeconomic volatility as well as uncertainty associated with

Note: The main authors of this box are M. Ayhan Kose and Marco Terrones.

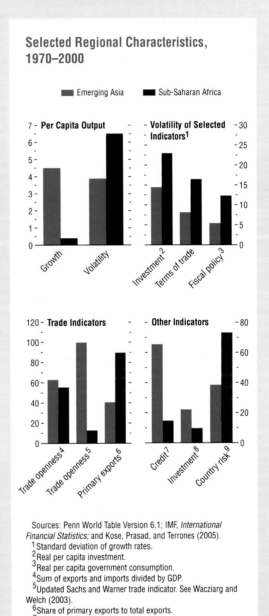

Selected Regional Characteristics, 1970–2000

Sources: Penn World Table Version 6.1; IMF, *International Financial Statistics;* and Kose, Prasad, and Terrones (2005).
[1] Standard deviation of growth rates.
[2] Real per capita investment.
[3] Real per capita government consumption.
[4] Sum of exports and imports divided by GDP.
[5] Updated Sachs and Warner trade indicator. See Wacziarg and Welch (2003).
[6] Share of primary exports to total exports.
[7] Credit to GDP ratio.
[8] Investment to GDP ratio.
[9] 100 – institutional investor index.

the scope and implementation of future government policies (see Azam and others, 2002). Not surprisingly, the typical measures of country risk indicate that investment is much riskier in sub-Saharan Africa than in other regions.

Box 1.5 *(concluded)*

Substantial growth benefits could be gained by stabilizing investment fluctuations in the region. For example, a reduction in investment volatility of the typical sub-Saharan African country to the level of a typical emerging Asian country—even if the average level is unchanged—would imply a ½ percentage point increase in annual per capita real GDP growth.[1]

Strength and Composition of Trade Linkages

Sub-Saharan Africa's trade linkages with the global economy remain relatively weak, limiting the region's ability to cope with the adverse impact of volatility on growth. Despite recent improvements in the region as a whole, the trade policy regimes of several countries in sub-Saharan Africa are highly restrictive, reflecting the presence of high and dispersed tariffs and widespread use of nontariff barriers. Several studies conclude that trade integration has a central role in helping achieve rapid growth in developing countries, including those in sub-Saharan Africa (see Krueger, 2004). Moreover, recent research shows that trade has a special role in mitigating the adverse impact of macro-economic volatility on growth. For example, trade integration could help a developing economy to export its way out of a recession since a given exchange rate depreciation could have a larger impact on that economy's export revenues than in an economy with weaker trade linkages. Stronger export revenues could also help in servicing external debt, which is quite substantial in a number of sub-Saharan African countries. There are significant growth benefits associated with further liberalizing trade regimes in sub-Saharan Africa: if the countries in the region were to raise the level of trade integration to the average of emerging Asia, their annual per capita real GDP growth would increase by about 1 percentage point.[2]

Sub-Saharan African economies depend on a narrow range of commodities for their export earnings. In particular, primary goods constitute close to 90 percent of total exports in sub-Saharan Africa, which is more than double that in emerging Asia. Mainly because of this, terms of trade fluctuations are very volatile in the sub-Saharan African countries, adversely affecting growth.[3]

Domestic Financial Sector and International Financial Integration

Having underdeveloped domestic financial systems and limited integration with global financial markets tends to magnify the negative impact of macroeconomic volatility on growth in the region. Total credit to the private sector as a ratio of GDP in the sub-Saharan African countries is roughly one-fifth of that in emerging Asian countries, implying that the financial sector plays only a minor role in these economies. Moreover, sub-Saharan Africa lags behind other developing regions in attracting capital flows (see Reinhart and Tokatlidis, 2003). Recent research finds that greater financial development not only significantly contributes to economic growth, but also dampens the adverse impact of volatility on economic growth. For example, if the level of financial sector development in sub-Saharan Africa increases to that of emerging Asia, this could increase the annual growth rate of per capita real GDP by ½ percentage point. International financial integration also appears to weaken the negative relationship between volatility and growth since it expands the set of risk-sharing opportunities.

---

impact of trade liberalization on fiscal balance, the sub-Saharan African countries would also need to implement fiscal reforms.

[3]Terms of trade shocks are an important channel transmitting the adverse effects of volatility on growth since they have a significant impact on savings and investment decisions (see Kose and Riezman, 2001; Belaney and Greenaway, 2001; and Calderon and others, 2004). Terms of trade shocks in sub-Saharan Africa are also highly persistent (see Cashin and others, 2004).

[1]The calculations reported in this box draw on Kose, Prasad, and Terrones (2005).

[2]To achieve this growth gain, however, reciprocal liberalization for key commodities in target markets will be needed. In addition, to mitigate the adverse

Nature of Macroeconomic Policies

Sub-Saharan African countries also suffer from the detrimental effects of highly volatile and procyclical fiscal policies on economic growth. Government revenues in sub-Saharan Africa are dependent on extremely volatile commodity exports, which results in large fluctuations in these revenues (Dehn, Gilbert, and Varangis, 2005). Meanwhile, inadequate expenditure control and the lack of a medium-term budget framework often mean that government expenditures move in tandem with revenues—leading to highly procyclical fiscal policy in most sub-Saharan African countries (Kaminsky, Reinhart, and Vegh, 2004). Recent research shows that highly volatile and procyclical fiscal policies often lead to an increase in the amplitude of macroeconomic fluctuations and lower economic growth (Fátas and Mihov, 2003).

In sum, economic growth in sub-Saharan Africa has strengthened in recent years, while volatility has fallen. Despite these welcome developments, however, growth is still below the rates that will be needed to achieve the Millennium Development Goals, and volatility remains the highest in the world. While macroeconomic stability is not a sufficient condition for economic growth in sub-Saharan Africa, recent research shows that it plays an important role. Without it, the impact of all other potential factors hindering economic growth in the region become much more damaging. This box—together with the analysis in Chapter II—suggests that creating a more attractive investment climate, expanding and diversifying exports, deepening the domestic financial sector, and designing prudent fiscal policies will all be important elements of the effort to further reduce economic volatility and enhance growth in the region.

growth is very rapid and unit labor costs are rising, raising the risk that without monetary tightening, the 3–6 percent inflation target may be missed. Notwithstanding the recent gains in employment, unemployment is likely to remain high unless reforms are implemented to reduce existing labor market rigidities.

In Nigeria, short-term economic performance continues to be greatly influenced by developments in the oil and gas sectors. The economy grew by 3.5 percent in 2004 and is expected to expand by 7.4 percent this year as a major offshore oil field and two new liquefaction trains come on stream. The adoption of more prudent macroeconomic policies has helped contain inflation, move the current account balance into a surplus, and increase international reserves sharply. Looking ahead, further reforms—centered around a strengthening of fiscal policy and monetary policy, civil service reform, and efforts to reduce corruption—together with sound macroeconomic policies are critical for the achievement of rapid and sustained eco-

nomic growth. The government should take advantage of the current favorable environment to implement other reforms, including trade liberalization, the unification of the exchange rate, and privatization to help increase the efficiency and resilience of the economy.

In the Maghreb region, the outlook remains positive notwithstanding an expected slowdown in output growth this year. In Algeria, the economy slowed in 2004—and is projected to slow further this year—reflecting a moderation in the expansion of hydrocarbon production. Fiscal policy has remained expansionary, as expenditures have been linked to hydrocarbon revenues. Starting with the 2005 budget, the government has begun the process of fiscal consolidation by delinking government spending from volatile hydrocarbon revenues. Financial sector reform, including the privatization of state-owned banks, and the pursuit of foreign trade liberalization are priorities to enhance economic growth and reduce the still-high levels of unemployment.

Table 1.11. Selected Middle Eastern Countries: Real GDP, Consumer Prices, and Current Account Balance
(Annual percent change unless otherwise noted)

	Real GDP				Consumer Prices[1]				Current Account Balance[2]			
	2003	2004	2005	2006	2003	2004	2005	2006	2003	2004	2005	2006
Middle East	**5.8**	**5.5**	**5.0**	**4.9**	**7.1**	**8.3**	**8.6**	**8.3**	**8.3**	**13.7**	**17.2**	**14.9**
Oil exporters[3]	**6.5**	**5.7**	**5.2**	**5.0**	**8.8**	**9.0**	**9.2**	**9.4**	**10.1**	**15.7**	**20.3**	**17.5**
I.R. of Iran	6.6	6.6	6.0	5.9	15.6	15.6	15.0	15.0	1.5	5.2	6.4	4.5
Saudi Arabia	7.2	5.3	4.1	3.3	0.6	0.2	1.0	1.0	13.8	19.8	27.7	25.1
Kuwait	9.7	7.2	3.2	3.2	1.0	1.8	1.8	1.8	17.5	29.1	37.8	34.7
Mashreq	**3.0**	**4.2**	**4.5**	**4.7**	**3.4**	**6.7**	**8.1**	**6.6**	**1.0**	**0.1**	**0.3**	**−0.4**
Egypt	3.1	4.1	4.8	5.0	3.2	8.1	9.9	8.0	2.4	4.4	4.5	3.4
Syrian Arab Republic	2.6	3.4	3.5	3.6	5.0	3.5	4.0	4.0	3.5	−0.4	−0.4	−2.9
Jordan	3.3	6.7	5.0	5.5	2.3	3.4	3.5	2.0	11.3	−0.8	−1.7	−5.0
Lebanon	3.0	5.0	4.0	3.5	1.3	3.0	2.0	2.5	−13.6	−16.1	−16.3	−12.9
Memorandum												
Israel	1.3	4.3	3.7	3.6	0.7	−0.4	1.0	2.0	0.1	0.1	−0.2	—

[1]In accordance with standard practice in the *World Economic Outlook*, movements in consumer prices are indicated as annual averages rather than as December/December changes during the year, as is the practice in some countries.
[2]Percent of GDP.
[3]Includes I.R. of Iran, Iraq, Kuwait, Libya, Oman, Qatar, Saudi Arabia, Syrian Arab Republic, and Yemen.

The Middle East: How Is the Recycling of Oil Revenues Affecting the Global Economy?

Oil-exporting countries in the Middle East have experienced a substantial increase in export earnings over the past two years as oil prices and oil production have risen. These revenues—together with sound financial policies and progress with structural reforms—have supported strong growth, which averaged 5.7 percent in 2004, and have underpinned large current account and fiscal surpluses. Growth in the non-oil-producing countries has also picked up as they have benefited from the strong growth in the oil producers and, in some cases, the positive impact of domestic reforms. Although growth is expected to slow, the outlook for the region remains positive with growth of 5 percent projected for 2005 (Table 1.11); indeed, with oil prices currently well above the baseline used in the World Economic Outlook forecasts, there is a clear upside risk to this projection. On the downside, continuing geopolitical uncertainties in the region could hurt growth. With the exchange rates of many countries in the region linked to the U.S. dollar, further dollar depreciation is not likely to have significant implications for most countries, unless it is associated with a slowing in global growth and a decline in oil prices.

Current expectations are that oil prices will remain high over the medium term. The prospect of a sustained period of high oil prices presents an important opportunity for oil exporters to press ahead with the reforms needed to boost medium-term growth prospects, increase employment prospects for the rapidly growing working age population, and reduce existing vulnerabilities, including from high public debt levels in a number of countries (see Box 1.6, "How Should Middle Eastern and Central Asian Oil Exporters Use Their Oil Revenues?"). Growth-enhancing reforms in the oil-exporting countries will also provide benefits to other countries in the region, particularly through trade links and remittance flows (see Chapter II for an assessment of the macroeconomic benefits of remittances).

From a global perspective, the behavior of the Middle Eastern oil-producing countries could have a bearing on how the current constellation of external imbalances unwinds. The combined current account surplus of these countries was larger (in dollar terms) than that in developing Asia last year. Over the medium term, it is likely that these surpluses will decline as increased domestic consumption and investment boosts imports. Further, while the impact on the global economy of the financial flows from the region has declined relative to earlier periods of high oil prices, these flows could have an impact on international financial markets, although it is difficult to know where the investments are directed (Figure 1.18).

Turning to individual countries, the economic outlook in the Islamic Republic of Iran remains favorable, with growth of 6 percent expected during 2005–06. The economy is benefiting from high oil prices and previously implemented reforms that have boosted the non-oil sector. Activity has also been underpinned by expansionary monetary and fiscal policies, but with inflation entrenched at about 15 percent, tighter macroeconomic policies are now required. Sustaining strong growth and reducing unemployment—which, although declining, remains high—is a policy priority, and this will require an acceleration of structural reforms, particularly in the labor market and financial sector.

Progress toward restoring economic stability in Iraq is continuing, although the recovery appears to be proceeding more slowly than had earlier been envisaged and inflation has risen sharply in recent months. A tightening of monetary policy is now required. With the elections completed, the government must focus its efforts on developing institutions to support a market-based economy, on reconstructing infrastructure, and on maintaining macroeconomic stability. The recent decision by the Paris Club to reduce their claims on Iraq by 80 percent is an important step toward achieving debt sustainability.

In Saudi Arabia, the economy expanded by 5.3 percent last year and inflation remained subdued. While oil sector output is projected to slow this year, the non-oil sector is expected to remain robust—supported by increased tourism and the continued expansion of the petrochemical sector—and overall GDP growth is projected at 4.1 percent. The sharp rise in oil revenues has underpinned a significant increase in the current account and fiscal surpluses and a

Figure 1.18. Middle East: How Are OPEC Members Using the Higher Oil Revenues?[1]

High oil prices have underpinned a considerable strengthening in the external position of Middle Eastern OPEC countries. Higher oil revenues have boosted imports and increased investment overseas. The impact on global financial markets, however, is more limited than during previous periods of high oil prices.

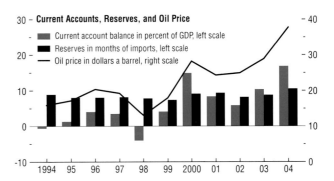

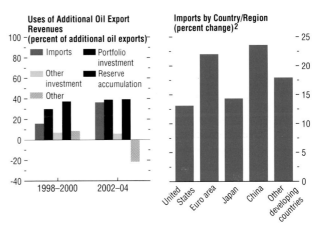

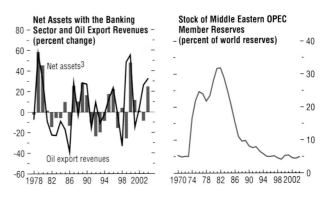

Sources: IMF, *Direction of Trade Statistics;* Bank of International Settlements; and IMF staff calculations.
[1]Consists of I.R. of Iran, Iraq, Kuwait, Libya, Qatar, Saudi Arabia, and the United Arab Emirates.
[2]First 11 months of 2004 over the same period of 2003.
[3]Net assets with the banking sector are defined as the stock of assets of Middle Eastern OPEC members vis-à-vis BIS reporting banks less liabilities to these banks. Data are fourth quarter over fourth quarter percent change. Data for 2004 are as of 2004Q3.

Box. 1.6. How Should Middle Eastern and Central Asian Oil Exporters Use Their Oil Revenues?

The rise in oil prices and the associated increase in oil earnings present a window of opportunity for oil-exporting countries to address their economic challenges. This box focuses on the Middle Eastern and central Asian oil-exporting countries, although the general analysis and implications are applicable to many oil-exporting developing countries. In particular, progress in generating employment for growing working-age populations and fostering the development of the private non-oil sectors can be facilitated by the increased financial resources now available. In principle, increased public spending accompanied by an acceleration of structural reforms, with due care to avoid low-return outlays seen during past oil booms in some countries, could place the economies on a higher sustained growth path and, by creating jobs, help improve social outcomes.[1]

Oil export receipts of Middle Eastern and central Asian oil-exporting countries increased by an estimated $100 billion in 2004. Most of the increase was due to higher oil prices, although some countries also expanded production significantly to meet rising global demand. While about two-thirds of oil export receipts constituted fiscal revenues in these countries on average, there were substantial cross-country variations owing to differences in production, extraction costs, the fiscal regime, and the extent of government ownership of oil fields and the distribution system. With oil prices expected to remain high in 2005, Middle Eastern and central Asian oil-exporting countries are likely to continue to earn substantial revenue from oil and must decide how much of this revenue should be spent and how much should be saved.

One obvious factor that will help guide this choice in all countries is how long the increase

in oil earnings is expected to last. If it is very temporary, then clearly more of the extra revenue should be saved. But the large increase in long-term futures prices of oil since mid-2003 suggests that a sizable portion of the rise in oil exporters' earnings is expected to persist over the medium term, implying that a higher level of spending could be sustainable and appropriate. The extent to which spending can and should be expanded depends on the circumstances of individual countries.

In countries where the social return on human capital development or infrastructure investment is high, there is a strong case for spending a larger part of the additional oil revenue in these areas.[2] For example, in countries where human development indicators are poor—such as Algeria, Sudan, Syria, Uzbekistan, and Yemen, as suggested by their ranking on the UN Human Development Index (see the table)—increased spending on education and health could be especially effective. Similarly, in countries where unemployment is a serious problem (e.g., Algeria, Bahrain, I.R. of Iran, Iraq, and Saudi Arabia), schemes to boost private sector employment—possibly through a combination of increased spending and tax cuts—may well carry high social returns. In other countries, infrastructure investment may offer high returns by enhancing the growth prospects of the private sector. Clearly in Iraq there are major infrastructure rebuilding requirements, but aging infrastructure also poses a constraint on growth elsewhere. As two widely used indices that measure the quality of the road network and the efficiency of the elec-

Note: The main authors of this box are Aasim Husain and Hamid Davoodi.

[1]The positive and significant direct impact of increased social spending on human capital accumulation and growth is supported by empirical studies. See, for example, Baldacci and others (2004).

[2]Increased investment spending in response to higher oil prices is supported by economic theory. Hotelling's rule for optimal exhaustible resource management indicates that if the return to public investment exceeds the world real interest rate—which in turn equals the return to holding oil in the ground over the long run—rates of oil extraction should rise and proceeds should be used to increase fixed investment. Similarly, higher earnings from a given rate of extraction, in such circumstances, should be used to finance higher investment.

Selected Economic and Social Indicators of Middle Eastern and Central Asian Oil-Exporting Countries

	Infrastructure Development				
	Human development Index rank[1] 2002	Paved roads (percent of all roads; 1995–2001)	Electric power losses (percent of output; 2001)	Proven oil reserves (billion barrels; end-2004)	Ratio of overall fiscal balance to GDP (percent, 2004)
Algeria	108	69	16	11.8	4.7
Azerbaijan	91	92	13	7.0	0.9
Bahrain	40	. . .	9	0.1	7.3
I.R. of Iran	101	56	16	125.8	2.7
Iraq	. . .	84	. . .	115.0	−43.0
Kazakhstan	78	94	17	9.0	2.7
Kuwait	44	81	3	101.5	21.0
Libya	58	57	. . .	39.0	18.8
Oman	74	30	17	5.5	7.7
Qatar	47	. . .	7	15.2	9.1
Saudi Arabia	77	30	8	261.9	7.4
Sudan	139	36	15	0.6	1.4
Syria	106	21	. . .	2.5	−5.7
Turkmenistan	86	81	13	0.5	−2.0
Uzbekistan	107	87	9	0.6	16.4
United Arab Emirates	49	100	9	97.8	−1.3
Yemen	149	12	26	4.0	−3.7
Memorandum					
World[2]					
High-income countries	22	93	6	. . .	. . .
Middle-income countries	78	52	11	. . .	. . .
Low-income countries	142	16	23	. . .	. . .

Sources: UNDP, *Human Development Report* (2004); World Bank, *World Development Indicators* (2004); Radler (2004); and IMF staff estimates.

[1]The rank represents a country's relative position out of 177 countries and is based on a composite index of life expectancy, enrollment rate, adult literacy rate, and per capita income.

[2]Simple average over country groups, based on the World Bank's income classification.

tricity distribution system suggest (see the table), Kazakhstan, Oman, Syria, and Yemen stand to gain substantially from improved infrastructure. In countries with a high incidence of poverty (e.g., Azerbaijan, Sudan, and Yemen), strengthening of social protection mechanisms is likely to take priority.

That said, overall macroeconomic conditions may affect some countries' ability to absorb additional public spending. In countries such as Azerbaijan, Iran, and Kazakhstan, where the non-oil sector is expanding rapidly, credit growth is high and persistent, and inflationary pressures are evident or emerging, the room for further relaxation of the budgetary position at present may be more limited. In countries where public spending has already been expanding at a rapid

pace, such as Algeria and Kuwait, further acceleration could lead to an erosion in its quality and effectiveness, and a withdrawal of fiscal stimulus may be needed. Countries that have accumulated significant public debt in the past may find that the value of paying down part of this debt, by reducing budgetary vulnerability to oil price declines and creating room for dissaving during possible bad times in the future, exceeds the benefits of additional spending now. Indeed, Saudi Arabia has reduced its domestic debt significantly over the past year.

The remaining stock of proven oil reserves and future profile of oil production will also need to guide the decision on the appropriate use of oil revenues, as the sustainability of spending depends on these factors. In countries

Box. 1.6 *(concluded)*

such as Oman and Yemen—whose oil revenues account for a large fraction of government revenues and which face aging oil fields and rising oil extraction costs, and which have recently witnessed large downward revisions in the size of their proven oil reserves—a larger share of additional oil revenue will need to be saved to avoid a disorderly adjustment of the fiscal position in the future. Indeed, these factors point to fiscal prudence and the adoption of measures to enhance non-oil revenues and rationalize spending. By contrast, there is clearly more room to relax the fiscal stance in countries with plentiful oil reserves, as well as in countries where a substantial rise in the volume of oil production is projected over the medium term (e.g., Azerbaijan and Kazakhstan), although other factors need to be considered in determining how much of an expansion in spending would be advisable.

Thus, these principles provide some general guidance on the use of oil revenues, but their appropriate use in a particular country will depend on each country's circumstances. Indeed, the general principles may well offer conflicting guidance, as in the case of a country with large social and/or infrastructure needs that is faced with emerging overheating pressures or diminishing oil revenue. In such cases, competing considerations for the optimal use of oil revenue will need to be carefully balanced and may, in some countries, imply the need to increase spending gradually or to shift the composition of spending to increase its productivity. Where increased spending is judged to be appropriate, an adequate public expenditure management system will need to be in place to ensure that the additional spending is of high quality, and basing such increases within a longer-term framework will help secure budget sustainability. And due caution will need to be exercised—by adopting appropriate macroeconomic policies and pressing ahead with structural reforms to enhance productivity—to avoid an erosion in the competitiveness of the non-oil sectors of the economy.

reduction in public debt. Efforts are needed, however, to contain current spending and increase non-oil revenues to strengthen the underlying structure of the budget. Structural reforms are continuing to move forward, with important progress being made in the legislative and financial sector areas.

The Egyptian economy gained momentum during 2004 owing to a strong export performance and a revival in domestic consumption, and growth of 4.8 percent is projected for 2005. Sentiment has been strengthened by the government's commitment to reforms—which include a major reform of the tariff system, plans for a comprehensive restructuring of the banking sector, and renewed impetus on privatization—and the stock market has risen to all-time highs. The fiscal position, however, needs to be strengthened and public debt reduced, and monetary policy tightened further to counter high inflation.

Elsewhere in the Mashreq, growth in Jordan strengthened to 6.7 percent in 2004 and is expected to remain robust this year. Exports have been boosted by strong growth in partner countries and exchange rate depreciation, while domestic demand has rebounded as confidence has returned after the Iraq war. Macroeconomic policies have imparted stability to the economy, while key structural reforms are proceeding, including in the area of privatization. In the Syrian Arab Republic, the economy has recovered slowly following the Iraq war. Although growth of 3.5 percent is expected in 2005, the balance of risks remains on the downside. A significant acceleration of reforms—including the liberalization of the trade and foreign exchange regimes and the strengthening of the financial sector—is required to raise growth potential. In Lebanon, the economy has benefited indirectly from the increase in oil prices through higher capital, remittance, and tourism inflows from elsewhere in the region, and this has boosted growth. Ongoing political developments, however, have increased financial market uncertainties, underscoring the benefits of pressing ahead with a strong economic reform program to maintain investor confidence.

In Israel, growth accelerated to 4.3 percent in 2004—supported by the favorable global environment and an improvement in the security situation—and is expected to be 3.7 percent this year. CPI inflation has remained very low, enabling the Bank of Israel to continue to reduce its policy interest rate, but is expected to return up into the target range of 1–3 percent during the course of this year. Regarding fiscal policy, the authorities have announced an ambitious agenda to reduce the size of government and public debt, and it is important that this be adhered to.

Appendix 1.1. Recent Developments in Commodity Markets

The main authors of this appendix are Sam Ouliaris and Hossein Samiei, with support from To-Nhu Dao and Paul Nicholson.

The overall index of primary commodity prices increased by about 11 percent in U.S. dollar terms (18 percent in SDR terms) between July 2004 and March 2005[9]—extending the robust boom in commodity prices that commenced in July 2002. Substantial increases in energy prices played a key role in strengthening the index. Oil prices stood at record highs in April 2005 owing to high oil consumption growth, a cold weather snap in the northern hemisphere, and uncertainties about OPEC's production plans. Led by beverages and metals prices, the index of nonenergy prices rose by about 3 percent in U.S. dollar and SDR terms. Nevertheless, nonenergy commodity price inflation eased considerably in the fourth quarter of

2004 owing to divergent movements in specific commodity prices and weakness in food and raw material prices in particular. Semiconductor markets posted significant gains in revenue during 2004; however, prospects for further revenue growth in 2005 appear limited owing to depressed prices and substantial gains in productive capacity.

Crude Oil

The average petroleum spot price[10] (APSP) rose to a record nominal high of $54.30 in early April 2005—a 73 percent increase relative to prices at the beginning of 2004 (Figure 1.19). Moreover, the rise in crude oil prices was broad based, with each component of the APSP reaching record highs. The increase in prices over the past year, which was largely unanticipated, reflected the combined influence of robust global demand for crude oil, temporary supply shocks, heightened geopolitical uncertainties, and limited spare capacity among OPEC producers. Futures markets in July 2004 implied that oil prices would ease for the rest of 2004 to average $32.50—about $5 less than the actual outcome of $37.65. The rise in prices was also accompanied by a considerable increase in volatility; the coefficient of variation of daily spot prices increased by over 79 percent relative to 2003 levels.

While the average U.S. dollar price of oil increased significantly during 2004, there were divergent movements in terms of non-U.S. currencies and specific grades of crude oil. The prices of heavier grades of crude oil were relatively subdued in the second half of 2004, while those of light sweet crudes surged, resulting in historically high spreads between light and heavy crudes. Also, the significant decline in the U.S. dollar during 2004 tempered the rise in domestic crude oil prices for many countries (e.g., EU member nations, where crude oil prices remain

---

[9]Unless otherwise stated, percentage changes and summary statistics apply to the July 2004–March 2005 period.

[10]The IMF average petroleum spot price is an equally weighted average of the West Texas Intermediate, Brent, and Dubai crude oil prices. Unless otherwise noted, all subsequent references to the oil price are to the APSP.

Figure 1.19. Oil Prices, Futures, and Production

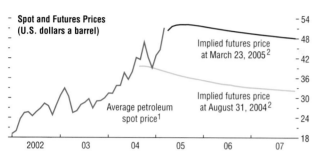

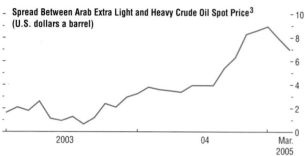

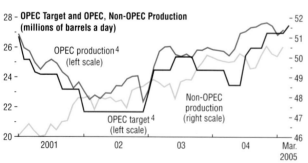

Sources: International Energy Agency; Bloomberg Financial Markets, LP; IMF, *International Financial Statistics;* and IMF staff calculations.

[1]Average petroleum spot price of West Texas Intermediate, U.K. Brent, and Dubai Fateh crude.

[2]Five-day weighted average of NYMEX Light Sweet Crude, IPE Dated Brent, and implied Dubai Fateh.

[3]Saudi Arabian crude oil deliverable in Asia. Arab Extra Light (Berri) has an API gravity of 37 and a sulphur content of 1.15. Arab Heavy (Safaniya) has an API gravity of 27 and a sulphur content of 2.8.

[4]Excluding Iraq.

Table 1.12. Global Oil Demand by Region
(Millions of barrels a day, mbd)

	Demand 2004	Annual Change	
		mbd	Percent
North America	25.18	0.61	2.5
Europe	16.47	0.26	1.6
OECD Pacific	8.62	−0.15	−1.8
China	6.38	0.86	15.6
Other Asia	8.55	0.45	5.6
CIS	3.71	0.14	3.8
Middle East	5.88	0.32	5.7
Africa	2.81	0.07	2.4
Latin America	4.91	0.18	3.8
World	82.51	2.73	3.4

Source: International Energy Agency, *Oil Market Report*, March 2005.

close to early 2003 levels in local currency terms; see Figure 1.19).

Turning to oil market fundamentals, the global consumption of crude oil increased by 2.73 million barrels a day (or 3.4 percent) during 2004—the fastest growth since 1976. The surge in consumption was largely unanticipated. For example, in January 2004, the International Energy Agency (IEA) forecast that global demand would increase by only 1.2 mbd (or 1.6 percent)—in line with a growth in non-OPEC output of approximately 1.2 mbd.

The key factor behind the robust growth in oil demand is the ongoing expansion of the global economy, with Asia (especially China) and North America leading the way (Table 1.12). China's consumption of crude oil increased by 0.86 mbd during 2004—contributing the most to the overall increase in consumption, and making it the second largest oil consumer after the United States—followed by North America (0.61 mbd) and other non-OECD Asian countries (e.g., India; 0.45 mbd). In the case of China, severe electrical power shortages encouraged the use of stand-alone, diesel-powered back-up generators, while expansion of pipeline and commercial oil storage absorbed substantial volumes of incremental crude and derivative products.

According to the IEA, average daily crude oil production from non-OPEC sources rose by about 1.1 mbd in 2004 (1.4 mbd including non-gas liquids)—similar to the growth recorded in

2003. Growth in non-OPEC output, however, was held back by significant declines in OECD production of about 0.35 mbd, arising from damaged oil infrastructure caused by Hurricane Ivan and structural declines in United Kingdom (0.2 mbd) and Norway output (0.1 mbd) of conventional crude. Despite ongoing tensions between OSA Yukos and the Russian government, crude oil output from CIS countries continued to rise, with Russia and Kazakhstan contributing more than half of the increase in non-OPEC output during 2004. Significant increases in synthetic crude oil production from Canada offset declines from more conventional sources, providing a net 0.1 mbd increase in non-OPEC supply. Early indicators compiled by the IEA suggest that non-OPEC output growth will slow to 0.9 mbd in 2005, owing in part to an unexpected shortfall in Russian output during the first two months of 2005.

The rise in non-OPEC output fell far short of the growth in global consumption during 2004, resulting in a significant increase in the demand for OPEC crude oil—the so-called call on OPEC. OPEC-10 members (OPEC excluding Iraq) adopted an accommodative stance toward the surge in demand, gradually raising official quotas from 23 mbd in April 2004 to 27 mbd in November 2004, and maintaining production close to full capacity levels until the end of 2004 (Figure 1.20). By the end of December 2004, actual OPEC-10 production was averaging 28 mbd for the year—about 1 mbd above official quotas, and a rise of nearly 2 mbd relative to 2003 levels. Notwithstanding frequent attacks on its oil infrastructure, oil production in Iraq recovered to about 2 mbd for 2004, supporting an overall increase in OPEC production in 2004 of 2.5 mbd—close to the growth in global demand. The significant increase in global production permitted a counterseasonal rise in OECD commercial inventories during the fourth quarter of 2004 to levels close to the average of the past decade. Crude oil inventories in the United States, however, despite a recent pickup, remain at the lower end of historical averages (Figure 1.20).

Figure 1.20. Commercial Oil Inventories and World Refinery Capacity

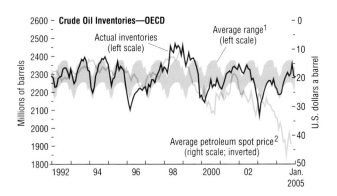

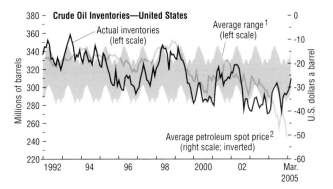

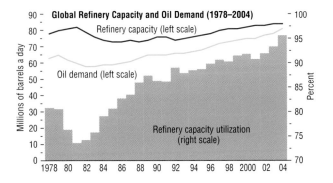

Sources: International Energy Agency; Bloomberg Financial, LP; and IMF staff calculations.
[1]Average of each calendar month during 1992–2004, plus a 40 percent confidence interval based on past deviations.
[2]Average petroleum spot price of West Texas Intermediate, U.K. Brent, and Dubai Fateh crude.

The sizable increase in commercial inventories and concerns about possible overproduction at the end of the cold season prompted OPEC-10 members to announce a cut in production of 1 mbd effective January 1, 2005, thereby reducing actual production closer to the official OPEC-10 quota as of November 2004. While actual OPEC-10 output remained above quota, crude oil prices rose significantly during the first three months of 2005 as colder weather hit the Northern Hemisphere and concerns about OPEC's production plans increased. Responding to significantly higher crude oil prices in March 2005, OPEC-10 members raised official quotas to a record high of 27.5 mbd on March 16, 2005, with the possibility of a further 0.5 mbd rise in official quotas before OPEC's next official meeting in June.

The surge in OPEC-10 output pushed upstream spare capacity to historical lows, increasing the sensitivity of spot prices to events that affect or threaten crude oil supplies. By the end of December 2004, however, with the addition of about 0.8 mbd capacity in Saudi Arabia, OPEC-10 spare capacity recovered from its historical low to about 1.4 mbd. Nevertheless, even this level of spare capacity—which is close to the 1.5–2.0 mbd target that OPEC has indicated it will aim for going forward—is unlikely to calm the oil market, especially if global demand continues to surge in 2005. According to the IEA, geopolitical tensions during the second half of 2004 threatened 1.5–3.0 mbd of crude oil output. Moreover, over 4 mbd were lost during the Middle East crisis of 1990–91, and the largest oil disruption since 1973 (Iranian revolution, 1978–79) resulted in a supply shortfall of approximately 5.6 mbd for six months. Spare capacity has averaged close to 5 mbd (8 percent of output) in the past three decades. Notwithstanding substantial precautionary inventories in OECD countries, higher spare capacity than currently is planned will be needed to reduce price volatility.

The erosion in spare capacity during 2004 highlighted structural imbalances in the oil sector, which led to higher spreads between light and heavy crudes in the second half of 2004.

- *While OPEC adopted an accommodative stance toward demand, the marginal barrel from OPEC— before the addition of the Qatif and Abu Sa'fah oil fields in Saudi Arabia at the end of 2004—was of the heavy sour type.* At the same time, hurricane-related damage to the U.S. pipeline network in the Gulf of Mexico in September shut in significant quantities of light sweet crude oil and disrupted the flow of imports to the mid-continent of the United States. The cumulative loss in U.S. output was about 40 million barrels by the end of 2004, causing price differentials between light sweet and heavy sour grades of crude oil to widen to historical highs.

- *The shortage of light sweet crude was also compounded by a structural imbalance in the refinery sector.* Global refinery capacity levels remain only slightly above 1980s levels, and utilization rates, which have risen gradually since 2002, remain over 90 percent. In addition, the majority of refinery capacity is simple distillation that is unable to process the heavier crudes. While such refineries can be modified to handle heavier crudes, the conversion process is costly and can take years to implement (Figure 1.20).

Looking forward, early April 2005 futures contract crude oil prices remain above the WEO baseline. Future contract prices imply that average annual prices will average around $52.23 for 2005 and $52.59 for 2006. Moreover, long-dated futures contract prices rose sharply in early 2005 and remain persistently higher—by about $23 relative to late 2002 levels—reflecting ongoing concerns about limited spare capacity relative to demand growth over the medium term (2007–10) that suggest a structural shift, despite ample reserves, toward permanently higher crude oil prices.

In addition, demand and supply conditions for 2005 point to high crude oil prices going forward. Early indicators for 2005 suggest that the demand for crude oil and derivative products continues to rise in North America, and there is little evidence of a slowdown in Chinese demand for diesel fuel in particular. Nevertheless, both the IEA and OPEC are predicting a decline in the growth of oil demand for 2005 to between 1.8 and 1.9 mbd—nearly a 33 percent reduction compared with the 2.73 mbd growth for 2004. This expectation is based on the assumption that oil consumption growth in China will halve in 2005 relative to 2004 levels as coal-based power generation capacity increases, inventory building eases, and GDP growth in China slows. It also assumes that the substantially higher prices of 2003 and 2004 will begin to temper the growth in global consumption. As for OPEC's supply, analysts appear divided regarding the ability of OPEC member countries to satisfy the incremental growth in demand. With non-OPEC supply predicted to rise by 0.9 mbd in 2005, growth in the call on OPEC in 2005 should slow considerably, reducing downward pressures on spare capacity. After allowing for growth in nongas liquids, both the IEA and OPEC are projecting marginal (0.5 mbd) growth for the call on OPEC during 2005.

That said, global growth for 2005—the main driver of oil demand—at 4.3 percent remains strong and there is little evidence, as yet, that oil demand growth in OECD countries is easing owing to higher crude oil prices. The main uncertainty remains in China, where electricity shortages could persist because power generation capability is lagging behind demand. Also, China's per capita consumption of oil (about 2 barrels a year) is less than 15 percent of that in more advanced Asian economies such as Japan, Korea, and Taiwan Province of China, and these economies experienced a rapid increase in absolute per capita oil consumption only *after* achieving China's current level of industrialization. More generally, price controls and generous tax subsidies continue to shield end-users from the full effect of crude oil prices in a number of developing countries. As such, the rise in global demand during 2005 could easily exceed 1.8 mbd, placing further upward pressure on the call on OPEC and possibly crude oil spot prices if OPEC cannot respond owing to limited spare capacity. For example, even after allowing for a slowing in demand from China, the U.S.

Energy Information Agency is predicting that global oil demand will grow by about 2.0 mbd in 2005.

Whatever the outcome for global demand growth in 2005, global spare capacity is likely to remain low, suggesting that prices will continue to be sensitive to ongoing geopolitical tensions. Moreover, the competitive nature of the non-OPEC sector suggests that non-OPEC producers are unlikely to play a strategic role in maintaining global spare capacity. As such, OPEC's capacity expansion plans will be the critical factor going forward. Given the sizable capital outlays involved and the irreversible nature of investments in oil infrastructure, OPEC may be inclined to adopt a "wait-and-see" attitude, possibly—in the absence of a global slowdown—allowing capacity to lag behind the growth in demand. The major risk OPEC faces is that the higher crude oil prices and concerns over the availability of future crude oil supplies encourages a permanent shift to other sources of energy, resulting in a permanent fall in the elasticity of crude oil demand with respect to global income.

On balance, the oil market in the near term is likely to remain dependent on all oil-exporting nations maintaining output at close to capacity, leaving the global economy exposed to the risk of significantly higher oil prices arising because of an unanticipated supply disruption. There also remains the pressing issue of limited downstream capacity (refinery, pipeline, and shipping infrastructure), which was pushed ever closer to its limits by early 2005. The latter contributed to bottlenecks in derivative product (gasoline, diesel) markets, weakening its ability to handle sudden shifts in the quality of crude oil available on the market, newer gasoline standards, and seasonal shifts in demand. More stringent environment standards, particularly in the United States and Europe, and public aversion to petroleum-related investments—especially in refinery capacity—have raised the cost of developing downstream capacity. Given that investments in the oil sector take two to four years to plan and implement, robust growth in oil

Table 1.13. Nonenergy Commodity Prices
(Percent change from July 2004 to March 2005)

	U.S. Dollar Terms	Contribution[1]	SDR Terms
Food	−3.6	38.1	−3.9
Beverages	35.3	21.9	38.2
Agricultural raw materials	−0.6	4.7	−3.5
Metals	10.4	35.3	10.7
Overall nonenergy	3.3	100.0	2.9

Sources: IMF, Primary Commodity Price Database; and IMF staff estimates.

[1]Contributions to change in overall nonenergy price index in U.S. dollar terms, in percent. Contributions to change in SDR terms are similar.

Figure 1.21. Nonenergy Commodities

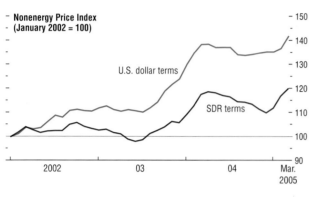

Nonenergy Price Index
(January 2002 = 100)

U.S. dollar terms

SDR terms

2002   03   04   Mar. 2005

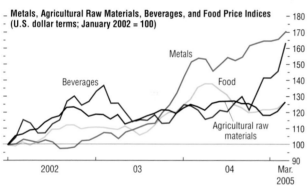

Metals, Agricultural Raw Materials, Beverages, and Food Price Indices
(U.S. dollar terms; January 2002 = 100)

Metals

Beverages

Food

Agricultural raw materials

2002   03   04   Mar. 2005

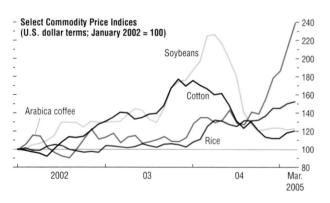

Select Commodity Price Indices
(U.S. dollar terms; January 2002 = 100)

Soybeans

Cotton

Arabica coffee

Rice

2002   03   04   Mar. 2005

Sources: IMF, *International Financial Statistics;* and IMF staff calculations.

demand in coming years will most likely keep the oil market close to capacity.

Nonenergy Commodity Prices

Overall nonenergy prices rose by 3 percent in U.S. dollar and SDR terms during July 2004–March 2005, with the beverage and metals components contributing the most to the rise (Table 1.13).[11] There were divergent movements in commodity prices during 2004, with cotton prices, for example, falling by 34 percent relative to end-2003 levels, soybeans prices easing by 21 percent, and sugar, rice, pork, and coffee prices all rising by at least 30 percent (Figure 1.21). Record harvests and slower demand growth—natural market responses to higher commodity prices, especially for the softer commodities—depressed food and agricultural raw materials prices during the second half of 2004. Looking forward, the ongoing global economic expansion is expected to support commodity prices in 2005. Nevertheless, on balance, the increase in overall nonenergy prices is expected to slow in 2005 owing to favorable harvests and weaker demand resulting from higher metals prices.

The overall index of food items fell by about 4 percent because of favorable harvests, and IMF staff expect further downward pressure on prices in 2005. While wheat, corn, and soybean prices

[11]Unless otherwise stated, percent changes in this section refer to March 2005 over July 2004 price movements.

all strengthened in March, large stocks and robust supply growth should reduce food prices for the remainder of 2005. Meat prices finished 2004 about 17 percent higher than 2003 levels because of the growing popularity of low-carbohydrate diets. However, they stabilized recently as BSE-related import bans on North American exports were removed, and are expected to fall further in 2005.

The index of beverage prices increased by 35 percent in U.S. dollar terms largely because of a substantial increase in coffee prices of 56 percent, reflecting significant production losses in Brazil and Vietnam. While cocoa and tea prices strengthened during the first quarter of 2005, cocoa prices remain sensitive to political situations in Côte d'Ivoire and a possibility of a smaller-than-expected crop in that country. Looking forward, the index of beverage prices is expected to rise in 2005 even as the supply of coffee beans from Brazil recovers and India's output of tea increases.

Agricultural raw materials fell by 1 percent between July 2004 and March 2005. Despite recent falls, softwood lumber prices ended 2004 about 35 percent higher owing to strong housing demand in both the United States and Canada, but recently stabilized. Cotton prices fell because of a sizable increase in global production, with the bulk of the price fall occurring in the second half of 2004. However, the drop in cotton prices reversed in early 2005 owing to stronger-than-expected demand and a projected fall in the 2005/06 harvest. Despite rising in the first half of the year, rubber prices ended 2004 about 4 percent lower than 2003 levels as slower global demand growth and surging production resulted in a 10 percent increase in global inventories. Demand for hides remained constant throughout 2004, keeping prices subdued. The overall agricultural raw materials index is expected to strengthen slightly in 2005 on strong demand for timber in particular.

Metals prices increased 10 percent, finishing the year 2004 up almost 25 percent owing to low inventories and strong demand, especially from China, which has been a main catalyst for the continued surge in metals prices. Copper prices increased 20 percent. However, increased mine operations are expected to bring more product to market in the second half of 2005 and help ease prices. Aluminum prices increased 17 percent but the surge in energy prices appears to be taking its toll and demand by refiners for the product may be limited as cost could begin affecting final demand. Looking forward, limited inventories in other key metals and continued demand strength should help increase metals prices slightly in 2005.

Semiconductor Markets

2004 was a record year for semiconductor sales, with revenues surging 30 percent relative to 2003 levels and by 5 percent compared with levels in 2000, the previous record year for sales (Figure 1.22). The Asia/Pacific region (excluding Japan) was responsible for the bulk of this increase, owing to a 44 percent increase in the consumption of semiconductors that supported further growth in technology manufacturing. By the end of 2004, the Asia/Pacific region was consuming nearly twice as many chips as the next largest market (Japan).

Countries appearing to benefit the most from the semiconductor boom are China, Korea, and Thailand, which have seen their exports of electronic goods grow by 236, 48, and 30 percent, respectively, since 2000. In addition, there are reports that as much as one-third of all venture capital spent inside of China in 2004 went toward the nation's chip industry. Additionally, Korea recorded its first year of net semiconductor exports since 2000.

Last year was also a record year for capacity expansion, with the semiconductor equipment sector experiencing 52 percent growth relative to 2003, mostly in the first half of the year. As a result, utilization in leading-edge technologies fell from over 97 percent utilization in early 2004 to almost 90 percent by the end of 2004. Utilization also fell because some firms have scaled back production to avoid unwanted inventory accumulation. While spending on semicon-

Figure 1.22. Semiconductor Market

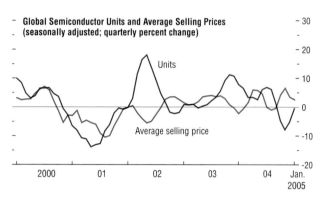

Global Semiconductor Units and Average Selling Prices
(seasonally adjusted; quarterly percent change)

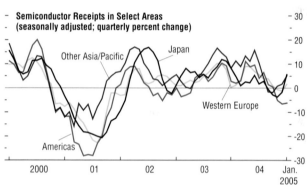

Semiconductor Receipts in Select Areas
(seasonally adjusted; quarterly percent change)

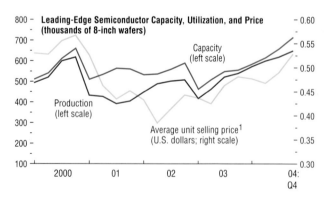

Leading-Edge Semiconductor Capacity, Utilization, and Price
(thousands of 8-inch wafers)

Sources: World Semiconductor Trade Statistics; Semiconductor International Capacity Statistics; and IMF staff calculations.
[1] Price refers to the average selling price for all semiconductors.

ductor equipment has recently fallen, pushing down the North American book-to-bill ratio to 0.78, bookings have bottomed out and further spending falls are not expected.

Notwithstanding the surge in capacity, unit prices for semiconductor equipment rose—in line with expectations—during the second half of 2004 owing to strong seasonal demand. As a result, some firms have reported strong earnings for 2004, and particular semiconductor stock indices have grown faster than the broader market. Nevertheless, during the fourth quarter of 2004, the number of earnings reports in the tech sector below expectations were 85 percent higher than the number above expectations, suggesting that growth may ease in 2005. Additionally, Dynamic Random Access Memory (DRAM) spot prices saw a 30 percent fall since the beginning of February.

Looking forward, industry analysts remain concerned about the large amounts of capacity coming on stream. This could create an incentive to keep production high as the year progresses which should lower prices. Lower prices are expected to reduce sales revenue growth significantly in 2005. However, consumer spending is expected to remain buoyant in several markets as prices for newer technologies continue to decline.

Forecasting Crude Oil Prices

Though the dependency of the global economy on crude oil has fallen steadily during the past 30 years, the oil price baseline assumption remains an important variable for the twice-yearly *World Economic Outlook* exercise. At the beginning of each WEO round, crude oil prices are forecast up to eight quarters ahead, and then a further three years on an annual basis. The crude oil baseline needs to be projected using a well-defined procedure—one that is easily understood and is verifiable by external users.

The forecasting process is complicated by the nonstationarity (and changing volatility) of crude oil spot prices and the apparent randomness of the daily movements in the spot price. In addition, crude oil spot prices have been subject to numerous unpredictable, yet significant, geopolitical events that typically have little to do with market fundamentals but have had a lasting impact on the level of crude oil prices.

For these reasons, a number of researchers recommend the so-called random walk (or "constant price") model to forecast crude oil prices. The random walk model uses the latest observable spot price to predict future crude oil prices. By construction, the random walk model implies that crude oil prices will not change throughout the forecast horizon. Though seemingly "naive," if the crude oil market were truly efficient, the latest spot price would embody all the relevant information about the market and the random walk model would yield the best possible prediction of the future spot price.

An alternative approach to forecasting crude oil prices, used, for example, by the International Monetary Fund and the European Central Bank, is to use futures contract prices. Futures trading of West Texas Intermediate (WTI) crude oil began in 1983 on the New York Mercantile Exchange (NYMEX), initially with a delivery period of up to six months. The delivery period was gradually extended to 24 months by 1995, in line with a substantial increase in the volume of contracts traded.

Futures markets provide an organized forum for traders to engage in hedging activity or speculation. The equilibrium prices of these contracts yield a summary or consensus view of future crude oil prices based on market trading. As such, a reasonable assumption is that the futures contract price is an unbiased predictor of the future spot prices. Provided the market is efficient and the volume of trading is sufficient, futures contract prices should reflect all available information about the crude oil market at a given point in time—much like the random walk model. They should also reflect traders' expectations of future developments in the crude oil market.

Of course, divergent opinions on future developments may produce future contract prices that are different from the random walk model.

An informal examination of futures contract prices suggests that this is especially true for longer-dated futures contracts, which are typically lower than the current spot price.

The forecasting performance of future crude oil contract prices is formally evaluated by Kumar (1992). Using futures prices spanning the 1986–92 period and a forecast horizon of nine months, Kumar concludes that (1) crude oil futures contract prices provide an unbiased predictor of future spot prices and (2) oil price forecasts based on future contracts yield slightly more accurate forecasts than the random walk model. In what follows, Kumar's analysis is updated using futures contract price data spanning 1989–2004.

Forecasting Framework

The ex post accuracy of crude oil futures prices is assessed by comparing the price of crude oil deliverable k periods ahead with the corresponding spot price. Specifically, the forecast error of a specific WTI contract at time t is given by $F_{t,t+k} - S_{t+k}$, where $F_{t,t+k}$ is the (end-of-month) future price of crude oil for delivery k periods ahead, and S_{t+k} is the (known) spot price for period $t + k$. The analysis is performed in terms of the logarithms of the spot and futures prices so that the forecast errors approximate percentage forecast errors, and then repeated for each month in the 1988:1–2004:6 period (a total of 198 months). This process generates a distribution of forecasting errors for each month in the 24-month forecast horizon, and for the overall sample.

The exercise is repeated for the random walk model, which has a forecast error of $S_t - S_{t+k}$, to provide a benchmark for assessing the marginal contribution of futures prices relative to the last known crude oil spot price.

Forecasting Performance

Forecasting accuracy is assessed using the mean absolute forecast error (MAE), while the variability of the forecast error is measured by

Figure 1.23. Forecasting Crude Oil Spot Prices

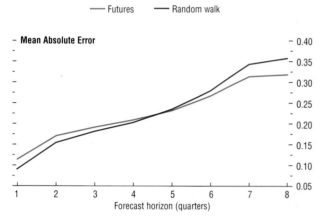

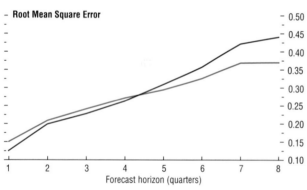

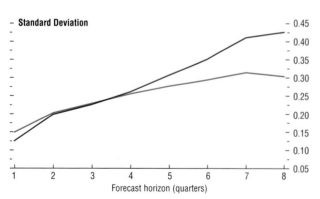

Table 1.14. Relative Forecasting Performance: Futures Versus Random Walk Model

Quarter	Mean Absolute Error	Root Mean Square Error	Standard Deviation of Forecast Error
1	1.27	1.21	1.05
2	1.11	1.05	0.91
3	1.06	1.06	1.00
4	1.03	1.04	0.99
5	0.99	0.95	0.91
6	0.96	0.91	0.87
7	0.92	0.88	0.81
8	0.89	0.84	0.75
Overall	1.01	0.96	0.92

Source: IMF staff estimates.

the root mean square error (RMSE) and standard deviation (SD). The mean absolute forecast error for the overall sample suggests a virtual tie between the random walk and futures model (Table 1.14). Nevertheless, futures-based forecasts appear to yield less volatile error sequences than the random walk model. However, the improvement in forecasting performance is rather slight, amounting to less than 5 percent of the RMSE (8 percent of the SD) of the random walk model, and not significant in a statistical sense. The near-identical performance for the overall sample reflects the fact that spot and futures prices, on average, tend to move together over time.

The analysis for the overall period masks the performance of the two models over specific forecast horizons. As short-term (1–12 month) spot and futures prices tend to react to the same underlying shocks, one might expect the two models to yield similar forecasting performances over the near term, and possibly diverge thereafter. The subperiod analysis confirms that this is indeed the case. Repeating the analysis for each three-month interval (or quarter) in the forecast horizon reveals that the random walk model yields a somewhat lower mean absolute error and root mean square error for the first four quarters (12 months) of the forecast horizon (Figure 1.23). Forecasts based on futures contract prices, however, do better thereafter, producing a lower root mean square error for the crude oil spot price—one that falls steadily as the length of the forecast horizon increases. Interestingly, the standard deviation of the futures model is also lower than the random walk model after four quarters, suggesting that futures based forecasts are less variable than those derived from the random walk model. In other words, this finding, which is consistent with the results reported in Bowman and Husain (2004) for nonfuel commodity prices, confirms that futures contract prices have some predictive content relative to the random walk model at longer time horizons, underscoring their usefulness for setting medium-term crude oil forecasts in particular.

References

Azam, Jean Paul, Agustin Fosu, and Njuguna S. Ndung'u, 2002, "Explaining Slow Growth in Africa," *African Development Review*, Vol. 14 (December), pp. 177–220.

Baldacci, Emanuele, Benedict Clements, Sanjeev Gupta, and Qiang Cui, 2004, "Social Spending, Human Capital, and Growth in Developing Countries: Implications for Achieving the MDGs," IMF Working Paper 04/217 (Washington: International Monetary Fund).

Belaney, Michael, and David Greenaway, 2001, "The Impact of Terms of Trade and Real Exchange Rate Volatility on Investment and Growth in Sub-Saharan Africa," *Journal of Development Economics*, Vol. 65 (August), pp. 491–500.

Bowman, Chakriya, and Aasim Husain, 2004, "Forecasting Commodity Prices: Futures versus Judgment," IMF Working Paper 04/41 (Washington: International Monetary Fund).

Calderón, César, Norman Loayza, and Klaus Schmidt-Hebbel, 2004, "External Conditions and Growth Performance," Working Papers of the Central Bank of Chile, No. 292 (Santiago, Chile: Central Bank of Chile).

Cashin, Paul, John Dermott, and Catherine Pattillo, 2004, "Terms of Trade Shocks in Africa: Are They Short-Lived or Long-Lived?" *Journal of Development Economics*, Vol. 73 (April), pp. 727–44.

Dehn, Jan, Christopher Gilbert, and Panos Varangis, 2005, "Commodity Price Variability" in *Managing Economic Volatility and Crises: A Practitioner's Guide*, ed. by Joshua Aizenman and Brian Pinto (Cambridge: Cambridge University Press, forthcoming).

Fátas, Antonio, and Ilian Mihov, 2003, "The Case for Restricting Fiscal Policy Discretion," *Quarterly Journal of Economics*, Vol. 118 (November), pp. 1419–47.

Fischer, Stanley, Ernesto Hernández-Catá, and Mohsin Khan, 1998, "Africa: Is This the Turning Point?" IMF Paper on Policy Analysis and Assessment 98/6 (Washington: International Monetary Fund).

Hertel, Thomas, 1997, *Global Trade Analysis—Modeling and Applications* (Cambridge: Cambridge University Press).

Hnatkovska, Viktoria, and Norman Loayza, 2005, "Volatility and Growth," in *Managing Economic Volatility and Crises: A Practitioner's Guide*, ed. by Joshua Aizenman and Brian Pinto (Cambridge: Cambridge University Press, forthcoming).

Kaminsky, Graciela, Carmen Reinhart, and Carlos Vegh, 2004, "When It Rains, It Pours: Procyclical Capital Flows and Macroeconomic Policies," NBER Working Paper No. 10780 (Cambridge, Massachusetts: National Bureau of Economic Research).

Kose, Ayhan, and Raymond Riezman, 2001, "Trade Shocks and Macroeconomic Fluctuations in Africa," *Journal of Development Economics*, Vol. 65 (June), pp. 55–80.

Kose, Ayhan, Eswar Prasad, and Marco Terrones, 2005, "Growth and Volatility in an Era of Globalization," *IMF Staff Papers* (Washington: International Monetary Fund, forthcoming).

Krueger, Anne O., 2004, "Expanding Trade and Unleashing Growth: The Prospects for Lasting Poverty Reduction," remarks at the IMF Seminar on Trade and Regional Integration, Dakar, Senegal, December 6. Available via the Internet: http://www.imf.org/external/np/speeches/2004/120604.htm.

———, 2005, "Shared Experience: What Reforming Economies Have in Common," remarks by the First Deputy Managing Director, International Monetary Fund, to the National Council of Applied Economic Research, Delhi, India, January 14. Available via the Internet: http://www.imf.org/external/np/speeches/2005/011405.htm.

Kumar, Manmohan S., 1992, "The Forecasting Accuracy of Crude Oil Futures Prices," *IMF Staff Papers*, Vol. 39 (June), pp. 432–61.

Laubach, Thomas, and John C. Williams, 2001, "Measuring the Natural Rate of Interest," Board of

Governors of the Federal Reserve System Finance and Economics Discussion Series No. 2001–56 (Washington).

OECD, 2004, *A New World Map in Textiles and Clothing—Adjusting to Change* (Paris: OECD).

Pallage, Stéphane, and Michel Robe, 2003, "On the Welfare Cost of Economic Fluctuations in Developing Countries," *International Economic Review*, Vol. 44 (May), pp. 677–98.

Radler, Marilyn, 2004, "Crude Oil Production Climbs as Reserves Post Modest Rise," *Oil and Gas Journal*, Vol. 102 (December), pp. 18–20.

Rajan, Raghuram, 2004, Remarks by Raghuram Rajan, Economic Counsellor and Director of the Research Department, IMF, at the Australasian Finance and Banking Conference, Sydney, Australia, December 15. Available via the Internet: http://www.imf.org/external/np/speeches/2004/121504.htm.

Reinhart, Carmen, and Ioannis Tokatlidis, 2003, "Financial Liberalisation: The African Experience," *Journal of African Economies*, Vol. 12 (October), pp. 53–88.

United Nations Development Program, 2004, *Human Development Report 2004: Cultural Liberty in Today's Diverse World* (New York).

UN Millennium Project, 2005, "Investing in Development: A Practical Plan to Achieve the Millennium Development Goals" (New York: United Nations). Available via the Internet: http://www.unmillenniumproject.org/reports/index.htm.

Wacziarg, Romain, and Karen H. Welch, 2003, "Trade Liberalization and Growth: New Evidence," NBER Working Paper No. 10152 (Cambridge, Massachusetts: National Bureau of Economic Research).

World Bank, 2004, *World Development Indicators 2004* (Washington).

TWO CURRENT ISSUES FACING DEVELOPING COUNTRIES

This chapter contains two essays focusing on developing countries. The first deals with the determinants and the implications of inflows of workers' remittances, while the second essay examines the sources of output volatility in these economies. The topics covered are of particular interest in light of the significant magnitude and rapid growth in remittances, and given that the present, relatively benign global macroeconomic conditions provide a window of opportunity to address some of the policy-driven sources of output fluctuations.

The first essay points out that remittances to developing countries have grown steadily over the past 30 years, and currently amount to about $100 billion a year. For many developing economies, remittances constitute the single largest source of foreign exchange, exceeding export revenues, foreign direct investment (FDI), and other private capital inflows. Moreover, remittances have proved remarkably resilient in the face of economic downturns. The essay finds that remittances can help improve a country's development prospects, maintain macroeconomic stability, mitigate the impact of adverse shocks, and reduce poverty. Remittances allow families to maintain or increase expenditure on basic consumption, housing, education, and small-business formation; they can also promote financial development in cash-based developing economies. The essay therefore argues that significant benefits might flow from measures to reduce the cost of sending remittances, for instance by removing barriers to entry and competition in the remittance market. The analysis also suggests that the potential negative impact on remittances provides further grounds to be wary of exchange rate and similar restrictions. On a cautionary note, remittance-service providers must be appro-

priately regulated to diminish the risk of money laundering or terrorist financing. However, regulatory frameworks must take into account, and where possible minimize, any adverse impact on the cost of sending remittances.

Volatility of output growth has negative effects on long-term growth, welfare, and income inequality, particularly in developing countries. The second essay observes that although output volatility has been on a downward trend in most emerging market and developing countries in recent years, it remains considerably higher than in industrial countries. Also, unlike in industrial countries, the lion's share of output volatility in emerging market and developing countries is driven by country-specific factors, underscoring the key role of domestic policies in reducing output volatility. Thus, the analysis suggests that while these countries have made important strides in strengthening macroeconomic and structural policies in recent years, more can and should be done to further reduce output volatility. A number of reform areas stand out as particularly important, particularly in sub-Saharan Africa and Latin America. These include improving the implementation of fiscal policy, making further progress in developing the financial sector, and carrying forward structural reforms to diversify the production base and reduce vulnerability to terms-of-trade shocks.

Workers' Remittances and Economic Development

Flows of workers' remittances to developing countries have grown steadily over the past 30 years, and currently amount to about $100 billion a year. This rising trend is likely to persist as population aging continues, and pressures for

Note: The main author of this essay is Nikola Spatafora, with support from Reena Aggarwal. Angela Cabugao provided research assistance.

migration from developing to advanced econo-mies increase. For many developing economies, remittances constitute the single largest source of foreign exchange, exceeding export revenues, FDI, and other private capital inflows. Moreover, remittances have proved remarkably resilient in the face of economic downturns and crises.

As a result, interest in remittances and their impact is rapidly growing, whether in policy circles including the G-8, among the research community, or indeed among potential remittance-service providers. Remittances are increasingly viewed as a relatively attractive source of external finance for developing coun-tries, one that can help foster development and smooth crises. At the same time there are con-cerns, chief among them that remittances can be abused to launder money and finance terrorism. Unfortunately, to date there has been little sys-tematic cross-country research on remittances. Against this background, this essay documents some key characteristics of remittances, discusses the available evidence on their determinants and impact, and highlights some of the most salient opportunities and policy challenges, including how to encourage and regulate remittances.

Growing workers' remittances are just one of the many channels through which rising global migration flows may affect developing country welfare. On the positive side, migrants themselves often find better opportunities in their destina-tion countries: they may also learn skills and gain experience that will prove valuable if they repatri-ate. Further, emigration may encourage the devel-opment of commercial networks, promote trade and investment flows, and lead to significant dias-pora philanthropy. Set against this, "brain drain" and the loss of specialized human capital may hamper the development prospects of those left behind, for instance by affecting the tax base. A broad discussion of migration, however, would go well beyond the scope of this essay.

Stylized Facts

Overall, workers' remittances constitute one of the largest sources of external finance for

Figure 2.1. Workers' Remittances and Other Foreign Exchange Flows to Developing Countries[1]
(1970–2003)

Remittances to developing countries have been rising steadily over time. Currently, they are almost comparable to FDI, and exceed both non-FDI private capital inflows and official aid in magnitude.

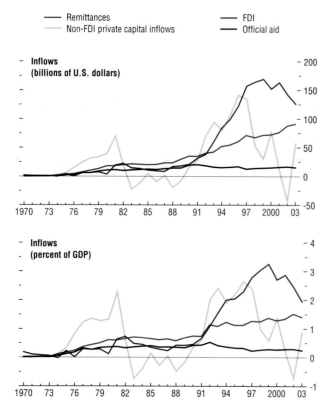

Sources: IMF, *Balance of Payments Statistics Yearbook;* and IMF staff calculations.
[1]For a detailed definition of the components of remittances, see Appendix 2.1.

developing countries. Total remittance inflows grew five-fold between 1980 and 2003 to reach $91 billion, or 1.6 percent of developing countries' GDP—an amount not far short of total inward FDI, and larger than all other private capital inflows (Figure 2.1).[1] These numbers, it should be noted, reflect official balance of payment statistics. As discussed in Appendix 2.1, there are severe problems with these data, which in particular are likely to exclude remittances occurring through informal channels (such as hawala, cash carried by friends and relatives, and in-kind remittances). As a result, actual remittances may be significantly underestimated.[2]

At a regional level, the Western Hemisphere and developing Asia in particular have experienced a major increase in remittance inflows, and currently account for the bulk of total remittance receipts (Figure 2.2). In absolute terms, the five single largest recipients of remittances during 1990–2003 were India, Mexico, the Philippines, Egypt, and Turkey (Figure 2.3). As a share of GDP, however, remittances are especially high among low-income, island, enclave, or generally small economies, such as Lesotho, Tonga, Samoa, Kiribati, and Cape Verde. In 24 countries, remittances during 1990–2003 amounted on average to more than 5 percent of GDP. In such countries, remittances are also very large relative to other sources of foreign exchange, such as aid or exports.

For remittance outflows, data are even patchier than for inflows. The main sources of recorded remittances are the United States, Saudi Arabia, Switzerland, Germany, and France (see Figure 2.2). Since the late 1990s, the United States has been by far the largest source of remit-

---

[1]See also Ratha (2003) for an analysis of recent trends.

[2]However, over the past two decades, data collection practices appear to have improved. Further, there may have been some shift of remittances from informal to formal channels, reflecting both a general easing of exchange rate restrictions, and increased regulation, especially in the wake of the terrorist attacks of September 11, 2001. As a result, while the actual level of remittances is likely still underestimated, their growth rate may be overestimated.

Figure 2.2. Remittances: Sources and Destinations[1]
(Billions of U.S. dollars; 1970–2003)

The United States is currently by far the largest single source of remittances. On the receiving end, among developing countries, those in the Western Hemisphere and developing Asia account for the bulk of remittance inflows.

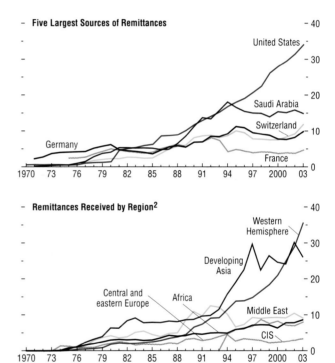

Sources: IMF, *Balance of Payments Statistics Yearbook;* and IMF staff calculations.
[1] For a detailed definition of the components of remittances, see Appendix 2.1.
[2] Regional groups are based on the current IMF *World Economic Outlook* country groupings. Only developing countries are included.

Figure 2.3. Developing Countries: 20 Largest Recipients of Remittances[1]

(1990–2003 average)

In absolute terms, India, Mexico, and the Philippines are the largest recipients of remittances. However, there are many small economies (typically small islands or enclaves) where remittances amount to 5 percent or more of GDP.

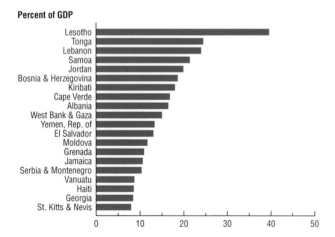

Billions of U.S. Dollars

India, Mexico, Philippines, Egypt, Turkey, Morocco, Lebanon, Russia, Brazil, Pakistan, Bangladesh, Jordan, Thailand, Serbia & Montenegro, China, Colombia, El Salvador, Yemen, Rep. of, I.R. of Iran, Dominican Rep.

0   2   4   6   8

Percent of GDP

Lesotho, Tonga, Lebanon, Samoa, Jordan, Bosnia & Herzegovina, Kiribati, Cape Verde, Albania, West Bank & Gaza, Yemen, Rep. of, El Salvador, Moldova, Grenada, Jamaica, Serbia & Montenegro, Vanuatu, Haiti, Georgia, St. Kitts & Nevis

0   10   20   30   40   50

Sources: IMF, *Balance of Payments Statistics Yearbook;* and IMF staff calculations.
[1]For a detailed definition of the components of remittances, see Appendix 2.1. Data refer to the average gross remittances for all available years over the period 1990–2003.

tances, accounting for $34 billion in 2003. Remittances from Saudi Arabia reflect its sizable employment of Asian migrant workers ever since the first oil-price boom, but there has been no growth in remittances since the mid-1990s.

Remittances are a relatively stable source of external finance, not exhibiting the fluctuations often associated with private capital inflows. Throughout the 1980s and 1990s, remittance receipts stayed within a small range of 1–1.6 percent of developing countries' GDP (see Figure 2.1). Non-FDI private capital inflows, exports, and even official aid and FDI all displayed greater volatility (Figure 2.4). In addition, remittances do not display the sharp procyclicality associated with non-FDI capital inflows; indeed, in many countries economic crises have been followed by sharp increases in remittances (e.g., Indonesia after 1997, Ecuador after 1999, and Argentina after 2001).

Development Impact of Remittances

At a very broad level, remittances help loosen the budget constraints of their recipients, allowing them to increase consumption of both durables and nondurables. Remittances also allow for increased human capital accumulation (through both education and health care), and for increased physical and financial investments (for example, in residential real estate or in starting up small businesses). In turn, these increased expenditures could affect a broad range of development outcomes.[3] For instance, long-run output growth could accelerate as a result of the additional investments in physical and human capital. Such an outcome might be especially likely where a well-developed financial system and institutions allow remittances to be effectively intermediated and efficiently used. Potentially offsetting this, significant remittances could weaken recipients' incentive to work (Chami, Fullenkamp, and Jahjah, 2003), or

[3]See Rapoport and Docquier (2005) for a fuller survey and discussion.

might lead to real exchange rate appreciation and a concomitant contraction of tradable sectors (the so-called Dutch disease).

Even where remittances only have a minimal growth effect, they could have a marked impact on welfare. To the extent that the poorer sections of society depend on remittances for their basic consumption needs, increased remittances would be associated with reductions in poverty, and possibly inequality.[4] Again, the relatively stable nature of remittances suggests that countries with access to significant remittance inflows may be less prone to damaging fluctuations, whether in output, consumption, or investment. In extreme cases, remittances might reduce the probability of financial crises. Such considerations are strengthened by the fact that remittances, unlike capital inflows, are unrequited transfers, which do not create future debt-servicing or other obligations.

As a first step, these hypotheses are tested using data on a broad sample of up to 101 countries, over the period 1970–2003. The sample and data are described in detail in Appendix 2.1. Results are also presented separately for a sub-sample of up to 50 economies that are relatively more dependent on remittances (specifically, where the average ratio of remittances to GDP exceeds 1 percent). Box 2.1 analyzes in greater detail the impact of remittances, and more generally of emigration, in the Caribbean countries, a group of small economies characterized by very large remittance inflows.

One important analytical consideration is that remittances may both influence and themselves be influenced by the economic variables of interest, such as output growth. In those countries and in time periods where growth is relatively weak, remittances may increase both because emigration increases and because workers

[4]Set against this, poorer and lower-skilled households may benefit relatively little from remittances, both because they are less able to meet the costs associated with emigrating in the first place (Chiquiar and Hanson, 2005) and because immigration policy in advanced economies often favors skilled workers with a permanent occupation (Carling, 2004).

Figure 2.4. Remittances and Other Foreign Exchange Flows: Volatility and Cyclicality[1]
(1980–2003)

Remittances to developing countries, as compared with other forms of inflows, are very stable and display relatively little procyclicality. This makes them an attractive source of external finance.

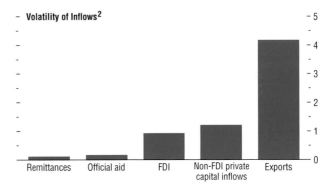

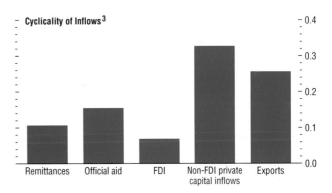

Sources: IMF, *Balance of Payments Statistics Yearbook;* and IMF staff calculations.
[1]For a detailed definition of the components of remittances, see Appendix 2.1.
[2]Volatility is defined as the standard deviation of the ratio of the relevant inflow to GDP.
[3]Cyclicality is defined as the correlation between the detrended relevant inflow and detrended GDP.

Box 2.1. Workers' Remittances and Emigration in the Caribbean

The Caribbean is the world's largest recipient of remittances, as a share of its GDP, and also has the highest emigration rate in the world, with evidence of massive brain drain.[1] The region therefore provides an excellent case study of the determinants and effects of remittances and emigration.

Over the past decade, remittance flows to the Caribbean region have steadily increased, while other sources of external funding have declined. As a result, remittances currently constitute the second largest source of external finance for the Caribbean, behind private capital flows. Between 1990 and 2002, remittances increased from 3 percent to 13 percent of the region's GDP (see the figure). In contrast, over the same period, foreign direct investment (FDI) declined from 11 percent to 7 percent, while official development assistance (ODA) decreased from 4 percent to 1 percent of GDP. As of 2002, 8 Caribbean countries (Haiti, Dominica, the Dominican Republic, Grenada, Guyana, Jamaica, St. Kitts and Nevis, and St. Vincent and the Grenadines) ranked among the world's top 30 recipients of remittances, relative to GDP.

Remittances to the Caribbean are an important source of finance for private investment. Mishra (2005b) uses data from 1980–2002 for 13 Caribbean countries to analyze the macroeconomic impact of remittances. The estimates (based on a panel-data regression model that allows for country- and year-specific fixed effects) show that remittances have a statistically and economically significant impact on private investment. A 1 percentage point increase in remittance inflows increases private investment by 0.6 percentage point (all measured relative to GDP). This result is striking, given the common perception that remittances are used largely for

Remittances, FDI, and ODA to the Caribbean[1]
(1990–2002; percent of GDP)

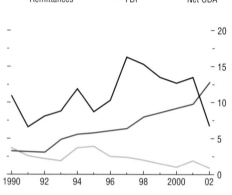

Sources: IMF, *Balance of Payments Statistics Yearbook* (BOP); World Bank, *World Development Indicators;* OECD; country authorities; and IMF staff calculations.
[1]Remittances are calculated as the sum of the following items from the BOP: workers' remittances, compensation of employees, and migrants' transfers. FDI is in terms of gross inflows.

Note: The author of this box is Prachi Mishra. The data quoted in this box are largely drawn from Mishra (2005a).
[1]The Caribbean region includes Antigua and Barbuda, Barbados, Belize, Dominica, the Dominican Republic, Grenada, Guyana, Haiti, Jamaica, St. Kitts and Nevis, St. Lucia, St. Vincent and the Grenadines, Suriname, and Trinidad and Tobago.

consumption purposes. It is, however, consistent with the micro-level studies discussed in the main text, which show that remittances have a strong impact on investment in real estate, small enterprises, and agriculture.

There is also evidence that, in countries with larger remittances, real private consumption is less volatile. Micro-level studies, again discussed in the main text, indicate that remittances act as insurance, increasing significantly in response to adverse shocks (the Caribbean region is one of the most vulnerable regions in the world to natural disasters; see Rasmussen, 2004). So far, few studies have confirmed this insurance hypothesis at the macroeconomic level. However, Mishra (2005b) finds that remittances to the Caribbean do increase after a negative output shock, although with a lag. A 1 percent decrease in real GDP is associated with an increase in remittances of about 3 percent after a two-year lag.

The magnitude of remittances to the Caribbean region is not surprising, given that the region has the highest emigration rates in the world: about 12 percent of its labor force has emigrated to OECD countries. The aggregate emigration rates, however, mask significant variation in the composition of emigrants by skill; in particular, the emigration rate is much higher among workers with more schooling. A majority of the Caribbean countries have lost more than half of their labor force in the tertiary education segment (with more than 12 years of schooling), and more than 30 percent of their labor force in the secondary education segment (9–12 years of schooling). The tertiary-educated labor force in Jamaica and Guyana decreased during 1970–2000 by 89 percent and 83 percent, respectively, owing to emigration to the OECD. In fact, almost all the Caribbean nations are among the top 20 countries in the world with the highest tertiary migration rates (Docquier and Marfouq, 2004; Mishra, 2005a). This likely reflects the combination of "pull" factors (higher wages abroad), "push" factors (limited domestic job opportunities for the highly educated), and low migration costs (not least because of the geographical proximity of the United States).

Mishra (2005a) finds that the costs of skilled-worker emigration are indeed significant. Calculations based on a labor demand-supply framework indicate that the changes in domestic labor supply and wages stemming from high-skill emigration lead to welfare losses for those workers and producers who stay in the country of origin. Adding to these losses are other costs to the economy, such as government expenditure on educating emigrants and the decline in productivity of those who stay behind. Set against this, of course, the migrants themselves experience large welfare increases.

There are two approaches the Caribbean countries could take with regard to migration and remittances: (1) introduce growth-enhancing reforms at home, thereby improving the investment climate and creating incentives that retain the highly skilled; and (2) seek to increase the benefits of emigration by adopting a "diaspora approach." This approach uses the diaspora to build networks for trade, tourism, and investment promotion; harnesses its knowledge, skills, and assets; and attracts increasingly efficient forms of remittances.

Highly skilled workers might be less likely to emigrate if the higher education system were reoriented toward providing skills demanded within the region, in particular by the service sectors that dominate these economies. Such reorientation could include, for example, the establishment of hotel management institutes designed to meet the needs of the tourism industry. Given the heavy subsidies to tertiary education, governments also need to design policies to ensure that migrants internalize the costs of their education.

There is also scope to increase the growth benefits from migration, for instance by encouraging remittances. As discussed in the main text, remittances can boost welfare and growth, including through their impact on physical and human capital investment. Using remittances to finance development presents both an opportunity and a challenge. On the one hand, remittances are large and increasing, whereas aid and FDI have been declining; this suggests that the importance of remittances as a source of investment financing can only increase. On the other hand, it is not straightforward to design policies to encourage remittances and to channel them toward productive uses. The evidence presented in this box suggests that remittances are already having an important positive impact on the Caribbean economies. It is important that governments continue to ensure a favorable climate for remittance flows, and where possible enhance it by reducing some of the barriers, such as high transaction costs and long delays in check clearance, that discourage remittances.[2]

---

[2]See Suki (2004) for an in-depth discussion, in the context of the Dominican Republic, of specific, micro-level reforms that governments could promote.

Table 2.1. Regression Results: Impact of Workers' Remittances

Dependent Variable	Impact of Workers' Remittances[4]	
	Full sample	Remittance-dependent[5]
Growth[1]		
Output growth	−0.30	−0.27
Education	−0.43	1.93
Investment	0.48	0.12
Poverty[2]		
Poverty headcount	**−0.02***	**−0.02***
Poverty gap	**−0.01***	**−0.01***
Volatility[3]		
Output volatility	**−0.29****	**−0.17****
Output worst drop	**−0.74****	**−0.63****
Consumption volatility	**−0.45****	**−0.19***
Investment volatility	**−1.31****	0.01
Credit ratings	**0.22****	**0.22****

[1]"Output growth" is measured in real, per capita terms. "Education" is measured using the secondary enrollment rate. "Investment" is measured using the investment/GDP ratio.

[2]All poverty measures are consumption based where available and income based otherwise, and are in logs. The poverty headcount is defined as the share of the population below the poverty line. The poverty gap is defined as the average percentage amount by which the poor lie below the poverty line. The poverty line is defined as $1.08 a day at 1993 international prices.

[3]All variables are measured in real, per capita terms. "Volatility" is defined as the standard deviation of the annual growth rate. "Worst drop" is defined as the largest annual percentage decrease.

[4]Workers' remittances are measured using the remittances/GDP ratio, except for the poverty regressions, where they are measured using logs of the remittances/GDP ratio. Coefficients are standardized: they indicate by how many standard deviations the dependent variable will change, if workers' remittances increase by one standard deviation. Bold-facing, followed by either * or **, denotes significance at the 10 percent or 5 percent level, respectively. See Appendix 2.1 for details of the additional control variables.

[5]"Remittance-dependent" economies are defined as those where the remittances/GDP ratio exceeds 1 percent.

already abroad increase their financial help to families back home. Such endogeneity would bias the results from any simple regression analysis. The essay tries to minimize this problem by employing instrumental variable techniques.[5] The main results of the analysis are as follows.

- Using a standard cross-country growth regression framework, there is no statistically significant direct link between real per capita *output growth* and remittances (Table 2.1).[6] Likewise, there is no significant relationship between remittances and some of the other variables, such as education levels and investment ratios, which are included as controls in the growth regression. Further, these results apply regardless of the level of financial development in the recipient economy. It has been argued that that the growth impact of remittances might be felt most strongly in certain sectors, including in particular residential real estate: migrants might be most willing to remit funds if these are used for purposes that reinforce their links to their home country (Bouhga-Hagbe, 2004). Indeed, there is some evidence that construction activity is correlated with remittance inflows, but the sample size here is very limited.

- Turning to the link between *poverty* and remittances, if remittances are used mainly to finance basic consumption, they may have an effect on poverty even though their growth impact may be minimal. The results indeed suggest a strong link between poverty, whether measured using the poverty headcount or the poverty gap, and remittances (see Table 2.1; Adams and Page, 2003, and Adams, 2004a, report similar results). The impact may seem to be economically small: on average, a 2½ percentage point increase in the remittances/GDP ratio[7] is associated with less than a ½ percentage point decrease in the share of people living in poverty. However, the analysis controls separately for the impact of average income and of inequality, as proxied by the

[5]As instruments for remittances, following Rajan and Subramanian (2005), we rely on two key geographic and cultural variables, which are both plausibly exogenous, and likely causally related to migration and hence to remittance flows. These variables are (1) the geographic distance between the country that is the recipient of remittances ("home country"), and the country that acts as host for the largest number of the source country's migrant workers ("host country"); and (2) the presence of a common language in home and host countries. Since these instruments do not allow for sufficient variation over time, it is impossible to estimate the impact of remittances using a panel specification.

[6]Faini (2002, 2004) finds a significant positive relationship between growth and remittances using cross-country data, but his results are not robust to alternative specifications. Chami, Fullenkamp, and Jahjah (2003) find a significant negative relationship between growth and remittances; however, the instruments they employ do not seem well placed to handle the endogeneity problem.

[7]Roughly the increase observed in Mexico during the past 25 years, and equal to one between-country standard deviation.

Gini coefficient, and these variables are themselves likely to be influenced by remittances.[8] As a result, the true impact of remittances on poverty may be substantially larger.

• As for the link between *volatility* and remittances, micro-level studies suggest that remittances play a critical role in reducing the vulnerability of individuals to shocks such as natural calamities or civil wars (Rapoport and Docquier, 2005). The results here indicate that the presence of remittances also reduces the volatility of aggregate output, consumption, and investment (Table 2.1).[9] Further, the impact is economically large: a 2½ percentage point increase in the remittances/GDP ratio is on average associated with a one-sixth decrease in output volatility. Of particular interest, an increase in remittances is associated with a reduction in the magnitude of the "worst drop" in output over the sample period, confirming that remittances may help dampen crises and recessions. Owing to data constraints, one cannot test the hypothesis that remittance inflows may help reduce the likelihood of balance of payments crises; however, remittances display a significant, positive association with credit ratings for sovereign debt. Overall, this provides strong evidence that remittance inflows help stabilize economic activity in recipient countries.

The impact of remittances, especially on output growth, may be hard to detect using macroeconomic data alone. First, as discussed, it is hard to disentangle the precise direction of the links, a problem that may not be fully solved by instrumental variable techniques. Further, some of the channels involved, such as those operating through human capital accumulation, may only be detectable over very long time periods. As a result, other studies that exploit household-level data, and usually draw on extensive surveys or on national censuses, may prove more convincing. Typically, these studies do find that households with access to remittances provide their children with significantly more education, engage in small-business formation on a greater scale, and accumulate more assets; further, the impact of remittances is especially large among poorer households, since these are subject to more severe credit constraints.[10] On the whole, there are good grounds to conclude that remittances may play an important role in fostering growth, although more research is needed to understand the precise channels through which this might occur.

Set against this, remittances, like any other foreign exchange inflow, may carry a potential for Dutch disease–type issues. They may, for instance, lead to real exchange rate appreciation and increases in property prices,[11] with

[8]Indeed, remittances must presumably influence poverty by changing either average income or inequality. Given that data on poverty, income, and remittances is measured relatively frequently, while data on inequality is only updated irregularly, the measured impact of remittances on poverty likely reflects some part of the effect that arises through the impact of remittances on inequality. See Adams and Page (2003) for more discussion.

[9]This chapter's other essay, "Output Volatility in Emerging Market and Developing Countries," provides a fuller discussion of output volatility. Here, given the different focus, a slightly different definition of volatility is adopted. Also, with a smaller sample, a more parsimonious specification is employed for the regression equations.

[10]The positive impact of remittances is confirmed inter alia by Adams (2004b) for education and real estate investment in Guatemala; Woodruff and Zenteno (2004) and Massey and Parrado (1998) for entrepreneurship in Mexico; Yang (2004) for education and entrepreneurship in the Philippines; Cox Edwards and Ureta (2003) for education in El Salvador; Hanson and Woodruff (2003) for education in Mexico; Taylor, Rozelle, and deBrauw (2003) and Rozelle, Taylor, and deBrauw (1999) for crop yields in China; McCormick and Wahba (2001) for entrepreneurship in Egypt; Adams (1991, 1998) for real estate investment in Egypt and Pakistan; Brown (1994) for business investment in Tonga and Western Samoa; and Lucas (1987) for crop productivity and cattle accumulation in Southern Africa. Set against this, Ahlburg (1991) finds that remittances to Tonga and Western Samoa result mainly in higher consumption, and rarely fund productive investments. However, Durand, Parrado, and Massey (1996) find that in Mexico even remittance-financed consumption increases can exert substantial multiplier effects on output.

[11]For instance, Bourdet and Falck (2003) argue that increases in remittances account for most of Cape Verde's 14 percent real appreciation over the past decade. Similarly, in Armenia, remittance inflows have recently had an extraordinary effect on the local housing market, with apartment prices in central Yerevan now comparable to North American prices.

negative effects on those not fortunate enough to receive remittances. Nevertheless, and consistent with our analysis, Rajan and Subramanian (2005) find that remittances, unlike official aid or natural resource revenues, do not have systematic, adverse effects on a country's competitiveness, including in labor-intensive, low-skilled, and tradable sectors. Part of the explanation may be that, since remittances accrue to private agents rather than to governments, they do not carry the same potential for stimulating corruption or wasteful spending. Also, given the relative stability of remittances, they seem unlikely to cause the real exchange rate volatility, or to require the difficult adjustments in other tradable sectors, that are often associated with fluctuations in natural resource exports.

The analysis so far has focused on historical outcomes. Looking ahead, remittance flows could also be exploited to accelerate *financial development* in recipient countries. In particular, to the extent that recipients can be persuaded to turn their remittances into deposits with financial institutions, remittances have the potential to bring a larger share of the population into contact with the formal financial system, expanding the availability of credit and saving products such as education loans, mortgages, and savings accounts ("banking the unbanked"). In turn, financial development will itself have positive effects on growth and development, both directly and by encouraging a more effective utilization of remittances. In a related vein, those banks involved in channeling remittance payments are increasingly finding that remittance flows (and the fees they generate for financial institutions) can be effectively securitized, like other future-flow receivables (Ketkar and Ratha, 2001). For instance, since 1994 there have been almost 40 issues of remittance-backed bonds in Latin America, accounting for over $5 billion. Such securitiza-

tion has been an attractive way for some developing country banks to achieve investment-grade ratings, significantly reducing their borrowing costs.

While remittances yield important economic benefits, there is also a risk that they could be used to facilitate *money laundering* and the financing of terrorism. These important concerns are examined in Box 2.2 (see also El-Qorchi, Maimbo, and Wilson, 2003), which in particular argues that informal remittance-service providers need to be brought into the formal arena through an appropriate regulatory framework. Regulations should be clear and simple, and should neither impede the flow of remittances nor drive remittance systems further underground.

Determinants of Remittances

Given the broadly positive impact of workers' remittances on the economy, it is important to identify what factors may encourage remittances. The existing literature on the determinants of remittances is therefore briefly summarized. Since this literature is typically limited to one-country studies, with little comprehensive analysis, the essay then analyzes data on a broad sample of countries.

Remittances can be analyzed using two broad approaches: the "altruism" approach, and the "portfolio" approach.[12] The altruism approach is based on the economics of the family; remittances are driven by migrant workers' concern for the income and consumption needs of family members left in the home country. Under the portfolio approach, in contrast, migrant workers earn income, and must then allocate their savings between home country and host country assets. Here, remittances are fundamentally driven by an investment motive. Many studies combine the two approaches in their empirical analysis.

---

[12]See Rapoport and Docquier (2005), Gupta (2004), Chami, Fullenkamp, and Jahjah (2003), Jadhav (2003), El-Sakka and McNabb (1999), Taylor (1999), Poirine (1997), Elbadawi and Rocha (1992), Russell (1986), and Lucas and Stark (1985) for fuller surveys and analyses of the determinants of remittances.

Box 2.2. Regulating Remittances

Remittance flows are an important source of financing for many countries. As discussed in the main text, a large proportion of remittances likely flow through informal remittance systems. The use of informal remittance-service providers may pose a particular risk of misuse for money laundering and financing of terrorism.[1] There is a need to deal with this risk by integrating informal remittance-service providers into the formal arena through a regulatory framework. Such a framework, however, must take into account, and where possible minimize, any adverse impact on the cost of sending remittances and on the cost of sending remittances and on the incentive to provide remittance services.

The regulatory framework, in both remitting and receiving countries, should focus on remittance-service providers that are not currently under any regulatory or prudential financial oversight, which includes compliance with Anti-Money Laundering and Combating Financing of Terrorism (AML/CFT) requirements. Banks and other financial institutions that conduct remittance operations but are already under the supervision of the relevant authorities, including for AML/CFT requirements would not need to be subject to this remittance regulatory framework.

For regulatory purposes, the Financial Action Task Force (FATF), the international standard setter advises in its Special Recommendation VI that countries should license or register money- or value-transfer providers, and that the latter should meet AML/CFT requirements. Countries will need to decide on a registration or licensing regime on the basis of domestic

circumstances and their accepted tradition for regulatory practices. FATF has recognized that government oversight should be flexible and commensurate with the risk of misuse.

Registration systems and licensing systems are alternative approaches to applying a regulatory framework to remittance-service providers, each consistent with FATF recommendations. Registration systems raise few barriers to participation in the financial system but require sufficient resources for ex post monitoring by the supervisors to ensure compliance with the supervisory and AML/CFT requirements, using the information acquired during the application process. Licensing systems filter participation at the application stage to ensure that the remittance-service providers are suitable; this can reduce the level of compliance oversight afterwards. Because licensing puts more of the emphasis on the application phase, the initial requirements can result in fewer providers signing up.

Remittance-service providers should be consulted before regulations and the associated requirements are issued. Remittance-service providers in general want to protect against flows from criminal proceeds, and even support adoption of a formal regulatory environment to avoid being associated with criminals who engage in money laundering or financing of terrorism activities. Consultation is also important when assessing whether a registration or licensing regime should be adopted, since it will allow the authorities to gauge whether informal providers will be amenable to participating in the selected framework. If there are preexisting remittance-service provider associations, this will make the authorities' task easier. If not, the authorities need to find different avenues for seeking the views of remitters to be regulated, including promoting the forming of associations and supporting self-regulation to ease providers into the formal system.

Requirements should be clear and simple, regardless of whether a registration or a licensing regime is adopted. This may include, depending on a country's choice of a registration or a licensing regime, an application process, the need for

Note: The main authors of this box are Chee Sung Lee and Maud Bökkerink.

[1]Kapur (2004) among others argues that ". . . remittances are an important mechanism to fund terrorism, civil wars, and liberation struggles. . . . In Somalia . . . a large portion of the remittances went to supply arms to the rural guerrillas who toppled the government in January 1991." Other examples include support in Sweden for the Free Aceh Movement, in Canada for the Liberation Tigers of Tamil Eelam, and in the United Kingdom for the Kashmiri cause.

Box 2.2 *(concluded)*

background checks, onsite and offsite monitoring, and compliance programs.

- As most remittance-service providers are small businesses, application procedures should be clear-cut and simple. Authorities should require an annual renewal of the authorization granted, so that regulators have at least yearly contact with providers. The authorities should be in a position to determine the principal provider but special attention needs to be focused on providers who are agents, franchise outlets, or subsidiaries of larger providers with extensive networks.
- Owners and managers of remittance-service providers need to be identified and subjected to at least a background check. Countries that choose a licensing regime may need to carry out thorough fit-and-proper tests to keep persons with criminal records from owning or managing a money transfer office. Applicants involved in financial crimes or possessing a history of insolvency should not be granted authorization.
- Countries should have onsite inspections and offsite monitoring to ensure compliance with regulatory requirements. For this purpose, remittance-service providers could be required to report and submit selected financial data and other information. This may help improve information on financial flows and the regulators' understanding of the remittance business.
- Under current circumstances, one important remaining vulnerability concerns the settlement of balances because remittance-service providers may continue to use formal and informal arrangements for this purpose. This area is likely to remain opaque to supervisors, and further work on understanding settlements is needed.
- If a risk-based assessment determines that the remittance sector is vulnerable to abuse for money laundering and the financing of terrorism, all the remittance-service providers should put in place an AML/CFT compliance program.

AML/CFT requirements include the need for appropriate customer identification, record keeping, and the reporting of suspicious transactions.

- Appropriate documentation to identify customers is a strict regulatory requirement for all financial sector activities, including remittance services. This requirement may pose difficulty for remittance-service providers' customers, who include undocumented or illegal migrant workers. Countries have addressed this difficulty in several ways. One practice is to set the cash threshold above which identification is needed at a level higher than average remittance amounts. Some countries allow the use of identification cards issued by a national consulate.
- Record keeping by remittance-service providers is essential and some countries have devised simple formats or provided software to assist providers. Guidelines are needed to ensure that transactions are transparent and traceable, to assist investigations when abuse is detected.
- The requirement for suspicious transaction reporting could pose difficulties for remittance-service providers. Awareness-raising, education, and training will be needed to improve the quality and number of suspicious transaction reporting.

Countries should impose sanctions for noncompliance with regulatory requirements. There are two levels of sanctions. First, the authorities must have the power to take actions against providers that choose not to register nor be licensed. Second, registered or licensed providers who do not comply with supervisory or AML/CFT requirements should be subject to sanctions similar to those imposed on other financial institutions, ranging from warnings and fines to revocation of permission to operate.

Some other important considerations for a regulatory framework are as follows.

- In developing countries, where beneficiaries are often in remote areas or otherwise have no access to banks and other financial institutions, customers may continue to rely mainly on informal remittance-service providers. In these countries, implementation of an effective regulatory framework will be especially difficult.

- Country authorities may employ consumer protection considerations to encourage customers to use registered or licensed providers. There are two main elements here. First, to deter fraudulent operations or scams, authorities should conduct awareness and education campaigns to inform consumers about choices, rights, and pitfalls when using the remittance system. The advantages of using a registered or licensed remittance-service provider compared with an informal one should be clearly presented. Second, authorities should ensure transparency of transaction fees and exchange rates.
- For a regulatory framework to be effective, supervisors must have the skills, capacity, and

resources to conduct oversight and enforcement. Further, if remittance-service providers are to be enticed to join the formal regulated system, the regulatory regime should not impose on them an excessive administrative and cost burden.

An effective regulatory framework for remittances will—especially in developing countries— increase the administrative burden on already stretched supervisory authorities. To the extent that the costs of financing the regulatory framework are entirely passed on to remittance-service providers, and thus to their users, this could contribute to the perseverance of the informal sector. The international community must therefore work with countries to help bring them into compliance with the international standards, especially by providing technical assistance.

At a broad level, remittance flows are clearly tied closely to migration patterns[13] (although a full joint analysis of remittances and migration is beyond the scope of this essay).[14] Drawing on the existing literature, the analysis here focuses on five broad groups of variables that could affect remittances (by changing either migrant stocks or the average remittances per migrant worker).

- *Economic activity in the migrant workers' host country.* Improved host country economic prospects increase migrants' employment chances and wages. This allows existing migrants to send more remittances, and may also encourage greater emigration from the home country, increasing future remittances.

Empirically, host country economic activity is measured using "world output,"[15] world oil prices are included as an additional control.

- *Economic activity in the migrant workers' home country.* Negative shocks to output, employment, and wages in the home country reduce the income of any family members left behind by the migrants. This may again encourage existing migrants to send more remittances, as well as push more people to emigrate. Home country economic activity is measured here using domestic GDP, lagged to minimize endogeneity problems.
- *Economic policies and institutions in the home country.* The presence of exchange rate restrictions and black market premia may discourage

[13]For a panel of 22 advanced economies during the period 1991–2000, remittance outflows are strongly and significantly correlated with the presence of foreign workers (after controlling for a time trend and country-specific fixed effects). A 2 percentage point (one within-group standard deviation) increase in the number of foreign workers as a share of the population is significantly associated with a ¼ percentage point (0.6 within-group standard deviation) increase in remittance outflows as a share of GDP. Likewise, Swamy (1981) reports a strong relationship between remittance inflows and the number of emigrants for Greece, Yugoslavia, and Turkey.

[14]Also, for many countries, data on the stock of migrant workers residing abroad, and their incomes, are very limited.

[15]Specifically, a weighted average of output in foreign countries, with weights equal to either (1) the share of migrant workers from the home country residing in each foreign country, where such data are available; or (2) the trade shares otherwise.

Table 2.2. Regression Results: Determinants of Workers' Remittances[1]

Explanatory Variables[2]	Models[3]		
	I	II	III
World output	1.44**	5.56**	1.47**
Home output	−2.52**	−3.20**	−2.11**
Dual exchange rates	−0.59**	. . .	−0.52**
Restrictions on foreign exchange deposits held abroad	. . .	−0.79**	. . .
Bank deposits to GDP	. . .	. . .	0.03

[1]Workers' remittances are measured using the remittances/GDP ratio.

[2]"World output" is the log of weighted average real GDP in partner countries with weights as described in the text. "Home output" is the log of lagged real GDP per capita (from the Penn World Tables). "Dual exchange rates" and "Restrictions on foreign exchange deposits held abroad" are indicators set equal to unity if such practices exist, and zero otherwise (from the IMF's *Annual Report on Exchange Arrangements and Exchange Restrictions*, 2003). Finally, "Bank deposits to GDP" are total demand, time, and saving deposits in deposit money banks as a share of GDP. Additional controls include political risk, and law and order (both from the International Country Risk Guide), the U.S. six-month LIBOR, world oil prices, country-specific fixed effects, and a time trend.

[3]Bold-facing, followed by either * or **, denotes significance at the 10 percent or 5 percent level, respectively.

migrants from sending remittances. In particular, it is likely to shift remittances away from formal channels, such as banks, toward informal and unrecorded channels; any remittances may also be kept in the form of foreign currency cash. Macroeconomic instability, as manifested in high inflation or real exchange rate overvaluation, may have similar effects. In contrast, greater financial sector development, by making remittances easier and cheaper to send and receive, may encourage remittances. Empirically, economic policies and institutions are measured here using an indicator of whether multiple exchange rate systems are present; an indicator of restrictions on holding foreign exchange deposits; black market premia; financial sector depth, as measured by the ratio of bank deposits, bank assets, or

stock market capitalization to GDP; and inflation.

- *General risks in the home country.* Political instability, or low levels of law and order, may discourage migrants from sending remittances, at least for investment purposes—for instance, because of the risk of expropriation or theft. Such risks are proxied here by the International Country Risk Guide measures of political risk and of law and order.

- *Investment opportunities.* Greater potential returns on host country assets as opposed to home country assets may encourage migrants to invest their savings in the host country, rather than sending them back as remittances. Investment opportunities on host country assets relative to home country assets are proxied here using the U.S. LIBOR.[16]

The analysis uses annual data on a panel of 87 countries during the period 1980–2003. The 1980s and the 1990s were also analyzed separately; since the results are similar to those for the full sample, they are not reported. The data are described in greater detail in Appendix 2.1. A panel regression is estimated, with workers' remittances as a share of recipient-country GDP as the dependent variable. Throughout, we control for country-specific fixed effects[17] and a time trend.

Overall, the regression results confirm that policies and regulations can play an important role in determining remittance inflows (Table 2.2). More specifically, world output has a statistically significant, positive impact on remittances: stronger economic activity in migrants' host countries increases the remittances sent to their home country.[18] Home country output has a significant negative impact on remittances, consis-

[16]For most developing countries, reliable measures of domestic rates of return are not available.

[17]These fixed effects may capture the impact on remittances of much of the cross-country variation in migration flows. However, their presence implies that we cannot estimate separately the impact of any largely time-invariant geographical, historical, or cultural factors affecting migration levels (such as geographical distance, or the presence of a common language, a shared border, or a single market between the host countries where migrants work and their home country).

[18]This suggests that, while remittances are typically relatively stable, they may nevertheless be subject to significant external shocks, especially where migrant workers are heavily concentrated in a single country and/or sector. In a dramatic illustration, the sharp drop in mining jobs in South Africa led to a collapse in remittances to Lesotho, from more than 50 percent of GDP in 1991–92 to less than 20 percent in 2003–04. In contrast, world oil prices have no significant effect on average remittances.

tent with the earlier finding that remittances help smooth fluctuations. The presence of multiple exchange rates also has a significant negative impact on remittances. Data on black market premia and on restrictions on holding foreign exchange deposits are only available for a limited number of countries, but within this subsample both variables likewise have a significant negative impact on remittances. Economically, the effects of policies and regulations are quite large: a full removal of all exchange rate distortions and restrictions is associated with an increase in remittances of 1–2 percentage points of GDP.[19] Financial development did not have a significant impact on remittances, nor did the broad measures of political risk or law and order.[20] Finally, relative investment opportunities, as proxied by the U.S. LIBOR, also had no significant effect on remittances; the fact that remittances are little affected by rate-of-return considerations may help explain their relative stability when compared with many types of capital flows.

It should be noted that remittance payments often incur significant transaction costs (involving both explicit fees and exchange rate spreads), and in some cases time delays. There are no systematic cross-country, time-series data on such costs (see Figure 2.5 for some estimates). However, the costs have drawn significant attention in the context of remittances from the United States to Latin America.[21] Overall, some key stylized facts and observations

[19]Owing to a lack of systematic data, this essay does not analyze the role of the tax treatment of remittances. However, anecdotal evidence suggests that incentives such as tax exemptions or preferential credits for migrants may affect significantly the share of remittances sent through the banking system. For instance, in Tajikistan, eliminating the taxation of remittances led to an increase in recorded remittances from $4 million in 2002Q1 to $56 million in 2004Q1.

[20]Results are only shown for the ratio of bank deposits to GDP, but the conclusion holds regardless of the precise measure of financial development employed.

[21]For analyses of remittances to Latin America, see Amuedo-Dorantes, Bansak, and Pozo (2004), DeSipio (2000), Lindsay Lowell and de La Garza (2000, 2002), Meyers (1998), Orozco (2000, 2003, 2004a, 2004b), Suki (2004), Suro (2003), and Suro and others (2002).

Figure 2.5. Cost of Sending $200 in Remittances from the United States

The cost of sending remittances displays significant variations across countries. Over the past 15 years, competition has increased and costs have been reduced—but in some cases remain very high.

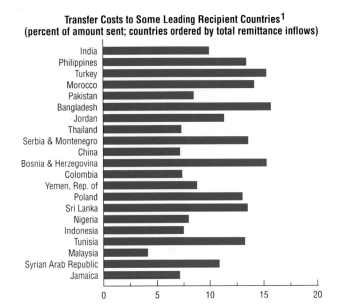

Transfer Costs to Some Leading Recipient Countries[1]
(percent of amount sent; countries ordered by total remittance inflows)

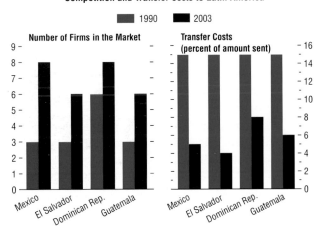

Competition and Transfer Costs to Latin America

Sources: Western Union; Women's World Banking; and IMF staff calculations.
[1]The cost of sending remittances is calculated as the percentage difference, as of February 2005, between the value of $200 in a country's local currency, converted using official exchange rates, and the actual payout from Western Union net of all service fees and exchange rate charges.

are as follows. First, transaction costs have declined significantly over the past few years, but often still amount to 5–10 percent or more of the sum remitted. Second, transaction costs display significant variation across countries. They seem to be especially low in some high-volume markets, such as remittances to Mexico; this may reflect greater intensity of competition among remittance-service providers, or the ability of such providers to spread fixed infrastructure costs over a larger volume of customers. Third, further reductions in transaction costs, even assuming no change in the volume of remittances sent, would automatically lead to increases in remittance receipts for developing countries. They could also encourage a shift in remittances away from informal, cash-based channels and toward formal channels.

Conclusions and Policy Challenges

For many developing countries, remittances are a very large source of foreign exchange, and have proved far more stable and less procyclical than other such sources. Remittances can help improve a country's development prospects, maintain macroeconomic stability, mitigate the impact of adverse shocks, and reduce poverty. Remittances allow families to maintain or increase expenditure on basic consumption including food, on housing, education, and small-business formation; they can also promote financial development in cash-based developing economies.

To maximize the benefits from potential remittance flows, however, a number of key policy challenges need to be tackled.

- While the cost of sending remittances has declined in recent years, it remains very variable, and in several cases is still high. To the extent possible, efforts must be undertaken to reduce the cost of sending remittances, including by removing barriers to entry and competition in the remittance market. For instance, authorities could publicize information about available options for money transfers and the associated costs.

- Different macroeconomic and exchange rate policies may act to encourage or discourage remittances, and especially those flowing through the formal financial system. This potential impact must be taken into account by authorities, particularly in those countries where remittance inflows (actual or potential) are significant. For instance, the analysis provides additional grounds to be wary of exchange rate restrictions, such as restrictions on personal payments or the presence of multiple exchange rate systems. To some extent, unstable macroeconomic policies and exchange rate misalignments may also deter remittances.

- Remittance receipts could be leveraged by households to obtain better access to banking and financial services. Such an outcome would be more likely if formal financial intermediaries, including banks and microfinance institutions, entered the remittance market more actively. Again, governments may help here by reducing entry barriers.

- Remittance-service providers must be appropriately regulated and supervised to minimize the potential risk of money laundering, terrorist financing, or consumer fraud. However, regulatory frameworks must take into account, and where possible minimize, any adverse impact on the cost of sending remittances, and the incentive to provide remittance services.

- Better information is needed on the magnitudes and sources of remittances, including both inflows and outflows. Without such information, other challenges (such as regulating remittances, or developing new financial products to serve the needs of remittance senders and recipients) will remain extremely difficult.

- Remittances, like any other foreign exchange inflow, carry a potential for Dutch disease–type issues. In general, this does not appear to have had major adverse effects on economic performance. However, it does suggest that, in the presence of significant changes in remittance inflows, authorities may need to accept a greater degree of exchange rate flexibility than would otherwise be the case.

Output Volatility in Emerging Market and Developing Countries

The main author of this essay is Dalia Hakura with consultancy support from Christopher Otrok. Stephanie Denis provided research assistance.

High output volatility can adversely affect economic growth, welfare, and poverty, particularly in developing countries (see Box 2.3). Although the volatility of output growth in emerging market and developing countries has declined over the past years, it remains differentiated between regions—it is much higher in sub-Saharan Africa than in Asia—and well above the levels in industrial countries, suggesting there is considerable scope to reduce it further (Figure 2.6). Understanding the determinants of output volatility in emerging market and developing countries could provide guidance on designing economic policies that would help in this task.

Against this background, this essay will examine key trends in the volatility of output growth in emerging market and developing countries and investigate the main drivers of these trends. In particular, it will address the following questions.

- To what extent has volatility declined across emerging market and developing country regions?
- To what extent are output fluctuations in emerging market and developing countries driven by global and regional economic events or by factors that are more specific to an individual country? Have the relative contributions of global and regional events become more important (for instance, as a result of increased trade and financial linkages between countries) and have these components of output volatility become more stable? Or have individual country factors become more stable, possibly as a result of stronger domestic economic policies and institutions?
- What policy and institutional variables are most important for explaining output volatility in emerging market and developing countries?

The essay uses a variety of new techniques to address the questions above. In addition,

Figure 2.6. Volatility of Output Growth

(Rolling 10-year standard deviations of per capita real output growth rates; mean for each group)[1]

The volatility of output growth in emerging market and developing countries, and industrial countries has declined markedly over the past decades, but it remains considerably higher in emerging market and developing countries.

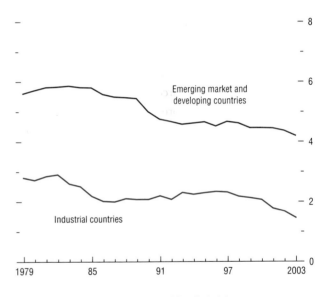

Sources: Penn World Tables Version 6.1; and IMF staff calculations.
[1]Data for 1979 refers to the standard deviation of per capita growth rates for the period 1970–79. Data for 1980 does the same for the period 1971–80, etc.

Box 2.3. Why Is Volatility Harmful?

Understanding the complex relationship between output volatility and long-term economic performance has been a challenge for economists. During the 1980s, the impact of volatility on economic growth and welfare was generally believed to be minor at most, and therefore not a major concern. Research in the 1990s reached a strikingly different conclusion—that output volatility may actually reduce long-term growth and could result in large welfare costs.[1] Moreover, the financial crises experienced by a number of emerging market and developing countries over the past two decades have highlighted the adverse impact of episodes of high volatility on income inequality and poverty. This box reviews some recent studies on the effects of output volatility on economic growth, welfare, and poverty.

Impact on Growth

Output volatility could have negative effects on economic growth through several channels.[2] One of the key channels linking volatility to growth is investment. For example, increased uncertainty about future returns associated with output volatility could reduce growth by lowering investment. Market imperfections associated with credit constraints and/or imperfect access to world financial markets could also magnify the negative impact of short-term volatility on long-term growth in emerging market and developing countries because these types of market imperfections severely limit the scope of financing options for long-term investment projects (Aghion and others, 2004).

Note: The main author of this box is Ayhan Kose.
[1]For recent surveys of the literature, see Kose, Prasad, and Terrones (2005) and Aizenman and Pinto (2005).
[2]Economic theory does not provide clear guidance on the impact of volatility on growth. Indeed, some theoretical studies argue that volatility could have beneficial effects on economic growth (Blackburn, 1999; Imbs, 2004; and Tornell, Westermann, and Martinez, 2004). For example, some of these theories emphasize that since potential profits associated with highly volatile and riskier investment projects could be larger than less volatile ones, they could translate into higher growth rates.

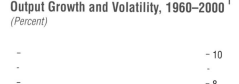

Output Growth and Volatility, 1960–2000[1]
(Percent)

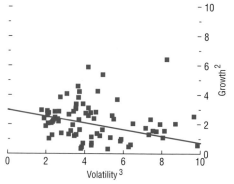

Source: Kose, Prasad, and Terrones (2005).
[1]Figure includes 85 countries, of which 22 are industrial countries.
[2]Average annual growth rate of real per capita GDP over the period 1960–2000.
[3]Standard deviation of real per capita GDP growth over the period 1960–2000.

Several empirical studies, using different methodologies and data sets, find a negative relationship between output volatility and economic growth (see the figure).[3] Kose, Prasad, and Terrones (2005) document that countries subject to higher output volatility show worse growth performance on average than more stable ones. Moreover, the negative relationship between volatility and growth is significant in terms of economic magnitudes: a 1 percentage point increase in the standard deviation of output growth is associated with a 0.16 percentage point decline in the average growth rate of a developing country.

The empirical relationship between volatility and growth is affected by several factors, including a country's structural characteristics, and the nature and origin of volatility.

[3]See Ramey and Ramey (1995), IDB (1995), Martin and Rogers (2000), Fatás (2002), Hnatkovska and Loayza (2005), and Kose, Prasad, and Terrones (2005).

- Developing countries with weaker institutions and less developed financial markets suffer more from the adverse impact of volatility on growth. The degree of trade integration with the global economy also affects the nature of the relationship between volatility and growth. Economies that are more open to trade flows with a diversified export base have the ability to withstand higher levels of volatility with less adverse effects on growth.[4]
- The source of volatility also matters. For example, volatility associated with discretionary fiscal policy could distort savings and investment decisions with particularly adverse effects on economic growth (Fatás and Mihov, 2003).

Impact on Welfare

Output volatility could result in large welfare costs through its impact on the dynamics of consumption since an important determinant of economic welfare is the stability of people's consumption patterns (Wolf, 2005). Output volatility could lead to an increase in the amplitude of consumption fluctuations, which in turn reduces economic welfare. Recent research shows that the volatility of consumption over the business cycle is indeed associated with large welfare costs, up to 8 percent of lifetime consumption, in developed countries (Barlevy, 2004). Moreover, the welfare costs of output volatility are much larger in developing countries, where volatility of consumption is on average two to three times higher than that in developed countries. Pallage and Robe (2003) report that the welfare cost of volatility in low-income countries could be 10–30 times larger than the estimates for a typical developed economy. In addition to being subject to a variety of highly volatile exter-

[4]It should be noted, however, that trade openness that leads to more product specialization could increase volatility and hurt growth.

nal and domestic shocks, the lack of developed financial markets coupled with developing countries' limited access to international financial markets magnify the welfare costs of consumption volatility in these countries.

Impact on Poverty

Output volatility could have a negative impact on poverty because the poor have the least access to financial markets, making it difficult for them to diversify the risk associated with their income, which is often based on a narrow set of sources, that is, mainly labor earnings and government transfers. Moreover, since the poor rely heavily on various public services, including education and health, they are directly affected by changes in government spending. Given that fiscal policy is procyclical in most developing countries, this magnifies the negative impact of volatility on poverty especially during crises. In addition, the poor often lack necessary education and skills, limiting their ability to move across sectors to adjust to changes in economic conditions.

Recent empirical research finds that volatility has a significantly negative and causal impact on poverty (Laursen and Mahajan, 2005). The adverse effect of volatility appears to be more pronounced in low-income developing countries in the Middle East and North Africa and sub-Saharan Africa. In addition, there has been an increase in poverty, with a concomitant worsening of the income distribution, in emerging market countries during the periods of extreme volatility associated with financial crises.

In sum, recent research demonstrates the harmful effects of volatility on economic growth, welfare, and poverty. These findings imply that stabilization policies aiming at reducing output volatility could have significant benefits in terms of improving long-term growth, increasing welfare, and reducing poverty in emerging market and developing countries.

the essay brings to the fore differences among emerging market and developing country regions in terms of both the factors driving output volatility and the impact of improvements in policies and institutions on volatility.

Figure 2.7. Volatility of Output Growth by Region
(Rolling 10-year standard deviations of per capita real output growth rates; mean for each group)

The volatility of output growth has declined in all regions, except for east Asia and Latin America.

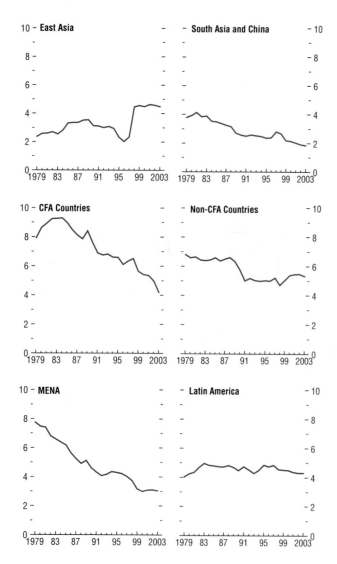

Sources: Penn World Tables Version 6.1; and IMF staff calculations.

Volatility: The Stylized Facts Across Emerging Market and Developing Country Regions

The volatility of output growth in emerging market and developing countries has declined over the past three decades. However, it remains considerably higher than in industrial countries. Moreover, the decline in volatility for all emerging market and developing countries taken together masks different trends among regions.[22] In particular, in south Asia and China, the Middle East and north Africa (MENA), and the CFA franc zone countries in sub-Saharan Africa, volatility has shown a sustained decline (Figure 2.7). In Latin America it has remained constant at a relatively high level, and in east Asia it has increased since 1997. Countries in Asia have, on average, had the lowest and countries in sub-Saharan Africa, the highest volatility of the various emerging market and developing country regions over the 1970–2003 period.

What explains these regional differences? To address this question, a dynamic factor model is estimated to decompose fluctuations in real per capita output growth. This technique identifies and estimates common movements or underlying forces (known as factors) that may be driving output fluctuations across countries (see Appendix 2.2 for further the details on the dynamic factor model). In particular, the dynamic factor model used in this essay decomposes output fluctuations into three factors:

---

[22]The essay groups emerging market and developing countries into regions primarily according to their geographic location: east Asia, south Asia and China, the Middle East and North Africa, Latin America, and sub-Saharan Africa. The latter region is further divided into CFA franc zone countries and non-CFA countries (see Appendix 2.2 for the countries included in each region). China is grouped with south Asia because its cycle moves more with south Asia than with east Asia. The results reported in the essay are, however, not sensitive to China's classification. Alternative country groupings were explored, including groupings based on the level of development and structure of production (e.g., emerging market economies, oil- and primary commodity–exporting countries) but these did not reveal regional cycles as pronounced as those captured here.

- an overall *global factor*, which captures events that affect real per capita output growth in all countries;
- a *regional factor*, which captures events that affect real per capita output growth in all countries in a particular region; and
- a *country-specific factor*, which captures events that specifically affect real per capita output growth in an individual country.

These factors capture movements in the underlying forces driving these economies (i.e., monetary and fiscal policy shocks, oil price shocks, productivity shocks, etc.), the relative importance of which changes over time and can vary across countries. For example, the co-movement across countries of variables affecting output growth, such as key international interest rates and oil prices, would be captured by the global factor. A shock that spills over from one country in a region to another owing to similarities in the quality of economic and political institutions or the stage of economic development would be captured by the regional factor. Changes in macroeconomic policy implementation or structural changes affecting output growth in a particular country would be captured by the country-specific factor.[23]

The estimate of the global factor picks up the key peaks and troughs in global GDP growth over the past 34 years, including the oil price shocks in the 1970s, the recessions in the early 1980s and 1990s, the high-tech investment bust in the early 2000s, and the recent global recovery (Figure 2.8). As is the case with actual global growth, the global factor is less volatile during the second half of the sample period.

The estimates of the regional factors also capture well-known cyclical fluctuations (Figure

---

Figure 2.8. Global Factor and Actual Global Growth
(Annual percentage change; de-meaned)

The estimate of the global factor picks up the key peaks and troughs in global GDP growth over the past 34 years, including the oil price shocks in the 1970s, the recessions in the early 1980s, the high-tech investment bust, and the recent global recovery.

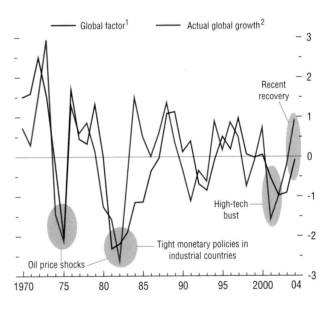

Sources: Penn World Tables Version 6.1; and IMF staff calculations.
[1]See Appendix 2.2 for further details on the estimation of the global factor. The global factor has been rescaled to have the same variance as the actual global growth.
[2]Actual global growth represents the purchasing-power-parity-weighted real per capita GDP growth rates for all countries in the study.

---

[23]It should be noted that if a country is heavily dependent on a commodity, either as an exporter or an importer, an externally driven change in the price of that commodity could be captured by the country-specific factor if this commodity does not have a significant impact on the global or regional economies.

Figure 2.9. Regional Factors[1]
(Annual percentage change; de-meaned)

The regional factors pick up well-known cyclical fluctuations, such as the 1997–98 crisis in east Asia, the debt crisis in the early 1980s in South America, and the recurrence of droughts and terms of trade shocks in the 1970s and early 1980s in CFA countries.

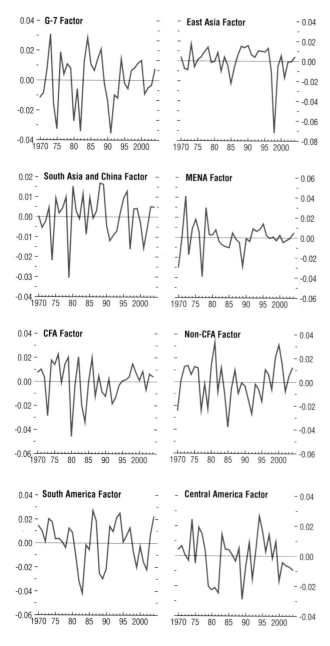

Sources: Penn World Tables Version 6.1; and IMF staff calculations.
[1]See Appendix 2.2 for further details on the estimation of the regional factors. An "other industrial countries factor" is also estimated but is not shown here.

2.9).[24] For example, the east Asia factor shows that the crisis in 1997–98 dominates the cycle in the region; the South America factor captures the debt crisis in the early 1980s and the problems of the late 1990s; and the CFA factor exhibits sharp swings in the 1970s and early 1980s, reflecting the recurrence of droughts and terms-of-trade shocks, but has been less volatile recently. Some of the other factors, on the other hand, exhibit no distinguishable regional cycles.

To investigate the importance of each of the three factors for explaining output volatility in each country, the share of the variance of real per capita output growth that is due to each is calculated. The results suggest that output fluctuations in emerging market and developing countries are driven more by country-specific factors than those in industrial countries (Figure 2.10). For example, the country-specific factor explains more than 60 percent of output volatility in about 90 percent of emerging market and developing countries, compared with only 40 percent of industrial countries. The global factor explains less than 10 percent of output fluctuations for more than 60 percent of the emerging market and developing countries, but between 10 and 20 percent of the output variation in nearly half the industrial countries.

An examination of the contributions of the factors to output volatility shows that in all the emerging market and developing country regions, except east Asia, at least 60 percent of output volatility is attributable to country-specific factors (Table 2.3). Also, unlike in industrial countries, in all emerging market and developing country regions the regional factor explains a greater fraction of volatility than the global factor. The contribution of the country-specific factor for explaining output fluctuations

[24]In addition to the regional groupings outlined earlier in the essay, for the purpose of estimation of the dynamic factor model Latin America is subdivided into Central America and the Caribbean, and South America, and the industrial countries are subdivided into G-7 and other industrial countries to capture differences in their regional cycles. Industrial countries were included in the sample to estimate the global factor properly.

Table 2.3. Contributors to Volatility in Real per Capita Output Growth[1]

(Averages for each group; percent)

	Global	Regional	Country
Sub-Saharan Africa			
CFA countries	5.7	18.2	76.1
Non-CFA countries	6.8	10.2	82.1
Middle East and North Africa	3.8	15.9	80.3
Latin America	12.6	13.7	73.7
South Asia and China	15.6	20.6	63.8
East Asia	11.0	41.8	47.2
East Asia (1970–96)	18.0	15.8	66.3
Emerging market and			
developing countries	9.3	16.9	73.8
Industrial countries	24.3	21.7	54.0

Source: IMF staff calculations.
[1]The table shows the fraction of the variance of output growth attributable to each factor.

in east Asia is about the same as for industrial countries, while the contribution of the regional factor is very large, largely reflecting the east Asian financial crisis, which resulted in large output losses simultaneously across the region. Indeed, estimating the model over the 1970–96 period suggests a more prominent role for the global factor and a less prominent role for the regional factor, making east Asia appear to share more of the attributes of industrial countries.

What accounts for the trend decline in output volatility in most of the emerging market and developing country regions? To address this question, the dynamic factor model is estimated over two periods: 1970–86 and 1987–2004.[25] The results suggest that the declines in output volatility in emerging market and developing country regions are mainly due to less volatile country-specific factors (Table 2.4).[26] In all regions except Latin America, at least 70 percent of the decline in the variance of output growth is

[25]These subperiods capture a break in output volatility (see Kose, Otrok, and Prasad, 2005).

[26]This table looks at countries where volatility has declined. It therefore differs from Figure 2.7, which shows average volatility for all countries in a region. This difference is particularly important for non-CFA countries, a number of which experienced large increases in volatility during the 1987–2004 period.

Figure 2.10. Contributors to Volatility in Real per Capita Output Growth, 1970–2004[1]

(Percent of countries on y-axis; x-axis as stated)

Output fluctuations in emerging market and developing countries are driven more by country-specific factors than in industrial countries. For example, the figure shows that the country-specific factor explains more than 60 percent of output volatility in about 90 percent of emerging market and developing countries, compared with only 40 percent of industrial countries.

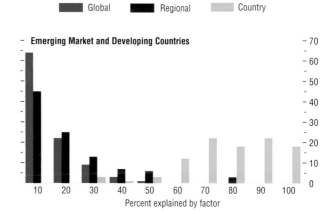

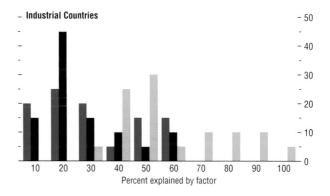

Sources: Penn World Tables Version 6.1; and IMF staff calculations.
[1]Twenty percent explained by a factor refers to countries for which between 10 and 20 percent of variations in output are explained by the factor; 30 percent refers to countries for which between 20 and 30 percent of variations are explained by the factor, and so on.

Table 2.4. What Explains the Declines in Output Volatility Between 1970–86 and 1987–2004?[1]

(Averages for each group; percentage change)

	Decline in Variance of Output Growth	Contribution of Factor to the Decline		
		Global	Regional	Country
Sub-Saharan Africa				
CFA countries	−40.0	−2.1	−5.8	−32.1
Non-CFA countries	−53.2	−6.9	−8.3	−38.0
Middle East and north Africa	−60.7	−0.5	−17.4	−42.7
Latin America	−12.1	−3.4	−2.8	−5.9
South Asia and China	−12.0	−0.9	−2.9	−8.2
Emerging market and developing countries	−34.2	−3.2	−6.8	−24.2
Industrial countries	−4.1	−1.1	−0.8	−2.3

Source: IMF staff calculations.

[1]Only countries that experienced a decline in volatility from the 1970–86 period to the 1987–2004 period are included in the calculations. For this reason, countries in east Asia are not included. The table shows the contribution of each factor to the decline in the variance of output growth from the 1970–86 period to the 1987–2004 period.

explained by the country-specific factor.[27] By contrast, for industrial countries, the corresponding share is about 50 percent.

Cross-Section Analysis of Output Volatility

This section examines the determinants of output volatility for a cross-section of 51 emerging market and developing countries. Unlike earlier studies of output volatility, the dependent variable in the regression is the standard deviation of the country-specific component of real per capita GDP growth for the 1970–2003 period

as derived from the estimates of the dynamic factor model. This abstracts from the effects of global and regional shocks and permits a better understanding of the importance of various domestic policies and institutions for explaining output volatility.

The determinants of output volatility that are considered can be broadly grouped into four categories.[28]

- *Stability of macroeconomic policies.* Higher volatility of fiscal policy—measured as the standard deviation of cyclically adjusted government spending—increases output volatility (Fatás and Mihov, 2003).[29] Similarly, a loose monetary policy that results in high inflation creates uncertainty, adversely affects investment, and contributes to volatility (Acemoglu and others, 2003). The results from the regression estimation—reported in Table 2.5—suggest that a more volatile fiscal policy and higher inflation are associated with increases in volatility, but only the fiscal effect is found to be significant.[30]
- *Trade and financial integration.* Theory does not provide a clear guide as to the effects of trade and financial integration on output volatility. While trade openness can contribute to lower volatility if it leads to more intra-industry specialization across countries and a larger volume of trade in intermediate inputs, it can also make countries vulnerable to external shocks if it leads to greater product specialization or if the country has weak

[27]Notwithstanding the overall relatively small contribution of the global factor, it should be noted that for some countries the global factor loading has risen. In fact, the changes in the factor loadings suggest that sensitivity to the global factor increased on average for CFA, MENA, and industrial countries. For Latin America, however, the contribution of the global factor has declined. This most likely reflects the large role the global factor played in explaining Latin American output volatility in the 1970–86 period; because the Latin American debt crisis coincided with the recession in the G-7 countries, the model identifies it as being part of the global factor.

[28]Depending on data availability, commonly used proxies for these explanatory variables were used in the empirical analysis. Appendix 2.2 provides further details. An instrumental variables estimation technique was used to account for possible endogeneity of some of the explanatory variables.

[29]A number of studies have found fiscal policy to be procyclical in many emerging market and developing countries, with government spending increasing in upturns and commodity price booms and falling with weakening economic growth, declining revenues, and a tightening of financing conditions (Chapter III, *World Economic Outlook*, September 2003, and Kaminsky, Reinhart, and Végh, 2004). The measure of fiscal policy volatility here adjusts for changes in macroeconomic conditions, past government spending and a time trend.

[30]Aid inflows, which have been found to be more volatile than fiscal revenue and to be procyclical (Bulíř and Hamann, 2001) can also be a source of country-specific output volatility. The effect of the volatility of aid inflows may be captured by the fiscal variable; to the extent that swings in government spending reflect the timing of aid disbursements, donors could help by reducing the volatility of their development assistance.

institutions or a nondiversified structure of production (Kose, Prasad, and Terrones, 2003). Trade openness is found to be positively and significantly associated with country-specific volatility in the regression analysis, although increased openness between 1970–86 and 1987–2003 only had a limited impact on volatility for the majority of emerging market and developing countries. Moreover, trade openness has been found to have important growth-enhancing effects (Berg and Krueger, 2003), and recent work shows that countries that are more open to trade can tolerate higher volatility without hurting their long-term growth (Kose, Prasad, and Terrones, 2005). The impact of current and capital account restrictions on output volatility were also investigated, but no significant relationship was found.

- *Financial sector development.* The results indicate that countries with more developed financial sectors, measured here as a higher initial ratio of private sector credit to GDP, have significantly lower output volatility.[31] This is consistent with better-developed financial systems contributing to an easing of financing constraints on firms particularly during downturns, thereby smoothing output volatility (see, for example, Easterly, Islam, and Stiglitz, 2000, and Raddatz, 2003).

- *Quality of institutions.* Poor-quality institutions conspire to weaken policies and undercut economies' resilience to exogenous shocks, thus increasing volatility and the risk of crises. In the analysis here, the institutional quality variable has the expected sign, but is not significant. This, however, does not mean that the quality of institutions is immaterial to volatility in emerging market and developing countries. Instrumental variables regressions

Table 2.5. Volatility Regression Results[1]

Explanatory Variables

Volatility of fiscal policy[2]	**1.67**
Inflation rate[3]	0.002
Institutional quality[4]	−0.26
Trade to GDP	***0.04***
Current and capital account restrictions	2.64
Initial level of financial sector development[5]	***−9.05***
Terms-of-trade volatility	**0.62**
Terms-of-trade volatility interacted with exchange regime flexibility[6]	**−0.29**
Exchange regime flexibility[6]	2.25
Initial relative income[7]	−2.25
Tropical climate	−1.53
R^2	0.44
Sargan test (*p*-value)[8]	0.93
Number of observations	51

Source: IMF staff calculations.

[1]The dependent variable is the standard deviation of the country component of real per capita GDP growth for the 1970–2003 period. The regression is estimated using an instrumental variables estimation technique in which the endogenous variables in the regression are the institutional quality and trade openness variables. Following the April 2003 *World Economic Outlook*, the fraction of the population speaking one of the major languages of western Europe, the fraction of the population speaking English, and ethnolinguistic fractionalization are used to instrument for the institutional quality variable. The predicted trade shares computed as for Frankel and Romer (1999) are used to instrument for trade openness. Bold values signify statistical significance at the 5 percent level and bold italics signify significance at the 10 percent level.

[2]Volatility of fiscal policy is measured as the standard deviation of the cyclically adjusted government spending, following Fatás and Mihov (2003).

[3]Inflation is the average annual inflation rate over 1970–2003.

[4]The institutional quality variable is measured as the average of three indices reported in the *International Country Risk Guide*.

[5]Financial sector development is measured as the ratio of private sector credit to GDP in 1970.

[6]Exchange regime flexibility is measured by an index which takes higher values the longer the period of time a country has been under a more flexible regime over the 1970–2001 period.

[7]Initial relative income is the level of real per capita GDP relative to that in the United States in 1970.

[8]This is the *p*-value from a Sargan test of the validity of the instruments used in the regression.

show that better-quality institutions are associated with more advanced financial sector development and lower fiscal volatility, suggesting that it is through these variables that institutional quality affects volatility.[32] Further,

---

[31]The private credit to GDP series are all stationary around a linear trend, and therefore, the initial period values can be taken as exogenous. In addition, the results reported in the essay are robust to using the ratio of average private credit to GDP over 1970–2003 as the explanatory variable (instrumented using indicators for French or English legal origin and life expectancy).

[32]See Acemoglu and Johnson (2003) on the importance of property rights institutions for financial development, investment, and long-run economic growth, and Satyanath and Subramanian (2004) on the effects of democratic institutions on monetary policy and macroeconomic stability.

Figure 2.11. Decompositions of Declines in Output Volatility Between 1970–86 and 1987–2003[1]

(Percent of change in volatility explained; a positive percentage indicates a reduction in volatility)

Improvements in financial sector development, volatility of fiscal policy, terms of trade volatility, and flexibility of the exchange rate regime have been the main contributors to the trend declines in volatility in emerging market and developing countries, although the relative importance of these factors varies across countries and regions.

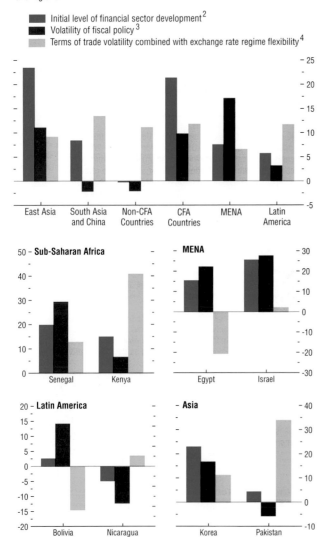

Sources: Beck, Demirgüç-Kunt, and Levine (1999); Fatás and Mihov (2003); Reinhart and Rogoff (2002); and IMF staff calculations.

[1]This figure shows the contribution of key variables to changes in the overall volatility of the country-specific components of output growth between the 1970–86 and 1987–2003 periods that can be explained by the cross-sectional regression estimates.

[2]Initial level of financial development is measured as the ratio of private sector credit to GDP in 1970 and 1987, respectively.

[3]Measured as the standard deviation of the cyclically adjusted government spending estimated for the 1960–86 and 1987–2000 periods, respectively (see Fatás and Mihov, 2003).

[4]Sum of the effects of changes in the terms of trade volatility and the interaction of the terms of trade volatility with exchange regime flexibility.

the April 2003 *World Economic Outlook* illustrates that sound macroeconomic policies, the quality of institutions, and output volatility are highly correlated.[33]

- *Other structural characteristics.* Terms-of-trade volatility is found to be associated with higher output volatility, although flexible exchange rates were found to have a dampening effect. While the exchange rate regime itself is not significant, the interaction of terms-of-trade volatility with a variable capturing the flexibility of the exchange rate regime during the sample period is negative and significant, confirming that the association between terms-of-trade shocks and output volatility is more pronounced under fixed than flexible exchange rate regimes (although, of course, fixed exchange rates may provide other benefits, including by fostering greater monetary and fiscal discipline).[34]

Improvements in key explanatory variables—financial sector development, volatility of fiscal policy, terms-of-trade volatility, and the flexibility of exchange rate regimes—have made an important contribution to the decline in volatility in many emerging market and developing countries. For the MENA countries, less volatile fiscal policy stands out as the key contributor to the decline in their output volatility between 1970–86 and 1987–2003, accounting for 17 percent of the overall decline in volatility (Figure

[33]Other studies, such as "Growth and Institutions," Chapter III, *World Economic Outlook*, April 2003, which have found better-quality institutions to be associated with lower volatility in a cross-section regression, have typically included industrial countries in the sample.

[34]Other variables in the regression include the level of real per capita income relative to the United States—which controls for the possibility that richer countries have less volatility because they have been able to diversify their economic base—and a dummy variable for countries in tropical climates to capture their tendency to have lower and more volatile per capita output. These variables are, however, not found to be statistically significant. In addition, indicators of political stability and conflict as well as the share of agricultural output in GDP were included but were insignificant—possibly because they are highly correlated with other variables in the regression such as the quality of institutions—and were dropped from the final regression reported here.

2.11).[35] For the CFA countries, the deepening of the financial sector accounts for as much as 21 percent of the overall decline in volatility. For south Asia and China and the non-CFA countries in sub-Saharan Africa, the main stabilizing factor appears to have been the reduction in the volatility of the terms of trade in combination with an increase in exchange rate flexibility. However, despite these improvements, terms-of-trade volatility remains a significant factor in the volatility of many countries in sub-Saharan Africa (Figure 2.12).

The key contributors to the decline in volatility in individual countries in each region are broadly consistent with those for the region as a whole. For example, in the case of Senegal, a reduction in the volatility of fiscal policy accounts for 30 percent of the decline in volatility, and financial sector development accounts for 20 percent of the decline. The findings are similar for Egypt and Israel, where reductions in the volatility of fiscal policy and developments in the financial sector account for between 40 and 50 percent of the changes in their volatility. For Kenya, on the other hand, the reduction in its terms-of-trade volatility combined with the increased flexibility of its exchange rate was the main factor contributing to lower volatility.

Many emerging market and developing country regions have made important progress in recent years in reducing economic volatility, yet much more can still be done. While efforts across a broad range of policy reforms will be necessary, the following stand out from the analysis as being particularly important. A more stable fiscal policy could play a significant role in reducing volatility in sub-Saharan Africa—a reduction in the volatility of cyclically adjusted government spending to the level in east Asia would reduce output volatility by 1.1 percentage points for countries in the CFA franc zone and by 0.9 percentage point for the non-CFA countries (Figure 2.13). This is equivalent to about 15 percent of the country-

Figure 2.12. Response of the Volatility of Output Growth to a One-Standard-Deviation Increase in Terms-of-Trade Volatility
(Percent)

In part because of the inflexibility of their exchange rate regime, terms-of-trade shocks over the 1970–2003 period had the largest impact on output volatility in CFA franc zone countries.

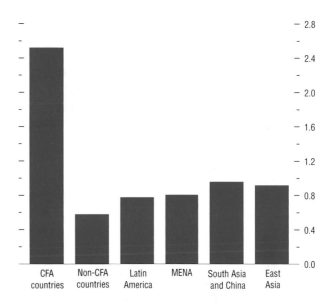

Source: IMF staff calculations.

[35]Percentages reported here refer to the contribution of a variable to the change in overall volatility that can be explained by the cross-sectional regression.

Figure 2.13. Output Volatility and Improvements in Policies[1]

Stability-oriented fiscal policies and improvements in the level of financial sector development would help to reduce volatility, particularly in sub-Saharan Africa and Latin America.

—— CFA countries   —— Non-CFA countries
—— Latin America   —— MENA
—— South Asia and China

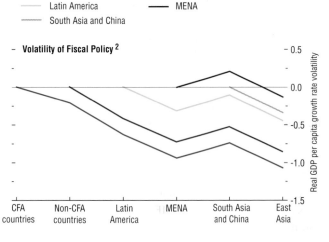

Volatility of Fiscal Policy[2]

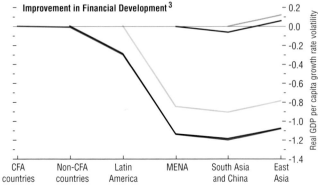

Improvement in Financial Development[3]

Source: IMF staff calculations.
[1]Figures show change in standard deviation of average annual real GDP per capita growth rate if a particular region improved its policies to match the quality of other regions.
[2]Measured as the standard deviation of the cyclically adjusted government spending estimated for the 1960–2000 period (see Fatás and Mihov, 2003).
[3]Measured by initial total private credit as a ratio of GDP (see Beck, Demirgüç-Kunt, and Levine, 1999).

specific output volatility. Countries in other regions (most notably in Latin America) also stand to gain from a more stable fiscal policy. Sub-Saharan African countries also would gain from further financial deepening. If they were able to raise the ratio of private sector credit to GDP to the average for the south Asia and China region, which has the highest initial level of financial sector development in the sample, output volatility in sub-Saharan Africa would fall by about 1.2 percentage points, or by about 20 percent of the country-specific output volatility.

Conclusions and Policy Recommendations

Output volatility has negative effects on long-term economic growth, welfare, and income inequality, particularly in developing countries, and therefore reducing such volatility can make an important contribution to improving growth and welfare. Although output volatility has been on a downward trend in most emerging market and developing country regions over the past three decades, it remains higher than in industrial countries. The analysis in this essay has shown that much of the output volatility in emerging market and developing countries is driven by country-specific factors, underscoring the key role of domestic policies. Thus, while emerging market and developing countries have made important strides in strengthening macroeconomic and structural policies in recent years, further progress is still needed.

The present favorable global economic environment provides an opportune time to address the sources of output volatility in emerging market and developing countries. While reforms across a broad range of areas will be needed to reduce volatility and improve growth performance, the following stand out from the analysis in this essay as being particularly important.

- Fiscal policies have tended to reinforce output fluctuations and hence increase volatility, particularly in sub-Saharan Africa and Latin America. To contain the volatility of fiscal policies, greater expenditure restraint is needed during cyclical upturns to raise budgetary surpluses and reduce debt. The strengthening of budgetary institutions would be helpful in this regard (see Chapter III, *World Economic Outlook*, September 2003, and Kaminsky, Reinhart, and Végh, 2004).

- The emerging market and developing country regions with the least developed financial sectors (sub-Saharan Africa and Latin America) have on average had higher output volatility. Progress in developing the financial sector, and ensuring that it is appropriately regulated and supervised, would help alleviate financing constraints, particularly during downturns, and thereby provide countries with additional scope to absorb shocks.

- Terms-of-trade volatility is associated with higher volatility of output growth. One way to reduce the incidence of terms-of-trade shocks is through structural reforms that promote diversification of the productive base, though this may also require a longer-term policy commitment. The essay also illustrates that exchange rate flexibility may cushion the impact of terms-of-trade shocks on output volatility.

Appendix 2.1. Workers' Remittances and Economic Development: Sample Composition, Data Sources, and Methods

The main author of this appendix is Angela Cabugao.

This appendix provides further details on the data used in the first essay, and in particular discusses the time series employed to construct a measure of workers' remittances.

The analysis of the impact of remittances uses a panel of up to 101 economies, both advanced and developing, during the period 1970–2003.[36] The analysis of the determinants of remittances uses a panel of up to 92 developing economies during the period 1980–2003. Throughout the essay, regional classifications follow the current WEO groupings.

Unless otherwise indicated, *total remittances* are constructed as the sum of three items in the IMF's *Balance of Payments Statistics Yearbook* (BOPSY): "Compensation of Employees," "Workers' Remittances," and "Migrants' Transfers."[37] Box 2.4 provides a fuller discussion of these three items and of the problems with the data. Following the country-specific notes in BOPSY, "Compensation of Employees" is excluded from total remittances for the following countries: Argentina, Australia, Azerbaijan, Barbados, Belize, Benin, Brazil, Cambodia, Cape Verde, China, Côte d'Ivoire, Dominican Republic, Ecuador, El Salvador, Guyana, Italy, Panama, Rwanda, Senegal, Seychelles, Turkey, and Venezuela.[38] In general, the "Other Current Transfers" item is not included in the definition of total remittances. However, BOPSY specifies explicitly that migrants' remittances are recorded under "Other Current Transfers" for Kenya, Malaysia, and the Syrian Arab Republic.

Additional adjustments or additions to the series for remittances were made on the basis of information received from IMF country desks and national authorities, as follows:

1.	Bosnia and Herzegovina:	Desk provided data for 1998–2003.
2.	Bulgaria:	Other current transfers are included in remittances.
3.	Caribbean:	Desk provided data for 1991–2002.[39]
4.	I.R. of Iran:	Other current transfers are used as figure for remittances.
5.	Lebanon:	Desk provided data for 1997–2003.
6.	Lesotho:	Desk provided data for 1982–2003.
7.	Macedonia, FYR:	Desk provided data for 1993–97.
8.	Moldova:	Desk provided data for 2000.
9.	Niger:	Desk provided data for 1995–2003.
10.	Romania:	Desk provided data for 2000–2003.
11.	Slovak Republic:	Desk provided data for 1999–2003.
12.	Tajikistan:	Desk provided data for 1997–2001.
13.	Ukraine:	Desk provided data for 2000.
14.	Venezuela:	Desk provided data for 1997–2003.

[36]The growth, poverty, and volatility regressions use, respectively, 101, 90, and 58 countries.
[37]Paola Giuliano and Marta Ruiz Arranz were instrumental in constructing the time series for remittances.
[38]For most of these countries, BOPSY states explicitly that no information on border and seasonal workers is included in this category.
[39]The Caribbean region is defined in Box 2.1. The data are taken from Mishra (2005b).

Box 2.4. Balance of Payments Data on Workers' Remittances

Data Concepts and Sources

There is no universally accepted definition of remittances. They are broadly thought of as unrequited transfers, sent by migrant workers back to relatives in their country of origin. In practice, data users and analysts have treated as remittances a variety of transactions that are initiated by individuals living or working outside their country of birth or origin (others have even mentioned donations sent by charitable organizations). Those components of balance of payments statistics most often specifically mentioned as constituting remittances are "Compensation of Employees" (part of the income component of the current account), "Workers' Remittances" (part of current transfers in the current account), and "Migrants' Transfers" (part of the capital account).[1]

According to the IMF's *Balance of Payments Manual, Fifth Edition* (IMF, 1993; henceforth *BPM5*), "Workers' Remittances" are current transfers made by migrants who are employed and *resident* in another economy. This typically includes those workers who move to an economy and stay, or are expected to stay, a year or longer. "Compensation of Employees" instead comprises wages, salaries, and other benefits (cash or in-kind) earned by *nonresident workers* for work performed for residents of other countries. Such workers typically include border and seasonal workers, together with some other categories, e.g., local embassy staff. Finally, "Migrants' Transfers" include financial items that arise from the migration (change of residence) of individuals from one economy to another. Data on these items are compiled by

relevant statistical authorities in IMF member countries. Using this source, the IMF's Statistics Department constructs the tables found in the *Balance of Payments Statistics Yearbook* (*BOPSY*).

Problems Faced by Data Users

Data are subject to variations in compilation on a national basis. This is partially due to different interpretations of the definitions and classifications set out in *BPM5*. Information of sources and methods used by member countries, illustrating the diversity of approaches, is published in *BOPSY*, Part 3.[2] In most cases, however, data weaknesses and omissions are due to the difficulties in obtaining all necessary data. For compiling all remittance-related flows, a variety of data sources would have to be used, some of which are difficult to capture. Transactions between households, particularly when using informal channels (e.g., sending cash through the mail or through systems such as hawala) are extremely hard to account for and are often omitted from official data. As a result, data are neither perfectly comparable nor equally comprehensive and reliable across countries. In some cases, actual remittances may be significantly underrecorded.[3]

There are some instances where the manner in which data users wish to access data, and the concepts of the balance of payments framework, are not ideally aligned. For example, migrants' accounts in their home country may be accessible by family members in the country of origin (e.g., through ATM cards). However, the migrants' deposits in these accounts are not seen as remittances. The IMF's *Balance of Payments Textbook* (IMF, 1996) states that "money

Note: The main author of this box is Jens Reinke.
This box is based on a paper ("Remittances in the Balance of Payments Framework") presented at the International Technical Meeting on Measuring Migrant Remittances, January 24–25, 2005, in Washington, DC.

[1]Data users frequently report that the concept of "workers' remittances" alone is too narrow. This box therefore considers transactions recorded under different headings and discusses the problems in using such data consistently.

[2]For example, some countries still consider their nationals working abroad for a year and longer to be domestic residents—and their earnings therefore as compensation of employees—because these nationals maintain strong links with their home country. However, most countries follow the one-year rule in principle.

[3]Studies for many countries, summarized in Puri and Ritzema (1999) find that informal transfers amount to 10–55 percent of total remittances.

remitted by a migrant for the purpose of making a deposit in his or her own account with a bank located abroad represents a financial investment . . . rather than a transfer" (p. 90) and is therefore not a remittance (but is instead recorded as an investment asset of the sending economy). It involves a quid pro quo since the sending party acquires a claim against the deposit-taking bank abroad. Withdrawals from such an account may constitute a remittance, yet it seems very unlikely that such transactions are accurately recorded.[4]

Similar caveats apply to some physical movements of goods across borders. Migrants visiting their home countries are considered visitors there. When they take personal effects with them on home country visits, these are not classified as exports in their country of residence nor imports in their country of origin. However, personal effects given as gifts to relatives living in the country of origin constitute remittances. It is unlikely that such transactions are sufficiently covered by customs data. The same applies to cash carried on home visits.

Data users are sometimes interested in the net income a country earns from seasonal and border workers abroad. Balance of payment statistics show under "Compensation of Employees" the gross remuneration paid by resident companies to nonresident employees and remuneration received by residents from nonresident employers. However, a part of these earnings will likely be spent in the host economy and will therefore not accrue to the home economy as net income. "Personal expenditures made by nonresident seasonal and border workers in the economies in which they are employed . . . are recorded under *travel*" (*BPM5*, paragraph 271). However, data reported under travel also include the personal expenditures made by other business and personal travelers. It is there-

fore difficult, at best, to identify the offset items needed to calculate the net income relating to seasonal and border workers.

Bilateral data on remittance flows are a key interest of some data users. Although classification of flows by partner country is possible, it is not a standard feature of the balance of payment framework and attempts to compile it may face practical limitations. Voluntary country classification as a supplemental item is outlined in *BPM5* and could be further encouraged, yet without widespread adoption this is unlikely to yield a global remittance matrix.

Improvements in Compilation Practices and Conceptual Guidance

Given the large size and steady growth in remittance flows, there is a need to improve data quality. Since many weaknesses in data on remittances are caused by the difficulties in identifying and using data sources, the improvement of data sourcing and compilation practices plays a key role in the effort to enhance data availability and quality. The IMF provides compilation guidance and technical assistance to member countries to support the continued improvement of balance of payments statistics.

Improving the conceptual basis for measuring remittances is equally important. *BPM5* did not define workers or migrants. According to the *Balance of Payments Textbook*, workers' remittances are "transfers made by migrants who are employed by entities of economies in which the workers are considered residents," whereas transfers made by self-employed migrants "are not classified as workers' remittances but as current transfers" (pp. 90–91). The focus on employment and the failure to define a migrant raise two questions.

- With increasing international mobility and the breakdown of traditional employment models, the focus on workers may be difficult to maintain. Should the focus perhaps be on all migrants, regardless of status of employment and source of income?
- There is no clear guidance on migrants, since *BPM5* distinguishes only residents and

---

[4]For instance, in India, nonresident rupee deposits (whose stock currently exceeds US$30 billion) are not currently recorded as remittances. Yet, since the rupee is not convertible, these deposits do not return to the nonresident depositor upon maturity.

Box 2.4 *(concluded)*

nonresidents (visitors). Is a clear definition of migrants needed, as the originating unit of remittances? Alternatively, should all household-to-household transfers be considered remittances, regardless of residence status?

These and other questions are currently being addressed in the context of ongoing work on the *Balance of Payments Manual* in the IMF Committee on Balance of Payments Statistics and in coordination with other forums, such as the UN Technical Sub-Group on the Movement of Natural Persons. Updated conceptual guidance will be tabled later this year. However, data users and their needs are diverse. Even outside

the balance of payments framework, there is no accepted definition of remittances, making it difficult to address data users' needs since they often appear a moving target. The IMF's Statistics Department is involved in consultative efforts with data users to better identify a common understanding of remittances and specific data needs.[5]

[5]The Statistics Department recently cohosted with the World Bank an international meeting on remittances, bringing together compilers and data users from around the world. Details are available via the Internet at www.worldbank.org/data/remittances.htm.

No data on remittances were available for the following countries, and they were therefore excluded from the analysis: I.S. of Afghanistan, Angola, the Bahamas, Bahrain, Bhutan, Brunei Darussalam, Burundi, Canada, Dem. Rep. of Congo, Iraq, Kuwait, Liberia, Libya, Qatar, Singapore, Taiwan Province of China, United Arab Emirates, Uzbekistan, Vietnam, and Zambia.

All regressions employ the ratio of remittances to GDP, except for the analyses of poverty and remittances, which employ logs of the ratio of remittances to GDP. Details of some other key variables are as follows.

- *Dual exchange rates.* This indicator specifies if a country has more than one exchange rate that may be used simultaneously for different purposes and/or by different entities. It comes from the IMF's *Annual Report on Exchange Arrangements and Exchange Restrictions, 2003* (AREAER).
- *Restrictions on foreign-currency deposits held abroad.* This indicator, also from the AREAER, specifies whether resident accounts that are maintained in foreign currency and held abroad are allowed.

All regressions include additional control variables as follows.

- *Output growth equation:* log of initial income, education, log of life expectancy, investment, inflation, budget balance, trade openness, and financial development.
- *Education and investment equations:* log of initial income, log of life expectancy, trade openness, and financial development.
- *Poverty equations:* log of average income and of the Gini coefficient.
- *Volatility equations:* log of initial income, share of agriculture in GDP, trade openness, real exchange rate overvaluation, and institutional quality.
- *Determinants of remittances equation:* political risk, law and order, the U.S. 6-month LIBOR, world oil prices, country-specific fixed effects, and a time trend.

Appendix 2.2. Output Volatility in Emerging Market and Developing Countries: Country Coverage, Methodology, and Data

The main author of this appendix is Dalia Hakura, with support from Christopher Otrok.

This appendix provides details on the regional groupings and country coverage, the dynamic factor model, and variable definitions and data sources used in the second essay.

Regional Groupings and Country Coverage

This section specifies the countries included in each regional grouping used in the essay. In addition to the regional groupings outlined in the essay, for the purpose of estimation of the dynamic factor model Latin America is divided into (1) Central America and the Caribbean and (2) South America, and the industrial countries are divided into (1) G-7 and (2) other industrial countries, to capture differences in their regional cycles. The grouping of the countries by region appears to be well-suited to identify a "regional factor" because countries that are geographically close to each other are likely to be affected by the same shocks, such as weather-related shocks or any given terms-of-trade shocks. In addition to the geographic aspect of the groupings, other factors such as trade and financial linkages or a degree of policy coordination (e.g., the longstanding peg of the CFA franc zone countries, initially to the French franc and now to the euro) can justify common regional cycles. The justification for grouping the industrial countries together is not based on geography but rather reflects the stage of economic development and the quality of institutions.

Industrial Countries

G-7 countries. Canada, France, Germany, Italy, Japan, the United Kingdom, and the United States.

Other industrial countries. Australia, Austria, Belgium, Denmark, Finland, Greece, the Netherlands, New Zealand, Norway, Portugal, Spain, Sweden, and Switzerland.

Latin America

Central America and the Caribbean. Costa Rica, Dominican Republic, El Salvador, Guatemala, Guyana, Haiti, Honduras, Mexico, Nicaragua, Panama, and Trinidad and Tobago.

South America. Argentina, Bolivia, Brazil, Chile, Colombia, Ecuador, Paraguay, Peru, Uruguay, and Venezuela.

Middle East and North Africa

Algeria, Egypt, Iran, Israel, Jordan, Morocco, Syria, Tunisia, and Turkey.

Sub-Saharan Africa

CFA franc zone countries. Burkina Faso, Cameroon, Republic of Congo, Côte d'Ivoire, Gabon, Guinea-Bissau, Mali, Niger, Senegal, and Togo.

Non-CFA countries. Botswana, Burundi, Ethiopia, Gambia, Ghana, Kenya, Madagascar, Malawi, Mozambique, Namibia, Nigeria, Sierra Leone, South Africa, Tanzania, Uganda, and Zambia.

South Asia and China

Bangladesh, China, India, Pakistan, and Sri Lanka.

East Asia

Korea, Indonesia, Malaysia, the Philippines, Singapore, and Thailand.

Dynamic Factor Model

Dynamic factor models are a generalization of the static factor models commonly used in psychology. The motivation underlying these models, which are gaining increasing popularity among economists, is that there are a few common factors that are driving fluctuations in large cross sections of macroeconomic time series. While these factors are unobservable and cannot be identified as clearly "productivity shocks" or "monetary shocks," the rationalization for these models is that a few aggregate shocks are the underlying driving forces for the economy. The unobserved factors are then indexes of common activity. These factors can capture common activity across the entire data set (e.g., global activity) or across subsets of the data (e.g., a particular region).

One goal of this literature is to extract estimates of these unobserved factors and use these estimated factors to quantify both the extent and nature of co-movement in a set of time-series data.[40] The dynamic factor model decomposes each observable variable—e.g., output growth in Nigeria—into components that are common across all observable variables or common across a subset of variables and idiosyncratic noise.

The model used in this essay has a block of equations for each region that is studied; each regional block contains an equation for output growth (Y) in each country decomposing output growth into a global component, a regional component, and a country-specific or idiosyncratic component. For example, the block of equations for the first region (G-7) is

$$Y_{US,t} = b_{US}^{Global} f_t^{Global} + b_{US}^{G-7} f_t^{G-7} + c_{US,t}$$

$$Y_{Japan,t} = b_{Japan}^{Global} f_t^{Global} + b_{Japan}^{G-7} f_t^{G-7} + c_{Japan,t}$$

$$\vdots$$

$$Y_{France,t} = b_{France}^{Global} f_t^{Global} + b_{France}^{G-7} f_t^{G-7} + c_{France,t}.$$

The same form is repeated for each of the nine regions in the system.

In this system, the global factor is the component common to all countries. The sensitivity of output growth in each country to the global factor depends on b, the factor loading. There is also a regional factor, which captures co-movement across the countries in a region.

The model captures dynamic co-movement by allowing the factors (fs) and country-specific terms (c) to be (independent) autoregressive processes. That is, each factor or country-specific term depends on lags of itself and an independent and identically distributed innovation to the variable (u_t):

$$f_t^{Global} = \phi(L) f_{t-1}^{Global} + u_t,$$

where $\phi(L)$ is a lag polynomial and u_t is normally distributed. All of the factor loadings (bs), and lag polynomials are independent of each other. The model is estimated using Bayesian

techniques as described in Kose, Otrok, and Whiteman (2003) and Otrok, Silos, and Whiteman (2003).[41]

To measure the importance of each factor for explaining the volatility of output growth, variance decompositions are calculated that decompose the volatility of output growth into components due to each factor. The formula for the variance decomposition is derived by applying the variance operator to each equation in the system. For example, for the first equation:

$$\mathrm{var}(Y_{US}) = (b_{US}^{Global})^2 \mathrm{var}(f^{Global})$$
$$+ (b_{US}^{G-7})^2 \mathrm{var}(f^{G-7}) + \mathrm{var}(c_{US}).$$

There are no cross-product terms between the factors because they are orthogonal to each other. The variance in real per capita output growth attributable to the global factor is then

$$\frac{(b_{US}^{Global})^2 \mathrm{var}(f^{Global})}{\mathrm{var}(Y_{US})}.$$

To address the question of what accounts for the trend declines in output volatility, the dynamic factor model is estimated over two periods: 1970–86 and 1987–2004. Each factor's contribution to the change in overall volatility is calculated. For instance, the contribution of the global factor to the decline in the variance of output growth, $\mathrm{var}(Y_{US,1987-04}) - \mathrm{var}(Y_{US,1970-86})$, is

$$[(b_{US,1987-04}^{Global})^2 \mathrm{var}(f_{1987-04}^{Global})]$$
$$- [(b_{US,1970-86}^{Global})^2 \mathrm{var}(f_{1970-86}^{Global})].$$

Data Definitions and Sources

This section describes the sources of the data on real per capita GDP used to estimate the dynamic factor model as well as the data used in

---

[40]The second major objective of this literature is using the information in the cross section of time series to forecast one time series.

[41]The innovation variance of the factors (error term in the factor autoregressive equation) is normalized. This normalization is based on the variance of the underlying series and determines the scale of the factor (i.e., 0.1 versus 0.01). This dependency on scaling is the reason for looking only at variance decompositions or appropriately scaled versions of the factors (factor times factor loading, as in the computation of the decline in variance shown below).

The model is estimated using de-meaned output growth data allowing for a break in 1986.

the cross-sectional regression that is estimated. The dynamic factor analysis cover data that include projections for 2004. The latter projections are not included in the cross-sectional regression analysis. The coverage of emerging market and developing countries in the cross-sectional regression estimated in the essay is limited to 51 countries owing to data availability.

Real per capita GDP growth is measured using data on real per capita GDP in constant dollars (international prices, base year 1996) obtained from the Penn World Tables (PWT), Version 6.1. The PWT data cover the 1970–2000 period. Real per capita GDP growth rates calculated using data from the WEO database were used to extend the series to 2004.

Volatility of country component of output growth is measured as the standard deviation of the growth rate of the country-component of real per capita GDP growth for the 1970–2003 period as derived from the estimates of the dynamic factor model.

Volatility of fiscal policy is measured as the standard deviation of cyclically adjusted government spending over 1960–2000 as estimated by Fatás and Mihov (2003). This is obtained as the standard deviation of the residual from an instrumental variables regression of the growth of government spending on output growth, the one-period lag of the growth of government spending as well as various controls for government spending and a time trend.

Inflation rate is the average annual growth of the Consumer Price Index over 1970–2004 (reflecting the availability of reliable data). The source of the data is the World Bank's *World Development Indicators* (WDI).

Institutional quality is constructed as the average of three indices reported by the International Country Risk Guide (ICRG) over 1984–2003. The indices are (1) corruption—the degree of all forms of corruption such as patronage, nepotism, and suspiciously close ties between politics and business; (2) rule of law—the strength and impartiality of the legal system and the extent of popular observance of the law; and (3) bureaucracy quality—the strength and

expertise of the bureaucracy to govern without drastic changes in policy or interruptions in government services. The indices are rescaled from 1 to 12, where high values indicate good institutions.

Trade openness is defined as the sum of imports and exports of goods and services (from balance of payments statistics), divided by GDP. The source of the data is the WDI.

Current and capital account restrictions is constructed as the average of four indices reported in the IMF's *Annual Report on Exchange Arrangements and Exchange Restrictions* for the 1970–2003 period. The indices are (1) current account restrictions; (2) capital account restrictions; (3) restrictions on export proceeds; and (4) multiple exchange rate regimes. Each index takes a value of one if the country has a restriction, and a value of zero otherwise.

Initial level of financial sector development is measured as the ratio of private credit to GDP in 1970 or the first year for which the data are available prior to 1990. The source of the data is Beck, Demirgüç-Kunt, and Levine (1999; 2003 database).

Terms-of-trade volatility is measured as the standard deviation of the annual change in the terms of trade over 1970–2003. The source of the data is the WEO database.

Exchange regime flexibility is constructed as the average over the 1970–2001 period of an index that takes a value of 1 in years in which a country is classified as having a fixed regime, a value of 2 in years in which a country is classified as having an intermediate regime, and a value of 3 in years in which a country is classified as having a free float. The de facto "Natural classification" developed by Reinhart and Rogoff (2004) is used to classify exchange rate regimes. The instances where countries were classified as having a free fall were replaced with the secondary classification as reported in Reinhart and Rogoff (2004).

Initial relative income is the ratio of real per capita GDP relative to that in the United States in 1970. The data on real per capita GDP in constant 1996 prices is obtained from PWT.

Tropical climate is a dummy variable for countries that are in tropical climate zones. The source of the data is the World Bank's Global Development Network Growth Database.

References

Acemoglu, Daron, and Simon Johnson, 2003, "Unbundling Institutions," NBER Working Paper No. 9934 (Cambridge, Massachusetts: National Bureau of Economic Research).

———, James Robinson, and Yunyong Thaicharoen, 2003, "Institutional Causes, Macroeconomic Symptoms: Volatility, Crises, and Growth," *Journal of Monetary Economics*, Vol. 50, No. 1, pp. 49–123.

Adams, Richard Jr., 1991, "The Effects of International Remittances on Poverty, Inequality, and Development in Rural Egypt," Research Report No. 86 (Washington: International Food Policy Research Institute).

———, 1998, "Remittances, Investment, and Rural Asset Accumulation in Pakistan," *Economic Development and Cultural Change*, Vol. 47, No. 1, pp. 155–73.

———, 2004a, "Remittances and Poverty in Guatemala," World Bank Policy Research Working Paper No. 3418 (Washington: World Bank).

———, 2004b, "Remittances, Household Expenditure and Investment in Guatemala" (unpublished; Washington: World Bank).

———, and John Page, 2003, "International Migration, Remittances, and Poverty in Developing Countries," World Bank Policy Research Working Paper No. 3179 (Washington: World Bank).

Aghion, Philippe, Angeletos George-Marios, Abhijit Banerjee, and Kalina Manova, 2004, "Volatility and Growth: Financial Development and the Cyclical Composition of Investment," MIT Working Paper (Cambridge, Massachusetts: MIT Press).

Ahlburg, Dennis, 1991, "Remittances and Their Impact: A Study of Tonga and Western Samoa," Pacific Policy Paper No. 7 (Canberra: Australian National University, National Centre for Development Studies).

Aizenman, Joshua, and Brian Pinto, 2005, *Managing Economic Volatility and Crises: A Practitioner's Guide* (Cambridge: Cambridge University Press, forthcoming).

Amuedo-Dorantes, Catalina, Cynthia Bansak, and Susan Pozo, 2004, "On the Remitting Patterns of Immigrants: Evidence from Mexican Survey Data," Department of Economics Working Paper, Department of Economics (San Diego, California: San Diego State University).

Barlevy, Gadi, 2004, "The Cost of Business Cycles and the Benefits of Stabilization: A Survey," NBER Working Paper No. 10926 (Cambridge, Massachusetts: National Bureau of Economic Research).

Beck, Thorsten, Asli Demirgüç-Kunt, and Ross Levine, 1999, "A New Database on Financial Development and Structure," World Bank Policy Research Working Paper No. 2146 (Washington: World Bank).

Berg, Andrew, and Anne Krueger, 2003, "Trade, Growth, and Poverty: A Selective Survey," IMF Working Paper 03/30 (Washington: International Monetary Fund).

Blackburn, Keith, 1999, "Can Stabilisation Policy Reduce Long-Run Growth?" *Economic Journal*, Vol. 109, No. 452, pp. 67–77.

Bouhga-Hagbe, Jacques, 2004, "A Theory of Workers' Remittances with An Application to Morocco," IMF Working Paper 04/194 (Washington: International Monetary Fund).

Bourdet, Yves, and Hans Falck, 2003, "Emigrants' Remittances and Dutch Disease in Cape Verde," Working Paper Series 11 (Kristianstad, Sweden: Kristianstad University College).

Brown, Richard P.C., 1994, "Migrants' Remittances, Savings, and Investment in the South Pacific," *International Labor Review*, Vol. 133, No. 3, pp. 347–67.

Bulíř, Aleš, and A. Javier Hamann, 2001, "How Volatile and Unpredictable Are Aid Flows, and What Are the Policy Implications?" IMF Working Paper 01/167 (Washington: International Monetary Fund).

Carling, Orgen J., 2004, "Emigration, Return, and Development in Cape Verde: The Impact of Closing Borders," *Population, Society, and Place*, Vol. 10, No. 2, pp. 113–32.

Chami, Ralph, Connel Fullenkamp, and Samir Jahjah, 2003, "Are Immigrant Remittance Flows a Source of Capital for Development?" IMF Working Paper 03/189 (Washington: International Monetary Fund).

Chiquiar, Daniel, and Gordon Hanson, 2005, "International Migration, Self-Selection, and the Distribution of Wages: Evidence from Mexico and the United States," *Journal of Political Economy* (forthcoming).

Cox Edwards, Alejandra, and Manuelita Ureta, 2003, "International Migration, Remittances, and Schooling: Evidence from El Salvador," *Journal of Development Economics,* Vol. 72, No. 2, pp. 429–61.

DeSipio, Louis, 2000, "Sending Money Home . . . For Now: Remittances and Immigrant Adaptation in the United States," IAD-TRPI Working Paper (Washington: Inter-American Dialogue).

Docquier, Frédéric, and Abdeslam Marfouk, 2004, "Measuring the International Mobility of Skilled Workers," World Bank Policy Research Working Paper No. 3381 (Washington: World Bank).

Durand, Jorge, Emilio A. Parrado, and Douglas S. Massey, 1996, "Migradollars and Development: A Reconsideration of the Mexican Case," *International Migration Review,* Vol. 30, No. 2, pp. 423–44.

Easterly, William, Roumeen Islam, and Joseph Stiglitz, 2000, "Shaken and Stirred: Explaining Growth Volatility," *Annual Bank Conference on Development Economics* (Washington: World Bank).

Elbadawi, Ibrahim, and Roberto de Rezende Rocha, 1992, "Determinants of Expatriate Workers' Remittances in North Africa and Europe," World Bank Policy Research Working Paper No. 1038 (Washington: World Bank).

El-Qorchi, Mohammed, Samuel Munzele Maimbo, and John Wilson, 2003, *"Informal Funds Transfer Systems: An Analysis of the Informal Hawala System,"* IMF Occasional Paper No. 222 (Washington: International Monetary Fund).

El-Sakka, M.I.T., and Robert McNabb, 1999, "The Macroeconomic Determinants of Emigrant Remittances," *World Development,* Vol. 27, No. 8, pp. 1493–1502.

Faini, Riccardo, 2002, "Development, Trade, and Migration," *Revue d'Économie et du Développement,* proceedings from the ABCDE Europe Conference, 1–2, pp. 85–116.

———, 2004, "Does the Brain Drain Boost Growth?" (unpublished; Rome: Università di Roma Tor Vergata).

Fatás, Antonio, 2002, "The Effects of Business Cycles on Growth," in *Economic Growth: Sources, Trends, and Cycles,"* ed. by Norman Loayza and Raimundo Soto (Santiago: Central Bank of Chile).

———, and Ilian Mihov, 2003, "The Case for Restricting Fiscal Policy Discretion," *Quarterly Journal of Economics,* Vol. 118, No. 4, pp. 1419–48.

Frankel, Jeffrey, and David Romer, 1999, "Does Trade Cause Growth?" *American Economic Review,* Vol. 89 (June), pp. 379–99.

Gupta, Poonam, 2004, "Microeconomic Determinants of Remittances: Evidence from India" (unpublished; Washington: International Monetary Fund).

Hanson, Gordon H., and Christopher Woodruff, 2003, "Emigration and Educational Attainment in Mexico" (unpublished; San Diego, California). Available via the Internet: http://irpshome.ucsd.edu/faculty/gohanson/emigration.pdf.

Hnatkovska, Viktoria, and Norman Loayza, 2005, "Volatility and Growth," in *Managing Economic Volatility and Crises: A Practitioner's Guide,* ed. by Joshua Aizenman and Brian Pinto (Cambridge: Cambridge University Press, forthcoming).

Imbs, Jean., 2004, "Why the Link Between Volatility and Growth Is Both Positive and Negative" (London: London Business School and Centre for Economic Policy Research).

Inter-American Development Bank, 1995, "Overcoming Volatility," 1995 Economic and Social Progress Report (Washington).

International Monetary Fund, 1993, *Balance of Payments Manual, Fifth Edition* (Washington).

———, 1996, *Balance of Payments Textbook* (Washington).

Jadhav, Narendra, 2003, "Maximizing Development Benefits of Migrant Remittances: The Indian Experience," Reserve Bank of India Working Paper (New Delhi: Reserve Bank of India).

Kaminsky, Graciela, Carmen Reinhart, and Carlos Végh, 2004, "When It Rains, It Pours: Procyclical Capital Flows and Macroeconomic Policies," NBER Working Paper No. 10780 (Cambridge, Massachusetts: National Bureau of Economic Research).

Kapur, Devesh, 2004, "Remittances: The New Development Mantra?" G-24 Discussion Paper No. 29, UN Conference on Trade and Development (Geneva: United Nations).

Ketkar, Suhas, and Dilip Ratha, 2001, "Development Financing During a Crisis: Securitization of Future Receivables," World Bank Policy Research Working Paper No. 2582 (Washington: World Bank).

Kose, M. Ayhan, Christopher Otrok, and Eswar S. Prasad, 2005, "Regionalization vs. Globalization: Explaining North-South Business Cycle Dynamics," IMF Working Paper (Washington: International Monetary Fund, forthcoming).

Kose, M. Ayhan, Christopher Otrok, and Charles Whiteman, 2003, "International Business Cycles: World, Region, and Country-Specific Factors," *American Economic Review,* Vol. 93, No. 4, pp. 1216–39.

Kose, M. Ayhan, Eswar S. Prasad, and Marco E. Terrones, 2003, "Financial Integration and

Macroeconomic Volatility," *IMF Staff Papers*, Vol. 50, Special Issues, pp. 119–42 (Washington: International Monetary Fund).

———, 2005, "How Do Trade and Financial Integration Affect the Relationship Between Growth and Volatility?" IMF Working Paper 05/19 (Washington: International Monetary Fund).

Laursen, Thomas, and Sandeep Mahajan, 2005, "Volatility, Income Distribution, and Poverty," in *Managing Economic Volatility and Crises: A Practitioner's Guide*, ed. by Joshua Aizenman and Brian Pinto (Cambridge: Cambridge University Press, forthcoming).

Lindsay Lowell, Briant, and Rodolfo O. de La Garza, 2000, "The Developmental Role of Remittances in U.S. Latino Communities and in Latin American Countries: A Final Project Report," reports for the TRPI and the IAD (Claremont, California, and Washington: Inter-American Dialogue).

———, 2002, eds. *Sending Money Home: Hispanic Remittances and Community Development* (Oxford: Rowman & Littlefield).

Lucas, Robert E. B., 1987, "Emigration to South Africa's Mines," *American Economic Review*, Vol. 77 (June), pp. 313–30.

———, and Oded Stark, 1985, "Motivations to Remit: Evidence from Botswana," *Journal of Political Economy*, Vol. 93 (October), pp. 901–18.

Martin, Philippe, and Carol Ann Rogers, 2000, "Long-Term Growth and Short-Term Economic Instability," *European Economic Review*, Vol. 44, No. 2, pp. 359–81.

Massey, Douglas S., and Emilio A. Parrado, 1998, "International Migration and Business Formation in Mexico," *Social Science Quarterly*, Vol. 79, No. 1, pp. 1–19.

McCormick, Barry, and Jackline Wahba, 2001, "Overseas Work Experience, Savings, and Entrepreneurship Amongst Return Migrants to LDCs," *Scottish Journal of Political Economy*, Vol. 48, No. 2, pp. 164–78.

Meyers, Deborah Waller, 1998, "Migrant Remittances to Latin America: Reviewing the Literature," IAD-TRPI Working Paper (Washington: Inter-American Dialogue).

Mishra, Prachi, 2005a, "Emigration and Brain Drain: Evidence from the Caribbean," IMF Working Paper (Washington: International Monetary Fund, forthcoming).

———, 2005b, "Macroeconomic Impact of Remittances in the Caribbean" (unpublished; Washington: International Monetary Fund).

Organization for Economic Cooperation and Development, 2004, *Working Abroad: The Benefits Flowing from Nationals Working in Other Economies* (Paris).

———, *Trends in International Migration: Annual Report* (Paris, various years).

Orozco, Manuel, 2000, "Remittances and Markets: New Players and Practices," IAD-TRPI Working Paper (Washington: Inter-American Dialogue).

———, 2003, "Worker Remittances in an International Scope," IAD Research Series, March 2003 (Washington: Inter-American Dialogue).

———, 2004a, "The Remittance Marketplace: Prices, Policy, and Financial Institutions," June 2004 (Washington: Institute for the Study of International Migration, Georgetown University). Available via the Internet: www.pewhispanic.org/site/docs/pdf/Remittances%20june%202004%20final.pdf.

———, 2004b, "Remittances to Latin America and the Caribbean: Issues and Perspectives on Development," IAD Working Paper, September 2004 (Washington: Inter-American Dialogue). Available via the Internet: www.frbatlanta.org/news/CONFEREN/payments04/orozco.pdf.

Otrok, Christopher, Pedro Silos, and Charles Whiteman, 2003, "Bayesian Dynamic Factor Models for Large Datasets: Measuring and Forecasting Macroeconomic Data" (unpublished; Charlottesville, Virginia: University of Virginia).

Pallage, Stéphane, and Michel Robe, 2003, "On The Welfare Cost of Economic Fluctuations in Developing Countries," *International Economic Review*, Vol. 44 (May), pp. 677–98.

Poirine, Bernard, 1997, "A Theory of Remittances as an Implicit Family Loan Arrangement," *World Development*, Vol. 25, No. 4, pp. 589–611.

Puri, Shivani, and Tineke Ritzema, 1999, "Migrant Worker Remittances, Micro-Finance, and the Informal Economy: Prospects and Issues," ILO Working Paper No. 21 (Geneva: International Labor Organization). Available via the Internet: www.ilo.org/public/english/employment/finance/download/wpap21.pdf.

Raddatz, Claudio, 2003, "Liquidity Needs and Vulnerability to Financial Underdevelopment," World Bank Policy Research Working Paper No. 3161 (Washington: World Bank).

Rajan, Raghuram, and Arvind Subramanian, 2005, "What Prevents Aid from Enhancing Growth?" (unpublished; Washington: International Monetary Fund).

Ramey, Garey, and Valerie Ramey, 1995, "Cross-Country Evidence on the Link Between Volatility and Growth," *American Economic Review,* Vol. 85, No. 5, pp. 1138–51.

Ranciere, Romain, Aaron Tornell, and Frank Westermann, 2005, "Systemic Crises and Growth," NBER Working Paper No. 11076 (Cambridge, Massachusetts: National Bureau of Economic Research).

Rapoport, Hillel, and Frédéric Docquier, 2005, "The Economics of Migrants' Remittances," in *Handbook on the Economics of Reciprocity, Giving, and Altruism,* ed. by Louis-Andre Gerard-Varet, Serge-Christophe Kolm, and Jean Mercier Ythier (Amsterdam: North Holland, forthcoming).

Rasmussen, Tobias, 2004, "Macroeconomic Implications of Natural Disasters in the Caribbean," IMF Working Paper 04/224 (Washington: International Monetary Fund).

Ratha, Dilip, 2003, "Workers' Remittances: An Important and Stable Source of External Development Finance," Chapter 7 in *Global Development Finance 2003—Striving for Stability in Development Finance* (Washington: World Bank), pp. 157–75.

Reinhart, Carmen, and Kenneth Rogoff, 2004, "The Modern History of Exchange Rate Arrangements: A Reinterpretation," *Quarterly Journal of Economics,* Vol. 119 (February), pp. 1–48.

Rozelle, Scott, J., Edward Taylor, and Alan deBrauw, 1999, "Migration, Remittances, and Agricultural Productivity in China," *American Economic Review,* Vol. 89 (May), pp. 287–91.

Russell, Sharon, 1986, "Remittances from International Migration: A Review in Perspective," *World Development,* Vol. 14, No. 6, pp. 677–96.

Satyanath, Shanker, and Arvid Subramanian, 2004, "What Determines Long-Run Macroeconomic Stability? Democratic Institutions," IMF Working Paper 04/215 (Washington: International Monetary Fund).

Stark, Oded, 1991, *The Migration of Labor* (Oxford: Basil Blackwell).

Suki, Lenora, 2004, "Financial Institutions and the Remittances Market in the Dominican Republic," Center on Globalization and Sustainable Development Working Paper Series (New York: Earth Institute at Columbia University). Available via the Internet: www.iadb.org/mif/v2/files/Suki_NYNov04.pdf.

Suro, Roberto, 2003, "Remittance Senders and Receivers: Tracking the Transnational Channels," PHC Report (Washington: Pew Hispanic Center). Available via the Internet: www.pewhispanic.org/site/docs/pdf/Remittances%20Senders%20and%20Receivers%20LAC%202003%20Final.pdf.

———, Sergio Bendixen, B. Lindsay Lowell, and Dulce C. Benavides, 2002, "Billions in Motion: Latino Immigrants, Remittances, and Banking," PHC Report (Washington: Pew Hispanic Center). Available via the Internet: www.pewhispanic.org/site/docs/pdf/billions_in_motion.pdf.

Swamy, Gurushri, 1981, "International Migrants Workers' Remittances: Issues and Prospects," World Bank Staff Working Paper No. 481 (Washington: World Bank).

Taylor, J. Edward, 1999, "The New Economics of Labor Migration and the Role of Remittances in the Development Process," *International Migration,* Vol. 37, No. 1, pp. 63–88.

———, Scott Rozelle, and Alan deBrauw, 2003, "Migration and Incomes in Source Communities: A New Economics of Migration Perspectives from China," *Economic Development and Cultural Change,* Vol. 52, No. 1, pp. 75–101.

Tornell, Aaron, Frank Westermann, and Lorenza Martinez, 2004, "The Positive Link Between Financial Liberalization, Growth and Crises," NBER Working Paper No.10293 (Cambridge, Massachusetts: National Bureau of Economic Research).

Wolf, Holger, 2005, "Volatility: Definitions and Consequences," in *Managing Economic Volatility and Crises: A Practitioner's Guide,* ed. by Joshua Aizenman and Brian Pinto (Cambridge: Cambridge University Press, forthcoming).

Woodruff, Christopher, and Rene M. Zenteno, 2004, "Remittances and Micro Enterprises in Mexico," Graduate School of International Relations and Pacific Studies Working Paper (unpublished; San Diego, California: University of California, San Diego, and ITESM).

World Bank, 2001, *World Development Report, 2000/01* (Washington: World Bank).

Yang, Dean, 2004, "International Migration, Human Capital, and Entrepreneurship: Evidence from Philippine Migrants' Exchange Rate Shocks," Ford School of Public Policy Working Paper No. 02–011 (unpublished; Ann Arbor, Michigan: University of Michigan).

GLOBALIZATION AND EXTERNAL IMBALANCES

External current account deficits or surpluses in some major economic areas—notably the United States and Asia—have reached record-high levels, and expectations are that they will stay large or increase for some time. Many observers, including IMF staff, have expressed concern that corrections to sustainable levels will likely require large exchange rate adjustments, especially against the U.S. dollar, with possibly disruptive effects on global financial markets and economic activity.[1] In contrast, other observers are less concerned, arguing that a benign resolution of global imbalances is likely with today's deep economic and financial integration.[2]

Some recent developments suggest that globalization—the increasingly global dimension of economic and financial transactions—has changed the environment for external imbalances and their adjustment. For instance, it may be argued that larger external current account deficits or surpluses are the natural outcome of the increased scope for cross-border trade in financial assets, and that higher trade openness and greater competition worldwide are likely to have facilitated adjustment of global imbalances. However, globalization has also brought new challenges and risks. Larger external positions raise economies' exposure to financial market disturbances, increasing the risks associated with an abrupt realignment in investors' expectations. Finally, the relationship between globalization and external adjustment can be more ambiguous than suggested by casual observation. Some aspects of globalization—including, for example, more specialization in production—

may, at least in theory, hinder rather than facilitate adjustment.

Against this background, this chapter will examine implications of globalization for external imbalances and their adjustment. The relationship between globalization and external imbalances is complex and encompasses many aspects. For tractability, the chapter will focus on aspects that are particularly relevant from the perspective of the unwinding of current imbalances, and the related risks. To this end, it is organized in three parts.

- The first part discusses the rapid expansion of two-way capital flows and the corresponding increases in gross external asset and liability positions and then examines the implications. The chapter finds that these developments have contributed to an environment in which large current account surpluses or deficits can emerge and be sustained and argues that this can be helpful insofar as it allows for gradual rebalancing. Moreover, while economies' exposure to market and exchange rate changes has increased with larger gross external positions, these valuation effects can, perhaps paradoxically, to some extent facilitate external adjustment among industrial countries, as they are, in effect, wealth transfers from countries with appreciating currencies to countries with depreciating currencies. The chapter notes, however, that these benefits could turn into a liability if policies are not consistent with a credible medium-term policy framework aimed at external and internal balances, as expectations may not be well anchored. In this case, investor preferences

---

Note: The main authors of this chapter are Thomas Helbling, Nicoletta Batini, and Roberto Cardarelli, with support from Douglas Laxton, Dirk Muir, Panagiotis Konstantinou, Philip Lane, and Linda Tesar. Nathalie Carcenac provided research assistance.

[1]See "How Worrisome Are External Imbalances?" Chapter II, *World Economic Outlook*, September 2002, and Obstfeld and Rogoff (2001, 2004).

[2]See Cooper (2001, 2004).

may quickly change and the fallout from disruptive financial market turbulence would likely be more elevated than it had been.

- In the second part, the chapter turns to real globalization and examines how a broad fall in trading costs has affected the magnitudes, composition, and direction of trade flows as well as other key determinants of external adjustment. It finds that trade shares have increased and the global distribution of trade flows has become more equal, as emerging markets have become more integrated, but it notes that the empirical evidence on how real globalization has affected price and demand elasticities of trade flows is inconclusive.

- In the third part of the chapter, simulations of the IMF's new multicountry Global Economic Model (GEM) are used to analyze the combined effects of real and financial globalization on the adjustment of external imbalances. The chapter finds that real and financial globalization should generally facilitate global rebalancing, provided financial conditions remain benign, reflecting, among other factors, the better burden sharing implied by the more even distribution of trade flows across the globe. It also shows, however, that globalization has not fundamentally changed the nature of adjustment, nor the magnitudes involved, and that larger net foreign asset positions raise the potential risks associated with unexpected changes in investor preferences.

Overall, the chapter concludes that policymakers need to be very mindful of the risks associated with global imbalances, while at the same time taking advantage of the scope that globalization provides to facilitate adjustment.

At the outset, two points should be noted.

- The chapter adopts a broad notion of globalization, its causes, and its impact. In particular, while using as a starting point the narrow defi-

nition of an acceleration in the pace of growth of international trade in goods, services, and financial assets relative to the rate of growth in domestic trade, the chapter also considers phenomena such as the integration of emerging market economies, greater competition, or reduced exchange rate pass-through, which—while related to globalization—also reflect other factors, including more credible monetary policy frameworks.

- The chapter is not intended to cover the specific policies needed for the orderly resolution of current imbalances, which are discussed in Chapter I, or how the current imbalances have emerged (see Chapter II, *World Economic Outlook,* September 2002, and Hunt and Rebucci, 2003, for recent discussions). Moreover, it focuses mostly on industrial and key emerging market countries that are highly integrated and likely to play a major role in the rebalancing.

Financial Globalization

Financial globalization—the global integration of capital markets—has accelerated noticeably since the early 1990s, as illustrated, for example, by the rapid simultaneous increase in many countries' foreign assets and liabilities (Figure 3.1).[3] The trend toward larger external assets and liabilities has been particularly relevant for industrial countries, where, relative to output, both average external assets and liabilities about tripled between 1990 and 2003, reaching levels of more than 200 percent by the end of the period.[4] While the broad trend for emerging market countries has been similar, average increases for these countries have been smaller since the mid-1990s and, on a global scale, their gross external positions remain relatively small compared with those of industrial countries (Table 3.1).

---

[3]See Lane and Milesi-Ferretti (2003, 2005a). There are other measures of financial globalization, including price-based measures or the correlation between saving and investment. See Obstfeld and Taylor (2004) for empirical evidence based on other measures that suggest similar broad trends.

[4]The data on gross foreign assets and liabilities used in this chapter are taken from the latest version of the database developed by Philip Lane and Gian Maria Milesi-Ferretti (and used in Lane and Milesi-Ferretti, 2005b).

The recent bout of financial globalization is partly associated with the decline in information processing and dissemination costs that have fostered cross-border trade in an expanding variety of financial instruments through decreasing transaction costs (Figure 3.2). Domestic and external financial liberalization have played a major role since the early 1970s when the current era of financial globalization began after a long period of financial disintegration (see Box 3.1 for a comparison of the current era of globalization with earlier ones).[5] Finally, real and financial globalization tend to stimulate each other. Increased trade flows, for example, tend to lead to larger gross capital flows, reflecting trade finance, among other factors.

This section will examine two issues related to the surge in international financial transactions. First, it will analyze whether investors' increased incentives for international portfolio diversification have reduced the extent to which financial markets still restrict net international borrowing (the financing need associated with current account deficits) and net foreign liabilities (the corresponding stock measure). Second, it will investigate the extent to which larger holdings of foreign assets and liabilities expose investors to greater valuation risks and what this means for external adjustment.

While data on external assets and liabilities have greatly improved so that more systematic empirical analysis is possible compared with some 10 years ago, important caveats nevertheless remain (see Box 3.2 on data issues).

Globalization and Net Foreign Assets

Traditionally, investors place the bulk of their financial wealth in domestic assets despite more favorable risk-return profiles—before transaction costs and taxes—of globally diversified portfolios

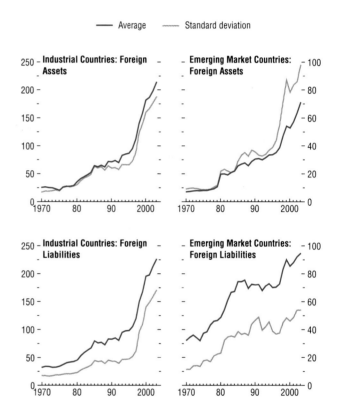

Figure 3.1. Financial Globalization Trends, 1970–2003
(Percent of GDP)

Global financial market integration has proceeded rapidly, especially in industrial countries, since the early 1990s.

Sources: IMF, *International Financial Statistics;* IMF, *Balance of Payments Statistics;* Lane and Milesi-Ferretti (2005b); and IMF staff calculations.

---

[5]See, among others, Edey and Hviding (1995) or Williamson and Mahar (1998). The end of the Bretton Woods regime of fixed but adjustable exchange rates also contributed, as trade in foreign exchange and related instruments began to spiral with floating rates.

Table 3.1. Gross Assets and Liabilities, 1980–2003

(Billions of U.S. dollars, excluding foreign assets held by central banks)

	1980	1985	1990	1995	2000	2003
External Assets						
Industrial countries	**2,287**	**3,975**	**9,701**	**15,334**	**26,810**	**36,039**
North America	668	1,310	2,331	4,107	7,914	8,454
United States	584	1,185	2,119	3,754	7,265	7,680
Europe	1,474	2,232	5,522	8,659	16,066	24,311
France	203	265	722	1,292	2,323	3,317
Germany	216	308	1,017	1,579	2,504	3,867
United Kingdom	519	838	1,695	2,342	4,400	6,293
Asia and Pacific	145	433	1,848	2,568	2,830	3,273
Japan	134	410	1,778	2,445	2,605	2,922
Emerging markets and other developing countries	**114**	**193**	**366**	**711**	**1,479**	**1,849**
Emerging Asia	28	72	166	384	948	1,193
China	. . .	18	25	47	225	273
Korea	4	7	17	58	103	127
Malaysia	4	7	5	13	39	53
Thailand	1	2	7	14	22	23
Latin America	55	80	126	214	325	386
Argentina	4	5	6	3	3	2
Brazil	10	19	29	51	74	96
Mexico	9	21	37	50	45	30
Others	31	42	74	113	206	270
External Liabilities						
Industrial countries	**2,485**	**4,186**	**10,531**	**16,139**	**28,419**	**39,039**
North America	708	1,464	2,909	4,849	9,741	11,452
United States	525	1,206	2,459	4,274	8,965	10,476
Europe	1,578	2,311	5,835	9,096	16,386	24,790
France	193	306	845	1,385	2,214	3,247
Germany	224	289	751	1,535	2,534	3,794
United Kingdom	508	755	1,762	2,426	4,497	6,429
Asia and Pacific	198	411	1,787	2,194	2,293	2,797
Japan	147	307	1,529	1,812	1,808	1,979
Emerging markets and other developing countries	**552**	**905**	**1,298**	**2,378**	**3,527**	**4,208**
Emerging Asia	138	284	493	1,125	1,626	2,116
China	. . .	27	77	255	479	659
Korea	33	59	55	147	195	293
Malaysia	12	31	31	81	101	115
Thailand	10	20	41	138	116	111
Latin America	267	395	492	819	1,247	1,310
Argentina	29	54	70	144	236	192
Brazil	90	121	153	241	403	420
Mexico	66	108	134	230	309	362
Others	147	226	313	435	654	782

Sources: Lane and Milesi-Ferretti (2005b); IMF, *International Financial Statistics,* and IMF staff calculations.

(the so-called *home bias* in asset holdings).[6] Clearly, with globalization, opportunities for international diversification have improved, as important obstacles, such as high cross-border transaction and information costs or regulatory barriers, have been reduced.[7] One would therefore expect that the home bias has decreased at the global level.

[6]Since asset returns are only partially correlated across countries, investors may reduce risks that are specific to their home country with international diversification (e.g., Solnik, 1974, or Obstfeld and Rogoff, 1996).

[7]Explanations of the home bias focus on factors reducing the incentives for international diversification, including high transaction costs in cross-border transactions compared with domestic transactions, problems of cross-border information dissemination, differences in regulatory regimes and regulatory barriers (e.g., regulations restricting foreign investment by pension funds), and differences in consumption baskets, owing to the presence of transport costs (nontraded goods), but

The decline in home bias matters for external imbalances and their adjustment because it determines the extent to which desired current account balances[8]—which depend on factors such as productivity growth differentials or demographic changes—are accommodated by international financial markets.[9] If home bias is strong, global demand for foreign assets will be low and price-inelastic. Large issuers of foreign liabilities will thus face high yields; this will discourage net external borrowing, and actual current account balances will likely be smaller than desired ones. On the other hand, if home bias is small, demand for foreign assets will be higher and more price-elastic, and larger net external liabilities will be less costly. That said, net external borrowing will remain limited by solvency considerations: countries need to be able to amortize external liabilities.

Over the past two decades, there is clear evidence that the home bias has declined and that restrictions on net external borrowing have eased.[10]

- Portfolio holdings of foreign bonds and equity in some major industrial countries, such as Canada, Germany, Japan, and the United Kingdom, have clearly increased compared with domestic market capitalization (Table 3.2).

- External current account deficits or surpluses (relative to domestic incomes) have, on

---

also differences in taste. See, among others, French and Poterba (1991), Tesar (1993), Tesar and Werner (1995), Baxter and Jermann (1997), Baxter, Jermann, and King (1998), or Obstfeld and Rogoff (2001).

[8]Defined as current account balances that would prevail with no restrictions on international capital market access and an infinitely elastic supply of capital.

[9]Financial globalization is a necessary condition for larger current account deficits or surpluses but not necessarily a main cause. For example, international risk diversification alone may not generate net external borrowing or lending: domestic investors can acquire foreign equity with the proceeds from selling domestic equity to foreign residents. Gross capital flows will increase, but inflows are exactly matched by outflows.

[10]Evidence on the degree of remaining restrictions is broadly similar for other measures. See also footnote 3.

Figure 3.2. Determinants of Financial Globalization

Decreasing communication and information costs and reduced restrictions on capital flows have fostered financial globalization.

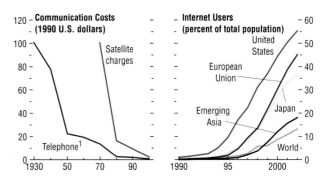

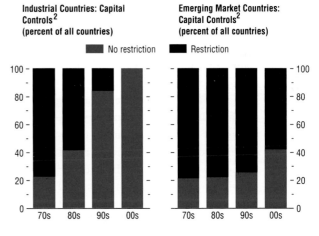

Sources: Busse (2003); IMF, *Annual Report on Exchange Arrangements and Exchange Restrictions* (2004); World Bank, *World Development Indicators;* and IMF staff calculations.
[1]Cost of a three-minute phone call from New York to London.
[2]Restrictions on international financial transactions.

Table 3.2. Overseas Portfolio Investment

(Percent of domestic market capitalization)

	1970	1975	1980	1985	1990	1995	2000	2003
Canada								
Portfolio investment	2.0	1.9	2.1	2.4	6.0	12.9	18.7	14.3
Equity	3.1	3.2	3.6	3.5	9.6	25.4	29.3	21.2
Bonds	0.7	0.6	0.4	1.3	1.9	2.2	3.2	3.6
Germany								
Portfolio investment	4.9	2.4	2.7	5.8	10.2	14.5	30.0	31.1
Equity	...	...	...	...	...	16.9	37.8	42.1
Bonds	...	...	...	...	...	13	23.0	25.7
Japan								
Portfolio investment	...	1.3	2.0	6.9	10.7	12.1	13.6	16.7
Equity	...	...	...	...	2.2	4.0	8.3	9.9
Bonds								
United Kingdom[1]								
Portfolio investment	9.5	8.6	11.4	27.5	34.0	37.1	42.6	48.1
Equity	...	...	...	...	33.1	33.5	40.9	52.4
Bonds	...	...	...	...	35.6	43.4	46.4	42.1
United States								
Portfolio investment	1.5	2.1	2.3	2.2	3.5	6.4	7.8	7.4
Equity	0.8	1.1	1.3	2.0	5.6	9.3	10.5	12.7
Bonds	2.7	3.1	3.3	2.4	2.1	3.5	3.8	2.3

Sources: Tesar and Werner (1995); Lane and Milesi-Ferretti (2005b); IMF, *Balance of Payments Statistics;* national flow of funds and balance sheet statistics; and IMF staff calculations.

Note: This table extends Table 2 in Tesar and Werner from 1990 to 2003 using similar but not necessarily identical data sources, replacing 1990 values with new data if available.

[1]1991 values rather than 1990.

average, increased while their dispersion across countries has widened in industrial countries and, to a lesser extent, in emerging market countries (Figure 3.3).

• Net external positions have, on average, widened also, as has their dispersion on account of the larger and more persistent current account deficits and surpluses.

A simple way to quantify the decline in home bias is to compare each country's actual share of foreign portfolio assets in its total portfolio asset holdings with the share of other countries' assets in the world total of assets (the world market portfolio). If the former is smaller than the latter, there is a home bias according to the so-called international capital asset pricing model (ICAPM).[11] While some of the underlying assumptions are clearly unrealistic, the model nevertheless provides useful benchmarks. The calculations shown in Table 3.3 suggest that between 1990 and 2003, the home bias in bond and equity portfolio holdings of most major industrial countries—except Japan[12]—has declined but not disappeared. This assessment is obviously tentative, given that the underlying evidence is model-specific and limited to patterns in major industrial countries only. Nevertheless, the broad conclusion is similar to that reached in other recent studies.[13]

[11]The ICAPM implies that investors should allocate their risky assets in proportion to the world market portfolio in equilibrium since other allocations involve idiosyncratic risks for which investors will not be compensated. See, among others, Adler and Dumas (1983), Branson and Henderson (1984), and Harvey (1991).

[12]In Japan, the home bias has increased despite the increase in the actual share of foreign assets, as the benchmark share implied by the ICAPM has risen even faster because of the relative decline of Japan's share in the world market portfolio.

[13]See, among others, Obstfeld (2004), Lane and Milesi-Ferretti (2004a), and Engel and Matsumoto (2004). In contrast, Heathcote and Perri (2004) argue that the home bias is much smaller than widely thought because their model implies a lower optimal allocation of financial wealth in foreign assets compared with other models.

Table 3.3. Portfolio Diversification: Actual Foreign Shares and Benchmark Foreign Shares Implied by Other Countries' Share in World Market Portfolio

(Percent)

	Equity				Bonds	
	1990	1995	2000	2003	2000	2003
Canada						
Actual	9.0	20.6	25.5	19.3	4.0	4.5
Benchmark	97.4	97.9	97.4	97.5	97.8	98.1
Germany						
Actual	13.2	13.6	23.9	26.3	20.6	22.9
Benchmark	96.2	96.8	96.1	97.1	92.7	92.2
Japan						
Actual	2.2	4.2	9.1	10.6	14.8	15.1
Benchmark	69.0	79.4	90.2	90.9	82.2	83.8
United Kingdom						
Actual	29.5	30.1	38.4	45.7	62.0	69.4
Benchmark	91.0	92.1	92.0	92.0	95.9	95.4
United States						
Actual	5.7	9.1	10.4	12.5	4.6	3.0
Benchmark	67.5	61.4	53.1	52.8	54.4	59.6

Sources: Lane and Milesi-Ferretti (2005b); IMF, *Balance of Payments Statistics Yearbook* and *Global Financial Stability Report,* various issues; national balance sheet statistics; Standard and Poors' *Emerging Markets Factbook,* various issues; and IMF staff calculations.

Note: The home bias can be gauged from the difference between actual shares of foreign assets in total asset holdings and the benchmark shares. Actual foreign shares are calculated as foreign securities held as a share of total securities held by domestic investors in each category. Benchmark foreign shares are based on foreign countries' share in total world market capitalization.

If risk diversification is an important motive for investors, one would expect that diversification across markets will be broad based. According to the ICAPM discussed earlier, investors should allocate their foreign assets across countries according to their shares in the world market portfolio. Table 3.4 compares major industrial countries' actual foreign equity allocations across countries with ICAPM benchmark allocations, taking the overall home bias as given.[14] The results suggest that diversification patterns are indeed broad based. However, as the example of European countries

[14]The results are based on data from the 1997 and 2002 *Coordinated Portfolio Investment Survey* conducted under the auspices of the IMF. The general lack of long time-series data prevents extensive historical analysis. Geographical patterns in holdings of long-term bonds are broadly similar.

Figure 3.3. External Current Account Balances and Net External Positions, 1970–2003

(Percent of GDP; absolute values)

On average, external current accounts and net foreign assets have increased in industrial and emerging market countries, suggesting that restrictions on net external borrowing and lending have eased.

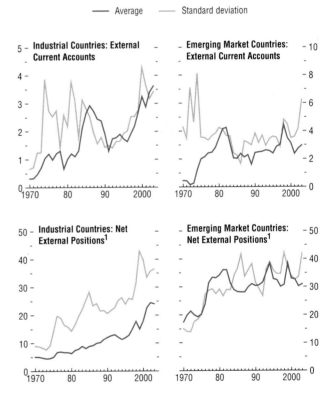

Sources: IMF, *International Financial Statistics;* IMF, *Balance of Payments Statistics;* Lane and Milesi-Ferretti (2005b); and IMF staff calculations.
[1]Net foreign assets as a percent of GDP.

Table 3.4. Geography of Cross-Border Portfolio Equity Holdings

(Percent of total foreign portfolio equity holdings; second row contains benchmark shares implied by international capital asset pricing model)

Destination	United States 1997	United States 2002	Canada 1997	Canada 2002	Japan 1997	Japan 2002	Euro area 2002	Germany 2002	United Kingdom 1997	United Kingdom 2002
United States	...	...	49.3	56.9	54.9	51.5	42.2	14.7	25.5	27.2
	...	...	50.2	48.4	54.1	52.0	55.3	48.7	53.5	51.3
Canada	5.9	5.0	...	...	1.5	1.4	0.4	—	0.8	—
	4.8	4.7	...	...	2.7	2.7	2.9	2.5	2.7	2.7
Japan	11.3	12.2	6.0	6.6	...	...	6.8	2.3	13.6	10.1
	18.8	17.2	9.8	9.3	...	...	10.6	9.4	10.5	9.9
Euro area	31.2	26.8	13.5	13.3	16.6	16.0	...	64.0	35.4	32.5
	24.9	27.5	13.0	14.9	14.1	16.0	...	11.9	13.9	15.8
Germany	5.4	2.9	...	...	5.5	2.3	...	...	6.4	4.4
	7.0	5.6	3.7	3.0	3.9	3.2	...	...	3.9	3.2
United Kingdom	18.0	23.9	1.2	11.0	11.9	12.6	23.0	10.3	...	...
	16.9	15.1	8.9	8.2	9.6	8.8	9.3	8.2	...	...
Industrial countries	79.2	78.5	87.5	93.2	91.2	87.3	92.7	97.9	87.7	80.9
	77.3	75.6	88.1	86.8	87.2	85.9	85.0	86.6	87.3	86.0

Sources: French and Poterba (1991); IMF, Coordinated Portfolio Survey database; Standard and Poors' *Emerging Stock Markets Factbook*, various issues; and IMF staff calculations.

Note: U.S. investors' holdings of Canadian equity amounted to 5.9 percent of their total foreign holdings in 1997. The benchmark allocation predicted by the ICAPM for a given total foreign allocation would have been 4.8 percent.

shows, forces of "gravity" are also relevant. Allocations to closely located countries or regions tend to exceed benchmark allocations, reflecting, among other factors, merchandise trade patterns and the fact that shorter distances and cultural similarities appear to facilitate financial transactions, possibly through their effects on transaction costs and information asymmetries.[15]

Despite growing U.S. net external liabilities, European countries tend to hold less U.S. equity than implied by the international capital asset pricing model benchmark. More generally, unlike in the 1980s, the share of U.S. portfolio equity liabilities in total foreign portfolio equity assets of other countries has been somewhat below ICAPM benchmarks in recent years (see also Bertaut and Kole, 2004). These observations suggest that more international financial diversification has led to increased gross capital inflows to the United States (in U.S. dollar terms)—given greater overall flows at the global level—but not to such an extent that investors are now overweight in U.S. equity (or bonds).[16]

[15]The so-called gravity model of international trade suggests that, everything else being equal, neighboring countries tend to have closer trade linkages than more distant countries (see Chapter II, *World Economic Outlook,* September 2002, for a more detailed discussion). Recent research has found that trade-style gravity equations also perform well in explaining bilateral investment patterns if augmented with financial market-specific variables (see Bertaut and Kole, 2004; Faruqee, Li, and Yan, 2004; and Lane and Milesi-Ferretti, 2004a).

[16]This could suggest that the United States has become a relatively less attractive destination for foreign investors for at least two reasons. First, with the weakening of business cycle linkages among major economic areas during the 1990s return correlations declined compared with the 1980s. This, in turn, has made broad-based diversification more attractive (see Heathcote and Perri, 2004). During the 1980s, diversifying internationally with U.S. assets only was perhaps more attractive, given (1) deep and well-developed U.S. markets and (2) smaller benefits of more broad-based diversification because of higher cross-country return correlations. Recently, however, return correlations have again increased. Second, on the supply side, other securities markets have developed rapidly, as manifested in the growth of outstanding issues, notably in the euro area. This has also increased the scope for broad-based diversification.

Naturally, these observations are based on the behavior of portfolio investment flows only, and general conclusions about the future willingness of investors to hold U.S. assets cannot be drawn.

Analyzing the long-run relationship between real interest rates on long-term government debt—a benchmark for rates of return in a country—and overall net external positions provides a useful complementary perspective. With home bias in asset demand, investors should only be willing to increase the share of foreign assets in their wealth if they are compensated with increasing returns. Accordingly, real interest rates in countries with net external liabilities should, on average, be higher than in countries with net external assets, suggesting a negative correlation between real interest rates and net foreign assets.[17] As noted earlier, if the home bias broadly declines, such portfolio balance effects should weaken, and the negative correlation between real interest rates and net foreign positions should decrease in absolute terms. The evidence shown in Figure 3.4 suggests that this has indeed happened. The correlation between the two variables during 1993–2002, while still negative, was clearly smaller than during 1982–92.

Overall, financial globalization has created an environment where net external borrowing and lending are less restricted and where maintaining larger net foreign liabilities appears to involve relatively lower costs. This can be helpful when it comes to external adjustment and global rebalancing. For example, everything else being equal, the United States now appears more likely to be able to sustain larger net foreign liabilities in the long run at a lower cost than, say, some 20 years ago. This could allow for a more gradual adjustment of the same

[17]See Lane and Milesi-Ferretti (2002b) for a recent empirical study presenting similar materials. Real exchange rate changes are another source of return differentials (in the home currency of the investor). See Branson and Henderson (1984) on the portfolio balance approach and the role of home bias therein.

Figure 3.4. Industrial Countries: Long-Term Real Interest Rates and Net Foreign Assets[1]

In industrial countries, during the past decades, the relationship between real interest rates and net foreign assets has weakened, as investors appear more willing to hold foreign assets.

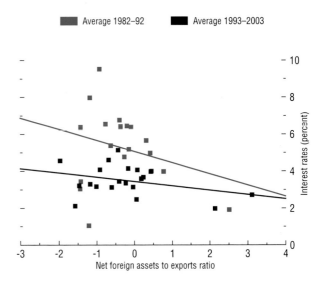

Sources: IMF, *International Financial Statistics;* Lane and Milesi-Ferretti (2005b); and IMF staff calculations.
[1] Real interest rate calculated as nominal long-term interest rate at end of year *t* minus the actual inflation rate at end of year *t* + 1.

Box 3.1. External Imbalances Then and Now

The current environment of globalized financial markets, which began in the 1970s for the advanced countries and in the 1980s for the emerging market countries, had an important precedent in the four decades before 1914—the era of the classical gold standard. Both eras of financial globalization share common features, including large net capital flows, but there are also important differences, including today's much larger two-way capital flows.[1] This box compares salient features of financial globalization during 1870–1914 with those of today, examines whether the large net capital flows in the earlier era represented a global imbalance comparable to that of today, and seeks to establish lessons from the earlier era.

Important common features in both eras of globalization include the following.

* *Large net capital flows and current account deficits and surpluses.* The 50 years before World War I saw massive net private flows of capital from the core countries of Western Europe to recent settlements overseas (mainly the rapidly developing Americas and Australasia). At the peak, the associated current account surpluses in Britain reached 9 percent of GDP and were almost as big in France, Germany, and the Netherlands (see the figure). For the principal capital importers in the late nineteenth century (Argentina, Australia, and Canada),[2] current account deficits exceeded 5 percent of GDP on average. By comparison, over the past two decades, current account surpluses and deficits have been, on average, increasing, as discussed in the main text, but they are still smaller than during the gold standard era, in industrial and emerging market countries alike. Another striking feature of the pre-1914 data is the high persistence in current account imbalances, even when compared with today's relatively persist-

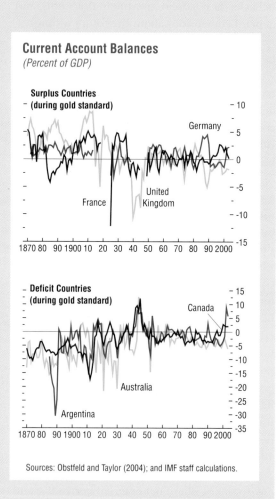

Current Account Balances
(Percent of GDP)

Surplus Countries
(during gold standard)

Germany

France

United
Kingdom

1870 80 90 1900 10 20 30 40 50 60 70 80 90 2000

Deficit Countries
(during gold standard)

Canada

Australia

Argentina

1870 80 90 1900 10 20 30 40 50 60 70 80 90 2000

Sources: Obstfeld and Taylor (2004); and IMF staff calculations.

Note: The main author of this box is Michael Bordo.
[1]See Bordo, Eichengreen, and Kim (1998), and Obstfeld and Taylor (2004).
[2]Earlier in the century, the United States experienced similar net inflows but by the end of the nineteenth century, the country began running current account surpluses.

ent ones (Bordo, Eichengreen, and Kim, 1998; and Obstfeld and Taylor, 2004).

* *Current account reversals.* Although current account imbalances were generally more long-lived in the pre-1914 era than in the recent period, they were punctuated in some countries by severe reversals, especially in the crisis-ridden 1890s (Bordo and Eichengreen, 1999). Current account reversals have reemerged in today's era of financial globalization. In fact, Bordo and others (2001) argue that the total incidence of financial crises has been greater during the post–Bretton Woods period than during the earlier period, although the output losses from crises were somewhat larger pre-1914.

There are also important differences between the two eras.

- *Distribution of current account deficits and surpluses.* Under the gold standard, countries of new settlement—the emerging markets of the time—ran current account deficits while the major European economies had surpluses. In the current era, core industrial countries run either persistent deficits or surpluses, with domestic saving-investment imbalances redistributed primarily among industrial countries rather than from the core to the periphery as in the earlier era.
- *Gross external positions are generally larger today.* Gross external positions were very close to net positions before 1914—that is, net creditors had large foreign asset positions whereas net debtors had large liabilities. In contrast, most major industrial countries today are both major creditors and debtors irrespective of their net position. The earlier pattern reflects the prevalence of long-term investment by the core countries in the countries of new settlement, seeking higher returns by financing railroads and other infrastructure as well as budget deficits (especially in the form of bonds but also in the form of foreign direct investment). The substantial growth of two-way flows between advanced countries since 1980 has been associated with both international financial diversification and intertemporal consumption smoothing, as discussed in the main text.
- *The adjustment mechanism is different.* The historical record shows that adjustment to the significant and persistent external imbalances in the pre-1914 era occurred largely through the Humean price-specie-flow mechanism of the classical gold standard (Bordo, 1984). Gold flows ensured that equilibrium was restored through changes in money supplies, the terms of trade, and real exchange rates. In contrast, the global economy is now on a managed floating exchange rate regime, and external adjustment depends no longer on gold flows but on changes in exchange rates and international reserves, along with relative price movements, short-term capital flows, and valuation effects (see Obstfeld, 2004).

Despite the fact that external imbalances were often larger and more persistent before 1914 than they are today, contemporaries in the earlier era did not view this as a problem for two broad reasons. First, they strongly believed that except in extreme situations (e.g., wars) the adjustment mechanism described above would always be stabilizing. Second, the nature of foreign investment was quite different. Most of the long-term flows were to countries with abundant natural resources and land on the one hand, and scarce labor and capital on the other. Returns on labor and capital were thus higher than in the more developed countries, with excellent prospects of sustained rapid long-term growth. The activities financed tended to be those in which information asymmetries could be most easily overcome: railroads and government (Bordo, Eichengreen, and Irwin, 1999). Many recipient countries tended to have sound institutions and sound fiscal fundamentals, further reducing the likelihood of default, and many adhered to the gold standard, which served as a signal of fiscal rectitude ("a Good Housekeeping seal of approval" (Bordo and Rockoff, 1996)). In addition, many recipient countries were part of the British Empire, with a de facto British government guarantee that virtually eliminated country risk. That said, not all of the recipients of foreign capital had such sound fundamentals. Many of the countries of peripheral Europe and Latin America were prone to fiscal and monetary instability. Their record of defaults and currency crises often attenuated the capital flows.

The large gross external asset positions among today's advanced countries with floating exchange rates have little precedence in the past, which suggests that exposure to market and exchange rate risks during external adjustment may be quite different. Nevertheless, with large imbalances in both eras of financial globalization, the earlier era may still provide relevant lessons. Most prominently, the generally remarkably smooth adjustment among the countries adhering to a stable and credible nominal anchor—the gold standard—underscores the important role of well-functioning and credible nominal anchors and sound financial policies in facilitating external adjustment.

Box. 3.2. Measuring a Country's Net External Position

The net external position of a country is the difference between the country's external assets—the claims of a country's residents on nonresidents—and its external liabilities—the claims of nonresidents on residents. These claims are divided in broad categories, which correspond to those in balance of payments statistics: foreign direct investment; portfolio equity securities; portfolio debt securities; other assets and liabilities (such as bank loans, trade credits, and currency deposits); and financial derivatives.[1] A country's claims on nonresidents also include the reserve holdings of the central bank, which are classified separately. Gross external debt is given by the sum of portfolio debt liabilities, debt liabilities in the direct investment category, and other liabilities.

Until a few years ago, data on external assets and liabilities (the so-called International Investment Position, or IIP) were reported by most industrial countries and few emerging markets. In recent years the number of reporting countries has increased exponentially and now totals about 100 (even though coverage for newly reporting countries is typically limited to the most recent period). The data used in this chapter, constructed by Lane and Milesi-Ferretti (2001, 2005b), combine country estimates of external assets and liabilities (as reported in their IIP) with estimates from alternative sources (such as the World Bank's debt database for external debt liabilities) or based on cumulative capital flows with appropriate valuation adjustments. The data cover 87 countries, including virtually all advanced and emerging economies, for the period 1970–2003.[2]

How do valuation adjustments work? For example, in the absence of information on foreigners' holdings of domestic equities, these can be approximated by cumulative net foreign purchases of domestic equity (which can be obtained from the widely available balance of payments data), adjusted each year for the change in the value of existing liabilities due to fluctuations in stock prices and exchange rates. These fluctuations in value, which can be approximated by the variation in a domestic stock price index, are not reported as investment returns in balance of payments statistics, which for equities only record the flow of dividends.[3]

As external assets and liabilities grow, these valuation changes become quantitatively very important—indeed, as discussed in the text, the relationship between the current account and the dynamics of the net external position has substantially weakened in recent years. For example, the U.S. net external position in 2003 was broadly unchanged as a ratio of GDP, since the large current account deficit was offset by a correspondingly large valuation gain, generated by increased dollar values of U.S. foreign assets as the dollar depreciated.

Valuation changes for portfolio equity and FDI can be particularly large. For example, between end-1998 and end-1999 the stock of

Note: The main author of this box is Gian Maria Milesi-Ferretti.

[1]The FDI category reflects a "lasting interest" of an entity resident in one economy in an enterprise resident in another economy (IMF, 1993). This includes greenfield investment as well as significant equity participation (typically set at above 10 percent), while remaining holdings of equity securities are classified under portfolio equity investment. This implies that in certain cases the distinction between these two categories can be blurred.

[2]A significant earlier contribution is Sinn (1990), who constructs estimates of external assets and liabilities for the period 1970–87 for an even larger sample of countries.

[3]Estimating valuation adjustments for the foreign assets of a country is a more complex endeavor. A precise calculation would require information on the geographical and currency distribution of the country's claims, which is available for only a few countries and typically for recent years. In the absence of such information, one can for example assume that the geographical distribution of assets follows the country's trade pattern, or, for stock or bond markets, relative market capitalization in the rest of the world.

Finnish portfolio equity liabilities increased from about US$80 billion to about US$220 billion, even though net purchases by foreigners during 1999 amounted to only US$10 billion! The underlying cause for this valuation change was the boom in the price of Finnish stocks—particularly Nokia—during 1999.

Particular difficulties are posed by the valuation of foreign direct investment. Most countries report the book value of their direct investment assets and liabilities, while others, such as France, Sweden, and the United States report estimates both at book and at market value. The difference can be significant, especially when corporate valuations change substantially. Finally, coverage of derivatives' contracts in international statistics is still very spotty, thereby limiting our knowledge on the extent of cross-country hedging.

With data on the stocks of external assets and liabilities and the underlying capital flows, it is possible to calculate the rate of return that a country earns on its external assets and pays out on its liabilities. These returns can be calculated by adding the yields on external claims (which are measured as investment income flows in the current account) and the capital gain (which can be approximated by the difference between the change in value of the claim and the underlying capital flow). On average, rates of return are larger and more volatile than yields, reflecting the fact that a significant component of equity returns takes the form of capital gains, rather than dividends (see the figure).

The availability of comprehensive data on external positions has enabled researchers to address a number of important issues in international macroeconomics, including the determinants of long-run net external positions (Lane and Milesi-Ferretti, 2002b), the link between net

United States: Rates of Return and Yields on Foreign Assets and Foreign Liabilities
(Percent 1983–2003)

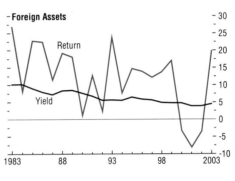

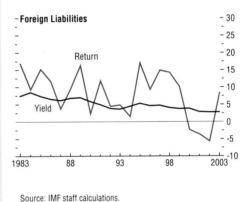

Source: IMF staff calculations.

external positions and real exchange rates (Lane and Milesi-Ferretti, 2004b), and changes in the extent of international risk sharing (Imbs, 2004; Huizinga and Zhu, 2004). Also, the sum of external assets and liabilities has been used as a volume-based measure of international financial integration when studying the effects of integration on macroeconomic performance (see, for example, Edison and others, 2002; and Prasad and others, 2003).

current account deficit, which could facilitate adjustment in production structures in the United States and other countries and, thereby, reduce the size of the overall exchange rate

adjustment (Obstfeld and Rogoff, 2000). On the other hand, this opportunity could also turn into a liability if macroeconomic policies do not remain consistent with a credible medium-term

Box 3.3. Financial Globalization and the Conduct of Macroeconomic Policies

Macroeconomic policies around the world have improved over the past two decades. The average budget deficit across both industrial and developing countries has declined from approximately 5 percent of GDP during the late 1970s to just over 2 percent of GDP recently. Similarly, with monetary policy increasingly focused on inflation control, inflation rates have been decreasing across the globe.

A widely quoted explanation for these developments is that financial globalization has exerted a disciplinary effect on the conduct of policies, because international capital flows adversely respond to imprudent macroeconomic policies (e.g., Fischer, 1997; or Stiglitz, 2000). This explanation is not universally accepted, however, and some have argued that global financial markets fail to discipline policies (e.g., Rodrik, 2001). Against this background, this box reexamines the foundations of the hypothesis of the disciplinary effects of financial globalization and assesses its empirical merits.

From a theoretical perspective, the incentives for host governments to conduct good policies depend on their rewards and costs. To the extent that good policies attract capital flows that help raise the domestic capital stock, the associated higher output is the reward. The costs of good policies to policymakers are related to political economy considerations. For example, the need to conduct prudent fiscal policy can limit politicians' scope for discretion related to their own narrow interest. If, on balance, the rewards are large enough to offset the costs, globalization will indeed be a disciplinary device. This in turn suggests two conclusions.

- The disciplinary effect of financial globalization may be stronger for some policies and weaker for others. In particular, if prudent fiscal policy exerts higher political economy costs than, say, monetary policy, one would expect the disciplinary effects of globalization to be stronger for monetary policy.

Note: The main author of this box is Irina Tytell.

Financial Globalization and Macroeconomic Policies[1]

Sources: Tytell and Wei (2004); and IMF staff calculations.
[1]For the period 1990–99.

- A critical issue regarding the benefits of capital flows concerns the possibility of changes in investor sentiments in international capital markets that are reflected in capital flow fluctuations unrelated to policies or developments in the host country. Through their potential to lower the benefits of good policies, they tend to weaken the disciplinary effect on policy conduct.

What does the empirical evidence for the recent era of globalization look like? A simple inspection of the relationship between a measure of financial globalization—the ratio of gross foreign assets and liabilities to GDP—and inflation rates and budget balances suggests the following (see the figure).

- The relationship between inflation and the extent of financial globalization is generally negative.
- The relationship between budget deficits and financial globalization is markedly weaker.

Such bivariate relationships can, of course, be misleading, since they do not control for other determinants of macroeconomic policies or other dimensions of globalization. For a more complete analysis, Tytell and Wei (2004) used two different econometric approaches.[1]

First, inflation rates and budget balances were simultaneously regressed on financial globalization (ratio of foreign assets and liabilities to GDP) and a number of other relevant variables, including indicators of exchange rate flexibility, central bank independence, government fragility and polarization, and trade openness. To isolate the effect of globalization on policies while mitigating problems of reverse causality (and measurement errors), the authors focused on the common component of international capital flows to countries in the same geographic region. The results confirm that the coefficient on financial openness in the inflation equation is negative and statistically significant (although fairly small in magnitude). The same coefficient in the equation for budget balances is statistically insignificant. These results are robust to various alternative specifications, different measures of financial openness, and alternative instrumental variables.

Tytell and Wei also use thresholds to classify policies as "good," "moderate," or "bad," to control for the fact that small fluctuations in inflation rates or budget balances are unlikely to

reflect changes in policymakers' attitudes.[2] This allows an investigation of whether the disciplinary effects differ depending on the economic situation and whether they work by inducing policy shifts between different states rather than affecting policies within a given state. The results lend support to the view that financial globalization has a positive and statistically significant effect on the probability of inflation decreasing from "bad" to "moderate" and from "moderate" to "good" and a negative effect on the probability of inflation increasing from "good" to "moderate." In contrast, the results do not provide support for the view that financial globalization exerts a disciplinary effect on government budgets.

Overall, while plausible from a theoretical perspective, the empirical evidence for the hypothesis that financial globalization exerts a disciplinary effect on the conduct of macroeconomic policies is rather mixed. There does appear to be a significant, albeit small, impact on monetary policy, but little on fiscal policy. This suggests that relying on financial globalization to act as a device for ensuring policy discipline is not enough. It also suggests that other factors must have played a role in the observed improvement of macroeconomic policies, some of which may have been related to globalization, although through channels other than the one discussed here. In this light, Box 3.4 examines the link between globalization and monetary policy from a broader perspective.

[1]The study covers a sample of 62 industrial and developing countries, which excludes major oil producers and very small countries.

[2]The thresholds are based on the relevant literature. For example, there is some agreement in the growth literature that inflation rates beyond 7 to 11 percent hurt growth in developing countries (e.g., Khan and Senhadji, 2000). Hence, inflation rates of 10 percent or less are classified as reflecting "good" monetary policy while inflation rates above 40 percent—a widely accepted benchmark for high inflation—are classified as "bad" policies.

policy framework aimed at external and internal balance. In this regard, it is important to note that globalization may not be as effective a disciplinary device for the conduct of macroeco-

nomic policies as is widely thought (see Box 3.3 for recent empirical evidence on the disciplinary effects of financial globalization on macroeconomic policies).

Figure 3.5. Valuation Effects on Net Foreign Assets
(Percent of GDP)

For larger industrial countries, annual valuation changes have become greater in the 1990s, even if the cumulative sums shown below tend to be small due to the frequent change in sign. For emerging market countries, magnitudes of valuation effects have generally increased over the past decade.

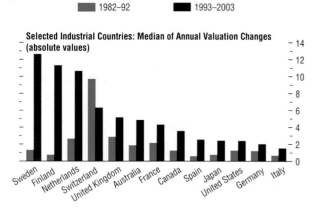

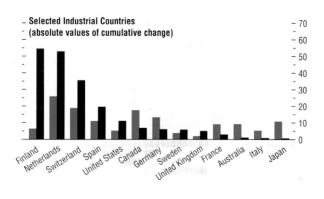

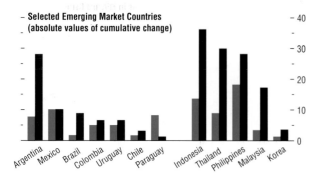

Sources: IMF, *Balance of Payments Statistics*; Lane and Milesi-Ferretti (2005b); and IMF staff calculations.

Valuation Effects and External Adjustment

A critical, and often underappreciated, implication of recent financial globalization is that with both foreign assets and foreign liabilities rising sharply, investors—and countries—are much more exposed to capital gains and losses owing to exchange rate and other asset price changes.[18] For example, if all foreign assets are denominated in foreign currency, a 10 percent exchange rate depreciation increases their domestic currency value by 5 percentage points of GDP if the stock of assets is 50 percent of GDP and by 10 percentage points if it is 100 percent. Higher gross positions also tend to generate larger valuation changes in net foreign assets, although structure and relative size of assets and liabilities also matter.

IMF staff estimates of valuation changes in industrial and key emerging market countries confirm that as a percent of GDP, annual and medium-term[19] valuation changes in net foreign assets generally increased in magnitude during the 1990s compared with the 1980s (Figure 3.5). The increase in medium-term valuation changes is particularly noteworthy in some smaller and relatively more open industrial countries that have seen rapid changes in gross or net positions (e.g., Finland, the Netherlands, and Switzerland) and in emerging market countries, particularly those that have faced large, one-off changes in exchange rates (e.g., Asian emerging market countries during the 1997–98 financial crises). In other countries, however, magnitudes have decreased, including in those that experienced larger exchange rate changes in the 1980s compared with the 1990s.

An important implication of persistent valuation changes is that external current account surpluses or deficits could become relatively less important determinants of net foreign asset positions (Obstfeld, 2004), as illustrated by the expe-

---

[18]See Lane and Milesi-Ferretti (2001, 2005a), Tille (2003, 2004), Gourinchas and Rey (2004), and Obstfeld (2004).

[19]Defined as the cumulative sum over a 10-year period.

rience of a number of industrial and emerging market countries during the 1990s (Figure 3.6). A key question, of course, is whether valuation effects can help in external adjustment. Given the prominent role of exchange rates in this regard, the focus will be on the exchange-rate-related valuation effects. (Historically, valuation effects arising from other asset price changes have also been large in some cases, including during times of sharply reduced asset return correlations.) Two factors are important in this regard. First, the nature of the exchange rate changes matters. If they are unexpected, valuation effects on net foreign assets are lasting, while those associated with anticipated changes are not, because the latter tend to be reflected in asset yields, which, in turn, offset the valuation effects through their impact on current accounts.[20]

Second, the general structure of external assets and liabilities—especially their currency composition but also the nature of the underlying financial instruments—also plays an important role in determining whether valuation effects contribute to external adjustment.

- In industrial countries, where foreign assets tend to be denominated in foreign currency and liabilities in domestic currency, valuation effects arising from unexpected exchange rate changes—including those related to portfolio preference disturbances—tend to facilitate adjustment because they can provide for burden sharing among countries. In countries with currency depreciation, the domestic currency value of foreign assets increases and—with the value of liabilities unchanged—net foreign assets improve; the reverse takes place in countries with appreciating currencies. If

[20]See Lane and Milesi-Ferretti (2005a) and Obstfeld (2004). Consider, for example, the case of an anticipated depreciation from the perspective of a foreign bond investor. Assuming unchanged risk preferences, the lower value of the principal (in foreign currency) due to the depreciation requires higher yields to preserve the present value of the investment. With anticipated exchange rate changes, return adjustments may be amplified by portfolio reallocation.

Figure 3.6. Valuation Effects, Current Accounts, and Net Foreign Assets

In the 1990s, the contribution of valuation effects to changes in net foreign assets was large relative to current account balances, especially in small open industrial economies and east Asian countries. More generally, the correlation between changes in net foreign assets and current account balances weakened.

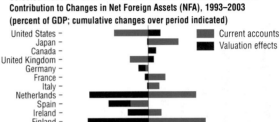

Selected Industrial Countries: Current Account and Valuation Effects Contribution to Changes in Net Foreign Assets (NFA), 1993–2003 (percent of GDP; cumulative changes over period indicated)

Selected Emerging Market Countries: Current Account and Valuation Effects Contribution to Changes in NFA, 1993–2003 (percent of GDP; cumulative changes over period indicated)

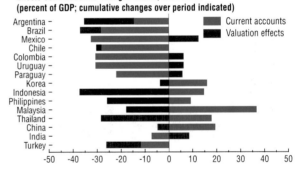

Rolling 10-Year Correlation Between Changes in NFA and Current Accounts (averages by country groups)

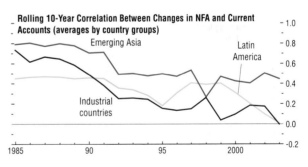

Sources: IMF, *Balance of Payments Statistics;* Lane and Milesi-Ferretti (2005b); and IMF staff calculations.

Figure 3.7. Valuation Changes in Net Foreign Assets and Real Effective Exchange Rates

Valuation effects on net foreign assets facilitated the external adjustment in the mid-1980s (as indicated by the ellipses).

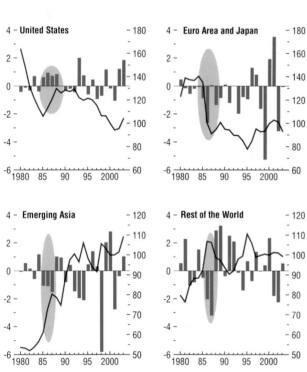

Sources: IMF, *Balance of Payments Statistics;* Lane and Milesi-Ferretti (2005b); and IMF staff calculations.

the direction of exchange rate changes matches that of external adjustment—that is, currency depreciation in countries where external balances have to improve (deficit countries) and appreciation in other countries—this is equivalent to a wealth transfer from surplus to deficit countries, which, everything else being equal, can help reduce the amount of trade adjustment needed (see Appendix 3.1).[21] This mechanism was evident during the U.S. current account correction of 1985–88, when the U.S. dollar depreciated by about 30 percent in real effective terms (Figure 3.7).[22] More recently, the valuation adjustments associated with the U.S dollar depreciation during 2002–03 have offset about three-fourths of the cumulative U.S. current account deficit over the same period.

• In emerging market countries, where some foreign liabilities, especially debt liabilities, tend to be denominated in foreign currency, valuation effects from unexpected exchange rate depreciations are likely to complicate external adjustment, given the increase in the domestic currency value of these liabilities. On the other hand, currency appreciation tends to have positive valuation effects and improve net external positions, as illustrated in Figure 3.8 for selected Latin American and East Asian countries.

For a systematic assessment of the role of the valuation channel in external adjustment, IMF

[21]It is, of course, possible to hedge at least partly against valuation effects by using financial derivatives, which may reduce the real impact of valuation effects, including those arising from the wealth transfer from surplus to deficit countries. This depends importantly on whether the hedging is undertaken within countries or across countries. In the case of the former, there are no aggregate hedging gains or losses at the country level because the gains from hedging for some residents are offset by hedging losses of other residents, and valuation effects have real aggregate effects. Cross-border hedging activities, however, affect the real impact of valuation changes.

[22]If the currency realignment of the mid-1980s had involved today's larger gross positions, U.S. valuation gains would have been more than twice as large as those in the 1980s, while the losses in Japan and the euro area countries would have been three times as large.

staff undertook an econometric investigation of the recent experience of 49 countries—21 industrial and 28 emerging market and developing countries—for the period 1970–2003 (see Appendix 3.2 for details and documentation of the results). Following Gourinchas and Rey (2004) and Corsetti and Kostantinou (2004), the approach was to examine the dynamic responses of trade balances (defined as the sum of net exports of goods and services) and net foreign assets to external imbalances. The intuition behind this approach is as follows. Because countries must ultimately be able to pay their debts—the so-called intertemporal external budget constraint—trade balances and net foreign assets are tied together in the long run. For example, a debtor country will need to have a trade surplus in the long run that is large enough to cover the cost of its net external liabilities.[23] While trade flows and net foreign assets can deviate from this long-run relationship in the short term, over time that relationship has to be restored through an adjustment in net exports, in net foreign assets (other than the changes arising from the adjustment in net exports), or a combination of both. If a significant part of the adjustment occurs through changes in net foreign assets, this is interpreted as evidence for the valuation channel contributing to external adjustment. The results can be summarized as follows.

- For the majority of emerging market countries, adjustment came entirely through trade (net foreign assets were not found to respond to deviations from the long-run relationship between the trade balance and net foreign assets). This finding does not mean that valuation effects are unimportant in these countries. On the contrary, the results imply, for example, that negative valuation shocks, such as those from a depreciation of the exchange rate, tend to permanently worsen net foreign asset positions in these countries and the

[23]Strictly speaking, the intertemporal budget constraint implies that the net present value of future trade surpluses (including current transfers) must be equal to current net external liabilities (see Appendix 3.1).

Figure 3.8. Selected Emerging Market Countries: Valuation Changes and Real Effective Exchange Rates

Exchange rate depreciations tend to have adverse valuation effects in emerging market countries.

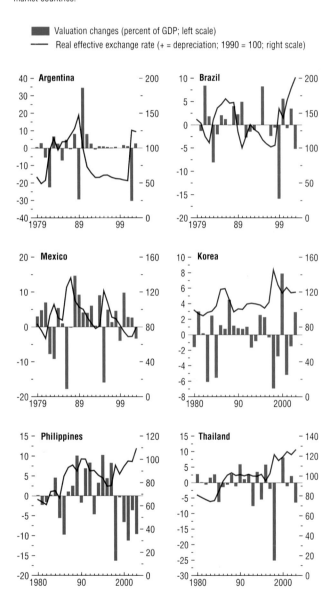

Sources: IMF, *Balance of Payments Statistics;* Lane and Milesi-Ferretti (2005b); and IMF staff calculations.

Figure 3.9. Determinants of Real Globalization

Declining trading costs and trade liberalization have driven real globalization.

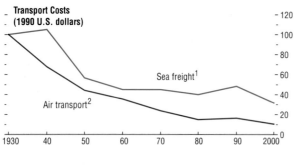

Transport Costs (1990 U.S. dollars)

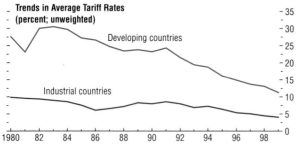

Trends in Average Tariff Rates (percent; unweighted)

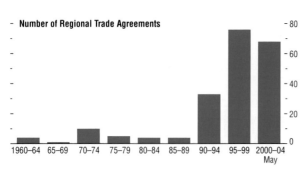

Number of Regional Trade Agreements

Sources: Busse (2003); World Trade Organization; and IMF staff calculations.
[1] Average ocean freight and port charges per short ton of import and export cargo.
[2] Average air transport revenue per passenger mile.

adjustment has to come from an improvement of net exports.

- In contrast, in a number of industrial countries, particularly the United States and Japan, valuation changes do appear to play a role, with changes in net foreign assets reacting systematically to deviations from the long-run relationship with net exports.

For major industrial countries, using quarterly data, the analysis was refined further by examining the extent to which deviations of trade balances and net foreign assets from their long-run relationship can predict other variables involved in external adjustment, especially net export growth and valuation changes. For all countries, the results show that adjustment came primarily through long-run changes in trade flows, but for the United States the evidence also suggests that valuation changes were helpful in the short term.[24]

Overall, these results suggest that, for all countries, exchange rate changes primarily affect medium- and long-term trade adjustment, although in the short term they appear to generate helpful valuation changes in some industrial countries, particularly the United States.[25] This may reflect the fact that short-run exchange rate changes in industrial countries tend to be unexpected and, hence, can have large valuation effects, whereas persistent exchange rate changes over the medium and long run have a larger anticipated component, with smaller valuation effects.

Naturally, these results are based on a period during most of which gross foreign positions were relatively small compared with exports or imports. One could therefore argue that analysis based on past data likely underestimates the role of valuation effects today.[26] Overall, the results

[24]For the United States, the findings match earlier ones by Gourinchas and Rey (2004) based on another data set.

[25]These results are consistent with—but not necessarily evidence for—the notion that the United States enjoys a reserve currency premium.

[26]In addition, there is the problem of using standard econometric methods in periods of rapid change, as parameters may change.

Table 3.5. Changes in Geographical Trade Patterns
(Extra-regional trade flows as a percent of world GDP; excluding intraregional trade)

| | Origin | | | | | | | | | |
| | Emerging Asia | | Euro area | | Japan | | Rest of world | | United States | |
Destination	1984	2003	1984	2003	1984	2003	1984	2003	1984	2003
Exports										
Emerging Asia	...	...	0.16	0.40	0.34	0.59	0.49	0.89	0.23	0.37
Euro area	0.18	0.65	...	...	0.12	0.16	2.37	2.65	0.31	0.31
Japan	0.28	0.45	0.06	0.11	...	...	0.16	0.21	0.19	0.14
Rest of world	0.27	0.41	2.19	2.96	0.42	0.24	...	...	1.03	1.18
United States	0.47	0.93	0.38	0.57	0.49	0.32	1.40	1.85	...	...
Total	**1.20**	**2.44**	**2.79**	**4.04**	**1.37**	**1.31**	**4.42**	**5.60**	**1.75**	**2.00**
Imports										
Emerging Asia	...	...	0.18	0.65	0.28	0.45	0.27	0.41	0.47	0.93
Euro area	0.16	0.40	...	...	0.06	0.11	2.19	2.96	0.39	0.53
Japan	0.34	0.59	0.16	0.21	...	...	0.42	0.24	0.49	0.33
Rest of world	0.49	0.89	2.37	2.65	0.54	0.33	...	...	1.40	1.80
United States	0.23	0.37	0.38	0.41	0.22	0.11	1.03	1.18	...	...
Total	**1.22**	**2.25**	**3.08**	**3.92**	**1.10**	**1.06**	**3.91**	**4.79**	**2.74**	**3.60**

Sources: IMF, *Direction of Trade Statistics*, and *International Finance Statistics;* and IMF staff calculations.

provide some evidence for the importance of the valuation channel facilitating short-term external adjustment in industrial countries, but also suggest that trade balance adjustment remains key to restoring external balance in the long term, so that trade balances and current account balances continue to be important as indicators of external balance.

Real Globalization

Besides financial markets, globalization has also profoundly affected markets for goods and services, with global trade[27] as a percent of GDP increasing from some 20 percent in the early 1970s to about 55 percent in 2003. A broad fall in costs of global trading—including declines in transport costs, costs of information gathering and sharing, and continued decreases in government-imposed trade barriers such as tariffs—has been the key driving force behind real globalization (Figure 3.9). Historically, the current era of real globalization began earlier than financial globalization, as liberalization of

external trade regimes started in the 1950s under the umbrella of the General Agreement on Tariffs and Trade (GATT). This section will document these changes and try to shed light on their implications for external adjustment.

Globalization and Changes in Trade Patterns

With the fall in trading costs over the last few decades, global trade patterns have changed markedly. First, geographical patterns of trade have changed (Table 3.5).[28] Arguably, in recent years, the most important feature in this respect has been the growing importance of emerging market economies in world trade, especially—but not only—the fast growing economies of emerging Asia, while trade shares of major industrial countries have decreased in relative terms. An important implication of these changes is that the trade adjustment associated with the resolution of global imbalances will be shared differently. In addition, as globalization has contributed to strong growth in many emerging market economies, relative economic

[27]Defined as the sum of exports and imports of goods and services.

[28]The changes in geographical trade patterns have partly emerged because of new regional trade agreements (e.g., the North American Free Trade Agreement) or the dismantling of old agreements (e.g., the Council for Mutual Economic Assistance, or COMECON).

Table 3.6. Trade Intensity
(Manufacturing trade as a fraction of manufacturing GDP)

	1970	1980	1990	2000–01[1]
United States	0.32	0.51	0.79	1.06
EU-15	0.38	0.50	0.70	0.89
Japan	0.66	0.75	0.66	0.88
Canada	1.36	1.79	2.51	2.93
Mexico	...	...	1.87	2.57
Canada and Mexico	...	...	2.24	2.75

Source: OECD.

[1]For Canada and EU-15 manufacturing GDP is only available through 1999. Ratios in the last column use trade data through 2001 but divide by 1999 value added. EU-15 refers to the member countries of the European Union prior to May 2004 when several eastern European countries joined the European Union.

sizes of major regions have changed, which has helped to spread the spillover of shocks originating in one region to other world regions—with potentially beneficial effects on external adjustment.

Magnitudes and composition of trade have also changed materially, with the following main observable changes.

- *Two-way intra-industry trade.* The bulk of trade now takes place within, not across, industries, as countries tend to specialize in varieties of particular goods, at the level of both final and intermediate goods, rather than in a particular industry. This partly reflects the fact that gains from lower trade barriers arise not only from lower prices, but also from the availability of a wider range of similar goods that better accommodate individual needs of consumers and firms. As a result, trade flows have increased rapidly relative to domestic production—reflected in higher trade shares—and more countries, especially industrial countries, now tend to be both large exporters and large importers within narrow industry categories.
- *Fragmentation in the production of manufactured goods.* With declining trading costs lowering

the costs of producing in multiple locations, firms have begun to divide the production process into multiple steps at different locations to take advantage of location-specific advantages in each step (e.g., low labor costs in the production of labor-intensive parts).[29] Because each step involves imports and re-exports of parts and intermediate goods up to the final assembly, manufacturing trade has increased dramatically compared with manufacturing GDP (Table 3.6).[30]

The ascent of multinational firms has played an important role in overall trade growth and in the changes in the composition of trade.[31] Foreign direct investment (FDI) inflows and outflows are good indicators of the increasingly international nature of firms (Table 3.7). Recently, the acquisition of existing firms in emerging markets, notably in Latin America and Asia, by firms headquartered in industrial countries, has been a prominent feature of FDI developments—mirroring changes in geographical trade patterns discussed earlier.

These changes in magnitudes and composition of trade related to real globalization may have affected external imbalances and their adjustment through a number of channels.

- *Trade shares, trade home biases, and spillovers.* With real globalization, trade shares (trade as a percent of domestic production) have generally been increasing. In many, but not all cases, this has been reflected in a declining share of domestically produced inputs utilized in production, a development sometimes referred to as the reduction of the home bias in production (as opposed to the home bias in international financial markets discussed earlier).[32] As a result, spillover effects from market to market are likely to have become larger, especially for sectoral disturbances, so that any

---

[29]Many terms are used to describe this phenomenon, including vertical specialization, production sharing, vertical production networks, and outsourcing. Hanson, Mataloni, and Slaughter (2003) find that, in a cross-section of countries, the location of vertical processing networks is sensitive to local labor costs.

[30]See Yi (2003) and Chen and Yi (2003).

[31]See, among others, Burstein, Kurz, and Tesar (2004).

[32]Similar considerations apply to domestic demand for final tradable goods, as the share of such goods produced domestically has generally also fallen (reduction in "consumption home bias").

Table 3.7. Foreign Direct Investment Flows
(Period averages, percent of total, unless otherwise noted)

	Outflows by Area of Origin			Inflows by Area of Destination		
	1970	1980	1990	1970	1980	1990
High-income countries						
United States	45.99	20.98	21.79	11.19	29.90	20.10
Europe	42.33	51.63	44.61	43.79	35.64	38.79
Japan	5.40	13.90	5.41	0.63	0.45	0.57
Oceania	0.91	2.17	1.08	5.97	4.71	2.33
Total	**98.98**	**93.84**	**87.5**	**75.93**	**75.19**	**65.23**
Developing and transition countries						
Latin America	0.32	0.93	2.19	12.66	9.02	11.10
Africa	0.41	1.44	0.50	4.29	2.32	1.75
Asia (excluding Japan)	0.29	3.76	9.34	6.60	13.00	18.66
Oceania	. . .	0.01	0.01	0.45	0.17	0.07
Central/eastern Europe	0.02	0.01	0.27	0.01	0.26	3.05
Total	**1.03**	**6.16**	**12.50**	**24.08**	**24.81**	**34.77**
World (millions of U.S. dollars)	23,678	124,407	523,293	20,956	113,917	530,174

Sources: Barba Navaretti and Venables (2004); and IMF staff calculations.

adjustment will have a magnified effect on trade flows. A contraction in demand for a particular final good, for example, will trigger a contraction in demand for imported intermediate inputs all along the production chain. Thus, trade flows will in general appear more elastic with respect to demand changes. Regarding net exports, however, implications are less clear-cut, partly because both exports and imports are generally affected.[33]

- *Price elasticity of trade flows.* The ability to purchase similar if not identical goods from domestic and foreign sources could raise the substitutability between foreign and domestically produced traded goods, which would tend to make bilateral trade flows more responsive to changes in prices, including those arising from exchange rate changes. For a given adjustment in quantities, relative prices will then have to change less. However, integrated production lines may have made some firms more dependent on particular foreign inputs that have no close substitutes, and their demand for foreign inputs may have

become more price-inelastic. Empirically, there is little evidence to date that the elasticity of substitution between foreign and domestically produced traded goods—which determines the price elasticity of trade flows—has changed (e.g., Ruhl, 2003).

- *Tradability and the share of nontradable goods in production.* With declining trading costs, one would expect the tradability of goods and services to have increased and the share of nontradable goods in demand and production to have decreased.[34] This would, everything else being equal, facilitate adjustment, as the required changes in tradables relative to nontradables output would be less and could occur with relatively smaller changes in the relative price of tradables compared to nontradables (the real exchange rate). Empirical evidence based on sectoral input-output tables, however, suggests that, unlike in many emerging market countries, the tradables sector share output in most industrial countries has actually fallen slightly in recent years because of the rapid expansion of service sectors.[35]

[33]Production-sharing links do not automatically imply tight links among national economies. If the contribution of local value added to the total value of trade is small, changes in trade volume could be large with very little impact on the local economy (see Burstein, Kurz, and Tesar, 2004).

[34]See, for example, Bayoumi and others (2004) or Bravo-Ortega and di Giovanni (2005) for recent studies.

[35]See Batini, Jackson, and Nickell (2002) on the methodology.

Figure 3.10. Degrees of Foreign Competition and Effective Exchange Rates in G-7 Countries

For the G-7 countries, foreign competition seems to have increased over time.

—— Ratio of other G-7 members' export deflators (PPP-weighted) to country GDP deflator (right scale)
—— Nominal effective exchange rate (+ = depreciation; left scale)

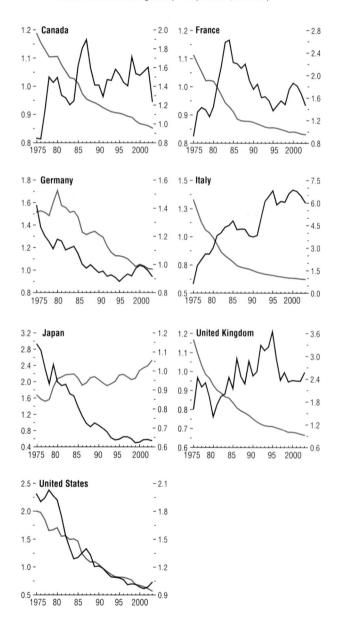

Sources: IMF, *International Financial Statistics;* and IMF staff calculations.

Other Implications of Real Globalization

There are a number of other factors partly linked to greater trade integration that may also affect the way external imbalances adjust. These include the following.

- *Greater international competition and lower markups.* Lower trading costs in recent decades have spurred product market competition by fostering the international supply of final and intermediate goods. At the same time, a wave of merger and acquisition activity, even in services industries (e.g., retailing, insurance, banking, and telecommunications) has brought international cost-cutting techniques and price competition into sectors that used to be isolated from such global pressures. Measuring competition is difficult, but the ratio of world export prices (in local currency terms) to the GDP deflator—a frequently used indicator for foreign competition—has decreased, which is consistent with the notion that foreign competition has intensified in G-7 countries even when changes in effective exchange rates are considered (Figure 3.10).[36] Evidence from sectoral markups partly supports this view (Martins and Scarpetta, 1999) even though the changes over the past two decades have, on average, been relatively small. The ongoing compression of markups puts a cap on global price levels and inflationary pressures from disturbances. This generally facilitates the task of delivering low and stable inflation for monetary policymakers (see Box 3.4).

- *Greater flexibility and lower rigidities.* Structural reforms over the past two decades—partly reflecting pressures from greater international

---

[36]World export prices in local currency terms depend on the nominal effective exchange rate by construction (see Bailliu and Fujii, 2004). This implies that the real price of exports can fall exclusively owing to an appreciation of the domestic currency. In the cases of Canada, France, Italy, and the United Kingdom, however, real prices of exports seem to have fallen—signaling an increase in foreign competition—even in the face of constant or depreciating nominal exchange rates. In Figure 3.10, world export prices for each country are approximated by export deflators of other G-7 countries.

competition—have enhanced economic flexibility, including by lowering real and nominal rigidities in product and labor markets, especially in industrial countries (see, for example, Chapter III, *World Economic Outlook*, April 2004). While recent empirical evidence,[37] at both the macroeconomic and the firm level, suggests that rigidities of both kinds are still present in most economies today, preliminary results obtained estimating aggregate pricing equations indicate that in most G-7 countries, nominal or real price rigidities or both have decreased somewhat since 1970 (Appendix 3.3 details these results). Other factors, such as the adoption of "just-in-time" technologies to reduce durables inventories relative to sales, have also contributed to enhancing flexibility. As result, economies are now believed to be in a better position to absorb and rebound from shocks, which would, by implication, also facilitate the rebalancing of global imbalances.

- *Reduced exchange rate pass-through and improved monetary policy credibility.* Empirical evidence suggests that the short-run pass-through of nominal exchange rate movements to domestic final goods prices has declined in many countries in recent years. This in part reflects more credible monetary policies and the associated transition to a lower inflation environment (see Taylor, 2000; Choudhri and Hakura, 2001; Devereux and Yetman, 2002; Gagnon and Ihrig, 2004; Bailliu and Fujii, 2004), as well as changes in pricing practices of firms engaged in trade—such as an increase in the prevalence of local currency pricing (see Devereux, Engel, and Storgaard, 2004). In contrast, the pass-through of exchange rate changes to prices of imports "at the dock" is higher, especially in the long run (e.g., Campa and Goldberg, 2002). While the extent and causes of the decline in the exchange rate pass-through to domestic consumer prices remain subject to debate (see, among others, Obstfeld, 2002), a lower pass-

through can have positive and negative consequences for external positions and their adjustment. On the one hand, it implies that economies are more insulated from external shocks, allowing growth to remain relatively stable in the face of high exchange rate volatility even in very open economies. On the other side, a lower pass-through may reduce the expenditure-switching effects of exchange rate changes, thereby complicating external adjustment. The fact that today a large portion of trade is intrafirm and intra-industry, and that the exchange rate pass-through to the prices of imported intermediates does not, in general, appear to have changed much over time, suggests however that the overall responsiveness of trade to changes in exchange rates may not have shifted dramatically, even if the exchange rate pass-through to final consumer goods prices has declined over the years.

In sum, real globalization has affected external imbalances and adjustment through a number of channels, although the extent and, in some cases, direction are yet to be established. Therefore, the chapter now turns to model simulations for a fuller and more integrated analysis of how real globalization has affected external adjustment.

The Effects of Globalization: An Integrated Perspective

To investigate the implications of globalization for the adjustment of external imbalances, this section uses simulations of the IMF's GEM.[38] GEM incorporates many trade linkages with an explicit microeconomic foundation, and is thus particularly well-suited to analyze the impact of real globalization discussed earlier. Moreover, while financial linkages in GEM are still cursory, the model nevertheless can mimic key aspects of financial globalization such as the apparent increasing willingness of investors

---

[37]See Angeloni and others (2004).
[38]See Bayoumi (2004) and Laxton and Pesenti (2003).

Box 3.4. Monetary Policy in a Globalized World

This box looks at the implications of globalization for monetary policy. The main conclusion is that although globalization has altered the environment in which central banks operate and made it more difficult to assess and predict economic developments, the objectives and instruments of monetary policy are no different in a more integrated world.

Effects of Globalization on Monetary Policy

Perhaps the most dramatic implication of financial integration and freer capital flows for monetary policy is the fact that it has become harder to simultaneously maintain fixed exchange rates and conduct an independent monetary policy dedicated to domestic objectives. If a country's exchange rate is pegged to the currency of another country, then its interest rates will have to follow closely those of the country to which its currency is pegged: any positive (negative) deviation would, in fact, trigger capital inflows (outflows) putting upward (downward) pressure on the exchange rate parity. The sheer increase in cross-border financial transactions in the past 20 years has made it harder for central banks to counter such pressures, even when they hold significant foreign exchange reserves. Of course, countries can decide to limit capital flows by imposing capital controls, but this implies that they have to forgo the benefits of capital integration, which puts them at a disadvantage relative to countries with floating exchange rates and free capital flows in tapping world saving. The conflicting nature of these policy options—fixed exchange rates, independent monetary policy, and free capital mobility—also known as the "impossible trinity," has pushed many countries in recent years to abandon exchange rate pegs altogether (see Fischer, 2001).

Globalization has also had numerous other important effects on monetary policy.

- *Greater international exposure.* By making economies more open, globalization has made economies more exposed to international shocks, thereby raising the challenges to which monetary policy must respond. For example, the fact that countries now trade more with each other in both final and intermediate goods and that production has become often geographically very fragmented implies that even the smallest demand and supply disturbances in a country can have repercussions for production and profitability in countries elsewhere. In addition, under globalization, financial markets are increasingly integrated with those abroad. Disturbances and policy decisions in one country are reflected swiftly in markets around the world.

- *Changes to the transmission of monetary policy.* There are two main ways in which this happened. First, while central banks can still control short-term interest rates under floating exchange rates with financial globalization (Boivin and Giannoni, 2002, 2003), deeper financial integration has made exchange rates more reactive to changes in interest rate differentials.[1] All things being equal, this means that changes in monetary instruments have a larger impact on exchange rates, reinforcing the exchange rate channel of monetary transmission. Second, globalization has influenced the way exchange rate changes affect aggregate demand, even though the overall direction of such influence on the exchange rate channel is yet unclear. On the one hand, trade globalization has boosted import and export volumes in many countries, and so changes in the exchange rate now affect a greater portion of aggregate demand. On the other hand, globalization may have contributed to weaken the link between exchange rates and the relative price of imports and exports (the third section of this chapter describes this process in more detail).

---

[1] Average correlations between (quarterly) changes in the U.S. dollar/euro bilateral exchange rate and nominal short-term interest rate U.S.–EU12, for example, have been strengthening since 1970. For a more general discussion, see, among others, Panigirtzoglou (2004) and Barnea and Djivre (2004).

Note: The main author of this box is Nicoletta Batini.

- *Compressed markups and wages.* Globalization has increased international competition, lessening markups and helping contain wage pressures. This has helped central banks attain their goals because it has lowered inflation expectations in many countries, keeping inflation subdued and, at the same time, allowing economies to operate at a higher degree of resource utilization with a lesser threat of rising inflation.
- *A more complex world.* Finally, as globalization has changed the behavior of consumers and firms and altered the nature and number of economic linkages across countries, historical data have become a less reliable yardstick for interpreting the present. On the whole, globalization has thus made it harder to model economies and predict economic developments. Central banks' increasing interest in how to operate under uncertainty, and the boom of analysis in this area in recent years (see Swiss National Bank, 2003) are testament to this fact.

How Should Monetary Policy Account for Globalization?

Does globalization introduce new objectives for monetary policy? Probably not. Although globalization has, in fact, reduced the ability of central banks to pursue inconsistent objectives, as exemplified by the dilemmas now posed by the "impossible trinity," it is generally agreed that central banks should continue using their sole policy instrument to achieve the primary goal of price stability. They should therefore refrain from pursuing additional objectives—for example, external balance or exchange rate stability—that may be perceived as playing a more prominent role in a globalized world but that cannot be directly controlled by monetary policy (Brash, 2001; Stevens, 2004; Greenspan, 2004).

Likewise, globalization does not seem to call for new instruments. As economies are more open, central banks may be tempted to influence demand and prices by making more intensive use of the exchange rate, either by affecting interest rate differentials or by directly buying and selling foreign currency to affect its value.

Clearly, with globalized economies the exchange rate has become a more pivotal indicator of monetary conditions and inflationary pressures. However, trying to control inflation and output by manipulating the exchange rate can be dangerous. Batini and Nelson (2000), for example, show that when uncovered interest parity holds, trying to move the exchange rate reduces exchange rate variability but actually increases the variability of inflation. The difficulties experienced by the Reserve Bank of New Zealand and the Bank of Canada with Monetary Condition Indices[2] (MCIs) are telling in this respect (see Batini and Turnbull, 2002).

On the other hand, monetary policy still needs to adjust to globalization in various ways. First, central banks should continue to work on refining their analytical toolkits to take into proper account developments from deeper financial and trade integration and the economic implications thereof. As discussed above and documented by Rogoff (2003), overall globalization seems to have helped reduce inflationary pressures in many countries, but the precise mechanism and the magnitude of such effect are still far from clear-cut, so more research is needed on this front. Second, when doing policy analysis and economic evaluation, central banks need to continue their efforts to move from models in which parameters depend heavily on historical estimates toward models in which parameters are less likely to change over time (see Sargent, 1999; and Pagan, 2003). Finally, central banks need to persevere in their efforts to exchange information on economic developments and discuss global economic issues within the many international forums that exist today. Given the growing interdependence of national economies and macroeconomic policies, the coordination of such policies has undoubtedly become more important.

[2]MCIs are fixed-weight weighted averages of interest rates and exchange rates. Their use as operating targets implies moving one of the rates or both to bring the average in line with some predetermined equilibrium that is assumed to be consistent with price stability and stable economic growth in the long run.

Table 3.8. Differences in Parameters in Vintage Calibrations, 1980s and 2000s

Description	Emerging Asia		Japan/Euro Area		Rest of World		United States	
	1980s	2000s	1980s	2000s	1980s	2000s	1980s	2000s
Home biases (percent)[1]								
Consumption goods	5	5	66	65	30	10	94	96
Investment goods	7	4	74	87	33	10	95	97
Tradable sector output (percent of total output)	57	61	33	30	35	42	32	32
Markups (percent)								
Tradables sector	15.4	14.3	23.5	21.3	19.0	17.5	16.7	15.0
Nontradables sector	28.6	26.7	41.7	40.0	34.5	32.9	31.3	27.9
Nominal rigidities (quarters)								
Average price contract lengths	4	4	5	4	5	4	5	4
Monetary policy reaction function								
Feedback parameters:								
Lagged interest rate	1.00	1.00	0.75	0.81	0.75	0.81	0.75	0.81
Inflation gap	—	—	0.44	0.52	0.44	0.52	0.44	0.52
Output gap level	—	—	0.19	0.10	0.19	0.10	1.19	0.10
Real growth	—	—	0.14	0.51	0.14	0.51	0.14	0.51

Source: IMF staff calculations.

[1]Weights of domestically produced tradable goods in the total input of tradable goods in the production of consumption or investment goods.

to hold foreign assets, and the connection between growing net foreign asset positions and risk premia.[39]

To conduct the simulations, a new four-bloc version of GEM was developed. The four-bloc partitioning, which involves (1) the United States; (2) the euro area plus Japan; (3) emerging Asia; and (4) the rest of the world, mirrors the geographical constellation of the current imbalances. In the simulation experiments, two versions of the model are used. One version replicates an environment of "low economic integration" based on data from the 1980s, while the second version portrays a "high economic integration" environment based on 2000 data. Key differences in the two model versions, resulting from or connected to globalization are summarized in Table 3.8 and Figure 3.11.[40] Compared with the "low economic integration" version, the "high economic integration" version (2000 calibration) portrays a generally more competitive and more flexible world economy

where, as discussed in the previous section, (1) trade flows are more evenly distributed across blocs; (2) trade shares are greater and home biases in consumption and production are generally smaller; (3) tradable sectors are larger in the rest of the world and emerging Asia and smaller in industrial countries; (4) mark-ups and nominal rigidities are somewhat lower; and, (5) the implications of exchange rate shocks for domestic inflation are smaller on account of more determined policy efforts to control inflation. Price and income elasticities in trade equations, however, are identical in the two calibrations, reflecting the unclear net overall effect of globalization on trade elasticities, as discussed earlier.

The simulations are illustrative in nature and should not be interpreted as forecasts by IMF staff of the resolution of actual imbalances. Their main purpose is to help explore the effects of globalization on external adjustment in the context of imbalances similar to the cur-

---

[39]These aspects of financial globalization are modeled broadly along the lines of Hunt and Rebucci (2003) and Ghironi, İşcan, and Rebucci (2005).

[40]Throughout, size is predicated on the value of nominal GDP in U.S. dollars given the difficulties in constructing world trade matrices with PPP exchange rates or other weights. Blocs are assumed to grow in real terms at different speeds, roughly reflecting growth assumptions for these blocs from the latest WEO forecast.

rent ones, assuming for simplicity that these are the result of a few stylized shocks and that policies follow simple, mechanical rules that do not respond directly to imbalances.[41] In this sense, the experiments below are meant to throw light on specific issues about the resolution of global imbalances—such as the implications of alternative financial market conditions for the adjustment—but are by no means an exhaustive analysis of possible resolution scenarios and policy options.

How Does Real Globalization Affect External Adjustment?

A first set of simulations looks at the effects of real sector globalization on external adjustment under the assumption that global investors continue to accumulate claims on the United States for a significant period. In this scenario, which also involves a moderate fiscal adjustment about the size proposed by the administration, U.S. net external liabilities stabilize at about 60 percent of GDP in the long run, well above current levels, and the U.S. current account deficit falls to a new long-run level of about 2.5 percent of GDP. The narrowing of the U.S. current account deficit is the result of a combination of higher U.S. real interest rates and higher U.S. saving ratios—hampering domestic demand—on the one hand, and a significantly weaker U.S. dollar—boosting net exports—on the other hand. In the short run, the net effect is a decline in output growth below trend. During the adjustment, the U.S. trade balance gradually goes into surplus to meet the additional costs of the higher long-run net foreign liabilities.

In the other blocs, the rebalancing involves opposite adjustment patterns. While the U.S.

[41]The simulations assume that in every bloc—excluding emerging Asia, which in the first set of simulations pegs its exchange rate to the U.S. dollar—monetary policy is implemented through an interest rate rule where rates are set in response to the extent to which inflation deviates from target and output deviates from potential. The exact specification of this monetary policy rule is described in Appendix 3.3.

Figure 3.11. Economies' Relative Sizes and Trade Patterns
(Percent of world GDP)

Economies in emerging Asia and the euro area and Japan are relatively larger in 2003 than they were in 1984, whereas the U.S. economy and economies in the rest of the world have become smaller over time.

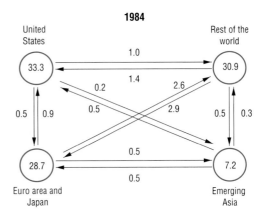

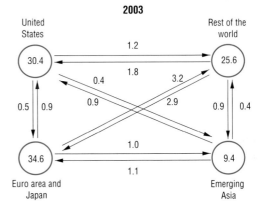

Sources: IMF, *International Financial Statistics;* IMF, *Direction of Trade Statistics;* and IMF staff calculations.

dollar depreciates, currencies elsewhere appreciate in real terms, and net export growth declines. At the same time, domestic demand in the other blocs strengthens, partly reflecting relatively lower real interest rates and higher income from larger net foreign assets. In the long run, the other blocs see their current account weaken in GDP terms (in the long run, in emerging Asia the current account to GDP ratio falls by about 4 percentage points; in Japan and the euro area it falls by about 1 percentage point). With the investment income from permanently larger net foreign asset positions, these blocs can afford to run small long-run trade deficits.

These fundamental adjustment patterns do not depend on the state of globalization; they follow from a country's long-run external budget constraint that ties trade balances and net foreign assets together. However, real sector globalization affects adjustment paths in this rebalancing scenario, as illustrated by the differences between the rebalancing responses of some key variables in the low- and high-integration versions of the model in Figure 3.12. The key results are as follows.

- With globalization, external adjustment can be achieved with a smaller real depreciation of the U.S. dollar and more contained real appreciations in the other blocs. Globalization also implies smaller increases in real interest rates in the United States and in other blocs during the adjustment.
- As a result, globalization also allows the adjustment to occur with smaller short-run declines in output growth in all blocs, apart from emerging Asia.
- The impact of globalization seems largest for the adjustment in emerging Asia, where output growth during the rebalancing is not as strong as in the absence of globalization.

The simulation results, therefore, suggest that real sector globalization broadly facilitates external adjustment. Which aspects of globalization matter most for this result?

- *Direction of trade and trade shares.* Trade today is more evenly distributed across blocs, helping to spread the adjustment in the U.S. current account deficit more evenly to other world regions. The positive effects of this, of course, vary among blocs. Today blocs other than emerging Asia, for example, are relatively less affected by negative U.S. developments compared with the 1980s while, at the same time, they benefit more from positive developments in emerging Asia, such as the region's strong growth. Emerging Asia, however, is now more internationally exposed with its higher trade share, so that the slowdown in growth necessary for the U.S. current account to rebalance has a correspondingly larger impact on this region compared with the 1980s.
- *Economic size of the various blocs.* In the 1980s, the relative economic size of the United States was bigger, while the economic sizes of emerging Asia, the euro area, and Japan were smaller, making it harder for them to absorb the same amount of U.S. assets. Given the increased economic size of emerging Asia, the euro area, and Japan in the high-integration version, an equal-sized increase in U.S. net foreign liabilities (as a percent of U.S. GDP) generates smaller increases in net foreign asset to GDP ratios in these blocs, other things being equal. In turn, these entail smaller external surpluses—that is, relatively smaller saving-investment balances, which can be attained through more limited real exchange rate changes and, especially in the short term, real interest rate changes, thereby allowing for higher growth, except in the case of emerging Asia, mostly for reasons noted above.

In addition, the results depend significantly on *differences in monetary policy strategies across time* (see Box 3.4 for a more detailed discussion of the links between globalization and monetary policy). Monetary policies today are more effective and credible, and thus require smaller interest rate changes to stabilize inflation following demand shocks and during adjustment, partly because of the lower exchange rate pass-through, as discussed earlier.

In contrast, other key elements, especially greater flexibility and greater international com-

Figure 3.12. Global Rebalancing Under Benign Financial Market Conditions

(Deviations between baseline responses in GEM 2000 and GEM 1980 calibrations; percentage points; x-axis in calendar quarters, 0 represents 2005Q1)

When financial market conditions are benign, globalization facilitates external adjustment, as this can now be achieved with smaller exchange rate changes and smaller increases in real interest rates. Under globalization, output losses are also smaller in the short run, except in emerging Asia.

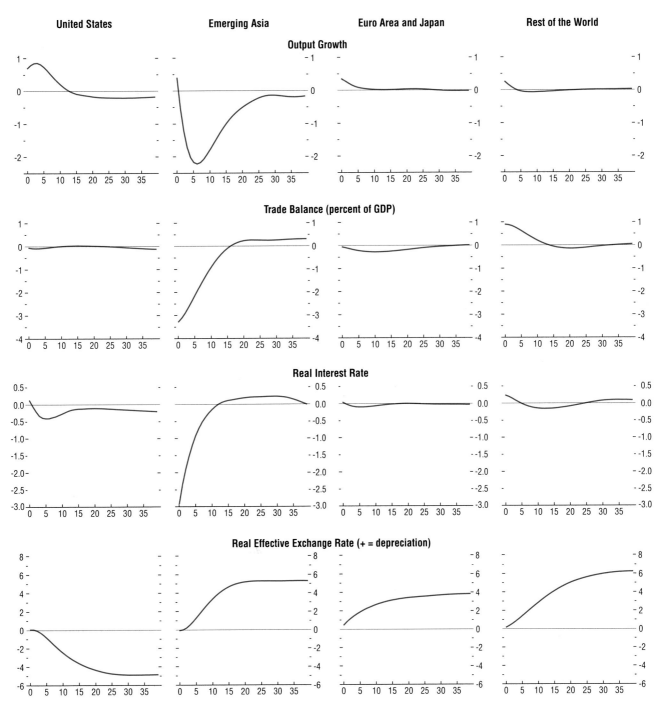

Source: IMF staff calculations.

petition, seem to play a minor role in explaining the result (see Appendix 3.3 for details).[42] This finding reflects two facts. First, given empirical evidence discussed earlier, mark-ups and rigidities differ only marginally across the two globalization environments, which is reflected in the two versions of the model. For example, as noted in Table 3.8, markups generally fell by less than 2 percentage points, implying relatively minor changes in price levels. Second, because empirical evidence suggests similar relative gains in flexibility and competition across blocs (although levels of competition and flexibility still differ), the related changes in price levels between the two globalization environments are similar also and, accordingly, changes in relative prices between blocs are minor. Hence, while greater competition and lower rigidities can facilitate adjustment from a unilateral perspective, they appear to have made less of difference so far from a global perspective.

What Are the Implications of Changes in Investor Preferences?

So far, the simulations have assumed—perhaps rather optimistically—that investors continue to accumulate U.S. assets for a considerable period. In practice, investor preferences can be highly volatile, arguably a greater concern in a globalized world where gross and net external positions are large and where large portions of foreign assets are often purchased and held by official investors for motives other than pure portfolio optimization. To explore the potential impact of a change in investor preferences, two alternative scenarios are considered, using the 2000 calibration of GEM.

- In the first scenario, investors in the euro area, Japan, and the rest of the world are unwilling to continue accumulating U.S. assets and begin to gradually reduce their desired

holdings of U.S. assets (back to 2001 levels by 2010). However, investment behavior in emerging Asia does not change, and currencies in the region remain closely linked to the U.S. dollar.

- In the second scenario, it is assumed that all investors outside the United States, including emerging Asia, gradually reduce their desired holdings of U.S. assets (back to 2001 levels by 2010). This scenario also assumes—for illustrative purposes only—that emerging Asia moves immediately to a floating exchange rate regime, with monetary policy determined by an interest rate rule broadly similar to that assumed for the other blocs.

Such changes in investor preferences clearly complicate global rebalancing. Compared with the previous scenario (2000 calibration), the key results are as follows (see Figure 3.13).

- Capital flows to the United States slow sharply, requiring a more abrupt adjustment in the U.S. current account. Correspondingly, U.S. interest rates rise relative to the baseline scenario, the U.S. dollar has to depreciate sooner and more sharply, and U.S. output slows more markedly. Unsurprisingly, all these effects are larger in the case where demand for U.S. assets falls in all regions.
- The depreciation of the U.S. dollar is matched by an appreciation of exchange rates—and lower trade and current account balances—in blocs with flexible exchange rates (Japan, the euro area, and the rest of the world). In emerging Asia, however, developments vary substantially across the two scenarios. In the former, the real exchange rate appreciates relatively less as the Asian currencies move down with the U.S. dollar. In contrast, when Asian currencies float, the exchange rate appreciates sharply. In this latter case, the appreciation in the other two blocs is somewhat less than under the first scenario, as the decline in

---

[42]Greater flexibility, competition, and lower pass-through (through a more credible monetary policy) generally tend to facilitate external adjustment in the sense that they push key variables in the direction required by the adjustment. The exception is emerging Asia, where, contrary to other blocs, monetary policy is assumed to have stayed the same between the 1980s and the 2000s.

Figure 3.13. Global Rebalancing Under Adverse Financial Market Conditions

(Shock minus control, where "shock" is adverse scenario and "control" is 2000 baseline under benign scenario; percentage points; x-axis in calendar quarter, 0 represents 2005Q1)

The effects of globalization when financial market conditions are adverse are more mixed. As capital flows to the United States dry up, the United States can only rebalance its external position through a sharper contraction and a bigger U.S. dollar depreciation. Other blocs largely benefit, as their saving need not rise to pay for additional purchases of U.S. assets.

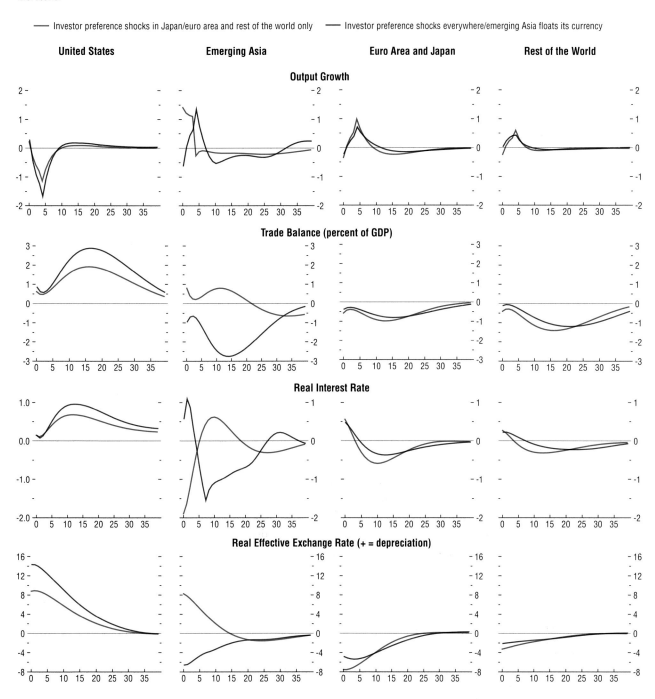

Source: IMF staff calculations.

emerging Asia's desire for foreign assets is accompanied by relatively faster domestic demand growth, which, unlike in the first scenario, contributes to the absorption of higher U.S. net exports.

- In both scenarios, real interest rates outside the United States fall, and—despite slower U.S. growth—GDP growth in the rest of the world rises moderately (or in emerging Asia stays broadly flat relative to the baseline in the first scenario). This rather benign outcome partly reflects the specification of the shift in investor preferences, as the decline in desired asset holdings in the rest of the world is accompanied by a reduction in desired savings, which boosts consumption.[43] In practice, demand outside the United States could fail to pick up—for example, because of adverse confidence effects—and GDP growth would correspondingly be weaker.

Overall, the simulations underscore the potential risks attendant on a reversal of investor preferences and of an abrupt, as opposed to a gradual, change in central bank behavior in Asia. Moreover, while the simulations do not take full account of some mitigating factors—notably positive valuation effects for the United States from a depreciating U.S. dollar, as discussed earlier[44]—on balance they probably underestimate the risks for a number of reasons. First, as noted above, growth in the rest of the world could well be weaker than suggested by the model. Second, large exchange rate changes may induce financial market turbulence, especially since investors may not always have the perfect foresight assumed in the model. Finally, GEM does not fully incorporate the effects of higher risk premia (since it only distinguishes

net foreign asset positions, not the underlying gross asset and liability positions). At current levels of U.S. external liabilities, a permanent 100 basis points increase in the risk premium on U.S. assets raises the required long-run trade surplus in the United States by 0.7 percentage point of GDP (Table 3.9), which would require a substantially larger depreciation of the U.S. dollar (and, of course, greater appreciations elsewhere). In contrast, the risk premium effect is less than half this size in the less globalized world of the 1980s, highlighting the importance of the buildup of gross assets and liabilities in recent years.

Summary and Policy Implications

Against the background of concerns about current global imbalances, the multidimensional relationship among globalization, external imbalances, and international adjustment has become of increasing interest to policymakers. Recent empirical evidence and theoretical considerations alike suggest that financial globalization has contributed to an environment in which large current account surpluses or deficits emerge and are sustained, partly reflecting the revealed willingness of investors to hold larger shares of foreign assets in their portfolios. Real sector globalization has clearly reshaped the magnitudes, composition, and direction of trade flows in the global economy. However, empirical evidence to date is ambiguous as to whether this has increased the sensitivity of the demand for traded goods and services to changes in relative prices or demand conditions.

As the simulations and related analysis above show, real and financial globalization should

---

[43]Simulation results from scenarios where the shift in investor preferences is reflected in a persistently higher risk premium on U.S. assets rather than in changes in desired net foreign asset positions suggest similar growth patterns during adjustment. In particular, the increase in the risk premium on U.S. assets leads to relatively lower real interest rates elsewhere, as capital leaves the United States and is invested elsewhere. This provides a boost to domestic demand that more than offsets the adverse growth impact of lower net export growth.

[44]In GEM, there is only one international bond, which is denominated in U.S. dollars. Hence, while emerging Asia, the euro area, Japan, and the rest of the world experience adverse valuation shocks when the U.S. dollar depreciates, there are no gains for the United States. Moreover, in GEM the valuation effects arise only on net foreign asset positions and not on gross positions.

Table 3.9. Impact of Risk Premium Shocks on Long-Run Trade Balances[1]

	Gross Foreign Assets (percent of GDP)	Changes in Long-Run Trade Balances (percent of GDP) After a Risk Premium Shock (in bps)[2]			
		$\rho = 100$	$\rho = 200$	$\rho = 300$	$\rho = 400$
United States					
Low integration (1984)	26.6	0.3	0.5	0.8	1.0
High integration (2003)	70.5	0.7	1.4	2.1	2.8
Emerging Asia					
Low integration (1984)	12.4	0.1	0.2	0.4	0.5
High integration (2003)	56.7	0.6	1.1	1.7	2.2
Japan and Europe					
Low integration (1984)	35.9	0.4	0.7	1.1	1.4
High integration (2003)	147.8	1.4	2.9	4.3	5.8

[1]In the long run, sustainable trade balances (i.e., trade balances consistent with stable ratio of net foreign assets to GDP) are obtained by adding to the long-run trade balances from GEM a term that captures the effect on the trade balance of changes in the value of gross foreign assets. This, in turn, depends proportionately on the interest rate differential (r^N) and the risk premium on those assets (ρ), as shown in (1) below:

$$tb = tb_{GEM} - \left(\frac{r^N - \rho}{1 + g}\right)\bar{a}, \tag{1}$$

where a is gross foreign assets (as a share of GDP) and g is the rate of output growth (see Appendix 3.1 for details). The gross asset positions used to calculate the trade balances in the two scenarios are the historical values reported in the table. In both scenarios, net foreign returns r^N are calculated as the averages for the period 1990–2003, and the long-run rate of output growth is taken to be 2 percent.

[2]Results reported in the table show how long-run trade balances change with different values for the risk premium in the two scenarios. For example, if net foreign returns for the United States decline (rise) by 400 bps in the high integration scenario, the trade balance required to stabilize U.S. net foreign assets increases (falls) by 2.8 percentage points of GDP. By contrast, in the low integration scenario, a similar fall in net foreign returns increases the long-run trade balance by 1 percent of GDP.

generally facilitate global rebalancing, provided financial conditions remain benign. With output levels in major economic blocs now more equal in size, the financing of the U.S. deficit requires relatively smaller surpluses elsewhere; the more even distribution of trade flows across the world contributes to better burden sharing among countries; and more credible monetary policies reduce the output cost of adjusting to shocks. That said, globalization has fundamentally changed neither the nature of adjustment nor the magnitudes involved: ultimately exchange rates and trade balances will need to adjust, and adjust substantially.

The analysis also suggests that while home bias in investor preferences and restrictions to net international borrowing have decreased, they have not disappeared. Accordingly, the accommodation of further increases in U.S. net external liabilities should not be taken for granted. If financial market conditions prove to be less benign, with only limited or perhaps temporary scope for further increases in U.S. net external liabilities, global rebalancing is

likely to involve greater risks. In particular, initial changes in real exchange and interest rates would be much larger, and the short-term output costs of a global rebalancing clearly higher, particularly in the United States. In an environment where gross assets and liabilities are substantially higher than they were in the past—a feature not fully captured in the simulations—the potential for large changes in exchange rates, interest rates, and risk premia to lead to disruptive financial market turbulence in the short term must be correspondingly elevated.

In sum, the central message of the chapter is that policy makers need to take advantage of the scope that globalization provides to facilitate adjustment, while remaining mindful that this adjustment must eventually take place, and of the potential risks associated with unexpected changes in investor preferences along the way. These simultaneous objectives would appear most likely to be achieved by the adoption of a credible medium-term policy framework consistent with achieving external and internal balance within a reasonable period of time, thereby anchoring expectations and reducing risks of reversals in investor preferences. This underscores the importance of implementing the cooperative strategy to address imbalances recommended by IMF Governors at the last IMFC meeting in October 2004. Unfortunately, as discussed in Chapter I, to date only moderate progress has been made.

Appendix 3.1. Net Foreign Assets, Valuation, and Adjustment: A Glossary of Terms

The main author of this appendix is Roberto Cardarelli.

Accounting for Changes in Net Foreign Assets

Changes in a country's net foreign asset position (NFA) are, by definition, described by the following accounting identity:

$$NFA_t - NFA_{t-1} \equiv NX_t + CT_t + IA_t + KA_t + EO_t + KG_t,$$

where *NX* denotes net exports of goods and services; *CT*, current transfers; *IA*, the investment income balance (with the sum of the three being the current account balance); *KA*, capital transfers; *EO*, errors and omissions; and *KG*, net capital gains (losses if negative).

Valuation Effects

Using lowercase letters to show net foreign assets and net exports as a share of GDP, excluding current and capital transfers on account of their relatively small size, ignoring errors and omissions, and assuming that returns on foreign assets are equal to returns on foreign liabilities, the accounting identity can be expressed as follows:

$$nfa_t - nfa_{t-1} \equiv nx_t + \frac{i_t - \gamma_t}{1 + \gamma_t} nfa_{t-1} + \frac{k_t}{1 + \gamma_t} nfa_{t-1},$$

where γ is the country's rate of nominal growth, *i* is the yield rate, and *k* is the rate of capital gain on external assets and liabilities. The last term on the right-hand side defines the *valua-*

tion effect shown in figures and tables in this chapter.

External Solvency

Because the accounting identity for net foreign assets holds in every period, it can be expressed on a cumulative basis—the so-called intertemporal budget constraint for a country—leading to the well-known proposition that a debtor country is *solvent* if the net present value of its future net exports equals the current period value of its net foreign liabilities.

External Sustainability and Imbalances

The intertemporal solvency condition serves only to exclude cases in which a country indulges in perpetual debt refinancing of its external imbalances (a so-called Ponzi game), but is otherwise consistent with many patterns for future net foreign assets, including one in which they increase exponentially at a rate lower than the difference between the yield on net external liabilities and the growth rate. A more operational definition of *sustainable* net exports consists in imposing that they *stabilize* the ratio of net foreign assets to GDP to a certain level. This could be its current level, or a level that is considered consistent with the international investors' willingness to lend to the country (which, in turn, may relate to their perception of the country's willingness and ability to meet its external obligations), or a level consistent with some optimal, theoretically predicted, benchmark. In this case, the level of net exports that a country needs to sustain in the long run to keep the ratio of net foreign assets to GDP constant at a level denoted with $\overline{nfa}$ can be written as

$$nx_t^* = \frac{r - g}{1 + g} \overline{nfa},$$

where *r* is the total real return (yield plus capital gains) on net foreign assets and *g* is the country's rate of real growth. In this framework, the difference between the current level of net exports and nx^* can be interpreted as a measure of the degree of external imbalances.

Financial Integration and External Adjustment

Introducing different rates of return on foreign assets and liabilities, the accumulation identity for net foreign assets can be written as

$$nfa_t - nfa_{t-1} \equiv nx_t + \frac{r_t^L - g_t}{1 + g_t} nfa_{t-1} + \frac{r_t^A - r_t^L}{1 + g_t} a_{t-1},$$

where r^L is the total real return (yield plus capital gains) on foreign liabilities, r^A is the total real return on foreign assets, and a denotes gross foreign assets (as a share of GDP). *Sustainable* net export levels can then be defined as

$$nx^* = \frac{r^L - g}{1 + g} \overline{nfa} - \frac{r^A - r^L}{1 + g} \overline{a}.$$

This expression shows that a larger (steady-state) stock of gross foreign assets imposes a bigger trade adjustment if the return differential $r^A - r^L$ is negative, highlighting the greater exposure arising from larger external positions. A numerical example of this effect is shown in Table 3.9, where the steady-state net exports derived from GEM are equal to the first term on the right-hand side of the expression above. Sustainable net export levels after a risk premium shock—modeled as increases in r^L while keeping r^A unchanged—are then obtained by adding the second term, taking the level in the year underlying the calibration as the steady-state ratio of gross foreign assets to GDP $\overline{a}$.

Appendix 3.2. Econometric Evidence on the Valuation Channel

The main author of this appendix is Roberto Cardarelli.

This appendix provides details on the econometric evidence discussed in the main text about

the role of the valuation channel in external adjustment.

Modeling and Econometric Strategy

The role of the valuation channel in the process of adjustment of external imbalances is assessed empirically by examining the dynamic responses of net exports and net foreign assets to shocks that move the two variables away from their long-run relationship implied by a country's intertemporal budget constraint. The latter is given by

$$NFA_t = \sum_{i=0}^{\infty} R_{t,t+i}(X_{t+i} - M_{t+i}), \qquad (1)$$

where NFA_t represents the real (based on GDP deflator) level of net foreign assets; X_t and M_t, the volumes of export and imports of goods and services, and $R_{t,s}$—the discount factor for period s net exports—is a function of the real returns on net foreign assets r_t (see also Appendix 3.1).[45]

Following Gourinchas and Rey (2004) and Corsetti and Konstantinou (2004), it is possible to derive the following log-linear approximation of equation (1):

$$\begin{aligned} x_t - \gamma m_t &+ (\gamma - 1)\,nfa_t \\ &= \sum_{i=1}^{\infty} \rho^i [\Delta x_{t+i} - \gamma \Delta m_{t+i} + (\gamma - 1)\, r_{t+i}], \qquad (2) \end{aligned}$$

where lowercase letters denote logarithms.[46] Under the assumptions that r_t, Δx_t, and Δm_t are stationary, expression (2) implies that x, m, and nfa should be cointegrated, and the left-hand side (the cointegration residual) represents deviations from the long-run relationship among the three variables. Expression (2) also implies that if the cointegrating residual is not a constant, it has to *predict* either changes in the future net exports or in net foreign returns or both. For example, if a country develops a larger trade deficit relative to what is consistent with its steady-state net foreign assets position, the deviation from the long-run relationship has to be

---

[45]In particular, $R_{t,s} = \prod_{i=0}^{s} \dfrac{1}{(1 + r_{t+i})}$.

[46]In expression (2), γ and ρ are constants related to the log-linearization of the country's intertemporal budget constraint (see Corsetti and Konstantinou, 2004).

corrected either by an increase in future net exports or by a future increase in net returns on the stock of its foreign assets and liabilities, or a combination of the two.

Based on this framework, the relevance of a valuation channel in the process of adjustment of external imbalances is assessed in two different ways.

- Using annual data from 1970 to 2003,[47] the following vector error correction model (VECM) representation of the three variables $Y = [x, m, nfa]$ was estimated for 21 industrial countries and 28 emerging market countries:[48]

$$\Delta Y_t = c + \alpha\beta'Y_{t-1} + \Gamma(L)\Delta Y_{t-1} + e_t,$$

where ΔY_t is the first difference of the vector Y_t; Γ is a coefficient matrix, $\beta'Y_{t-1}$ is the last period's deviation from the long-run relationship (cointegrating residual in period $t-1$), L is the lag operator, and α is a vector of adjustment coefficients that determines how each variable adjusts to restore the long-run relationship if the cointegration residual signals a deviation from that relationship.

If the coefficient α in the equation for net foreign assets is statistically significant, this implies that changes in net foreign assets play a role in the adjustment to restore the long-run relationship among the three variables x, m, and nfa (see Lettau and Ludvigson, 2004, and Corsetti and Konstantinou, 2004). In fact, that role varies with the value of α. The larger the value of α in the equation for net foreign assets, the bigger the role played by changes in that variable in the overall adjustment. Moreover, using cointegration results (and assuming orthogonality between shocks), one can distinguish between permanent and transitory

shocks on the variables in Y.[49] In particular, it has been shown that variables that participate significantly in the adjustment are assigned a relatively large (small) weight in the transitory (permanent) innovations. A large value of α in the equation for net foreign assets, therefore, implies that a significant share of the variation in net foreign assets is explained by transitory movements. These, in turn, can be interpreted as exchange-rate- or asset-price-related valuation effects that force the stock of net foreign assets to temporarily deviate from its trend to help restore the long-run relationship with net exports.

If, on the other hand, the coefficient α in the equation for net foreign assets is not significantly different from zero, net foreign assets do not play a role in the adjustment process. In this case, the adjustment has to come exclusively from trade flows and any shock has permanent effects on net foreign assets, which will follow a random walk process. This, in turn, is interpreted as evidence against the notion that the valuation channel facilitates the adjustment of external imbalances.

- Using quarterly data on net foreign assets and returns, the implication that deviations from the long-run relationship may predict future changes in net foreign returns was formally tested for G-7 countries. In particular, in-sample forecasts were performed by regressing the changes between t and $t+k$ of export, import, net foreign returns, and real exchange rates on the estimated cointegrating residuals (see Gourinchas and Rey, 2004). For example, the regression for export growth between t and $t+k$ ahead takes the form

$$X_{t+k} - X_t = c + \delta(\hat{\beta}'Y_{t-1}) + e_t.$$

---

[47]For some countries, the sample period is slightly shorter, especially for emerging market countries, where data tend to start from the mid-1970s.

[48]The industrial countries are Australia, Austria, Belgium, Canada, Denmark, Finland, France, Germany, Iceland, Ireland, Italy, Japan, the Netherlands, New Zealand, Norway, Portugal, Spain, Sweden, Switzerland, the United Kingdom, and the United States. The emerging market countries are Argentina, Brazil, Chile, People's Republic of China, Colombia, Costa Rica, Côte d'Ivoire, Ecuador, Egypt, Hungary, India, Indonesia, Jordan, Korea, Malaysia, Mexico, Morocco, Pakistan, Peru, the Philippines, Poland, Singapore, South Africa, Taiwan Province of China, Thailand, Turkey, Uruguay, and Venezuela.

[49]Methodologies to decompose transitory and permanent components based on the cointegration results have been described by King and others (1991), Gonzalo and Granger (1995), Gonzalo and Ng (2001), and Warne (1993).

Results

For each of the 49 countries considered, the existence of cointegration among the logarithm of real exports, imports, and net foreign assets was tested using Johansen's trace test.[50] For the vast majority of countries (37), the results supported the null hypothesis of one cointegrating relationship among the three variables at a 5 percent confidence level. However, since the intertemporal budget constraint is an identity that needs to hold in the long run, cointegration was imposed for all countries in the subsequent analysis, as was the condition that the cointegrating vector is of the form $\beta = [1, -\gamma, (\gamma - 1)]$ (formal tests suggested rejection of that restriction in about one-half of the countries).

The subsequent estimates of the VECM show that the adjustment coefficient α in the equation for Δnfa_t was significantly different from zero for a number of industrial countries (8 out of 21), including Japan and the United States, for which about one-half of the variation in net foreign assets was explained by transitory shocks. On the contrary, the adjustment coefficient in the equation of net foreign assets was statistically significant for only 4 of the 28 emerging market and developing countries (net foreign assets were found weakly exogenous to the system for all other countries).

The difference between the two sets of countries emerges from Table 3.10, showing the arithmetic average of the countries' variance decompositions (mean group estimator).[51] On average, the share of the variation in net foreign assets explained by transitory shocks at a one-year horizon is about twice for the 21 industrial countries as much as that for the 28 emerging market countries considered.

The ability of deviations from trend to predict future changes in net foreign returns was

Table 3.10. Panel VECM: Forecast Variance Decomposition[1]
(Percent)

| | Industrial Countries | | | | | |
| | X | | M | | NFA | |
Horizon	P	T	P	T	P	T
1	86	14	70	30	79	21
2	87	13	74	26	81	19
3	89	11	79	21	83	17
4	89	11	84	16	85	15
10	95	5	92	8	90	10

| | Emerging Markets | | | | | |
| | X | | M | | NFA | |
Horizon	P	T	P	T	P	T
1	82	18	48	52	90	10
2	85	15	58	42	93	7
3	87	13	65	35	95	5
4	90	10	70	30	96	4
10	96	4	85	15	99	1

Source: IMF staff calculations.
[1]Fraction of the variance of the *h*-year ahead forecasts error of exports (*X*), imports (*M*), and net foreign assets (*NFA*) that is explained by the two permanent (*P*) shocks combined and the single transitory (*T*) shock. Values reported are the averages across countries.

assessed through in-sample forecasts only for the G-7 countries, for which quarterly series on net foreign assets and net foreign returns were constructed (see below). Evidence of cointegration was found only for Canada, Germany, Japan, and the United States, so Table 3.11 shows the results only for these countries. In all four countries, cointegrating residuals have substantial predictive power (reflected in a high relative value of the R^2 of the regressions) for export and/or import growth over relatively long horizons. The coefficients generally have the expected sign (negative for export growth and positive for import growth), and tend to be statistically significant for long horizons. By contrast, cointegrating residuals do not seem to have the same general ability to predict future net foreign returns. In these regressions,

---

[50]The number of lags in the VECM specification was chosen in accordance with standard lag order selection criteria (such as the Akaike and Hannan-Quinn information criteria). However, given the limited number of time-series observations available, a more parsimonious choice was often preferred, as long as it resulted in normally distributed and serially uncorrelated errors.

[51]See Pesaran and Smith (1995) and Rebucci (2003), for a description of the properties of this estimator.

Table 3.11. Predictive Ability of Cointegrating Residuals

	Forecast Horizon (quarter)											
	United States						Japan					
	1	2	4	8	12	24	1	2	4	8	12	24
	Real Export Growth						Real Export Growth					
	0.00	0.00	−0.02	−0.05	−0.12	**−0.38**	**−0.07**	**−0.16**	**−0.35**	**−0.50**	**−0.43**	**−0.59**
R^2	0.00	0.00	0.01	0.02	0.03	0.13	0.08	0.16	0.32	0.39	0.32	0.53
	Real Import Growth						Real Import Growth					
	0.00	0.00	0.01	0.11	**0.24**	0.24	−0.01	−0.02	0.00	0.26	**0.63**	**1.14**
R^2	0.00	0.00	0.00	0.04	0.12	0.05	0.00	0.00	0.00	0.06	0.23	0.56
	Real Net Foreign Return						Real Net Foreign Return					
	−0.02	**−0.02**	**−0.02**	**−0.01**	−0.01	0.00	0.01	0.01	0.00	−0.01	−0.02	−0.01
R^2	0.04	0.07	0.08	0.06	0.02	0.00	0.00	0.00	0.00	0.01	0.02	0.01
	Real Effective Exchange Rate (+ = appreciation)						Real Effective Exchange Rate (+ = appreciation)					
	0.02	0.04	0.08	0.15	0.20	0.26	0.06	0.11	0.25	**0.64**	**0.81**	**0.71**
R^2	0.04	0.05	0.09	0.11	0.08	0.04	0.01	0.02	0.04	0.15	0.16	0.12

	Germany						Canada					
	1	2	4	8	12	24	1	2	4	8	12	24
	Real Export Growth						Real Export Growth					
	−0.06	−0.12	−0.19	−0.30	**−0.39**	**−0.90**	0.00	0.02	−0.01	−0.23	**−0.51**	**−0.59**
R^2	0.02	0.04	0.05	0.08	0.11	0.41	0.00	0.00	0.00	0.04	0.16	0.23
	Real Import Growth						Real Import Growth					
	0.01	0.01	0.08	0.21	0.17	0.18	**0.10**	**0.22**	**0.42**	**0.46**	**0.45**	0.26
R^2	0.00	0.00	0.02	0.05	0.02	0.02	0.07	0.13	0.19	0.14	0.12	0.03
	Real Net Foreign Return						Real Net Foreign Return					
	0.03	0.03	0.03	0.03	0.02	−0.02	−0.02	−0.02	0.00	0.05	0.07	0.04
R^2	0.01	0.01	0.01	0.03	0.01	0.02	0.00	0.00	0.00	0.04	0.12	0.10
	Real Effective Exchange Rate (+ = appreciation)						Real Effective Exchange Rate (+ = appreciation)					
	0.00	0.01	0.03	0.12	0.18	**0.51**	0.02	0.04	0.07	0.14	0.36	**0.46**
R^2	0.00	0.00	0.00	0.02	0.06	0.24	0.00	0.01	0.01	0.02	0.10	0.15

Source: IMF staff calculations.

Note: For each variable, the table shows (1) the coefficient δ of regressions of the form: $Y_{t+k} - Y_t = c + \delta(\hat{\beta} Y_{t-1}) + e_t$, where the left-hand side denotes the change in the variable between $t + k$ and t, and the independent variable is the deviation of net exports and net foreign assets from their long-run relationship (cointegration residual) and (2) the R^2 of the regression. Bold values denote coefficients that are significant at a 5 percent level (based on Newey-West robust standard errors).

the coefficients have the expected negative sign and are statistically significant only for the United States. Finally, deviations from trend seem to have some predictive power for real exchange rates only for medium and long horizons, when coefficients are generally found to be statistically significant (the United States again being the exception). This is consistent with the adjustment taking place more through long-term (exchange-rate-related) realignments of trade flows, rather than through short-term valuation changes in the stock of foreign assets.

Data

Exports and imports: Annual and quarterly data from the OECD (*Economic Outlook*).

Net foreign assets: Annual data from Lane and Milesi-Ferretti (2005b). Quarterly data on the stocks of foreign assets and liabilities were obtained by interpolating the Lane and

Milesi-Ferretti annual data, using the quarterly path of capital inflows and outflows (from the IMF's *International Financial Statistics*).

Quarterly returns on foreign assets and liabilities: Following the methodology adopted by Gourinchas and Rey (2004) to estimate the returns on foreign assets and liabilities for the United States, quarterly rates of return of foreign assets and liabilities were constructed for the G-7 countries as weighted averages of the returns on four different subcategories of the financial accounts (equity, FDI, debt, and other assets and liabilities), with weights given by their relative shares in the total stock of assets and liabilities.

Returns were estimated as follows. For equity assets, returns were calculated as the weighted average of quarterly (dollar) returns on the Morgan Stanley Capital International (MSCI) indexes for the major countries of nonresident issuers, with weights from the geographical allocation of foreign equity assets as reported in the IMF's 2001 *Coordinated Portfolio Investment Survey* (CPIS). For FDI assets, the same returns were used but the weights reflected the geographical allocation of FDI assets, as reported by the OECD's *International Direct Investment* database. For debt assets, the returns were calculated as a weighted average of the (dollar) long-term interest rates on government bonds (from the OECD's *Economic Outlook*), with weights derived from the geographical allocation of long-term debt assets reported in the 2001 CPIS. For other assets, the returns were calculated as a weighted average of the (dollar) short-term interest rates (from the OECD's, *Economic Outlook*), with weights from the 2001 CPIS foreign geographical allocation of short-term debt assets. For each country, the returns on equity and FDI liabilities were estimated as the return on their MSCI indexes (in U.S. dollars), while returns on debt and other liabilities were estimated as the national long- and short-term interest rates (in U.S. dollars). Conversion into U.S. dollars was obtained using end-of-period exchange rates from the OECD's *Main Economic Indicators*. Nominal returns were then deflated using the U.S. GDP deflators, and converted into local currencies using bilateral real exchange rates against the U.S. dollar.

Appendix 3.3. Details on Rigidities and Monetary Policy Rule Used in the GEM Simulation

The author of this appendix is Nicoletta Batini.

Preliminary Estimates of Nominal and Real Rigidities

To examine whether nominal and real rigidities have changed in the past three decades, IMF staff estimated structural equations for inflation using data from G-7 countries. These equations, known in the literature as New Keynesian Phillips Curves (NKPC) (see Sbordone, 2005), describe the evolution of aggregate inflation with respect to marginal costs faced by firms in the production of goods and services, and capture the fact that prices are set in a forward-looking way. The extent of nominal and real rigidities can be gauged by looking at reduced-form parameter estimates that, in turn, depend nonlinearly on structural parameters in the equations.

For the standard specification of the NKPC, it is assumed that steady-state inflation is zero, and that the world is "hybrid" in the sense that a fraction of firms are forward-looking and set prices in a staggered fashion as in Calvo (1983) while the rest are myopic and set their prices equal to the average price in the previous period. The NKPC can then be written as follows (variables are expressed in log deviation from their steady-state values):

$$\pi_t = \lambda mc_t + \gamma_f E_t\{\pi_{t+1}\} + \gamma_b\pi_{t-1}, \qquad (1)$$

where π_t is inflation, mc_t is the real marginal cost, and E_t is the expectational operator based on information at time t. The marginal cost is unobservable and, thus, it is usually proxied by an appropriate measure of the unit labor cost. The parameters λ, γ_f, and γ_b are functions of the probability faced by firms of resetting their

Table 3.12. Estimates of Nominal and Real Rigidities in an Earlier and a Later Sample

	Degree of Nominal Rigidity (D)		Degree of Real Rigidity (λ)	
	Earlier sample	Later sample	Earlier sample	Later sample
Canada	9.92	3.12	0.25	0.09
France	2.31	12.50	0.01	0.00
Germany	3.12	3.84	0.25	0.18
Italy	1.47	11.00	0.45	0.06
Japan	10.45	9.00	0.009	0.009
United Kingdom	2.81	2.17	0.23	0.00
United States	3.41	2.86	0.16	0.00

Source: IMF staff calculations.

prices in each period $(1 - \theta)$, the fraction of myopic firms (ω), and the discount rate (β).

The degree of nominal rigidity, or price inertia, is typically captured by $D = (1/1 - \theta)(1/1 - \omega)$, which measures the average duration of price contracts when a fraction of firms are myopic (see Galí, Gertler, and López-Salido, 2001). The degree of real rigidity is usually captured by λ, where $\lambda \equiv (1 - \omega)(1 - \theta)(1 - \beta\theta)\phi^{-1}$, and where, in turn, $\phi \equiv \theta + \omega[1 - \theta(1 - \beta)]$ (see Coenen and Levin, 2004).

Table 3.12 reports values of D and λ from preliminary results obtained by estimating equation (1) for a group of G-7 countries with the General Method of Moments, using quarterly data over two different samples: an earlier sample covering the 1970s up to the mid-1980s, and a later sample covering the second half of the 1980s to the present.[52] Results indicate that real rigidities seem to have diminished over time, while the direction of nominal rigidities has been more mixed, especially in the case of European countries, in line with findings in Batini (2002) and Khan (2004).

Monetary Policy Rule Used in the Simulations

The simulations shown in the chapter use the same specification for the monetary policy rule for the interest rate as that of a policy rule esti-

mated by Orphanides (2003) for the United States. The properties of inflation-forecast-based rules like this, with and without output terms, are discussed in Batini and Haldane (1999). The exact specification used in the chapter is as follows:

$$i_t = \theta_0 + \theta_i i_{t-1} + \theta_\pi i^a_{t+3} + \theta_{\Delta y}\Delta^\alpha y_{t+3} + \theta_y y_{t-1}, \quad (2)$$

where i_t is the short-term nominal interest rate; $\pi^a_{t+3} = [(p_{t+3} - p_{t+1}) - \pi^T_t$ is the one-year-ahead forecast of inflation starting at $t - 1$; $y_{t-1} = q_{t-1} - q^*_{t-1}$ is the output gap in period $t - 1$; and $\Delta^\alpha y_{t+3} = y_{t+3} - y_{t+1} = \Delta^\alpha q_{t+3} - \Delta^\alpha q^*_{t+3}$ is the one-year-ahead growth forecast relative to potential growth. In the model simulations, price inflation used in the rule is taken to be consumer price inflation.

π^T_t is the annual inflation target. This is set to 2½ percent for the United States and 2 percent for Japan and the euro area and the rest of the world. In the simulation with adverse global financial market conditions (Figure 3.13), emerging Asia is assumed to float its currency and move to a rule like (2), with an inflation target that is gradually reduced to 2½ percent by 2007. Details of the remaining parameters used in the rule in the two vintage model calibrations of GEM are given in Table 3.8 in the main text.

Decomposition of Differences in Two GEM Calibrations

Table 3.13 shows a breakdown of the contribution by various groups of parameters to the differences in the response paths of output growth, inflation and interest rates, and real exchange rates at various horizons between the less globalized and more globalized environment. The table illustrates that while the economic size of various blocs, a more equal distribution of trade, and differences in monetary policy are key in explaining differences across simulations between the "low integration" and the "high integration" worlds, greater flexibility and greater international competition seem to play a

---

[52]Exact sample periods are slightly different for each country to maximize individual fits.

Table 3.13. Decomposition of Differences in Response Paths by Parameter Groups
(Differences in percentage points)

	Total	Trade	Markups	Flexibility Contracting[1]	Monetary Policies	Cross Effects
Decomposition for emerging Asia						
First two years						
Output growth	−2.11	−2.46	0.02	−0.26	0.28	0.30
Year-on-year inflation	0.16	−0.74	−0.03	−0.30	1.15	0.08
Real short-term interest rate	−0.44	0.92	0.24	1.28	−2.49	−0.39
Real effective exchange rate	0.82	0.82	0.06	0.39	−0.13	−0.32
First five years						
Output growth	−1.46	−1.56	0.01	−0.00	0.01	0.09
Year-on-year inflation	−0.74	−1.34	−0.05	−0.06	0.70	0.02
Real short-term interest rate	1.85	2.97	0.19	0.31	−1.58	−0.05
Real effective exchange rate	2.72	3.27	0.19	0.31	−0.36	−0.68
Long run						
Output growth	−0.02	−0.03	−0.00	0.02	0.00	−0.01
Year-on-year inflation	−0.01	−0.01	0.00	0.01	0.00	−0.00
Real short-term interest rate	−0.05	−0.03	−0.00	−0.01	−0.01	0.01
Real effective exchange rate	6.04	7.79	0.69	−0.21	−1.12	−1.12
Decomposition for Japan/euro area						
First two years						
Output growth	0.07	0.06	−0.01	−0.00	0.05	−0.03
Year-on-year inflation	−0.09	−0.08	−0.01	0.01	0.01	−0.02
Real short-term interest rate	0.20	0.18	0.02	−0.01	−0.06	0.06
Real effective exchange rate	1.44	1.56	−0.03	−0.13	−0.09	0.13
First five years						
Output growth	0.03	0.05	−0.01	−0.02	0.00	0.00
Year-on-year inflation	−0.09	−0.08	−0.00	0.01	−0.01	−0.00
Real short-term interest rate	0.20	0.21	0.01	−0.04	0.01	0.02
Real effective exchange rate	2.31	2.29	−0.06	−0.07	−0.05	0.20
Long run						
Output growth	−0.00	−0.00	0.00	0.00	0.00	−0.00
Year-on-year inflation	−0.00	−0.00	−0.00	−0.00	0.00	−0.00
Real short-term interest rate	−0.02	−0.01	0.00	−0.00	−0.01	0.00
Real effective exchange rate	3.55	3.04	−0.12	0.08	0.30	0.25
Decomposition for the United States						
First two years						
Output growth	0.66	0.11	0.00	0.02	0.50	0.02
Year-on-year inflation	0.97	0.11	−0.01	0.01	1.01	−0.15
Real short-term interest rate	−2.93	−0.33	0.00	0.05	−3.04	0.39
Real effective exchange rate	−0.57	−0.55	−0.03	−0.12	0.02	0.12
First five years						
Output growth	0.18	0.09	0.01	0.03	0.08	−0.02
Year-on-year inflation	0.54	0.04	−0.00	−0.04	0.68	−0.13
Real short-term interest rate	−1.69	−0.14	0.01	0.13	−2.04	0.35
Real effective exchange rate	−2.25	−1.90	−0.05	−0.14	−0.26	0.10
Long run						
Output growth	0.01	0.01	−0.00	0.00	0.00	−0.00
Year-on-year inflation	0.00	0.00	0.00	0.00	−0.00	−0.00
Real short-term interest rate	−0.12	−0.11	−0.00	−0.00	−0.00	0.00
Real effective exchange rate	−4.59	−2.92	−0.20	−0.17	−1.16	−0.14

Source: IMF staff calculations.
Note: The table shows the approximate differences between response paths of output growth, inflation, real interest rates, and real exchange rates at three time horizons. The values shown in the first column reflect the total difference between the response paths in the high integration version (2003 calibration) and response paths in the low integration version (1984 calibration). Values in the second to the fifth columns show differences attributable to changes in each parameter group for all four blocks (holding all other parameters constant).
[1]Difference in average contract length.

minor role. This finding reflects two facts: first, the calibrations allow for similar gains in flexibility and competition in all blocs, dampening the relative effect of these changes in parameters across the versions of the model; and second, empirical evidence suggests that in fact mark-ups and rigidities differ only marginally across the two globalization environments (see also Table 3.8 in the main text).

References

Adler, Michael, and Bernard Dumas, 1983, "International Portfolio Choice and Corporation Finance: A Synthesis," *Journal of Finance*, Vol. 38, No. 3, pp. 925–84.

Angeloni, Ignazio, and others, 2004, "Inflation Persistence in the Euro Area," presented at the conference on Inflation Persistence in the Euro Area, Frankfurt, December 10–11. Available via the Internet: http://www.ecb.int/events/conferences/html/inflationpersistence.en.html.

Bailliu, Jeannine, and Eiji Fujii, 2004, "Exchange-Rate Pass-Through and the Inflation Environment in Industrialized Countries: An Empirical Investigation," Bank of Canada Working Paper No. 2004–21 (Ottawa: Bank of Canada).

Barba Navaretti, Giorgio, and Anthony J. Venables, 2004, *Multinational Firms in the World Economy* (Princeton, New Jersey: Princeton University Press).

Barnea, Ami, and Joseph Djivre, 2004, "Changes in Monetary and Exchange Rate Policies and the Transmission Mechanism in Israel, 1989.IV–2002.I," Bank of Israel Discussion Paper No. 2004.13 (Jerusalem: Bank of Israel).

Batini, Nicoletta, 2002, "Euro Area Inflation Persistence," ECB Working Paper No. 201 (Frankfurt: European Central Bank).

———, and Andrew G. Haldane, 1999, "Forward-Looking Rules for Monetary Policy," in *Monetary Policy Rules*, ed. by J.B. Taylor (Chicago, Illinois: University of Chicago Press).

Batini, Nicoletta, Brian Jackson, and Stephen Nickell, 2002, "The Pricing Behaviour of UK Firms," Bank of England External MPC Unit Discussion Paper No. 9 (London: Bank of England).

Batini, Nicoletta, and Edward Nelson, 2000, "When the Bubble Bursts: Monetary Policy Rules and Exchange Rate Market Behavior" (unpublished;

Washington and St. Louis, Missouri: IMF and Federal Reserve Bank of St. Louis).

Batini, Nicoletta, and Kenny Turnbull, 2002, "A Dynamic Monetary Condition Index for the UK," *Journal of Policy Modeling*, Vol. 24 (June), pp. 257–81.

Baxter, Marianne, and Urban J. Jermann, 1997, "The International Diversification Puzzle Is Worse Than You Think," *American Economic Review*, Vol. 87 (March), pp. 70–80.

———, and Robert G. King, 1998, "Nontraded Goods, Nontraded Factors, and International Non-diversification," *Journal of International Economics*, Vol. 44 (April), pp. 211–29.

Bayoumi, Tamim, 2004, *GEM: A New International Macroeconomic Model*, IMF Occasional Paper No. 239 (Washington: International Monetary Fund).

———, and others, 2004, "Exchange Rate Regimes, International Linkages, and the Macroeconomic Performance of the New Member States," paper presented at the IMF Jacques Polak Annual Research Conference, November 4–5 (Washington: International Monetary Fund).

Bertaut, Carol C., and Linda S. Kole, 2004, "What Makes Investors Over or Underweight? Explaining International Appetites for Foreign Equities," FRB International Finance Discussion Paper No. 819 (Washington: Board of Governors of the Federal Reserve System).

Boivin, Jean, and Mark Giannoni, 2002, "Has Monetary Policy Become Less Powerful?" Federal Reserve Bank of New York Staff Report No. 144 (New York: Federal Reserve Bank of New York). Available via the Internet: http://www.newyorkfed.org/research/staff reports/sr144.html.

———, 2003, "Has Monetary Policy Become More Effective?" NBER Working Paper No. 9459 (Cambridge, Massachusetts: National Bureau of Economic Research).

Bordo, Michael D., 1984, "The Gold Standard: The Traditional Approach," in *A Retrospective on the Classical Gold-Standard, 1821–1931*, ed. by Michael D. Bordo and Anna J. Schwartz (Chicago, Illinois: University of Chicago Press).

———, and Barry Eichengreen, 1999, "Is Our International Economic Environment Unusually Crisis Prone?" in *International Financial System Conference Proceedings: Capital Flows and the Reserve Bank of Australia*, ed. by David Gruen and Luke Gower (Sydney: Reserve Bank of Australia).

———, and Douglas A. Irwin, 1999, "Is Globalization Today Really Different from Globalization a

Hundred Years Ago? in *Brookings Trade Forum,* ed. by Susan Collins and Robert Lawrence (Washington: Brookings Institution Press).

Bordo, Michael D., Barry Eichengreen, and Jongwoo Kim, 1998, "Was There Really an Earlier Period of International Financial Integration Comparable to Today?" in *Conference Proceedings: The Implications of the Globalization of World Financial Markets* (Seoul, South Korea: Bank of Korea), pp. 27–75.

Bordo, Michael D., and Hugh Rockoff, 1996, "The Gold Standard as a 'Good Housekeeping Seal of Approval,'" *Journal of Economic History,* Vol. 56 (June), pp. 389–428.

Bordo, Michael, and others, 2001, "Is the Crisis Problem Growing More Severe?" *Economic Policy,* Vol. 16 (April), pp. 51–82.

Branson, William H., and Dale W. Henderson, 1984, "The Specification and Influence of Asset Markets," in *Handbook of International Economics,* Vol. 2, ed. by Ronald W. Jones and Peter B. Kenen (Amsterdam: North-Holland), pp. 749–805.

Brash, Donald T., 2001, "Central Banks: What They Can and Cannot Do," speech to the Trans-Tasman Business Circle, Sydney, Australia, March.

Bravo-Ortega, Claudio, and Julian di Giovanni, 2005, "Trade Costs and Real Exchange Rate Volatility: The Role of Ricardian Comparative Advantage," IMF Working Paper 05/5 (Washington: International Monetary Fund).

Burstein, Ariel, Christopher J. Kurz, and Linda Tesar, 2004, "Trade, Production Sharing, and the International Transmission of Business Cycles" (unpublished; New York: Federal Reserve Bank of New York).

Busse, Matthias, 2003, "Tariffs, Transport Costs, and the WTO Doha Round: The Case of Developing Countries," *Journal of International Law and Trade Policy,* Vol. 4, No. 1, pp. 15–31.

Calvo, Guillermo, 1983, "Staggered Prices in a Utility-Maximizing Framework," *Journal of Monetary Economics,* Vol. 12 (September), pp. 383–98.

———, and Carmen Reinhart, 2002, "Fear of Floating," *Quarterly Journal of Economics,* Vol. 117 (May), pp. 379–408.

Campa, José Manuel, and Linda Goldberg, 2002, "Exchange Rate Pass-Through into Import Prices," NBER Working Paper No. 8934 (Cambridge, Massachusetts: National Bureau of Economic Research).

Chen, Hogan, and Kei-Mu Yi, 2003, "Vertical Specialization and Trends in U.S. International Trade" (unpublished).

Choudhri, Ehsan U., and Dalia S. Hakura, 2001, "Exchange Rate Pass-Through to Domestic Prices: Does the Inflationary Environment Matter?" IMF Working Paper 01/194 (Washington: International Monetary Fund).

Coenen, Günther, and Andrew Levin, 2004, "Identifying the Influences of Nominal and Real Rigidities in Aggregate Price-Setting Behavior," ECB Working Paper No. 418 (Frankfurt: European Central Bank).

Cooper, Richard N., 2001, "Is the U.S. Current Account Deficit Sustainable? Will It Be Sustained?" *Brookings Papers on Economic Activity: 1,* Brookings Institution, pp. 217–26.

———, 2004, "How Big Is the Hole in the Economy?" *Financial Times,* November 1, p. 15.

Corsetti, Giancarlo, and Panagiotis Konstantinou, 2004, "Current Account Theory and the Dynamics of U.S. Net Foreign Liabilities" (unpublished; Rome: University of Rome).

Devereux, Michael B., Charles Engel, and Peter E. Storgaard, 2004, "Endogenous Exchange Rate Pass-Through When Nominal Prices Are Set in Advance," *Journal of International Economics,* Vol. 63 (June), pp. 263–91.

Devereux, Michael B., and James Yetman, 2002, "Menu Costs and the Long-Run Output-Inflation Trade-Off," *Economics Letters,* Vol. 76 (June), pp. 95–100.

Edey, Malcolm, and Ketil Hviding, 1995, "An Assessment of Financial Reform in OECD Countries," Economics Department Working Paper No. 154 (Paris: Organization for Economic Cooperation and Development).

Edison, Hali, and others, 2002, "International Financial Integration and Economic Growth," *Journal of International Money and Finance,* Vol. 21 (November), pp. 749–76.

Engel, Charles, and Akito Matsumoto, 2004, "Home Bias in Equities Under New Open Economy Macroeconomics," presented at the Joint ECB/IMF Workshop, Washington, November.

Faruqee, Hamid, Shujing Li, and Isabel K. Yan, 2004, "The Determinants of International Portfolio Holdings and Home Bias," IMF Working Paper 04/34 (Washington: International Monetary Fund).

Fischer, Stanley, 1997, "Capital Account Liberalization and the Role of the IMF," speech made at the IMF Annual Meetings seminar on "Asia and the IMF," September 19, 1997. Available via the Internet:

http://www.imf.org/external/np/speeches/1997/091997.htm.

———, 2001, "Exchange Rate Regimes: Is the Bipolar View Correct?" *Journal of Economic Perspectives,* Vol. 15 (Spring), pp. 3–24.

French, Kenneth, R., and James M. Poterba, 1991, "Investor Diversification and International Equity Markets," *American Economic Review,* Vol. 81, No. 2, pp. 222–26.

Gagnon, Joseph E., and Jane Ihrig, 2004, "Monetary Policy and Exchange Rate Pass-Through," *International Journal of Finance and Economics,* Vol. 9 (October), pp. 315–38.

Galí, Jordi, Mark Gertler, and David López-Salido, 2001, "European Inflation Dynamics," *European Economic Review,* Vol. 45, No. 7, pp. 1237–70.

Ghironi, Fabio, Talan B. İşan, and Alessandro Rebucci, 2005, "Net Foreign Asset Positions and Consumption Dynamics in the International Economy," IMF Working Paper (Washington: International Monetary Fund, forthcoming).

Gonzalo, Jesús, and Clive W.J. Granger, 1995, Estimation of Common Long-Memory Components in Cointegrated Systems," *Journal of Business and Economic Statistics,* Vol. 13, No. 1, pp. 27–35.

Gonzalo, Jesús, and Serena Ng, 2001, "A Systematic Framework for Analyzing the Dynamic Effects of Permanent and Transitory Shocks," *Journal of Economic Dynamics and Control,* Vol. 25, No. 10, pp. 1527–46.

Gourinchas, Pierre-Olivier, and Hélène Rey, 2004, "International Financial Adjustment" (unpublished; Princeton, New Jersey: Princeton University).

Greenspan, Alan, 2004, "Globalization and Innovation," remarks at the Conference on Bank Structure and Competition, sponsored by the Federal Reserve Bank of Chicago, Chicago, Illinois, May 6.

Hanson, Gordon H., Raymond J. Mataloni, and Matthew J. Slaughter, 2003, "Vertical Production Networks in Multinational Firms," NBER Working Paper No. 9723 (Cambridge, Massachusetts: National Bureau of Economic Research).

Harvey, Campbell R., 1991, "The World Price of Covariance Risk," *Journal of Finance,* Vol. 46 (March), pp. 111–57.

Heathcote, Jonathan, and Fabrizio Perri, 2004, "Financial Globalization and Real Regionalization," *Journal of Economic Theory,* Vol. 119 (November), pp. 207–43.

Huizinga, Harry, and Dantao Zhu, 2004, "Domestic and International Finance: How Do They Affect Consumption Smoothing?" CEPR Discussion Paper No. 4677 (London: Centre for Economic Policy Research).

Hunt, Benjamin, and Alessandro Rebucci, 2003, "The U.S. Dollar and the Trade Deficit: What Accounts for the Late 1990s?" IMF Working Paper 03/194 (Washington: International Monetary Fund).

Imbs, Jean, 2004, "The Real Effects of Financial Integration," CEPR Discussion Paper No. 4335 (London: Centre for Economic Policy Research).

International Monetary Fund, 1993, *Balance of Payments Statistics Manual, Fifth Edition* (Washington).

Khan, Hashmat, 2004, "Price-Setting Behaviour, Competition, and Mark-Up Shocks in the New Keynesian Model," Bank of England Working Paper No. 240 (London: Bank of England).

Khan, Mohsin S., and Abdelhak S. Senhadji, 2000, "Threshold Effects in the Relationship Between Inflation and Growth," IMF Working Paper 00/110 (Washington: International Monetary Fund).

King, Robert G., and others, 1991, "Stochastic Trends and Economic Fluctuations," *American Economic Review,* Vol. 81, No. 4, pp. 819–40.

Lane, Philip, R., and Gian Maria Milesi-Ferretti, 2001, "The External Wealth of Nations: Measures of Foreign Assets and Liabilities for Industrial and Developing Countries," *Journal of International Economics,* Vol. 55, No. 2, pp. 263–94.

———, 2002a, "External Wealth, the Trade Balance, and the Real Exchange Rate," *European Economic Review,* Vol. 46 (June), pp. 1049–71.

———, 2002b, "Long-Term Capital Movements," in *NBER Macroeconomics Annual,* Vol. 16, ed. by Ben S. Bernanke and Kenneth Rogoff (Cambridge, Massachusetts: MIT Press), pp. 73–116.

———, 2003, "International Financial Integration," *IMF Staff Papers,* Vol. 50, Special Issue, pp. 82–113.

———, 2004a, "International Investment Patterns," IMF Working Paper 04/134 (Washington: International Monetary Fund).

———, 2004b, "The Transfer Problem Revisited: Net Foreign Assets and Real Exchange Rates," *Review of Economics and Statistics,* Vol. 86, No. 4, pp. 841–57.

———, 2005a, "Financial Globalization and Exchange Rates," IMF Working Paper 05/3 (Washington: International Monetary Fund).

———, 2005b, "The External Wealth of Nations Mark II: Revised and Extended Estimates of Foreign

Assets and Liabilities, 1970–2003" (unpublished; Washington: International Monetary Fund).

Laxton, Douglas, and Paolo Pesenti, 2003, "Monetary Rules for Small, Open, Emerging Economies," *Journal of Monetary Economics*, Vol. 50, No. 5, pp. 1109–46.

Lettau, Martin, and Sydney Ludvigson, 2004, "Understanding Trend and Cycle in Asset Values: Reevaluating the Wealth Effect on Consumption," *American Economic Review*, Vol. 94, No. 1, pp. 276–99.

Martins, Joaquim Oliveira, and Stefano Scarpetta, 1999, "The Levels and Cyclical Behaviour of Mark-Ups Across Countries and Market Structures," OECD Economics Department Working Paper No. 213 (Paris: Organization for Economic Cooperation and Development).

Obstfeld, Maurice, 2002, "Exchange Rates and Adjustment: Perspectives from the New Open-Economy Macroeconomics," *Bank of Japan Monetary and Economic Studies*, Vol. 20 (December).

———, 2004, "External Adjustment," NBER Working Paper No. W10843 (Cambridge, Massachusetts: National Bureau of Economic Research).

———, and Kenneth S. Rogoff, 1996, *Foundations of International Macroeconomics* (Cambridge, Massachusetts: MIT Press).

———, 2000, "Perspectives on OECD Economic Integration: Implications for U.S. Current Account Adjustment," in *Global Economic Integration: Opportunities and Challenges* (Kansas City, Missouri: Federal Reserve Bank of Kansas City).

———, 2001, "The Six Major Puzzles in International Macroeconomics: Is There a Common Cause?" in *NBER Macroeconomics Annual 2000*, Vol. 15, ed. by Ben S. Bernanke and Kenneth Rogoff (Cambridge, Massachusetts: MIT Press), pp. 338–90.

———, 2004, "The Unsustainable US Current Account Position Revisited," NBER Working Paper No. 10869 (Cambridge, Massachusetts: National Bureau of Economic Research).

Obstfeld, Maurice, and Alan M. Taylor, 2004, *Global Capital Markets: Integration, Crisis, and Growth* (Cambridge, Massachusetts: Cambridge University Press).

Organization for Economic Cooperation and Development, 2002, "Intra-Industry and Intra-Firm Trade and the Internationalization of Production," Economic Outlook No. 71 (Paris), pp. 159–70.

Orphanides, Athanasios, 2003, "Historical Monetary Analysis and the Taylor Rule," *Journal of Monetary Economics*, Vol. 50, No. 5, pp. 983–1022.

———, 2004, "Monetary Policy Rules, Macroeconomic Stability, and Inflation: A View from the Trenches," *Journal of Money, Credit and Banking*, Vol. 36 (May), pp. 151–75.

Pagan, Adrian, 2003, "Report on Modelling and Forecasting at the Bank of England" (London: Bank of England).

Panigirtzoglou, Nikolaos, 2004, "Implied Foreign Exchange Risk Premia," *European Financial Management*, Vol. 10 (June), pp. 321–38.

Pesaran, M. Hashem, and Ron Smith, 1995, "Estimating Long-Run Relationships from Dynamic Heterogeneous Panels," *Journal of Econometrics*, Vol. 68, No. 1, pp. 79–113.

Prasad, Eswar S., and others, 2003, *Effects on Financial Globalization on Developing Countries: Some Empirical Evidence*, IMF Occasional Paper No. 220 (Washington: International Monetary Fund).

Rebucci, Alessandro, 2003, "On the Heterogeneity Bias of Pooled Estimators in Stationary VAR Specifications," IMF Working Paper 03/73 (Washington: International Monetary Fund).

Rodrik, Dani, 2001, "The Developing Countries' Hazardous Obsession with Global Integration," Kennedy School of Government, Harvard University (Cambridge, Massachusetts: Harvard University).

Rogoff, Kenneth, 2003, "Globalization and Global Disinflation," paper prepared for the Federal Reserve Bank of Kansas City conference on Monetary Policy and Uncertainty: Adapting to a Changing Economy, Jackson Hole, Wyoming, August.

Ruhl, Kim J., 2003, "Solving the Elasticity Puzzle in International Economics" (unpublished; Minneapolis, Minnesota: University of Minnesota).

Sargent, Thomas, 1999, *The Conquest of American Inflation* (Princeton: New Jersey: Princeton University Press).

Sbordone, Argia, 2005, "Do Expected Marginal Costs Drive Inflation Dynamics?" *Journal of Monetary Economics* (forthcoming).

Sinn, Stefan, 1990, "Net External Asset Positions of 145 Countries," Kieler Studien No. 224, Institut für Weltwirtschaft an der Universität Kiel (Tübingen, Germany: J.C.B. Mohr).

Solnik, Bruno, 1974, "Why Not Diversify Internationally Rather Than Domestically?" *Financial Analyst Journal*, Vol. 30 (July–August), pp. 48–54.

Stevens, Glenn, 2004, "Recent Issues for the Conduct of Monetary Policy," speech by the Reserve Bank of Australia Deputy Governor, February 17.

Stiglitz, Joseph, 2000, "Capital Account Liberalization, Economic Growth, and Instability," *World Development*, Vol. 28, No. 5, pp. 1075–86.

Swiss National Bank, 2003, "Study Center Gerzensee Conference on Monetary Policy Under Incomplete Information (Gerzensee, Switzerland, October 12, 2000)," *Journal of Monetary Economics*, Vol. 50 (April), pp. 497–720.

Taylor, John B., 2000, "Low Inflation, Pass-Through, and the Pricing Power of Firms," *European Economic Review* (The Netherlands), Vol. 44 (June), pp. 1389–408.

Tesar, Linda L., 1993, "International Risk Sharing and Non-Traded Goods," *Journal of International Economics*, Vol. 35 (August), pp. 69–89.

———, and Ingrid M. Werner, 1995, "Home Bias and High Turnover," *Journal of International Money and Finance*, Vol. 14 (August), pp. 467–92.

Tille, Cedric, 2003, "The Impact of Exchange Rate Movements on U.S. Foreign Debt," *Federal Reserve Bank of New York, Current Issues in Economics and Finance*, Vol. 9 (January) pp. 1–7.

———, 2004, "Financial Integration and the Wealth Effect of Exchange Rate Fluctuations" (unpublished; New York: Federal Reserve Bank of New York).

Tytell, Irina, and Shang-Jin Wei, 2004, "Does Financial Globalization Induce Better Macroeconomic Policies?" paper presented at the Fifth Annual IMF Research Conference, Washington, November 4.

Warne, Anders, 1993, "A Common Trends Model: Identification, Estimation, and Inference," International Economic Studies Paper No. 555 (Stockholm: University of Stockholm, Institute for International Economic Studies).

Williamson, John, and Molly Mahar, 1998, "A Survey of Financial Liberalization," Essays in International Finance No. 211 (Princeton, New Jersey: Princeton University, Department of Economics, International Economics Section).

Yi, Kei-Mu, 2003, "Can Vertical Specialization Explain the Growth of World Trade?" *Journal of Political Economy*, Vol. 111, No. 1, pp. 52–102.

WILL THE OIL MARKET CONTINUE TO BE TIGHT?

During most of the 1990s, real crude oil prices (expressed in 2003 dollars) fluctuated about $20 a barrel. Moreover, the oil market experienced periods of high volatility only during the Middle East conflict in 1990–91 and during the Asian currency crisis in 1997–98. Crude oil prices started edging up with the economic recovery and production cuts at the end of the decade, but the upward price pressures became pronounced only during 2003–04. Synchronized global growth, high oil demand (especially from China), and a series of supply disruptions eroded spare capacity of producers and pushed the annual real average price of oil close to $40 a barrel in 2004 (Figure 4.1). Average oil prices increased further to about $50 a barrel in March 2005.

Should policymakers be concerned about developments in the oil market? While the percentage increase in the real oil price has been much smaller than during the 1970s,[1] Chapter I of this *World Economic Outlook* suggests that the recent oil price increases may still have a non-negligible impact on the world economy—GDP growth is expected to slow by 0.7–0.8 percentage points in 2005–06 relative to 2004, with oil prices being one of the contributing factors. The impact could be yet stronger in the developing countries and emerging markets that face external financial constraints. IMF staff analysis suggests that the relationship between oil price and output is nonlinear: particularly high oil prices may trigger a rapid fall in consumer and business confidence with a strong negative impact

Figure 4.1. Oil Market as a Source of Shocks
(1970–2004)

Periods of low spare capacity tend to be associated with rising and volatile prices.

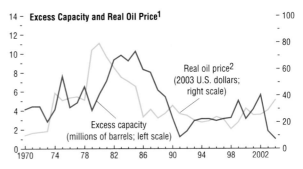

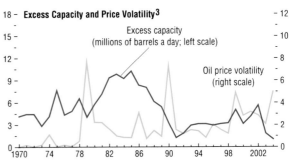

Sources: International Energy Agency; U.S. Department of Energy; and IMF staff calculations.
[1]Excess capacity is defined as spare capacity of OPEC producers in millions of barrels a day.
[2]Simple average of West Texas Intermediate, Brent, and Dubai oil prices.
[3]Volatility is defined as the standard deviation of monthly real oil prices.

Note: The main author of this chapter is Martin Sommer, with support from Dermot Gately. Paul Atang provided research assistance.

[1]The real average oil price rose by 74 percent between June 2003 and March 2005, compared with the 185 percent increase during 1974 and the 158 percent increase between June 1978 and November 1979.

Figure 4.2. Oil Consumption
(1971–2004)

Oil consumption declined in response to price shocks of the 1970s but has since grown steadily. The United States, European Union, and Japan account for half of total demand. Almost half of oil is used in transport.

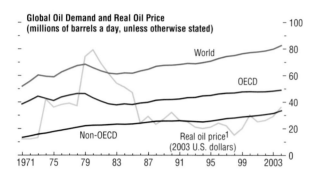

Global Oil Demand and Real Oil Price
(millions of barrels a day, unless otherwise stated)

Consumption by Countries and Regions, 2004

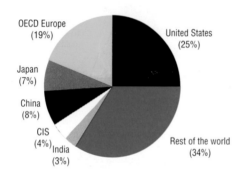

OECD Europe (19%)
Japan (7%)
China (8%)
CIS (4%)
India (3%)
United States (25%)
Rest of the world (34%)

Consumption by Products, 2002

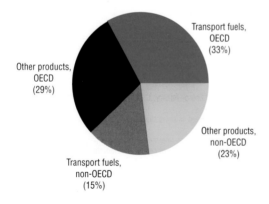

Transport fuels, OECD (33%)
Other products, OECD (29%)
Other products, non-OECD (23%)
Transport fuels, non-OECD (15%)

Sources: International Energy Agency; and IMF staff calculations.
[1]Simple average of West Texas Intermediate, Brent, and Dubai oil prices.

on economic activity. Besides generating price volatility (see Box 4.1), the current lack of spare production capacity also makes oil-importing economies, especially in the non-OECD region, vulnerable to supply disruptions.

Recent developments in the oil market are analyzed in detail in Appendix 1.1 of this *World Economic Outlook* and in the April 2005 edition of the IMF's *Global Financial Stability Report.* The purpose of this chapter is to assess longer-run oil market prospects, focusing on the following questions.

- What is the medium- and long-term outlook for the oil market, and what are the relevant risk factors on the demand and supply sides?
- Will there be enough spare production capacity going forward to satisfy demand in periods of unexpectedly strong growth or supply disruptions?
- In the long run, will the level of oil prices that has been typical until recently ($20–30 a barrel) be sufficient to provide the main producers with incentives to increase capacity and meet growing demand?
- How can policymakers reduce the risks arising from tight market conditions? How much insurance should they take out and in what form?

Basic Stylized Facts

Oil Demand

The main consumers of oil continue to be the advanced economies; the United States, OECD Europe, and Japan together consume about half of annual oil output (Figure 4.2). But consumption in the emerging market and developing countries has been increasing at a faster pace, as these economies grow rapidly and their use of energy including oil in the transport, industry, and residential sector expands. China and India contributed 35 percent to incremental oil consumption between 1990 and 2003, even though the two countries produced only 15 percent of world output over the period. By sectors, demand for transport fuels is the most important,

BASIC STYLIZED FACTS

Box 4.1. Should Countries Worry About Oil Price Fluctuations?

Despite a consistent fall in global oil intensity, crude oil remains an important commodity and events in the oil market continue to play a significant role in shaping global economic and political developments. Oil accounted for 8 percent of global trade in goods and services and about 2.5 percent of world activity in 2004—higher than any other commodity, although well below 1980 levels. Moreover, given the distribution of oil reserves and the structure of supply and demand, geopolitical factors play an important role in the oil market.

Over the past 30 years, oil prices have moved in the range of US$8–96 (in constant 2003 dollars), and have lacked any meaningful trend (see the first figure). After a period of sharp movements in the 1970s and the first half of the 1980s, prices were more stable through 1997—except for the spike during the first Middle East crisis in 1990–91. Since that time, however, volatility has increased markedly, reflecting a combination of declining excess capacity, which is held almost entirely in OPEC countries; lower private stocks; changes in OPEC production levels, including disruptions to Iraq's production; and geopolitical uncertainties. Volatility may well have been exacerbated by persistently low oil prices between the late 1980s and the late 1990s, which encouraged a relatively cautious approach to investment.

How much of a concern is oil price volatility?[1] If it were possible to clearly distinguish a temporary oil shock from a permanent one, and for all economic agents to borrow/lend as necessary to smooth the effects, the economic impact of price volatility should be rather limited. In practice, however, neither of these conditions hold. Of the 2.5 percent volatility (defined as the standard deviation) of the median of GDP growth across the globe over the past 35 years, rough estimates suggest that volatility in oil prices has

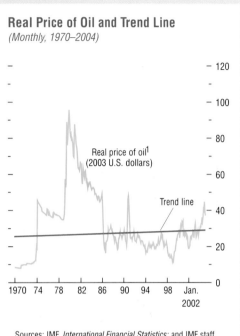

Real Price of Oil and Trend Line
(Monthly, 1970–2004)

Real price of oil[1]
(2003 U.S. dollars)

Trend line

Sources: IMF, *International Financial Statistics;* and IMF staff calculations.
[1]Simple average of West Texas Intermediate, Brent, and Dubai oil prices.

contributed about 0.3 percentage point. Based on the results in the literature on the impact of volatility on growth[2] reducing such volatility by, say, 50 percent could increase global GDP, on average, by about 0.03 percentage point or $12 billion a year. The impact of volatility is, of course, likely to vary significantly across countries.

- Industrial countries are likely to be best placed to manage oil price volatility, aided by credible monetary policy frameworks—reducing the need for an interest rate response to higher oil prices; well-developed domestic financial markets, allowing consumers to smooth expenditure in response to shocks; and access to international capital markets, so that the balance of payments impact can be more readily financed. Even in this relatively

Note: The authors of this box are Sam Ouliaris and Hossein Samiei.
[1]Note that the focus of this box is on the impact of volatility and price uncertainty per se, as distinguished from the impact of higher prices.

[2]See, for example, Ramey and Ramey (1995).

Box 4.1 *(concluded)*

benign environment, it remains very difficult to distinguish temporary from permanent shocks; and uncertainties related to large changes in oil prices can have significant effects on consumer confidence, and thereby on growth.[3]

- The impact is likely to be significantly greater in oil-importing developing countries, especially where policy frameworks are weak, foreign exchange reserves are low, and access to international capital markets is limited. This is particularly so for many of the poorest developing countries, where even a temporary period of higher oil prices can force a substantial adjustment in domestic consumption, at a considerable cost to growth and poverty reduction. The fiscal impact can also be significant when domestic petroleum product prices are administered.

- Price volatility can also cause significant problems for oil exporters. For many, volatility and unpredictability of prices are a potential source of fiscal vulnerability, and an impediment to sound expenditure planning—especially as government expenditures tend to increase with the price of oil (see the second figure). This is, in particular, true for countries that do not operate within a longer-term framework.

The unpredictability and volatility of oil prices also has deleterious effects on investment in the oil sector. Higher volatility and uncertainty—other things being equal—generally lead to conservative future oil price assumptions and higher required rates of return (to compensate for the higher risk), while the difficulty of distinguishing between transitory and permanent price shifts complicates the task of predicting future cash flows. Given the huge up-front capital outlays involved and the irreversible nature of investment in the oil sector, it could also

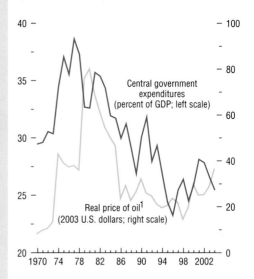

OPEC-10 Central Government Expenditures and Real Oil Price
(Annual, 1970–2004)

Sources: IMF, *International Financial Statistics;* and IMF staff calculations.
[1]Simple average of West Texas Intermediate, Brent, and Dubai oil prices.

encourage delays in decision making. The impact of price volatility on investment could generate a vicious circle whereby low or delayed investment activity could in turn add to price volatility.

How can the costs of oil price volatility be reduced? Clearly, one important way—discussed in detail in the main text—is to reduce oil price volatility itself. One key issue is maintenance of adequate spare capacity as a public good. The costs and benefits of doing so are obviously difficult to calculate. Rough calculations, however, suggest that additional spare capacity (relative to current levels) on the order of 5 mbd may reduce price volatility by over 50 percent. Based on IEA estimates of exploration and development costs, the up-front costs of such additional capacity for OPEC countries are about $20 billion, with an average estimated depreciation costs on the order of $2 billion a

[3]In the United States, for example, the loss of consumer confidence accompanying the two shocks of the 1970s was in the range of 30–40 percent, estimated to reduce GDP by 0.5–1 percentage point.

year. Given the benefits of lower volatility for world activity—as noted above—the world as a whole can clearly benefit from higher spare capacity. Devising mechanisms that would allow the potential benefits of lower volatility to finance the cost of creating spare capacity is, however, not an easy task. There is a role for enhanced consumer-producer dialogue in this regard, although, as noted above, oil producers on their own also have some incentive to increase price stability.

Beyond these steps, efforts could focus on mitigating the impact of volatility. First, given the difficulties of distinguishing temporary from permanent shocks, greater transparency in oil markets and enhanced dialogue between producers and consumers will allow markets to assess developments in fundamentals more clearly (see Box 4.2); this also underscores the importance of allowing changes in world prices to flow through to domestic prices. Second, both importers and exporters can reduce price risks by actively engaging in hedging markets. Finally, oil price shocks—like other shocks—are more easily managed in countries with credible domestic policy frameworks.

accounting for 48 percent of oil products consumption in 2002.

As is apparent from Figure 4.2, demand for oil has grown steadily in the past, only marginally reacting to year-on-year price fluctuations. However, oil consumption responded very strongly to the oil price hikes of the 1970s, especially in the advanced countries that subsequently imposed high taxes on energy consumption. On average, oil intensity, or use of oil per unit of output, halved over the past 30 years in advanced countries and declined by about one-third in developing countries (Figure 4.3). The group of developing countries and emerging markets is less oil efficient than the advanced economies when output is measured at market exchange rates. But oil intensity is similar in the two groups when output is adjusted for differences in national price levels.

Oil Supply

Proven oil reserves (see Figure 4.4) are sufficient to meet world demand at current levels for over 40 years.[2] However, this figure significantly underestimates the volume of oil resources that may be eventually recoverable with improved technology or at higher oil prices. On this basis, the International Energy Agency (2004b) calculates that remaining oil resources could cover 70 years of average annual consumption between 2003 and 2030.

For the purposes of this analysis, oil producers can broadly be divided into two categories.

- *Producers from OPEC* (Organization of the Petroleum Exporting Countries),[3] which own about 70 percent of proven oil reserves. The OPEC countries are highly dependent on oil revenues and try to coordinate their production targets to influence prices on the world oil market.

- *Producers from non-OPEC countries*, which mainly invest and produce based on current and expected market prices, subject to cost, technological, and regulatory constraints.

OPEC members currently produce 40 percent of total world oil output and supply about 55 percent of oil traded internationally. Their output market share used to be higher—about 50 percent in the 1970s. However, the oil shocks of

---

[2]Proven reserves are the oil resources that can be extracted profitably with at least 90 percent probability.

[3]The OPEC member countries are Algeria, Indonesia, I.R. of Iran, Iraq, Kuwait, Libya, Nigeria, Qatar, Saudi Arabia, the United Arab Emirates, and Venezuela.

Figure 4.3. Oil Consumption per Unit of Output
(Kilograms per unit of real PPP-adjusted GDP, unless otherwise stated; 1971–2004)

Over the past three decades, the use of oil per unit of output has fallen by about half in OECD and by one-third in non-OECD countries. Oil intensity is comparable between the two groups in purchasing-power-parity (PPP) terms though the intensity is much higher in the non-OECD countries at market exchange rates.

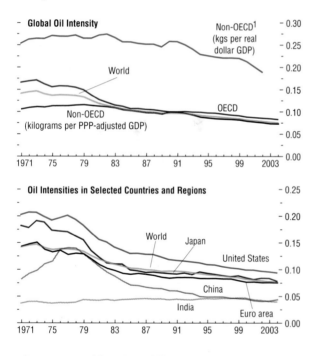

Sources: International Energy Agency; OECD analytical database; and IMF staff calculations.
[1]Data for this series are available only through 2002.

the 1970s reduced demand and OPEC, in particular Saudi Arabia, responded in the early 1980s by cutting production to stabilize prices. This had the side effect of creating significant spare capacity, with several consequences for the world economy. The financial position of many OPEC members deteriorated. At the same time, the existence of spare capacity provided oil consumers with a buffer against supply disruptions (such as during the Middle East conflict in 1991); but it also deterred some oil extraction projects in the non-OPEC regions. Over the past two years, spare production capacity has been eroded by surging oil demand. OPEC now produces close to its capacity, which, for comparison, is lower than its peak capacity in the 1970s (Figure 4.5).

Proven reserves in the non-OPEC region account for only 30 percent of the world total. Moreover, unit exploration, development, and production costs are much higher than in the OPEC region (Table 4.1). Despite lower and more expensive endowments, non-OPEC supply has grown steadily, though the price collapse of the mid-1980s combined with OPEC excess capacity slowed down growth. Most of the recent increases in non-OPEC production have been from the Commonwealth of Independent States (CIS) (see Figure 4.5). Many fields in the non-OPEC region are now mature and have high decline rates. Canada holds almost one-half of non-OPEC proven reserves in the form of non-conventional oil contained in its oil sands. The production costs of such oil have fallen considerably over the past decades, in many areas to about $10–15 a barrel including producer taxes (National Energy Board, 2004). However, achieving high output from the fields is a complex and time-consuming task since significant investment in extracting and refining infrastructure is needed, together with large quantities of water and natural gas.

Medium- and Long-Term Projections

This section presents projections of oil demand and supply, and identifies the main risk factors, focusing on medium- and long-term developments. It is important to keep in mind that the projections are sensitive to specific assumptions about economic growth, efficiency gains, use of alternative fuels, and new oil discoveries. But important conclusions about the market dynamics can be drawn even without the benefit of perfect foresight.

The section is organized as follows. First, projections of oil supply and demand are presented assuming that:

- Global growth averages 3.6 percent in purchasing-power-parity-adjusted (PPP-adjusted) terms between 2003 and 2030.[4] Annual growth rates for each country are based on *World Economic Outlook* estimates and forecasts for 2004–09 and the U.S. Department of Energy projections thereafter.
- Oil prices move as projected in futures markets (as of end-February 2005) through 2010, and thereafter stay constant in real terms. This implies that the real average oil price falls from $45 a barrel in 2005 to approximately $34 a barrel in 2010 and beyond.[5] This long-term price level is $3–10 higher than that assumed by other institutions (see Department of Energy, 2004a, for a detailed price comparison).

Second, we make a comparison of the initial demand and supply projections, and assess whether the starting assumption of a long-term $34 a barrel real oil price is realistic. Finally, we use an oil market model to calculate the price that will balance supply and demand over the long run.

Oil Demand

The analysis of oil demand is based on a simple model estimated using disaggregated data for advanced economies and emerging market

[4]Global GDP growth is assumed to be 3 percent between 2003 and 2030 based on market exchange rates.
[5]The average oil price is defined as the simple average of West Texas Intermediate, Brent, and Dubai oil prices.

Figure 4.4. Oil Production and Reserves
(1965–2004)

In the 1980s, non-OPEC countries surpassed OPEC as the dominant producers of oil. The proven oil reserves, however, are much higher in the OPEC region, especially in the Middle East.

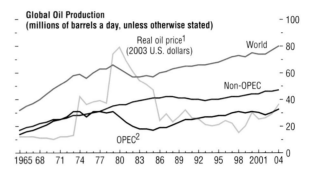

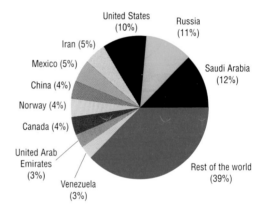

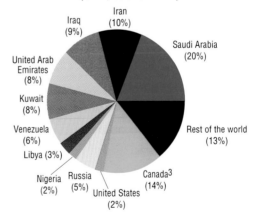

Sources: International Energy Agency; *British Petroleum Review; Oil and Gas Journal* (2003); and IMF staff calculations.
[1]Simple average of West Texas Intermediate, Brent, and Dubai oil prices.
[2]Members of OPEC (Organization of the Petroleum Exporting Countries) are Algeria, Indonesia, I.R. of Iran, Iraq, Kuwait, Libya, Nigeria, Qatar, Saudi Arabia, United Arab Emirates, and Venezuela.
[3]Includes nonconventional oil.

Figure 4.5. OPEC and Non-OPEC Oil Supply

In the past several years, Russia and several other CIS members have contributed most to growth in non-OPEC production. OPEC countries now produce very close to their capacity.

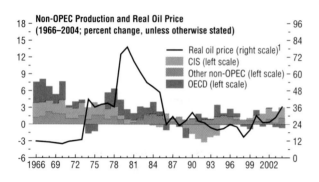

Non-OPEC Production and Real Oil Price
(1966–2004; percent change, unless otherwise stated)

— Real oil price (right scale)[1]
  CIS (left scale)
  Other non-OPEC (left scale)
  OECD (left scale)

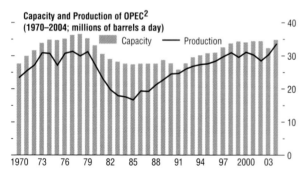

Capacity and Production of OPEC[2]
(1970–2004; millions of barrels a day)

  Capacity   — Production

Sources: International Energy Agency; *British Petroleum Review;* U.S. Department of Energy; and IMF staff calculations.
[1]Simple average of West Texas Intermediate, Brent, and Dubai oil prices, expressed in 2003 U.S. dollars.
[2]Includes crude oil and other liquids.

and developing countries over the past three decades. The model distinguishes between consumption of different types of oil products: transport fuels, other fuels for industry and residential sectors, and heavy fuel oil (used mainly for electricity generation). The demand for transport fuel is primarily modeled as a function of the number of motor vehicles in each economy; the number of vehicles is in turn estimated as a nonlinear function of income. Consumption of other fuels is directly related to the level of income; and consumption of the heavy fuel oil is assumed to stay constant or grow slowly, depending on each country's historical pattern. Details of the model are discussed in Appendix 4.1.

The model finds that in both groups of countries, consumption of oil products is closely linked to the level of economic activity and vehicle ownership. These two variables in fact explain the bulk of oil consumption growth over time. In contrast, oil demand is fairly unresponsive to price changes as long as the level of real oil prices remains well below its historical peak—a 10 percent a barrel increase in prices reduces demand by only about 1 percent. However, large price changes, such as the ones experienced in the 1970s, have substantial—up to five times stronger—effects, in part because they can trigger a significant adjustment of technology and oil consumption. Both insights are consistent with the intuition built from the aggregated data in Figure 4.2.[6]

Table 4.2 presents the baseline oil demand projections using the estimated coefficients and the above price and growth assumptions. (Figure 4.6 examines the sensitivity of the demand projections to these assumptions, and Table 4.3 summarizes the average income elasticities over the forecasting period.) The baseline scenario

---

[6]In many advanced economies, taxes make up a large proportion of end-user prices of oil products. Owing to limited availability of comparable cross-country products' price data, the analysis in this chapter mostly focuses on the crude oil prices. In countries with large specific oil consumption taxes (such as in the European Union), the sensitivity of oil demand to price could be lower than assumed in this chapter.

Table 4.1. Unit Costs of Oil Production
(Dollars a barrel)

	Exploration and Development Cost	Production Cost	Implied Tax Cost[1]	Differential to Brent[2]	Total[3]
Non-OPEC[4]					
Africa	2.9	2.2	9.0	2.6	16.8
Asia	2.9	3.3	8.3	2.0	16.5
Asia-Pacific	2.7	2.2	7.8	2.3	15.1
Europe	4.0	2.7	8.0	1.2	15.9
Latin America	3.2	3.1	6.1	3.3	15.8
Middle East	2.6	2.6	9.7	1.7	16.6
North America	3.7	6.0	4.2	—	13.9
OPEC					
Saudi Arabia	1–2	<2	Markup to revenue[5]	. . .	. . .

Sources: Goldman Sachs; and International Energy Agency.
[1]Combined income tax, production tax, and royalty fees. The tax components vary with revenue and profit a barrel. Here they are calibrated for the revenue of about $20 a barrel.
[2]Difference between the average revenue a barrel (oil and gas combined) and the Brent crude oil price.
[3]Total unit cost structure, on a Brent oil equivalent after-tax basis. Excludes any profit (return) from invested capital. According to Goldman Sachs estimates, oil price of $20 a barrel would cover the cost structure of the industry while offering an 8 percent nominal rate of return.
[4]Based on 100 largest recent oil and gas projects.
[5]Most oil revenues are surrendered to the government.

projects oil consumption to grow from an average of 82.4 million barrels a day (mbd) in 2004 to 92.0 mbd in 2010, and 138.5 mbd in 2030. The main contributor to the consumption increase is transport demand, which is expected to account for over 60 percent of the total oil consumption increase. Demand for other oil products will contribute about one-third to demand growth, and heavy fuel oil, less than 5 percent.

Looking across regions, advanced countries will only account for 25 percent of the increase in world oil demand. Most of demand growth will come from developing countries, with transport demand in the non-OECD region almost tripling from 16 mbd to 45 mbd between 2003 and 2030, driven by a six-fold increase in vehicle ownership. Much of this is expected to take place in the rapidly growing Asian economies—particularly in China, where income per capita has reached the level at which vehicle ownership rates rise quickly. Demand for other products will more than double in developing countries, from an estimated 10 mbd in 2003 to 22 mbd in 2030.

As can be seen from the above, vehicle ownership plays a key role in oil demand growth; transport demand in emerging market and developing countries is projected to contribute almost half of the total oil demand increase over the next three decades. To provide a perspective on the importance of fast transport growth, Figure 4.7 compares the vehicle ownership rates across countries over the past three decades (see Appendix 4.1 for a formal model of vehicle ownership). Both OECD and non-OECD countries started to experience rapid vehicle ownership growth at income levels of about $2,500 per capita in PPP terms. Growth in vehicles continued to be much faster than GDP growth until about $10,000 of per capita income. The projections suggest that China, as a fast-growing developing country, could see its vehicle ownership rates jump from 16 vehicles per 1,000 people in 2002 to 267 vehicles per 1,000 people in 2030. This is actually slightly below the vehicle ownership rates seen in other countries at similar PPP per capita income levels (between 300–600 vehicles per 1,000 people—see Figure 4.7).[7] If

[7]The predicted vehicle ownership rate for China is below the historical range because, for the purposes of vehicles projection, the country is divided into three areas with different initial income levels.

Figure 4.6. Long-Term Projections of Oil Demand
(2000–30; millions of barrels a day, unless otherwise stated)

Oil demand is projected to grow as economies and vehicle ownership expand. Projections are sensitive to underlying assumptions about growth and oil price.

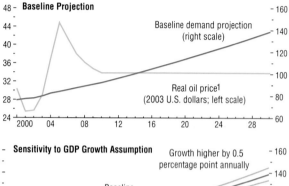

Baseline Projection

Baseline demand projection (right scale)

Real oil price¹ (2003 U.S. dollars; left scale)

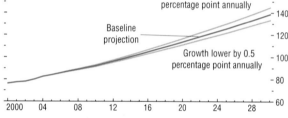

Sensitivity to GDP Growth Assumption

Growth higher by 0.5 percentage point annually

Baseline projection

Growth lower by 0.5 percentage point annually

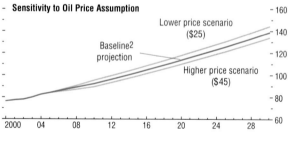

Sensitivity to Oil Price Assumption

Lower price scenario ($25)

Baseline² projection

Higher price scenario ($45)

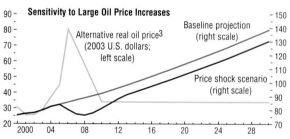

Sensitivity to Large Oil Price Increases

Alternative real oil price³ (2003 U.S. dollars; left scale)

Baseline projection (right scale)

Price shock scenario (right scale)

Sources: International Energy Agency; U.S. Department of Energy; and IMF staff calculations.
¹Simple average of West Texas Intermediate, Brent, and Dubai oil prices.
²According to the futures markets, the real price of oil expressed in 2003 dollars is expected to fall from $45 a barrel in 2005 to about $34 a barrel in 2010. The real price of oil is assumed by the IMF staff to stay at this level after 2010.
³Real oil price is assumed to jump to $80 a barrel in 2006 and then gradually fall to the baseline price of about $34 a barrel in 2010.

Table 4.2. Oil Demand Projection
(Millions of barrels a day unless otherwise stated)

	Estimate		Projection		
	2003	2004	2010	2020	2030
Total demand	**79.8**	**82.4**	**92.0**	**113.5**	**138.5**
OECD and NIEs¹	48.9	49.5	52.0	57.9	63.7
Other non-OECD	30.9	32.9	40.0	55.6	74.7
Of which: China	5.5	6.4	8.6	13.6	18.7
Transport demand²	**46.3**	...	**54.3**	**67.6**	**82.8**
OECD and NIEs	30.4	...	32.5	35.6	38.3
Other non-OECD	15.9	...	21.8	31.9	44.5
Other nonresidual demand³	**23.0**	...	**27.1**	**34.3**	**42.9**
OECD and NIEs	13.6	...	14.9	17.7	20.8
Other non-OECD	9.5	...	12.2	16.6	22.0
Residual demand⁴	**10.5**	...	**10.6**	**11.6**	**12.8**
OECD and NIEs	4.6	...	4.6	4.6	4.6
Other non-OECD	5.9	...	6.0	7.0	8.2
Memorandum					
Number of vehicles					
(millions of units)	**751⁵**	...	**939**	**1,255**	**1,660**
OECD and NIEs	625⁵	...	720	827	920
Other non-OECD	126⁵	...	219	429	741
Of which: China	21⁵	...	80	209	387

Sources: International Energy Agency; United Nations Yearbook; and IMF staff calculations.
¹Newly industrialized Asian economies (NIEs) include Hong Kong SAR, Korea, Singapore, and Taiwan Province of China. Korea is also an OECD member.
²Includes gasoline, jet fuel, and gas/diesel (including light heating oil).
³Includes liquefied petroleum gas, naphtha, kerosene, and other products except heavy fuel oil.
⁴Heavy fuel oil.
⁵Year 2002.

China's economic growth is sustained, and the cross-country experience is at least a partial guide for its vehicle ownership rates, the country would contribute almost one-fourth of total world incremental oil demand between 2003 and 2030. But even if annual growth rates of vehicle ownership in China were only at one-half of what is predicted based on the past experience of other countries, world oil demand would still be about 132 mbd in 2030—a significant increase over the current 82 mbd.⁸ Additional sensitivity tests are reported in Figure 4.6.

⁸Similarly, if we stipulated that vehicle ownership would saturate in all developing countries at levels that are much lower than in the advanced economies (for example, at about one-half), oil demand could be lower by as much as 10 mbd relative to the baseline in 2030. However, the experience of many emerging market economies has not been consistent with this assumption.

Table 4.3. Average Income Semi-Elasticities, 2003–30[1]

	OECD and NIEs[2]	Other Non-OECD
Transport fuel	0.32	0.85
Other products	0.60	0.70
Heavy fuel	—	0.37
Total demand	0.38	0.74

Source: IMF staff calculations.

[1]Semi-elasticity is defined as average growth of oil consumption over average growth of purchasing power parity adjusted income. The semi-elasticity includes the impact of oil price changes on oil consumption.

[2]Newly industrialized Asian economies (NIEs) include Hong Kong SAR, Korea, Singapore, and Taiwan Province of China. Korea is also an OECD member.

Oil Supply

Against this background, we now turn to prospects for oil supply in both OPEC and non-OPEC regions. We start by analyzing the outlook for non-OPEC oil production. Given projections of demand and non-OPEC supply, we will subsequently assess the expected demand for OPEC oil at the baseline real price path.

Non-OPEC Oil Production

Expansion of non-OPEC production will be constrained by the declining potential of many traditional fields and, relative to OPEC, by limited and high-cost reserves. Capacity additions are planned in Africa, the CIS, and Latin America in the medium term. However, it is not clear whether non-OPEC production growth can be sustained in the long run.

Non-OPEC supply projections in this section rely primarily on estimates by the International Energy Agency (IEA) and the United States Department of Energy (DoE).[9] IEA (2004b) expects non-OPEC oil production to rise from 50 mbd in 2004 to 57 mbd in 2010 (including non-conventional oil and processing gains), and stay broadly constant thereafter as falling production

[9]Oil supply is inherently difficult to estimate using simple regression models owing to long time lags between price signals and investment decisions, technological and reserve constraints, and changes in policy frameworks.

Figure 4.7. Vehicle Ownership and per Capita Income
(1971–2002)

Vehicle ownership starts to grow quickly when countries reach income of about $2,500 per capita in purchasing-power-parity (PPP) terms. Rapid growth continues until income per capita reaches about $10,000. Saturation level is at about 850 vehicles per 1,000 people.

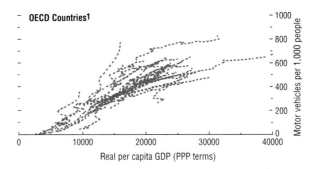

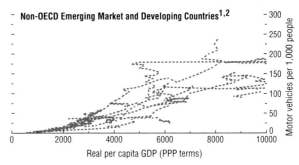

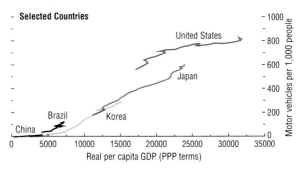

Sources: United Nations Statistical Yearbook; OECD analytical database; and IMF staff calculations.

[1]Only data fitting the scale are shown.

[2]This group of countries includes Argentina, Brazil, Chile, China, Colombia, Dominican Republic, Ecuador, Egypt, Morocco, South Africa, Israel, India, Indonesia, Malaysia, Thailand, Pakistan, and Syrian Arab Republic.

Table 4.4. Projections of Non-OPEC Oil Supply[1]
(Millions of barrels a day)

	International Energy Agency (IEA)					U.S. Department of Energy (DoE)				
	2002	2004	2010	2020	2030	2002	2010	2020	2025	2030[2]
United States and Canada[3]	10.5	. . .	11.0	9.1	7.6	11.1	11.3	10.5	. . .	9.9
Mexico	3.7	. . .	4.4	4.2	3.0	3.7	4.2	4.6	. . .	5.0
OECD Europe	6.9	. . .	5.0	3.2	2.3	6.8	6.4	5.5	. . .	4.6
Russia	8.0	. . .	10.8	11.1	11.4	7.6	10.0	10.9	. . .	11.3
Other transition economies	2.0	. . .	4.4	4.9	5.5	1.8	3.5	5.6	. . .	8.0
China	3.5	. . .	3.4	2.8	2.3	3.3	3.6	3.5	. . .	3.3
Other Asia	2.6	. . .	2.4	1.9	1.2	2.5	2.6	2.7	. . .	2.5
Central and South America	3.8	. . .	4.9	5.8	6.4	3.8	4.5	5.9	. . .	6.9
Africa	3.1	. . .	4.8	5.1	4.6	2.9	3.8	5.4	. . .	8.1
Rest of world	3.0	. . .	2.4	2.0	1.6	2.9	3.3	3.6	. . .	4.0
Nonconventional oil[4]	1.7	. . .	3.9	6.8	10.7	1.5	2.8	5.0	. . .	5.4
Total	48.8	50.4	57.2	56.9	56.6	48.0	56.0	63.2	65.0	69.0

Sources: International Energy Agency (2004a, 2004b); U.S. Department of Energy (2004a); and IMF staff calculations.
[1]Projections of IEA and DoE at their baseline oil prices (including processing gains).
[2]IMF staff estimate based on DoE projections for 2020 and 2025.
[3]Excludes nonconventional oil.
[4]Includes heavy oil from Venezuela (OPEC member).

of conventional oil is offset by rising nonconventional oil production in Canada (Table 4.4). The U.S. Department of Energy (2004a) is more optimistic about non-OPEC prospects and expects production to continue to grow over the projection period, from 50 mbd in 2004 to 56 mbd in 2010, and about 65 mbd in 2025.[10]

The responsiveness of non-OPEC supply to prices is the key unknown in the projection. While most analysts would agree that the high prices of the 1970s stimulated non-OPEC investment (and the price collapse of 1986 dampened it), the range of quantitative estimates is very wide. Gately (2004) constructs a model where the long-term elasticity of non-OPEC supply to prices varies from 0.15 to 0.58.[11] Such a broad range of elasticities captures a complex mix of uncertainties: the speed of declines in traditional regions such as the United States and OECD Europe, the timing and level of the production peak in the CIS,

and the output of nonconventional oil in Canada. Canada's oil sands make up about half of non-OPEC's proven reserves and potential for output growth from this source is in principle very high. However, according to IEA estimates it takes five to seven years for investment in oil sands projects to come on-stream, and therefore the speed of price responsiveness may be slow.

OPEC Oil Production

Given the baseline demand and non-OPEC supply projections, we can calculate the residual demand for OPEC oil (the so-called "call on OPEC"). This is the hypothetical amount of oil that OPEC would need to produce to close the gap between total demand and non-OPEC supply, and maintain prices at their assumed path. Initially (by about 2010), the call on OPEC is expected to stay roughly unchanged at current 32 mbd.[12] Over the next decades, however, the

[10]IEA's projections assume that the real price of oil (expressed in 2003 prices) will fall to $23.5 a barrel by 2010 and then rise gradually to $31 in 2030. In the DoE baseline scenario, the real oil price rises from $25 in 2010 to about $28 in 2025. The IEA and DoE long-term price projections (made earlier in a period of slack market) are lower than this chapter's assumption of $33.73 a barrel for 2010–30, though the price differences narrow down in the long term to $3–5 a barrel.
[11]Moroney and Berg (1999) estimate the long-term elasticity of oil supply with respect to real prices at 0.1–0.2, while Dahl and Duggan (1996) estimate it at 0.6 using U.S. data.
[12]Excluding global inventory changes.

call on OPEC is projected to grow significantly at the baseline price path, to about 61–74 mbd in 2030, implying a more than doubling of OPEC oil production. Such a production increase would require a significant amount of investment spending, both in the form of initial investment (about $5,000 a barrel of daily capacity) and follow-up spending to offset natural declines in fields. The increase in production and capacity would have to be provided mainly by the Middle East OPEC members because these countries have the largest oil reserves.

The actual OPEC response to demand pressures is difficult to predict, but the choices faced by OPEC can be evaluated under the assumption that OPEC, acting as one entity, bases its production decisions on the net present value of future profits. Using parameter values estimated in this chapter, Gately (2005) calculates the OPEC's net present value of profits for different choices of its market share. In the model, OPEC seeks to balance the gains from higher output expansion against the losses from the resulting lower prices, taking into account investment and extraction costs (for details of the model, see Appendix 4.1). The model results suggest that OPEC's optimal market share is between 41 and 46 percent (see Figure 4.8), which corresponds to OPEC output of 52–59 mbd in 2030, well below the initial hypothetical call on OPEC of 61–74 mbd. The simulation model also suggests the market share in the range of 41–46 percent is optimal for OPEC under many different assumptions about income and vehicle elasticities; consequently, OPEC may not have an incentive to significantly increase its current market share of just below 40 percent even if oil demand turns out to be different from the baseline scenario.

All this suggests that once non-OPEC production peaks, there will likely be a strong upward pressure on prices. If OPEC's production decisions were to be broadly along the lines described above, oil prices expressed in 2003

Figure 4.8. Profitability of Various OPEC Market Strategies

According to the model of Gately (2005), the Net Present Value (NPV) of OPEC profits is highest for OPEC market shares between 41 and 46 percent. This is in contrast with the 50–58 percent OPEC market share projected in the baseline scenario in Table 4.5.

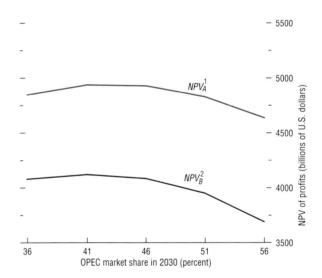

Source: Gately (2005).
[1]NPV_A corresponds to the NPV of discounted profits in the baseline scenario, with the International Energy Agency non-OPEC supply path.
[2]NPV_B corresponds to the NPV of discounted profits in the baseline scenario, with the U.S. Department of Energy non-OPEC supply path.

Table 4.5. Projected Oil Demand, Non-OPEC Supply, and Call on OPEC
(Millions of barrels a day)

	2003 Actual	2004 Estimate	2010	2020	2025	2030
Baseline demand projection	79.8	82.4	92.0	113.5	125.5	138.5
Non-OPEC supply[1]						
Lower bound	49.0	50.4	59.3	64.4	64.5	64.1
Upper bound	49.0	50.4	61.4	70.1	73.9	77.2
Call on OPEC[2]						
Lower bound	30.7	32.0	30.6	43.5	51.6	61.3
Upper bound	30.7	32.0	32.7	49.2	61.0	74.4
Memorandum						
Oil demand projection by agency						
IEA (2004b)	79.8	. . .	90.4	106.7	. . .	121.3
DoE (2004a)	79.8	. . .	91.1	110.0	120.6	. . .
OPEC Secretariat (2004)	79.8	. . .	88.7	105.8	114.6	. . .
Call on OPEC by agency:						
IEA (2004b)	30.7	. . .	33.3	49.8	. . .	64.8
DoE (2004a)	30.7	. . .	35.7	47.8	56.0	. . .
OPEC Secretariat (2004)	30.7	. . .	34.1	48.9	58.3	. . .

Sources: International Energy Agency; United States Department of Energy; OPEC Secretariat; and IMF staff calculations.

[1]Non-OPEC supply are projections of the International Energy Agency (IEA, 2004b) and the United States Department of Energy (DoE, 2004a), adjusted for the difference between the IMF's, IEA's, and DoE's baseline price paths. Includes nonconventional oil and processing gains. See Appendix 4.1 for details.

[2]Call on OPEC is the hypothetical amount of oil that OPEC would need to produce to close the gap between total demand and non-OPEC supply at the long-term real oil price of $33.73; excludes global inventory changes.

dollars would range between $39 and $56 a barrel in 2030, with the shortfall in OPEC production of 12.5 mbd relative to the baseline offset by lower oil demand (about 8.5 mbd) and higher non-OPEC supply (roughly 4 mbd). This scenario would still require significant investment in oil extraction capacity by OPEC, about $350 billion until 2030.[13] While the figure is a small fraction of overall OPEC export profits over the period (only about 5 percent, net of domestic consumption), it is important to keep in mind that most of the oil profits accrue to governments who face other competing priorities for spending.[14]

Conclusions and Policy Recommendations

Over the past two decades, oil-importing countries have enjoyed the benefits of double insurance against oil shocks: considerable spare production capacity in OPEC, and sizable emergency stocks held by OECD countries. However, spare capacity is now reduced to historically low levels and there are significant risks that the oil market will continue to be tight going forward. The analysis set out above—which is qualitatively consistent with forecasts of other institutions, including IEA, DoE, and OPEC Secretariat (Table 4.5)[15]—suggests that future

[13]IEA (2004b) estimates global investment needs of the oil sector at $3 trillion between 2003 and 2030. This figure includes investment in refining capacity. Also, unit investment costs in the non-OPEC region are considerably higher that in OPEC countries. Finally, IEA's call on OPEC is higher than suggested by the equilibrium model above.

[14]See Box 1.6 for a detailed discussion.

[15]For 2010, the forecasts of IEA, DoE, and OPEC Secretariat range between 89–91 mbd for total demand, and between 33 and 36 mbd for the call on OPEC. These forecasts are similar to the baseline projection of this chapter. In 2030, the IEA's call on OPEC is within the range of the baseline scenario (65 mbd compared with the 61–74 mbd interval), although it is higher than actual OPEC production suggested by our equilibrium model. Looking at long-term demand projections, IEA and DoE forecasts for 2025–30 are about 5–17 mbd lower than projected by the IMF staff in the baseline scenario, mainly reflecting a lower projection for transportation demand in developing countries, and to some extent also growth of demand for other products.

oil market developments could fall into two main phases.

- During the period through about 2010, the high—though gradually decreasing—oil prices currently predicted by the futures market will keep the oil market broadly in balance, with incremental oil demand being met mostly by higher non-OPEC production. However, since the prospects for higher spare capacity are unfavorable,[16] the market will likely remain tight and vulnerable to shocks. Oil prices will continue to be subject to the risk of large, unexpected price changes.
- From 2010 onward, the call on OPEC may increase significantly as non-OPEC production peaks while global demand continues to rise. With global dependence on oil production from OPEC countries rising, much would depend on OPEC supply response; most likely, however, there would be growing upside risks to prices. While projected increases of the size described above would appear manageable if they took place over a long period,[17] this would add to the risk of volatility looking forward.

As past experience underscores, long-run forecasts for oil supply and demand are subject to substantial uncertainties.[18] Beyond the future pace of global growth—which is clearly critical—two appear to be of particular importance.

- *Technological progress could exceed expectations.* The demand projection assumes a continued reduction in oil intensity measured as oil consumption per unit of output—by 1.6 percent annually in OECD and 1.1 percent annually in

non-OECD countries—broadly in line with the average over the past 30 years. It is possible that the spread of new fuel-efficient vehicles, including hybrid cars, or efficiency-enhancing policy measures could produce more rapid reductions, especially if the market went through a period of sustained large price increases. However, the overall efficiency savings incorporated in the projections are already quite large.[19]

- *Non-OPEC production could increase more rapidly than expected.* Output of nonconventional oil might increase more rapidly than assessed above, changing the projected balance between production of OPEC and non-OPEC producers. Output of nonconventional oil would also respond to high prices, although—as noted above—with significant lags. Upward pressures on prices could also be reduced by competition from gas and other fuels, whose endowments are more equally distributed around the world.

Against this background, how should policymakers respond? While the macroeconomic risks from oil price volatility have declined in recent years, they remain a significant concern for both oil importers and exporters (Box 4.1). To reduce these risks, actions in three broad areas could be considered.

Making Oil Markets Work Better

A variety of constraints/rigidities hinder the efficient operation of the oil market, adding to uncertainty and volatility. The priorities include the following.

---

[16]The non-OPEC producers do not have the incentive to maintain spare capacity as they individually lack the necessary market power to influence oil prices. The OPEC producers have indicated that they plan to maintain some level of spare capacity (about 1.5–2 mbd in the case of Saudi Arabia). However, the historical data in Figure 4.1 suggest that spare capacity in the range of 3–5 mbd would provide much better protection against supply disruptions and demand shocks.

[17]The increase in real oil prices from $34 in 2010 to $56 in 2030 would imply average annual price growth of 2.5 percent.

[18]For example, on April 2, 2004, the oil futures markets expected the nominal price of oil to fall gradually from $32 to $26 by the end of 2006 (see Appendix 1.1, *World Economic Outlook*, April 2004).

[19]The use of oil per vehicle is projected to fall by 0.5 percent annually in OECD and 2.5 percent annually in non-OECD regions by 2030, equivalent to a saving of 50 mbd. Even a complete replacement of the existing and projected global vehicle stock by hybrid cars would reduce world oil demand by at most 20 mbd by 2030 (about 40 percent of the savings already factored into the scenario).

Box 4.2. Data Quality in the Oil Market

Recent developments in the oil market, the most widely traded commodity, have highlighted the need for more timely and accurate oil market data. Limited or incorrect information about oil demand, supply, stocks, and trade can increase perceptions of risk, reduce willingness to invest in new capacity, and increase price volatility. Indeed, price fluctuations in 2004 have likely been exacerbated by data inadequacies. For example, successive upward revisions in estimates of demand by the International Energy Agency (IEA)—in part reflecting limited available information on emerging market countries—added to market uncertainties, when spare capacity in the oil market was approaching historical lows. Underestimation of demand together with overly optimistic assessment of the level of inventory building may have also been responsible for OPEC's decision to cut official quotas in early 2004, thus contributing to higher prices.

The main source of international monthly oil market data is the IEA, which publishes a wide range of oil market indicators for over 130 countries. The data are compiled from questionnaires and market information. Annual questionnaires are sent to OECD and non-OECD countries, whereas monthly questionnaires are sent only to OECD countries. These have recently been supplemented by the Joint Oil Data Initiative (JODI) reporting (see below). Key indicators on demand, supply, trade, stocks, prices, and refining of oil (largely in physical units) are published by area and product. The main publications are the monthly *Oil Market Report* and the *Annual Statistical Supplement*. Annual compendiums on energy balances are also available with a substantial delay.

Within the limits of the data provided by countries, the IEA does a laudable job in providing oil statistics. Yet, a number of weaknesses still exist, with their root in the uneven and inadequate data reporting by individual countries. The problem many countries face is to satisfy reporting requirements with limited resources and short-

age of experienced staff. Further, there is room for improved governance to enhance data quality through greater transparency.

Demand data are dominated by information from OECD countries, which are mostly net importers of oil. However, emerging market countries are increasingly significant in the oil market and the quality of data reported by such major consumers as China is of particular concern. Even for OECD countries, there are substantial time lags. Final annual estimates are only available 16–20 months after the reference year, and the initial estimates are not very reliable. The initial monthly estimates (published with a nine-week lag) are based on surveys of OECD countries, market information, and past trends. Monthly data on oil stocks are limited to primary industry and strategic government holdings for OECD countries. Non-OECD stocks held in smaller OECD facilities without reporting requirements are not captured by the data collection system. The average price data for individual petroleum products in OECD countries are adequate for most analyses but are neither defined nor reported consistently for non-OECD countries.

The accuracy and timeliness of data on supply and exports are weaker than those related to demand and prices. This largely reflects the quality of data sources, with current data compiled from a mixture of monthly direct reporting from OECD countries, and market information combined with past trends for non-OECD countries. The latter countries, which account for almost three-fourths of oil supply, have no obligation to report data to the IEA. Production and reserve data from non-OECD countries are particularly lacking, as reporting can be hampered by factors such as the proprietary nature of the data, the existence of production agreements, and sensitivities related to data on the size of oil funds. Hence, these data have to be estimated for a number of countries. Since a dominant share of oil is produced by non-OECD countries, information on global oil production and reserve data are, thus, not as reliable. The limited availability of timely data

Note: The author of this box is Paul Armknecht.

on the breakdown by different types of crude oil—the prices of which have moved differently—is also a concern.

Against this background, the international community has called for additional efforts to improve data quality, including transparency, in the oil market. In October 2004, the G-7 Ministers asked international organizations to strengthen their effort toward transparency, and the International Monetary and Financial Committee stressed the importance of further progress to improve oil market information and transparency. In November 2004, the G-20 Ministers urged cooperation between oil producers and consumers to enhance oil market transparency.

The JODI, which started in 2001 and is coordinated by the International Energy Forum (IEF), is a monthly exercise to improve the coverage and transparency of oil market data and extend the monthly reporting to non-OECD countries but with less detail than the IEA monthly oil survey. This initiative has led to some improvement in the coverage of data, which increased from about 70 percent at its initiation to about 95 percent now, representing data from 93 countries. However, quality remains weak: only 56 out of the 93 participating countries submit data regularly. In several cases, the data are of questionable accuracy owing, in part, to lack of experience of the respondents with oil market data. A comprehensive review of the data is expected to be undertaken during the first half of 2005.

The Extractive Industries Transparency Initiative (EITI), launched by the United Kingdom in 2003, is a multi-stakeholder initiative involving governments, companies, and NGOs that aims at voluntary disclosure of natural resource–related revenue by governments

and payments by companies. The reconciliation and verification of government receipts and company payments is expected to substantially improve the accuracy of these data for participating countries. The initiative has led to increased awareness of the importance of transparency in this area. If major oil-producing countries become convinced that increased fiscal transparency is useful in their own resource management, this could have significant positive implications for the quality of global oil data.

The IMF is exploring ways to support the JODI through technical assistance to member countries on statistical legislation and organization. The IMF is also encouraging its members to embrace and accelerate their participation in the IMF's data-related initiatives. These include the Special Data Dissemination Standard (SDDS), the General Data Dissemination System (GDDS), Reports on the Observance of Standards and Codes on statistical data (data ROSCs), and the Coordinated Portfolio Investment Survey (CPIS). Through their focus on data transparency, the SDDS and GDDS could pave the way for better reporting and monitoring of oil reserves, production, and consumption by individual countries.

Besides the international initiatives, individual countries should take steps to contribute to improved oil data. Many national statistical agencies do not have adequate resources to comply with the increasing requirements on oil data, and new staff need to be trained in energy statistics production. Standard definitions and terminology are critical in obtaining data that are consistent internally and conceptually comparable across countries. Statistical laws need to be reviewed and strengthened to support data reporting, and links between industry and government need to be established to identify data reporting requirements.

- *Strengthening transparency*, particularly by improving the timeliness and reliability of data on oil demand, supply, and inventories, which are now very weak (Box 4.2). Improved data on available excess capacity and

planned investment—particularly for OPEC producers—would also be helpful.
- *Participation in the hedging markets*. In principle, oil consumers and producers could protect themselves against increased volatility

by hedging on futures and derivative markets. Daniel (2001) shows that the oil producers (and the oil-rich governments) can use simple hedging techniques to diminish the oil price risk without significantly reducing return, with the added benefits of greater predictability and certainty. The study also finds that companies and governments often do not operate on the hedging markets because of the concerns about the possible political costs of hedging (i.e., failure to benefit from price rises), lack of institutional capacity, and limited market depth. The success story of the state of Texas and the positive experience of Mexico during the episode of market instability in the early 1990s suggest, however, that producers and oil-rich governments should explore possibilities for hedging their own price risk, especially given prospects for increased oil price volatility.[20]

- *Ensuring that taxation and regulatory frameworks are stable, transparent, and do not add to volatility.* Abrupt changes and unexpected raises in taxes and royalty rates should be avoided.[21] Regulatory issues—such as the differences in emissions regulations across U.S. states, as well as tight limitations on refinery investment— should also be reviewed.[22] Moreover, a shift from ad valorem to specific taxation of oil products would tend to reduce price volatility of end products.

Reducing Obstacles to Investment

As can be seen from the discussion above, securing adequate oil supplies and spare capacity would be one possible way of reducing volatility. That said, there are many obstacles to investment in the oil sector. Some of them,

such as fluctuating world oil prices and political risks (including embargos) are exogenous to most oil producers. However, in many countries—both inside and outside OPEC—regulatory frameworks are an additional impediment. Some countries limit, or even forbid, participation of foreign investors in oil sector projects. While this may be seen as desirable in part for strategic reasons, it could lead to slower development of fields and reduce access to the latest technological advances, know-how, and financing (though well-defined service contracts can help mitigate these potential drawbacks). Investment by national oil companies is in some countries constrained by surrender requirements for oil revenues and by competing demands for social and infrastructure expenditures. Moreover, the access to external financing is often in such cases limited by a lack of transparency about financial performance. Making policy frameworks more friendly toward investment would be an important step toward creating conditions for further capacity expansion and ensuring orderly developments in the oil market.

Is There an Additional Role for Government?

Since high and volatile oil prices can have significant adverse spillovers for the economy at large, there is in principle an argument for government intervention to reduce volatility. While such arguments have to be assessed very carefully—not least because such measures can be expensive, and because government intervention can in practice have quite the reverse effect—three areas appear worth considering.

- *Both oil exporters and importers could benefit from increasing spare production capacity* (see Box

---

[20]For a more detailed analysis of hedging on commodities markets, see the April 2005 *Global Financial Stability Report.*

[21]For example, after recent tax changes that included an increase in export duties on crude oil and refined products, most oil companies in Russia make little additional profit when oil prices rise above $25 a barrel (IEA, 2004b).

[22]The lack of refining capacity has increased premia on easy-to-process light crudes with a negative impact on the light-crude oil importers. Moreover, to the extent that most of the incremental OPEC production has been of the heavy kind, bottlenecks in the refinery sector can impede stabilization of the crude oil market.

4.1). Countries highly dependent on oil imports could also consider protecting themselves from the risk of supply disruptions by gradually boosting strategic reserves, especially in the non-OECD region, where reserve ratios are currently low.[23] Enhanced consumer-producer dialogue would be helpful in striking the right balance between building spare capacity (with costs to oil producers) and building stocks (with costs to oil consumers).

- *Energy conservation remains a priority.* As noted above, oil intensity has been falling, partly in response to services-biased growth and price signals, but also reflecting explicit government policies such as energy taxes, efficiency standards, and support of public transport and alternative sources of energy. While faster reduction in oil intensity can require substantial up-front expenditures,[24] countries whose oil import dependency is expected to rise over the projection period should consider oil-saving measures very carefully.

- *Increased multilateral cooperation could also play a role,* both to facilitate understanding of oil market developments, and to move forward a number of the initiatives described above. The Joint Oil Data Initiative is a good example of what can be achieved through cooperation (see Box 4.2). Looking forward, enhanced dialogue between oil consumers and producers could bring benefits to all

stakeholders as it would reduce the currently perceived risks of tight oil supplies or unexpected policy actions to curb long-term oil demand.

Appendix 4.1. Oil Market Prospects: Data and Modeling Strategy

The main authors of this appendix are Martin Sommer and Dermot Gately. Paul Atang provided research assistance.

The analysis in the main text of this chapter is based on three integrated models of oil demand, oil supply, and vehicle ownership. This appendix provides a description of each model.

Model of Oil Demand

Oil Demand Data

The model of oil demand is estimated separately for a panel of advanced economies, and for a panel of emerging markets and developing countries over 1971–2002 (a total of 51 countries).

- The first panel consists of the 30 OECD members and the three other newly industrialized economies (NIEs).[25]
- The second panel consists of 18 non-OECD emerging markets and developing countries. This group includes Argentina, Brazil, Chile,

---

[23]Some major non-OECD countries, including China and India, have been proactive on this front. However, any reserve accumulation would need to be well-timed to avoid additional demand pressures on the market. If all non-OECD countries decided to raise their emergency stocks by five days of annual consumption a year, this would represent additional demand of about 0.5 million barrels a day. According to Downstream B.V. Rotterdam, the necessary infrastructure could cost roughly $1.5 billion annually, or 0.02 percent of non-OECD gross domestic product at market exchange rates. OECD countries already have a significant amount of protection against supply disruptions as their emergency stocks cover over 110 days of net imports and the member governments have well-defined plans for emergency situations under the IEA framework.

[24]IEA (2004b) estimates that OECD countries would need to invest about $30 billion annually (0.1 percent of GDP), and non-OECD countries would be required to invest about $10 billion annually (above 0.1 percent of GDP) to reduce oil intensity of their transport systems by 10 percent in 2030 beyond the efficiency gains projected by the IEA. The 10 percent efficiency gain would correspond to about 7 mbd world oil demand in the IEA Reference Scenario, currently valued at about $100 billion annually. The initial gains from adopting the more radical policies would be smaller—about one-third in 2010.

[25]The group of NIEs consists of Hong Kong SAR, Korea, Singapore, and Taiwan Province of China. Korea is also an OECD member.

Figure 4.9. Oil Demand in Advanced Economies[1]
(1971–2003; per capita, 1985 = 100)

Transport demand and demand for other nonresidual oil have been increasing in proportion to the number of vehicles and GDP, respectively. Residual fuel demand dropped off in the 1980s and has not on average recovered.

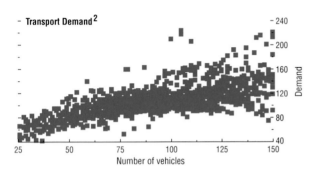

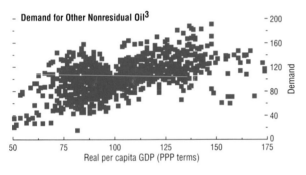

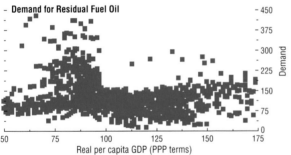

Sources: International Energy Agency; United Nations Statistical Yearbook; OECD analytical database; and IMF staff calculations.

[1]Advanced economies defined here as OECD countries and newly industrialized Asian economies (Hong Kong SAR, Singapore, and Taiwan Province of China). All variables were expressed in per capita terms and indexed for each country at 1985 = 100. Only data fitting the scale are shown.

[2]Transport demand is defined as consumption of gasoline, jet fuel, and gas/diesel oil (including light heating oil).

[3]Other nonresidual demand is defined as consumption of naphtha, liquefied petroleum gas, kerosene, and other products except residual fuel oil.

China, Colombia, the Dominican Republic, Ecuador, Egypt, Morocco, South Africa, Israel, India, Indonesia, Malaysia, the Philippines, Thailand, Pakistan, and the Syrian Arab Republic.

Oil demand is modeled for three different groups of products:

- transport demand, defined as consumption of gasoline, jet fuel, and gas/diesel oil;
- other nonresidual demand, which includes naphtha, liquefied petroleum gas, kerosene, and other products other than residual fuel oil; and
- residual (heavy) fuel oil.

Figures 4.9 and 4.10 illustrate the basic stylized facts about demand for the three product groups. The data for each country is expressed in per capita terms and indexed at 1985 = 100 to distinguish between the periods before and after adjustment of economies to the oil price shocks of the 1970s. Transport demand is in the long run strongly related to the number of vehicles, while the demand for other nonresidual products is correlated with the gross domestic product. Demand for residual fuel has been falling in advanced economies as many oil-based power generation plants switched to alternative fuels in the 1980s. Demand for the residual fuel oil continues to grow in some emerging markets and developing countries.

The measure of transport demand contains gas/diesel oil, whose subcomponents are diesel, light heating oil, and other gas oil. Light heating oil and other gas oil are not, strictly speaking, transport fuels. However, IEA does not provide decomposition of gas/diesel oil into its components for the period prior to 1993. Figure 4.2 in the main text is based on the strict definition of transport demand—that is, excluding light heating oil and other gas oil. All other calculations and projections consider all gas/diesel fuels as transport fuels.

Oil Price Data

The estimation was carried out with two alternative measures of historical oil prices: end-user prices and the U.S. refineries crude oil acquisition cost. The advantage of using end-user prices is that they capture changes in taxation, transport costs, and refiner's margins over time. However, the series is available on a consistent basis only for a subgroup of 11 OECD countries. The oil prices are expressed in U.S. dollar terms. Estimation results change only marginally when prices are expressed in local currency. Using the U.S. dollar prices simplifies oil demand projections.

Equation Specification

The estimated equation for *transport demand* takes the following form:

$$D_{i,t}^{transport} = k_{1i} + \mu V_{i,t} + \beta_{T,m} P_{max,t-1} + \beta_{T,d} P_{decline,t-1} + \beta_{T,r} P_{recovery,t-1} + \varepsilon_{i,t},$$

where $D_{i,t}^{transport}$ is the natural logarithm of transport demand per capita in country i at time t; $V_{i,t}$ denotes the log of number of vehicles per capita in country i at time t; P_{max} denotes the natural logarithm of historical real oil price maximum; $P_{decline}$ denotes cumulative decreases in the natural logarithm of real oil price; and $P_{recovery}$ denotes cumulative increases in the logarithm of real oil price. For simplicity, transport demand is modeled only as a function of vehicles and prices; business cycle fluctuations in utilization are abstracted from in this medium-term model. The decomposition of prices into the three elements follows the approach of Gately and Huntington (2002). This approach helps to distinguish between the impact of large and small price changes on oil demand, and test for any asymmetries between the impact of price increases and price decreases. Figure 4.11 illustrates how the decomposition is made in practice. Formally, the decomposition can be characterized as follows (all variables are expressed in natural logarithms):

$$P_t = P_{max,t} + P_{decline,t} + P_{recovery,t}$$

if $P_t \geq P_{max,t}$: $P_{max,t} = P_t$; otherwise $P_{max,t} = P_{max,t-1}$

Figure 4.10. Oil Demand in Emerging Market and Developing Countries[1]
(1971–2002; per capita, 1985 = 100)

As in advanced economies, transport and other nonresidual demand have been increasing steadily. Unlike in OECD countries, demand for residual fuel continues to grow on average.

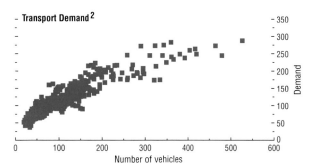

Transport Demand[2]

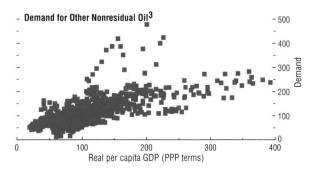

Demand for Other Nonresidual Oil[3]

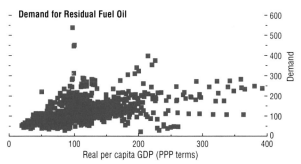

Demand for Residual Fuel Oil

Sources: International Energy Agency; OECD analytical database; United Nations Statistical Yearbook; and IMF staff calculations.
[1]This group of countries includes Argentina, Brazil, Chile, China, Colombia, Dominican Republic, Ecuador, Egypt, Morocco, South Africa, Israel, India, Indonesia, Malaysia, Philippines, Thailand, Pakistan, and Syrian Arab Republic. All variables were expressed in per capita terms and indexed for each country at 1985 = 100. Only data fitting the scale are shown.
[2]Transport demand is defined as consumption of gasoline, jet fuel, and gas/diesel oil (including light heating oil).
[3]Other nonresidual demand is defined as consumption of naphtha, liquefied petroleum gas, kerosene, and other products except residual fuel oil.

if $P_t < P_{max,t}$ and $P_t < P_{t-1}$: $P_{decline,t}$
   $= P_{decline,t-1} + (P_t - P_{t-1})$;
   otherwise $P_{decline,t} = P_{decline,t-1}$.

if $P_t < P_{max,t}$ and $P_t > P_{t-1}$: $P_{recovery,t}$
   $= P_{recovery,t-1} + (P_t - P_{t-1})$;
   otherwise $P_{recovery,t} = P_{recovery,t-1}$.

The equation for *other nonresidual oil* takes the following form:

$$D_{i,t}^{other} = k_{2i} + \gamma Y_{i,t} + \beta_{NT,m} P_{max,t-1} + \beta_{NT,d} P_{decline,t-1}$$
$$+ \beta_{NT,r} P_{recovery,t-1} + \eta_{i,t},$$

where $D_{i,t}^{other}$ is the natural logarithm of other nonresidual oil demand per capita in country i at time t; and $Y_{i,t}$ denotes the log of real purchasing power parity GDP per capita in country i at time t.

No equation for *residual fuel oil* was estimated.

Estimation Results

Table 4.6 presents the estimation results. The coefficients on vehicles and income in the demand equations are all highly statistically significant. Large negative coefficients on the P_{max} price term suggest that oil consumption in OECD countries responded strongly to the price shocks of the 1970s. The estimated elasticities are particularly high when using the end-user prices. By contrast, the oil consumption in developing countries did not seem to respond much since the P_{max} variable was insignificant. Therefore, only results for a specification without the three-way decomposition of prices is reported for the panel of developing countries. The estimation results suggest that price elasticity of oil demand is small for minor price fluctuations. Overall, the econometric estimates are qualitatively similar to the evidence presented in Gately and Huntington (2002).

The estimation results should be interpreted with two caveats: the estimated relationships capture only the long-run dynamics of oil demand; and, as discussed in the main text of this chapter, the parameter values embed historical trends in oil intensity in the form of reduced estimates of income and vehicle elasticities.

Figure 4.11. Decomposition of Oil Price Movements
(1970–2004)

Movements in the real price of oil can be decomposed into three components: historical maximum (P_{max}), cumulative increases ($P_{recovery}$), and cumulative decreases ($P_{decline}$).[1]

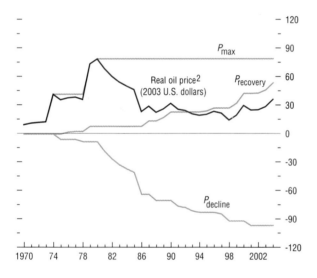

Source: IMF staff calculations.
[1]Current oil price P_t equals the sum of $P_{max,t}$, $P_{decline,t}$, and $P_{recovery,t}$.
[2]Simple average of West Texas Intermediate, Brent, and Dubai oil prices.

Table 4.6. Estimated Demand Elasticities

	Transport Demand			Other Nonresidual Demand		
	OECD 11	OECD and NIEs	Other non-OECD	OECD 11	OECD and NIEs	Other non-OECD
GDP				0.63**	1.10**	0.73**
Vehicles	0.70**	0.51**	0.55**			
Crude oil price			−0.07**			−0.10**
Crude oil price (max)		−0.10**			−0.09**	
Crude oil price (decline)		−0.03			−0.01	
Crude oil price (recovery)		—			−0.06*	
End-user price (max)	−0.50**			−0.48**		
End-user price (decline)	−0.03			−0.14**		
End-user price (recovery)	−0.11**			−0.07		

Source: IMF staff estimates.
Note: Oil demand, gross domestic product, and vehicles are expressed in per capita terms. ** and * denote significance at the 1 and 5 percent level, respectively. Crude oil price (max) denotes the maximum historical real price. Price (decline) denotes cumulative decrease, while price (recovery) denotes cumulative increase in real price. Regressions contain country-specific constants.

Calibration of Elasticities in the Oil Demand Model

The choice of elasticities for demand projections was closely linked to the estimated coefficients. The calibrated parameters are reported in Table 4.7. The demand for residual fuel oil was calibrated based on an expert judgment.

Main Assumptions Underlying Oil Demand Projections

Long-term projections of oil demand are sensitive to assumptions about economic growth and efficiency improvements. Sensitivity to price is a less important factor for small price changes.

Economic Growth

The average world growth rate is 3.6 percent in PPP terms over 2003–30, and 3.0 percent at market exchange rates. GDP projections set out in the September 2004 *World Economic Outlook* were used for 2004–09. For 2010–30, we used the U.S. Department of Energy (DoE) *International Energy Outlook April 2004* projections. An adjustment was made to the DoE growth projection for China and India. In both cases, the long-term growth rates were reduced by 1 percentage point. The adjustment was made for two reasons: to build in a conservative bias into the oil demand projections for Asia and to reduce the PPP-weighted world growth rate closer to its historical average.

The sensitivity analysis in the middle panel of Figure 4.6 is based on a model where growth rates for each country are higher or lower by 0.5 percentage point annually over 2004–30. The projected demand is 91.3–92.9 mbd in 2010 (compared with the baseline of 92.0 mbd), and 133.2–144.6 mbd (compared with the baseline of 138.5 mbd).

Table 4.7. Demand Elasticities Used for Projections

	Transport Demand		Other Nonresidual Demand		Residual Fuel Demand	
	OECD and NIEs[1]	Other non-OECD	OECD and NIEs[1]	Other non-OECD	OECD and NIEs[1]	Other non-OECD
GDP	. . .	. . .	0.6	0.7	—	0.3
Vehicles	0.6	0.55	. . .	. . .	. . .	. . .
World oil price	−0.1	−0.1	−0.3	−0.1	−0.1	−0.1

Source: IMF staff calculations.
[1]Newly industrialized Asian economies (NIEs) include Hong Kong SAR, Korea, Singapore, and Taiwan Province of China. Korea is also an OECD member.

Baseline Price Path

The baseline price path is the *World Economic Outlook* forecast of the simple average of West Texas Intermediate, Brent, and Dubai oil prices. The average is expected to fall in nominal terms from $46.5 in 2005 to $38.8 a barrel in 2010. The series is converted into constant 2003 prices assuming annual inflation of 2 percent. The real price of oil therefore falls from estimated $44.7 in 2005 to $33.7 a barrel in 2010, and is assumed to stay constant at this level until 2030.

The sensitivity analysis in the bottom panel of Figure 4.6 is based on a model where real prices are assumed constant at either $25 or $45 a barrel over 2005–30. The projected demand is 89.3–95.2 mbd in 2010 (compared with the baseline of 92.0 mbd), and 133.7–144.0 mbd (compared with the baseline of 138.5 mbd).

Efficiency Gains

The demand model was estimated over a period of significant declines in oil intensity, in both advanced and developing countries. The estimated coefficients, therefore, carry over the historical trend in efficiency gains into the projection.

The actual future improvements in oil intensity could be different from the ones estimated from the historical data. Services-biased growth in the advanced countries, graduation of some developing countries and emerging markets into the group of advanced countries, and government policies to promote energy efficiency could all reduce oil intensity beyond the projected gains (1.6 percent annually for advanced countries and 1.1 percent for the other economies). By contrast, the baseline oil price remains in real terms well below the historical maximum in the 1970s, which was one of the main triggers of the past technological adjustment. A detailed assessment of efficiency gains taking into account forward-looking trends and policies would be beyond the scope of this study.

Oil Demand Projection

Oil demand is projected for each of 51 countries in the sample. The projections were converted from per capita terms to overall levels using population data from the United Nations. Various simplifying assumptions are taken for countries that are not in the estimation sample.

The first projection year of the model is 2004. The actual growth in 2004 demand was unexpectedly strong and overperforms the model. Moreover, most industry analysts expect demand growth to be strong again in 2005. In reconciling the model's forecasts with actual data, it is assumed that 2004–05 is a period of unusually strong oil demand and that, by 2010, oil demand will gradually converge to the path predicted by the model. In all figures in the main text, the oil demand data for 2004 and 2005 are the *IEA Oil Market Report* estimates from January 2005.

Model of Oil Supply

Non-OPEC Supply

Non-OPEC oil supply is defined as total non-OPEC output plus world output of nonconventional oil and processing gains. The lower bound projection corresponds to the forecast of non-OPEC output path from the IEA *World Energy Outlook 2004*. The upper bound projection is a forecast of the DoE from *International Energy Outlook April 2004*. Since the baseline IMF, IEA, and DoE price paths are different, the methodology of Gately (2004) is used to adjust the IEA and DoE paths:

$$S_t^{non\text{-}OPEC,adj.} = S_t^{non\text{-}OPEC,IEA}\left(\frac{S_{t-1}^{non\text{-}OPEC,adj.}}{S_{t-1}^{non\text{-}OPEC,IEA}}\right)^{1-\alpha}\left(\frac{P_t^{IMF}}{P_t^{IEA}}\right)^{\alpha},$$

where α captures elasticity of non-OPEC supply. Following Gately (2004), the parameter is calibrated at 0.03, which for permanent price changes implies the long-run elasticity of supply of about 0.5 (by 2030). For comparison, Moroney and Berg (1999) estimate the long-term elasticity of oil with respect to real price at 0.1–0.2, while Dahl and Duggan (1996) estimate it at 0.6 using the U.S. data. At baseline prices, the IMF upper- and lower-bound projections of non-OPEC supply in Table 4.5 are higher by about 8 mbd than DoE and IEA projections in Table 4.4.

OPEC's Incentives to Increase Output

This section evaluates OPEC capacity expansion strategies in a profit-maximization framework. The methodology follows Gately (2004, 2005). Gately's model calculates OPEC profits for various target market shares, and solves for the associated market-clearing prices together with oil demand and non-OPEC supply. The different market shares are then ranked based on the discounted net present value of profits (the required real rate of return is assumed at 5 percent).

The baseline version of the model was calibrated using parameter values estimated in this chapter but the actual simulation was carried out over 50 alternative parameter sets. In the model, OPEC's decision to increase output is mainly based on the price elasticity of demand, elasticity of non-OPEC supply, and investment costs. The higher the elasticities of demand and non-OPEC supply, the higher the incentive of OPEC to avoid high oil prices. When the real oil price exceeds $63 a barrel (this is the historical maximum of the real U.S. refineries crude oil acquisition cost), oil demand of OECD is assumed to become highly responsive to price with elasticity of –0.5. The investment costs are twofold: the capacity expansion cost is assumed at about $4,000–6,000 a barrel of incremental daily capacity; and the investment to offset natural declines in fields is approximated at 5 percent of total capacity, evaluated also at $4,000–6,000 a barrel, depending on the country. The latter assumption is important because the costs of maintaining capacity can over time be much larger than current investment.

The results presented in Figure 4.8 suggest that the optimal strategy for OPEC is to let its market share grow slowly, to about 41–46 percent by 2030. This is well below the share implied by the baseline projection in Table 4.5. In the baseline scenario, the call on OPEC was predicted at 61.3–74.4 mbd and oil demand at 138.5 mbd in 2030. The implied long-term OPEC market share was therefore up to 54 percent. But the simulation results suggest that OPEC may lack incentives to increase its market share from the current 39 percent to as much as implied by the baseline scenario.

The model solves for the price path associated with the profit-maximizing solution. In 2030, the price range is $39–56 a barrel expressed in 2003 dollars (compared with the baseline of $33.7). Total oil demand is in the range of about 126–134 mbd in 2030 and the OPEC supply is between 52 and 59 mbd, depending on the parameter set.

Model of Vehicle Ownership

For the purposes of this chapter, vehicles are defined according to the UN methodology; the main components are motor cars seating less than eight persons, trucks, buses, and tractors.

The relationship between vehicle ownership and income in Figure 4.7 suggests that income per capita is the main determinant of vehicle ownership across time and across countries. The relationship is highly nonlinear: vehicle ownership grows very slowly at low and high income levels; but grows at much faster rates than income when countries reach per capita income of about $2,500 dollars in PPP terms.

The estimation methodology follows closely Dargay and Gately (1999) except that the PPP-adjusted GDP is used as a measure of income. The model is also estimated over a broader set of countries and contains 10 most recent annual observations for each country (the actual sample is 1971–2002).

The estimated equation is

$$V_{i,t} = (1 - \theta) V_{i,t-1} + \theta(\gamma e^{\alpha e^{\beta_i Y_{i,t}}}) + \upsilon_{i,t},$$

where $V_{i,t}$ is the number of vehicles per 1,000 people; $Y_{i,t}$ denotes the real PPP-adjusted

Table 4.8. Vehicle Ownership and Income

Estimated equation: $V_{i,t} = (1 - \theta)V_{i,t-1} + \theta\,(\gamma e^{\alpha e^{\beta_i/Y_i}}) + \upsilon_{i,t}$

Parameter	Value	Country Group
γ	850	Calibrated parameter
θ	0.062**	All
α	−5.513**	All
β_1	−0.221**	United States, Canada, Australia, New Zealand, Taiwan Province of China
β_2	−0.153**	Austria, Belgium, Denmark, France, Finland, Greece, Iceland, Ireland, Israel, Italy, Luxembourg, the Netherlands, Norway, Sweden, Switzerland, United Kingdom
β_3	−0.188**	Chile, Czech Republic, Hungary, Poland, Portugal, Slovakia, South Africa, Spain
β_4	−0.158**	Argentina, Brazil, China, Colombia, Dominican Republic, Ecuador, Egypt, India, Indonesia, Malaysia, Mexico, Morocco, Pakistan, Syria, Thailand
β_5	−0.174**	Japan, Korea
β_6	−0.045	Hong Kong SAR, Singapore

Source: IMF staff estimates.
Note: **denotes significance at the 1 percent level.

income per capita; γ represents the saturation level for vehicle ownership (calibrated at 850 vehicles per 1,000 people in line with Dargay and Gately, 1999); θ is the speed of adjustment to the desired vehicle level; α is related to the speed of vehicle ownership growth at high incomes; and β is related to the speed of vehicle ownership growth at low income levels (β is allowed to vary across countries to allow for different speed of vehicles penetration).

The coefficient estimates together with the country groupings are reported in Table 4.8. All coefficients are highly statistically significant with the exception of β for Hong Kong SAR and Singapore, where vehicle ownership grows very slowly owing to geographical factors and restrictive regulatory frameworks.

Urbanization and population density were not significant in the estimated equation as income per capita already explains a large fraction of vehicle ownership variability. The example of Hong Kong SAR and Singapore illustrates that the geographical and institutional factors can to some extent be captured by allowing β to vary across countries.

Table 4.9 presents vehicle projections in absolute as well as per capita terms. China was for the purposes of vehicle projections split into three regions according to their current level of per capita income (high-, middle-, and low-

Table 4.9. Vehicle Ownership Projections

	Millions of Vehicles				Per 1,000 People			
	2002	2010	2020	2030	2002	2010	2020	2030
World	751	939	1,255	1,660	. . .	. . .	. . .	. . .
OECD	625	720	827	920	. . .	. . .	. . .	. . .
United States	234	260	288	312	812	826	837	843
Germany	48	54	60	63	586	655	725	774
France	35	40	46	50	576	650	725	777
Italy	37	39	41	41	656	697	752	793
United Kingdom	31	37	44	50	515	616	711	771
Japan	76	87	95	96	599	682	753	796
Korea	14	22	31	36	293	442	610	718
Australia	12	15	18	19	632	715	778	812
Other OECD	137	164	205	252	. . .	. . .	. . .	. . .
Non-OECD	126	219	429	741	. . .	. . .	. . .	. . .
Africa	11	15	23	33	. . .	. . .	. . .	. . .
Brazil	21	27	42	71	121	139	200	320
Other Latin America	12	19	33	54	. . .	. . .	. . .	. . .
China	21	80	209	387	16	59	146	267
Other Asia	58	72	113	184	. . .	. . .	. . .	. . .
Rest of world	4	6	8	11	. . .	. . .	. . .	. . .

Sources: United Nations Yearbook; and IMF staff calculations.
Note: Vehicles are defined according to the United Nations methodology; the main components are motor cars seating less than eight persons, trucks, buses, and tractors.

income regions). Income growth rate was assumed to be the same in all three regions. Given the current data on vehicle stock by provinces, a separate vehicle forecast was prepared for each region, and then aggregated into the total for China.

References

Dahl, C., and T. Duggan, 1996, "U.S. Energy Product Supply Elasticities: A Survey and Application to the U.S. Oil Market," *Resource and Energy Economics*, Vol. 18, No. 3, pp. 243–63.

Daniel, James A., 2001, "Hedging Government Oil Price Risk," IMF Working Paper 01/185 (Washington: International Monetary Fund).

Dargay, Joyce, and Dermot Gately, 1999, "Income's Effect on Car and Vehicle Ownership, Worldwide: 1960–2015," *Transportation Research*, Vol. 33, No. 2, pp. 101–38.

Department of Energy, 2004a, *International Energy Outlook 2004* (Washington: Energy Information Administration).

———, 2004b, *Short-Term Energy Outlook* (Washington: Energy Information Administration, various issues).

Gately, Dermot, 2004, "OPEC's Incentives for Faster Output Growth," *Energy Journal*, Vol. 25, No. 2, pp. 75–96.

———, 2005, "OPEC's Incentives for Faster Output Growth—An Update" (unpublished; New York: New York University).

———, and Hillard G. Huntington, 2002, "The Asymmetric Effects of Changes in Price and Income on Energy and Oil Demand," *Energy Journal*, Vol. 23, No. 1, pp. 19–55.

Goldman Sachs, 2005, *Global Energy: 100 Projects to Change the World* (London).

International Energy Agency, 2004a, *Oil Market Report* (Paris, various issues).

———, 2004b, *World Energy Outlook 2004* (Paris).

International Monetary Fund, 2005, *Global Financial Stability Report, April 2005* (Washington).

Moroney, John R., and M. Douglas Berg, 1999, "An Integrated Model of Oil Production," *Energy Journal*, Vol. 20, No. 1, pp. 105–24.

National Energy Board, 2004, *Canada's Oil Sands: Opportunities and Challenges to 2015* (Calgary).

Oil and Gas Journal, 2003, "Worldwide Look at Reserves and Production" (December) (Tulsa, Oklahoma: Penwell Corporation).

Organization of the Petroleum Exporting Countries Secretariat, 2004, "Oil Outlook to 2025," OPEC Review Paper (Vienna).

Ramey, Garey, and Valerie A. Ramey, 1995, "Cross-Country Evidence on the Link Between Volatility and Growth," *American Economic Review*, Vol. 85 (December), pp. 1138–51.

The following remarks by the Acting Chair were made at the conclusion of the Executive Board's discussion of the World Economic Outlook on March 23, 2005.

Executive Directors noted that the global expansion remains broadly on track, underpinned by generally supportive macroeconomic policies and notably benign financial market conditions. Following last year's performance—the strongest in three decades—growth is expected to moderate to a more sustainable pace in 2005. At the same time, Directors observed that the expansion has become less balanced. Growth has been strong in the United States, China, and most emerging market and developing countries, and disappointing in Europe and Japan.

Globally, inflationary pressures remain relatively subdued. With monetary tightening cycles under way in most cyclically advanced economies and generally moderate inflationary expectations, inflation should remain well contained. Directors considered that inflation risks will nevertheless need careful monitoring, with due regard to rising unit labor costs in many industrial countries as labor markets tighten, and to monetary policy implementation in a number of emerging markets receiving strong external inflows that, in the absence of greater exchange rate flexibility, may lead to inflationary pressures.

Looking forward, Directors were of the view that the slower but solid global growth in 2005 will be underpinned by still accommodative—albeit to a lesser degree—macroeconomic policies, improving corporate balance sheets, supportive financial market conditions, a gradual rise in employment, and continued strong growth in China. Given improving corporate and household balance sheets, a stronger cyclical rebound cannot be ruled out. Nevertheless,

most Directors assessed the balance of risks to be tilted to the downside. The key risks to the short-term outlook include: (1) the increasingly unbalanced nature of the expansion, with global growth significantly dependent on the United States and China; (2) a significant tightening of financial market conditions, which can adversely affect domestic demand in the United States, prompt financial market deleveraging and asset price corrections more broadly, and lead to a deterioration in emerging market financing conditions; and (3) a further sharp increase in oil prices.

Directors welcomed the staff's analysis of the oil market. Noting that currently oil prices are already significantly higher than staff projections, Directors agreed that conditions in the oil market are likely to remain tight for the foreseeable future, as demand continues to rise and non-OPEC oil production peaks. Directors underlined the importance of stability in oil markets, and considered that measures to promote stability should include steps to increase transparency in oil markets; eliminate overly restrictive regulatory frameworks that impede investment in the oil sector; promote energy sustainability and efficiency; and enhance dialogue between oil producers and consumers.

Directors expressed concern that global current account imbalances have widened further over the past year. A number of Directors cautioned that this may increase the risk of abrupt movements in exchange rates. Directors noted that the strategy to support an orderly adjustment in global imbalances has been broadly agreed. Among the key elements of this strategy are fiscal consolidation in the United States;

steps toward greater exchange rate flexibility, supported by continued financial sector reform, in emerging Asia; and continued structural reforms to boost growth and domestic demand in Japan and Europe. Directors recognized that, while these policies will have varying economic impacts in different countries and regions, the pursuit of this agenda will lead to more sustainable external positions and stronger medium-term growth. Several Directors noted that the euro area was in external balance, and that structural reform was needed primarily for exploiting euro area countries' economic growth potential. Directors reiterated the collective responsibility of the membership to ensure that the strategy is implemented in a timely and effective manner. Several Directors underlined the key role of the Fund, through its multilateral and bilateral surveillance, in monitoring and encouraging the implementation of this strategy. Referring to risks of abrupt movements in exchange rates, several Directors drew attention to the currency composition of official reserves of member countries and the importance of adequate statistics in this area for the Fund to assess those risks and possible policy implications.

Directors welcomed the staff's analysis of globalization and external imbalances. They agreed that the evolving trends of financial and real globalization should ultimately facilitate global rebalancing. At the same time, they stressed that the nature of adjustment, and the magnitudes involved, have not fundamentally changed because of globalization—in particular, exchange rates and trade balances still need to adjust. Many Directors noted that, with investors now willing to hold larger shares of foreign assets in their portfolios, globalization may have contributed to the persistence of current account imbalances, and in this sense, provided policymakers with the option of more gradual adjustment. Directors cautioned, however, that the increased flexibility should not be an excuse to delay difficult policy actions, as continued delays can sharply increase the risk of a sudden and disorderly unwinding of global imbalances. In particular, it was suggested that the risk of

rapid changes in global investor preferences for U.S. dollar–denominated assets places an even greater premium on the adoption of sound policies in all key industrial and emerging market countries to achieve internal and external balance.

Directors identified a number of key medium-term issues that in their view need to be addressed.

- First, fiscal positions in many countries remain very difficult, particularly against the backdrop of global population aging, and pose a threat to medium-term macroeconomic stability. Directors noted that fiscal deficits remain high in the largest industrial countries—with the exception of Canada. Projected improvements are modest, and in many cases not underpinned by sufficiently ambitious consolidation measures. In emerging markets, fiscal indicators have generally improved, but many countries still have a long way to go to bring public debt ratios down to sustainable levels.

- Second, structural reforms need to be advanced to remove rigidities and enable domestic economies to take full advantage of the opportunities provided by globalization.

- Third, successful and appropriately ambitious trade liberalization on the part of all countries under the Doha Round, including improved market access for developing countries, will be critical to support medium-term global growth. Directors noted that in agriculture, key issues remain to be resolved, and faster progress is needed in the area of services. They stressed that translating the mid-2004 framework agreements into a viable policy package—to be taken up at the December 2005 WTO Ministerial Conference—should be a key priority for the coming months.

- Fourth, Directors noted that 2005 is a critical year for the Millennium Development Goals (MDGs). Despite the improved growth performance of recent years, meeting the MDGs will be an enormous challenge for most developing countries. Directors called on the developing countries to press ahead with policy and governance reforms to strengthen the investment environment and private sector–led growth, and on the advanced economies to support these efforts with substantially higher assistance. A number of Directors considered that increased official development assistance will be most effective in support of countries with the strongest policies and the most severe poverty.

Industrial Countries

Directors welcomed the continued strong performance of the *U.S.* economy. With most forward-looking indicators remaining solid, the expansion is set to continue in 2005. With household saving close to zero, however, a retrenchment in private consumption remains a risk, particularly if house price increases are to slow. Against the background of relatively benign inflationary pressures, Directors agreed that a measured pace of monetary tightening remains appropriate, although incoming data will need to be monitored carefully in view of possible upside risks to the inflation outlook from pressures in the labor market or further oil price increases. Directors underscored the need for significant fiscal consolidation, with a view to ensuring medium-term sustainability and facilitating an orderly unwinding of global current account imbalances. In this connection, Directors underscored the importance of fully achieving the expenditure restraint envisaged in the current budget proposal. Many Directors were of the view that the Administration's fiscal plans remain insufficiently ambitious, and noted that a number of likely future budgetary costs are not included in current fiscal projections.

Directors expressed disappointment that the *euro area* economy lost momentum during the second half of 2004, although they expected a strengthening of growth in the period ahead. Further appreciation of the euro and high and volatile oil prices remain the key risks to the regional outlook. With inflationary pressures well contained, Directors agreed that monetary policy should remain firmly on hold until a self-sustaining recovery is in place. A few Directors

suggested that an easing of monetary policy would need to be considered if downside risks to growth materialize or the euro further appreciates significantly. Regarding fiscal policy, Directors viewed existing policy settings as insufficient to deliver the budgetary adjustments required to cope with the fiscal pressures of population aging. They emphasized that a faster pace of fiscal consolidation is particularly needed in countries with weak budgetary positions. Underscoring that a strong fiscal framework is an integral part of monetary union in Europe, Directors noted that reform of the Stability and Growth Pact should be implemented in a way that does not lead to a weakening of fiscal discipline. Directors also stressed the importance of making further progress in implementing structural reforms to improve the region's growth performance, with a greater focus on addressing distortions in labor markets and promoting competition in product markets. In this connection, they looked forward to the revitalization of the Lisbon agenda, with a focus on reforms to spur efficiency, flexibility, innovation, and productivity. It was recognized that the scope of required actions varies across countries, and that several countries have already made significant headway on structural reforms.

Directors noted that the *Japanese* economy stalled in the last three quarters of 2004—reflecting weak global demand for IT products and a decline in consumption spending—but that recent data have been more encouraging. With bank and corporate balance sheets now in better shape, Directors believed that growth should regain some momentum in 2005, although they acknowledged the downside risks from high oil prices and the possible adverse impact on exports of a sharp appreciation of the yen. While deflationary pressures have eased in recent years, Directors urged the Bank of Japan to maintain a very accommodative monetary policy stance until deflation is decisively beaten. Against the background of high public debt and intensifying demographic pressures, Directors considered that fiscal consolidation remains a priority. They also stressed the need to continue with efforts to strengthen the bank and corporate sectors and to accelerate structural reforms—including measures to increase competition and improve labor market flexibility—to pave the way for sustained medium-term growth.

Emerging Market and Developing Countries

Directors welcomed the strong economic performance in *emerging Asia,* although growth has slowed noticeably in most countries during the course of last year—with the important exception of China. In 2005, growth in the region is expected to be slightly weaker, with upside risks from higher-than-anticipated growth in China, and downside risks from a more protracted correction in the IT sector or sluggish demand from Japan and Europe. Directors expressed their profound sympathy at the devastating loss of life and property from the recent catastrophic tsunami. They noted that reconstruction costs—and the impact on fiscal and external imbalances—will be very substantial; however, in most cases, excepting the Maldives and Sri Lanka, GDP growth will be only modestly affected. Directors noted that policy challenges facing the region vary. Monetary tightening cycles in most countries—with the exception of Korea, where domestic demand growth remains weak—are already under way, and in the view of most Directors further tightening will be facilitated in many countries by greater exchange rate flexibility. While budget positions have generally improved, public debt levels remain high in a number of countries, and further fiscal consolidation will be needed. In addition, structural reforms are required in several countries to reduce vulnerabilities in the bank and corporate sectors and to boost investment, which remains unusually low.

Growth in *Latin America* has exceeded expectations. While the favorable external environment has supported activity, Directors observed that domestic demand is now leading growth. While Directors saw a number of downside risks

to the outlook—including unexpected increases in global interest rates or a prolonged slowdown in key export markets—they believed that the region will continue to grow robustly this year. Directors were encouraged by the improved fiscal performance in many Latin American economies, although they noted that public debt, while declining, generally remains high. They therefore stressed the need for fiscal consolidation and more general measures to improve public debt sustainability, including structural reforms to boost growth. Directors agreed that the tightening of monetary policy in a number of countries in response to the recent uptick in inflation has been appropriate, and noted that exchange rate flexibility has played a key role in supporting monetary policy frameworks and improving the region's resilience to shocks.

Directors noted that *emerging Europe* is experiencing its strongest growth since the beginning of transition—with the recovery broadening across the region and moving beyond consumption to the export sector—and welcomed the expected moderation in the pace of activity to more sustainable levels. Two key risks facing emerging Europe are a prolonged slowdown in western Europe and a further appreciation of the euro. Many Directors observed that strong domestic demand has led to a general widening of current account deficits, a key regional vulnerability. They noted, however, that the policy requirements to reduce these external deficits vary across countries. In the Baltics and southern and southeastern Europe, containing credit growth and improving private saving will be key, while in central Europe ambitious fiscal consolidation and structural reforms will be needed, particularly in those countries that aim to adopt the euro in the relatively near future. In the view of many Directors, the rapid growth of credit in the region underscores the importance of strengthening banking supervision.

In the *Commonwealth of Independent States,* growth has been buoyant on the back of strong domestic demand and high energy and metals prices. While growth is expected to moderate in

2005, Directors viewed the outlook as generally favorable, but cautioned about the risks to inflation and growth from capacity constraints and inadequate investment in a number of countries. Against the background of strong capital inflows, Directors were concerned that the pace of disinflation in the region may be slowing, and stressed the need for policymakers to manage the revenue gains from oil and commodity exports prudently, while also allowing greater flexibility in exchange rates.

Directors welcomed the strong growth in the oil exporting countries of the *Middle East*, underpinned by increased export earnings from oil, sound financial policies, and progress with structural reforms. Directors urged policymakers to use the window of opportunity provided by high oil prices to press ahead with the reforms that are needed to boost medium-term growth and employment prospects and reduce vulnerabilities, including from high public debt levels in some countries. Directors noted that increased public spending on high-return human capital development and infrastructure outlays, accompanied by an acceleration of structural reforms, could help to place these economies on a higher sustained growth path and, by creating jobs, help improve social outcomes. Non-oil-producing countries in the region have also benefited from the positive impact of domestic reforms, as well as the strong growth in oil-exporting countries in the region.

Directors were encouraged by the highest growth seen in a decade in *sub-Saharan Africa*. This was underpinned by the strength of the global economy, high commodity prices, improved macroeconomic policies, and progress with structural reforms. Directors viewed the prospects for growth as generally favorable, but cautioned that there are a number of downside risks. A less benign global economy and a further sharp depreciation of the U.S. dollar would adversely affect a number of countries. While higher oil prices would be beneficial for some, they would not be so for other countries. Moreover, many countries would need to adjust to the elimination of world textile trade quotas. To sustain the improved growth performance in sub-Saharan Africa, Directors urged governments to further their reform efforts by promoting private sector investment, developing infrastructure, and strengthening institutions (including better transparency, governance, and property rights). They also called on the international community to support these policies with increased aid, debt relief, and improved market access.

Directors welcomed the two staff essays on output volatility and remittances in developing countries. Directors agreed with the staff's analysis that output volatility has negative effects on long-term economic growth, and encouraged policymakers to address the sources of output volatility. In particular, they noted the contribution that more stable fiscal policies and further steps to develop financial sectors and diversify the production base can make to reduce output volatility. Directors noted the positive impact that remittances have on recipient economies, particularly in terms of imparting macroeconomic stability and helping reduce poverty. They encouraged governments to enact policies to increase remittance flows, particularly by reducing transactions costs and implementing policies to promote formal financial sector participation in the remittance market. Several Directors stressed that remittances should not be seen as a substitute for aid flows.

STATISTICAL APPENDIX

The statistical appendix presents historical data, as well as projections. It comprises five sections: Assumptions, What's New, Data and Conventions, Classification of Countries, and Statistical Tables.

The assumptions underlying the estimates and projections for 2005–06 and the medium-term scenario for 2007–10 are summarized in the first section. The second section presents a brief description of changes to the database and statistical tables. The third section provides a general description of the data, and of the conventions used for calculating country group composites. The classification of countries in the various groups presented in the *World Economic Outlook* is summarized in the fourth section.

The last, and main, section comprises the statistical tables. Data in these tables have been compiled on the basis of information available through end-March 2005. The figures for 2005 and beyond are shown with the same degree of precision as the historical figures solely for convenience; since they are projections, the same degree of accuracy is not to be inferred.

Assumptions

Real effective *exchange rates* for the advanced economies are assumed to remain constant at their average levels during the period January 31–February 28, 2005. For 2005 and 2006, these assumptions imply average U.S. dollar/SDR conversion rates of 1.522 for both years, U.S. dollar/euro conversion rate of 1.31 for both years, and yen/U.S. dollar conversion rates of 105.2 and 104.4, respectively.

It is assumed that the *price of oil* will average $46.50 a barrel in 2005 and $43.75 a barrel in 2006.

Established *policies* of national authorities are assumed to be maintained. The more specific policy assumptions underlying the projections for selected advanced economies are described in Box A1.

With regard to *interest rates*, it is assumed that the London interbank offered rate (LIBOR) on six-month U.S. dollar deposits will average 3.3 percent in 2005 and 4.1 percent in 2006, that three-month euro deposits will average 2.3 percent in 2005 and 2.9 percent in 2006, and that six-month Japanese yen deposits will average 0.1 percent in 2005 and 0.4 percent in 2006.

With respect to *introduction of the euro*, on December 31, 1998, the Council of the European Union decided that, effective January 1, 1999, the irrevocably fixed conversion rates between the euro and currencies of the member states adopting the euro are as follows.

1 euro	=	13.7603	Austrian schillings
	=	40.3399	Belgian francs
	=	1.95583	Deutsche mark
	=	5.94573	Finnish markkaa
	=	6.55957	French francs
	=	340.750	Greek drachma[1]
	=	0.787564	Irish pound
	=	1,936.27	Italian lire
	=	40.3399	Luxembourg francs
	=	2.20371	Netherlands guilders
	=	200.482	Portuguese escudos
	=	166.386	Spanish pesetas

See Box 5.4 in the October 1998 *World Economic Outlook* for details on how the conversion rates were established.

What's New

- The country composition of the analytical groups has been revised to reflect the periodic update of the classification criteria.

---

[1]The conversion rate for Greece was established prior to inclusion in the euro area on January 1, 2001.

Box A1. Economic Policy Assumptions Underlying the Projections for Selected Advanced Economies

The short-term *fiscal policy assumptions* used in the *World Economic Outlook* are based on officially announced budgets, adjusted for differences between the national authorities and the IMF staff regarding macroeconomic assumptions and projected fiscal outturns. The medium-term fiscal projections incorporate policy measures that are judged likely to be implemented. In cases where the IMF staff has insufficient information to assess the authorities' budget intentions and prospects for policy implementation, an unchanged structural primary balance is assumed, unless otherwise indicated. Specific assumptions used in some of the advanced economies follow (see also Tables 12–14 in the Statistical Appendix for data on fiscal and structural balances).[1]

United States. The fiscal projections are based on the Administration's FY2006 Budget projections (February 7, 2005) adjusted to take into account: (1) differences in macroeconomic assumptions; (2) IMF staff assumptions about Alternative Minimum Tax (AMT) relief; and (3) IMF staff assumptions about additional defense spending using analysis by the Congressional Budget Office.

Japan. The medium-term fiscal projections assume that expenditure and revenue of the general government (excluding social security) are adjusted in line with the current govern-

ment target to achieve a primary fiscal balance by the early 2010s.

Germany. Fiscal projections for 2005–10 are based on IMF staff macroeconomic assumptions and estimates of fiscal adjustment measures and structural reforms.

France. The projections for 2005 are based on the initial budget adjusted for the IMF staff macroeconomic assumptions and IMF staff projected overruns in social security expenditures. For 2006–08, the projections are based on the intentions underlying the 2006–08 Stability Program Update adjusted for the IMF staff macroeconomic assumptions and lower projections of nontax revenue. For 2009–10, the staff assumes unchanged tax policies and real expenditure growth as in the Stability Program Update for 2008.

Italy. The 2005 projection is based on the IMF staff macroeconomic assumptions and its assessment of the authorities' budget. Beyond 2005, projections start with the assumption of constant structural primary balance, and are then adjusted for the savings from the ongoing pension reform (impact starting from 2008).

United Kingdom. The fiscal projections are based on information provided in the December 2004 Pre-Budget Report. Additionally, the projections incorporate the most recent statistical releases from the Office for National Statistics, including provisional budgetary outturns through 2004:Q4.

Canada. Projections are based on the 2004 budget, and updated with the 2004 Economic and Fiscal Update, released in November 2004. The federal government balance is the desk's estimate of the planning surplus (budgetary balance less contingency and economic reserves).

Australia. The fiscal projections through the fiscal year 2007/08 are based on the 2004/05 Mid-Year Economic and Fiscal Outlook published in December 2004. Subsequently, the IMF staff assumes no change in policies.

Austria. Fiscal figures for 2004 are based on the authorities' estimated outturn. Projections for 2005–06 are based on the budgets for 2005 and 2006. Projections for 2007–08 are based on

---

[1]The output gap is actual less potential output, as a percent of potential output. Structural balances are expressed as a percent of potential output. The structural budget balance is the budgetary position that would be observed if the level of actual output coincided with potential output. Changes in the structural budget balance consequently include effects of temporary fiscal measures, the impact of fluctuations in interest rates and debt-service costs, and other noncyclical fluctuations in the budget balance. The computations of structural budget balances are based on IMF staff estimates of potential GDP and revenue and expenditure elasticities (see the October 1993 *World Economic Outlook*, Annex I). Net debt is defined as gross debt less financial assets of the general government, which include assets held by the social security insurance system. Estimates of the output gap and of the structural balance are subject to significant margins of uncertainty.

the Austrian Stability Program (2004–08). For 2009–10, projections assume unchanged overall and structural balances from those in 2008.

Belgium. Fiscal projections for 2005 and the subsequent years are based on current government policies and historical expenditure trends, adjusted for the IMF staff macroeconomic assumptions.

Denmark. Projections for 2005 are aligned with the latest official projections and budget, adjusted for the IMF staff macroeconomic projections. For 2006–10, projections are in line with the authorities' medium-term framework— adjusted for the IMF staff macroeconomic projections—targeting an average budget surplus of 1.5–2.5 percent of GDP, supported by a ceiling on real public consumption growth.

Greece. The fiscal projections assume (1) constant ratios of tax and other nontax revenues to GDP; (2) EU transfers falling in the medium term; (3) continuation of recent trend in the increase in social contributions until 2007 (constant ratio to GDP thereafter); (4) continuation of recent trends for wage growth, social spending, and operational spending; (5) a gradual decline in investment spending from peak levels in 2003–04 owing to the 2004 Olympic games; and (6) a constant ratio to GDP for other spending.

Korea. For 2005, it is assumed that the fiscal outcome will be in line with the budget. In the medium term, fiscal policy is assumed consistent with achieving a balanced budget excluding social security funds.

Netherlands. The fiscal projections for 2005 and beyond build on the 2005 budget and the latest Stability Program, adjusted for IMF staff macroeconomic assumptions.

New Zealand. The fiscal projections through the fiscal year 2008–09 are based on the 2004 December Economic and Fiscal Update published in December 2004. For the remainder of the projection period, the IMF staff assumes unchanged policies.

Portugal. Fiscal projections for 2005 build on the preliminary figures for the 2004 deficit and the authorities' 2005 targets (including the 2005 budget for one-off measures), adjusted for the

IMF staff macroeconomic projections for 2005. Projections for 2006 and beyond assume a constant structural primary balance.

Spain. Fiscal projections through 2008 are based on the policies outlined in the national authorities' updated Stability Program of December 2004. These projections have been adjusted for the IMF staff macroeconomic scenario. In subsequent years, the fiscal projections assume no significant changes in these policies.

Sweden. The fiscal projections are based on information provided in the budget, presented on September 20, 2004. Additionally, the projections incorporate the most recent statistical releases from Statistics Sweden, including provisional budgetary outturns throughout December 2004.

Switzerland. Estimates for 2004 and projections for 2005–10 are based on IMF staff calculations, which incorporate measures to restore balance in the Federal accounts.

Monetary policy assumptions are based on the established policy framework in each country. In most cases, this implies a nonaccommodative stance over the business cycle: official interest rates will therefore increase when economic indicators suggest that prospective inflation will rise above its acceptable rate or range, and they will decrease when indicators suggest that prospective inflation will not exceed the acceptable rate or range, that prospective output growth is below its potential rate, and that the margin of slack in the economy is significant. On this basis, LIBOR on six-month U.S. dollar deposits is assumed to average 3.3 percent in 2005 and 4.1 percent in 2006. The projected path for U.S. dollar short-term interest rates reflects the assumption implicit in prevailing forward rates that the U.S. Federal Reserve will continue to raise interest rates in 2005–06. The rate on three-month euro deposits is assumed to average 2.3 percent in 2005 and 2.9 percent in 2006. The interest rate on six-month Japanese yen deposits is assumed to average 0.1 percent in 2005 and 0.4 percent in 2006, with the current monetary policy framework being maintained. Changes in interest rate assumptions compared with the September 2004 *World Economic Outlook* are summarized in Table 1.1.

- The purchasing-power-parity (PPP) weights have been updated to reflect the most up-to-date PPP conversion factor provided by the World Bank.

Data and Conventions

Data and projections for 175 countries form the statistical basis for the *World Economic Outlook* (the World Economic Outlook database). The data are maintained jointly by the IMF's Research Department and area departments, with the latter regularly updating country projections based on consistent global assumptions.

Although national statistical agencies are the ultimate providers of historical data and definitions, international organizations are also involved in statistical issues, with the objective of harmonizing methodologies for the national compilation of statistics, including the analytical frameworks, concepts, definitions, classifications, and valuation procedures used in the production of economic statistics. The World Economic Outlook database reflects information from both national source agencies and international organizations.

The comprehensive revision of the standardized *System of National Accounts 1993 (SNA),* the IMF's *Balance of Payments Manual, Fifth Edition (BPM5),* the *Monetary and Financial Statistics Manual (MFSM),* and the *Government Finance Statistics Manual 2001 (GFSM 2001)* represented important improvements in the standards of economic statistics and analysis.[2] The IMF was actively involved in all projects, particularly the new *Balance of Payments Manual,* which reflects the IMF's special interest in countries' external positions. Key changes introduced with the new *Manual* were summarized in Box 13 of the May 1994 *World Economic Outlook.* The process of adapting country balance of payments data to the definitions of the new *BPM5* began with the May 1995 *World Economic Outlook.* However, full concordance with the *BPM5* is ultimately dependent on the provision by national statistical compilers of revised country data, and hence the *World Economic Outlook* estimates are still only partially adapted to the *BPM5.*

The members of the European Union have adopted a harmonized system for the compilation of the national accounts, referred to as ESA 1995. All national accounts data from 1995 onward are presented on the basis of the new system. Revision by national authorities of data prior to 1995 to conform to the new system has progressed, but has in some cases not been completed. In such cases, historical *World Economic Outlook* data have been carefully adjusted to avoid breaks in the series. Users of EU national accounts data prior to 1995 should nevertheless exercise caution until such time as the revision of historical data by national statistical agencies has been fully completed. See Box 1.2, "Revisions in National Accounts Methodologies," in the May 2000 *World Economic Outlook.*

Composite data for country groups in the *World Economic Outlook* are either sums or weighted averages of data for individual countries. Unless otherwise indicated, multiyear averages of growth rates are expressed as compound annual rates of change. Arithmetically weighted averages are used for all data except inflation and money growth for the other emerging market and developing country group, for which geometric averages are used. The following conventions apply.

- Country group composites for exchange rates, interest rates, and the growth rates of monetary aggregates are weighted by GDP converted to U.S. dollars at market exchange rates (averaged over the preceding three years) as a share of group GDP.

---

[2]Commission of the European Communities, International Monetary Fund, Organization for Economic Cooperation and Development, United Nations, and World Bank, *System of National Accounts 1993* (Brussels/Luxembourg, New York, Paris, and Washington, 1993); International Monetary Fund, *Balance of Payments Manual, Fifth Edition* (Washington, 1993); International Monetary Fund, *Monetary and Financial Statistics Manual* (Washington, 2000); and International Monetary Fund, *Government Finance Statistics Manual* (Washington, 2001).

Table A. Classification by World Economic Outlook Groups and Their Shares in Aggregate GDP, Exports of Goods and Services, and Population, 2004[1]

(Percent of total for group or world)

	Number of Countries	GDP		Exports of Goods and Services		Population	
		Advanced economies	World	Advanced economies	World	Advanced economies	World
Advanced economies	**29**	**100.0**	**54.6**	**100.0**	**71.8**	**100.0**	**15.3**
United States		38.2	20.9	14.4	10.4	30.5	4.7
Euro area	12	28.0	15.3	43.4	31.1	32.1	4.9
Germany		7.9	4.3	13.2	9.5	8.6	1.3
France		5.7	3.1	6.7	4.8	6.4	1.0
Italy		5.3	2.9	5.3	3.8	6.0	0.9
Spain		3.2	1.7	3.4	2.4	4.3	0.7
Japan		12.6	6.9	8.0	5.7	13.3	2.0
United Kingdom		5.7	3.1	6.6	4.7	6.2	1.0
Canada		3.5	1.9	4.8	3.4	3.3	0.5
Other advanced economies	13	12.1	6.6	22.8	16.4	14.6	2.2
Memorandum							
Major advanced economies	7	78.8	43.0	59.0	42.3	74.3	11.4
Newly industrialized Asian economies	4	6.4	3.5	13.4	9.6	8.6	1.3
		Other emerging market and developing countries	World	Other emerging market and developing countries	World	Other emerging market and developing countries	World
Other emerging market and developing countries	**146**	**100.0**	**45.4**	**100.0**	**28.2**	**100.0**	**84.7**
Regional groups							
Africa	48	7.2	3.3	7.8	2.2	14.8	12.5
Sub-Sahara	45	5.6	2.5	5.7	1.6	13.4	11.4
Excluding Nigeria and South Africa	43	2.9	1.3	2.8	0.8	9.9	8.4
Central and eastern Europe	15	7.5	3.4	15.1	4.3	3.5	2.9
Commonwealth of Independent States[2]	13	8.3	3.8	9.5	2.7	5.2	4.4
Russia		5.7	2.6	6.5	1.8	2.7	2.3
Developing Asia	23	54.2	24.6	39.0	11.0	61.8	52.3
China		29.0	13.2	20.9	5.9	24.4	20.7
India		13.0	5.9	3.5	1.0	20.4	17.3
Excluding China and India	21	12.2	5.5	14.5	4.1	17.0	14.4
Middle East	14	6.2	2.8	13.6	3.8	4.8	4.1
Western Hemisphere	33	16.5	7.5	15.0	4.2	10.0	8.4
Brazil		5.8	2.6	3.5	1.0	3.3	2.8
Mexico		4.0	1.8	4.3	1.2	2.0	1.7
Analytical groups							
By source of export earnings							
Fuel	18	7.1	3.2	14.3	4.0	7.6	6.5
Nonfuel	128	92.9	42.2	85.7	24.2	92.4	78.2
of which, primary products	23	2.2	1.0	2.5	0.7	5.2	4.4
By external financing source							
Net debtor countries	126	56.4	25.6	51.7	14.6	67.6	57.3
of which, official financing	50	12.9	5.8	9.0	2.5	22.4	19.0
Net debtor countries by debt-servicing experience							
Countries with arrears and/or rescheduling during 1999–2003	56	12.2	5.6	10.9	3.1	23.7	20.1
Other net debtor countries	70	44.2	20.1	40.8	11.5	43.9	37.2
Other groups							
Heavily indebted poor countries	28	1.9	0.9	1.1	0.3	7.6	6.4
Middle East and north Africa	20	8.2	3.7	15.8	4.5	6.9	5.8

[1]The GDP shares are based on the purchasing-power-parity (PPP) valuation of country GDPs. The number of countries comprising each group reflects those for which data are included in the group aggregates.

[2]Mongolia, which is not a member of the Commonwealth of Independent States, is included in this group for reasons of geography and similarities in economic structure.

Table B. Advanced Economies by Subgroup

Major Currency Areas	Euro area		Other Subgroups			
			Newly industrialized Asian economies	Major advanced economies	Other advanced economies	
United States	Austria	Ireland	Hong Kong SAR[1]	Canada	Australia	Korea
Euro area	Belgium	Italy	Korea	France	Cyprus	New Zealand
Japan	Finland	Luxembourg	Singapore	Germany	Denmark	Norway
	France	Netherlands	Taiwan Province	Italy	Hong Kong SAR[1]	Singapore
	Germany	Portugal	of China	Japan	Iceland	Sweden
	Greece	Spain		United Kingdom	Israel	Switzerland
				United States		Taiwan Province of China

[1]On July 1, 1997, Hong Kong was returned to the People's Republic of China and became a Special Administrative Region of China.

- Composites for other data relating to the domestic economy, whether growth rates or ratios, are weighted by GDP valued at purchasing power parities (PPPs) as a share of total world or group GDP.[3]
- Composites for data relating to the domestic economy for the euro area (12 member countries throughout the entire period unless otherwise noted) are aggregates of national source data using weights based on 1995 ECU exchange rates.
- Composite unemployment rates and employment growth are weighted by labor force as a share of group labor force.
- Composites relating to the external economy are sums of individual country data after conversion to U.S. dollars at the average market exchange rates in the years indicated for balance of payments data and at end-of-year market exchange rates for debt denominated in currencies other than U.S. dollars. Composites of changes in foreign trade volumes and prices, however, are arithmetic averages of percentage changes for individual countries weighted by the U.S. dollar value of exports or imports as a share of total world or

group exports or imports (in the preceding year).

For central and eastern European countries, external transactions in nonconvertible currencies (through 1990) are converted to U.S. dollars at the implicit U.S. dollar/ruble conversion rates obtained from each country's national currency exchange rate for the U.S. dollar and for the ruble.

Classification of Countries

Summary of the Country Classification

The country classification in the *World Economic Outlook* divides the world into two major groups: advanced economies and other emerging market and developing countries.[4] Rather than being based on strict criteria, economic or otherwise, this classification has evolved over time with the objective of facilitating analysis by providing a reasonably meaningful organization of data. A few countries are presently not included in these groups, either because they are not IMF members and their economies are not monitored by the IMF, or because databases have not yet been

---

[3]See Box A2 of the April 2004 *World Economic Outlook* for a summary of the revised PPP-based weights and Annex IV of the May 1993 *World Economic Outlook*. See also Anne-Marie Gulde and Marianne Schulze-Ghattas, "Purchasing Power Parity Based Weights for the *World Economic Outlook*," in *Staff Studies for the World Economic Outlook* (International Monetary Fund, December 1993), pp. 106–23.

[4]As used here, the term "country" does not in all cases refer to a territorial entity that is a state as understood by international law and practice. It also covers some territorial entities that are not states, but for which statistical data are maintained on a separate and independent basis.

Table C. European Union

Austria	France	Latvia	Portugal
Belgium	Germany	Lithuania	Slovak Republic
Cyprus	Greece	Luxembourg	Slovenia
Czech Republic	Hungary	Malta	Spain
Denmark	Ireland	Netherlands	Sweden
Estonia	Italy	Poland	United Kingdom
Finland			

fully developed. Because of data limitations, group composites do not reflect the following countries: Afghanistan, Bosnia and Herzegovina, Brunei Darussalam, Eritrea, Liberia, Serbia and Montenegro, Somalia, and Timor-Leste. Cuba and the Democratic People's Republic of Korea are examples of countries that are not IMF members, whereas San Marino, among the advanced economies, is an example of an economy for which a database has not been completed.

Each of the two main country groups is further divided into a number of subgroups. Among the advanced economies, the seven largest in terms of GDP, collectively referred to as the major advanced countries, are distinguished as a subgroup, and so are the 12 members of the euro area, and the four newly industrialized Asian economies. The other emerging market and developing countries are classified by region, as well as into a number of analytical and other groups. Table A provides an overview of these standard groups in the *World Economic Outlook*, showing the number of countries in each group and the average 2004 shares of groups in aggregate PPP-valued GDP, total exports of goods and services, and population.

General Features and Composition of Groups in the *World Economic Outlook* Classification

Advanced Economies

The 29 advanced economies are listed in Table B. The seven largest in terms of GDP—the United States, Japan, Germany, France, Italy, the United Kingdom, and Canada—constitute the

Table D. Other Emerging Market and Developing Countries by Region and Main Source of Export Earnings

	Fuel	Nonfuel, of Which Primary Products
Africa		
Sub-Sahara	Angola Congo, Rep. of Equatorial Guinea Gabon Nigeria	Botswana Burkina Faso Burundi Chad Congo, Dem. Rep. of Côte d'Ivoire Ghana Guinea Guinea-Bissau Malawi Mauritania Namibia Niger Sierra Leone Uganda Zambia Zimbabwe
North Africa	Algeria	
Commonwealth of Independent States	Azerbaijan Turkmenistan	Tajikistan Uzbekistan
Developing Asia		Papua New Guinea Solomon Islands
Middle East	Iran, I.R. of Iraq Kuwait Libya Oman Qatar Saudi Arabia Syrian Arab Republic Yemen	
Western Hemisphere	Venezuela	Chile Suriname

subgroup of *major advanced economies,* often referred to as the Group of Seven (G-7) countries. The euro area (12 countries) and the *newly industrialized Asian economies* are also distinguished as subgroups. Composite data shown in the tables for the euro area cover the current members for all years, even though the membership has increased over time.

In 1991 and subsequent years, data for *Germany* refer to west Germany *and* the eastern Länder (i.e., the former German Democratic

Table E. Other Emerging Market and Developing Countries by Region and Net External Position

Countries	Net Creditor	Net Debtor[1]	Countries	Net Creditor	Net Debtor[1]
Africa			**Central and eastern Europe**		
Sub-Sahara			Albania		★
Angola		★	Bulgaria	★	
Benin		•	Croatia		★
Botswana	★		Czech Republic		★
Burkina Faso		•	Estonia		★
Burundi		•	Hungary		★
Cameroon		★	Latvia		★
Cape Verde		★	Lithuania		★
Central African Republic		•	Macedonia, FYR		★
Chad		•	Malta		★
Comoros		•	Poland		★
Congo, Dem. Rep. of		•	Romania		★
Congo, Rep. of		•	Slovak Republic		★
Côte d'Ivoire		•	Slovenia	★	
Djibouti		•	Turkey		★
Equatorial Guinea		★	**Commonwealth of Independent States**[2]		
Ethiopia		•	Armenia		★
Gabon		•	Azerbaijan		★
Gambia, The		★	Belarus		★
Ghana		•	Georgia		★
Guinea		•	Kazakhstan		★
Guinea-Bissau		•	Kyrgyz Republic		•
Kenya		•	Moldova		★
Lesotho		★	Mongolia		•
Madagascar		•	Russia	★	
Malawi		•	Tajikistan		★
Mali		•	Turkmenistan	★	
Mauritania		★	Ukraine	★	
Mauritius		★	Uzbekistan		★
Mozambique, Rep. of		★	**Developing Asia**		
Namibia	★		Bangladesh		•
Niger		•	Bhutan		•
Nigeria		★	Cambodia		•
Rwanda		•	China	★	
São Tomé and Príncipe		★	Fiji		★
Senegal		★	India		★
Seychelles		★	Indonesia		•
Sierra Leone		•	Kiribati	★	
Somalia		★	Lao PDR		★
South Africa		★	Malaysia	★	
Sudan		★	Maldives		★
Swaziland		★	Myanmar		★
Tanzania		•	Nepal		•
Togo		•	Pakistan		•
Uganda		★	Papua New Guinea		•
Zambia		•	Philippines		★
Zimbabwe		★	Samoa		★
North Africa			Solomon Islands		•
Algeria	★		Sri Lanka		•
Morocco		★	Thailand		★
Tunisia		★	Tonga		★
			Vanuatu		•
			Vietnam		•

Table E *(concluded)*

Countries	Net Creditor	Net Debtor[1]	Countries	Net Creditor	Net Debtor[1]
Middle East			Costa Rica		★
Bahrain		★	Dominica		★
Egypt		★	Dominican Republic		•
Iran, I.R. of	★				
			Ecuador		★
Iraq		★	El Salvador		•
Jordan		★	Grenada		•
Kuwait	★				
			Guatemala		★
Lebanon		•	Guyana		★
Libya	★		Haiti		•
Oman	★				
			Honduras		•
Qatar	★		Jamaica		★
Saudi Arabia	★		Mexico		★
Syrian Arab Republic		★			
			Netherlands Antilles		★
United Arab Emirates	★		Nicaragua		★
Yemen	★		Panama		★
Western Hemisphere			Paraguay		•
Antigua and Barbuda		★	Peru		★
Argentina		•	St. Kitts and Nevis		★
Bahamas, The		★			
			St. Lucia		•
Barbados		★	St. Vincent and the Grenadines		★
Belize		★	Suriname		★
Bolivia		•			
			Trinidad and Tobago		★
Brazil		★	Uruguay		•
Chile		★	Venezuela	★	
Colombia		•			

[1]Dot instead of star indicates that the net debtor's main external finance source is official financing.

[2]Mongolia, which is not a member of the Commonwealth of Independent States, is included in this group for reasons of geography and similarities in economic structure.

Republic). Before 1991, economic data are not available on a unified basis or in a consistent manner. Hence, in tables featuring data expressed as annual percent change, these apply to west Germany in years up to and including 1991, but to unified Germany from 1992 onward. In general, data on national accounts and domestic economic and financial activity through 1990 cover west Germany only, whereas data for the central government and balance of payments apply to west Germany through June 1990 and to unified Germany thereafter.

Table C lists the member countries of the European Union, not all of which are classified as advanced countries in the *World Economic Outlook.*

Other Emerging Market and Developing Countries

The group of other emerging market and developing countries (146 countries) includes all countries that are not classified as advanced economies.

The *regional breakdowns* of other emerging market and developing countries—*Africa, central and eastern Europe, Commonwealth of Independent States, developing Asia, Middle East, and Western Hemisphere*—largely conform to the regional breakdowns in the IMF's *International Financial Statistics.* In both classifications, Egypt and the Libyan Arab Jamahiriya are included in the *Middle East* region rather than in Africa. Three additional regional groupings—two of them constituting part of Africa and one a subgroup of Asia—are included in the *World Economic Outlook* because of their analytical significance. These are *sub-Sahara, sub-Sahara excluding Nigeria and South Africa,* and *Asia excluding China and India.*

Other emerging market and developing countries are also classified according to *ana-*

lytical criteria and into *other groups*. The analytical criteria reflect countries' composition of export earnings and other income from abroad, a distinction between net creditor and net debtor countries, and, for the net debtor countries, financial criteria based on external financing source and experience with external debt servicing. Included as "other groups" are the heavily indebted poor countries (HIPCs), and Middle East and north Africa (MENA). The detailed composition of other emerging market and developing countries in the regional, analytical, and other groups is shown in Tables D through F.

The first analytical criterion, by *source of export earnings*, distinguishes between categories: *fuel* (Standard International Trade Classification—SITC 3) and nonfuel and then focuses on *nonfuel primary products* (SITC 0, 1, 2, 4, and 68).

The financial criteria focus on *net creditor* and *net debtor countries*. Net debtor countries are further differentiated on the basis of two additional financial criteria: by *official external financing* and by *experience with debt servicing*.[5]

The *other groups* of developing countries constitute the HIPCs and MENA countries. The first group comprises the countries considered by the IMF and the World Bank for their debt initiative, known as the HIPC Initiative.[6] Middle East and north Africa, also referred to as the MENA countries, is a *World Economic Outlook* group, whose composition straddles the Africa and Middle East regions. It is defined as the Arab League countries plus the Islamic Republic of Iran.

[5]During 1999–2003, 56 countries incurred external payments arrears or entered into official or commercial bank debt-rescheduling agreements. This group of countries is referred to as *countries with arrears and/or rescheduling during 1999–2003*.

[6]See David Andrews, Anthony R. Boote, Syed S. Rizavi, and Sukwinder Singh, *Debt Relief for Low-Income Countries: The Enhanced HIPC Initiative*, IMF Pamphlet Series, No. 51 (Washington: International Monetary Fund, November 1999)

Table F. Other Developing Country Groups

Countries	Heavily Indebted Poor Countries	Middle East and North Africa
Africa		
Sub-Sahara		
Benin	•	
Burkina Faso	•	
Cameroon	•	
Chad	•	
Congo, Dem. Rep. of	•	
Djibouti		•
Ethiopia	•	
Gambia, The	•	
Ghana	•	
Guinea	•	
Guinea-Bissau	•	
Madagascar	•	
Malawi	•	
Mali	•	
Mauritania	•	•
Mozambique, Rep. of	•	
Niger	•	
Rwanda	•	
São Tomé and Príncipe	•	
Senegal	•	
Sierra Leone	•	
Sudan		•
Tanzania	•	
Uganda	•	
Zambia	•	
North Africa		
Algeria		•
Morocco		•
Tunisia		•
Middle East		
Bahrain		•
Egypt		•
Iran, I.R. of		•
Iraq		•
Jordan		•
Kuwait		•
Lebanon		•
Libya		•
Oman		•
Qatar		•
Saudi Arabia		•
Syrian Arab Republic		•
United Arab Emirates		•
Yemen		•
Western Hemisphere		
Bolivia	•	
Guyana	•	
Honduras	•	
Nicaragua	•	

List of Tables

Output

Inflation

Financial Policies

Foreign Trade

Current Account Transactions

Table 1. Summary of World Output[1]

(Annual percent change)

	Ten-Year Averages		1997	1998	1999	2000	2001	2002	2003	2004	2005	2006
	1987–96	1997–2006										
World	**3.3**	**3.9**	**4.2**	**2.8**	**3.7**	**4.6**	**2.5**	**3.0**	**4.0**	**5.1**	**4.3**	**4.4**
Advanced economies	**3.0**	**2.7**	**3.4**	**2.6**	**3.5**	**3.8**	**1.2**	**1.6**	**2.0**	**3.4**	**2.6**	**3.0**
United States	2.9	3.4	4.5	4.2	4.4	3.7	0.8	1.9	3.0	4.4	3.6	3.6
Euro area	. . .	2.0	2.4	2.8	2.8	3.6	1.6	0.9	0.5	2.0	1.6	2.3
Japan	3.2	0.9	1.7	−1.1	—	2.4	0.2	−0.3	1.4	2.6	0.8	1.9
Other advanced economies[2]	3.8	3.3	4.1	1.8	4.7	5.2	1.8	3.2	2.3	3.8	3.1	3.4
Other emerging market and developing countries	**3.9**	**5.3**	**5.3**	**3.0**	**4.0**	**5.8**	**4.2**	**4.7**	**6.4**	**7.2**	**6.3**	**6.0**
Regional groups												
Africa	2.2	4.0	3.2	3.0	2.8	3.2	4.0	3.6	4.6	5.1	5.0	5.4
Central and eastern Europe	0.9	3.6	4.2	2.8	0.4	4.9	0.2	4.4	4.6	6.1	4.5	4.5
Commonwealth of Independent States[3]	. . .	5.2	1.1	−3.5	5.1	9.1	6.4	5.4	7.9	8.2	6.5	6.0
Developing Asia	7.8	6.6	6.5	4.1	6.2	6.5	5.8	6.5	8.1	8.2	7.4	7.1
Middle East	3.4	4.5	4.8	4.0	2.1	5.4	3.3	4.1	5.8	5.5	5.0	4.9
Western Hemisphere	2.8	2.8	5.2	2.3	0.4	3.9	0.5	−0.1	2.2	5.7	4.1	3.7
Memorandum												
European Union	2.2	2.4	2.8	3.0	2.9	3.7	1.8	1.2	1.2	2.5	2.1	2.5
Analytical groups												
By source of export earnings												
Fuel	2.6	4.5	4.2	3.2	0.9	4.7	3.7	3.6	6.1	6.9	5.8	6.2
Nonfuel	4.0	5.3	5.3	3.0	4.3	5.9	4.2	4.8	6.4	7.2	6.3	6.0
of which, primary products	3.2	3.4	3.7	2.8	1.3	1.9	2.9	2.9	3.1	5.4	4.8	5.3
By external financing source												
Net debtor countries	3.5	4.1	4.6	2.1	2.9	4.4	2.6	3.2	4.9	6.0	5.3	5.2
of which, official financing	4.4	3.4	5.0	−0.5	1.0	3.2	2.2	1.5	5.2	5.9	5.4	5.2
Net debtor countries by debt-servicing experience												
Countries with arrears and/or rescheduling during 1999–2003	4.0	3.9	5.3	−0.5	1.7	3.6	2.9	2.1	5.8	6.3	5.8	5.8
Memorandum												
Median growth rate												
Advanced economies	3.1	3.0	3.8	3.6	3.8	4.2	1.7	1.9	1.9	3.2	2.8	2.8
Other emerging market and developing countries	3.2	4.2	4.6	3.7	3.4	4.2	3.5	3.5	4.8	5.1	4.4	4.5
Output per capita												
Advanced economies	2.3	2.1	2.8	2.0	2.9	3.2	0.6	1.0	1.5	2.9	2.1	2.5
Other emerging market and developing countries	2.1	3.9	3.7	1.5	2.6	4.4	2.8	3.4	5.1	5.9	5.0	4.8
World growth based on market exchange rates	**2.6**	**2.9**	**3.5**	**2.2**	**3.1**	**4.0**	**1.4**	**1.8**	**2.7**	**4.0**	**3.2**	**3.4**
Value of world output in billions of U.S. dollars												
At market exchange rates	23,744	35,274	29,768	29,529	30,638	31,455	31,195	32,410	36,327	40,671	44,168	46,573
At purchasing power parities	28,778	49,104	38,351	39,790	41,827	44,729	46,866	49,015	51,824	55,655	59,560	63,420

[1]Real GDP.
[2]In this table, "other advanced economies" means advanced economies excluding the United States, euro area countries, and Japan.
[3]Mongolia, which is not a member of the Commonwealth of Independent States, is included in this group for reasons of geography and similarities in economic structure.

Table 2. Advanced Economies: Real GDP and Total Domestic Demand

(Annual percent change)

	Ten-Year Averages		1997	1998	1999	2000	2001	2002	2003	2004	2005	2006	Fourth Quarter[1]		
	1987–96	1997–2006											2004	2005	2006
Real GDP															
Advanced economies	**3.0**	**2.7**	**3.4**	**2.6**	**3.5**	**3.8**	**1.2**	**1.6**	**2.0**	**3.4**	**2.6**	**3.0**	. . .	. . .	. . .
United States	2.9	3.4	4.5	4.2	4.4	3.7	0.8	1.9	3.0	4.4	3.6	3.6	3.9	3.6	3.7
Euro area	. . .	2.0	2.4	2.8	2.8	3.6	1.6	0.9	0.5	2.0	1.6	2.3	1.6	2.3	2.2
Germany	2.5	1.3	1.4	2.0	2.0	2.9	0.8	0.1	−0.1	1.7	0.8	1.9	0.6	2.1	1.8
France	2.0	2.3	1.9	3.6	3.2	4.2	2.1	1.1	0.5	2.3	2.0	2.2	2.2	2.1	2.3
Italy	1.9	1.5	2.0	1.8	1.7	3.0	1.8	0.4	0.3	1.2	1.2	2.0	0.8	2.1	2.0
Spain	2.9	3.3	4.0	4.3	4.2	4.4	2.8	2.2	2.5	2.7	2.8	3.0	2.7	2.7	3.1
Netherlands	2.7	2.2	3.8	4.3	4.0	3.5	1.4	0.6	−0.9	1.3	1.5	2.2	1.0	2.3	2.3
Belgium	2.2	2.3	3.8	2.1	3.2	3.7	0.9	0.9	1.3	2.7	2.1	2.3	2.6	1.9	2.5
Austria	2.5	2.1	1.6	3.9	2.7	3.4	0.7	1.2	0.8	2.0	2.1	2.3	2.5	2.3	2.1
Finland	1.3	3.5	6.3	5.0	3.4	5.1	1.1	2.2	2.4	3.7	3.1	3.0	3.6	3.0	3.1
Greece	1.4	3.8	3.6	3.4	3.4	4.5	4.3	3.8	4.7	4.2	3.0	3.0	4.2	2.5	3.2
Portugal	4.0	2.2	4.0	4.6	3.8	3.4	1.7	0.4	−1.2	1.0	1.8	2.3	0.8	2.6	2.4
Ireland	5.2	7.1	10.8	8.9	11.1	9.9	6.0	6.1	3.7	5.1	4.8	4.6	3.4	4.8	4.6
Luxembourg	5.2	5.0	8.3	6.8	7.3	9.2	2.2	2.3	2.4	4.4	3.5	3.4	. . .	. . .	. . .
Japan	3.2	0.9	1.7	−1.1	—	2.4	0.2	−0.3	1.4	2.6	0.8	1.9	1.0	1.6	1.9
United Kingdom	2.4	2.8	3.3	3.1	2.9	3.9	2.3	1.8	2.2	3.1	2.6	2.6	2.9	2.6	2.5
Canada	2.2	3.5	4.2	4.1	5.5	5.2	1.8	3.4	2.0	2.8	2.8	3.0	3.0	2.9	3.1
Korea	8.4	4.2	4.7	−6.9	9.5	8.5	3.8	7.0	3.1	4.6	4.0	5.2	2.8	4.8	5.1
Australia	3.6	3.6	3.9	5.3	4.3	3.2	2.5	4.0	3.4	3.2	2.6	3.3	1.5	3.4	3.2
Taiwan Province of China	7.6	4.1	6.4	4.3	5.3	5.8	−2.2	3.9	3.3	5.7	4.0	4.3	3.2	4.4	4.4
Sweden	1.5	2.8	2.4	3.6	4.6	4.3	1.0	2.0	1.5	3.5	3.0	2.5	2.8	3.3	2.5
Switzerland	1.4	1.5	1.9	2.8	1.3	3.6	1.0	0.3	−0.4	1.7	1.2	2.0	1.2	1.6	1.9
Hong Kong SAR	5.9	3.5	5.1	−5.0	3.4	10.2	0.5	1.9	3.2	8.1	4.0	4.0	6.4	3.1	4.8
Denmark	1.5	2.0	3.0	2.5	2.6	2.8	1.6	1.0	0.4	2.3	2.2	1.9	3.2	1.0	2.5
Norway	2.9	2.6	5.2	2.6	2.1	2.8	2.7	1.1	0.4	2.9	3.7	2.8	2.9	4.2	2.0
Israel	5.5	2.9	3.5	3.7	2.5	8.0	−0.9	−0.7	1.3	4.3	3.7	3.6	8.2	0.6	5.4
Singapore	9.4	4.3	8.6	−0.8	6.8	9.6	−2.0	3.2	1.4	8.4	4.0	4.5	6.5	3.2	4.8
New Zealand	2.8	3.1	1.9	−0.1	4.3	3.6	2.6	4.7	3.4	5.0	2.8	2.6	4.7	2.4	2.6
Cyprus	5.8	3.7	2.3	5.0	4.8	5.0	4.1	2.1	1.9	3.7	3.8	4.0	. . .	. . .	. . .
Iceland	1.6	4.0	4.7	5.5	4.2	5.7	2.2	−0.5	4.3	5.7	5.4	2.5	. . .	. . .	. . .
Memorandum															
Major advanced economies	2.7	2.5	3.2	2.8	3.1	3.4	1.0	1.2	2.0	3.3	2.5	2.9	2.7	2.8	2.9
Newly industrialized Asian economies	7.9	4.2	5.5	−2.6	7.3	7.9	1.3	5.3	3.1	5.5	4.0	4.8	4.0	4.8	5.3
Real total domestic demand															
Advanced economies	**2.9**	**2.8**	**3.2**	**3.0**	**4.1**	**3.8**	**1.0**	**1.7**	**2.1**	**3.4**	**2.7**	**2.9**	. . .	. . .	. . .
United States	2.7	3.8	4.8	5.3	5.3	4.4	0.9	2.5	3.3	4.8	3.8	3.4	4.5	3.3	3.5
Euro area	. . .	2.0	1.8	3.6	3.5	2.9	1.0	0.4	1.2	2.0	1.6	2.1	1.9	1.7	2.3
Germany	2.5	0.8	0.6	2.4	2.8	1.9	−0.8	−1.9	0.5	0.5	0.4	1.6	−0.1	0.8	2.2
France	1.8	2.6	0.7	4.2	3.7	4.5	2.0	1.5	1.3	3.5	2.3	2.0	3.6	1.8	2.2
Italy	1.6	1.9	2.7	3.1	3.2	2.3	1.4	1.3	1.2	1.1	1.2	1.9	1.0	1.7	2.0
Spain	3.3	4.0	3.5	5.7	5.6	4.6	2.9	2.8	3.2	4.2	4.0	3.7	4.5	3.5	3.7
Japan	3.5	0.6	0.6	−1.5	0.2	1.9	0.7	−0.9	0.8	1.9	0.8	1.6	0.9	1.4	1.7
United Kingdom	2.4	3.4	3.5	4.8	3.9	3.8	2.9	2.9	2.4	3.8	3.0	2.8	3.3	2.6	2.8
Canada	1.8	3.6	5.7	2.4	4.1	4.9	1.3	3.4	4.4	3.6	3.7	2.9	4.6	2.4	3.1
Other advanced economies	5.5	2.9	3.7	−1.6	5.5	5.2	0.6	3.5	1.1	3.7	3.3	4.1	. . .	. . .	. . .
Memorandum															
Major advanced economies	2.6	2.7	3.1	3.5	3.8	3.6	1.0	1.4	2.3	3.4	2.6	2.7	3.1	2.5	2.8
Newly industrialized Asian economies	9.0	2.6	4.2	−8.2	7.8	7.5	—	4.1	−0.3	3.5	3.4	5.4	2.5	5.8	6.2

[1]From fourth quarter of preceding year.

Table 3. Advanced Economies: Components of Real GDP
(Annual percent change)

	Ten-Year Averages		1997	1998	1999	2000	2001	2002	2003	2004	2005	2006
	1987–96	1997–2006										
Private consumer expenditure												
Advanced economies	**3.0**	**2.8**	**2.8**	**3.0**	**4.0**	**3.7**	**2.2**	**2.2**	**2.0**	**2.6**	**2.4**	**2.7**
United States	2.9	3.8	3.8	5.0	5.1	4.7	2.5	3.1	3.3	3.8	3.6	3.0
Euro area	. . .	1.9	1.6	3.0	3.5	2.8	1.9	0.7	1.0	1.3	1.6	2.1
Germany	2.7	1.0	0.6	1.8	3.7	2.0	1.7	−0.7	—	−0.3	0.2	1.2
France	1.6	2.4	0.2	3.6	3.5	2.9	2.8	1.8	1.6	2.3	2.5	2.3
Italy	1.9	1.9	3.2	3.2	2.6	2.7	0.8	0.5	1.3	1.0	1.4	1.9
Spain	2.8	3.5	3.2	4.4	4.7	4.1	2.8	2.9	2.9	3.5	3.3	3.3
Japan	3.2	0.6	0.7	−0.2	—	0.5	1.1	0.5	0.2	1.5	0.1	1.4
United Kingdom	2.8	3.3	3.6	3.9	4.4	4.6	2.9	3.3	2.3	3.3	2.5	2.4
Canada	2.2	3.3	4.6	2.8	3.8	4.0	2.7	3.4	3.1	3.5	2.4	2.6
Other advanced economies	5.2	3.1	4.0	−1.0	5.9	5.4	2.6	3.7	1.0	2.5	2.5	4.3
Memorandum												
Major advanced economies	2.7	2.7	2.6	3.4	3.7	3.4	2.2	2.0	2.1	2.7	2.4	2.4
Newly industrialized Asian economies	8.2	3.1	4.9	−5.5	8.2	7.4	3.3	4.9	−0.6	1.1	2.4	5.8
Public consumption												
Advanced economies	**2.0**	**2.3**	**1.4**	**1.8**	**2.8**	**2.5**	**2.9**	**3.5**	**2.3**	**2.1**	**1.6**	**2.0**
United States	1.1	2.4	1.8	1.6	3.1	1.7	3.1	4.0	2.9	1.7	1.6	2.3
Euro area	. . .	1.8	1.4	1.4	1.7	2.4	2.4	3.1	1.6	1.6	1.1	1.4
Germany	1.5	0.8	0.3	1.9	0.8	1.1	1.0	1.9	0.1	0.4	−0.2	0.8
France	2.3	2.3	2.1	−0.1	1.5	3.0	2.9	4.6	2.5	2.6	1.9	1.7
Italy	1.1	1.3	0.3	0.3	1.4	1.7	3.8	1.9	2.2	0.6	0.6	0.4
Spain	4.3	4.0	2.9	3.7	4.2	5.6	3.5	4.1	3.9	4.9	4.3	3.4
Japan	3.4	2.5	1.1	2.2	4.8	4.9	3.0	2.6	1.2	2.7	1.4	1.0
United Kingdom	1.0	2.7	−0.4	1.2	3.5	2.3	2.6	3.8	3.2	4.7	3.0	3.0
Canada	1.3	2.6	−1.0	3.2	2.1	3.1	3.7	2.8	3.8	2.5	3.0	3.2
Other advanced economies	4.6	2.4	2.8	2.7	1.5	1.9	2.9	3.8	2.1	1.7	2.1	2.9
Memorandum												
Major advanced economies	1.6	2.2	1.2	1.5	2.9	2.4	2.9	3.4	2.3	2.0	1.5	1.9
Newly industrialized Asian economies	6.6	2.5	3.7	2.8	0.3	2.3	3.3	4.2	2.2	1.6	1.7	3.2
Gross fixed capital formation												
Advanced economies	**3.6**	**3.3**	**5.3**	**5.1**	**5.5**	**5.2**	**−1.0**	**−1.9**	**2.2**	**5.4**	**3.9**	**4.0**
United States	3.3	4.9	8.0	9.1	8.2	6.1	−1.7	−3.1	4.5	8.9	4.9	4.8
Euro area	. . .	2.2	2.5	4.9	5.9	5.2	−0.2	−2.5	−0.6	1.8	2.5	3.4
Germany	2.9	—	0.6	3.0	4.1	2.7	−4.2	−6.4	−2.2	−0.7	1.0	3.0
France	1.8	3.4	−0.2	7.2	8.3	8.4	2.1	−1.8	0.2	3.3	3.7	3.8
Italy	1.6	2.3	2.1	4.0	5.0	6.9	1.9	1.2	−2.1	0.5	1.1	2.2
Spain	4.2	5.1	5.0	10.0	8.8	5.7	3.0	1.7	3.2	4.6	5.1	4.7
Japan	3.9	−0.3	0.2	−4.2	−0.8	2.0	−1.6	−5.7	1.1	1.5	2.2	2.8
United Kingdom	3.0	4.7	6.8	12.7	1.6	3.6	2.6	2.7	2.3	5.6	5.8	3.7
Canada	2.0	5.6	15.2	2.4	7.3	4.7	4.1	2.4	4.9	6.3	5.2	4.2
Other advanced economies	7.0	3.1	5.3	−1.4	3.1	6.9	−3.7	3.7	1.8	6.4	4.7	4.3
Memorandum												
Major advanced economies	3.1	3.3	5.1	5.7	5.6	5.0	−0.9	−2.8	2.4	5.5	3.8	4.0
Newly industrialized Asian economies	11.8	1.9	4.1	−10.0	2.7	10.6	−6.5	1.9	1.1	7.3	4.0	5.8

Table 3 (concluded)

	Ten-Year Averages		1997	1998	1999	2000	2001	2002	2003	2004	2005	2006
	1987–96	1997–2006										
Final domestic demand												
Advanced economies	**3.0**	**2.8**	**3.0**	**3.1**	**4.1**	**3.8**	**1.6**	**1.6**	**2.1**	**3.1**	**2.6**	**2.8**
United States	2.7	3.8	4.3	5.3	5.4	4.5	1.8	2.1	3.4	4.4	3.6	3.2
Euro area	. . .	2.0	1.7	3.1	3.6	3.3	1.5	0.5	0.8	1.5	1.7	2.2
Germany	2.5	0.8	0.5	2.1	3.2	2.0	0.2	−1.5	−0.4	−0.2	0.3	1.5
France	1.8	2.5	0.6	3.3	4.0	4.1	2.7	1.7	1.5	2.5	2.6	2.5
Italy	1.7	1.8	2.4	2.8	2.9	3.4	1.6	0.9	0.7	0.8	1.2	1.7
Spain	3.3	4.0	3.5	5.5	5.5	4.7	3.0	2.8	3.1	4.0	3.9	3.7
Japan	3.4	0.7	0.7	−1.0	0.5	1.6	0.7	−0.7	0.6	1.7	0.9	1.7
United Kingdom	2.4	3.4	3.3	4.8	3.8	4.0	2.8	3.3	2.5	3.9	3.1	2.8
Canada	2.0	3.6	5.4	2.8	4.2	4.0	3.2	3.1	3.6	3.8	3.1	3.1
Other advanced economies	5.9	2.9	4.1	−1.4	4.4	5.4	1.1	3.9	1.5	3.3	2.8	4.3
Memorandum												
Major advanced economies	2.6	2.7	2.8	3.4	3.9	3.6	1.6	1.3	2.2	3.1	2.5	2.6
Newly industrialized Asian economies	9.0	2.6	4.3	−6.3	5.3	7.6	0.7	4.0	0.4	2.6	2.7	5.4
Stock building[1]												
Advanced economies	**—**	**—**	**0.2**	**—**	**—**	**—**	**−0.6**	**0.1**	**0.1**	**0.4**	**0.1**	**0.1**
United States	0.1	0.1	0.5	—	—	−0.1	−0.9	0.4	−0.1	0.5	0.2	0.3
Euro area	. . .	—	—	0.5	−0.1	−0.3	−0.6	−0.1	0.4	0.5	−0.1	−0.1
Germany	—	—	—	0.3	−0.4	−0.1	−1.0	−0.4	0.9	0.7	0.1	0.1
France	—	—	0.1	0.8	−0.2	0.4	−0.6	−0.2	−0.2	0.9	−0.3	−0.5
Italy	−0.1	0.1	0.3	0.3	0.3	−1.1	−0.1	0.5	0.5	0.2	—	0.3
Spain	—	—	—	0.2	0.1	−0.1	−0.1	—	0.1	0.2	—	—
Japan	—	−0.1	−0.1	−0.5	−0.4	0.3	0.1	−0.2	0.2	0.2	−0.1	—
United Kingdom	—	—	0.3	0.1	0.2	−0.1	0.1	−0.4	—	−0.2	−0.1	—
Canada	0.1	0.2	0.7	−0.3	0.1	0.8	−1.9	0.6	0.9	—	0.7	−0.2
Other advanced economies	—	—	−0.3	−0.6	1.0	−0.1	−0.4	−0.1	−0.3	0.4	0.3	—
Memorandum												
Major advanced economies	—	—	0.3	—	−0.1	—	−0.6	0.1	0.1	0.4	0.1	0.1
Newly industrialized Asian economies	0.1	—	−0.2	−1.9	2.1	−0.1	−0.6	0.1	−0.6	0.7	0.6	—
Foreign balance[1]												
Advanced economies	**—**	**−0.1**	**0.2**	**−0.3**	**−0.5**	**—**	**0.1**	**−0.1**	**−0.2**	**−0.1**	**−0.2**	**0.1**
United States	0.2	−0.6	−0.3	−1.2	−1.0	−0.9	−0.2	−0.7	−0.4	−0.6	−0.3	—
Euro area	. . .	0.1	0.7	−0.7	−0.7	0.8	0.7	0.5	−0.6	0.1	—	0.2
Germany	—	0.6	0.8	−0.4	−0.7	1.0	1.6	1.9	−0.6	1.2	0.4	0.4
France	0.2	−0.2	1.2	−0.5	−0.4	−0.2	0.1	−0.4	−0.8	−1.2	−0.3	0.2
Italy	0.3	−0.4	−0.6	−1.2	−1.4	0.8	0.3	−0.9	−0.9	0.2	—	0.1
Spain	−0.4	−0.8	0.6	−1.3	−1.4	−0.3	−0.2	−0.6	−0.8	−1.7	−1.4	−1.0
Japan	−0.2	0.3	1.0	0.4	−0.2	0.5	−0.6	0.6	0.6	0.8	—	0.3
United Kingdom	—	−0.7	−0.3	−1.6	−1.0	−0.1	−0.7	−1.2	−0.4	−0.8	−0.5	−0.3
Canada	0.2	−0.1	−1.7	1.7	1.4	0.6	0.7	−0.1	−2.4	−0.9	−0.8	0.3
Other advanced economies	−0.3	0.8	0.8	2.5	0.3	0.8	0.9	0.3	1.3	1.0	0.1	—
Memorandum												
Major advanced economies	0.1	−0.2	0.1	−0.7	−0.7	−0.2	—	−0.2	−0.4	−0.2	−0.2	0.1
Newly industrialized Asian economies	−1.0	1.7	1.3	6.0	0.3	0.6	1.2	1.2	3.2	2.7	0.8	−0.1

[1]Changes expressed as percent of GDP in the preceding period.

Table 4. Advanced Economies: Unemployment, Employment, and Real Per Capita GDP

(Percent)

	Ten-Year Averages[1]		1997	1998	1999	2000	2001	2002	2003	2004	2005	2006
	1987–96	1997–2006										
Unemployment rate												
Advanced economies	**6.8**	**6.3**	**6.8**	**6.7**	**6.4**	**5.8**	**5.9**	**6.4**	**6.6**	**6.3**	**6.1**	**6.0**
United States[2]	6.1	5.0	4.9	4.5	4.2	4.0	4.8	5.8	6.0	5.5	5.3	5.2
Euro area	. . .	8.9	10.6	10.0	9.2	8.2	7.8	8.2	8.7	8.8	8.7	8.4
Germany	7.3	8.9	9.7	9.1	8.4	7.8	7.9	8.7	9.6	9.2	9.4	9.2
France	10.4	9.7	11.5	11.1	10.5	9.1	8.4	8.9	9.5	9.7	9.5	8.9
Italy	11.3	9.7	11.7	11.8	11.4	10.6	9.5	9.0	8.7	8.3	8.0	7.6
Spain	20.0	13.3	20.8	18.7	15.7	13.9	10.5	11.4	11.3	10.8	10.3	9.9
Netherlands	6.5	3.9	5.0	3.8	3.2	2.9	2.5	2.7	3.8	4.6	5.3	5.0
Belgium	8.4	7.9	9.2	9.3	8.6	6.9	6.7	7.3	7.9	7.8	7.8	7.7
Austria	3.4	4.2	4.4	4.5	4.0	3.7	3.6	4.3	4.4	4.5	4.5	4.2
Finland	9.7	9.7	12.6	11.4	10.2	9.8	9.1	9.1	9.0	8.8	8.4	8.1
Greece	8.4	10.2	9.8	11.0	12.1	11.4	10.8	10.3	9.7	8.9	8.8	8.8
Portugal	5.8	5.6	6.7	5.0	4.4	3.9	4.1	5.1	6.4	6.8	6.8	6.8
Ireland	14.5	5.3	10.3	7.6	5.6	4.3	3.8	4.4	4.6	4.5	4.1	4.0
Luxembourg	2.0	3.6	3.6	3.1	2.9	2.6	2.6	3.0	3.8	4.4	4.8	5.2
Japan	2.6	4.6	3.4	4.1	4.7	4.7	5.0	5.4	5.3	4.7	4.5	4.4
United Kingdom	8.5	5.4	7.1	6.3	6.0	5.5	5.1	5.2	5.0	4.8	4.7	4.7
Canada	9.5	7.6	9.2	8.4	7.6	6.9	7.2	7.7	7.6	7.2	7.2	7.1
Korea	2.5	4.1	2.6	7.0	6.4	4.2	3.8	3.1	3.4	3.5	3.6	3.3
Australia	8.4	6.4	8.2	7.7	6.9	6.3	6.8	6.4	6.1	5.5	5.1	5.3
Taiwan Province of China	1.7	3.9	2.7	2.7	2.9	3.0	4.6	5.2	5.0	4.6	4.3	4.2
Sweden	4.7	5.3	8.1	6.5	5.6	4.7	4.0	4.0	4.9	5.5	5.1	4.4
Switzerland	2.1	3.0	4.5	3.4	2.4	1.7	1.6	2.3	3.4	3.5	3.7	3.5
Hong Kong SAR	1.9	5.6	2.2	4.7	6.2	5.0	5.1	7.3	7.9	6.8	5.7	4.9
Denmark	9.8	5.7	7.8	6.4	5.5	5.1	4.9	4.9	5.8	5.9	5.6	5.5
Norway	4.9	3.8	4.1	3.2	3.2	3.4	3.5	3.9	4.5	4.4	4.0	4.0
Israel	8.4	9.4	7.7	8.5	8.9	8.7	9.3	10.3	10.8	10.4	9.8	9.5
Singapore	2.6	3.5	1.8	3.2	3.5	3.1	3.3	4.4	4.7	4.0	3.6	3.4
New Zealand	7.5	5.4	6.6	7.4	6.8	6.0	5.3	5.2	4.6	3.9	3.8	4.2
Cyprus	2.6	3.3	3.4	3.4	3.6	3.4	2.9	3.2	3.5	3.4	3.2	3.0
Iceland	2.8	2.4	3.9	2.8	1.9	1.3	1.4	2.5	3.3	3.1	2.3	1.7
Memorandum												
Major advanced economies	6.6	6.2	6.5	6.3	6.1	5.7	5.9	6.6	6.7	6.3	6.2	6.0
Newly industrialized Asian economies	2.2	4.1	2.6	5.4	5.3	3.9	4.1	4.1	4.3	4.1	4.0	3.7
Growth in employment												
Advanced economies	**1.1**	**1.1**	**1.5**	**1.1**	**1.4**	**2.1**	**0.7**	**0.3**	**0.6**	**1.0**	**1.2**	**1.1**
United States	1.5	1.3	2.3	1.5	1.5	2.5	—	−0.3	0.9	1.1	1.9	1.5
Euro area	1.1	0.8	1.9	1.8	2.2	1.3	0.5	0.2	0.9	0.9	1.0	
Germany	0.4	0.6	−0.2	1.1	1.2	1.8	0.4	−0.6	−1.0	1.4	0.9	0.6
France	0.4	1.0	0.4	1.5	2.0	2.7	1.7	0.7	—	−0.2	0.5	1.0
Italy	−0.4	1.2	0.4	1.1	1.3	1.9	2.1	1.5	1.0	0.8	0.7	0.9
Spain	1.7	3.4	3.3	4.1	5.5	5.5	3.7	2.0	2.7	2.5	2.4	2.1
Japan	1.0	−0.2	1.1	−0.7	−0.8	−0.2	−0.5	−1.3	−0.2	0.2	−0.1	0.2
United Kingdom	0.4	1.0	1.8	1.0	1.4	1.2	0.8	0.8	0.9	0.9	0.6	0.5
Canada	1.2	2.0	1.6	2.5	2.7	2.6	1.3	2.4	2.3	1.8	1.3	1.3
Other advanced economies	1.9	1.3	1.3	−0.9	1.6	2.9	1.1	1.6	0.6	1.6	1.6	1.4
Memorandum												
Major advanced economies	0.9	0.9	1.4	1.0	1.1	1.8	0.4	−0.1	0.5	0.9	1.1	1.0
Newly industrialized Asian economies	2.6	1.2	1.8	−2.9	1.5	3.5	1.0	2.0	0.3	1.8	1.6	1.7

Table 4 *(concluded)*

	Ten-Year Averages[1]		1997	1998	1999	2000	2001	2002	2003	2004	2005	2006
	1987–96	1997–2006										
Growth in real per capita GDP												
Advanced economies	**2.3**	**2.1**	**2.8**	**2.0**	**2.9**	**3.2**	**0.6**	**1.0**	**1.5**	**2.9**	**2.1**	**2.5**
United States	1.7	2.3	3.3	3.0	3.3	2.5	−0.3	0.9	2.0	3.4	2.6	2.6
Euro area	. . .	1.8	2.1	2.6	2.5	3.3	1.2	0.5	0.1	1.7	1.3	2.0
Germany	1.8	1.2	1.2	2.0	2.0	2.7	0.7	−0.1	−0.3	1.5	0.7	1.9
France	1.5	1.9	1.5	3.2	2.8	3.7	1.6	0.6	—	1.9	1.6	1.8
Italy	1.8	1.5	1.9	1.7	1.6	3.0	1.8	0.4	0.4	1.0	1.0	1.9
Spain	2.7	2.7	3.8	4.1	3.8	3.2	2.2	1.6	1.9	2.1	2.1	2.5
Japan	2.9	0.8	1.4	−1.4	−0.2	2.2	−0.1	−0.5	1.2	2.6	0.7	1.9
United Kingdom	2.1	2.3	3.1	2.8	2.5	3.6	1.6	1.3	1.7	2.6	2.1	2.1
Canada	0.9	2.5	3.2	3.2	4.7	4.3	0.7	2.3	1.1	1.8	1.6	1.8
Other advanced economies	4.0	2.8	3.4	−0.4	4.5	5.1	0.7	3.1	1.8	3.7	2.8	3.3
Memorandum												
Major advanced economies	2.0	2.0	2.6	2.2	2.5	2.9	0.4	0.7	1.4	2.8	2.0	2.4
Newly industrialized Asian economies	6.8	3.3	4.3	−3.7	6.3	7.0	0.4	4.5	2.4	4.9	3.4	4.2

[1]Compound annual rate of change for employment and per capita GDP; arithmetic average for unemployment rate.
[2]The projections for unemployment have been adjusted to reflect the survey techniques adopted by the U.S. Bureau of Labor Statistics in January 1994.

Table 5. Other Emerging Market and Developing Countries: Real GDP

(Annual percent change)

	Ten-Year Averages		1997	1998	1999	2000	2001	2002	2003	2004	2005	2006
	1987–96	1997–2006										
Other emerging market and developing countries	**3.9**	**5.3**	**5.3**	**3.0**	**4.0**	**5.8**	**4.2**	**4.7**	**6.4**	**7.2**	**6.3**	**6.0**
Regional groups												
Africa	2.2	4.0	3.2	3.0	2.8	3.2	4.0	3.6	4.6	5.1	5.0	5.4
Sub-Sahara	2.3	4.0	3.9	2.2	2.8	3.4	3.9	3.6	4.2	5.1	5.2	5.6
Excluding Nigeria and South Africa	2.4	4.6	5.0	3.7	3.4	2.5	4.9	4.1	3.7	6.4	5.5	6.8
Central and eastern Europe	0.9	3.6	4.2	2.8	0.4	4.9	0.2	4.4	4.6	6.1	4.5	4.5
Commonwealth of Independent States[1]	...	5.2	1.1	−3.5	5.1	9.1	6.4	5.4	7.9	8.2	6.5	6.0
Russia	...	4.7	1.4	−5.3	6.3	10.0	5.1	4.7	7.3	7.1	6.0	5.5
Excluding Russia	...	6.0	0.6	0.7	2.2	6.8	9.3	6.9	9.1	10.5	7.7	7.0
Developing Asia	7.8	6.6	6.5	4.1	6.2	6.5	5.8	6.5	8.1	8.2	7.4	7.1
China	10.0	8.3	8.8	7.8	7.1	8.0	7.5	8.3	9.3	9.5	8.5	8.0
India	5.9	5.9	5.2	5.6	6.9	4.7	4.8	4.4	7.5	7.3	6.7	6.4
Excluding China and India	6.4	3.9	3.9	−4.5	3.8	5.4	3.2	4.7	5.7	5.9	5.6	5.9
Middle East	3.4	4.5	4.8	4.0	2.1	5.4	3.3	4.1	5.8	5.5	5.0	4.9
Western Hemisphere	2.8	2.8	5.2	2.3	0.4	3.9	0.5	−0.1	2.2	5.7	4.1	3.7
Brazil	2.1	2.5	3.3	0.1	0.8	4.4	1.3	1.9	0.5	5.2	3.7	3.5
Mexico	2.5	3.5	6.8	5.0	3.6	6.6	—	0.6	1.6	4.4	3.7	3.3
Analytical groups												
By source of export earnings												
Fuel	2.6	4.5	4.2	3.2	0.9	4.7	3.7	3.6	6.1	6.9	5.8	6.2
Nonfuel	4.0	5.3	5.3	3.0	4.3	5.9	4.2	4.8	6.4	7.2	6.3	6.0
of which, primary products	3.2	3.4	3.7	2.8	1.3	1.9	2.9	2.9	3.1	5.4	4.8	5.3
By external financing source												
Net debtor countries	3.5	4.1	4.6	2.1	2.9	4.4	2.6	3.2	4.9	6.0	5.3	5.2
of which, official financing	4.4	3.4	5.0	−0.5	1.0	3.2	2.2	1.5	5.2	5.9	5.4	5.2
Net debtor countries by debt-servicing experience												
Countries with arrears and/or rescheduling during 1999–2003	4.0	3.9	5.3	−0.5	1.7	3.6	2.9	2.1	5.8	6.3	5.8	5.8
Other groups												
Heavily indebted poor countries	1.8	4.5	4.0	3.6	3.6	2.9	5.1	4.1	4.2	6.5	5.4	6.1
Middle East and north Africa	3.1	4.5	4.1	4.5	2.4	4.8	3.6	4.0	5.9	5.4	5.0	5.1
Memorandum												
Real per capita GDP												
Other emerging market and developing countries	2.1	3.9	3.7	1.5	2.6	4.4	2.8	3.4	5.1	5.9	5.0	4.8
Africa	−0.5	1.7	0.8	0.6	0.5	0.9	1.7	1.3	2.4	2.9	2.8	3.2
Central and eastern Europe	0.2	3.2	3.7	2.3	−0.1	4.4	−0.2	3.9	4.2	5.7	4.1	4.1
Commonwealth of Independent States[1]	...	5.4	1.3	−3.3	5.3	9.3	6.6	5.6	8.1	8.4	6.7	6.2
Developing Asia	6.1	5.3	5.1	2.7	4.8	5.2	4.5	5.2	6.8	7.0	6.2	6.0
Middle East	0.8	2.3	2.6	1.9	—	3.2	1.1	1.9	3.7	3.3	2.9	2.8
Western Hemisphere	0.9	1.3	3.6	0.7	−1.2	2.4	−1.0	−1.5	0.7	4.2	2.7	2.3

[1]Mongolia, which is not a member of the Commonwealth of Independent States, is included in this group for reasons of geography and similarities in economic structure.

Table 6. Other Emerging and Developing Countries—by Country: Real GDP[1]
(Annual percent change)

	Average 1987–96	1997	1998	1999	2000	2001	2002	2003	2004	2005	2006
Africa	**2.2**	**3.2**	**3.0**	**2.8**	**3.2**	**4.0**	**3.6**	**4.6**	**5.1**	**5.0**	**5.4**
Algeria	0.8	1.1	5.1	3.2	2.1	2.6	4.0	6.9	5.3	4.6	4.7
Angola	−0.1	7.9	6.8	3.2	3.0	3.1	14.4	3.4	11.2	13.8	24.5
Benin	2.9	5.7	4.6	4.7	5.8	5.0	6.0	4.8	3.0	5.0	6.0
Botswana	7.6	6.7	5.9	5.5	7.6	5.2	5.0	6.6	5.2	4.2	3.5
Burkina Faso	4.7	6.9	8.4	4.2	3.1	6.7	5.2	8.0	4.8	3.1	4.2
Burundi	2.5	0.4	4.8	−1.0	−0.9	2.1	4.5	−1.2	5.5	5.0	5.0
Cameroon[2]	−2.3	5.1	5.0	4.4	4.2	5.3	6.5	4.5	4.3	3.9	4.6
Cape Verde	4.8	8.5	8.0	10.9	8.1	6.1	5.0	5.3	4.0	6.0	7.0
Central African Republic	−1.7	7.5	3.9	3.6	1.8	0.3	−0.6	−7.0	0.9	3.5	4.0
Chad	3.6	4.2	7.7	−1.7	−0.6	9.9	9.9	11.3	30.5	10.0	5.6
Comoros	0.8	4.2	1.2	1.9	2.4	2.3	2.3	2.1	1.9	3.0	3.5
Congo, Dem. Rep. of	−4.3	−5.4	−1.7	−4.3	−6.9	−2.1	3.5	5.7	6.8	7.0	7.0
Congo, Rep. of	5.0	−0.6	3.7	−3.0	8.2	3.6	5.4	0.8	4.0	9.2	4.7
Côte d'Ivoire	2.8	5.7	4.7	1.5	−2.2	0.1	−1.5	−1.6	−0.9	−1.4	2.0
Djibouti	−1.5	−0.7	0.1	2.2	0.7	1.9	2.6	3.5	3.0	3.9	4.3
Equatorial Guinea	7.3	82.0	22.6	27.0	18.0	40.5	9.6	18.3	34.2	4.8	4.6
Eritrea	. . .	7.9	1.8	—	−13.1	9.2	0.6	3.0	1.8	0.7	0.1
Ethiopia	3.1	5.1	−1.4	6.0	5.4	7.7	1.6	−3.9	11.6	5.7	4.6
Gabon	2.5	5.7	3.5	−8.9	−1.9	2.0	—	2.6	1.9	1.6	1.1
Gambia, The	3.3	4.9	6.5	6.4	5.5	5.8	−3.2	6.7	7.7	5.0	4.8
Ghana	4.7	4.2	4.7	4.4	3.7	4.2	4.5	5.2	5.5	5.6	5.9
Guinea	4.2	4.9	4.8	4.7	1.9	4.0	4.2	1.2	2.5	3.2	4.8
Guinea-Bissau	3.5	6.5	−27.2	7.6	7.5	0.2	−7.2	0.6	4.3	2.4	2.6
Kenya	3.4	2.2	1.6	1.3	—	1.1	1.1	1.6	3.1	3.3	3.7
Lesotho	6.1	4.8	−3.5	0.5	1.9	3.3	4.5	5.2	2.3	2.4	3.0
Madagascar	1.2	3.7	3.9	4.7	4.7	6.0	−12.7	9.8	5.3	6.4	7.0
Malawi	3.4	6.6	1.1	3.5	0.8	−4.1	2.1	3.9	4.3	4.8	5.1
Mali	3.3	5.3	8.4	3.0	−3.2	12.1	4.3	7.4	2.2	5.8	5.8
Mauritania	3.1	2.8	3.9	5.2	5.2	4.4	4.1	6.6	5.2	5.8	47.0
Mauritius	6.8	5.7	5.9	4.4	6.1	7.1	3.4	3.0	4.4	3.7	2.9
Morocco	3.0	−2.2	7.7	−0.1	1.0	6.3	3.2	5.2	3.5	3.0	3.8
Mozambique, Rep. of	5.3	11.0	12.6	7.5	1.6	13.0	7.4	7.1	7.8	7.3	6.5
Namibia	3.3	4.2	3.3	3.4	3.5	2.2	2.5	3.7	4.4	3.6	3.8
Niger	1.3	2.8	10.4	−0.6	−1.4	7.1	3.0	5.3	0.9	4.2	4.2
Nigeria	3.6	3.2	0.3	1.5	5.4	3.1	1.5	10.7	3.5	7.4	5.8
Rwanda	−3.9	13.8	8.9	7.6	6.0	6.7	9.4	0.9	4.0	4.0	4.3
São Tomé and Príncipe	0.9	1.0	2.5	2.5	3.0	4.0	5.0	5.5	6.0	7.0	9.1
Senegal	2.4	3.3	4.5	6.2	3.0	4.7	1.1	6.5	6.0	6.4	5.2
Seychelles	5.3	12.2	2.5	1.9	4.3	−2.2	1.3	−6.3	−2.0	−4.0	3.0
Sierra Leone	−4.2	−17.6	−0.8	−8.1	3.8	18.1	27.5	8.6	7.4	7.5	7.1
South Africa	1.7	2.6	0.5	2.4	4.2	2.7	3.6	2.8	3.7	4.0	3.5
Sudan	3.3	9.3	5.7	6.5	6.9	6.1	6.0	6.0	7.3	8.3	8.6
Swaziland	5.7	3.8	3.3	3.5	2.0	1.7	2.8	2.4	2.1	2.0	1.7
Tanzania	3.6	3.5	3.7	3.5	5.1	6.2	7.2	7.1	6.3	6.5	7.0
Togo	2.0	3.5	−2.3	2.4	−0.4	0.6	4.5	4.4	2.9	3.0	3.0
Tunisia	4.3	5.4	4.8	6.1	4.7	4.9	1.7	5.6	5.8	5.0	5.9
Uganda	6.4	5.5	3.6	8.1	5.6	4.9	6.8	4.7	5.9	5.2	6.4
Zambia	−0.3	3.3	−1.9	2.2	3.6	4.9	3.3	5.1	5.0	5.0	5.0
Zimbabwe	3.6	1.4	0.1	−3.6	−7.3	−2.7	−6.0	−10.0	−4.8	−1.6	—

Table 6 *(continued)*

	Average 1987–96	1997	1998	1999	2000	2001	2002	2003	2004	2005	2006
Central and eastern Europe[3]	**0.9**	**4.2**	**2.8**	**0.4**	**4.9**	**0.2**	**4.4**	**4.6**	**6.1**	**4.5**	**4.5**
Albania	−0.8	−10.2	12.7	10.1	7.3	7.2	3.4	6.0	5.9	6.0	6.0
Bosnia and Herzegovina	. . .	29.9	15.6	9.6	5.5	4.3	5.3	4.0	5.2	4.5	5.1
Bulgaria	−4.8	−5.6	4.0	2.3	5.4	4.1	4.9	4.3	5.7	5.5	5.5
Croatia	. . .	6.8	2.5	−0.9	2.9	4.4	5.2	4.3	3.8	3.8	4.5
Czech Republic	. . .	−0.8	−1.0	0.5	3.3	2.6	1.5	3.7	4.0	4.0	3.9
Estonia	. . .	10.5	5.2	−0.1	7.8	6.4	7.2	5.1	6.2	6.0	5.5
Hungary	−0.9	4.6	4.9	4.2	5.2	3.8	3.5	3.0	4.0	3.7	3.8
Latvia	. . .	8.3	4.7	3.3	6.9	8.0	6.4	7.5	8.0	7.3	6.2
Lithuania	. . .	7.0	7.3	−1.7	3.9	6.4	6.8	9.7	6.6	7.0	6.8
Macedonia, FYR	. . .	1.4	3.4	4.4	4.5	−4.5	0.9	3.2	2.3	3.7	3.5
Malta	5.9	4.9	3.4	4.1	9.9	−1.7	2.2	−1.8	1.5	1.5	1.8
Serbia and Montenegro	. . .	—	2.5	−18.0	5.0	5.5	3.8	2.7	7.2	4.6	4.8
Poland	1.8	6.8	4.8	4.1	4.0	1.0	1.4	3.8	5.3	3.5	3.7
Romania	−1.8	−6.1	−4.8	−1.2	2.1	5.7	5.1	5.2	8.3	5.5	5.0
Slovak Republic	. . .	4.6	4.2	1.5	2.0	3.8	4.6	4.5	5.5	4.8	4.9
Slovenia	. . .	4.8	3.6	5.6	3.9	2.7	3.4	2.5	4.4	4.0	4.0
Turkey	4.4	7.6	3.1	−4.7	7.4	−7.5	7.9	5.9	8.0	5.0	5.0
Commonwealth of Independent States[3,4]	**. . .**	**1.1**	**−3.5**	**5.1**	**9.1**	**6.4**	**5.4**	**7.9**	**8.2**	**6.5**	**6.0**
Russia	. . .	1.4	−5.3	6.3	10.0	5.1	4.7	7.3	7.1	6.0	5.5
Excluding Russia	. . .	0.6	0.7	2.2	6.8	9.3	6.9	9.1	10.5	7.7	7.0
Armenia	. . .	3.3	7.3	3.3	6.0	9.6	13.2	13.9	10.1	8.0	6.0
Azerbaijan	. . .	6.1	8.6	7.9	10.3	9.6	9.7	10.8	10.1	21.6	38.3
Belarus	. . .	11.4	8.4	3.4	5.8	4.7	5.0	6.8	11.0	7.1	6.0
Georgia	. . .	10.6	2.9	3.0	1.9	4.7	5.5	11.1	8.5	6.0	5.0
Kazakhstan	. . .	1.6	−1.9	2.7	9.8	13.5	9.8	9.3	9.4	8.0	7.7
Kyrgyz Republic	. . .	9.9	2.1	3.7	5.4	5.3	—	6.9	6.0	5.0	5.9
Moldova	. . .	1.6	−6.5	−3.4	2.1	6.1	7.8	6.3	7.0	5.0	4.0
Mongolia	−0.2	4.0	3.5	3.2	1.1	1.0	3.9	5.3	6.0	5.5	5.5
Tajikistan	. . .	1.8	5.2	3.8	8.3	10.2	9.1	10.2	10.6	8.0	7.0
Turkmenistan	. . .	−11.3	6.7	16.4	18.6	20.4	19.8	16.9	7.5	7.0	6.5
Ukraine	. . .	−3.0	−1.9	−0.2	5.9	9.2	5.2	9.6	12.1	7.0	4.0
Uzbekistan	. . .	2.5	2.1	3.4	3.2	4.1	3.1	1.5	7.1	3.5	2.5

Table 6 *(continued)*

	Average 1987–96	1997	1998	1999	2000	2001	2002	2003	2004	2005	2006
Developing Asia	**7.8**	**6.5**	**4.1**	**6.2**	**6.5**	**5.8**	**6.5**	**8.1**	**8.2**	**7.4**	**7.1**
Afghanistan, I.S. of	...	...	...	...	...	...	28.6	15.7	7.5	10.1	9.7
Bangladesh	4.2	5.3	5.0	5.4	5.6	4.8	4.9	5.4	5.4	5.5	5.9
Bhutan	6.2	7.2	6.4	7.7	5.5	7.1	6.7	6.5	7.0	7.4	11.5
Brunei Darussalam	...	2.6	−4.0	2.6	2.8	3.1	2.8	3.1	1.1	1.6	1.3
Cambodia	...	6.8	3.7	10.8	7.0	5.7	5.5	5.2	4.3	1.9	4.3
China	10.0	8.8	7.8	7.1	8.0	7.5	8.3	9.3	9.5	8.5	8.0
Fiji	3.5	−2.3	1.2	9.2	−2.8	2.7	4.3	4.8	4.7	3.1	2.3
India	5.9	5.2	5.6	6.9	4.7	4.8	4.4	7.5	7.3	6.7	6.4
Indonesia	7.0	4.5	−13.1	0.8	4.9	3.8	4.4	4.9	5.1	5.5	6.0
Kiribati	2.4	1.9	12.6	9.5	1.6	1.8	1.0	2.5	1.8	1.5	1.5
Lao PDR	5.2	6.9	4.0	7.3	5.8	5.8	5.8	5.3	6.0	7.0	6.5
Malaysia	9.1	7.3	−7.4	6.1	8.9	0.3	4.1	5.3	7.1	6.0	6.2
Maldives	7.5	10.4	9.8	7.2	4.8	3.5	6.5	8.4	8.8	1.0	9.0
Myanmar	2.5	5.7	5.8	10.9	13.7	11.3	12.0	13.8	5.0	4.5	3.5
Nepal	5.5	5.3	2.9	4.5	6.1	5.5	−0.6	3.1	3.5	3.5	5.0
Pakistan	4.9	1.8	3.1	4.0	3.4	2.7	3.2	5.6	6.5	6.7	6.3
Papua New Guinea	5.1	−3.9	−3.8	7.6	−1.2	−2.3	−0.8	2.7	2.5	2.9	2.3
Philippines	3.7	5.2	−0.6	3.4	4.4	1.8	4.3	4.7	6.1	4.7	4.5
Samoa	2.5	0.8	2.4	2.6	6.9	6.2	1.8	3.1	3.2	3.2	3.2
Solomon Islands	5.7	−1.4	1.8	−0.5	−14.3	−9.0	−1.6	5.0	6.0	4.3	5.2
Sri Lanka	4.3	6.4	4.7	4.3	6.0	−1.5	4.0	5.9	5.2	5.3	6.0
Thailand	9.5	−1.4	−10.5	4.4	4.8	2.2	5.3	6.9	6.1	5.6	6.2
Timor-Leste, Dem. Rep. of	...	...	...	...	15.4	14.6	3.0	−2.7	1.0	1.5	2.3
Tonga	1.5	−3.0	3.6	2.5	5.5	0.9	2.7	1.9	1.0	1.3	2.0
Vanuatu	3.5	8.4	4.5	−3.2	2.7	−2.7	−4.9	2.4	3.0	2.8	2.6
Vietnam	7.1	8.2	5.8	4.8	6.8	6.9	7.1	7.3	7.7	7.2	7.0
Middle East	**3.4**	**4.8**	**4.0**	**2.1**	**5.4**	**3.3**	**4.1**	**5.8**	**5.5**	**5.0**	**4.9**
Bahrain	4.5	3.1	4.8	4.3	5.3	4.5	5.1	5.7	5.5	5.3	5.2
Egypt	2.8	5.9	7.5	6.1	5.4	3.5	3.2	3.1	4.1	4.8	5.0
Iran, I.R. of	3.1	3.4	2.7	1.9	5.1	3.7	7.5	6.6	6.6	6.0	5.9
Iraq	...	...	...	...	...	...	...	...	...	...	...
Jordan	3.0	3.3	3.0	3.1	4.1	4.9	4.8	3.3	6.7	5.0	5.5
Kuwait	1.8	2.5	3.7	−1.8	1.9	0.7	−0.5	9.7	7.2	3.2	3.2
Lebanon	−2.5	4.0	3.0	1.0	−0.5	2.0	2.0	3.0	5.0	4.0	3.5
Libya	−0.3	4.3	−1.3	0.4	2.4	2.9	3.7	5.3	0.9	4.3	4.4
Oman	4.4	6.2	2.7	−0.2	5.5	7.5	1.7	1.4	2.5	3.6	5.3
Qatar	1.4	31.1	11.7	4.5	9.1	4.5	7.3	8.5	9.9	5.1	5.7
Saudi Arabia	3.0	2.6	2.8	−0.7	4.9	0.5	0.1	7.2	5.3	4.1	3.3
Syrian Arab Republic	5.8	5.0	6.8	−3.6	0.6	3.8	4.2	2.6	3.4	3.5	3.6
United Arab Emirates	6.3	8.3	1.4	4.4	12.3	3.5	1.9	7.0	5.7	4.5	4.0
Yemen	...	6.4	5.3	3.5	4.4	4.6	3.9	3.1	2.7	2.9	2.7

Table 6 (concluded)

	Average 1987–96	1997	1998	1999	2000	2001	2002	2003	2004	2005	2006
Western Hemisphere	**2.8**	**5.2**	**2.3**	**0.4**	**3.9**	**0.5**	**−0.1**	**2.2**	**5.7**	**4.1**	**3.7**
Antigua and Barbuda	3.9	5.6	5.0	4.0	3.5	2.1	2.4	4.9	4.1	2.4	2.6
Argentina	2.6	8.1	3.8	−3.4	−0.8	−4.4	−10.9	8.8	9.0	6.0	3.6
Bahamas, The	1.2	3.3	3.0	5.9	4.9	−3.1	−0.1	1.9	3.3	3.5	3.5
Barbados	0.7	4.6	6.2	0.5	2.4	−3.4	−0.5	2.2	3.0	2.5	2.5
Belize	7.5	3.6	3.7	8.8	12.3	4.9	4.3	9.4	3.0	3.3	4.6
Bolivia	3.8	5.0	5.0	0.4	2.3	1.5	2.8	2.5	3.8	4.4	4.5
Brazil	2.1	3.3	0.1	0.8	4.4	1.3	1.9	0.5	5.2	3.7	3.5
Chile	7.9	6.6	3.2	−0.8	4.5	3.4	2.2	3.3	6.0	6.1	5.4
Colombia	4.2	3.4	0.6	−4.2	2.9	1.5	1.9	4.0	4.0	4.0	4.0
Costa Rica	4.8	5.6	8.4	8.2	1.8	1.0	2.9	6.5	4.2	3.2	2.7
Dominica	3.3	2.0	2.8	1.6	1.4	−4.2	−4.7	—	1.0	2.0	1.5
Dominican Republic	3.8	8.3	7.3	8.1	7.8	4.0	4.3	−1.6	2.0	2.5	4.3
Ecuador	2.7	4.1	2.1	−6.3	2.8	5.1	3.4	2.7	6.6	3.9	3.7
El Salvador	4.3	4.2	3.7	3.4	2.2	1.7	2.2	1.8	1.5	2.5	3.0
Grenada	3.5	4.4	7.9	7.3	7.0	−4.4	−0.4	5.7	−3.2	1.3	7.4
Guatemala	3.9	4.4	5.0	3.8	3.6	2.3	2.2	2.2	2.6	3.1	3.5
Guyana	3.5	6.2	−1.7	3.0	−1.3	2.3	1.1	−0.7	1.6	0.4	1.2
Haiti	−1.0	2.7	2.2	2.7	0.9	−1.0	−0.5	0.4	−3.5	2.5	3.0
Honduras	3.6	5.0	2.9	−1.9	5.7	2.6	2.7	3.5	4.2	4.0	4.5
Jamaica	1.7	−1.4	−0.6	1.1	0.8	1.0	1.9	2.0	2.5	2.5	2.8
Mexico	2.5	6.8	5.0	3.6	6.6	—	0.6	1.6	4.4	3.7	3.3
Netherlands Antilles	2.8	−0.5	0.7	−0.7	−2.0	0.6	0.4	1.4	1.0	1.5	2.0
Nicaragua	0.1	4.0	3.7	7.0	4.2	3.0	1.0	2.3	4.0	3.5	4.0
Panama	2.7	6.4	7.4	4.0	2.7	0.6	2.2	4.3	6.0	3.5	4.0
Paraguay	3.7	2.6	−0.4	0.5	−0.4	2.7	−2.3	2.6	2.1	2.5	3.0
Peru	1.5	6.8	−0.7	0.9	2.9	0.2	4.9	3.8	5.1	4.5	4.5
St. Kitts and Nevis	5.2	6.8	1.1	3.7	4.4	2.6	1.6	2.1	5.1	3.7	3.0
St. Lucia	4.6	0.6	3.4	2.8	0.1	−4.3	—	2.3	2.0	1.5	1.0
St. Vincent and the Grenadines	4.4	3.9	5.2	3.0	1.3	0.9	1.1	2.2	2.8	3.3	3.3
Suriname	0.5	5.7	1.6	−0.9	−0.1	4.5	3.0	5.3	4.6	4.8	3.3
Trinidad and Tobago	0.3	2.8	7.8	4.4	7.3	4.3	6.8	13.2	6.2	6.3	13.9
Uruguay	3.6	5.0	4.5	−2.8	−1.4	−3.4	−11.0	2.5	12.0	5.0	3.5
Venezuela	2.3	6.4	0.3	−6.0	3.7	3.4	−8.9	−7.7	17.3	4.6	3.8

[1]For many countries, figures for recent years are IMF staff estimates. Data for some countries are for fiscal years.

[2]The percent changes in 2002 are calculated over a period of 18 months, reflecting a change in the fiscal year cycle (from July–June to January–December).

[3]Data for some countries refer to real net material product (NMP) or are estimates based on NMP. For many countries, figures for recent years are IMF staff estimates. The figures should be interpreted only as indicative of broad orders of magnitude because reliable, comparable data are not generally available. In particular, the growth of output of new private enterprises of the informal economy is not fully reflected in the recent figures.

[4]Mongolia, which is not a member of the Commonwealth of Independent States, is included in this group for reasons of geography and similarities in economic structure.

Table 7. Summary of Inflation
(Percent)

	Ten-Year Averages 1987–96	Ten-Year Averages 1997–2006	1997	1998	1999	2000	2001	2002	2003	2004	2005	2006
GDP deflators												
Advanced economies	**3.3**	**1.6**	**1.7**	**1.3**	**0.9**	**1.5**	**1.9**	**1.6**	**1.5**	**1.6**	**1.9**	**1.7**
United States	2.8	1.9	1.7	1.1	1.4	2.2	2.4	1.7	1.8	2.1	2.3	2.0
Euro area	...	1.8	1.6	1.7	1.1	1.4	2.4	2.5	2.0	1.9	1.9	1.8
Japan	1.0	−0.9	0.4	−0.2	−1.3	−1.5	−1.3	−1.3	−1.4	−1.2	−0.8	−0.6
Other advanced economies[1]	4.6	2.0	2.6	2.0	1.0	2.0	2.0	1.8	2.0	2.0	2.6	2.3
Consumer prices												
Advanced economies	**3.5**	**1.8**	**2.0**	**1.5**	**1.4**	**2.2**	**2.1**	**1.5**	**1.8**	**2.0**	**2.0**	**1.9**
United States	3.7	2.4	2.3	1.5	2.2	3.4	2.8	1.6	2.3	2.7	2.7	2.4
Euro area[2]	...	1.8	1.6	1.1	1.1	2.1	2.4	2.3	2.1	2.2	1.9	1.7
Japan	1.3	−0.1	1.7	0.6	−0.3	−0.9	−0.7	−1.0	−0.2	—	−0.2	—
Other advanced economies	4.5	1.9	2.2	2.3	1.2	1.8	2.1	1.7	1.8	1.8	2.0	2.1
Other emerging market and developing countries	**56.6**	**7.4**	**11.5**	**11.1**	**10.2**	**7.1**	**6.7**	**6.0**	**6.0**	**5.7**	**5.5**	**4.6**
Regional groups												
Africa	28.5	10.1	13.4	9.0	11.6	13.0	12.1	9.8	10.6	7.7	7.7	5.9
Central and eastern Europe	61.3	18.1	51.4	32.7	22.9	22.7	19.4	14.7	9.2	6.6	5.2	4.0
Commonwealth of Independent States[3]	...	20.2	18.1	23.7	69.6	24.6	20.3	13.8	12.0	10.3	11.4	8.8
Developing Asia	11.0	3.6	4.9	7.9	2.6	1.9	2.7	2.1	2.6	4.2	3.9	3.4
Middle East	15.3	7.6	8.6	8.4	8.5	5.9	5.4	6.5	7.1	8.3	8.6	8.3
Western Hemisphere	182.3	7.7	11.5	8.6	7.3	6.7	6.1	8.9	10.6	6.5	6.0	5.2
Memorandum												
European Union	9.6	2.2	2.6	2.1	1.7	2.5	2.5	2.2	2.0	2.2	2.0	1.9
Analytical groups												
By source of export earnings												
Fuel	27.0	11.2	15.7	13.1	12.7	10.0	9.6	10.3	11.1	10.3	9.8	9.4
Nonfuel	59.7	7.1	11.2	11.0	10.0	6.9	6.5	5.6	5.6	5.4	5.2	4.3
of which, primary products	62.6	18.0	24.1	11.8	24.0	29.0	26.1	15.5	18.3	11.9	12.2	8.6
By external financing source												
Net debtor countries	65.5	8.8	13.5	15.1	10.3	8.7	8.3	8.4	7.6	5.9	5.9	4.9
of which, official financing	42.8	8.6	8.8	17.9	9.9	6.1	7.2	9.4	7.8	6.8	6.9	5.7
Net debtor countries by debt-servicing experience												
Countries with arrears and/or rescheduling during 1999–2003	50.5	11.2	10.6	19.9	12.0	8.4	10.9	13.7	11.1	9.3	8.9	7.4
Memorandum												
Median inflation rate												
Advanced economies	3.5	2.0	1.8	1.6	1.4	2.7	2.5	2.1	2.1	1.9	2.0	2.0
Other emerging market and developing countries	10.3	4.7	7.0	6.3	4.1	4.3	4.8	3.3	4.3	4.7	4.4	4.0

[1]In this table, "other advanced economies" means advanced economies excluding the United States, euro area countries, and Japan.
[2]Based on Eurostat's harmonized index of consumer prices.
[3]Mongolia, which is not a member of the Commonwealth of Independent States, is included in this group for reasons of geography and similarities in economic structure.

Table 8. Advanced Economies: GDP Deflators and Consumer Prices

(Annual percent change)

	Ten-Year Averages		1997	1998	1999	2000	2001	2002	2003	2004	2005	2006	Fourth Quarter[1]		
	1987–96	1997–2006											2004	2005	2006
GDP deflators															
Advanced economies	**3.3**	**1.6**	**1.7**	**1.3**	**0.9**	**1.5**	**1.9**	**1.6**	**1.5**	**1.6**	**1.9**	**1.7**	...	...	...
United States	2.8	1.9	1.7	1.1	1.4	2.2	2.4	1.7	1.8	2.1	2.3	2.0	2.4	2.3	2.0
Euro area	...	1.8	1.6	1.7	1.1	1.4	2.4	2.5	2.0	1.9	1.9	1.8	1.7	1.9	1.9
Germany	3.5	0.9	0.7	1.1	0.5	−0.3	1.3	1.5	1.1	0.6	0.8	1.2	0.3	1.4	1.2
France	2.5	1.4	1.3	0.8	0.4	0.7	1.7	2.4	1.5	1.8	1.8	1.8	1.7	2.0	1.8
Italy	5.7	2.4	2.4	2.7	1.6	2.2	2.6	3.1	2.9	2.7	2.2	1.9	2.3	2.0	1.9
Spain	5.7	3.5	2.3	2.4	2.8	3.4	4.2	4.5	4.0	4.4	3.9	3.2	4.7	3.4	3.1
Netherlands	1.6	2.4	2.0	1.7	1.6	3.9	5.2	3.1	3.0	1.0	1.5	1.4	1.5	0.9	1.7
Belgium	2.6	1.8	1.4	1.7	1.4	1.3	1.8	1.8	2.0	2.3	2.1	2.0	2.3	2.5	1.7
Austria	2.7	1.4	0.9	0.5	0.7	1.4	2.1	1.5	1.8	2.0	1.8	1.8	2.1	1.8	1.8
Finland	3.7	1.5	2.1	3.5	−0.2	3.2	3.0	1.3	−0.2	0.8	0.7	1.1	1.2	0.6	2.0
Greece	14.4	3.9	6.8	5.2	3.0	3.4	3.5	4.0	3.5	3.4	3.1	3.0	4.1	0.5	4.7
Portugal	8.5	3.3	3.8	3.8	3.1	3.5	4.3	4.4	2.3	2.5	2.9	2.9	3.2	3.5	2.1
Ireland	2.7	3.9	4.4	6.4	3.8	4.8	5.7	4.5	1.6	3.1	2.7	2.3	3.1	3.2	1.9
Luxembourg	2.7	2.4	2.7	2.8	2.6	4.0	1.3	1.2	2.6	2.2	2.4	2.6	...	...	...
Japan	1.0	−0.9	0.4	−0.2	−1.3	−1.5	−1.3	−1.3	−1.4	−1.2	−0.8	−0.6	−0.4	−1.1	−0.4
United Kingdom	4.7	2.5	2.9	2.8	2.3	1.3	2.2	3.2	3.2	2.2	2.1	2.8	2.1	2.6	3.0
Canada	2.7	2.0	1.2	−0.4	1.7	4.1	1.1	1.0	3.2	3.3	2.5	1.9	4.2	1.8	2.0
Korea	7.7	2.9	4.6	5.8	−0.1	0.7	3.5	2.8	2.3	3.4	3.5	3.0	3.2	3.6	3.0
Australia	3.4	2.6	1.4	0.4	0.6	4.3	3.8	2.7	3.1	3.4	3.9	2.0	3.9	3.1	2.0
Taiwan Province of China	2.6	0.1	1.7	2.7	−1.4	−1.7	0.5	−0.9	−2.1	−1.9	2.6	1.8	−1.6	2.4	2.2
Sweden	4.8	1.6	1.6	0.8	0.7	1.3	2.3	1.7	2.1	0.8	2.2	2.3	0.9	2.8	2.3
Switzerland	2.5	0.8	−0.1	−0.3	0.7	0.8	0.6	1.7	0.9	0.9	1.2	1.2	1.0	1.2	1.2
Hong Kong SAR	8.0	−1.8	5.7	0.2	−5.9	−6.2	−1.9	−3.6	−5.2	−2.8	1.2	1.4	−2.1	2.8	0.7
Denmark	3.0	1.9	2.2	1.0	1.8	3.0	2.1	1.6	2.2	1.5	1.6	1.6	0.6	2.2	1.3
Norway	3.2	3.6	2.9	−0.7	6.6	15.9	1.1	−1.6	2.4	4.9	4.9	0.7	7.5	2.3	0.2
Israel	15.3	3.3	9.2	6.4	5.7	1.0	2.2	5.9	1.5	−1.1	1.0	2.0	1.0	1.7	2.0
Singapore	3.0	0.2	0.4	−2.3	−4.6	4.1	−1.7	−0.4	0.4	3.5	1.5	1.5	6.5	1.2	1.5
New Zealand	3.5	2.1	1.5	1.6	0.7	2.7	4.7	0.2	2.0	3.2	2.0	2.3	3.3	2.2	2.4
Cyprus	4.3	2.9	2.8	2.4	2.3	3.7	3.2	2.2	4.8	2.2	2.5	2.5	...	...	...
Iceland	9.7	3.8	3.5	5.0	2.8	2.8	9.9	5.3	−0.3	4.5	2.3	2.7	...	...	...
Memorandum															
Major advanced economies	2.9	1.4	1.4	1.0	0.9	1.2	1.6	1.4	1.5	1.5	1.6	1.6	1.7	1.6	1.6
Newly industrialized Asian economies	6.0	1.4	3.6	3.7	−1.4	−0.6	1.7	0.8	—	1.1	2.8	2.4	1.4	3.1	2.5
Consumer prices															
Advanced economies	**3.5**	**1.8**	**2.0**	**1.5**	**1.4**	**2.2**	**2.1**	**1.5**	**1.8**	**2.0**	**2.0**	**1.9**	...	...	...
United States	3.7	2.4	2.3	1.5	2.2	3.4	2.8	1.6	2.3	2.7	2.7	2.4	3.4	2.4	2.5
Euro area[2]	...	1.8	1.6	1.1	1.1	2.1	2.4	2.3	2.1	2.2	1.9	1.7	2.4	1.9	1.7
Germany	2.6	1.3	1.5	0.6	0.6	1.4	1.9	1.3	1.0	1.8	1.5	1.2	2.1	1.5	1.0
France	2.6	1.6	1.3	0.7	0.6	1.8	1.8	1.9	2.2	2.3	2.0	1.9	2.3	2.1	1.8
Italy	5.2	2.2	1.9	2.0	1.7	2.6	2.3	2.6	2.8	2.3	1.8	1.8	2.2	1.8	1.8
Spain	5.4	2.8	1.9	1.8	2.2	3.5	2.8	3.6	3.1	3.1	3.1	2.7	3.5	3.0	2.7
Japan	1.3	−0.1	1.7	0.6	−0.3	−0.9	−0.7	−1.0	−0.2	—	−0.2	—	0.6	−0.6	0.3
United Kingdom[2]	4.2	1.4	1.8	1.6	1.4	0.8	1.2	1.3	1.4	1.3	1.7	2.0	1.4	1.9	1.9
Canada	3.1	2.0	1.6	1.0	1.7	2.7	2.5	2.3	2.7	1.8	2.1	1.9	2.3	1.9	2.0
Other advanced economies	5.1	2.1	2.6	3.0	0.9	2.0	2.4	1.7	1.8	1.9	2.1	2.2	...	...	...
Memorandum															
Major advanced economies	3.2	1.7	2.0	1.2	1.4	2.1	1.9	1.3	1.7	2.0	1.9	1.8	2.4	1.7	1.8
Newly industrialized Asian economies	5.3	2.1	3.4	4.6	—	1.2	2.0	1.0	1.5	2.4	2.2	2.3	2.5	2.2	2.4

[1]Annual data are calculated from seasonally adjusted quarterly data.
[2]Based on Eurostat's harmonized index of consumer prices.

Table 9. Advanced Economies: Hourly Earnings, Productivity, and Unit Labor Costs in Manufacturing

(Annual percent change)

	Ten-Year Averages		1997	1998	1999	2000	2001	2002	2003	2004	2005	2006
	1987–96	1997–2006										
Hourly earnings												
Advanced economies	**4.9**	**3.7**	**3.1**	**3.4**	**3.0**	**5.6**	**3.0**	**4.0**	**4.9**	**3.0**	**3.6**	**3.5**
United States	3.4	5.1	2.6	5.8	3.9	9.0	2.5	6.7	8.5	3.6	4.5	4.0
Euro area	. . .	2.9	3.1	1.5	2.4	4.0	3.4	3.2	2.9	2.3	2.9	3.1
Germany	5.9	2.4	1.9	1.5	2.3	5.2	3.0	2.0	1.7	0.5	2.5	3.0
France	3.8	2.9	2.1	0.6	1.0	4.3	2.5	3.7	2.7	3.7	4.0	4.0
Italy	6.8	2.5	4.2	−1.4	2.3	3.1	3.3	2.3	3.1	2.8	2.7	2.6
Spain	6.6	3.7	4.5	3.3	2.7	2.8	4.0	5.2	5.1	3.2	3.0	3.0
Japan	3.7	0.6	3.1	0.9	−0.7	—	1.0	−1.1	0.8	0.3	0.9	0.9
United Kingdom	6.8	4.0	4.2	4.6	4.0	4.7	4.3	3.5	3.6	3.7	3.8	4.1
Canada	3.8	3.1	2.2	3.7	3.4	3.3	3.6	3.3	1.2	3.7	3.6	3.1
Other advanced economies	9.2	4.7	4.9	3.1	5.5	5.7	5.5	3.1	4.4	4.9	4.8	5.0
Memorandum												
Major advanced economies	4.3	3.6	2.8	3.5	2.7	5.8	2.5	4.1	5.1	2.7	3.5	3.3
Newly industrialized Asian economies	14.0	5.8	5.7	2.5	7.8	6.7	6.7	3.1	6.3	6.5	6.3	6.4
Productivity												
Advanced economies	**3.1**	**3.3**	**3.9**	**2.3**	**3.5**	**5.2**	**0.7**	**4.5**	**3.9**	**4.2**	**2.8**	**2.5**
United States	2.9	4.3	3.6	4.8	3.5	4.6	2.3	7.6	5.0	5.0	3.9	3.0
Euro area	. . .	2.5	4.4	2.6	1.9	4.5	0.5	1.7	2.2	2.9	2.1	2.2
Germany	3.6	2.6	4.1	1.6	0.2	5.1	−0.3	2.4	2.9	4.5	2.8	2.8
France	3.5	4.1	5.6	5.5	2.9	7.2	2.2	2.3	3.2	3.8	4.1	4.0
Italy	2.8	0.6	2.7	−0.6	1.5	3.8	−0.8	−2.0	−0.9	0.4	0.4	1.2
Spain	2.9	1.5	2.7	1.4	1.4	0.4	−0.1	2.2	4.2	2.5	0.3	0.3
Japan	2.7	2.4	5.0	−3.6	3.2	6.8	−3.1	3.6	5.4	5.4	0.9	1.2
United Kingdom	3.4	3.4	1.5	1.3	4.5	6.3	3.4	1.5	5.5	5.4	2.9	2.0
Canada	2.3	3.0	3.4	3.6	5.4	5.9	−1.7	3.9	—	3.0	3.0	3.0
Other advanced economies	4.0	3.6	4.4	1.3	7.2	6.7	−0.4	4.2	3.6	3.1	2.6	3.5
Memorandum												
Major advanced economies	3.0	3.4	3.8	2.4	3.1	5.3	0.8	4.7	4.1	4.5	3.0	2.6
Newly industrialized Asian economies	6.8	5.1	4.8	−0.1	11.2	10.8	−1.4	6.2	5.7	4.5	4.3	5.4
Unit labor costs												
Advanced economies	**1.9**	**0.4**	**−0.7**	**1.1**	**−0.4**	**0.4**	**2.3**	**−0.4**	**0.9**	**−1.1**	**0.8**	**0.9**
United States	0.5	0.8	−0.9	1.0	0.4	4.2	0.2	−0.8	3.3	−1.3	0.7	1.0
Euro area	. . .	0.4	−1.2	−1.0	0.5	−0.5	2.8	1.5	0.6	−0.5	0.8	0.9
Germany	2.3	−0.2	−2.1	—	2.1	0.1	3.3	−0.4	−1.2	−3.8	−0.3	0.2
France	0.3	−1.2	−3.3	−4.7	−1.8	−2.7	0.3	1.4	−0.5	−0.1	−0.1	—
Italy	3.9	1.9	1.5	−0.8	0.8	−0.7	4.1	4.4	4.0	2.4	2.3	1.4
Spain	3.6	2.1	1.7	1.9	1.2	2.3	4.1	2.9	0.9	0.7	2.7	2.7
Japan	1.0	−1.8	−1.8	4.6	−3.8	−6.4	4.2	−4.5	−4.4	−4.8	—	−0.3
United Kingdom[1]	3.3	0.6	2.6	3.3	−0.4	−1.5	0.9	2.0	−1.9	−1.6	0.9	2.0
Canada	1.5	0.1	−1.2	—	−1.9	−2.5	5.4	−0.6	1.1	0.7	0.6	—
Other advanced economies	5.0	1.0	0.6	2.2	−1.3	−1.1	5.7	−1.1	0.4	1.4	2.0	1.3
Memorandum												
Major advanced economies	1.3	0.2	−1.0	1.1	−0.4	0.5	1.7	−0.6	0.9	−1.7	0.5	0.7
Newly industrialized Asian economies	6.6	0.5	1.2	3.1	−2.8	−3.9	7.5	−2.9	−0.1	1.3	1.6	0.7

[1]Data refer to unit wage cost.

Table 10. Other Emerging Market and Developing Countries: Consumer Prices
(Annual percent change)

	Ten-Year Averages		1997	1998	1999	2000	2001	2002	2003	2004	2005	2006
	1987–96	1997–2006										
Other emerging market and developing countries	**56.6**	**7.4**	**11.5**	**11.1**	**10.2**	**7.1**	**6.7**	**6.0**	**6.0**	**5.7**	**5.5**	**4.6**
Regional groups												
Africa	28.5	10.1	13.4	9.0	11.6	13.0	12.1	9.8	10.6	7.7	7.7	5.9
Sub-Sahara	33.8	12.3	16.3	10.5	14.6	16.7	15.0	12.2	13.3	9.1	9.2	6.8
Excluding Nigeria and South Africa	52.5	17.4	24.2	13.3	23.6	28.0	21.4	14.1	18.7	13.4	11.1	7.8
Central and eastern Europe	61.3	18.1	51.4	32.7	22.9	22.7	19.4	14.7	9.2	6.6	5.2	4.0
Commonwealth of Independent States[1]	. . .	20.2	18.1	23.7	69.6	24.6	20.3	13.8	12.0	10.3	11.4	8.8
Russia	. . .	21.7	14.8	27.7	85.7	20.8	21.5	15.8	13.7	10.9	11.8	9.7
Excluding Russia	. . .	17.0	26.3	15.3	37.0	34.2	17.6	9.3	8.3	9.1	10.6	6.7
Developing Asia	11.0	3.6	4.9	7.9	2.6	1.9	2.7	2.1	2.6	4.2	3.9	3.4
China	11.9	1.1	2.8	−0.8	−1.4	0.4	0.7	−0.8	1.2	3.9	3.0	2.5
India	9.5	5.2	7.2	13.2	4.7	4.0	3.8	4.3	3.8	3.8	4.0	3.6
Excluding China and India	10.9	7.1	6.6	20.9	8.7	2.9	5.9	6.3	4.5	5.3	6.0	5.2
Middle East	15.3	7.6	8.6	8.4	8.5	5.9	5.4	6.5	7.1	8.3	8.6	8.3
Western Hemisphere	182.3	7.7	11.5	8.6	7.3	6.7	6.1	8.9	10.6	6.5	6.0	5.2
Brazil	656.6	6.9	6.9	3.2	4.9	7.1	6.8	8.4	14.8	6.6	6.5	4.6
Mexico	36.7	9.0	20.6	15.9	16.6	9.5	6.4	5.0	4.5	4.7	4.6	3.7
Analytical groups												
By source of export earnings												
Fuel	27.0	11.2	15.7	13.1	12.7	10.0	9.6	10.3	11.1	10.3	9.8	9.4
Nonfuel	59.7	7.1	11.2	11.0	10.0	6.9	6.5	5.6	5.6	5.4	5.2	4.3
of which, primary products	62.6	18.0	24.1	11.8	24.0	29.0	26.1	15.5	18.3	11.9	12.2	8.6
By external financing source												
Net debtor countries	65.5	8.8	13.5	15.1	10.3	8.7	8.3	8.4	7.6	5.9	5.9	4.9
of which, official financing	42.8	8.6	8.8	17.9	9.9	6.1	7.2	9.4	7.8	6.8	6.9	5.7
Net debtor countries by debt-servicing experience												
Countries with arrears and/or rescheduling during 1999–2003	50.5	11.2	10.6	19.9	12.0	8.4	10.9	13.7	11.1	9.3	8.9	7.4
Other groups												
Heavily indebted poor countries	65.4	12.2	18.9	9.2	18.8	24.7	18.6	6.5	8.6	6.8	7.0	4.9
Middle East and north Africa	16.1	6.7	8.7	7.7	7.3	5.0	4.8	5.7	6.1	7.2	7.4	7.1
Memorandum												
Median												
Other emerging market and developing countries	10.3	4.7	7.0	6.3	4.1	4.3	4.8	3.3	4.3	4.7	4.4	4.0
Africa	10.4	5.0	6.1	5.4	4.3	5.0	4.9	3.6	5.3	4.5	5.5	5.0
Central and eastern Europe	50.9	4.7	8.8	8.2	3.3	6.2	5.5	3.3	2.3	3.5	3.1	2.8
Commonwealth of Independent States[1]	. . .	11.2	17.4	9.4	23.5	18.7	11.6	5.9	5.6	7.1	7.6	5.5
Developing Asia	8.6	4.7	6.2	8.3	4.2	2.5	3.8	3.3	3.8	5.5	5.0	4.0
Middle East	7.1	2.4	3.3	3.0	2.1	1.0	1.6	1.4	2.3	3.7	3.3	2.5
Western Hemisphere	12.6	4.3	6.9	4.8	3.5	4.6	3.6	4.2	4.5	4.4	3.7	3.2

[1]Mongolia, which is not a member of the Commonwealth of Independent States, is included in this group for reasons of geography and similarities in economic structure.

Table 11. Other Emerging Market and Developing Countries—by Country: Consumer Prices[1]
(Annual percent change)

	Average 1987–96	1997	1998	1999	2000	2001	2002	2003	2004	2005	2006
Africa	**28.5**	**13.4**	**9.0**	**11.6**	**13.0**	**12.1**	**9.8**	**10.6**	**7.7**	**7.7**	**5.9**
Algeria	18.2	5.7	5.0	2.6	0.3	4.2	1.4	2.6	3.6	3.5	3.5
Angola	313.3	221.5	107.4	248.2	325.0	152.6	108.9	98.3	43.6	20.1	11.7
Benin	6.4	3.8	5.8	0.3	3.0	4.0	2.4	1.5	2.6	3.0	3.0
Botswana	11.6	8.9	6.5	7.8	8.5	6.6	8.1	8.7	6.3	6.8	5.8
Burkina Faso	3.7	2.4	5.0	−1.1	−0.3	4.9	2.3	2.0	−0.4	2.0	2.0
Burundi	11.3	31.1	12.5	3.4	24.3	9.3	−1.3	10.7	7.9	8.2	5.3
Cameroon[2]	4.4	4.1	3.9	2.9	0.8	2.8	6.3	0.6	0.3	2.0	2.0
Cape Verde	6.7	8.6	4.4	3.9	−2.4	3.8	1.8	1.2	−1.9	2.0	2.0
Central African Republic	2.6	1.6	−1.9	−1.4	3.2	3.8	2.3	4.2	−2.2	2.5	2.5
Chad	4.7	5.6	4.3	−8.4	3.8	12.4	5.2	−1.8	−4.8	3.0	3.0
Comoros	3.1	1.5	1.2	1.1	4.6	5.9	3.3	4.4	4.3	3.0	3.0
Congo, Dem. Rep. of	776.8	199.0	29.1	284.9	550.0	357.3	25.3	12.8	3.9	12.7	5.2
Congo, Rep. of	3.3	13.1	1.8	3.1	0.4	0.8	3.1	1.5	2.0	2.0	2.0
Côte d'Ivoire	6.2	4.2	4.5	0.7	2.5	4.4	3.1	3.3	1.5	2.0	2.0
Djibouti	5.1	2.5	2.2	2.0	2.4	1.8	0.6	2.0	3.0	3.0	2.2
Equatorial Guinea	4.9	4.5	3.7	6.0	6.5	7.3	5.9	7.0	8.0	8.0	8.0
Eritrea	. . .	3.7	9.5	8.4	19.9	14.6	16.9	22.7	21.4	20.4	18.8
Ethiopia	7.1	−6.4	3.6	4.8	6.2	−5.2	−7.2	15.1	9.0	5.4	5.0
Gabon	3.9	4.1	2.3	−0.7	0.4	2.1	0.2	2.1	1.0	2.0	2.0
Gambia, The	8.8	2.8	1.1	3.8	0.9	4.5	8.6	17.0	14.6	7.1	5.2
Ghana	31.1	27.9	14.6	12.4	25.2	32.9	14.8	26.7	12.6	14.5	8.4
Guinea	8.4	1.9	5.1	4.6	6.8	5.4	3.0	12.9	17.5	22.6	9.6
Guinea-Bissau	55.9	49.1	8.0	−2.1	8.6	3.3	3.3	3.0	3.0	3.0	3.0
Kenya	16.1	11.9	6.7	5.8	10.0	5.8	2.0	9.8	11.5	6.6	3.6
Lesotho	12.4	8.5	7.8	8.6	6.1	6.9	11.2	7.6	5.5	5.5	5.5
Madagascar	19.7	4.5	6.2	8.1	10.7	6.9	16.2	−1.1	13.8	5.5	5.0
Malawi	27.9	9.1	29.8	44.8	29.6	27.2	14.9	9.6	11.6	12.3	9.0
Mali	2.9	−0.7	4.1	−1.2	−0.7	5.2	2.4	−1.3	−3.1	2.5	2.5
Mauritania	6.9	4.5	8.0	4.1	3.3	4.7	3.9	5.5	10.4	14.2	6.0
Mauritius	7.5	6.4	7.0	6.9	5.5	4.8	5.9	5.2	4.4	5.1	5.0
Morocco	4.8	1.0	2.7	0.7	1.9	0.6	2.8	1.2	2.0	2.0	2.0
Mozambique, Rep. of	56.1	6.4	0.6	2.9	12.7	9.0	16.8	13.4	12.6	6.5	7.0
Namibia	11.9	8.8	6.2	8.6	9.3	9.3	11.3	7.2	5.5	5.8	5.0
Niger	3.2	2.9	4.5	−2.3	2.9	4.0	2.7	−1.8	0.4	2.4	2.0
Nigeria	35.9	8.5	10.0	6.6	6.9	18.0	13.7	14.0	15.0	14.8	7.3
Rwanda	15.5	11.7	6.8	−2.4	3.9	3.4	2.0	7.4	12.0	7.0	4.0
São Tomé and Príncipe	37.1	69.0	42.1	16.3	11.0	9.5	9.2	9.6	12.8	14.6	12.4
Senegal	3.1	1.8	1.1	0.8	0.7	3.0	2.3	—	0.5	1.6	1.9
Seychelles	1.7	0.6	2.7	6.3	4.2	1.9	0.2	3.2	4.0	10.0	5.0
Sierra Leone	58.5	14.6	36.0	34.1	−0.9	2.6	−3.7	8.2	13.7	8.5	7.4
South Africa	12.1	8.6	6.9	5.2	5.4	5.7	9.2	5.8	1.4	4.5	5.0
Sudan	84.8	46.7	17.1	16.0	8.0	4.9	8.3	7.7	8.4	7.5	7.0
Swaziland	11.5	7.9	7.5	5.9	7.2	7.5	11.7	7.4	3.5	5.5	5.8
Tanzania	27.6	15.4	13.2	9.0	6.2	5.2	4.6	4.5	4.6	4.3	4.0
Togo	5.3	5.3	1.0	−0.1	1.9	3.9	3.1	−0.9	1.2	1.5	2.0
Tunisia	6.2	3.7	3.1	2.7	3.0	1.9	2.8	2.8	3.6	2.5	2.5
Uganda	50.1	5.8	0.2	5.8	4.5	−2.0	5.7	5.1	5.9	3.5	3.5
Zambia	85.5	24.4	24.5	26.8	26.1	21.7	22.2	21.5	18.0	16.2	12.3
Zimbabwe	20.6	18.8	31.7	58.5	55.9	76.7	140.0	431.7	282.4	187.2	103.7

Table 11 *(continued)*

	Average 1987–96	1997	1998	1999	2000	2001	2002	2003	2004	2005	2006
Central and eastern Europe[3]	**61.3**	**51.4**	**32.7**	**22.9**	**22.7**	**19.4**	**14.7**	**9.2**	**6.6**	**5.2**	**4.0**
Albania	28.4	32.1	20.9	0.4	—	3.1	5.2	2.4	2.9	2.4	3.0
Bosnia and Herzegovina	...	5.6	−0.4	2.9	5.0	3.2	0.3	0.6	0.8	1.9	2.0
Bulgaria	63.2	1,061.2	18.8	2.6	10.4	7.5	5.8	2.3	6.1	4.0	3.5
Croatia	...	3.6	5.7	4.1	6.2	4.9	2.2	1.8	2.1	2.7	2.5
Czech Republic	...	8.5	10.6	2.1	3.9	4.7	1.8	0.1	2.8	2.5	2.7
Estonia	...	11.2	8.2	3.3	4.0	5.8	3.6	1.3	3.0	3.7	2.7
Hungary	21.8	18.3	14.3	10.0	9.8	9.2	5.3	4.7	6.8	4.0	3.8
Latvia	...	8.4	4.6	2.4	2.6	2.5	1.9	2.9	6.3	5.7	5.3
Lithuania	...	8.8	5.1	0.8	1.0	1.3	0.3	−1.2	1.2	2.9	3.0
Macedonia, FYR	...	2.6	−0.1	−2.0	6.2	5.3	2.4	1.2	−0.3	1.5	2.0
Malta	2.4	3.1	3.8	2.2	3.1	2.5	2.7	1.9	2.7	2.4	1.9
Poland	78.2	14.9	11.8	7.3	10.1	5.5	1.9	0.8	3.5	3.1	2.5
Romania	76.8	154.8	59.1	45.8	45.7	34.5	22.5	15.3	11.9	8.2	5.7
Serbia and Montenegro	...	...	29.5	42.1	69.9	91.1	21.2	11.3	9.5	14.2	7.8
Slovak Republic	...	6.1	6.7	10.7	12.0	7.3	3.3	8.5	7.5	3.6	2.8
Slovenia	...	8.4	7.9	6.2	8.9	8.4	7.5	5.6	3.6	2.3	2.0
Turkey	70.9	85.0	83.6	63.5	54.3	53.9	44.8	25.3	10.6	9.0	6.1
Commonwealth of Independent States[3,4]	...	**18.1**	**23.7**	**69.6**	**24.6**	**20.3**	**13.8**	**12.0**	**10.3**	**11.4**	**8.8**
Russia	...	14.8	27.7	85.7	20.8	21.5	15.8	13.7	10.9	11.8	9.7
Excluding Russia	...	26.3	15.3	37.0	34.2	17.6	9.3	8.3	9.1	10.6	6.7
Armenia	...	14.0	8.6	0.6	−0.8	3.1	1.1	4.7	7.0	2.0	3.0
Azerbaijan	...	3.7	−0.8	−8.5	1.8	1.5	2.8	2.2	8.1	7.6	5.0
Belarus	...	63.8	73.0	293.7	168.6	61.1	42.6	28.4	18.1	13.0	11.0
Georgia	...	7.0	3.6	19.1	4.0	4.7	5.6	4.8	5.7	6.8	4.0
Kazakhstan	...	17.4	7.3	8.4	13.3	8.3	5.9	6.4	6.9	7.3	6.5
Kyrgyz Republic	...	23.4	−18.6	35.9	18.7	6.9	2.1	3.1	4.1	4.0	3.7
Moldova	...	11.8	7.7	39.3	31.3	9.8	5.3	11.7	12.3	10.0	8.1
Mongolia	50.0	36.6	9.4	7.6	11.6	11.6	6.3	0.9	5.0	5.0	5.0
Tajikistan	...	88.0	43.2	27.5	32.9	38.6	12.2	16.4	7.1	5.7	5.5
Turkmenistan	...	83.7	16.8	23.5	8.0	11.6	8.8	5.6	5.9	8.1	5.0
Ukraine	...	15.9	10.6	22.7	28.2	12.0	0.8	5.2	9.0	12.5	5.9
Uzbekistan	...	70.9	16.7	44.6	49.5	47.5	44.3	14.8	8.8	14.1	13.0

Table 11 *(continued)*

	Average 1987–96	1997	1998	1999	2000	2001	2002	2003	2004	2005	2006
Developing Asia	**11.0**	**4.9**	**7.9**	**2.6**	**1.9**	**2.7**	**2.1**	**2.6**	**4.2**	**3.9**	**3.4**
Afghanistan, I.S. of	...	...	...	...	...	...	52.3	10.3	13.0	10.0	5.0
Bangladesh	7.4	5.0	8.6	6.2	2.2	1.5	3.8	5.4	6.1	5.7	4.5
Bhutan	9.8	9.0	9.0	9.2	3.6	3.6	2.7	1.8	4.5	5.0	5.0
Brunei Darussalam	...	1.7	−0.4	—	1.2	0.6	−2.3	0.3	0.9	1.6	1.5
Cambodia	...	8.6	17.3	4.2	−0.8	0.2	3.3	1.2	2.0	2.9	2.5
China	11.9	2.8	−0.8	−1.4	0.4	0.7	−0.8	1.2	3.9	3.0	2.5
Fiji	5.4	3.4	5.9	2.0	1.1	4.3	0.8	4.2	2.4	2.7	2.5
India	9.5	7.2	13.2	4.7	4.0	3.8	4.3	3.8	3.8	4.0	3.6
Indonesia	8.4	6.2	58.0	20.7	3.8	11.5	11.8	6.8	6.1	7.0	6.5
Kiribati	1.8	2.2	3.7	1.8	0.4	6.0	3.2	1.4	2.3	2.5	2.5
Lao PDR	11.2	19.5	90.1	128.4	23.2	7.8	10.6	15.5	11.2	7.8	5.0
Malaysia	3.0	2.7	5.3	2.7	1.5	1.4	1.8	1.1	1.4	2.5	2.5
Maldives	10.1	7.6	−1.4	3.0	−1.2	0.7	0.9	−2.9	6.4	6.8	2.8
Myanmar	24.3	33.9	49.1	10.9	−1.7	34.5	58.1	24.9	9.0	17.5	27.5
Nepal	10.6	8.1	8.3	11.4	3.4	2.4	2.9	4.7	4.0	4.1	4.0
Pakistan	9.7	11.4	6.5	4.1	4.4	3.1	3.2	2.9	6.7	7.9	6.5
Papua New Guinea	6.7	3.9	13.6	14.9	15.6	9.3	11.8	14.7	7.4	6.0	4.5
Philippines	9.9	5.9	9.7	6.7	4.3	6.1	2.9	3.0	5.5	6.8	4.9
Samoa	5.7	6.9	2.2	0.3	1.0	3.8	8.1	4.2	2.4	2.4	2.2
Solomon Islands	12.1	8.0	12.3	8.0	6.9	7.6	9.4	10.1	6.8	3.8	4.7
Sri Lanka	12.1	9.6	9.4	4.7	6.2	14.2	9.6	6.3	7.6	12.0	7.5
Thailand	4.8	5.6	8.1	0.3	1.6	1.7	0.6	1.8	2.7	2.9	2.1
Timor-Leste, Dem. Rep. of	...	...	...	...	63.6	3.6	4.8	7.1	4.1	3.2	3.0
Tonga	5.7	−31.2	3.0	3.9	5.3	6.9	10.4	11.1	11.0	10.0	7.0
Vanuatu	2.7	2.8	3.3	2.2	2.5	3.7	2.0	3.0	2.8	3.7	2.7
Vietnam	71.0	3.2	7.7	4.2	−1.6	−0.4	4.0	3.2	7.7	5.5	4.0
Middle East	**15.3**	**8.6**	**8.4**	**8.5**	**5.9**	**5.4**	**6.5**	**7.1**	**8.3**	**8.6**	**8.3**
Bahrain	0.6	4.6	−0.4	−1.3	−3.6	−1.2	−0.5	1.6	4.9	3.7	1.7
Egypt	15.3	6.2	4.7	3.7	2.8	2.4	2.4	3.2	8.1	9.9	8.0
Iran, I.R. of	25.5	17.3	18.1	20.1	12.6	11.4	15.8	15.6	15.6	15.0	15.0
Iraq	...	...	...	...	...	...	...	...	...	...	...
Jordan	5.4	3.0	3.1	0.6	0.7	1.8	1.8	2.3	3.4	3.5	2.0
Kuwait	3.1	0.8	0.6	3.1	1.6	1.4	0.8	1.0	1.8	1.8	1.8
Lebanon	72.8	7.7	4.5	0.2	−0.4	−0.4	1.8	1.3	3.0	2.0	2.5
Libya	7.2	3.6	3.7	2.6	−2.9	−8.8	−9.9	−2.1	−1.0	1.8	2.4
Oman	2.1	−0.5	−0.5	0.5	−1.2	−1.1	−0.6	−0.4	1.6	0.6	0.8
Qatar	3.5	1.1	2.9	2.2	1.7	1.4	1.0	2.3	7.5	3.0	2.8
Saudi Arabia	1.1	−0.4	−0.2	−1.3	−0.6	−0.8	0.2	0.6	0.2	1.0	1.0
Syrian Arab Republic	18.1	1.9	−1.0	−3.7	−3.9	3.0	0.6	5.0	3.5	4.0	4.0
United Arab Emirates	4.2	2.9	2.0	2.1	1.4	2.8	3.1	2.8	3.8	1.9	1.8
Yemen	38.1	4.6	11.5	8.0	10.9	11.9	12.2	10.8	12.5	14.2	14.8

Table 11 *(concluded)*

	Average 1987–96	1997	1998	1999	2000	2001	2002	2003	2004	2005	2006
Western Hemisphere	**182.3**	**11.5**	**8.6**	**7.3**	**6.7**	**6.1**	**8.9**	**10.6**	**6.5**	**6.0**	**5.2**
Antigua and Barbuda	4.4	0.2	3.4	1.1	−1.7	0.2	2.2	1.0	−1.3	—	—
Argentina	193.3	0.5	0.9	−1.2	−0.9	−1.1	25.9	13.4	4.4	7.7	6.7
Bahamas, The	4.0	0.5	1.3	1.3	1.6	2.0	2.1	2.8	1.5	2.0	2.0
Barbados	3.6	7.7	−1.3	1.6	2.4	2.8	0.2	1.5	1.5	2.0	2.0
Belize	2.9	1.0	−0.9	−1.2	0.6	1.2	2.2	2.5	2.7	2.2	1.0
Bolivia	13.5	4.7	7.7	2.2	4.6	1.6	0.9	3.3	4.4	3.7	3.2
Brazil	656.6	6.9	3.2	4.9	7.1	6.8	8.4	14.8	6.6	6.5	4.6
Chile	15.3	6.1	5.1	3.3	3.8	3.6	2.5	2.8	1.1	2.5	3.1
Colombia	25.0	18.5	18.7	10.9	9.2	8.0	6.3	7.1	5.9	5.2	4.8
Costa Rica	18.7	13.2	11.7	10.0	11.0	11.3	9.2	9.4	12.3	10.5	9.5
Dominica	3.3	2.4	1.0	1.2	−7.3	1.6	0.1	1.6	2.3	1.5	1.5
Dominican Republic	21.8	8.3	4.8	6.5	7.7	8.9	5.2	27.4	51.5	8.9	8.4
Ecuador	2.9	4.1	−0.6	−29.2	−7.7	37.7	12.6	7.9	2.7	2.0	2.0
El Salvador	16.0	4.5	2.5	−1.0	4.3	1.4	2.8	2.5	4.5	2.8	2.5
Grenada	2.8	1.3	1.4	0.5	2.2	1.7	1.1	2.2	2.3	2.5	2.0
Guatemala	13.7	9.2	6.6	4.9	5.1	8.9	6.3	5.9	7.0	5.0	4.0
Guyana	36.1	3.6	4.7	7.4	6.1	2.7	5.4	6.0	4.7	5.7	4.2
Haiti	17.2	16.2	12.7	8.1	11.5	16.8	8.7	32.5	27.1	16.6	10.4
Honduras	16.7	20.2	13.7	11.6	11.0	9.7	7.7	7.7	8.1	7.8	5.9
Jamaica	27.5	9.1	8.1	6.3	7.7	8.0	6.5	12.9	11.5	7.9	6.4
Mexico	36.7	20.6	15.9	16.6	9.5	6.4	5.0	4.5	4.7	4.6	3.7
Netherlands Antilles	2.8	3.1	1.2	0.8	5.0	1.8	0.4	1.9	2.5	2.5	2.5
Nicaragua	644.7	9.2	13.0	11.2	11.5	7.4	4.0	5.2	8.2	6.5	4.8
Panama	0.9	1.3	0.6	1.3	1.4	0.3	1.0	1.0	0.5	2.4	1.8
Paraguay	20.8	7.0	11.6	6.8	9.0	7.3	10.5	14.2	5.2	5.3	5.3
Peru	287.4	8.5	7.3	3.5	3.8	2.0	0.2	2.3	3.7	2.1	2.4
St. Kitts and Nevis	2.6	8.7	3.7	3.4	2.1	2.1	2.1	2.3	2.4	2.3	2.1
St. Lucia	3.7	—	2.8	3.5	3.6	2.1	−0.2	1.0	1.0	1.0	1.0
St. Vincent and the Grenadines	3.4	0.5	2.1	1.0	0.2	0.8	1.0	0.3	2.0	2.0	2.0
Suriname	63.8	7.3	19.1	98.7	58.6	39.8	15.5	23.1	9.0	8.6	6.6
Trinidad and Tobago	7.9	3.6	5.6	3.4	3.5	5.5	4.2	3.8	3.9	3.1	3.0
Uruguay	64.0	19.8	10.8	5.7	4.8	4.4	14.0	19.4	9.2	7.0	6.2
Venezuela	49.0	50.0	35.8	23.6	16.2	12.5	22.4	31.1	21.7	18.2	25.0

[1]For many countries, figures for recent years are IMF staff estimates. Data for some countries are for fiscal years.

[2]The percent changes in 2002 are calculated over a period of 18 months, reflecting a change in the fiscal year cycle (from July–June to January–December).

[3]For many countries, inflation for the earlier years is measured on the basis of a retail price index. Consumer price indices with a broader and more up-to-date coverage are typically used for more recent years.

[4]Mongolia, which is not a member of the Commonwealth of Independent States, is included in this group for reasons of geography and similarities in economic structure.

Table 12. Summary Financial Indicators

(Percent)

	1997	1998	1999	2000	2001	2002	2003	2004	2005	2006
Advanced economies										
Central government fiscal balance[1]										
Advanced economies	−1.6	−1.1	−1.1	0.2	−1.0	−2.4	−3.0	−2.9	−2.8	−2.8
United States	−0.6	0.5	1.2	2.0	0.5	−2.4	−3.3	−3.3	−3.4	−3.4
Euro area	−2.6	−2.5	−1.6	−0.4	−1.6	−2.0	−2.3	−2.0	−2.0	−2.0
Japan	−4.0	−3.8	−8.5	−6.9	−6.3	−6.9	−7.1	−7.0	−7.0	−7.0
Other advanced economies[2]	−0.4	−0.2	0.2	2.2	0.6	−0.3	−0.7	−0.5	−0.3	−0.1
General government fiscal balance[1]										
Advanced economies	−1.9	−1.4	−1.0	—	−1.5	−3.4	−3.9	−3.5	−3.5	−3.4
United States	−1.1	0.1	0.6	1.3	−0.7	−4.0	−4.6	−4.3	−4.4	−4.2
Euro area	−2.7	−2.3	−1.3	−1.0	−1.8	−2.4	−2.8	−2.7	−2.6	−2.6
Japan	−3.8	−5.5	−7.2	−7.5	−6.1	−7.9	−7.8	−7.1	−6.9	−6.5
Other advanced economies[2]	−0.7	−0.2	0.6	2.6	0.4	−0.7	−1.1	−0.6	−0.6	−0.5
General government structural balance[3]										
Advanced economies	−1.8	−1.5	−1.3	−1.2	−1.7	−3.2	−3.3	−3.1	−3.2	−3.1
Growth of broad money[4]										
Advanced economies	5.0	6.7	5.9	5.0	8.7	5.8	5.3	5.1	. . .	. . .
United States	5.6	8.5	6.3	6.1	10.2	6.7	5.3	5.2	. . .	. . .
Euro area[5]	4.5	4.8	5.4	4.2	11.2	6.7	6.5	6.2	. . .	. . .
Japan	3.9	4.0	2.7	1.9	3.3	1.8	1.6	1.8	. . .	. . .
Other advanced economies[2]	6.1	9.4	9.0	6.9	7.3	6.2	6.9	6.1	. . .	. . .
Short-term interest rates[6]										
United States	5.2	4.9	4.8	6.0	3.5	1.6	1.0	1.4	2.7	3.7
Euro area[5]	4.4	4.1	3.0	4.4	4.2	3.3	2.4	2.1	2.7	3.2
Japan	0.3	0.2	0.0	0.2	0.0	0.0	0.0	0.0	0.2	0.7
LIBOR	5.9	5.6	5.5	6.6	3.7	1.9	1.2	1.8	3.3	4.1
Other emerging market and developing countries										
Central government fiscal balance[1]										
Weighted average	−2.9	−3.8	−3.9	−2.9	−3.3	−3.6	−3.0	−1.9	−1.6	−1.5
Median	−2.5	−3.0	−3.2	−2.7	−3.7	−3.8	−3.1	−2.7	−2.7	−2.3
General government fiscal balance[1]										
Weighted average	−3.8	−4.9	−4.8	−3.6	−4.1	−4.5	−3.8	−2.6	−2.2	−2.0
Median	−2.5	−3.3	−3.3	−3.1	−3.6	−3.9	−3.0	−2.5	−2.5	−2.3
Growth of broad money										
Weighted average	19.4	17.1	18.2	15.0	14.5	17.3	16.7	16.6	14.3	12.4
Median	17.3	11.3	13.2	13.6	14.0	13.1	12.7	12.0	10.6	9.9

[1]Percent of GDP.

[2]In this table, "other advanced economies" means advanced economies excluding the United States, euro area countries, and Japan.

[3]Percent of potential GDP.

[4]M2, defined as M1 plus quasi-money, except for Japan, for which the data are based on M2 plus certificates of deposit (CDs). Quasi-money is essentially private term deposits and other notice deposits. The United States also includes money market mutual fund balances, money market deposit accounts, overnight repurchase agreements, and overnight Eurodollars issued to U.S. residents by foreign branches of U.S. banks. For the euro area, M3 is composed of M2 plus marketable instruments held by euro-area residents, which comprise repurchase agreements, money market fund shares/units, money market paper, and debt securities up to two years.

[5]Excludes Greece prior to 2001.

[6]For the United States, three-month treasury bills; for Japan, three-month certificates of deposit; for the euro area, a weighted average of national three-month money market interest rates through 1998 and three-month EURIBOR thereafter; and for LIBOR, London interbank offered rate on six-month U.S. dollar deposits.

Table 13. Advanced Economies: General and Central Government Fiscal Balances and Balances Excluding Social Security Transactions[1]

(Percent of GDP)

	1997	1998	1999	2000	2001	2002	2003	2004	2005	2006
General government fiscal balance										
Advanced economies	**−1.9**	**−1.4**	**−1.0**	**—**	**−1.5**	**−3.4**	**−3.9**	**−3.5**	**−3.5**	**−3.4**
United States	−1.1	0.1	0.6	1.3	−0.7	−4.0	−4.6	−4.3	−4.4	−4.2
Euro area	−2.7	−2.3	−1.3	−1.0	−1.8	−2.4	−2.8	−2.7	−2.6	−2.6
Germany	−2.7	−2.2	−1.5	1.3	−2.8	−3.7	−3.8	−3.7	−3.5	−3.4
France[2]	−3.0	−2.7	−1.8	−1.4	−1.4	−3.2	−4.2	−3.7	−3.1	−3.1
Italy	−2.7	−2.8	−1.7	−0.6	−3.0	−2.6	−2.9	−3.0	−3.5	−4.3
Spain	−3.2	−3.0	−1.2	−0.9	−0.5	−0.3	0.3	−0.3	0.3	0.3
Netherlands	−1.1	−0.8	0.7	2.2	−0.1	−1.9	−3.2	−2.5	−2.0	−1.7
Belgium	−2.0	−0.7	−0.4	0.2	0.6	0.1	0.4	—	−0.4	−1.4
Austria[3]	−2.0	−2.5	−2.4	−1.7	0.1	−0.4	−1.3	−1.4	−2.0	−1.8
Finland	−1.3	1.6	2.2	7.1	5.2	4.3	2.3	1.9	1.7	1.9
Greece	−6.6	−4.3	−3.4	−4.1	−3.6	−4.1	−5.2	−6.1	−4.1	−4.1
Portugal	−3.0	−2.6	−2.8	−2.9	−4.4	−2.7	−2.8	−2.9	−2.8	−2.5
Ireland[4]	1.5	2.3	2.5	4.4	0.9	−0.4	0.2	1.3	−0.7	−0.6
Luxembourg	3.2	3.2	3.7	6.0	6.4	2.8	0.8	−1.4	−1.6	−1.8
Japan	−3.8	−5.5	−7.2	−7.5	−6.1	−7.9	−7.8	−7.1	−6.9	−6.5
United Kingdom	−2.2	0.1	1.0	3.9	0.8	−1.7	−3.3	−3.0	−3.1	−2.9
Canada	0.2	0.1	1.6	2.9	1.1	0.3	0.6	1.4	1.3	1.2
Korea[5]	−1.5	−3.9	−3.0	1.1	0.6	2.3	2.8	2.0	2.1	2.7
Australia[6]	−0.1	0.3	1.4	1.9	0.9	1.0	1.2	0.7	0.5	0.7
Taiwan Province of China	−3.8	−3.4	−6.0	−4.7	−6.7	−4.3	−4.0	−3.3	−3.0	−2.8
Sweden	−1.0	1.9	2.3	5.1	2.9	−0.3	0.5	0.7	0.6	0.4
Switzerland	−3.2	−1.7	−0.3	2.7	0.9	−0.7	−1.8	−2.4	−2.3	−1.8
Hong Kong SAR	6.5	−1.8	0.8	−0.6	−5.0	−4.9	−3.2	−0.9	−0.7	0.5
Denmark	0.4	1.1	3.2	2.5	2.8	1.6	1.2	1.3	1.4	1.4
Norway	7.7	3.6	6.2	15.6	13.6	9.3	7.7	11.5	11.9	10.9
Israel	−4.5	−3.7	−4.2	−2.1	−4.1	−4.5	−6.1	−4.4	−3.9	−3.5
Singapore	9.2	3.6	4.6	7.9	4.8	4.0	5.8	5.2	4.5	4.2
New Zealand[7]	2.2	2.1	1.5	1.3	1.6	1.7	3.5	4.5	3.9	3.6
Cyprus	−5.1	−4.2	−4.4	−2.4	−2.3	−4.5	−6.3	−4.2	−3.0	−2.8
Iceland	—	0.5	2.4	2.5	0.2	−0.4	−1.6	0.5	1.6	1.9
Memorandum										
Major advanced economies	−2.0	−1.5	−1.2	−0.2	−1.8	−4.1	−4.6	−4.2	−4.2	−4.1
Newly industrialized Asian economies	0.3	−2.2	−3.2	−2.2	−4.8	−3.4	−2.6	−1.6	−1.5	−1.2
Fiscal balance excluding social security transactions										
United States	−1.5	−0.6	−0.4	0.2	−1.5	−4.4	−5.0	−4.5	−4.7	−4.7
Japan	−5.5	−6.9	−8.2	−8.0	−6.2	−7.7	−7.9	−7.0	−6.7	−6.1
Germany	−2.8	−2.4	−1.8	1.3	−2.6	−3.4	−3.5	−3.2	−3.0	−3.0
France	−2.6	−2.6	−2.1	−1.9	−1.7	−3.0	−3.5	−2.8	−2.2	−2.4
Italy	−0.7	1.3	2.7	3.4	1.0	1.6	1.4	1.4	1.0	0.3
Canada	3.0	2.7	3.9	4.8	2.8	1.8	2.0	2.8	2.7	2.6

Table 13 *(concluded)*

	1997	1998	1999	2000	2001	2002	2003	2004	2005	2006
Central government fiscal balance										
Advanced economies	**−1.6**	**−1.1**	**−1.1**	**0.2**	**−1.0**	**−2.4**	**−3.0**	**−2.9**	**−2.8**	**−2.8**
United States[8]	−0.6	0.5	1.2	2.0	0.5	−2.4	−3.3	−3.3	−3.4	−3.4
Euro area	−2.6	−2.5	−1.6	−0.4	−1.6	−2.0	−2.3	−2.0	−2.0	−2.0
Germany[9]	−1.6	−1.8	−1.5	1.4	−1.4	−1.7	−1.9	−1.6	−1.5	−1.5
France	−3.6	−3.9	−2.5	−2.4	−2.2	−3.9	−4.0	−3.2	−3.1	−2.6
Italy	−2.9	−2.7	−1.5	−1.1	−2.7	−2.6	−2.4	−2.5	−2.7	−3.2
Spain	−2.7	−2.4	−1.1	−1.0	−0.6	−0.5	−0.3	−1.3	−0.5	−0.4
Japan[10]	−4.0	−3.8	−8.5	−6.9	−6.3	−6.9	−7.1	−7.0	−7.0	−7.0
United Kingdom	−2.2	0.1	1.0	3.9	0.8	−1.7	−3.6	−3.2	−3.0	−3.0
Canada	0.7	0.8	0.9	1.9	1.3	0.8	0.4	0.3	0.5	0.5
Other advanced economies	0.2	−0.8	−0.4	1.3	0.3	0.1	0.5	0.6	0.8	1.1
Memorandum										
Major advanced economies	−1.7	−1.0	−1.2	0.1	−1.1	−3.0	−3.6	−3.5	−3.5	−3.5
Newly industrialized Asian economies	0.7	−1.2	−1.1	0.8	−0.8	−0.3	0.2	0.3	0.4	0.9

[1]On a national income accounts basis except as indicated in footnotes. See Box A1 for a summary of the policy assumptions underlying the projections.
[2]Adjusted for valuation changes of the foreign exchange stabilization fund.
[3]Based on ESA95 methodology, according to which swap income is not included.
[4]To maintain comparability, data exclude the impact of discharging future pension liabilities of the formerly state-owned telecommunications company at a cost of 1.8 percent of GDP in 1999.
[5]Data cover the consolidated central government including the social security funds but excluding privatization.
[6]Data exclude net advances (primarily privatization receipts and net policy-related lending).
[7]Government balance is revenue minus expenditure plus balance of state-owned enterprises, excluding privatization receipts.
[8]Data are on a budget basis.
[9]Data are on an administrative basis and exclude social security transactions.
[10]Data are on a national income basis and exclude social security transactions.

Table 14. Advanced Economies: General Government Structural Balances[1]

(Percent of potential GDP)

	1997	1998	1999	2000	2001	2002	2003	2004	2005	2006
Structural balance										
Advanced economies	**−1.8**	**−1.5**	**−1.3**	**−1.2**	**−1.7**	**−3.2**	**−3.3**	**−3.1**	**−3.2**	**−3.1**
United States	−1.2	−0.3	−0.1	0.5	−0.6	−3.3	−3.7	−3.7	−3.9	−3.9
Euro area[2,3]	−1.8	−2.0	−1.5	−1.9	−2.5	−2.6	−2.4	−2.0	−1.9	−1.9
Germany[2]	−2.3	−2.1	−1.9	−2.5	−3.9	−3.7	−3.5	−3.1	−2.5	−2.3
France[2]	−1.1	−1.8	−1.4	−2.0	−2.1	−3.2	−3.2	−2.7	−2.6	−2.3
Italy[2]	−1.9	−2.8	−1.6	−2.3	−3.6	−3.5	−2.6	−2.6	−3.0	−3.5
Spain[2]	−1.8	−2.3	−1.0	−1.4	−1.0	—	0.9	1.1	1.0	0.9
Netherlands[2]	−1.1	−1.4	−0.7	−0.2	−1.1	−2.5	−2.4	−1.3	−0.6	−0.4
Belgium[2]	−2.0	−0.7	−1.0	−1.6	−0.7	−0.1	−1.0	0.1	−0.2	−1.4
Austria[2]	−1.7	−2.5	−2.7	−2.9	—	0.2	−0.2	−0.5	−1.2	−1.4
Finland	−1.8	—	0.3	6.0	5.2	4.6	2.8	2.0	1.4	1.4
Greece	−3.9	−2.5	−2.0	−3.8	−3.8	−4.5	−6.1	−7.1	−4.9	−4.7
Portugal[2]	−2.7	−2.8	−3.3	−4.0	−4.7	−3.6	−3.4	−2.6	−2.2	−0.9
Ireland[2]	0.7	1.9	1.0	2.4	−0.5	−1.2	0.6	1.6	−0.7	−0.6
Japan	−4.3	−5.3	−6.5	−7.2	−5.5	−6.8	−6.8	−6.7	−6.4	−6.3
United Kingdom[2]	−2.2	−0.1	0.9	1.3	0.2	−1.9	−3.0	−2.7	−3.0	−2.9
Canada	0.7	0.5	1.3	1.9	0.8	—	0.8	1.6	1.5	1.4
Other advanced economies	−0.9	−0.5	—	0.7	0.5	—	0.7	0.8	0.7	0.6
Australia[4]	−1.8	−1.6	−0.7	−0.3	−0.6	−0.2	0.6	0.8	0.9	0.8
Sweden	0.7	2.8	2.0	4.1	3.0	0.1	1.6	1.8	1.0	0.6
Denmark	−0.1	0.8	2.2	2.2	2.4	1.6	2.1	1.9	1.7	1.5
Norway[5]	−2.6	−3.9	−3.1	−1.8	−1.8	−3.0	−3.0	−1.8	−1.8	−1.8
New Zealand[6]	1.7	1.8	0.9	1.2	2.1	3.3	4.4	4.1	3.9	3.6
Memorandum										
Major advanced economies	−1.9	−1.5	−1.4	−1.3	−1.9	−3.6	−3.8	−3.7	−3.7	−3.7

[1]On a national income accounts basis. The structural budget position is defined as the actual budget deficit (or surplus) less the effects of cyclical deviations of output from potential output. Because of the margin of uncertainty that attaches to estimates of cyclical gaps and to tax and expenditure elasticities with respect to national income, indicators of structural budget positions should be interpreted as broad orders of magnitude. Moreover, it is important to note that changes in structural budget balances are not necessarily attributable to policy changes but may reflect the built-in momentum of existing expenditure programs. In the period beyond that for which specific consolidation programs exist, it is assumed that the structural deficit remains unchanged.

[2]Excludes one-off receipts from the sale of mobile telephone licenses equivalent to 2.5 percent of GDP in 2000 for Germany, 0.1 percent of GDP in 2001 and 2002 for France, 1.2 percent of GDP in 2000 for Italy, 2.4 percent of GDP in 2000 for the United Kingdom, 0.1 percent of GDP in 2000 for Spain, 0.7 percent of GDP in 2000 for the Netherlands, 0.2 percent of GDP in 2001 for Belgium, 0.4 percent of GDP in 2000 for Austria, 0.3 percent of GDP in 2000 for Portugal, and 0.2 percent of GDP in 2002 for Ireland. Also excludes one-off receipts from sizable asset transactions, in particular 0.5 percent of GDP for France in 2005.

[3]Excludes Luxembourg.

[4]Excludes commonwealth government privatization receipts.

[5]Excludes oil.

[6]Government balance is revenue minus expenditure plus balance of state-owned enterprises, excluding privatization receipts.

Table 15. Advanced Economies: Monetary Aggregates[1]
(Annual percent change)

	1997	1998	1999	2000	2001	2002	2003	2004
Narrow money[2]								
Advanced economies	**4.5**	**5.8**	**8.2**	**2.6**	**9.8**	**9.1**	**7.7**	**6.0**
United States	−1.2	2.0	1.9	−1.7	7.0	3.3	6.6	5.5
Euro area[3]	7.3	10.6	11.0	5.3	9.7	9.9	9.6	8.1
Japan	8.6	5.0	11.7	3.5	13.7	23.5	4.5	4.0
United Kingdom	6.3	5.8	11.7	4.5	8.0	6.1	7.3	5.8
Canada[4]	10.6	8.7	8.9	14.4	15.3	4.6	11.1	11.5
Memorandum								
Newly industrialized Asian economies	−3.9	0.9	19.9	4.6	11.4	13.4	13.9	5.1
Broad money[5]								
Advanced economies	**5.0**	**6.7**	**5.9**	**5.0**	**8.7**	**5.8**	**5.3**	**5.1**
United States	5.6	8.5	6.3	6.1	10.2	6.7	5.3	5.2
Euro area[3]	4.5	4.8	5.4	4.2	11.2	6.7	6.5	6.2
Japan	3.9	4.0	2.7	1.9	3.3	1.8	1.6	1.8
United Kingdom	5.8	8.4	4.1	8.4	6.6	7.0	7.2	8.5
Canada[4]	−1.3	1.4	4.3	6.9	5.9	5.0	6.2	6.3
Memorandum								
Newly industrialized Asian economies	11.6	20.0	17.3	14.5	7.3	5.7	6.8	3.5

[1]End-of-period based on monthly data.

[2]M1 except for the United Kingdom, where M0 is used here as a measure of narrow money; it comprises notes in circulation plus bankers' operational deposits. M1 is generally currency in circulation plus private demand deposits. In addition, the United States includes traveler's checks of nonbank issues and other checkable deposits and excludes private sector float and demand deposits of banks. Canada excludes private sector float.

[3]Excludes Greece prior to 2001.

[4]Average of Wednesdays.

[5]M2, defined as M1 plus quasi-money, except for Japan, and the United Kingdom, for which the data are based on M2 plus certificates of deposit (CDs), and M4, respectively. Quasi-money is essentially private term deposits and other notice deposits. The United States also includes money market mutual fund balances, money market deposit accounts, overnight repurchase agreements, and overnight Eurodollars issued to U.S. residents by foreign branches of U.S. banks. For the United Kingdom, M4 is composed of non-interest-bearing M1, private sector interest-bearing sterling sight bank deposits, private sector sterling time bank deposits, private sector holdings of sterling bank CDs, private sector holdings of building society shares and deposits, and sterling CDs less building society of banks deposits and bank CDs and notes and coins. For the euro area, M3 is composed of M2 plus marketable instruments held by euro-area residents, which comprise repurchase agreements, money market fund shares/units, money market paper, and debt securities up to two years.

Table 16. Advanced Economies: Interest Rates

(Percent a year)

	1997	1998	1999	2000	2001	2002	2003	2004	February 2005
Policy-related interest rate[1]									
United States	5.5	4.7	5.3	6.4	1.8	1.2	1.0	2.2	2.5
Euro area[2]	...	...	3.0	4.8	3.3	2.8	2.0	2.0	2.0
Japan	0.4	0.3	0.0	0.2	0.0	0.0	0.0	0.0	0.0
United Kingdom	7.3	6.3	5.5	6.0	4.0	4.0	3.8	4.8	4.8
Canada	4.3	5.0	4.8	5.8	2.3	2.8	2.8	2.5	2.5
Short-term interest rate[3]									
Advanced economies	**4.1**	**4.1**	**3.4**	**4.4**	**3.2**	**2.0**	**1.6**	**1.8**	**2.3**
United States	5.2	4.9	4.8	6.0	3.5	1.6	1.0	1.4	2.6
Euro area[2]	4.4	4.1	3.0	4.4	4.2	3.3	2.4	2.1	2.1
Japan	0.3	0.2	0.0	0.2	0.0	0.0	0.0	0.0	0.0
United Kingdom	6.9	7.4	5.5	6.1	5.0	4.0	3.7	4.6	4.9
Canada	3.2	4.7	4.7	5.5	3.9	2.6	2.9	2.2	2.5
Memorandum									
Newly industrialized Asian economies	9.3	10.6	4.6	4.6	3.7	0.7	3.0	3.8	3.1
Long-term interest rate[4]									
Advanced economies	**5.5**	**4.5**	**4.7**	**5.0**	**4.4**	**4.2**	**3.7**	**3.9**	**3.7**
United States	6.4	5.3	5.6	6.0	5.0	4.6	4.0	4.3	4.2
Euro area[2]	6.1	4.8	4.7	5.5	5.0	4.9	4.2	4.2	3.6
Japan	2.1	1.3	1.7	1.7	1.3	1.3	1.0	1.5	1.5
United Kingdom	6.8	5.1	5.2	5.0	5.0	4.8	4.5	4.8	4.5
Canada	6.1	5.3	5.6	5.9	5.5	5.3	4.8	4.6	4.3
Memorandum									
Newly industrialized Asian economies	8.9	9.7	6.8	6.9	5.0	4.9	4.8	5.0	3.3

[1]Annual data are end of period. For the United States, federal funds rate; for Japan, overnight call rate; for the euro area, main refinancing rate; for the United Kingdom, base lending rate; and for Canada, overnight money market financing rate.

[2]Excludes Greece prior to 2001.

[3]Annual data are period average. For the United States, three-month treasury bill market bid yield at constant maturity; for Japan, three-month bond yield with repurchase agreement; for the euro area, a weighted average of national three-month money market interest rates through 1998 and three-month EURIBOR thereafter; for the United Kingdom, three-month London interbank offered rate; and for Canada, three-month treasury bill yield.

[4]Annual data are period average. For the United States, 10-year treasury bond yield at constant maturity; for Japan, 10-year government bond yield; for the euro area, a weighted average of national 10-year government bond yields through 1998 and 10-year euro bond yield thereafter; for the United Kingdom, 10-year government bond yield; and for Canada, government bond yield of 10 years and over.

Table 17. Advanced Economies: Exchange Rates

	1997	1998	1999	2000	2001	2002	2003	2004	Exchange Rate Assumption 2005
				U.S. dollars per national currency unit					
U.S. dollar nominal exchange rates									
Euro	. . .	. . .	1.067	0.924	0.896	0.944	1.131	1.243	1.314
Pound sterling	1.638	1.656	1.618	1.516	1.440	1.501	1.634	1.832	1.887
				National currency units per U.S. dollar					
Japanese yen	120.8	130.4	113.5	107.7	121.5	125.2	115.8	108.1	105.2
Canadian dollar	1.384	1.482	1.486	1.485	1.548	1.569	1.397	1.299	1.240
Swedish krona	7.628	7.948	8.257	9.132	10.314	9.707	8.068	7.338	6.971
Danish krone	6.597	6.691	6.967	8.060	8.317	7.870	6.577	5.985	5.667
Swiss franc	1.451	1.447	1.500	1.687	1.686	1.554	1.346	1.242	1.183
Norwegian krone	7.059	7.544	7.797	8.782	8.989	7.932	7.074	6.730	6.417
Israeli new sheqel	3.447	3.786	4.138	4.077	4.205	4.735	4.548	4.481	4.439
Icelandic krona	70.89	70.94	72.30	78.28	96.84	91.19	76.64	70.07	62.74
Cyprus pound	0.513	0.517	0.542	0.621	0.643	0.609	0.517	0.468	0.448
Korean won	931.5	1,389.2	1,188.4	1,130.3	1,290.8	1,249.0	1,191.2	1,144.1	1,164.1
Australian dollar	1.344	1.589	1.550	1.717	1.932	1.839	1.534	1.358	1.291
New Taiwan dollar	28.622	33.434	32.263	31.216	33.787	34.571	34.441	33.440	31.554
Hong Kong dollar	7.742	7.745	7.757	7.791	7.799	7.799	7.787	7.788	7.799
Singapore dollar	1.485	1.674	1.695	1.724	1.792	1.791	1.742	1.690	1.638
									Percent change from previous assumption[2]
				Index, 2000 = 100					
Real effective exchange rates[1]									
United States	87.0	92.4	92.1	100.0	108.8	107.3	94.3	86.7	2.0
Japan	87.1	81.5	92.8	100.0	88.7	80.6	78.2	78.6	0.3
Euro[3]	123.8	120.4	113.4	100.0	99.2	102.2	112.8	115.5	−1.6
Germany	113.7	110.9	107.2	100.0	98.8	99.4	103.3	103.9	−0.8
France	107.3	106.8	105.3	100.0	98.7	99.8	103.5	104.4	−0.7
United Kingdom	88.4	93.6	95.4	100.0	99.6	101.7	98.0	103.3	0.2
Italy	107.5	105.5	104.6	100.0	99.1	101.0	105.6	107.2	−0.7
Canada	107.0	100.4	99.5	100.0	96.2	95.6	106.6	114.0	−0.9
Spain	99.6	101.6	101.6	100.0	102.1	104.9	109.8	112.0	−0.5
Netherlands	103.6	104.8	103.5	100.0	101.8	105.1	109.4	110.1	−0.7
Belgium	110.0	109.2	104.6	100.0	100.9	100.3	103.5	104.0	−0.6
Sweden	106.3	104.4	101.2	100.0	90.9	93.1	98.7	101.2	−1.7
Austria	107.5	105.6	103.2	100.0	99.3	100.2	103.3	104.6	−0.4
Denmark	103.3	104.9	104.4	100.0	101.1	103.1	108.4	110.8	−0.6
Finland	111.3	110.0	105.6	100.0	100.1	99.8	102.6	102.5	−0.6
Greece	107.6	103.8	104.3	100.0	100.0	103.2	108.3	111.2	−0.5
Portugal	99.3	100.8	101.1	100.0	102.3	105.1	109.9	112.3	−0.4
Ireland	132.5	120.2	112.0	100.0	98.7	99.5	105.6	106.3	−1.1
Switzerland	96.7	101.7	101.4	100.0	104.6	110.5	112.4	114.6	−1.4
Norway	93.8	94.7	99.0	100.0	105.5	118.5	119.0	118.0	−1.5
Australia	114.8	101.8	105.2	100.0	93.2	97.8	107.6	114.9	3.3
New Zealand	129.7	112.6	111.3	100.0	96.2	105.0	120.5	129.7	0.8

[1]Defined as the ratio, in common currency, of the normalized unit labor costs in the manufacturing sector to the weighted average of those of its industrial country trading partners, using 1999–2001 trade weights.

[2]In nominal effective terms. Average December 6, 2004–January 3, 2005 rates compared with January 31, 2005–February 28, 2005 rates.

[3]A synthetic euro for the period prior to January 1, 1999 is used in the calculation of real effective exchange rates for the euro. See Box 5.5 in the *World Economic Outlook*, October 1998.

Table 18. Other Emerging Market and Developing Countries: Central Government Fiscal Balances

(Percent of GDP)

	1997	1998	1999	2000	2001	2002	2003	2004	2005	2006
Other emerging market and developing countries	**-2.9**	**-3.8**	**-3.9**	**-2.9**	**-3.3**	**-3.6**	**-3.0**	**-1.9**	**-1.6**	**-1.5**
Regional groups										
Africa	-2.8	-3.8	-3.5	-1.3	-2.1	-2.5	-1.9	-0.7	—	0.2
Sub-Sahara	-3.5	-3.7	-3.9	-2.4	-2.6	-2.7	-2.5	-1.1	-0.8	-0.6
Excluding Nigeria and South Africa	-3.7	-3.3	-4.9	-4.5	-2.8	-3.4	-3.1	-2.0	-1.8	-1.2
Central and eastern Europe	-3.9	-3.9	-5.7	-5.4	-7.6	-8.6	-6.5	-5.0	-4.3	-3.7
Commonwealth of Independent States[1]	-6.9	-5.3	-4.0	0.3	1.8	1.0	1.2	2.7	4.8	3.5
Russia	-7.7	-6.0	-4.2	0.8	2.7	1.3	1.5	4.3	7.5	5.9
Excluding Russia	-4.6	-3.2	-3.3	-1.4	-0.7	0.2	0.2	-1.6	-2.7	-3.1
Developing Asia	-2.7	-3.7	-4.3	-4.3	-4.1	-4.1	-3.5	-3.1	-2.9	-2.6
China	-1.9	-3.0	-4.0	-3.6	-3.1	-3.3	-2.8	-2.4	-2.0	-1.7
India	-4.7	-5.3	-5.5	-5.7	-6.2	-6.1	-5.3	-4.8	-5.0	-4.7
Excluding China and India	-2.2	-3.1	-3.2	-4.5	-4.2	-3.5	-3.3	-2.9	-3.0	-2.6
Middle East	-1.7	-5.1	-1.8	4.2	-0.5	-2.3	-0.2	3.4	4.7	3.8
Western Hemisphere	-1.9	-3.4	-2.9	-2.4	-2.6	-3.1	-3.1	-1.6	-2.1	-2.1
Brazil	-2.6	-5.4	-2.7	-2.3	-2.1	-0.8	-4.0	-1.5	-2.6	-2.7
Mexico	-1.9	-2.3	-2.2	-1.6	-1.3	-1.6	-1.6	-0.4	-1.5	-1.3
Analytical groups										
By source of export earnings										
Fuel	-1.0	-5.9	-2.3	6.3	0.2	-1.8	1.0	5.3	7.6	6.4
Nonfuel	-3.1	-3.7	-4.0	-3.6	-3.5	-3.7	-3.3	-2.5	-2.3	-2.1
of which, primary products	-2.2	-2.2	-3.7	-4.5	-2.8	-3.0	-3.0	-1.4	-1.2	-1.0
By external financing source										
Net debtor countries	-3.2	-3.9	-4.1	-4.0	-4.3	-4.5	-4.0	-3.1	-3.2	-3.0
of which, official financing	-3.0	-3.3	-3.7	-4.2	-4.1	-4.7	-3.1	-2.7	-2.9	-2.5
Net debtor countries by debt-servicing experience										
Countries with arrears and/or rescheduling during 1999–2003	-2.7	-3.0	-3.2	-3.2	-3.4	-4.0	-2.4	-1.4	-1.3	-1.0
Other groups										
Heavily indebted poor countries	-3.2	-3.3	-4.4	-5.3	-4.1	-4.4	-4.5	-3.4	-2.8	-2.0
Middle East and north Africa	-1.4	-4.7	-1.8	3.6	-0.5	-2.1	-0.2	2.7	4.2	3.6
Memorandum										
Median										
Other emerging market and developing countries	-2.5	-3.0	-3.2	-2.7	-3.7	-3.8	-3.1	-2.7	-2.7	-2.3
Africa	-2.6	-3.3	-3.3	-2.9	-3.4	-4.0	-3.1	-2.6	-2.8	-2.7
Central and eastern Europe	-2.0	-2.9	-3.2	-2.5	-3.5	-5.1	-3.6	-3.0	-3.4	-2.5
Commonwealth of Independent States[1]	-4.7	-4.4	-3.7	-1.0	-1.5	-0.6	-0.7	-1.3	-2.0	-2.1
Developing Asia	-3.0	-2.3	-3.6	-4.3	-4.4	-4.2	-3.2	-3.1	-3.5	-3.0
Middle East	-2.4	-4.8	-1.3	5.2	0.4	-1.4	-0.3	1.6	2.6	2.3
Western Hemisphere	-2.5	-2.3	-2.9	-2.6	-4.3	-4.6	-4.0	-3.0	-2.5	-1.8

[1]Mongolia, which is not a member of the Commonwealth of Independent States, is included in this group for reasons of geography and similarities in economic structure.

Table 19. Other Emerging Market and Developing Countries: Broad Money Aggregates
(Annual percent change)

	1997	1998	1999	2000	2001	2002	2003	2004	2005	2006
Other emerging market and developing countries	**19.4**	**17.1**	**18.2**	**15.0**	**14.5**	**17.3**	**16.7**	**16.6**	**14.3**	**12.4**
Regional groups										
Africa	19.2	18.7	19.2	19.7	18.8	21.1	21.6	19.1	16.3	12.5
Sub-Sahara	20.8	17.3	21.3	22.3	19.3	24.5	25.0	22.2	18.1	13.2
Central and eastern Europe	51.8	37.1	37.1	24.0	30.6	12.3	11.7	12.7	12.2	10.9
Commonwealth of Independent States[1]	31.8	20.9	60.2	61.2	40.9	64.0	38.7	31.4	33.5	21.5
Russia	30.0	19.8	57.2	62.4	40.1	77.3	39.4	33.7	33.2	22.8
Excluding Russia	39.0	24.8	70.3	58.2	43.0	34.3	36.6	24.7	34.5	17.3
Developing Asia	18.2	18.8	14.4	12.2	13.1	15.4	16.1	14.5	13.2	12.7
China	19.6	14.8	14.7	12.3	14.8	19.7	19.6	14.5	13.0	12.0
India	17.6	20.2	18.6	16.2	13.9	15.1	15.9	17.3	15.5	15.8
Excluding China and India	17.1	22.4	11.5	9.7	9.5	8.5	10.3	12.3	12.0	11.8
Middle East	10.0	8.3	10.7	12.5	13.2	15.7	13.0	18.7	12.9	11.4
Western Hemisphere	12.1	11.1	10.1	7.1	6.5	13.6	15.0	15.9	11.1	9.8
Brazil	−7.3	5.5	7.8	3.3	13.3	23.6	3.7	19.3	12.0	9.5
Mexico	28.3	25.1	19.6	12.9	16.0	11.0	13.4	12.3	8.4	6.9
Analytical groups										
By source of export earnings										
Fuel	18.9	14.2	16.2	19.0	14.2	18.6	20.8	23.2	15.9	15.2
Nonfuel	19.5	17.4	18.4	14.6	14.5	17.2	16.2	15.8	14.1	12.1
of which, primary products	24.1	17.4	20.2	22.5	21.4	21.9	26.8	29.9	19.8	11.4
By external financing source										
Net debtor countries	18.2	18.3	16.8	12.7	13.0	13.9	13.9	14.9	12.9	11.3
of which, official financing	23.8	22.4	10.5	10.1	−0.6	10.0	20.6	13.4	12.9	12.0
Net debtor countries by debt-servicing experience										
Countries with arrears and/or rescheduling during 1999–2003	25.5	24.2	12.7	14.6	0.7	14.2	27.3	18.3	16.8	14.7
Other groups										
Heavily indebted poor countries	22.0	20.1	23.4	30.5	22.4	18.8	15.5	15.3	12.9	12.2
Middle East and north Africa	11.0	10.8	11.3	12.6	14.0	15.3	13.1	17.6	12.9	11.5
Memorandum										
Median										
Other emerging market and developing countries	17.3	11.3	13.2	13.6	14.0	13.1	12.7	12.0	10.6	9.9
Africa	14.2	8.6	12.6	14.1	14.8	17.3	14.3	9.8	10.4	10.0
Central and eastern Europe	34.1	13.0	14.2	16.5	21.4	10.4	10.9	11.8	9.9	9.0
Commonwealth of Independent States[1]	33.9	19.8	32.1	40.1	36.4	34.1	29.8	16.1	18.4	14.4
Developing Asia	17.6	11.7	14.7	12.3	11.7	13.4	14.6	13.5	12.8	11.9
Middle East	9.9	8.3	11.3	10.2	13.4	10.9	9.4	12.6	9.6	8.2
Western Hemisphere	14.0	11.7	10.8	8.5	8.1	7.5	9.8	10.3	8.1	7.2

[1]Mongolia, which is not a member of the Commonwealth of Independent States, is included in this group for reasons of geography and similarities in economic structure.

Table 20. Summary of World Trade Volumes and Prices

(Annual percent change)

	Ten-Year Averages		1997	1998	1999	2000	2001	2002	2003	2004	2005	2006
	1987–96	1997–2006										
Trade in goods and services												
World trade[1]												
Volume	6.5	6.6	10.5	4.6	5.8	12.4	0.2	3.3	4.9	9.9	7.4	7.6
Price deflator												
In U.S. dollars	3.2	0.8	−5.9	−5.7	−1.9	−0.5	−3.4	1.1	10.7	9.4	5.2	0.2
In SDRs	1.0	0.3	−0.8	−4.3	−2.6	3.1	0.1	−0.6	2.4	3.4	2.4	0.2
Volume of trade												
Exports												
Advanced economies	6.6	5.7	10.6	4.2	5.6	11.7	−0.7	2.2	2.8	8.1	5.9	6.8
Other emerging market and developing countries	6.8	9.1	12.8	5.9	4.3	14.4	3.4	6.7	10.7	13.8	9.9	9.7
Imports												
Advanced economies	6.5	6.1	9.4	5.9	8.1	11.7	−0.8	2.6	3.6	8.5	6.5	6.3
Other emerging market and developing countries	6.4	8.3	11.8	0.1	0.3	15.2	3.4	6.1	8.9	15.5	12.0	11.0
Terms of trade												
Advanced economies	0.1	—	−0.6	1.3	−0.3	−2.5	0.2	1.0	0.8	−0.4	0.3	−0.1
Other emerging market and developing countries	−0.4	0.5	−0.4	−6.8	3.7	6.6	−2.9	1.0	−0.5	3.3	2.2	−0.9
Trade in goods												
World trade[1]												
Volume	6.6	6.9	11.1	4.9	5.6	13.2	−0.3	3.5	5.3	10.7	7.9	8.0
Price deflator												
In U.S. dollars	3.2	0.7	−6.5	−6.6	−1.4	0.1	−3.7	0.6	10.7	9.6	5.6	−0.1
In SDRs	1.1	0.2	−1.3	−5.3	−2.2	3.8	−0.3	−1.1	2.3	3.6	2.8	—
World trade prices in U.S. dollars[2]												
Manufactures	4.2	0.6	−9.0	−3.8	−2.5	−5.7	−3.2	2.5	13.4	8.8	6.2	1.3
Oil	3.7	7.9	−5.4	−32.1	37.5	57.0	−13.8	2.5	15.8	30.7	23.2	−5.9
Nonfuel primary commodities	2.7	−0.2	−2.9	−14.5	−6.9	4.5	−4.1	0.8	7.1	18.8	3.8	−5.1
World trade prices in SDRs[2]												
Manufactures	2.0	0.1	−4.0	−2.5	−3.3	−2.2	0.3	0.7	4.9	2.9	3.4	1.3
Oil	1.5	7.4	−0.2	−31.2	36.4	62.8	−10.7	0.8	7.1	23.6	19.8	−5.9
Nonfuel primary commodities	0.5	−0.7	2.4	−13.3	−7.6	8.3	−0.7	−0.9	−1.0	12.3	1.1	−5.0
World trade prices in euros[2]												
Manufactures	1.6	0.2	1.8	−2.6	2.4	8.9	−0.1	−2.8	−5.3	−1.0	0.5	1.4
Oil	1.1	7.6	5.8	−31.3	44.4	81.3	−11.1	−2.8	−3.3	18.9	16.5	−5.9
Nonfuel primary commodities	0.1	−0.6	8.6	−13.4	−2.2	20.6	−1.1	−4.4	−10.5	8.0	−1.7	−5.0

Table 20 (concluded)

	Ten-Year Averages		1997	1998	1999	2000	2001	2002	2003	2004	2005	2006
	1987–96	1997–2006										
Trade in goods												
Volume of trade												
Exports												
Advanced economies	6.6	5.7	11.1	4.4	5.2	12.5	−1.4	2.1	2.9	8.6	5.8	7.0
Other emerging market and developing countries	6.8	9.1	12.7	5.9	3.3	15.5	3.1	7.0	10.3	13.7	10.4	9.9
Fuel exporters	5.9	4.4	7.2	2.6	−1.4	6.9	1.5	1.5	10.0	4.9	5.3	5.7
Nonfuel exporters	6.9	9.9	13.8	6.4	3.9	16.9	3.5	8.0	10.4	15.3	11.3	10.7
Imports												
Advanced economies	6.7	6.5	10.3	6.0	8.5	12.4	−1.5	2.7	4.3	9.3	7.0	6.6
Other emerging market and developing countries	6.2	8.9	11.7	1.4	−0.9	15.8	3.4	6.6	10.3	16.9	13.0	11.9
Fuel exporters	−0.5	8.7	15.9	2.9	1.4	11.1	12.8	8.6	3.7	13.1	11.5	6.6
Nonfuel exporters	7.3	8.9	11.3	1.2	−1.1	16.3	2.5	6.4	11.0	17.2	13.2	12.4
Price deflators in SDRs												
Exports												
Advanced economies	1.0	−0.1	−2.2	−3.9	−3.4	0.4	−0.1	−0.8	3.2	3.0	3.0	0.3
Other emerging market and developing countries	1.6	1.8	0.9	−10.9	4.8	13.5	−1.7	0.1	2.2	7.3	4.5	−1.2
Fuel exporters	0.7	5.6	−1.0	−30.2	39.9	50.5	−10.1	0.8	3.0	18.9	12.4	−5.2
Nonfuel exporters	1.9	1.1	1.2	−7.6	0.4	7.4	0.1	—	2.1	5.2	3.0	−0.4
Imports												
Advanced economies	0.7	−0.2	−1.8	−5.1	−3.4	3.6	−0.5	−1.8	1.9	3.0	2.1	0.3
Other emerging market and developing countries	2.4	0.8	0.9	−4.8	−0.7	5.8	1.5	−0.9	1.3	3.2	2.0	−0.3
Fuel exporters	0.7	−0.2	−1.6	−1.6	−2.0	1.6	2.5	−1.2	0.3	−0.1	−0.5	1.0
Nonfuel exporters	2.6	0.9	1.1	−5.1	−0.6	6.3	1.5	−0.9	1.4	3.5	2.2	−0.4
Terms of trade												
Advanced economies	0.3	0.1	−0.5	1.3	0.1	−3.1	0.4	1.0	1.3	—	0.9	—
Other emerging market and developing countries	−0.7	1.0	−0.1	−6.5	5.6	7.2	−3.2	1.0	0.9	4.0	2.5	−0.9
Fuel exporters	0.1	5.7	0.6	−29.1	42.7	48.1	−12.3	2.0	2.8	19.0	12.9	−6.2
Nonfuel exporters	−0.7	0.2	0.1	−2.7	1.0	1.0	−1.3	0.8	0.6	1.7	0.7	—
Memorandum												
World exports in billions of U.S. dollars												
Goods and services	4,654	9,029	6,899	6,788	7,032	7,828	7,567	7,936	9,216	11,069	12,503	13,447
Goods	3,721	7,240	5,520	5,387	5,583	6,295	6,032	6,304	7,352	8,902	10,129	10,900

[1]Average of annual percent change for world exports and imports.

[2]As represented, respectively, by the export unit value index for the manufactures of the advanced economies; the average of U.K. Brent, Dubai, and West Texas Intermediate crude oil spot prices; and the average of world market prices for nonfuel primary commodities weighted by their 1995–97 shares in world commodity exports.

Table 21. Nonfuel Commodity Prices[1]
(Annual percent change; U.S. dollar terms)

	Ten-Year Averages 1987–96	1997–2006	1997	1998	1999	2000	2001	2002	2003	2004	2005	2006
Nonfuel primary commodities	**2.7**	**−0.2**	**−2.9**	**−14.5**	**−6.9**	**4.5**	**−4.1**	**0.8**	**7.1**	**18.8**	**3.8**	**−5.1**
Food	2.3	−1.7	−8.9	−11.0	−11.4	1.8	2.1	1.3	5.9	14.5	−4.7	−3.4
Beverages	−4.0	−1.2	31.1	−13.2	−21.3	−15.1	−16.1	16.5	4.9	3.0	12.7	−2.3
Agricultural raw materials	5.9	−0.9	−4.7	−16.7	1.2	4.4	−4.9	1.8	3.7	6.0	0.9	1.4
Metals	3.2	2.5	1.2	−17.7	−1.1	12.2	−9.8	−2.7	11.9	36.4	14.7	−10.2
Advanced economies	**3.2**	**—**	**−3.6**	**−15.8**	**−5.6**	**5.4**	**−5.6**	**1.4**	**8.2**	**20.8**	**4.9**	**−5.6**
Other emerging market and developing countries	**2.8**	**−0.1**	**−1.5**	**−16.1**	**−7.0**	**4.4**	**−6.6**	**1.7**	**8.5**	**21.1**	**4.6**	**−5.6**
Regional groups												
Africa	2.5	−0.2	−1.7	−14.7	−6.7	2.5	−6.5	4.0	8.2	15.0	4.8	−3.6
Sub-Sahara	2.5	−0.1	−1.4	−14.8	−6.5	2.5	−6.9	4.2	8.4	15.0	5.2	−3.6
Central and eastern Europe	3.3	0.4	−2.6	−16.6	−4.3	6.3	−6.7	0.5	8.5	23.6	6.9	−6.6
Commonwealth of Independent States[2]	...	1.3	−1.8	−17.9	−2.5	9.8	−8.4	−0.8	10.5	30.1	10.3	−8.5
Developing Asia	3.0	−0.6	−3.5	−13.5	−7.2	2.1	−5.8	2.2	6.9	16.8	2.8	−4.0
Middle East	3.1	0.1	−2.6	−15.4	−6.8	6.3	−6.7	0.3	9.9	22.0	5.6	−6.3
Western Hemisphere	2.3	−0.4	1.0	−18.4	−9.6	4.4	−6.6	1.9	9.3	22.9	3.1	−6.2
Analytical groups												
By source of export earnings												
Fuel	3.2	0.9	−1.1	−17.0	−4.4	8.1	−8.1	−0.8	10.8	26.8	8.9	−7.6
Nonfuel	2.8	−0.2	−1.6	−16.1	−7.1	4.2	−6.5	1.7	8.4	20.9	4.5	−5.6
of which, primary products	2.6	0.2	−1.3	−16.8	−7.5	4.5	−7.3	3.8	9.4	23.7	5.0	−6.0
By source of external financing												
Net debtor countries	2.7	−0.3	−1.2	−16.1	−7.8	3.7	−6.5	2.1	8.4	20.3	4.1	−5.4
of which, official financing	2.0	−0.6	−1.7	−12.9	−9.8	0.3	−6.6	3.9	8.2	15.9	4.0	−3.6
Net debtor countries by debt-servicing experience												
Countries with arrears and/or rescheduling during 1999–2003	2.1	−0.3	—	−15.4	−9.3	2.5	−6.8	3.0	8.9	19.1	4.1	−5.1
Other groups												
Heavily indebted poor countries	0.7	−0.6	0.7	−13.7	−12.2	−2.6	−7.2	9.2	9.7	12.4	3.9	−2.7
Middle East and north Africa	2.9	−0.1	−3.1	−14.9	−7.2	5.2	−5.7	0.8	9.1	19.9	4.3	−5.5
Memorandum												
Average oil spot price[3]	3.7	7.9	−5.4	−32.1	37.5	57.0	−13.8	2.5	15.8	30.7	23.2	−5.9
In U.S. dollars a barrel	18.26	28.47	19.27	13.08	17.98	28.24	24.33	24.95	28.89	37.76	46.50	43.75
Export unit value of manufactures[4]	4.2	0.6	−9.0	−3.8	−2.5	−5.7	−3.2	2.5	13.4	8.8	6.2	1.3

[1]Averages of world market prices for individual commodities weighted by 1995–97 exports as a share of world commodity exports and total commodity exports for the indicated country group, respectively.
[2]Mongolia, which is not a member of the Commonwealth of Independent States, is included in this group for reasons of geography and similarities in economic structure.
[3]Average of U.K. Brent, Dubai, and West Texas Intermediate crude oil spot prices.
[4]For the manufactures exported by the advanced economies.

231

Table 22. Advanced Economies: Export Volumes, Import Volumes, and Terms of Trade in Goods and Services

(Annual percent change)

	Ten-Year Averages		1997	1998	1999	2000	2001	2002	2003	2004	2005	2006
	1987–96	1997–2006										
Export volume												
Advanced economies	**6.6**	**5.7**	**10.6**	**4.2**	**5.6**	**11.7**	**−0.7**	**2.2**	**2.8**	**8.1**	**5.9**	**6.8**
United States	9.1	4.5	11.9	2.4	4.3	8.7	−5.4	−2.3	1.9	8.5	7.2	9.5
Euro area	5.5	5.8	10.6	7.2	5.3	12.1	3.4	1.7	0.1	5.8	5.8	6.4
Germany	4.0	7.1	11.2	7.0	5.5	13.5	5.7	4.1	1.8	8.2	6.9	7.6
France	5.6	5.4	12.0	8.4	4.2	13.4	1.9	1.7	−2.5	3.2	5.3	7.5
Italy	6.2	2.5	6.4	3.4	0.1	9.7	1.6	−3.4	−3.9	3.2	4.2	4.8
Spain	7.8	6.3	15.3	8.2	7.7	10.1	3.6	1.2	2.6	4.5	4.7	5.5
Japan	4.2	5.7	11.4	−2.3	1.5	12.2	−6.0	7.2	9.1	14.4	5.6	5.6
United Kingdom	5.2	4.1	8.4	2.8	4.3	9.4	2.9	0.1	0.9	3.0	4.6	5.0
Canada	6.4	4.8	8.3	9.1	10.7	8.9	−2.8	1.1	−2.4	4.9	4.3	6.6
Other advanced economies	8.7	7.2	10.3	2.4	8.4	14.8	−2.3	5.9	8.2	12.6	6.1	6.7
Memorandum												
Major advanced economies	6.0	5.0	10.5	3.9	4.2	10.8	−1.1	1.0	1.3	7.2	5.9	7.2
Newly industrialized Asian economies	12.1	8.7	10.8	1.4	9.2	17.1	−4.4	9.4	12.9	17.1	7.2	8.0
Import volume												
Advanced economies	**6.5**	**6.1**	**9.4**	**5.9**	**8.1**	**11.7**	**−0.8**	**2.6**	**3.6**	**8.5**	**6.5**	**6.3**
United States	6.1	7.7	13.6	11.6	11.5	13.1	−2.7	3.4	4.4	9.9	7.0	6.3
Euro area	5.4	6.0	9.1	9.9	7.6	11.2	1.7	0.6	1.8	6.0	6.1	6.3
Germany	4.1	5.9	8.3	9.1	8.4	10.6	1.0	−1.6	4.0	5.7	6.8	7.7
France	4.8	6.5	7.2	11.5	6.1	15.2	1.6	3.3	0.2	7.4	6.1	6.7
Italy	5.3	4.2	10.1	8.9	5.6	7.1	0.5	−0.2	−0.6	2.6	4.4	4.4
Spain	9.9	8.5	13.3	13.2	12.6	10.5	3.9	3.1	4.8	9.0	8.0	7.1
Japan	8.5	2.9	0.7	−6.7	3.6	8.5	−0.7	1.2	3.8	8.9	6.9	4.1
United Kingdom	5.4	6.3	9.8	9.3	7.9	9.1	4.9	4.1	1.9	5.2	5.5	5.2
Canada	6.0	5.7	14.2	5.1	7.8	8.1	−5.0	1.4	3.8	8.2	7.4	6.6
Other advanced economies	9.2	6.2	8.7	−2.3	7.2	14.0	−4.1	5.8	6.8	13.0	6.7	7.4
Memorandum												
Major advanced economies	5.7	6.1	9.4	7.8	8.3	11.1	−0.6	2.0	3.2	7.5	6.5	6.1
Newly industrialized Asian economies	14.3	6.6	8.2	−8.2	8.2	17.4	−6.4	8.1	9.1	15.8	7.3	9.4
Terms of trade												
Advanced economies	**0.1**	**—**	**−0.6**	**1.3**	**−0.3**	**−2.5**	**0.2**	**1.0**	**0.8**	**−0.4**	**0.3**	**−0.1**
United States	−0.2	0.4	2.1	3.4	−1.2	−2.2	2.4	0.6	−1.3	−2.1	1.4	0.8
Euro area	−0.3	−0.1	−1.0	1.3	0.2	−3.6	0.7	1.6	0.8	−0.2	−0.3	−0.2
Germany	−1.4	−0.2	−1.7	2.1	1.2	−4.3	0.3	1.6	1.6	−0.2	−1.0	−1.6
France	−0.4	0.2	−0.5	1.4	0.3	−3.8	1.2	2.2	−0.1	1.5	−0.3	0.7
Italy	0.5	−0.3	−1.5	2.0	0.3	−7.2	0.6	2.3	1.3	−1.1	0.3	0.5
Spain	1.2	0.3	−0.3	0.9	−0.8	−2.2	2.8	2.5	1.0	−2.4	1.1	—
Japan	0.4	−1.8	−4.3	3.4	−0.2	−5.3	−2.4	0.1	−2.0	−3.7	−1.8	−2.1
United Kingdom	0.4	0.9	3.3	2.1	0.6	−0.9	−0.6	2.7	0.9	0.3	0.7	—
Canada	0.4	0.8	−0.7	−3.9	1.4	4.0	−1.6	−2.5	6.1	4.4	2.2	−0.6
Other advanced economies	0.4	−0.4	−1.0	−0.4	−0.9	−0.9	−0.4	0.2	−0.3	−0.8	0.3	−0.1
Memorandum												
Major advanced economies	−0.1	0.1	−0.4	2.1	—	−3.2	0.3	1.2	1.3	−0.3	0.3	−0.2
Newly industrialized Asian economies	0.3	−1.2	−1.3	0.2	−2.4	−3.3	−0.5	0.2	−1.7	−2.7	−0.6	0.4
Memorandum												
Trade in goods												
Advanced economies												
Export volume	6.6	5.7	11.1	4.4	5.2	12.5	−1.4	2.1	2.9	8.6	5.8	7.0
Import volume	6.7	6.5	10.3	6.0	8.5	12.4	−1.5	2.7	4.3	9.3	7.0	6.6
Terms of trade	0.3	0.1	−0.5	1.3	0.1	−3.1	0.4	1.0	1.3	—	0.9	—

Table 23. Other Emerging Market and Developing Countries—by Region: Total Trade in Goods

(Annual percent change)

	Ten-Year Averages		1997	1998	1999	2000	2001	2002	2003	2004	2005	2006
	1987–96	1997–2006										
Other emerging market and developing countries												
Value in U.S. dollars												
Exports	10.0	11.2	7.4	−7.1	7.9	25.6	−2.1	8.8	22.0	28.4	18.3	8.6
Imports	9.9	10.1	6.6	−4.7	−1.7	18.0	1.3	7.5	20.9	27.1	18.4	11.5
Volume												
Exports	6.8	9.1	12.7	5.9	3.3	15.5	3.1	7.0	10.3	13.7	10.4	9.9
Imports	6.2	8.9	11.7	1.4	−0.9	15.8	3.4	6.6	10.3	16.9	13.0	11.9
Unit value in U.S. dollars												
Exports	3.8	2.2	−4.4	−12.2	5.6	9.5	−5.1	1.8	10.6	13.4	7.4	−1.2
Imports	4.6	1.3	−4.3	−6.1	—	2.1	−2.0	0.8	9.6	9.1	4.8	−0.3
Terms of trade	−0.7	1.0	−0.1	−6.5	5.6	7.2	−3.2	1.0	0.9	4.0	2.5	−0.9
Memorandum												
Real GDP growth in developing country trading partners	3.5	3.2	4.0	1.8	3.5	4.8	1.6	2.2	2.8	4.5	3.4	3.6
Market prices of nonfuel commodities exported by other emerging market and developing countries	2.8	−0.1	−1.5	−16.1	−7.0	4.4	−6.6	1.7	8.5	21.1	4.6	−5.6
Regional groups												
Africa												
Value in U.S. dollars												
Exports	6.3	9.0	3.0	−13.8	7.6	28.2	−7.0	2.8	25.5	28.6	19.0	4.9
Imports	5.8	8.2	4.9	−2.3	0.6	4.2	1.8	8.7	21.5	26.2	14.2	6.2
Volume												
Exports	3.8	5.1	5.6	2.2	1.5	11.1	0.5	1.3	6.6	6.9	7.4	8.2
Imports	3.1	6.3	9.0	4.3	2.2	2.2	5.7	7.5	6.6	9.6	8.9	6.9
Unit value in U.S. dollars												
Exports	2.7	3.8	−2.3	−15.8	6.5	15.3	−7.4	1.6	18.1	20.4	11.2	−3.0
Imports	3.1	2.1	−3.8	−6.3	−1.4	2.3	−3.4	1.5	14.2	15.3	5.1	−0.6
Terms of trade	−0.3	1.8	1.6	−10.1	8.0	12.7	−4.1	0.1	3.4	4.4	5.8	−2.4
Sub-Sahara												
Value in U.S. dollars												
Exports	6.0	8.7	3.0	−14.1	6.3	25.7	−7.4	3.1	26.2	29.9	18.4	5.4
Imports	5.8	8.4	7.8	−4.9	−0.4	4.2	1.8	7.7	23.8	26.3	15.8	5.9
Volume												
Exports	4.1	5.0	5.2	1.4	−0.7	12.3	0.4	0.7	6.7	7.1	9.0	9.1
Imports	3.4	6.1	10.7	2.1	1.4	1.3	6.3	6.6	7.9	8.5	10.2	6.5
Unit value in U.S. dollars												
Exports	2.0	3.7	−2.0	−15.4	7.6	11.7	−7.0	2.5	18.9	21.3	9.0	3.2
Imports	2.7	2.4	−2.5	−6.8	−1.6	3.3	−4.0	1.5	15.3	16.5	5.6	−0.5
Terms of trade	−0.7	1.2	0.6	−9.3	9.4	8.2	−3.8	1.0	3.1	4.1	3.2	−2.7

Table 23 *(continued)*

	Ten-Year Averages		1997	1998	1999	2000	2001	2002	2003	2004	2005	2006
	1987–96	1997–2006										
Central and eastern Europe												
Value in U.S. dollars												
Exports	7.3	13.9	7.9	6.4	−2.5	13.3	10.8	13.9	28.7	31.0	21.1	12.4
Imports	9.4	12.8	9.1	5.9	−4.2	16.0	−0.4	13.5	29.5	31.2	21.1	11.2
Volume												
Exports	4.0	11.1	13.1	9.5	0.9	16.1	10.1	8.1	13.7	16.2	12.7	11.7
Imports	7.0	10.3	16.8	11.6	−2.5	16.1	1.5	8.9	13.5	16.0	11.7	11.0
Unit value in U.S. dollars												
Exports	4.1	2.6	−4.4	−2.9	−3.2	−2.5	1.2	5.4	13.5	13.0	7.3	0.5
Imports	4.8	2.3	−6.3	−5.0	−1.6	—	−2.1	4.6	14.4	13.5	8.3	—
Terms of trade	−0.7	0.2	2.0	2.3	−1.7	−2.5	3.3	0.7	−0.8	−0.4	−0.9	0.5
Commonwealth of Independent States[1]												
Value in U.S. dollars												
Exports	...	10.6	−1.4	−14.0	0.1	37.0	−0.9	6.3	26.8	35.5	25.2	4.4
Imports	...	7.4	4.0	−15.9	−25.8	14.2	15.0	9.7	26.5	26.6	21.9	12.1
Volume												
Exports	...	5.9	1.6	0.7	−1.1	9.2	4.0	6.7	11.8	11.5	7.6	8.1
Imports	...	7.0	12.7	−13.5	−22.1	14.6	16.8	8.5	14.5	21.1	15.7	11.4
Unit value in U.S. dollars												
Exports	...	4.6	−1.8	−14.0	1.0	24.7	−4.8	−0.5	13.5	21.9	16.6	−3.3
Imports	...	0.6	−6.8	−3.1	−4.7	−0.3	−1.6	1.6	10.7	5.0	5.5	0.7
Terms of trade	...	4.0	5.4	−11.3	5.9	25.1	−3.3	−2.0	2.6	16.1	10.6	−4.0
Developing Asia												
Value in U.S. dollars												
Exports	17.1	13.2	12.2	−2.4	8.5	22.3	−1.8	14.0	23.0	27.8	18.2	14.4
Imports	15.7	12.0	1.0	−13.7	9.0	27.7	−0.7	12.8	26.1	30.5	20.3	14.9
Volume												
Exports	12.6	12.8	18.5	7.8	5.8	22.5	1.4	12.7	12.7	19.5	15.1	13.7
Imports	11.7	10.9	6.1	−5.0	5.8	22.4	2.0	12.3	15.1	21.5	16.4	16.0
Unit value in U.S. dollars												
Exports	4.1	0.7	−5.1	−9.3	4.5	0.1	−3.1	1.2	9.0	7.3	2.7	0.6
Imports	4.0	1.3	−4.6	−9.3	6.0	4.8	−2.3	0.4	9.4	7.7	3.5	−0.8
Terms of trade	0.1	−0.7	−0.5	0.1	−1.5	−4.5	−0.8	0.8	−0.4	−0.4	−0.7	1.4
Excluding China and India												
Value in U.S. dollars												
Exports	16.6	7.4	7.4	−4.2	10.3	18.9	−9.4	6.1	11.5	18.5	11.5	6.7
Imports	17.9	5.3	−1.0	−23.4	6.3	24.3	−6.8	6.2	11.8	22.5	14.2	8.6
Volume												
Exports	11.9	6.3	10.9	9.4	3.4	15.8	−6.3	5.9	4.9	8.0	6.4	5.8
Imports	14.1	3.8	1.8	−14.7	−0.7	20.3	−6.9	7.0	6.0	12.5	8.6	8.1
Unit value in U.S. dollars												
Exports	4.4	1.5	−3.1	−12.2	10.2	2.8	−3.1	0.3	6.4	10.0	4.8	1.0
Imports	3.7	2.1	−2.6	−10.3	12.3	3.4	0.2	−0.7	5.4	9.4	5.3	0.5
Terms of trade	0.7	−0.6	−0.5	−2.1	−1.9	−0.6	−3.3	1.1	0.9	0.5	−0.4	0.5

Table 23 *(concluded)*

	Ten-Year Averages		1997	1998	1999	2000	2001	2002	2003	2004	2005	2006
	1987–96	1997–2006										
Middle East												
Value in U.S. dollars												
Exports	9.5	9.7	1.6	−26.0	31.8	45.4	−8.0	5.7	21.3	27.4	17.3	−0.8
Imports	5.0	7.2	5.2	−0.9	−1.5	9.3	8.7	8.4	12.4	14.8	9.9	6.9
Volume												
Exports	7.5	4.7	8.0	1.8	1.0	7.1	3.4	3.6	10.1	3.8	4.6	3.7
Imports	1.5	7.6	13.2	3.9	2.5	12.1	10.3	9.3	3.3	8.8	7.5	5.9
Unit value in U.S. dollars												
Exports	2.4	5.0	−6.0	−26.8	30.9	36.5	−11.0	2.5	10.0	23.2	12.4	−4.3
Imports	3.9	−0.3	−7.2	−4.5	−3.8	−2.4	−1.5	−0.7	8.8	5.7	2.2	0.9
Terms of trade	−1.4	5.4	1.3	−23.4	36.0	39.8	−9.7	3.3	1.1	16.6	10.0	−5.2
Western Hemisphere												
Value in U.S. dollars												
Exports	10.9	7.3	9.9	−3.8	4.0	19.8	−4.1	1.1	11.1	24.1	11.6	3.0
Imports	13.2	6.6	18.6	4.8	−6.8	14.8	−1.4	−8.5	4.2	22.1	15.6	7.1
Volume												
Exports	8.6	6.5	15.4	7.1	4.1	11.5	3.0	−0.1	3.3	10.5	5.0	5.7
Imports	9.6	5.5	18.7	8.8	−4.0	12.4	−0.3	−7.6	0.7	12.5	9.6	7.3
Unit value in U.S. dollars												
Exports	3.7	1.0	−4.4	−10.3	1.5	7.8	−6.9	1.4	7.6	12.1	6.4	−2.5
Imports	4.5	1.0	0.1	−3.6	−3.0	2.1	−1.2	−1.1	3.5	8.6	5.3	−0.3
Terms of trade	−0.8	—	−4.5	−7.0	4.6	5.6	−5.8	2.5	4.0	3.2	1.0	−2.3

[1]Mongolia, which is not a member of the Commonwealth of Independent States, is included in this group for reasons of geography and similarities in economic structure.

Table 24. Other Emerging Market and Developing Countries—by Source of Export Earnings: Total Trade in Goods
(Annual percent change)

| | Ten-Year Averages | | 1997 | 1998 | 1999 | 2000 | 2001 | 2002 | 2003 | 2004 | 2005 | 2006 |
	1987–96	1997–2006										
Fuel												
Value in U.S. dollars												
Exports	8.4	10.4	−0.1	−29.6	37.4	55.2	−11.8	3.6	22.6	31.5	21.2	—
Imports	2.0	9.0	8.3	0.2	0.3	9.0	11.6	8.3	13.0	19.1	14.1	7.6
Volume												
Exports	5.9	4.4	7.2	2.6	−1.4	6.9	1.5	1.5	10.0	4.9	5.3	5.7
Imports	−0.5	8.7	15.9	2.9	1.4	11.1	12.8	8.6	3.7	13.1	11.5	6.6
Unit value in U.S. dollars												
Exports	2.9	6.1	−6.2	−31.2	41.0	45.2	−13.3	2.5	11.4	25.7	15.5	−5.2
Imports	2.8	0.3	−6.7	−3.0	−1.2	−2.0	−1.1	0.5	8.5	5.6	2.3	1.0
Terms of trade	0.1	5.7	0.6	−29.1	42.7	48.1	−12.3	2.0	2.8	19.0	12.9	−6.2
Nonfuel												
Value in U.S. dollars												
Exports	10.4	11.4	8.8	−3.1	4.1	20.6	−0.1	9.8	21.9	27.8	17.7	10.2
Imports	11.2	10.2	6.5	−5.1	−1.9	19.0	0.3	7.4	21.8	27.9	18.9	11.9
Volume												
Exports	6.9	9.9	13.8	6.4	3.9	16.9	3.5	8.0	10.4	15.3	11.3	10.7
Imports	7.3	8.9	11.3	1.2	−1.1	16.3	2.5	6.4	11.0	17.2	13.2	12.4
Unit value in U.S. dollars												
Exports	4.1	1.5	−4.1	−8.9	1.1	3.6	−3.4	1.7	10.4	11.3	5.8	−0.4
Imports	4.8	1.3	−4.1	−6.4	0.2	2.5	−2.1	0.9	9.7	9.4	5.0	−0.4
Terms of trade	−0.7	0.2	0.1	−2.7	1.0	1.0	−1.3	0.8	0.6	1.7	0.7	—
Primary products												
Value in U.S. dollars												
Exports	7.5	5.4	2.6	−9.7	2.1	4.7	−6.3	2.9	18.6	36.5	9.2	0.5
Imports	8.8	4.3	4.9	−6.7	−11.9	5.4	−0.8	0.5	14.4	25.0	11.9	4.9
Volume												
Exports	6.0	4.7	5.3	3.2	6.1	1.6	2.0	0.1	4.0	14.3	5.6	5.7
Imports	6.2	4.9	9.5	3.2	−8.3	3.0	4.3	2.9	6.0	13.7	9.1	7.5
Unit value in U.S. dollars												
Exports	2.8	0.8	−2.6	−12.0	−3.6	3.2	−7.9	2.9	14.1	18.5	3.4	−4.5
Imports	2.9	−0.3	−4.1	−9.5	−3.9	2.9	−4.6	−2.3	8.6	10.4	2.9	−2.2
Terms of trade	−0.1	1.1	1.6	−2.7	0.3	0.3	−3.5	5.3	5.0	7.3	0.4	−2.3

Table 25. Summary of Payments Balances on Current Account
(Billions of U.S. dollars)

	1997	1998	1999	2000	2001	2002	2003	2004	2005	2006
Advanced economies	**81.6**	**35.8**	**−108.1**	**−250.9**	**−201.6**	**−218.1**	**−231.9**	**−327.8**	**−381.0**	**−394.1**
United States	−136.0	−209.6	−296.8	−413.5	−385.7	−473.9	−530.7	−665.9	−724.5	−749.8
Euro area[1]	99.7	64.3	30.5	−28.5	13.1	53.5	25.8	35.6	50.1	52.2
Japan	96.6	119.1	114.5	119.6	87.8	112.6	136.2	171.8	157.2	173.1
Other advanced economies[2]	21.4	62.0	43.7	71.4	83.1	89.7	136.7	130.7	136.1	130.4
Memorandum										
Newly industrialized Asian economies	5.9	64.6	57.9	40.1	50.6	59.3	84.5	89.6	92.2	90.7
Other emerging market and										
developing countries	**−85.6**	**−115.1**	**−17.4**	**88.2**	**40.8**	**85.0**	**149.1**	**246.6**	**303.4**	**255.2**
Excluding Asian countries in surplus[3]	−106.7	−172.0	−65.6	43.6	8.6	30.1	78.5	149.7	203.6	152.2
Regional groups										
Africa	−6.2	−19.4	−15.3	6.5	−1.3	−8.0	−1.7	1.1	6.5	4.2
Central and eastern Europe	−21.1	−19.3	−26.6	−32.7	−16.6	−24.5	−37.0	−50.6	−56.0	−55.8
Commonwealth of Independent States[4]	−8.8	−9.6	20.7	46.3	32.8	32.2	36.2	64.4	91.2	76.8
Developing Asia	7.7	49.3	48.7	46.3	40.8	72.2	85.8	103.3	97.1	96.9
Middle East	9.5	−25.5	11.9	69.5	39.1	29.4	59.3	112.5	160.8	145.8
Western Hemisphere	−66.7	−90.5	−56.7	−47.8	−53.9	−16.4	6.6	15.9	3.8	−12.7
Memorandum										
European Union	93.7	48.9	−17.1	−73.0	−20.1	24.7	3.0	−6.0	−6.5	−5.7
Analytical groups										
By source of export earnings										
Fuel	16.0	−32.3	11.3	88.6	45.0	33.4	67.6	122.5	178.8	162.0
Nonfuel	−101.6	−82.7	−28.7	−0.4	−4.2	51.6	81.5	124.1	124.7	93.1
of which, primary products	−7.6	−7.5	−2.5	−2.7	−4.2	−3.2	−2.3	−0.1	−0.7	−3.6
By external financing source										
Net debtor countries	−132.8	−128.7	−85.6	−77.0	−67.4	−33.8	−26.0	−42.1	−70.3	−90.9
of which, official financing	−39.5	−32.7	−17.8	−11.8	−8.0	10.2	9.3	−0.2	−13.4	−20.5
Net debtor countries by debt-										
servicing experience										
Countries with arrears and/or										
rescheduling during 1999–2003	−31.2	−34.9	−22.5	−2.1	−7.3	2.1	4.3	1.2	−3.2	−12.6
Total[1]	**−4.0**	**−79.3**	**−125.5**	**−162.7**	**−160.8**	**−133.1**	**−82.8**	**−81.2**	**−77.6**	**−138.9**
Memorandum										
In percent of total world current										
account transactions	—	−0.6	−0.9	−1.0	−1.1	−0.8	−0.4	−0.4	−0.3	−0.5
In percent of world GDP	—	−0.3	−0.4	−0.5	−0.5	−0.4	−0.2	−0.2	−0.2	−0.3

[1]Reflects errors, omissions, and asymmetries in balance of payments statistics on current account, as well as the exclusion of data for international organizations and a limited number of countries. Calculated as the sum of the balance of individual euro area countries. See "Classification of Countries" in the introduction to this Statistical Appendix.
[2]In this table, "other advanced economies" means advanced economies excluding the United States, euro area countries, and Japan.
[3]Excludes China, Malaysia, the Philippines, and Thailand.
[4]Mongolia, which is not a member of the Commonwealth of Independent States, is included in this group for reasons of geography and similarities in economic structure.

Table 26. Advanced Economies: Balance of Payments on Current Account

	1997	1998	1999	2000	2001	2002	2003	2004	2005	2006
					Billions of U.S. dollars					
Advanced economies	**81.6**	**35.8**	**−108.1**	**−250.9**	**−201.6**	**−218.1**	**−231.9**	**−327.8**	**−381.0**	**−394.1**
United States	−136.0	−209.6	−296.8	−413.5	−385.7	−473.9	−530.7	−665.9	−724.5	−749.8
Euro area[1]	99.7	64.3	30.5	−28.5	13.1	53.5	25.8	35.6	50.1	52.2
Germany	−8.6	−11.8	−24.0	−25.7	1.6	43.1	51.8	96.4	110.5	102.7
France	39.8	38.6	42.0	18.0	21.5	14.5	5.0	−5.4	−9.9	−1.5
Italy	32.4	20.0	8.1	−5.8	−0.7	−6.7	−21.9	−24.8	−23.9	−18.1
Spain	2.5	−2.9	−14.0	−19.4	−16.4	−15.9	−23.6	−49.2	−54.3	−63.7
Netherlands	25.1	13.0	15.6	7.2	9.8	12.8	15.1	19.4	26.2	29.6
Belgium	13.8	13.3	12.9	9.0	8.9	14.1	13.3	14.9	16.8	17.1
Austria	−6.5	−5.2	−6.8	−4.9	−3.7	0.3	−2.3	−2.0	−3.3	−3.7
Finland	6.8	7.3	7.8	9.2	8.6	8.9	6.8	8.4	9.5	10.5
Greece	−4.8	−3.6	−4.8	−7.8	−7.7	−9.7	−10.8	−8.4	−8.1	−7.9
Portugal	−6.0	−7.8	−9.8	−11.1	−10.4	−8.9	−8.0	−13.3	−13.2	−13.5
Ireland	2.5	1.0	0.5	−0.1	−0.6	−1.5	−2.1	−2.7	−3.5	−3.1
Luxembourg	2.6	2.6	2.7	3.0	2.3	2.4	2.6	2.3	3.3	3.8
Japan	96.6	119.1	114.5	119.6	87.8	112.6	136.2	171.8	157.2	173.1
United Kingdom	−1.5	−6.6	−39.5	−36.5	−32.2	−26.4	−30.6	−47.0	−53.9	−57.8
Canada	−8.2	−7.7	1.7	19.7	16.1	14.4	17.0	26.0	28.3	29.1
Korea	−8.3	40.4	24.5	12.3	8.0	5.4	12.1	26.8	26.1	23.1
Australia	−12.7	−18.0	−22.2	−15.3	−8.2	−16.6	−30.2	−39.4	−38.9	−41.7
Taiwan Province of China	7.1	3.4	8.4	8.9	18.2	25.6	29.3	19.0	22.6	21.8
Sweden	10.3	9.7	10.7	9.9	9.7	12.1	23.0	28.0	23.5	28.0
Switzerland	25.5	26.1	29.4	30.7	20.0	23.3	42.4	42.9	42.8	44.3
Hong Kong SAR	−7.7	2.5	10.3	7.1	9.9	12.6	16.2	15.9	16.3	17.0
Denmark	0.7	−1.5	3.0	2.3	4.9	3.5	6.3	3.5	5.0	4.7
Norway	10.0	0.1	8.5	26.1	26.2	24.4	28.3	34.4	46.3	43.1
Israel	−3.8	−1.4	−1.6	−1.7	−2.1	−1.8	0.2	0.1	−0.3	−0.1
Singapore	14.9	18.3	14.8	11.9	14.4	15.7	27.0	27.9	27.2	28.7
New Zealand	−4.3	−2.2	−3.5	−2.5	−1.2	−2.2	−3.3	−6.0	−6.9	−7.4
Cyprus	−0.3	−0.6	−0.2	−0.5	−0.3	−0.5	−0.5	−0.6	−0.6	−0.5
Iceland	−0.1	−0.6	−0.6	−0.9	−0.3	0.1	−0.4	−0.7	−1.6	−1.8
Memorandum										
Major advanced economies	14.4	−58.0	−193.9	−324.2	−291.6	−322.4	−373.2	−448.9	−516.1	−522.4
Euro area[2]	56.8	22.0	−31.0	−71.7	−9.8	54.5	24.7	52.6	39.8	41.5
Newly industrialized Asian economies	5.9	64.6	57.9	40.1	50.6	59.3	84.5	89.6	92.2	90.7

Table 26 *(concluded)*

	1997	1998	1999	2000	2001	2002	2003	2004	2005	2006
					Percent of GDP					
Advanced economies	**0.3**	**0.2**	**−0.4**	**−1.0**	**−0.8**	**−0.8**	**−0.8**	**−1.0**	**−1.1**	**−1.1**
United States	−1.6	−2.4	−3.2	−4.2	−3.8	−4.5	−4.8	−5.7	−5.8	−5.7
Euro area[1]	1.5	1.0	0.5	−0.5	0.2	0.8	0.3	0.4	0.5	0.5
Germany	−0.4	−0.5	−1.1	−1.4	0.1	2.2	2.2	3.6	3.8	3.4
France	2.8	2.7	2.9	1.4	1.6	1.0	0.3	−0.3	−0.4	−0.1
Italy	2.8	1.7	0.7	−0.5	−0.1	−0.6	−1.5	−1.5	−1.3	−0.9
Spain	0.5	−0.5	−2.3	−3.4	−2.8	−2.4	−2.8	−5.0	−4.8	−5.4
Netherlands	6.6	3.3	3.9	2.0	2.5	3.1	2.9	3.4	4.2	4.5
Belgium	5.6	5.3	5.1	3.9	3.9	5.7	4.4	4.2	4.3	4.2
Austria	−3.2	−2.5	−3.2	−2.6	−1.9	0.2	−0.9	−0.7	−1.0	−1.1
Finland	5.6	5.6	6.1	7.7	7.1	6.7	4.2	4.5	4.7	5.0
Greece	−4.0	−3.0	−3.8	−6.9	−6.6	−7.2	−6.2	−4.1	−3.5	−3.2
Portugal	−5.7	−6.9	−8.5	−10.4	−9.5	−7.3	−5.5	−7.9	−7.1	−6.9
Ireland	3.1	1.1	0.6	−0.1	−0.6	−1.3	−1.4	−1.5	−1.7	−1.4
Luxembourg	14.9	13.7	13.4	15.1	11.7	11.2	9.4	7.1	9.2	10.1
Japan	2.2	3.0	2.6	2.5	2.1	2.8	3.2	3.7	3.3	3.5
United Kingdom	−0.1	−0.5	−2.7	−2.5	−2.3	−1.7	−1.7	−2.2	−2.3	−2.4
Canada	−1.3	−1.2	0.3	2.7	2.3	2.0	2.0	2.6	2.6	2.5
Korea	−1.6	11.6	5.5	2.4	1.7	1.0	2.0	3.9	3.6	2.9
Australia	−3.1	−5.0	−5.7	−4.1	−2.3	−4.1	−5.9	−6.4	−5.6	−5.7
Taiwan Province of China	2.4	1.3	2.9	2.9	6.5	9.1	10.2	6.2	6.6	5.9
Sweden	4.2	3.9	4.3	4.1	4.4	5.0	7.6	8.1	6.1	7.0
Switzerland	9.7	9.7	11.1	12.4	8.0	8.4	13.2	12.0	11.1	11.3
Hong Kong SAR	−4.4	1.5	6.4	4.3	6.1	7.9	10.3	9.6	9.4	9.3
Denmark	0.4	−0.9	1.8	1.5	3.1	2.0	3.0	1.4	1.9	1.7
Norway	6.3	—	5.4	15.6	15.4	12.8	12.8	13.7	16.2	14.9
Israel	−3.7	−1.4	−1.5	−1.5	−1.9	−1.8	0.1	0.1	−0.2	—
Singapore	15.6	22.3	17.9	12.9	16.8	17.8	29.2	26.1	23.4	22.9
New Zealand	−6.5	−4.0	−6.2	−4.8	−2.4	−3.7	−4.2	−6.2	−6.4	−6.6
Cyprus	−3.8	−6.4	−2.3	−5.3	−3.3	−4.5	−3.4	−4.1	−3.4	−2.7
Iceland	−1.8	−6.9	−7.0	−10.1	−4.0	1.1	−4.1	−5.2	−10.1	−11.8
Memorandum										
Major advanced economies	0.1	−0.3	−0.9	−1.5	−1.4	−1.5	−1.6	−1.7	−1.9	−1.8
Euro area[2]	0.9	0.3	−0.5	−1.2	−0.2	0.8	0.3	0.6	0.4	0.4
Newly industrialized Asian economies	0.5	7.5	5.9	3.7	5.0	5.5	7.4	7.1	6.8	6.2

[1]Calculated as the sum of the balances of individual euro area countries.
[2]Corrected for reporting discrepancies in intra-area transactions.

Table 27. Advanced Economies: Current Account Transactions
(Billions of U.S. dollars)

	1997	1998	1999	2000	2001	2002	2003	2004	2005	2006
Exports	4,234.0	4,191.6	4,294.0	4,677.2	4,448.3	4,580.4	5,249.7	6,202.6	6,935.9	7,433.6
Imports	4,153.0	4,129.6	4,362.2	4,898.4	4,635.1	4,754.9	5,457.9	6,493.4	7,284.9	7,781.4
Trade balance	81.0	62.0	−68.2	−221.2	−186.8	−174.5	−208.2	−290.8	−349.0	−347.8
Services, credits	1,102.6	1,132.3	1,188.3	1,249.4	1,245.2	1,323.9	1,513.0	1,742.2	1,899.5	2,025.0
Services, debits	1,018.3	1,055.0	1,118.1	1,175.2	1,181.9	1,244.9	1,421.6	1,648.5	1,789.9	1,905.1
Balance on services	84.3	77.4	70.2	74.1	63.3	79.0	91.4	93.7	109.5	119.9
Balance on goods and services	165.3	139.4	2.0	−147.1	−123.5	−95.5	−116.7	−197.1	−239.5	−227.9
Income, net	29.3	23.6	16.4	32.2	44.7	18.9	61.1	66.7	55.3	42.4
Current transfers, net	−112.9	−127.3	−126.5	−136.0	−122.8	−141.5	−176.3	−197.4	−196.8	−208.6
Current account balance	**81.6**	**35.8**	**−108.1**	**−250.9**	**−201.6**	**−218.1**	**−231.9**	**−327.8**	**−381.0**	**−394.1**
Balance on goods and services										
Advanced economies	**165.3**	**139.4**	**2.0**	**−147.1**	**−123.5**	**−95.5**	**−116.7**	**−197.1**	**−239.5**	**−227.9**
United States	−108.2	−164.9	−263.3	−378.3	−362.7	−421.7	−496.5	−617.1	−654.7	−644.5
Euro area[1]	163.3	147.2	105.5	49.5	101.4	169.1	176.9	192.7	194.6	201.8
Germany	27.6	29.5	20.4	9.3	40.5	91.0	106.7	146.5	151.5	144.4
France	44.9	42.3	36.3	16.5	21.4	24.7	16.0	5.5	0.2	10.0
Italy	47.6	39.8	24.5	10.5	15.5	13.2	8.3	7.3	8.7	13.1
Spain	6.6	1.3	−7.5	−12.5	−8.3	−7.6	−12.0	−33.2	−44.2	−53.0
Japan	47.3	73.2	69.2	69.0	26.5	51.7	72.5	93.8	82.4	83.5
United Kingdom	1.8	−14.1	−25.8	−29.6	−39.5	−46.7	−52.4	−71.1	−81.0	−86.2
Canada	12.1	11.8	23.8	41.3	40.5	32.1	33.8	43.2	45.6	46.2
Other advanced economies	48.9	86.2	92.5	101.1	110.3	120.0	148.9	161.4	173.5	171.3
Memorandum										
Major advanced economies	73.2	17.7	−114.8	−261.3	−257.8	−255.7	−311.4	−391.8	−447.3	−433.5
Newly industrialized Asian economies	4.5	63.0	57.0	40.9	46.9	59.0	80.5	85.0	88.0	85.7
Income, net										
Advanced economies	**29.3**	**23.6**	**16.4**	**32.2**	**44.7**	**18.9**	**61.1**	**66.7**	**55.3**	**42.4**
United States	12.6	3.8	13.2	20.6	23.6	7.2	33.3	24.1	−8.2	−40.2
Euro area[1]	−16.3	−31.1	−27.3	−30.6	−39.3	−64.5	−81.5	−80.2	−63.4	−63.8
Germany	−5.7	−11.0	−17.7	−8.8	−14.4	−21.5	−22.4	−16.7	2.7	3.3
France	7.9	8.7	19.0	15.5	15.0	4.0	7.8	9.6	11.1	11.5
Italy	−11.2	−12.3	−11.1	−12.0	−10.3	−14.6	−22.1	−22.4	−21.7	−19.9
Spain	−6.8	−7.5	−9.5	−8.3	−9.7	−10.6	−12.0	−15.9	−15.7	−16.6
Japan	58.1	54.7	57.4	60.4	69.2	65.8	71.2	85.7	85.4	100.8
United Kingdom	6.4	21.4	−1.8	7.9	16.8	33.1	37.9	44.0	48.4	51.0
Canada	−20.9	−20.0	−22.6	−22.3	−25.4	−18.3	−17.0	−17.3	−16.9	−16.7
Other advanced economies	−10.7	−5.1	−2.5	−3.8	−0.1	−4.4	17.2	10.4	9.9	11.2
Memorandum										
Major advanced economies	47.2	45.2	36.4	61.2	74.4	55.6	88.7	107.1	100.7	89.9
Newly industrialized Asian economies	5.8	2.5	3.9	4.1	9.8	7.5	12.5	14.0	14.9	16.7

[1]Calculated as the sum of the individual euro area countries.

Table 28. Other Emerging Market and Developing Countries: Payments Balances on Current Account

	1997	1998	1999	2000	2001	2002	2003	2004	2005	2006
					Billions of U.S. dollars					
Other emerging market and developing countries	**−85.6**	**−115.1**	**−17.4**	**88.2**	**40.8**	**85.0**	**149.1**	**246.6**	**303.4**	**255.2**
Regional groups										
Africa	−6.2	−19.4	−15.3	6.5	−1.3	−8.0	−1.7	1.1	6.5	4.2
Sub-Sahara	−9.0	−17.7	−14.7	−1.3	−9.2	−13.1	−11.4	−9.7	−7.7	−10.1
Excluding Nigeria and South Africa	−8.6	−12.4	−10.9	−6.0	−10.6	−8.7	−7.9	−6.4	−8.1	−8.9
Central and eastern Europe	−21.1	−19.3	−26.6	−32.7	−16.6	−24.5	−37.0	−50.6	−56.0	−55.8
Commonwealth of Independent States[1]	−8.8	−9.6	20.7	46.3	32.8	32.2	36.2	64.4	91.2	76.8
Russia	−2.6	−2.1	22.2	44.6	33.4	30.9	35.4	59.6	85.9	74.9
Excluding Russia	−6.3	−7.6	−1.5	1.7	−0.6	1.3	0.8	4.8	5.2	2.0
Developing Asia	7.7	49.3	48.7	46.3	40.8	72.2	85.8	103.3	97.1	96.9
China	34.4	31.6	15.9	20.5	17.4	35.4	45.9	70.0	76.5	81.3
India	−3.0	−6.9	−3.2	−4.6	1.4	7.1	6.9	2.1	−2.5	−2.6
Excluding China and India	−23.8	24.6	36.0	30.4	22.0	29.7	33.1	31.3	23.1	18.2
Middle East	9.5	−25.5	11.9	69.5	39.1	29.4	59.3	112.5	160.8	145.8
Western Hemisphere	−66.7	−90.5	−56.7	−47.8	−53.9	−16.4	6.6	15.9	3.8	−12.7
Brazil	−30.3	−33.3	−25.4	−24.2	−23.2	−7.6	4.2	11.7	8.0	2.8
Mexico	−7.7	−16.1	−14.0	−18.2	−18.2	−13.7	−8.6	−8.7	−9.8	−12.2
Analytical groups										
By source of export earnings										
Fuel	16.0	−32.3	11.3	88.6	45.0	33.4	67.6	122.5	178.8	162.0
Nonfuel	−101.6	−82.7	−28.7	−0.4	−4.2	51.6	81.5	124.1	124.7	93.1
of which, primary products	−7.6	−7.5	−2.5	−2.7	−4.2	−3.2	−2.3	−0.1	−0.7	−3.6
By external financing source										
Net debtor countries	−132.8	−128.7	−85.6	−77.0	−67.4	−33.8	−26.0	−42.1	−70.3	−90.9
of which, official financing	−39.5	−32.7	−17.8	−11.8	−8.0	10.2	9.3	−0.2	−13.4	−20.5
Net debtor countries by debt-servicing experience										
Countries with arrears and/or rescheduling during 1999–2003	−31.2	−34.9	−22.5	−2.1	−7.3	2.1	4.3	1.2	−3.2	−12.6
Other groups										
Heavily indebted poor countries	−6.5	−7.2	−8.6	−7.0	−7.2	−7.7	−7.0	−7.7	−9.2	−9.5
Middle East and north Africa	10.8	−29.0	9.6	75.5	44.7	32.9	67.3	121.5	173.4	158.0

Table 28 *(concluded)*

	Ten-Year Averages 1987–96	1997–2006	1997	1998	1999	2000	2001	2002	2003	2004	2005	2006
	Percent of exports of goods and services											
Other emerging market and developing countries	**−7.5**	**2.5**	**−5.5**	**−7.9**	**−1.1**	**4.6**	**2.2**	**4.2**	**6.1**	**7.9**	**8.3**	**6.4**
Regional groups												
Africa	−8.6	−3.1	−4.6	−16.2	−11.9	4.1	−0.9	−5.2	−0.9	0.4	2.3	1.4
Sub-Sahara	−9.5	−8.7	−8.8	−19.6	−15.4	−1.1	−8.4	−11.7	−8.1	−5.4	−3.7	−4.6
Excluding Nigeria and South Africa	−22.0	−14.9	−17.4	−27.5	−22.6	−11.0	−20.1	−15.2	−11.6	−7.4	−8.3	−8.3
Central and eastern Europe	−1.5	−9.9	−10.0	−8.5	−12.5	−13.6	−6.4	−8.5	−10.1	−10.7	−9.9	−8.8
Commonwealth of Independent States[1]	. . .	15.2	−6.0	−7.6	16.7	28.1	19.9	18.1	16.1	21.6	24.7	19.9
Russia	. . .	22.9	−2.5	−2.4	26.2	38.9	29.7	25.7	23.3	29.4	33.1	27.7
Excluding Russia	. . .	−1.9	−13.6	−18.7	−3.9	3.3	−1.2	2.3	1.1	5.0	4.7	1.7
Developing Asia	−8.1	7.1	1.4	9.2	8.4	6.6	5.9	9.2	9.0	8.5	6.8	5.9
China	3.1	10.0	16.6	15.2	7.2	7.3	5.8	9.7	9.5	10.7	9.6	8.6
India	−21.7	−1.7	−6.7	−15.1	−6.3	−7.7	2.3	10.0	8.3	1.9	−1.8	−1.7
Excluding China and India	−11.1	6.0	−7.6	8.6	11.7	8.5	6.7	8.5	8.6	6.9	4.6	3.4
Middle East	−9.7	15.0	4.6	−16.0	5.8	24.5	14.7	10.5	17.5	26.4	32.4	29.4
Western Hemisphere	−13.3	−10.2	−22.3	−31.0	−18.8	−13.3	−15.6	−4.7	1.7	3.4	0.7	−2.4
Brazil	−7.5	−21.1	−50.6	−56.4	−46.0	−37.5	−34.4	−10.9	5.0	10.7	6.5	2.2
Mexico	−24.2	−11.3	−9.0	−18.6	−14.3	−15.4	−16.0	−12.0	−7.2	−6.5	−6.5	−7.8
Analytical groups												
By source of export earnings												
Fuel	−9.4	16.0	7.8	−21.6	5.6	29.3	16.7	11.9	19.7	27.4	33.1	29.9
Nonfuel	−7.1	0.2	−7.5	−6.3	−2.1	—	−0.3	2.9	3.9	4.6	4.0	2.7
of which, primary products	−12.6	−6.6	−14.8	−15.8	−5.2	−5.4	−8.9	−6.5	−4.1	−0.2	−0.9	−4.3
By external financing source												
Net debtor countries	−11.9	−6.8	−14.6	−14.4	−9.3	−7.2	−6.4	−3.0	−2.0	−2.6	−3.8	−4.5
of which, official financing	−18.1	−5.8	−19.8	−17.1	−9.4	−5.4	−3.8	4.7	3.9	−0.1	−4.4	−6.4
Net debtor countries by debt-servicing experience												
Countries with arrears and/or rescheduling during 1999–2003	−17.6	−4.8	−14.7	−17.8	−11.0	−0.8	−3.0	0.8	1.5	0.4	−0.8	−3.0
Other groups												
Heavily indebted poor countries	−31.7	−28.7	−29.7	−32.2	−40.3	−30.7	−30.1	−31.5	−24.4	−21.6	−23.3	−23.1
Middle East and north Africa	−10.1	14.0	4.5	−15.3	4.0	23.0	14.5	10.1	17.2	24.6	30.0	27.1
Memorandum												
Median												
Other emerging market and developing countries	−13.2	−10.1	−12.2	−16.2	−11.1	−9.6	−10.0	−9.5	−7.5	−7.4	−9.2	−8.7

[1]Mongolia, which is not a member of the Commonwealth of Independent States, is included in this group for reasons of geography and similarities in economic structure.

Table 29. Other Emerging Market and Developing Countries—by Region: Current Account Transactions

(Billions of U.S. dollars)

	1997	1998	1999	2000	2001	2002	2003	2004	2005	2006
Other emerging market and developing countries										
Exports	1,285.8	1,195.0	1,288.9	1,618.3	1,583.6	1,723.1	2,102.6	2,699.5	3,192.7	3,466.7
Imports	1,273.4	1,213.9	1,193.8	1,409.0	1,427.2	1,533.6	1,854.7	2,357.9	2,792.9	3,114.9
Trade balance	12.4	−18.9	95.1	209.2	156.4	189.5	247.8	341.7	399.8	351.8
Services, net	−55.2	−45.5	−47.1	−57.1	−59.6	−58.3	−64.9	−63.2	−69.1	−69.9
Balance on goods and services	−42.8	−64.4	48.0	152.1	96.8	131.3	182.9	278.5	330.7	281.9
Income, net	−95.0	−99.7	−118.4	−120.2	−120.8	−131.2	−145.1	−160.2	−159.6	−152.6
Current transfers, net	52.1	49.0	52.9	56.3	64.8	84.9	111.3	128.3	132.3	125.9
Current account balance	**−85.6**	**−115.1**	**−17.4**	**88.2**	**40.8**	**85.0**	**149.1**	**246.6**	**303.4**	**255.2**
Memorandum										
Exports of goods and services	1,562.5	1,464.2	1,549.9	1,901.7	1,873.5	2,032.0	2,453.3	3,124.1	3,667.9	3,988.5
Interest payments	126.8	138.0	135.2	140.2	137.3	125.5	124.7	143.1	159.2	173.8
Oil trade balance	159.3	102.4	157.8	255.6	210.8	222.3	280.4	371.9	455.9	438.8
Regional groups										
Africa										
Exports	113.9	98.2	105.6	135.4	125.9	129.4	162.4	208.9	248.6	260.8
Imports	103.4	100.9	101.6	105.8	107.8	117.2	142.3	179.6	205.1	217.7
Trade balance	10.6	−2.7	4.1	29.6	18.1	12.3	20.1	29.3	43.6	43.1
Services, net	−10.4	−11.7	−11.1	−11.3	−11.7	−11.9	−13.5	−16.1	−19.9	−22.3
Balance on goods and services	0.2	−14.4	−7.1	18.3	6.4	0.3	6.6	13.2	23.7	20.8
Income, net	−17.4	−16.2	−18.3	−23.4	−20.7	−26.3	−31.0	−34.3	−40.2	−39.8
Current transfers, net	11.0	11.2	10.1	11.6	12.9	18.0	22.7	22.2	23.1	23.2
Current account balance	**−6.2**	**−19.4**	**−15.3**	**6.5**	**−1.3**	**−8.0**	**−1.7**	**1.1**	**6.5**	**4.2**
Memorandum										
Exports of goods and services	135.2	119.7	128.0	157.5	149.1	153.6	192.0	242.7	284.6	298.7
Interest payments	15.5	15.6	15.3	14.8	16.6	12.8	13.4	14.1	15.2	15.8
Oil trade balance	29.0	18.6	26.0	45.8	37.8	39.9	54.4	76.0	100.3	104.7
Central and eastern Europe										
Exports	151.8	161.5	157.5	178.4	197.7	225.1	289.8	379.6	459.8	516.9
Imports	197.2	208.9	200.1	232.0	231.1	262.3	339.7	445.7	539.8	600.4
Trade balance	−45.4	−47.4	−42.5	−53.5	−33.4	−37.2	−49.9	−66.1	−80.0	−83.5
Services, net	19.1	21.6	11.2	14.8	14.0	12.1	15.1	19.5	22.8	25.2
Balance on goods and services	−26.3	−25.7	−31.3	−38.7	−19.3	−25.1	−34.8	−46.6	−57.2	−58.3
Income, net	−5.3	−6.4	−6.7	−5.8	−8.4	−11.7	−15.4	−19.3	−18.8	−20.7
Current transfers, net	10.6	12.8	11.3	11.8	11.2	12.4	13.1	15.3	20.0	23.1
Current account balance	**−21.1**	**−19.3**	**−26.6**	**−32.7**	**−16.6**	**−24.5**	**−37.0**	**−50.6**	**−56.0**	**−55.8**
Memorandum										
Exports of goods and services	211.7	227.7	213.6	240.7	259.4	288.2	366.7	471.7	564.5	630.4
Interest payments	11.7	11.5	11.8	12.9	14.1	14.3	16.8	20.0	23.0	26.5
Oil trade balance	−17.5	−14.3	−14.1	−20.4	−19.5	−19.4	−23.8	−28.5	−31.8	−32.3

Table 29 (concluded)

	1997	1998	1999	2000	2001	2002	2003	2004	2005	2006
Commonwealth of Independent States[1]										
Exports	125.0	107.4	107.5	147.2	145.9	155.0	196.6	266.3	333.4	347.9
Imports	118.3	99.5	73.8	84.3	96.9	106.3	134.5	170.3	207.6	232.7
Trade balance	6.7	7.9	33.7	63.0	48.9	48.7	62.1	96.0	125.8	115.3
Services, net	−4.7	−3.7	−3.8	−7.0	−10.2	−11.0	−13.2	−17.6	−20.6	−25.0
Balance on goods and services	2.0	4.2	29.9	55.9	38.8	37.7	48.9	78.4	105.2	90.2
Income, net	−12.0	−15.2	−11.5	−11.9	−8.1	−8.4	−16.1	−17.3	−17.2	−16.7
Current transfers, net	1.2	1.3	2.3	2.3	2.1	3.0	3.4	3.3	3.2	3.3
Current account balance	**−8.8**	**−9.6**	**20.7**	**46.3**	**32.8**	**32.2**	**36.2**	**64.4**	**91.2**	**76.8**
Memorandum										
Exports of goods and services	147.1	127.2	123.6	164.8	165.2	178.0	224.0	298.2	369.3	386.1
Interest payments	13.9	17.0	12.7	12.9	10.5	9.3	9.6	17.8	18.9	20.4
Oil trade balance	20.4	13.5	20.0	39.0	36.8	42.3	56.4	84.7	119.3	125.2
Developing Asia										
Exports	466.5	455.4	493.9	604.2	593.5	676.6	832.0	1,063.1	1,256.6	1,437.1
Imports	449.6	387.8	422.8	540.1	536.4	605.2	763.3	996.3	1,198.7	1,377.2
Trade balance	16.8	67.5	71.1	64.0	57.0	71.4	68.7	66.9	57.9	59.8
Services, net	−11.1	−12.3	−8.0	−10.6	−10.7	−7.1	−13.3	−6.3	−4.4	1.0
Balance on goods and services	5.8	55.3	63.0	53.4	46.3	64.3	55.5	60.6	53.5	60.9
Income, net	−26.3	−27.8	−40.1	−35.6	−38.2	−33.3	−24.7	−25.2	−21.5	−20.7
Current transfers, net	28.2	21.9	25.7	28.5	32.7	41.1	55.1	67.9	65.1	56.7
Current account balance	**7.7**	**49.3**	**48.7**	**46.3**	**40.8**	**72.2**	**85.8**	**103.3**	**97.1**	**96.9**
Memorandum										
Exports of goods and services	564.8	538.3	579.0	696.9	689.8	785.2	950.4	1,218.3	1,434.7	1,642.0
Interest payments	28.0	33.2	33.2	33.3	31.2	29.2	27.7	31.6	37.4	44.2
Oil trade balance	−20.6	−12.4	−19.5	−37.4	−34.8	−39.5	−50.8	−82.3	−115.9	−127.8
Middle East										
Exports	178.9	132.4	174.5	253.7	233.5	246.7	299.3	381.3	447.4	444.0
Imports	134.1	132.9	130.9	143.1	155.6	168.7	189.5	217.6	239.2	255.6
Trade balance	44.8	−0.5	43.6	110.6	77.9	78.0	109.7	163.7	208.3	188.4
Services, net	−33.2	−24.2	−23.6	−30.7	−26.7	−30.9	−32.1	−33.8	−35.2	−35.3
Balance on goods and services	11.7	−24.7	20.0	79.9	51.2	47.2	77.7	130.0	173.0	153.0
Income, net	12.7	15.3	9.0	9.5	8.3	1.8	0.5	3.8	7.8	14.4
Current transfers, net	−14.9	−16.2	−17.2	−19.9	−20.4	−19.6	−18.9	−21.3	−19.9	−21.6
Current account balance	**9.5**	**−25.5**	**11.9**	**69.5**	**39.1**	**29.4**	**59.3**	**112.5**	**160.8**	**145.8**
Memorandum										
Exports of goods and services	204.5	159.2	203.7	283.9	265.5	280.8	337.9	425.8	496.5	496.2
Interest payments	7.3	7.3	6.5	7.0	6.7	7.0	4.9	5.1	6.0	6.3
Oil trade balance	122.7	80.8	120.6	188.3	160.3	166.3	207.1	271.1	323.2	312.1
Western Hemisphere										
Exports	249.8	240.2	249.9	299.3	287.1	290.3	322.5	400.2	446.8	460.1
Imports	270.8	284.0	264.6	303.7	299.3	273.9	285.4	348.4	402.6	431.3
Trade balance	−21.0	−43.8	−14.8	−4.4	−12.2	16.4	37.1	51.8	44.2	28.7
Services, net	−15.0	−15.3	−11.7	−12.4	−14.3	−9.4	−8.0	−9.0	−11.8	−13.5
Balance on goods and services	−36.0	−59.1	−26.5	−16.8	−26.5	6.9	29.1	42.9	32.4	15.3
Income, net	−46.7	−49.5	−50.8	−53.0	−53.7	−53.3	−58.4	−68.0	−69.6	−69.2
Current transfers, net	16.1	18.0	20.6	22.0	26.3	29.9	35.9	41.0	41.0	41.3
Current account balance	**−66.7**	**−90.5**	**−56.7**	**−47.8**	**−53.9**	**−16.4**	**6.6**	**15.9**	**3.8**	**−12.7**
Memorandum										
Exports of goods and services	299.3	292.1	302.1	358.0	344.5	346.2	382.4	467.5	518.2	535.0
Interest payments	50.3	53.5	55.6	59.3	58.1	53.0	52.4	54.6	58.7	60.5
Oil trade balance	25.4	16.1	24.9	40.3	30.1	32.8	37.0	50.9	60.9	57.0

[1]Mongolia, which is not a member of the Commonwealth of Independent States, is included in this group for reasons of geography and similarities in economic structure.

Table 30. Other Emerging Market and Developing Countries—by Analytical Criteria: Current Account Transactions
(Billions of U.S. dollars)

	1997	1998	1999	2000	2001	2002	2003	2004	2005	2006
By source of export earnings										
Fuel										
Exports	191.2	134.6	184.9	287.1	253.1	262.1	321.5	422.7	512.4	512.5
Imports	114.3	114.5	114.9	125.2	139.7	151.4	171.1	203.8	232.6	250.3
Trade balance	76.9	20.1	70.1	161.9	113.4	110.8	150.4	218.9	279.8	262.2
Services, net	−44.4	−35.6	−37.7	−44.0	−41.2	−44.5	−49.0	−57.8	−63.1	−66.3
Balance on goods and services	32.4	−15.5	32.4	118.0	72.1	66.3	101.3	161.1	216.6	195.9
Income, net	−1.6	−0.7	−3.6	−9.5	−7.3	−13.9	−16.3	−20.7	−21.3	−16.8
Current transfers, net	−14.8	−16.1	−17.6	−19.9	−19.8	−19.0	−17.4	−17.9	−16.6	−17.0
Current account balance	**16.0**	**−32.3**	**11.3**	**88.6**	**45.0**	**33.4**	**67.6**	**122.5**	**178.8**	**162.0**
Memorandum										
Exports of goods and services	205.1	149.5	199.7	302.8	270.2	281.4	343.8	447.6	539.6	541.4
Interest payments	15.0	15.4	13.3	14.1	14.0	13.7	11.9	13.8	14.2	14.5
Oil trade balance	161.7	106.7	155.8	249.7	213.2	219.0	269.7	358.2	438.8	433.4
Nonfuel exports										
Exports	1,094.6	1,060.4	1,104.0	1,331.2	1,330.5	1,461.0	1,781.1	2,276.9	2,680.3	2,954.2
Imports	1,159.1	1,099.4	1,079.0	1,283.9	1,287.5	1,382.2	1,683.6	2,154.1	2,560.3	2,864.6
Trade balance	−64.4	−39.0	25.0	47.3	43.0	78.8	97.5	122.8	120.0	89.6
Services, net	−10.8	−9.8	−9.4	−13.1	−18.3	−13.8	−15.8	−5.4	−6.0	−3.6
Balance on goods and services	−75.2	−48.8	15.6	34.2	24.7	65.0	81.6	117.4	114.0	86.0
Income, net	−93.4	−99.1	−114.8	−110.7	−113.5	−117.3	−128.8	−139.6	−138.3	−135.8
Current transfers, net	67.0	65.2	70.5	76.2	84.6	103.8	128.7	146.2	148.9	142.9
Current account balance	**−101.6**	**−82.7**	**−28.7**	**−0.4**	**−4.2**	**51.6**	**81.5**	**124.1**	**124.7**	**93.1**
Memorandum										
Exports of goods and services	1,357.4	1,314.7	1,350.3	1,599.0	1,603.3	1,750.6	2,109.5	2,676.6	3,128.3	3,447.0
Interest payments	111.8	122.6	121.9	126.1	123.3	111.8	112.8	129.3	144.9	159.2
Oil trade balance	−2.3	−4.3	2.0	5.9	−2.4	3.3	10.8	13.6	17.1	5.5
Nonfuel primary products										
Exports	43.5	39.3	40.1	42.0	39.3	40.5	48.0	65.5	71.6	71.9
Imports	43.8	40.9	36.0	37.9	37.6	37.8	43.3	54.1	60.6	63.5
Trade balance	−0.3	−1.6	4.1	4.1	1.7	2.7	4.7	11.4	11.0	8.4
Services, net	−3.9	−4.0	−4.0	−3.8	−3.8	−4.1	−4.2	−4.7	−5.8	−6.2
Balance on goods and services	−4.2	−5.6	0.1	0.3	−2.1	−1.4	0.6	6.8	5.2	2.2
Income, net	−6.2	−4.9	−5.5	−6.2	−5.8	−6.2	−8.4	−14.0	−13.0	−12.6
Current transfers, net	2.8	3.0	3.0	3.2	3.7	4.4	5.5	7.1	7.0	6.8
Current account balance	**−7.6**	**−7.5**	**−2.5**	**−2.7**	**−4.2**	**−3.2**	**−2.3**	**−0.1**	**−0.7**	**−3.6**
Memorandum										
Exports of goods and services	51.2	47.1	47.7	49.5	47.2	48.7	57.7	77.0	83.1	84.0
Interest payments	4.5	4.6	4.6	5.0	4.5	4.5	4.3	3.9	4.7	5.2
Oil trade balance	−1.8	−1.7	−2.0	−3.0	−2.9	−2.9	−3.4	−3.4	−3.5	−3.9

Table 30 *(continued)*

	1997	1998	1999	2000	2001	2002	2003	2004	2005	2006
By external financing source										
Net debtor countries										
Exports	709.1	694.6	724.5	860.0	851.8	906.0	1,065.6	1,327.6	1,538.7	1,658.7
Imports	833.5	809.4	789.4	914.5	899.6	932.1	1,092.6	1,374.8	1,616.5	1,762.1
Trade balance	−124.4	−114.8	−64.9	−54.5	−47.8	−26.0	−27.0	−47.2	−77.8	−103.3
Services, net	−2.4	−4.7	−0.6	−0.2	−5.1	−0.9	0.7	10.7	10.5	12.9
Balance on goods and services	−126.8	−119.5	−65.4	−54.8	−52.9	−27.0	−26.3	−36.5	−67.3	−90.4
Income, net	−73.6	−75.7	−87.8	−94.1	−94.0	−101.9	−115.3	−130.8	−135.6	−139.6
Current transfers, net	67.6	66.5	67.6	71.9	79.5	95.1	115.6	125.3	132.7	139.1
Current account balance	**−132.8**	**−128.7**	**−85.6**	**−77.0**	**−67.4**	**−33.8**	**−26.0**	**−42.1**	**−70.3**	**−90.9**
Memorandum										
Exports of goods and services	909.1	893.7	916.7	1,066.8	1,058.4	1,119.0	1,306.6	1,616.0	1,858.7	2,005.8
Interest payments	95.0	99.1	102.6	106.8	105.1	94.1	94.6	101.3	110.4	118.1
Oil trade balance	−2.1	−1.4	10.8	20.9	13.8	17.6	22.5	26.7	33.4	34.5
Official financing										
Exports	163.0	156.7	154.8	182.0	172.2	178.1	200.5	235.7	257.9	269.3
Imports	181.7	169.3	156.0	176.4	166.6	159.4	183.5	226.7	258.6	279.1
Trade balance	−18.7	−12.6	−1.2	5.7	5.5	18.7	17.0	9.0	−0.6	−9.7
Services, net	−19.9	−21.5	−11.7	−13.6	−12.8	−9.8	−12.3	−14.3	−17.5	−17.6
Balance on goods and services	−38.6	−34.1	−12.9	−7.9	−7.2	8.9	4.7	−5.3	−18.1	−27.4
Income, net	−18.1	−16.8	−25.1	−25.4	−25.2	−31.0	−33.2	−31.4	−33.8	−33.1
Current transfers, net	17.2	18.2	20.1	21.5	24.5	32.3	37.9	36.5	38.5	40.1
Current account balance	**−39.5**	**−32.7**	**−17.8**	**−11.8**	**−8.0**	**10.2**	**9.3**	**−0.2**	**−13.4**	**−20.5**
Memorandum										
Exports of goods and services	199.4	190.9	189.8	218.3	210.3	216.0	241.3	282.0	306.6	322.1
Interest payments	26.5	29.8	30.8	32.3	32.9	26.5	26.0	26.3	29.4	30.5
Oil trade balance	3.0	3.2	4.1	4.5	1.6	1.4	0.8	0.4	−2.1	−6.6
Net debtor countries by debt-servicing experience										
Countries with arrears and/or rescheduling during 1999–2003										
Exports	175.9	162.8	172.8	221.1	207.8	214.7	246.4	297.5	341.8	361.7
Imports	176.6	165.7	161.5	184.1	180.8	184.0	212.7	259.1	299.0	325.3
Trade balance	−0.8	−2.9	11.3	36.9	27.0	30.7	33.7	38.4	42.8	36.4
Services, net	−24.4	−26.5	−17.8	−19.6	−21.1	−18.9	−22.4	−26.9	−32.1	−34.7
Balance on goods and services	−25.2	−29.4	−6.5	17.3	5.9	11.8	11.3	11.5	10.7	1.7
Income, net	−22.7	−22.1	−31.7	−36.4	−32.5	−38.4	−42.3	−43.7	−48.6	−49.5
Current transfers, net	16.7	16.6	15.7	17.0	19.4	28.6	35.2	33.4	34.8	35.3
Current account balance	**−31.2**	**−34.9**	**−22.5**	**−2.1**	**−7.3**	**2.1**	**4.3**	**1.2**	**−3.2**	**−12.6**
Memorandum										
Exports of goods and services	211.6	196.5	205.5	256.1	243.3	250.8	285.3	340.9	388.1	412.1
Interest payments	28.7	32.9	34.2	35.9	35.6	28.6	28.6	29.1	32.5	34.1
Oil trade balance	26.4	20.7	32.5	53.0	48.0	47.8	57.8	74.1	90.5	94.0

Table 30 *(concluded)*

	1997	1998	1999	2000	2001	2002	2003	2004	2005	2006
Other groups										
Heavily indebted poor countries										
Exports	16.9	16.7	15.5	16.5	17.4	17.5	20.8	26.5	29.6	31.1
Imports	21.9	23.3	24.2	24.2	25.3	27.1	31.1	37.5	41.5	43.7
Trade balance	−5.0	−6.6	−8.7	−7.7	−8.0	−9.6	−10.3	−11.0	−11.8	−12.6
Services, net	−2.7	−3.0	−2.5	−2.3	−2.7	−2.5	−2.7	−2.7	−3.1	−3.3
Balance on goods and services	−7.7	−9.6	−11.2	−10.1	−10.6	−12.1	−13.0	−13.7	−15.0	−15.9
Income, net	−3.2	−2.5	−2.5	−2.7	−3.2	−2.8	−2.8	−4.3	−5.0	−4.1
Current transfers, net	4.4	4.9	5.1	5.9	6.7	7.2	8.8	10.3	10.8	10.4
Current account balance	**−6.5**	**−7.2**	**−8.6**	**−7.0**	**−7.2**	**−7.7**	**−7.0**	**−7.7**	**−9.2**	**−9.5**
Memorandum										
Exports of goods and services	21.9	22.2	21.5	22.7	23.8	24.3	28.6	35.6	39.3	41.2
Interest payments	3.0	3.3	2.8	2.7	2.6	2.5	2.3	2.4	2.4	2.4
Oil trade balance	−1.0	−1.1	−1.5	−2.0	−2.0	−2.1	−2.4	−1.3	−0.8	−1.2
Middle East and north Africa										
Exports	206.4	156.4	201.4	290.9	268.4	282.5	343.5	437.1	516.3	516.5
Imports	160.6	161.1	159.9	173.4	186.9	203.4	229.5	268.5	295.7	316.8
Trade balance	45.8	−4.7	41.5	117.5	81.5	79.1	113.9	168.7	220.7	199.8
Services, net	−32.1	−23.3	−22.9	−30.0	−25.5	−29.5	−30.3	−32.5	−34.5	−34.8
Balance on goods and services	13.7	−28.0	18.6	87.5	56.0	49.5	83.7	136.1	186.2	164.9
Income, net	7.3	10.2	3.6	3.2	3.2	−3.4	−5.6	−3.7	−3.5	3.6
Current transfers, net	−10.2	−11.2	−12.6	−15.2	−14.5	−13.1	−10.8	−10.9	−9.3	−10.5
Current account balance	**10.8**	**−29.0**	**9.6**	**75.5**	**44.7**	**32.9**	**67.3**	**121.5**	**173.4**	**158.0**
Memorandum										
Exports of goods and services	238.4	189.8	237.5	327.9	308.5	325.1	392.2	493.5	578.2	582.5
Interest payments	−12.3	−12.0	−11.1	−12.2	−11.0	−10.8	−8.8	−9.6	−11.1	−12.0
Oil trade balance	134.2	89.4	131.3	208.6	178.0	183.8	230.4	302.5	365.7	356.7

Table 31. Other Emerging Market and Developing Countries—by Country: Balance of Payments on Current Account
(Percent of GDP)

	1997	1998	1999	2000	2001	2002	2003	2004	2005	2006
Africa	**−1.4**	**−4.5**	**−3.6**	**1.5**	**−0.3**	**−1.7**	**−0.3**	**0.2**	**0.8**	**0.5**
Algeria	7.2	−1.9	—	16.8	12.9	7.8	13.3	13.3	15.4	14.7
Angola	−11.5	−28.8	−27.5	8.7	−14.8	−2.9	−5.2	6.5	3.3	4.7
Benin	−7.4	−5.7	−7.6	−8.0	−6.7	−9.0	−8.5	−8.5	−8.5	−8.3
Botswana	13.9	4.1	12.3	10.4	11.5	2.2	6.5	6.3	8.1	7.7
Burkina Faso	−9.6	−8.6	−10.8	−12.2	−10.2	−9.1	−6.9	−8.5	−9.0	−8.2
Burundi	−2.8	−7.5	−6.1	−10.0	−6.8	−6.5	−6.1	−23.8	−23.1	−18.2
Cameroon	−2.8	−2.5	−4.3	−1.7	−4.1	−7.0	−2.4	−1.7	−0.6	−0.8
Cape Verde	−6.0	−11.0	−12.4	−11.2	−9.9	−10.9	−9.1	−7.9	−8.0	−7.9
Central African Republic	−3.0	−6.1	−1.6	−3.0	−2.5	−2.8	−4.6	−4.8	−4.1	−3.9
Chad	−9.0	−9.8	−15.9	−18.0	−35.1	−51.8	−40.1	−17.7	−6.8	−5.0
Comoros	−19.9	−8.4	−6.8	−1.7	1.1	−4.0	−6.2	−3.0	−4.2	−4.1
Congo, Dem. Rep. of	−3.1	−9.0	−2.6	−4.6	−4.9	−2.8	−1.5	−2.5	−4.8	−6.7
Congo, Rep. of	−12.9	−20.6	−17.1	7.9	−3.2	−0.3	—	7.2	10.5	10.9
Côte d'Ivoire	−1.8	−2.7	−1.4	−2.8	−1.1	6.1	3.9	3.1	4.1	3.5
Djibouti	−2.3	−0.6	−0.4	−7.2	−5.8	−9.2	−8.8	−10.7	−9.4	−15.5
Equatorial Guinea	−37.5	−78.5	−58.7	−27.7	−51.2	−67.0	−29.2	−14.6	−16.9	−7.8
Eritrea	2.1	−23.6	−28.0	−11.6	—	0.3	−15.1	−11.9	−5.7	−2.2
Ethiopia	−3.0	−1.6	−7.9	−5.1	−3.6	−5.7	−2.7	−6.1	−8.1	−7.5
Gabon	10.0	−13.8	8.4	19.7	11.0	5.2	9.6	10.4	10.5	8.3
Gambia, The	−3.7	−2.4	−2.8	−3.1	−2.6	−2.8	−4.8	−4.4	−10.6	−6.3
Ghana	−14.4	−5.0	−11.6	−8.4	−5.3	0.5	1.7	1.2	−1.3	−0.6
Guinea	−7.0	−8.5	−6.9	−6.4	−2.7	−4.3	−3.3	−4.9	−4.1	−3.2
Guinea-Bissau	−8.7	−13.2	−12.0	−5.6	−22.4	−11.5	−1.0	1.6	−12.2	−13.1
Kenya	−4.2	−4.9	−2.2	−2.1	−3.5	2.4	−0.2	−3.7	−4.9	−5.7
Lesotho	−30.9	−25.0	−22.8	−18.2	−13.2	−16.9	−12.3	−1.0	−6.2	−5.5
Madagascar	−5.5	−7.5	−5.6	−5.6	−1.3	−6.0	−4.9	−8.5	−8.2	−6.4
Malawi	−11.4	−0.4	−8.3	−5.3	−6.8	−11.2	−10.3	−7.6	−7.7	−7.6
Mali	−6.5	−6.8	−8.8	−10.0	−10.4	−3.1	−4.6	−4.7	−6.0	−7.7
Mauritania	1.7	−0.7	3.0	−2.7	−10.8	1.5	−9.6	−21.6	−25.9	−15.1
Mauritius	0.4	−2.8	−1.6	−5.5	−2.1	2.2	2.0	0.6	−0.8	−2.6
Morocco	−0.3	−0.4	−0.5	−1.4	4.8	4.1	3.6	1.2	—	0.3
Mozambique, Rep. of	−12.5	−14.4	−22.4	−19.3	−21.4	−22.3	−16.8	−12.4	−16.9	−15.4
Namibia	1.7	2.4	6.9	9.3	1.7	3.8	4.0	5.5	4.4	3.6
Niger	−7.2	−6.9	−6.5	−6.2	−4.8	−6.5	−6.0	−5.9	−7.2	−6.9
Nigeria	5.1	−8.9	−8.4	10.5	3.0	−11.0	−3.7	2.8	7.8	5.1
Rwanda	−9.5	−9.6	−7.7	−5.0	−5.9	−6.7	−7.8	−2.6	−9.6	−7.3
São Tomé and Príncipe	−30.9	−30.8	−52.4	−20.9	−22.8	−22.1	−18.8	−26.8	−32.1	−33.9
Senegal	−4.2	−4.1	−5.6	−5.1	−4.6	−5.9	−6.5	−6.2	−5.6	−5.0
Seychelles	−10.7	−16.5	−19.8	−7.2	−23.5	−16.3	−0.9	−4.9	−10.6	−24.4
Sierra Leone	−0.4	−2.6	−11.1	−15.2	−16.2	−4.8	−7.6	−9.0	−9.3	−7.2
South Africa	−1.5	−1.8	−0.5	−0.1	—	0.6	−0.9	−2.5	−3.0	−2.6
Sudan	−13.6	−14.9	−15.8	−15.1	−15.5	−9.6	−8.2	−6.8	−4.5	−5.5
Swaziland	−0.2	−6.9	−2.6	−5.4	−4.5	6.0	0.6	−0.6	−2.5	−2.6
Tanzania	−5.3	−11.0	−9.9	−5.3	−5.3	−3.8	−2.4	−5.8	−5.4	−6.6
Togo	−11.3	−8.8	−8.1	−10.5	−13.0	−9.7	−12.9	−12.4	−12.3	−12.3
Tunisia	−3.1	−3.4	−2.2	−4.2	−4.3	−3.5	−2.9	−2.1	−2.5	−2.5
Uganda	−4.0	−7.0	−8.7	−6.5	−5.6	−5.9	−6.2	−1.9	−4.4	−6.0
Zambia	−6.1	−16.7	−13.7	−18.2	−20.0	−15.4	−15.2	−11.5	−10.3	−11.0
Zimbabwe	−8.0	−4.7	2.5	0.2	−3.5	−1.8	−5.0	−5.3	−2.7	−3.7

Table 31 *(continued)*

	1997	1998	1999	2000	2001	2002	2003	2004	2005	2006
Central and eastern Europe	**−3.6**	**−3.0**	**−4.3**	**−5.3**	**−2.7**	**−3.6**	**−4.4**	**−5.0**	**−4.7**	**−4.4**
Albania	−8.7	−3.9	−3.9	−4.4	−3.4	−6.9	−5.6	−5.0	−5.2	−5.0
Bosnia and Herzegovina	. . .	−8.6	−9.2	−12.8	−16.8	−21.9	−17.6	−17.3	−16.8	−15.5
Bulgaria	10.1	−0.5	−5.0	−5.6	−7.3	−5.6	−9.3	−7.4	−7.6	−6.9
Croatia	−12.5	−6.7	−7.0	−2.5	−3.7	−8.4	−6.1	−5.4	−5.0	−4.4
Czech Republic	−6.2	−2.0	−2.5	−4.9	−5.4	−5.6	−6.2	−5.2	−4.8	−4.4
Estonia	−11.4	−8.6	−4.4	−5.5	−5.6	−10.2	−13.2	−13.8	−11.0	−9.7
Hungary	−4.5	−7.1	−7.9	−8.7	−6.2	−7.2	−9.0	−9.0	−8.6	−8.1
Latvia	−4.7	−9.0	−9.0	−4.6	−7.6	−6.7	−8.2	−12.3	−10.9	−9.8
Lithuania	−7.9	−11.7	−11.0	−5.9	−4.7	−5.2	−7.0	−8.6	−9.5	−9.3
Macedonia, FYR	−7.9	−7.5	−0.9	−2.1	−6.8	−8.5	−3.0	−6.0	−6.0	−5.7
Malta	−6.0	−6.3	−3.3	−12.3	−4.4	0.3	−5.8	−10.3	−4.0	−3.0
Poland	−3.7	−4.1	−7.6	−6.0	−2.9	−2.6	−1.9	−1.5	−2.1	−2.5
Romania	−5.4	−7.1	−4.1	−4.6	−6.5	−4.4	−6.8	−7.5	−6.9	−6.3
Serbia and Montenegro	. . .	−4.8	−7.5	−3.9	−4.6	−8.9	−7.5	−13.1	−10.8	−11.6
Slovak Republic	−9.2	−9.6	−4.8	−3.5	−8.4	−8.0	−0.9	−3.4	−6.0	−4.6
Slovenia	0.3	−0.6	−3.3	−2.8	0.2	1.4	0.1	−0.6	−1.4	−2.2
Turkey	−1.1	1.0	−0.7	−4.8	2.2	−0.8	−3.4	−5.2	−4.5	−3.7
Commonwealth of Independent States[1]	**−1.7**	**−2.5**	**7.1**	**13.0**	**7.9**	**7.0**	**6.4**	**8.5**	**9.4**	**6.8**
Armenia	−16.6	−20.8	−16.6	−14.6	−9.5	−6.2	−6.8	−5.8	−5.5	−5.5
Azerbaijan	−23.1	−30.7	−13.1	−3.6	−0.9	−12.3	−28.3	−27.3	−7.8	6.0
Belarus	−6.1	−6.7	−1.6	−2.6	−3.5	−2.6	−2.9	−3.0	−3.4	−3.3
Georgia	−10.5	−10.2	−7.8	−4.4	−6.5	−5.8	−7.2	−7.5	−8.1	−6.0
Kazakhstan	−3.5	−5.5	−0.1	4.2	−4.0	−3.5	−0.2	2.3	1.8	−0.8
Kyrgyz Republic	−8.3	−22.3	−14.8	−4.3	−1.5	−2.6	−2.8	−3.0	−6.3	−4.6
Moldova	−14.2	−19.7	−5.8	−8.9	−4.6	−3.1	−7.3	−7.1	−6.1	−5.9
Mongolia	9.0	−5.8	−4.7	−5.7	−7.6	−7.1	−5.6	−3.3	−2.8	−3.9
Russia	−0.6	−0.8	11.3	17.2	10.9	9.0	8.2	10.2	11.4	8.7
Tajikistan	−5.0	−8.3	−3.4	−6.3	−6.6	−2.7	−1.3	−3.9	−4.2	−4.2
Turkmenistan	−21.6	−32.7	−14.8	8.4	1.7	6.7	4.2	4.3	5.1	3.8
Ukraine	−3.0	−3.1	2.6	4.7	3.7	7.5	5.8	11.0	7.2	2.5
Uzbekistan	−4.0	−0.8	−0.8	1.6	−1.0	1.2	8.9	0.8	4.5	3.9

Table 31 *(continued)*

	1997	1998	1999	2000	2001	2002	2003	2004	2005	2006
Developing Asia	**0.4**	**2.6**	**2.4**	**2.1**	**1.8**	**2.9**	**3.1**	**3.3**	**2.8**	**2.5**
Afghanistan, I.S. of	...	...	...	...	...	−3.5	1.7	1.8	−1.7	−3.1
Bangladesh	−1.5	−1.1	−0.9	−1.4	−0.8	0.3	0.1	−1.2	−2.4	−2.5
Bhutan	8.3	5.6	0.9	−1.6	−1.1	−2.0	−2.0	−2.0	−2.0	2.0
Brunei Darussalam	35.7	44.7	48.1	81.7	83.7	70.7	78.9	76.3	80.8	74.2
Cambodia	−8.0	−5.9	−5.2	−3.0	−1.2	−1.0	−3.2	−2.3	−5.2	−4.4
China	3.8	3.3	1.6	1.9	1.5	2.8	3.2	4.2	4.2	4.0
Fiji	1.6	−0.3	−3.8	−5.8	−3.3	−3.5	−10.2	−5.9	−4.9	−4.1
India	−0.7	−1.7	−0.7	−1.0	0.3	1.4	1.2	0.3	−0.3	−0.3
Indonesia	−1.6	3.8	3.7	4.9	4.2	3.9	3.0	2.8	2.2	0.9
Kiribati	22.0	35.2	12.4	13.3	3.2	7.7	−21.5	−12.5	−13.6	−14.5
Lao PDR	−10.5	−4.6	−4.0	−1.4	−3.7	−5.4	−5.5	−8.5	−7.9	−10.5
Malaysia	−5.9	13.2	15.9	9.4	8.3	8.4	12.9	13.3	13.6	12.2
Maldives	−6.2	−4.1	−13.4	−8.2	−9.4	−5.6	−4.6	−11.8	−25.1	−21.4
Myanmar	−10.6	−10.9	−6.3	4.2	−3.7	1.7	0.2	−0.4	−0.7	−1.1
Nepal	−1.0	−1.0	4.3	3.2	4.9	4.5	2.1	2.5	0.9	0.6
Pakistan	−4.2	−3.2	−2.8	−1.9	0.4	4.5	4.1	0.3	−1.2	−0.8
Papua New Guinea	−5.4	0.6	2.8	8.7	7.0	−0.7	11.2	16.2	10.0	5.0
Philippines	−5.3	2.3	9.5	8.4	1.9	5.8	4.3	4.6	2.6	2.0
Samoa	−3.6	−3.4	−8.6	−6.1	−11.7	−8.1	−1.9	−1.1	−0.3	0.1
Solomon Islands	−5.6	−1.6	3.1	−10.6	−12.5	−6.1	0.4	7.8	−14.2	−5.8
Sri Lanka	−2.6	−1.4	−3.6	−6.4	−1.1	−1.4	−0.4	−3.2	−5.3	−4.2
Thailand	−2.1	12.8	10.2	7.6	5.4	5.5	5.6	4.5	2.0	1.4
Timor-Leste, Dem. Rep. of	...	...	2.1	14.9	14.0	11.6	12.7	12.3	8.9	10.7
Tonga	−0.9	−10.5	−0.6	−5.9	−9.2	4.9	−2.9	0.8	−0.5	−0.3
Vanuatu	−1.0	2.5	−4.9	2.0	2.0	−6.0	−8.5	−3.6	−4.5	−4.3
Vietnam	−6.2	−3.9	4.5	2.1	2.1	−1.2	−4.7	−4.6	−4.9	−3.7
Middle East	**1.7**	**−5.0**	**2.1**	**11.0**	**6.1**	**4.6**	**8.3**	**13.7**	**17.2**	**14.9**
Bahrain	−0.5	−12.5	−1.4	10.4	2.8	−6.1	−0.5	8.1	11.4	9.5
Egypt	0.2	−2.9	−1.9	−1.2	—	0.7	2.4	4.4	4.5	3.4
Iran, I.R. of	2.1	−2.2	6.3	12.9	5.2	3.1	1.5	5.2	6.4	4.5
Iraq	...	...	...	...	...	...	...	...	...	...
Jordan	0.4	0.3	5.0	0.7	−0.1	3.8	11.3	−0.8	−1.7	−5.0
Kuwait	25.9	8.5	16.6	39.8	24.4	12.1	17.5	29.1	37.8	34.7
Lebanon	−34.6	−29.1	−19.5	−19.0	−22.7	−14.9	−13.6	−16.1	−16.3	−12.9
Libya	5.8	−1.2	7.0	22.5	12.3	0.6	15.4	25.7	33.5	32.7
Oman	−1.2	−22.3	−3.1	16.1	9.9	8.7	6.6	11.0	7.0	6.9
Qatar	−25.6	−21.5	6.8	18.0	19.9	16.5	29.0	42.0	40.2	37.8
Saudi Arabia	−0.1	−9.0	0.3	7.6	5.1	6.3	13.8	19.8	27.7	25.1
Syrian Arab Republic	1.9	−0.3	0.6	4.4	4.8	6.7	3.5	−0.4	−0.4	−2.9
United Arab Emirates	10.1	1.8	1.6	17.3	9.4	4.9	8.5	16.9	17.8	16.6
Yemen	1.6	−2.8	2.7	13.2	5.3	5.4	1.1	1.0	2.6	−1.7

Table 31 *(concluded)*

	1997	1998	1999	2000	2001	2002	2003	2004	2005	2006
Western Hemisphere	**−3.3**	**−4.5**	**−3.2**	**−2.4**	**−2.8**	**−1.0**	**0.4**	**0.8**	**0.2**	**−0.5**
Antigua and Barbuda	−14.7	−10.8	−8.9	−9.7	−9.2	−15.2	−13.7	−13.2	−13.1	−13.8
Argentina	−4.2	−4.9	−4.2	−3.2	−1.4	8.5	5.8	2.0	−1.2	−2.9
Bahamas, The	−16.9	−23.8	−5.3	−10.5	−11.9	−6.8	−8.1	−8.8	−11.6	−11.6
Barbados	−2.2	−2.4	−6.0	−5.6	−3.7	−6.6	−7.8	−10.0	−7.7	−6.7
Belize	−3.5	−6.0	−10.4	−20.6	−22.6	−20.2	−19.5	−14.7	−11.1	−8.6
Bolivia	−7.0	−7.9	−5.9	−5.3	−3.4	−4.2	0.4	2.7	2.6	2.4
Brazil	−3.8	−4.2	−4.8	−4.0	−4.6	−1.7	0.8	1.9	1.1	0.4
Chile	−4.4	−5.0	0.1	−1.2	−1.6	−0.9	−1.6	1.5	0.9	−1.3
Colombia	−5.4	−4.9	0.8	0.9	−1.4	−1.7	−1.5	−1.1	−2.6	−2.6
Costa Rica	−4.8	−5.3	−5.2	−4.4	−4.5	−5.7	−5.3	−4.8	−4.2	−3.8
Dominica	−16.4	−9.0	−12.9	−19.5	−18.2	−15.0	−18.1	−15.0	−12.1	−8.6
Dominican Republic	−1.1	−2.1	−2.4	−5.1	−3.4	−3.7	6.3	5.8	2.0	0.5
Ecuador	−3.0	−9.3	4.6	5.3	—	−4.9	−1.7	−0.5	0.8	1.2
El Salvador	−0.8	−0.8	−1.6	−2.9	−0.9	−2.5	−4.3	−4.4	−4.0	−4.2
Grenada	−24.5	−23.5	−14.6	−21.5	−26.6	−32.3	−33.1	−11.4	−41.4	−39.7
Guatemala	−3.5	−5.2	−5.5	−5.4	−5.9	−5.3	−4.3	−4.4	−3.9	−3.6
Guyana	−14.2	−13.7	−11.4	−15.3	−18.5	−14.8	−11.4	−12.2	−25.1	−24.4
Haiti	−0.3	0.5	−1.0	−1.0	−2.0	−1.0	−0.1	0.4	0.9	−0.3
Honduras	−3.1	−2.4	−4.4	−4.0	−4.0	−3.2	−4.4	−5.8	−3.6	−3.0
Jamaica	−5.2	−2.0	−3.4	−4.9	−9.8	−14.9	−10.6	−13.2	−12.4	−11.8
Mexico	−1.9	−3.8	−2.9	−3.1	−2.9	−2.1	−1.3	−1.3	−1.4	−1.6
Netherlands Antilles	−2.6	−3.6	−9.2	−2.7	−5.5	−2.2	0.2	−3.1	−2.2	−2.8
Nicaragua	−21.2	−19.3	−25.2	−20.1	−19.9	−20.2	−19.6	−21.4	−20.6	−19.3
Panama	−5.0	−9.3	−10.1	−5.9	−1.5	−0.5	−3.2	−1.7	−1.1	−0.1
Paraguay	−6.8	−1.9	−2.1	−2.1	−3.9	2.3	2.5	1.3	0.2	—
Peru	−5.7	−5.9	−2.8	−2.9	−2.2	−2.0	−1.8	−0.1	0.5	0.2
St. Kitts and Nevis	−21.1	−14.3	−21.7	−19.7	−29.0	−36.8	−29.6	−23.9	−21.8	−21.5
St. Lucia	−11.8	−11.8	−12.5	−12.5	−9.1	−12.7	−18.8	−10.2	−10.1	−10.0
St. Vincent and the Grenadines	−28.5	−29.7	−21.8	−8.4	−11.8	−11.8	−12.4	−13.1	−13.9	−15.7
Suriname	−6.4	−14.3	−19.0	−3.8	−15.2	−6.3	−13.8	−13.2	−12.3	−8.7
Trinidad and Tobago	−9.9	−10.6	0.5	6.6	5.0	0.9	12.8	7.3	4.8	6.7
Uruguay	−1.3	−2.1	−2.4	−2.8	−2.9	1.6	0.7	−0.3	−0.2	−0.6
Venezuela	4.3	−4.9	2.2	10.1	1.6	8.2	13.6	13.5	12.0	8.4

[1]Mongolia, which is not a member of the Commonwealth of Independent States, is included in this group for reasons of geography and similarities in economic structure.

Table 32. Summary of Balance of Payments, Capital Flows, and External Financing
(Billions of U.S. dollars)

	1997	1998	1999	2000	2001	2002	2003	2004	2005	2006
Other emerging market and developing countries										
Balance of payments[1]										
Balance on current account	−85.6	−115.1	−17.4	88.2	40.8	85.0	149.1	246.6	303.4	255.2
Balance on goods and services	−42.8	−64.4	48.0	152.1	96.8	131.3	182.9	278.5	330.7	281.9
Income, net	−95.0	−99.7	−118.4	−120.2	−120.8	−131.2	−145.1	−160.2	−159.6	−152.6
Current transfers, net	52.1	49.0	52.9	56.3	64.8	84.9	111.3	128.3	132.3	125.9
Balance on capital and financial account	140.0	160.5	84.3	−37.0	11.6	−38.6	−179.5	−267.8	−288.9	−249.0
Balance on capital account[2]	19.8	6.6	9.9	9.0	9.7	8.6	6.8	9.1	11.6	11.6
Balance on financial account	120.1	153.8	74.4	−46.0	1.9	−47.2	−186.3	−277.0	−300.6	−260.6
Direct investment, net	149.9	159.5	158.2	156.3	177.2	153.5	141.7	167.3	199.8	203.5
Portfolio investment, net	46.9	28.5	23.0	−36.4	−59.3	−36.0	−37.5	4.3	−28.0	−7.3
Other investment, net	11.6	−30.7	−70.3	−88.1	−29.3	−14.1	6.9	−12.3	−10.2	−6.6
Reserve assets	−88.2	−3.5	−36.6	−77.8	−86.8	−150.7	−297.3	−436.3	−462.2	−450.2
Errors and omissions, net	−54.4	−45.4	−66.8	−51.2	−52.4	−46.3	30.4	21.3	−14.5	−6.2
Capital flows										
Total capital flows, net[3]	208.4	157.3	110.9	31.8	88.7	103.4	111.1	159.3	161.6	189.6
Net official flows	7.9	56.3	38.2	−34.6	13.5	12.7	−52.2	−48.3	−58.3	−49.9
Net private flows[4]	212.5	107.5	59.0	45.6	74.9	87.0	162.6	192.4	197.0	212.1
Direct investment, net	149.9	159.5	158.2	156.3	177.2	153.5	141.7	167.3	199.8	203.5
Private portfolio investment, net	58.0	22.6	9.2	−9.5	−49.4	−38.0	10.7	52.7	30.5	44.6
Other private flows, net	4.6	−74.7	−108.4	−101.3	−52.9	−28.5	10.2	−27.6	−33.3	−36.0
External financing[5]										
Net external financing[6]	360.1	281.9	239.9	232.1	169.1	187.4	249.8	356.0	381.9	397.0
Non-debt-creating flows	197.7	171.8	174.4	170.4	171.4	152.0	152.2	203.8	226.5	231.6
Capital transfers[7]	19.8	6.6	9.9	9.0	9.7	8.6	6.8	9.1	11.6	11.6
Foreign direct investment and equity security liabilities[8]	177.9	165.2	164.5	161.4	161.7	143.4	145.4	194.6	214.8	220.0
Net external borrowing[9]	162.4	110.1	65.5	61.6	−2.3	35.3	97.6	152.3	155.4	165.4
Borrowing from official creditors[10]	13.0	47.3	31.3	2.8	23.5	12.6	−3.7	7.7	11.7	15.8
of which, credit and loans from IMF[11]	3.3	14.0	−2.4	−10.9	19.0	13.4	1.7	−14.1	. . .	. . .
Borrowing from banks[10]	9.6	6.5	−16.5	−11.7	−6.0	−5.9	27.1	51.5	64.0	67.1
Borrowing from other private creditors[10]	139.9	56.3	50.7	70.6	−19.8	28.7	74.2	93.0	79.7	82.5
Memorandum										
Balance on goods and services in percent of GDP[12]	−0.7	−1.1	0.8	2.5	1.5	2.0	2.5	3.3	3.4	2.7
Scheduled amortization of external debt	253.4	262.7	295.3	307.9	313.5	328.1	340.1	332.3	349.2	352.1
Gross external financing[13]	613.6	544.7	535.2	539.9	482.6	515.4	589.9	688.3	731.1	749.1
Gross external borrowing[14]	415.9	372.8	360.8	369.5	311.3	363.4	437.7	484.5	504.7	517.5
Exceptional external financing, net	−10.3	33.6	24.4	8.0	21.7	44.1	33.3	17.0	24.1	10.7
Of which,										
Arrears on debt service	−27.0	12.5	9.8	−17.8	2.0	3.4	16.0	8.7	. . .	. . .
Debt forgiveness	13.6	2.0	0.8	2.1	−0.4	3.1	0.9	2.1	. . .	. . .
Rescheduling of debt service	3.0	8.2	10.5	2.0	8.8	13.1	6.5	6.9	. . .	. . .

[1]Standard presentation in accordance with the 5th edition of the International Monetary Fund's *Balance of Payments Manual* (1993).

[2]Comprises capital transfers—including debt forgiveness—and acquisition/disposal of nonproduced, nonfinancial assets.

[3]Comprise net direct investment, net portfolio investment, and other long- and short-term net investment flows, including official and private borrowing. In the standard balance of payments presentation above, total net capital flows are equal to the balance on financial account minus the change in reserve assets.

[4]Because of limitations on the data coverage for net official flows, the residually derived data for net private flows may include some official flows.

[5]As defined in the *World Economic Outlook* (see footnote 6). It should be noted that there is no generally accepted standard definition of external financing.

[6]Defined as the sum of—with opposite sign—the goods and services balance, net income and current transfers, direct investment abroad, the change in reserve assets, the net acquisition of other assets (such as recorded private portfolio assets, export credit, and the collateral for debt-reduction operations), and the net errors and omissions. Thus, net external financing, according to the definition adopted in the *World Economic Outlook*, measures the total amount required to finance the current account, direct investment outflows, net reserve transactions (often at the discretion of the monetary authorities), the net acquisition of nonreserve external assets, and the net transactions underlying the errors and omissions (not infrequently reflecting capital flight).

[7]Including other transactions on capital account.

[8]Debt-creating foreign direct investment liabilities are not included.

[9]Net disbursement of long- and short-term credits, including exceptional financing, by both official and private creditors.

[10]Changes in liabilities.

[11]Comprise use of International Monetary Fund resources under the General Resources Account, Trust Fund, and Poverty Reduction and Growth Facility (PRGF). For further detail, see Table 36.

[12]This is often referred to as the "resource balance" and, with opposite sign, the "net resource transfer."

[13]Net external financing plus amortization due on external debt.

[14]Net external borrowing plus amortization due on external debt.

Table 33. Other Emerging Market and Developing Countries—by Region: Balance of Payments and External Financing[1]
(Billions of U.S. dollars)

	1997	1998	1999	2000	2001	2002	2003	2004	2005	2006
Africa										
Balance of payments										
Balance on current account	−6.2	−19.4	−15.3	6.5	−1.3	−8.0	−1.7	1.1	6.5	4.2
Balance on capital account	8.0	4.1	5.0	4.2	5.0	5.8	5.5	6.6	6.3	6.0
Balance on financial account	−0.3	16.7	13.0	−10.9	−5.2	2.2	−5.0	−16.9	−13.9	−12.1
Change in reserves (− = increase)	−11.3	1.7	−2.8	−12.8	−11.9	−8.1	−19.2	−33.1	−34.3	−32.1
Other official flows, net	−4.5	2.9	1.1	−0.2	−2.6	3.8	2.8	−0.5	−1.4	0.7
Private flows, net	14.3	10.8	11.5	−1.7	7.6	6.9	12.3	11.4	15.6	13.5
External financing										
Net external financing	30.7	29.8	32.4	15.7	19.4	21.7	23.0	27.6	29.6	29.6
Non-debt-creating inflows	24.1	20.8	24.2	13.8	22.5	20.4	21.3	26.5	26.5	26.2
Net external borrowing	6.6	9.0	8.2	1.9	−3.1	1.3	1.7	1.0	3.1	3.4
From official creditors	−3.9	3.5	2.8	1.7	−1.7	3.6	2.4	2.1	1.8	3.6
of which, credit and loans from IMF	−0.5	−0.4	−0.2	−0.2	−0.4	−0.1	−0.8	−0.7	. . .	. . .
From banks	0.8	−1.3	2.3	0.1	0.8	1.7	−0.1	−0.5	−1.7	−0.5
From other private creditors	9.7	6.8	3.1	0.1	−2.1	−4.0	−0.5	−0.6	3.0	0.3
Memorandum										
Exceptional financing	10.2	9.9	9.5	7.3	5.9	7.1	6.9	1.8	6.0	4.6
Sub-Sahara										
Balance of payments										
Balance on current account	−9.0	−17.7	−14.7	−1.3	−9.2	−13.1	−11.4	−9.7	−7.7	−10.1
Balance on capital account	7.9	4.0	4.7	4.2	4.9	5.6	5.4	6.5	6.2	5.9
Balance on financial account	4.4	15.7	11.4	−3.1	2.8	7.3	4.5	−4.9	0.5	3.1
Change in reserves (− = increase)	−6.3	0.6	−3.2	−6.1	−1.9	−3.7	−9.9	−22.2	−18.6	−16.2
Other official flows, net	−2.7	4.3	2.6	2.1	−0.4	6.3	5.0	1.8	0.2	2.5
Private flows, net	13.7	11.2	10.6	—	5.5	7.6	12.2	13.0	15.0	13.9
External financing										
Net external financing	29.0	28.3	29.7	14.6	15.5	20.0	21.7	26.4	27.3	27.1
Non-debt-creating inflows	22.2	19.1	22.2	12.2	17.9	18.0	17.7	23.6	23.1	23.5
Net external borrowing	6.8	9.2	7.4	2.4	−2.4	2.0	3.9	2.8	4.2	3.6
From official creditors	−2.9	4.0	3.3	2.6	−0.6	4.9	3.5	3.0	2.2	4.0
of which, credit and loans from IMF	−0.5	−0.3	−0.1	—	−0.2	0.2	−0.4	−0.3	. . .	. . .
From banks	—	−1.3	0.9	−0.2	0.2	0.8	−0.9	−0.7	−1.6	−0.7
From other private creditors	9.7	6.5	3.2	—	−2.0	−3.7	1.3	0.4	3.7	0.3
Memorandum										
Exceptional financing	6.6	8.8	8.9	7.2	5.8	7.0	6.9	1.8	6.0	4.6
Central and eastern Europe										
Balance of payments										
Balance on current account	−21.1	−19.3	−26.6	−32.7	−16.6	−24.5	−37.0	−50.6	−56.0	−55.8
Balance on capital account	10.2	0.4	0.3	0.5	0.7	0.7	0.4	2.0	4.0	4.3
Balance on financial account	6.2	18.4	23.0	38.2	25.7	36.9	34.8	39.7	53.2	48.8
Change in reserves (− = increase)	−10.7	−9.5	−11.3	−2.9	7.4	−10.5	−11.4	−12.9	−6.9	−5.1
Other official flows, net	−3.3	0.3	−2.6	1.5	5.5	−7.6	−5.5	−6.9	−5.0	−3.3
Private flows, net	20.2	27.2	36.7	39.1	12.2	55.3	52.0	60.6	65.8	57.7
External financing										
Net external financing	40.1	33.9	47.1	52.7	27.8	46.2	55.0	74.7	76.0	72.9
Non-debt-creating inflows	23.8	21.1	21.5	24.8	25.1	25.3	17.4	26.5	34.4	35.4
Net external borrowing	16.3	12.8	25.6	27.9	2.7	20.9	37.6	48.2	41.6	37.5
From official creditors	−3.3	0.5	−2.5	1.7	5.9	−7.7	−5.6	−7.5	−5.4	−3.5
of which, credit and loans from IMF	0.4	−0.5	0.5	3.3	9.9	6.1	—	−3.8	. . .	. . .
From banks	1.2	2.6	2.0	4.0	−7.3	2.8	8.7	9.9	9.8	8.2
From other private creditors	18.4	9.7	26.0	22.2	4.1	25.9	34.6	45.8	37.1	32.8
Memorandum										
Exceptional financing	0.2	0.4	0.6	0.3	0.1	0.1	0.3	0.1	—	—

Table 33 *(continued)*

	1997	1998	1999	2000	2001	2002	2003	2004	2005	2006
Commonwealth of Independent States[2]										
Balance of payments										
Balance on current account	−8.8	−9.6	20.7	46.3	32.8	32.2	36.2	64.4	91.2	76.8
Balance on capital account	−0.9	—	−0.2	−0.5	−0.7	−0.5	−0.9	−1.0	−0.9	−0.9
Balance on financial account	21.0	21.0	−10.8	−36.2	−21.1	−23.6	−27.6	−54.6	−80.3	−67.4
Change in reserves (− = increase)	−4.3	7.5	−2.7	−17.2	−11.3	−11.8	−33.8	−55.5	−69.8	−70.7
Other official flows, net	8.6	10.0	0.1	−4.3	−4.5	−1.7	−5.2	−1.0	−5.4	−1.7
Private flows, net	19.9	6.7	−6.4	−13.0	−1.8	−9.5	16.4	2.9	−6.4	2.7
External financing										
Net external financing	54.9	31.4	10.7	3.0	−5.1	11.6	35.5	39.9	30.0	43.3
Non-debt-creating inflows	6.8	5.7	4.6	2.7	3.2	3.3	10.2	10.0	11.5	14.3
Net external borrowing	48.1	25.7	6.0	0.2	−8.2	8.3	25.3	29.9	18.4	29.0
From official creditors	7.0	8.4	−0.8	−5.2	−5.0	−2.0	−2.2	−0.1	−3.2	0.2
of which, credit and loans from IMF	2.1	5.8	−3.6	−4.1	−4.0	−1.8	−2.3	−2.1	. . .	. . .
From banks	15.7	0.1	−1.4	0.9	3.3	10.9	23.1	20.2	26.1	28.2
From other private creditors	25.4	17.2	8.2	4.5	−6.5	−0.6	4.5	9.9	−4.4	0.5
Memorandum										
Exceptional financing	−20.9	7.4	7.3	5.7	1.6	1.7	−1.9	−0.9	0.1	0.2
Developing Asia										
Balance of payments										
Balance on current account	7.7	49.3	48.7	46.3	40.8	72.2	85.8	103.3	97.1	96.9
Balance on capital account	0.8	0.7	0.6	0.4	0.5	0.4	0.4	0.4	0.5	0.5
Balance on financial account	34.7	−28.0	−26.1	−22.4	−30.2	−76.1	−104.9	−119.6	−94.5	−94.4
Change in reserves (− = increase)	−28.4	−21.0	−31.5	−18.0	−60.9	−114.0	−165.0	−261.7	−248.7	−249.9
Other official flows, net	11.5	19.0	19.7	8.9	4.1	4.2	−6.4	19.1	26.2	25.3
Private flows, net	51.6	−26.0	−14.3	−13.2	26.5	33.6	66.5	123.0	128.0	130.1
External financing										
Net external financing	105.7	40.8	56.0	69.5	46.6	64.6	88.3	171.1	198.6	196.7
Non-debt-creating inflows	62.4	53.0	54.7	62.9	53.7	60.5	68.7	93.8	106.5	108.7
Net external borrowing	43.4	−12.2	1.3	6.6	−7.1	4.0	19.5	77.3	92.0	88.0
From official creditors	11.5	19.0	19.7	8.9	4.1	4.2	−6.4	19.1	26.2	25.3
of which, credit and loans from IMF	5.0	6.6	1.7	0.9	−2.2	−2.7	−0.6	−1.1	. . .	. . .
From banks	13.5	−12.5	−11.8	−22.3	−6.4	−8.3	0.4	22.1	30.3	30.1
From other private creditors	18.4	−18.7	−6.6	20.0	−4.8	8.1	25.5	36.0	35.5	32.6
Memorandum										
Exceptional financing	0.5	14.5	7.0	5.5	6.6	7.5	6.2	3.1	10.0	2.6
Excluding China and India										
Balance of payments										
Balance on current account	−23.8	24.6	36.0	30.4	22.0	29.7	33.1	31.3	23.1	18.2
Balance on capital account	0.8	0.7	0.6	0.5	0.6	0.5	0.5	0.5	0.5	0.5
Balance on financial account	33.6	−19.9	−28.9	−18.0	−17.0	−26.1	−33.6	−22.6	−20.5	−15.8
Change in reserves (− = increase)	12.1	−11.9	−17.0	−1.5	−4.8	−19.6	−22.3	−29.8	−19.0	−20.2
Other official flows, net	9.9	13.4	12.7	9.4	3.1	3.0	−1.8	−0.8	2.8	1.9
Private flows, net	11.6	−21.4	−24.6	−25.9	−15.4	−9.5	−9.5	8.1	−4.4	2.5
External financing										
Net external financing	26.7	−1.7	1.9	0.7	−4.3	0.9	0.8	11.9	22.5	22.4
Non-debt-creating inflows	10.7	10.1	13.8	7.1	3.1	7.9	7.2	17.4	9.0	9.3
Net external borrowing	16.0	−11.8	−11.8	−6.4	−7.5	−6.9	−6.4	−5.4	13.5	13.1
From official creditors	9.9	13.4	12.7	9.4	3.1	3.0	−1.8	−0.8	2.8	1.9
of which, credit and loans from IMF	5.7	7.0	2.1	0.9	−2.2	−2.7	−0.6	−1.1	. . .	. . .
From banks	6.2	−15.4	−9.8	−15.7	−6.5	−10.4	−6.6	0.8	7.3	7.2
From other private creditors	−0.1	−9.8	−14.7	−0.1	−4.1	0.5	2.0	−5.4	3.3	4.0
Memorandum										
Exceptional financing	0.5	14.5	7.0	5.5	6.6	7.5	6.2	3.1	10.0	2.6

Table 33 *(concluded)*

	1997	1998	1999	2000	2001	2002	2003	2004	2005	2006
Middle East										
Balance of payments										
Balance on current account	9.5	−25.5	11.9	69.5	39.1	29.4	59.3	112.5	160.8	145.8
Balance on capital account	0.3	−0.3	0.9	1.4	1.5	1.7	0.1	−0.7	0.1	0.8
Balance on financial account	−8.3	34.9	16.5	−56.1	−21.5	−2.7	−68.8	−109.6	−160.6	−147.3
Change in reserves (− = increase)	−7.2	10.7	—	−28.6	−11.8	−4.1	−32.1	−51.2	−81.3	−79.2
Other official flows, net	−9.7	7.2	14.4	−33.1	−15.4	−5.7	−46.7	−51.7	−64.2	−60.3
Private flows, net	6.9	17.9	−7.2	−6.2	2.6	−2.6	0.3	−18.1	−28.4	−22.1
External financing										
Net external financing	16.0	27.9	5.0	25.2	−2.2	9.6	5.2	1.0	−1.4	1.1
Non-debt-creating inflows	4.2	5.7	5.1	−0.9	2.0	0.2	—	0.5	2.0	1.8
Net external borrowing	11.8	22.3	—	26.1	−4.2	9.4	5.2	0.6	−3.4	−0.7
From official creditors	0.4	0.6	4.3	0.1	−3.0	−1.1	0.2	−0.1	−0.3	−0.6
of which, credit and loans from IMF	0.2	0.1	0.1	−0.1	0.1	—	−0.1	−0.2	. . .	. . .
From banks	0.1	2.1	1.2	—	—	0.2	0.2	1.1	0.2	1.2
From other private creditors	11.3	19.5	−5.5	26.0	−1.2	10.3	4.7	−0.5	−3.3	−1.3
Memorandum										
Exceptional financing	0.3	0.4	0.2	0.3	0.3	0.6	2.5	0.4	0.3	0.3
Western Hemisphere										
Balance of payments										
Balance on current account	−66.7	−90.5	−56.7	−47.8	−53.9	−16.4	6.6	15.9	3.8	−12.7
Balance on capital account	1.5	1.8	3.4	2.9	2.5	0.5	1.3	1.9	1.7	1.0
Balance on financial account	66.9	90.8	58.7	41.4	54.2	16.1	−14.8	−15.9	−4.5	11.9
Change in reserves (− = increase)	−26.4	7.0	11.8	1.6	1.6	−2.3	−35.8	−21.9	−21.3	−13.2
Other official flows, net	5.4	16.9	5.5	−7.4	26.4	19.8	8.7	−7.3	−8.3	−10.5
Private flows, net	99.6	70.8	38.7	40.5	27.8	3.3	15.2	12.7	22.4	30.3
External financing										
Net external financing	112.7	118.0	88.6	66.1	82.6	33.7	42.8	41.8	49.2	53.5
Non-debt-creating inflows	76.4	65.6	64.2	67.2	64.9	42.4	34.6	46.5	45.5	45.3
Net external borrowing	36.3	52.5	24.4	−1.1	17.7	−8.7	8.2	−4.7	3.7	8.2
From official creditors	1.3	15.2	7.8	−4.5	23.3	15.4	7.9	−5.8	−7.4	−9.3
of which, credit and loans from IMF	−4.0	2.5	−0.9	−10.7	15.6	11.9	5.6	−6.3	. . .	. . .
From banks	−21.8	15.5	−8.9	5.6	3.7	−13.2	−5.2	−1.3	−0.8	−0.1
From other private creditors	56.8	21.8	25.5	−2.2	−9.2	−10.9	5.5	2.4	11.9	17.5
Memorandum										
Exceptional financing	−0.6	0.9	−0.3	−11.0	7.2	27.0	19.4	12.5	7.6	3.1

[1]For definitions, see footnotes to Table 32.

[2]Mongolia, which is not a member of the Commonwealth of Independent States, is included in this group for reasons of geography and similarities in economic structure.

Table 34. Other Emerging Market and Developing Countries—by Analytical Criteria: Balance of Payments and External Financing[1]

(Billions of U.S. dollars)

	1997	1998	1999	2000	2001	2002	2003	2004	2005	2006
By source of export earnings										
Fuel										
Balance of payments										
Balance on current account	16.0	−32.3	11.3	88.6	45.0	33.4	67.6	122.5	178.8	162.0
Balance on capital account	0.5	0.6	1.7	3.3	4.0	3.5	2.8	2.7	1.8	1.3
Balance on financial account	−20.8	36.7	9.3	−89.6	−35.0	−7.9	−71.9	−127.6	−180.8	−164.3
Change in reserves (− = increase)	−28.9	17.9	5.1	−42.3	−16.3	−3.1	−41.7	−72.5	−110.0	−101.5
Other official flows, net	−4.8	8.4	7.0	−32.7	−14.1	2.5	−32.8	−39.3	−47.0	−44.2
Private flows, net	12.1	14.5	−14.7	−37.6	−10.9	−15.1	−4.2	−30.3	−43.8	−42.3
External financing										
Net external financing	25.4	15.9	9.4	4.9	7.6	12.0	10.5	2.3	0.5	2.0
Non-debt-creating inflows	12.3	13.8	9.4	10.3	14.2	14.1	17.1	20.2	18.0	18.0
Net external borrowing	13.1	2.1	—	−5.3	−6.7	−2.2	−6.5	−17.9	−17.5	−16.0
From official creditors	3.5	3.1	3.0	0.7	−0.4	1.5	1.6	−2.1	0.7	0.8
of which, credit and loans from IMF	−0.1	−0.5	−0.4	−0.7	−0.3	−0.4	−0.5	−0.4	. . .	. . .
From banks	−2.3	0.3	−0.3	−1.6	−1.9	−1.2	−1.6	−1.5	−1.7	−1.1
From other private creditors	11.8	−1.4	−2.8	−4.4	−4.3	−2.5	−6.5	−14.4	−16.4	−15.6
Memorandum										
Exceptional financing	7.9	6.1	4.5	2.8	2.2	2.6	2.4	−2.4	2.0	1.3
Nonfuel										
Balance of payments										
Balance on current account	−101.6	−82.7	−28.7	−0.4	−4.2	51.6	81.5	124.1	124.7	93.1
Balance on capital account	19.4	6.1	8.2	5.7	5.7	5.1	3.9	6.4	9.8	10.3
Balance on financial account	140.9	117.1	65.1	43.6	36.9	−39.4	−114.3	−149.3	−119.8	−96.2
Change in reserves (− = increase)	−59.3	−21.4	−41.6	−35.6	−70.5	−147.6	−255.6	−363.8	−352.2	−348.7
Other official flows, net	12.7	48.0	31.2	−1.9	27.7	10.2	−19.4	−9.0	−11.2	−5.7
Private flows, net	200.3	92.9	73.7	83.2	85.7	102.1	166.8	222.8	240.8	254.4
External financing										
Net external financing	334.8	266.0	230.5	227.1	161.5	175.4	239.2	353.8	381.4	395.0
Non-debt-creating inflows	185.4	158.0	165.0	160.1	157.1	137.9	135.1	183.6	208.4	213.6
Net external borrowing	149.4	108.0	65.5	67.0	4.4	37.5	104.1	170.2	172.9	181.4
From official creditors	9.4	44.1	28.2	2.1	24.0	11.0	−5.3	9.8	11.0	15.0
of which, credit and loans from IMF	3.4	14.5	−2.0	−10.2	19.3	13.8	2.3	−13.6	. . .	. . .
From banks	11.9	6.2	−16.2	−10.1	−4.1	−4.8	28.7	53.0	65.7	68.2
From other private creditors	128.1	57.7	53.5	75.0	−15.4	31.2	80.7	107.4	96.2	98.2
Memorandum										
Exceptional financing	−18.2	27.5	19.8	5.2	19.4	41.5	31.0	19.4	22.1	9.4
By external financing source										
Net debtor countries										
Balance of payments										
Balance on current account	−132.8	−128.7	−85.6	−77.0	−67.4	−33.8	−26.0	−42.1	−70.3	−90.9
Balance on capital account	20.8	6.9	9.5	6.9	7.2	7.7	6.6	10.3	12.4	12.4
Balance on financial account	122.9	124.8	91.1	85.7	76.5	42.2	9.7	24.0	63.0	77.7
Change in reserves (− = increase)	−26.2	−15.4	−23.7	−13.2	−13.4	−54.7	−97.7	−92.7	−71.1	−63.2
Other official flows, net	6.8	33.4	21.9	8.8	29.0	13.3	−4.1	−17.0	−13.3	−11.0
Private flows, net	151.7	107.2	88.5	88.0	62.2	82.7	109.9	127.9	140.2	143.6
External financing										
Net external financing	210.5	209.8	190.7	150.8	134.8	121.9	156.9	185.7	210.7	209.8
Non-debt-creating inflows	139.8	120.9	134.7	117.5	126.8	105.2	95.6	123.5	137.4	140.6
Net external borrowing	70.7	88.9	56.0	33.4	7.9	16.7	61.3	62.2	73.3	69.2
From official creditors	3.3	33.7	25.6	8.9	27.5	11.2	−1.4	−11.6	−8.5	−7.5
of which, credit and loans from IMF	1.3	8.8	1.4	−6.9	23.3	15.5	4.3	−11.6	. . .	. . .
From banks	−12.4	2.2	−13.6	−4.2	−9.0	−17.0	−1.4	11.9	15.2	15.8
From other private creditors	79.8	53.0	44.0	28.7	−10.6	22.5	64.1	61.9	66.6	61.0
Memorandum										
Exceptional financing	7.1	25.0	16.7	2.1	20.0	42.5	35.3	18.1	24.1	10.6

Table 34 *(continued)*

	1997	1998	1999	2000	2001	2002	2003	2004	2005	2006
Official financing										
Balance of payments										
Balance on current account	−39.5	−32.7	−17.8	−11.8	−8.0	10.2	9.3	−0.2	−13.4	−20.5
Balance on capital account	9.3	4.6	5.7	5.2	6.4	4.6	3.8	4.6	4.8	4.0
Balance on financial account	32.9	24.8	14.0	7.1	2.3	−12.2	−11.7	−4.0	8.5	14.6
Change in reserves (− = increase)	−12.1	−9.9	−6.1	−2.1	8.3	−6.5	−22.6	−14.3	−2.7	−9.1
Other official flows, net	−1.3	10.7	17.7	15.1	17.8	15.1	12.9	−0.7	5.8	4.7
Private flows, net	46.1	24.5	1.3	−6.1	−22.5	−14.2	3.9	10.7	5.4	19.1
External financing										
Net external financing	67.4	43.3	38.6	29.0	9.5	9.7	25.6	16.8	39.2	38.3
Non-debt-creating inflows	27.5	18.2	16.4	17.1	18.6	18.7	15.1	18.4	20.4	20.3
Net external borrowing	39.9	25.1	22.2	11.9	−9.1	−9.0	10.5	−1.6	18.8	18.0
From official creditors	−0.7	10.2	18.9	15.5	18.8	10.2	10.5	0.7	5.7	3.5
of which, credit and loans from IMF	2.6	5.4	0.8	1.7	8.2	—	0.5	−2.5	. . .	. . .
From banks	12.0	0.4	−0.7	−8.9	−4.6	−10.1	−3.7	−0.3	6.4	9.0
From other private creditors	28.6	14.5	4.0	5.2	−23.3	−9.2	3.7	−2.0	6.7	5.5
Memorandum										
Exceptional financing	2.0	18.3	10.7	7.9	8.7	23.3	25.1	17.0	26.2	15.3
Net debtor countries by debt-servicing experience										
Countries with arrears and/or rescheduling during 1997–2001										
Balance of payments										
Balance on current account	−31.2	−34.9	−22.5	−2.1	−7.3	2.1	4.3	1.2	−3.2	−12.6
Balance on capital account	8.8	4.2	7.1	5.2	5.1	5.3	4.2	5.7	5.8	5.3
Balance on financial account	26.5	32.0	20.0	−0.2	3.6	−2.4	−6.5	−10.9	−4.0	5.4
Change in reserves (− = increase)	−15.8	−6.9	−5.1	−11.4	6.2	−5.6	−17.2	−23.3	−20.2	−20.2
Other official flows, net	−3.1	11.9	18.0	14.9	15.1	6.3	5.5	−2.0	−2.3	−1.7
Private flows, net	45.1	29.3	6.3	−4.2	−16.0	−1.5	6.5	12.5	15.5	24.7
External financing										
Net external financing	64.2	54.7	49.6	38.2	15.1	31.9	34.3	31.8	55.9	56.6
Non-debt-creating inflows	28.0	23.5	21.7	24.8	24.3	29.2	26.3	32.2	34.6	37.4
Net external borrowing	36.2	31.2	27.9	13.4	−9.3	2.7	7.9	−0.4	21.3	19.2
From official creditors	−3.0	10.8	18.4	15.2	14.3	5.5	4.9	−1.1	−0.7	−0.4
of which, credit and loans from IMF	3.1	5.3	1.1	1.9	8.1	−1.5	−0.2	−2.9	. . .	. . .
From banks	11.2	−1.5	−0.4	−8.8	−4.6	−9.5	−4.8	−0.4	6.0	8.6
From other private creditors	27.9	21.9	9.9	7.0	−18.9	6.7	7.9	1.1	16.0	11.0
Memorandum										
Exceptional financing	8.2	24.4	17.3	12.1	12.6	30.3	27.8	21.6	30.2	18.5
Other groups										
Heavily indebted poor countries										
Balance of payments										
Balance on current account	−6.5	−7.2	−8.6	−7.0	−7.2	−7.7	−7.0	−7.7	−9.2	−9.5
Balance on capital account	7.8	4.2	5.1	3.5	4.0	1.9	3.8	3.6	4.4	4.6
Balance on financial account	−0.1	4.7	4.0	2.5	2.6	6.2	3.2	4.2	5.0	5.6
Change in reserves (− = increase)	−1.2	−0.2	−0.9	−0.6	−0.8	−2.5	−2.0	−2.2	−1.1	−0.8
Other official flows, net	−4.3	1.5	1.1	1.4	−0.3	3.1	1.8	5.5	1.0	3.0
Private flows, net	5.0	2.8	3.3	1.2	3.7	5.9	3.6	1.4	5.0	3.4
External financing										
Net external financing	9.3	9.6	10.2	6.8	7.5	10.5	9.7	10.3	11.1	11.3
Non-debt-creating inflows	9.9	6.3	8.0	5.9	6.7	5.8	7.6	7.2	8.1	8.3
Net external borrowing	−0.6	3.3	2.2	0.9	0.7	4.7	2.1	3.1	3.0	3.0
From official creditors	−4.1	1.8	1.4	1.8	−0.3	3.0	1.7	5.2	1.1	3.0
of which, credit and loans from IMF	—	0.2	0.3	0.1	—	0.2	−0.2	−0.1	. . .	. . .
From banks	0.5	−0.1	1.3	0.6	—	0.6	0.1	0.2	0.3	0.2
From other private creditors	3.0	1.7	−0.5	−1.5	1.0	1.1	0.4	−2.4	1.7	−0.2
Memorandum										
Exceptional financing	1.0	2.6	3.3	3.3	2.8	4.8	2.7	2.7	3.1	2.4

Table 34 *(concluded)*

	1997	1998	1999	2000	2001	2002	2003	2004	2005	2006
Middle East and north Africa										
Balance of payments										
Balance on current account	10.8	−29.0	9.6	75.5	44.7	32.9	67.3	121.5	173.4	158.0
Balance on capital account	0.4	−0.2	1.1	1.5	1.7	1.9	0.2	−0.5	0.3	1.0
Balance on financial account	−11.7	37.7	19.5	−62.7	−28.1	−6.8	−76.9	−120.1	−173.5	−160.5
Change in reserves (− = increase)	−12.3	11.8	0.3	−35.3	−21.8	−8.8	−41.9	−62.8	−98.1	−95.6
Other official flows, net	−10.4	7.0	14.2	−34.1	−16.7	−7.4	−48.1	−53.4	−65.0	−61.4
Private flows, net	7.7	18.4	−5.9	−7.6	5.5	−2.3	1.7	−18.2	−25.9	−20.5
External financing										
Net external financing	19.1	31.2	9.1	27.6	3.0	12.5	8.3	4.6	3.5	6.3
Non-debt-creating inflows	6.4	8.0	7.3	0.9	7.3	3.3	4.8	5.2	7.5	6.6
Net external borrowing	12.7	23.1	1.9	26.7	−4.3	9.2	3.5	−0.6	−4.0	−0.3
From official creditors	0.5	1.2	4.9	0.4	−3.4	−1.8	−0.3	−0.3	—	−0.3
of which, credit and loans from IMF	0.3	−0.1	—	−0.3	−0.2	−0.3	−0.6	−0.6	. . .	. . .
From banks	0.9	2.2	2.6	0.3	0.5	1.0	1.0	1.4	0.2	1.4
From other private creditors	11.3	19.7	−5.7	26.0	−1.4	10.0	2.8	−1.6	−4.1	−1.4
Memorandum										
Exceptional financing	5.3	2.9	2.3	1.8	1.3	1.5	3.3	1.2	1.1	1.1

[1]For definitions, see footnotes to Table 32.

Table 35. Other Emerging Market and Developing Countries: Reserves[1]

	1997	1998	1999	2000	2001	2002	2003	2004	2005	2006
					Billions of U.S. dollars					
Other emerging market and developing countries	**701.3**	**700.8**	**728.2**	**818.9**	**915.7**	**1,095.5**	**1,419.8**	**1,856.0**	**2,318.2**	**2,768.4**
Regional groups										
Africa	43.8	41.5	42.4	54.5	64.7	73.0	91.3	124.4	158.7	190.8
Sub-Sahara	29.5	28.1	29.6	35.5	35.9	37.0	41.1	63.2	81.8	98.1
Excluding Nigeria and South Africa	16.9	16.4	17.6	19.2	19.1	23.5	27.2	33.0	37.2	41.2
Central and eastern Europe	77.4	89.7	94.9	97.3	98.9	132.0	160.9	173.8	180.7	185.8
Commonwealth of Independent States[2]	22.3	15.1	16.5	33.2	44.2	58.2	92.6	148.2	217.9	288.6
Russia	13.7	8.5	9.1	24.8	33.1	44.6	73.8	121.4	183.1	248.2
Excluding Russia	8.6	6.6	7.4	8.4	11.1	13.5	18.8	26.7	34.8	40.4
Developing Asia	249.6	274.5	307.7	321.8	380.4	496.9	670.1	931.8	1180.5	1430.4
China	143.4	149.8	158.3	168.9	216.3	292.0	409.2	615.8	825.8	1035.8
India	25.3	27.9	33.2	38.4	46.4	68.2	99.5	124.7	144.4	164.1
Excluding China and India	80.9	96.8	116.1	114.5	117.8	136.7	161.5	191.3	210.2	230.4
Middle East	137.6	126.6	123.2	155.9	168.2	174.2	208.6	259.8	341.1	420.2
Western Hemisphere	170.6	153.4	143.4	156.1	159.2	161.3	196.2	218.0	239.3	252.5
Brazil	51.0	34.4	23.9	31.5	35.8	37.7	49.1	52.8	61.7	62.1
Mexico	28.8	31.8	31.8	35.5	44.8	50.6	59.0	63.0	68.8	74.5
Analytical groups										
By source of export earnings										
Fuel	133.8	118.0	111.5	157.6	173.1	175.8	221.5	294.0	404.0	505.5
Nonfuel	567.5	582.7	616.7	661.2	742.5	919.8	1,198.2	1,562.0	1,914.2	2,262.9
of which, primary products	29.3	27.5	26.6	27.1	26.7	29.6	31.9	34.0	36.1	38.9
By external financing source										
Net debtor countries	395.6	404.5	422.3	446.0	470.6	550.0	667.4	760.0	831.2	894.4
of which, official financing	77.2	85.7	94.2	94.4	87.3	95.9	119.7	134.0	136.7	145.9
Net debtor countries by debt-servicing experience										
Countries with arrears and/or rescheduling during 1999–2003	78.1	84.8	92.8	100.7	93.9	99.8	116.6	139.8	160.1	180.3
Other groups										
Heavily indebted poor countries	8.8	8.5	9.4	9.9	10.8	13.8	15.7	17.8	18.9	19.7
Middle East and north Africa	152.3	140.4	136.5	175.4	197.5	211.1	260.2	323.1	421.1	516.8

Table 35 *(concluded)*

	1997	1998	1999	2000	2001	2002	2003	2004	2005	2006
	\multicolumn{10}{c}{*Ratio of reserves to imports of goods and services[3]*}									
Other emerging market and developing countries	**43.7**	**45.8**	**48.5**	**46.8**	**51.5**	**57.6**	**62.5**	**65.2**	**69.5**	**74.7**
Regional groups										
Africa	32.5	31.0	31.4	39.1	45.4	47.6	49.3	54.2	60.8	68.7
Sub-Sahara	28.0	27.3	28.9	33.6	33.2	32.1	29.0	36.4	40.9	46.1
Excluding Nigeria and South Africa	29.8	28.6	30.7	33.5	31.3	36.5	36.0	35.7	35.7	36.4
Central and eastern Europe	32.5	35.4	38.7	34.8	35.5	42.1	40.1	33.5	29.1	27.0
Commonwealth of Independent States[2]	15.4	12.3	17.6	30.5	35.0	41.5	52.9	67.4	82.5	97.6
Russia	14.9	11.5	17.2	40.6	45.4	53.7	71.5	94.7	114.8	135.7
Excluding Russia	16.2	13.6	18.2	17.6	20.7	23.7	26.1	29.2	33.3	35.8
Developing Asia	44.6	56.8	59.6	50.0	59.1	68.9	74.9	80.5	85.5	90.5
China	87.2	91.6	83.4	67.4	79.7	89.0	91.1	101.6	111.3	117.6
India	43.4	47.0	52.9	52.6	65.0	90.0	106.0	98.8	91.5	91.6
Excluding China and India	24.1	37.2	44.1	35.8	39.1	43.1	45.9	45.0	43.7	44.2
Middle East	71.4	68.8	67.1	76.4	78.5	74.6	80.2	87.8	105.4	122.4
Western Hemisphere	50.9	43.7	43.7	41.7	42.9	47.5	55.5	51.4	49.3	48.6
Brazil	66.0	45.4	37.6	43.5	49.2	61.1	77.2	66.0	62.2	56.5
Mexico	33.8	33.4	30.3	27.6	35.2	40.1	45.8	42.8	42.1	43.3
Analytical groups										
By source of export earnings										
Fuel	77.5	71.5	66.6	85.3	87.4	81.7	91.4	102.6	125.1	146.3
Nonfuel	39.6	42.7	46.2	42.3	47.0	54.6	59.1	61.0	63.5	67.3
of which, primary products	53.0	52.3	55.9	55.1	54.3	59.1	55.8	48.4	46.3	47.6
By external financing source										
Net debtor countries	38.2	39.9	43.0	39.8	42.3	48.0	50.1	46.0	43.2	42.7
of which, official financing	32.4	38.1	46.5	41.8	40.1	46.3	50.6	46.6	42.1	41.7
Net debtor countries by debt-servicing experience										
Countries with arrears and/or rescheduling during 1999–2003	33.0	37.6	43.8	42.2	39.5	41.8	42.5	42.4	42.4	43.9
Other groups										
Heavily indebted poor countries	29.6	26.6	28.8	30.1	31.3	37.7	37.7	36.1	34.7	34.4
Middle East and north Africa	67.8	64.5	62.4	73.0	78.2	76.6	84.3	90.4	107.4	123.7

[1]In this table, official holdings of gold are valued at SDR 35 an ounce. This convention results in a marked underestimate of reserves for countries that have substantial gold holdings.
[2]Mongolia, which is not a member of the Commonwealth of Independent States, is included in this group for reasons of geography and similarities in economic structure.
[3]Reserves at year-end in percent of imports of goods and services for the year indicated.

Table 36. Net Credit and Loans from IMF[1]
(Billions of U.S. dollars)

	1996	1997	1998	1999	2000	2001	2002	2003	2004
Advanced economies	**−0.1**	**11.3**	**5.2**	**−10.3**	**—**	**−5.7**	**—**	**—**	**—**
Newly industrialized Asian economies	—	11.3	5.2	−10.3	—	−5.7	—	—	—
Other emerging market and developing countries	**0.7**	**3.3**	**14.0**	**−2.4**	**−10.9**	**19.0**	**13.4**	**1.7**	**−14.5**
Regional groups									
Africa	0.6	−0.5	−0.4	−0.2	−0.2	−0.4	−0.1	−0.8	−0.7
Sub-Sahara	0.1	−0.5	−0.3	−0.1	—	−0.2	0.2	−0.4	−0.3
Excluding Nigeria and South Africa	0.1	−0.1	0.1	−0.1	—	−0.2	0.2	−0.4	−0.3
Central and eastern Europe	−0.8	0.4	−0.5	0.5	3.3	9.9	6.1	—	−3.8
Commonwealth of									
Independent States[2]	4.5	2.1	5.8	−3.6	−4.1	−4.0	−1.8	−2.3	−2.1
Russia	3.2	1.5	5.3	−3.6	−2.9	−3.8	−1.5	−1.9	−1.7
Excluding Russia	1.3	0.5	0.5	—	−1.2	−0.2	−0.3	−0.4	−0.5
Developing Asia	−1.7	5.0	6.6	1.7	0.9	−2.2	−2.7	−0.6	−1.9
China	—	—	—	—	—	—	—	—	—
India	−1.3	−0.7	−0.4	−0.3	−0.1	—	—	—	—
Excluding China and India	−0.4	5.7	7.0	2.1	0.9	−2.2	−2.7	−0.6	−1.9
Middle East	0.1	0.2	0.1	0.1	−0.1	0.1	—	−0.1	0.3
Western Hemisphere	−2.0	−4.0	2.5	−0.9	−10.7	15.6	11.9	5.6	−6.3
Brazil	−0.1	—	4.6	4.1	−6.7	6.7	11.2	5.2	−4.4
Mexico	−2.1	−3.4	−1.1	−3.7	−4.3	—	—	—	—
Analytical groups									
By source of export earnings									
Fuel	0.9	−0.1	−0.5	−0.4	−0.7	−0.3	−0.4	−0.5	—
Nonfuel	−0.1	3.4	14.5	−2.0	−10.2	19.3	13.8	2.3	−14.5
of which, primary products	0.1	−0.1	0.2	−0.1	−0.2	−0.2	0.1	−0.3	−0.3
By external financing source									
Net debtor countries	−3.9	1.3	8.8	1.4	−6.9	23.3	15.5	4.3	−12.0
of which, official financing	0.3	2.6	5.4	0.8	1.7	8.2	—	0.5	−3.3
Net debtor countries by debt-servicing experience									
Countries with arrears and/or rescheduling during 1999–2003	0.6	3.1	5.3	1.1	1.9	8.1	−1.5	−0.2	−3.4
Other groups									
Heavily indebted poor countries	—	—	0.2	0.3	0.1	—	0.2	−0.2	−0.1
Middle East and north Africa	0.6	0.3	−0.1	—	−0.3	−0.2	−0.3	−0.6	−0.1
Memorandum									
Total									
Net credit provided under:									
General Resources Account	0.291	14.355	18.811	−12.856	−10.741	13.213	12.832	1.741	−14.276
PRGF	0.325	0.179	0.374	0.194	−0.148	0.106	0.567	0.009	−0.175
Disbursements at year-end under:[3]									
General Resources Account	51.396	62.301	84.541	69.504	55.368	66.448	85.357	95.323	84.992
PRGF	8.379	8.037	8.775	8.749	8.159	7.974	9.222	10.108	10.426

[1]Includes net disbursements from programs under the General Resources Account and Poverty Reduction and Growth Facility (formerly ESAF—Enhanced Structural Adjustment Facility). The data are on a transactions basis, with conversion to U.S. dollar values at annual average exchange rates.
[2]Mongolia, which is not a member of the Commonwealth of Independent States, is included in this group for reasons of geography and similarities in economic structure.
[3]Converted to U.S. dollar values at end-of-period exchange rates.

Table 37. Summary of External Debt and Debt Service

	1997	1998	1999	2000	2001	2002	2003	2004	2005	2006
					Billions of U.S. dollars					
External debt										
Other emerging market and developing countries	**2,318.1**	**2,519.6**	**2,560.7**	**2,502.3**	**2,497.9**	**2,559.5**	**2,762.8**	**2,896.1**	**3,046.5**	**3,207.3**
Regional groups										
Africa	284.4	283.3	281.7	267.9	256.4	263.5	283.5	281.9	283.6	282.7
Central and eastern Europe	236.3	269.4	286.6	309.8	315.1	372.0	459.9	499.8	531.4	558.6
Commonwealth of Independent States[1]	199.1	222.8	218.9	198.9	193.3	196.9	222.2	241.5	256.3	283.7
Developing Asia	659.6	695.9	693.0	663.8	668.4	665.1	696.1	771.8	869.4	970.4
Middle East	259.3	283.9	294.3	294.7	295.5	301.0	320.5	320.8	318.2	317.5
Western Hemisphere	679.3	764.4	786.1	767.2	769.2	761.0	780.5	780.3	787.4	794.5
Analytical groups										
By external financing source										
Net debtor countries	1,789.4	1,935.7	1,977.1	1,953.4	1,936.6	1,997.4	2,138.1	2,183.3	2,243.2	2,295.7
of which, official financing	516.2	555.8	559.2	551.2	564.8	547.5	572.7	585.5	613.0	631.3
Net debtor countries by debt-servicing experience										
Countries with arrears and/or rescheduling during 1999–2003	661.8	703.8	712.2	700.1	715.5	708.6	732.0	740.7	765.2	782.0
Debt-service payments[2]										
Other emerging market and developing countries	**361.5**	**387.5**	**409.0**	**426.0**	**432.2**	**406.8**	**438.8**	**436.5**	**475.2**	**495.3**
Regional groups										
Africa	32.3	27.4	26.8	27.1	27.9	23.5	27.4	28.4	25.3	27.3
Central and eastern Europe	40.8	55.0	58.4	64.3	74.3	75.8	90.8	102.8	108.0	118.1
Commonwealth of Independent States[1]	25.5	29.7	27.0	27.8	32.9	32.1	28.9	29.9	48.6	40.8
Developing Asia	84.7	99.3	93.9	97.5	100.8	110.0	109.1	102.6	115.1	126.8
Middle East	27.1	24.0	24.0	24.0	26.6	19.8	25.9	27.4	30.9	31.8
Western Hemisphere	151.2	152.1	178.9	185.2	169.7	145.7	156.8	145.4	147.2	150.4
Analytical groups										
By external financing source										
Net debtor countries	283.1	301.5	325.0	342.5	338.8	320.2	348.6	340.6	351.0	368.8
of which, official financing	80.1	84.2	79.0	89.3	90.6	75.7	77.0	66.3	62.3	64.1
Net debtor countries by debt-servicing experience										
Countries with arrears and/or rescheduling during 1999–2003	78.5	82.4	76.6	87.7	89.9	69.8	74.4	68.1	62.1	65.2

Table 37 (concluded)

	1997	1998	1999	2000	2001	2002	2003	2004	2005	2006
					Percent of exports of goods and services					
External debt[3]										
Other emerging market and developing countries	**148.4**	**172.1**	**165.2**	**131.6**	**133.3**	**126.0**	**112.6**	**92.7**	**83.1**	**80.4**
Regional groups										
Africa	210.4	236.7	220.2	170.1	172.0	171.5	147.7	116.2	99.6	94.7
Central and eastern Europe	111.6	118.3	134.2	128.7	121.5	129.1	125.4	106.0	94.1	88.6
Commonwealth of Independent States[1]	135.4	175.2	177.2	120.7	117.0	110.7	99.2	81.0	69.4	73.5
Developing Asia	116.8	129.3	119.7	95.3	96.9	84.7	73.2	63.3	60.6	59.1
Middle East	126.8	178.2	144.5	103.8	111.3	107.2	94.9	75.3	64.1	64.0
Western Hemisphere	227.0	261.7	260.2	214.3	223.3	219.8	204.1	166.9	151.9	148.5
Analytical groups										
By external financing source										
Net debtor countries	196.8	216.6	215.7	183.1	183.0	178.5	163.6	135.1	120.7	114.5
of which, official financing	258.9	291.1	294.6	252.5	268.6	253.4	237.3	207.7	200.0	196.0
Net debtor countries by debt-servicing experience										
Countries with arrears and/or rescheduling during 1999–2003	312.8	358.2	346.5	273.4	294.1	282.5	256.6	217.3	197.2	189.8
Debt-service payments										
Other emerging market and developing countries	**23.1**	**26.5**	**26.4**	**22.4**	**23.1**	**20.0**	**17.9**	**14.0**	**13.0**	**12.4**
Regional groups										
Africa	23.9	22.9	21.0	17.2	18.7	15.3	14.3	11.7	8.9	9.2
Central and eastern Europe	19.3	24.2	27.3	26.7	28.7	26.3	24.7	21.8	19.1	18.7
Commonwealth of Independent States[1]	17.3	23.4	21.9	16.9	19.9	18.0	12.9	10.0	13.2	10.6
Developing Asia	15.0	18.4	16.2	14.0	14.6	14.0	11.5	8.4	8.0	7.7
Middle East	13.2	15.1	11.8	8.5	10.0	7.0	7.7	6.4	6.2	6.4
Western Hemisphere	50.5	52.1	59.2	51.7	49.3	42.1	41.0	31.1	28.4	28.1
Analytical groups										
By external financing source										
Net debtor countries	31.1	33.7	35.5	32.1	32.0	28.6	26.7	21.1	18.9	18.4
of which, official financing	40.2	44.1	41.6	40.9	43.1	35.0	31.9	23.5	20.3	19.9
Net debtor countries by debt-servicing experience										
Countries with arrears and/or rescheduling during 1999–2003	37.1	41.9	37.3	34.2	37.0	27.8	26.1	20.0	16.0	15.8

[1]Mongolia, which is not a member of the Commonwealth of Independent States, is included in this group for reasons of geography and similarities in economic structure.
[2]Debt-service payments refer to actual payments of interest on total debt plus actual amortization payments on long-term debt. The projections incorporate the impact of exceptional financing items.
[3]Total debt at year-end in percent of exports of goods and services in year indicated.

Table 38. Other Emerging Market and Developing Countries—by Region: External Debt, by Maturity and Type of Creditor
(Billions of U.S. dollars)

	1997	1998	1999	2000	2001	2002	2003	2004	2005	2006
Other emerging market and developing countries										
Total debt	**2,318.1**	**2,519.6**	**2,560.7**	**2,502.3**	**2,497.9**	**2,559.5**	**2,762.8**	**2,896.1**	**3,046.5**	**3,207.3**
By maturity										
Short-term	352.4	349.1	325.6	305.9	318.4	305.4	373.8	418.9	465.2	508.9
Long-term	1,964.3	2,168.7	2,233.1	2,194.2	2,177.6	2,252.4	2,387.5	2,475.9	2,580.2	2,697.4
By type of creditor										
Official	947.2	1,007.2	1,010.0	968.3	976.2	1,005.2	1,026.4	1,020.5	1,027.1	1,023.7
Banks	715.8	746.5	748.8	703.1	676.2	674.5	727.2	788.0	853.8	921.6
Other private	650.5	758.6	794.2	822.1	836.5	867.0	989.0	1,066.0	1,142.2	1,236.9
Regional groups										
Africa										
Total debt	**284.4**	**283.3**	**281.7**	**267.9**	**256.4**	**263.5**	**283.5**	**281.9**	**283.6**	**282.7**
By maturity										
Short-term	36.1	38.7	40.1	18.8	17.2	19.6	19.9	23.3	25.6	26.8
Long-term	248.3	244.6	241.7	249.1	239.2	243.9	263.7	258.6	258.0	255.9
By type of creditor										
Official	203.9	206.9	204.2	197.7	195.8	202.5	217.0	212.9	211.6	206.8
Banks	50.9	48.0	47.8	42.3	39.5	38.8	42.9	42.9	42.3	43.0
Other private	29.6	28.3	29.7	27.8	21.1	22.2	23.6	26.1	29.7	32.8
Sub-Sahara										
Total debt	**222.6**	**220.6**	**221.8**	**213.2**	**206.1**	**211.4**	**227.1**	**227.9**	**231.5**	**232.0**
By maturity										
Short-term	34.2	36.3	37.2	16.0	14.5	16.8	17.6	19.8	22.1	23.2
Long-term	188.5	184.4	184.6	197.1	191.6	194.6	209.6	208.1	209.3	208.8
By type of creditor										
Official	158.6	160.4	160.2	157.1	158.3	162.3	172.9	170.5	170.8	167.3
Banks	40.7	37.0	35.7	31.0	28.6	27.8	30.6	31.2	30.9	31.9
Other private	23.4	23.2	25.9	25.0	19.3	21.4	23.6	26.1	29.7	32.8
Central and eastern Europe										
Total debt	**236.3**	**269.4**	**286.6**	**309.8**	**315.1**	**372.0**	**459.9**	**499.8**	**531.4**	**558.6**
By maturity										
Short-term	48.8	56.4	60.1	65.7	56.4	63.9	90.1	100.4	108.1	113.4
Long-term	187.5	213.0	226.5	244.1	258.7	308.1	369.8	399.4	423.3	445.2
By type of creditor										
Official	77.1	79.5	75.8	77.6	83.1	76.6	73.4	66.5	61.0	57.1
Banks	78.5	94.3	101.9	114.1	99.7	127.6	154.5	168.3	178.4	183.7
Other private	76.1	88.3	101.2	109.3	123.2	155.1	211.8	243.5	268.7	292.6
Commonwealth of Independent States[1]										
Total debt	**199.1**	**222.8**	**218.9**	**198.9**	**193.3**	**196.9**	**222.2**	**241.5**	**256.3**	**283.7**
By maturity										
Short-term	14.9	23.8	15.3	15.5	15.9	15.9	23.0	23.5	23.6	23.5
Long-term	182.9	197.2	201.7	181.2	175.5	179.4	197.6	216.7	231.6	259.3
By type of creditor										
Official	102.6	113.8	113.6	106.0	101.0	96.7	91.7	87.1	82.2	69.4
Banks	56.4	49.9	49.7	18.2	22.4	21.2	44.0	64.0	90.1	118.4
Other private	40.1	59.0	55.6	74.6	69.9	79.0	86.4	90.4	84.0	95.9

Table 38 *(concluded)*

	1997	1998	1999	2000	2001	2002	2003	2004	2005	2006
Developing Asia										
Total debt	**659.6**	**695.9**	**693.0**	**663.8**	**668.4**	**665.1**	**696.1**	**771.8**	**869.4**	**970.4**
By maturity										
Short-term	99.3	88.7	70.1	59.2	88.7	87.1	107.1	138.2	173.6	208.4
Long-term	560.3	607.2	623.0	604.6	579.7	578.0	589.0	633.6	695.8	761.9
By type of creditor										
Official	274.9	296.8	303.0	286.1	280.9	287.7	293.1	310.6	335.2	360.5
Banks	209.9	202.5	197.1	182.5	178.1	168.4	161.5	183.4	213.3	243.1
Other private	174.9	196.6	192.9	195.2	209.4	209.0	241.5	277.8	320.9	366.7
Middle East										
Total debt	**259.3**	**283.9**	**294.3**	**294.7**	**295.5**	**301.0**	**320.5**	**320.8**	**318.2**	**317.5**
By maturity										
Short-term	34.7	47.0	49.4	46.9	47.7	45.5	61.2	58.5	55.3	55.3
Long-term	224.6	236.9	244.9	247.8	247.8	255.4	259.3	262.3	263.0	262.2
By type of creditor										
Official	132.6	134.6	136.6	136.1	137.2	143.8	146.6	145.8	144.7	143.6
Banks	106.2	121.9	127.2	129.1	126.4	124.8	140.5	142.4	140.9	140.4
Other private	20.6	27.3	30.6	29.5	32.0	32.4	33.4	32.6	32.7	33.5
Western Hemisphere										
Total debt	**679.3**	**764.4**	**786.1**	**767.2**	**769.2**	**761.0**	**780.5**	**780.3**	**787.4**	**794.5**
By maturity										
Short-term	118.6	94.6	90.7	99.8	92.5	73.4	72.4	75.0	79.0	81.4
Long-term	560.7	669.8	695.4	667.4	676.7	687.6	708.2	705.3	708.5	713.1
By type of creditor										
Official	156.2	175.5	176.9	164.7	178.3	197.9	204.6	197.7	192.4	186.2
Banks	213.8	229.8	225.0	216.9	210.1	193.7	183.7	187.0	188.8	193.0
Other private	309.3	359.1	384.2	385.7	380.9	369.4	392.2	395.6	406.2	415.3

[1]Mongolia, which is not a member of the Commonwealth of Independent States, is included in this group for reasons of geography and similarities in economic structure.

Table 39. Other Emerging Market and Developing Countries—by Analytical Criteria: External Debt, by Maturity and Type of Creditor
(Billions of U.S. dollars)

	1997	1998	1999	2000	2001	2002	2003	2004	2005	2006
By source of export earnings										
Fuel										
Total debt	**315.5**	**338.2**	**346.3**	**343.8**	**340.9**	**345.8**	**364.1**	**355.9**	**349.2**	**345.2**
By maturity										
Short-term	49.4	55.4	57.1	34.7	35.7	34.8	51.7	51.2	47.4	46.7
Long-term	264.7	281.0	287.1	306.9	303.4	309.3	310.8	303.4	300.7	297.6
By type of creditor										
Official	164.6	168.5	172.6	172.6	173.7	183.0	189.2	184.0	181.8	179.8
Banks	99.1	112.1	114.5	113.8	109.4	104.5	117.5	115.9	110.6	106.5
Other private	51.8	57.7	59.2	57.4	57.9	58.4	57.4	56.0	56.9	58.8
Nonfuel										
Total debt	**2,002.6**	**2,181.4**	**2,214.4**	**2,158.5**	**2,157.0**	**2,213.7**	**2,398.7**	**2,540.2**	**2,697.3**	**2,862.1**
By maturity										
Short-term	303.0	293.7	268.4	271.2	282.7	270.6	322.1	367.7	417.8	462.2
Long-term	1,699.7	1,887.6	1,946.0	1,887.2	1,874.2	1,943.1	2,076.6	2,172.5	2,279.5	2,399.9
By type of creditor										
Official	782.6	838.7	837.4	795.7	802.5	822.2	837.2	836.5	845.4	843.9
Banks	616.7	634.4	634.3	589.3	566.8	570.0	609.7	672.1	743.3	815.0
Other private	598.7	701.0	735.0	764.7	778.6	808.7	931.6	1,010.0	1,085.3	1,178.1
Nonfuel primary products										
Total debt	**97.9**	**100.8**	**103.7**	**104.9**	**106.8**	**107.8**	**111.8**	**113.1**	**114.3**	**113.1**
By maturity										
Short-term	11.1	7.8	6.8	8.2	7.1	7.9	9.9	10.5	11.1	11.7
Long-term	86.8	93.0	96.9	96.8	99.6	99.9	101.9	102.5	103.2	101.4
By type of creditor										
Official	60.7	62.7	62.9	61.5	62.2	61.3	62.5	62.1	61.3	56.1
Banks	20.4	19.8	21.5	21.3	21.8	22.1	21.9	22.0	21.2	23.4
Other private	16.7	18.3	19.3	22.1	22.8	24.4	27.4	28.9	31.9	33.6
By external financing source										
Net debtor countries										
Total debt	**1,789.4**	**1,935.7**	**1,977.1**	**1,953.4**	**1,936.6**	**1,997.4**	**2,138.1**	**2,183.3**	**2,243.2**	**2,295.7**
By maturity										
Short-term	271.0	258.5	247.9	232.3	211.6	195.6	222.1	241.0	258.8	270.5
Long-term	1,518.3	1,677.2	1,729.2	1,721.1	1,725.0	1,801.9	1,916.0	1,942.3	1,984.4	2,025.3
By type of creditor										
Official	750.0	796.0	805.1	782.7	796.5	823.2	841.7	821.2	811.5	799.4
Banks	563.3	584.8	579.1	568.2	542.6	546.5	564.3	586.9	608.8	629.5
Other private	471.6	547.7	585.1	593.8	588.5	614.9	711.8	753.6	799.6	841.7
Official financing										
Total debt	**516.2**	**555.8**	**559.2**	**551.2**	**564.8**	**547.5**	**572.7**	**585.5**	**613.0**	**631.3**
By maturity										
Short-term	64.0	64.4	59.4	61.1	55.0	39.6	43.5	46.8	49.5	52.0
Long-term	452.2	491.4	499.8	490.1	509.8	507.9	529.2	538.7	563.5	579.4
By type of creditor										
Official	256.5	267.8	277.5	269.2	276.5	288.7	304.9	301.9	300.8	292.8
Banks	100.1	106.7	105.5	100.9	101.9	94.1	95.0	97.1	107.0	118.3
Other private	159.6	181.2	176.2	181.1	186.4	164.7	172.8	186.5	205.2	220.2
Net debtor countries by debt-servicing experience										
Countries with arrears and/or rescheduling during 1999–2003										
Total debt	**661.8**	**703.8**	**712.2**	**700.1**	**715.5**	**708.6**	**732.0**	**740.7**	**765.2**	**782.0**
By maturity										
Short-term	71.9	66.2	63.4	43.2	35.7	26.9	29.7	32.6	34.4	35.8
Long-term	589.9	637.6	648.8	656.8	679.8	681.8	702.3	708.2	730.8	746.2
By type of creditor										
Official	387.8	404.0	418.2	411.3	419.6	430.8	447.7	441.9	439.8	432.8
Banks	134.8	139.6	139.5	132.2	134.8	127.1	126.6	128.8	135.9	145.3
Other private	139.2	160.2	154.5	156.5	161.1	150.7	157.7	170.1	189.5	203.9

Table 39 *(concluded)*

	1997	1998	1999	2000	2001	2002	2003	2004	2005	2006
Other groups										
Heavily indebted poor countries										
Total debt	**98.0**	**99.9**	**100.1**	**96.2**	**95.0**	**90.5**	**92.4**	**94.8**	**96.2**	**91.6**
By maturity										
Short-term	1.3	2.8	2.9	3.0	2.8	2.9	2.6	2.8	2.9	3.0
Long-term	96.7	97.1	97.2	93.2	92.2	87.5	89.8	92.0	93.2	88.7
By type of creditor										
Official	93.2	95.1	93.2	90.0	89.8	86.7	89.2	91.5	92.8	88.2
Banks	4.2	3.6	4.7	3.6	3.5	2.5	2.3	2.1	2.0	2.0
Other private	0.6	1.2	2.2	2.7	1.7	1.2	0.9	1.2	1.3	1.4
Middle East and north Africa										
Total debt	**344.6**	**371.3**	**379.4**	**371.8**	**369.1**	**378.8**	**405.0**	**403.5**	**399.5**	**399.3**
By maturity										
Short-term	36.9	49.6	52.3	49.6	50.4	48.3	63.6	62.0	58.8	59.0
Long-term	307.7	321.7	327.1	322.2	318.7	330.5	341.5	341.5	340.8	340.3
By type of creditor										
Official	196.2	200.4	200.3	195.8	194.4	206.1	214.7	212.5	210.3	209.6
Banks	120.4	137.3	143.4	143.0	140.1	138.7	156.2	157.6	155.6	155.2
Other private	27.9	33.6	35.6	33.0	34.6	34.0	34.2	33.4	33.7	34.5

Table 40. Other Emerging Market and Developing Countries: Ratio of External Debt to GDP[1]

	1997	1998	1999	2000	2001	2002	2003	2004	2005	2006
Other emerging market and developing countries	**37.7**	**43.1**	**44.9**	**40.4**	**39.8**	**39.9**	**38.3**	**34.3**	**31.6**	**30.7**
Regional groups										
Africa	64.1	66.4	65.7	60.8	58.4	56.8	50.5	41.5	36.7	34.3
Sub-Sahara	64.9	68.4	68.5	64.0	62.4	60.2	53.3	43.8	39.3	36.9
Central and eastern Europe	40.5	42.4	46.5	50.2	52.2	54.1	54.6	49.2	44.9	43.9
Commonwealth of Independent States[2]	38.0	58.2	75.2	56.0	46.7	42.6	39.1	31.9	26.4	25.3
Developing Asia	32.2	37.0	34.0	30.5	29.5	27.1	25.1	24.4	24.7	25.1
Middle East	47.6	55.8	52.7	46.6	46.0	46.9	44.9	39.0	34.1	32.4
Western Hemisphere	33.9	38.1	44.5	38.9	40.2	44.9	44.5	39.1	35.1	33.4
Analytical groups										
By source of export earnings										
Fuel	54.2	62.8	58.9	50.9	48.7	51.0	47.6	38.5	32.6	30.4
Nonfuel	36.0	41.1	43.3	39.1	38.7	38.6	37.2	33.8	31.5	30.7
of which, primary products	56.4	61.0	65.5	68.3	70.8	63.5	68.4	57.8	52.0	48.6
By external financing source										
Net debtor countries	43.7	49.0	52.2	48.4	48.9	50.3	48.2	42.8	38.9	37.1
of which, official financing	52.7	65.5	64.2	62.3	65.1	73.1	68.1	61.9	58.6	56.2
Net debtor countries by debt-servicing experience										
Countries with arrears and/or rescheduling during 1999–2003	74.2	92.0	89.0	83.6	84.6	93.3	85.6	76.6	70.4	66.5
Other groups										
Heavily indebted poor countries	101.3	102.0	102.5	102.7	98.3	88.1	78.7	71.3	64.8	57.5
Middle East and north Africa	52.4	59.3	56.2	49.4	48.1	49.1	46.7	40.1	34.9	33.1

[1]Debt at year-end in percent of GDP in year indicated.
[2]Mongolia, which is not a member of the Commonwealth of Independent States, is included in this group for reasons of geography and similarities in economic structure.

Table 41. Other Emerging Market and Developing Countries: Debt-Service Ratios[1]

(Percent of exports of goods and services)

	1997	1998	1999	2000	2001	2002	2003	2004	2005	2006
Interest payments[2]										
Other emerging market and developing countries	**7.6**	**9.6**	**8.8**	**7.5**	**7.3**	**5.7**	**4.9**	**4.3**	**4.1**	**4.1**
Regional groups										
Africa	9.2	8.7	7.9	6.2	6.8	4.9	4.3	3.1	2.7	2.9
Sub-Sahara	8.3	7.6	7.0	5.6	6.6	4.4	4.1	2.7	2.4	2.7
Central and eastern Europe	5.6	10.1	10.2	9.8	9.9	8.8	8.3	6.6	6.2	5.9
Commonwealth of Independent States[3]	9.4	13.3	10.3	7.9	6.4	5.2	4.3	5.9	5.1	5.4
Developing Asia	5.0	6.2	5.4	4.6	4.1	3.3	2.6	2.6	2.4	2.7
Middle East	3.1	3.9	3.1	2.4	2.3	1.9	1.7	1.1	1.2	1.2
Western Hemisphere	15.5	17.1	17.9	15.9	16.2	12.3	10.6	9.0	9.0	9.0
Analytical groups										
By source of export earnings										
Fuel	5.1	6.5	5.2	3.5	4.0	2.8	2.5	1.6	1.6	1.8
Nonfuel	8.0	9.9	9.3	8.2	7.8	6.2	5.2	4.7	4.5	4.5
of which, primary products	6.0	6.6	7.1	8.3	7.8	6.1	4.8	2.8	3.4	3.9
By external financing source										
Net debtor countries	10.0	11.7	11.4	10.3	10.1	7.9	7.0	5.9	5.5	5.6
of which, official financing	13.3	14.6	13.9	13.3	11.9	7.9	6.5	6.0	5.4	6.3
Net debtor countries by debt-servicing experience										
Countries with arrears and/or rescheduling during 1999–2003	12.4	14.0	12.8	11.3	10.8	6.1	5.2	4.4	3.8	4.7
Other groups										
Heavily indebted poor countries	12.3	6.5	6.0	7.3	6.8	4.6	4.3	3.1	3.3	3.0
Middle East and north Africa	4.3	5.2	4.1	3.1	2.9	2.5	2.1	1.5	1.5	1.6
Amortization[2]										
Other emerging market and developing countries	**15.5**	**16.9**	**17.6**	**14.9**	**15.8**	**14.3**	**13.0**	**9.7**	**8.9**	**8.3**
Regional groups										
Africa	14.7	14.2	13.1	11.0	11.9	10.4	10.0	8.6	6.2	6.3
Sub-Sahara	14.1	12.1	10.7	9.8	11.1	8.6	8.6	6.9	4.9	4.9
Central and eastern Europe	13.7	14.0	17.2	16.9	18.8	17.5	16.4	15.2	12.9	12.8
Commonwealth of Independent States[3]	8.0	10.0	11.6	9.0	13.5	12.8	8.6	4.1	8.0	5.2
Developing Asia	10.0	12.3	10.8	9.4	10.5	10.7	8.9	5.8	5.6	5.0
Middle East	10.1	11.1	8.7	6.1	7.7	5.1	6.0	5.4	5.0	5.2
Western Hemisphere	35.0	34.9	41.4	35.9	33.1	29.8	30.4	22.1	19.4	19.2
Analytical groups										
By source of export earnings										
Fuel	15.6	17.9	13.6	9.1	9.2	8.3	9.6	8.5	6.3	6.1
Nonfuel	15.5	16.8	18.2	16.0	16.9	15.3	13.6	9.9	9.3	8.6
of which, primary products	11.1	11.6	13.3	15.6	15.8	18.8	15.4	11.8	9.1	8.1
By external financing source										
Net debtor countries	21.1	22.0	24.1	21.8	21.9	20.7	19.7	15.1	13.4	12.8
of which, official financing	26.8	29.5	27.7	27.6	31.2	27.1	25.4	17.5	14.9	13.6
Net debtor countries by debt-servicing experience										
Countries with arrears and/or rescheduling during 1999–2003	24.7	27.9	24.4	22.9	26.1	21.7	20.9	15.5	12.2	11.1
Other groups										
Heavily indebted poor countries	32.1	16.1	12.1	14.0	15.2	10.6	8.5	7.9	6.5	6.2
Middle East and north Africa	11.0	12.6	10.2	7.1	8.6	6.4	7.1	6.4	5.7	5.9

[1]Excludes service payments to the International Monetary Fund.

[2]Interest payments on total debt and amortization on long-term debt. Estimates through 2004 reflect debt-service payments actually made. The estimates for 2005 and 2006 take into account projected exceptional financing items, including accumulation of arrears and rescheduling agreements. In some cases, amortization on account of debt-reduction operations is included.

[3]Mongolia, which is not a member of the Commonwealth of Independent States, is included in this group for reasons of geography and similarities in economic structure.

Table 42. IMF Charges and Repurchases to the IMF[1]

(Percent of exports of goods and services)

	1997	1998	1999	2000	2001	2002	2003	2004
Other emerging market and developing countries	**0.6**	**0.6**	**1.2**	**1.2**	**0.7**	**1.1**	**1.2**	**0.8**
Regional groups								
Africa	0.9	1.1	0.5	0.2	0.3	0.4	0.3	0.2
Sub-Sahara	0.7	0.8	0.2	0.1	0.1	0.2	—	0.1
Excluding Nigeria and South Africa	0.4	0.5	0.4	0.3	0.3	0.5	0.1	0.1
Central and eastern Europe	0.3	0.4	0.4	0.3	0.8	2.7	0.8	1.3
Commonwealth of Independent States[2]	0.9	1.7	4.9	3.2	3.1	1.2	1.1	0.8
Russia	1.1	1.9	5.9	3.1	3.8	1.4	1.3	0.9
Excluding Russia	0.5	1.2	2.9	3.4	1.4	0.7	0.6	0.5
Developing Asia	0.2	0.2	0.2	0.2	0.6	0.6	0.3	0.2
Excluding China and India	0.2	0.2	0.3	0.4	1.2	1.4	0.8	0.5
Middle East	—	—	0.1	0.1	0.1	—	—	—
Western Hemisphere	1.9	1.1	3.2	4.2	0.6	2.0	5.3	2.6
Analytical groups								
By source of export earnings								
Fuel	0.5	0.8	0.5	0.3	0.2	0.2	0.2	0.1
Nonfuel	0.7	0.6	1.3	1.4	0.8	1.3	1.4	0.9
By external financing source								
Net debtor countries	0.8	0.6	1.3	1.6	0.8	1.8	2.0	1.3
of which, official financing	0.6	0.8	0.9	1.1	1.9	2.2	3.7	3.0
Net debtor countries by debt-servicing experience								
Countries with arrears and/or rescheduling during 1999–2003	0.7	0.9	1.0	1.0	1.8	1.9	3.1	2.4
Other groups								
Heavily indebted poor countries	0.5	0.5	0.2	0.2	0.3	1.0	0.1	—
Middle East and north Africa	0.3	0.4	0.3	0.1	0.1	0.1	0.2	0.1
Memorandum								
Total, billions of U.S. dollars								
General Resources Account	9.986	8.809	18.531	22.863	13.849	22.352	29.425	23.578
Charges	2.200	2.510	2.829	2.846	2.638	2.806	3.020	3.384
Repurchases	7.786	6.300	15.702	20.017	11.211	19.546	26.405	20.193
PRGF[3]	0.866	0.881	0.855	0.835	1.042	1.214	1.225	1.427
Interest	0.039	0.040	0.042	0.038	0.038	0.040	0.046	0.050
Repayments	0.827	0.842	0.813	0.798	1.005	1.174	1.179	1.377

[1]Excludes advanced economies. Charges on, and repurchases (or repayments of principal) for, use of International Monetary Fund credit.
[2]Mongolia, which is not a member of the Commonwealth of Independent States, is included in this group for reasons of geography and similarities in economic structure.
[3]Poverty Reduction and Growth Facility (formerly ESAF—Enhanced Structural Adjustment Facility).

Table 43. Summary of Sources and Uses of World Saving
(Percent of GDP)

	Averages										Average
	1983–90	1991–98	1999	2000	2001	2002	2003	2004	2005	2006	2007–10
World											
Saving	22.9	22.9	23.2	23.9	23.2	23.1	23.9	24.9	25.4	25.5	26.0
Investment	24.2	24.0	23.2	23.6	23.2	22.9	23.5	24.6	25.2	25.6	26.0
Advanced economies											
Saving	22.1	21.1	21.5	21.7	20.6	19.4	19.1	19.4	19.2	19.4	20.3
Investment	22.7	21.6	21.9	22.2	20.9	20.0	20.0	20.7	21.0	21.2	21.5
Net lending	−0.6	−0.5	−0.4	−0.5	−0.3	−0.6	−0.9	−1.3	−1.8	−1.8	−1.3
Current transfers	−0.3	−0.4	−0.5	−0.5	−0.5	−0.5	−0.6	−0.6	−0.5	−0.5	−0.5
Factor income	−0.3	−0.5	0.1	0.6	0.5	0.1	0.1	—	−0.4	−0.5	−0.1
Resource balance	—	0.4	—	−0.6	−0.3	−0.2	−0.4	−0.7	−0.8	−0.8	−0.6
United States											
Saving	17.5	16.1	18.1	18.0	16.4	14.2	13.5	13.6	12.6	13.0	15.1
Investment	20.2	18.5	20.6	20.8	19.1	18.4	18.4	19.6	19.8	20.2	20.8
Net lending	−2.8	−2.4	−2.6	−2.7	−2.8	−4.2	−4.9	−6.0	−7.2	−7.2	−5.6
Current transfers	−0.5	−0.4	−0.5	−0.6	−0.5	−0.6	−0.6	−0.6	−0.5	−0.5	−0.5
Factor income	0.1	−0.8	0.8	1.7	1.3	0.4	0.2	−0.1	−1.4	−1.8	−0.8
Resource balance	−2.4	−1.2	−2.8	−3.9	−3.6	−4.0	−4.5	−5.3	−5.3	−4.9	−4.3
Euro area											
Saving	...	21.4	21.8	21.8	21.3	20.9	20.3	20.9	20.9	21.0	21.3
Investment	...	21.1	21.4	21.9	20.9	19.9	19.5	20.2	20.2	20.3	20.5
Net lending	...	0.3	0.4	−0.1	0.5	0.9	0.7	0.7	0.8	0.8	0.8
Current transfers[1]	−0.4	−0.6	−0.6	−0.7	−0.7	−0.7	−0.8	−0.8	−0.7	−0.8	−0.8
Factor income[1]	−0.5	−0.5	−0.5	−0.3	−0.4	−0.8	−0.9	−0.9	−0.7	−0.7	−0.6
Resource balance[1]	1.2	1.3	1.4	0.6	1.4	2.3	2.0	1.9	1.7	1.7	1.8
Germany											
Saving	23.9	21.8	20.5	20.3	19.4	19.5	19.6	21.3	21.1	20.9	19.5
Investment	20.9	22.7	21.7	21.6	19.4	17.3	17.5	17.7	17.3	17.4	17.1
Net lending	3.1	−0.9	−1.1	−1.4	0.1	2.2	2.2	3.6	3.8	3.4	2.4
Current transfers	−1.5	−1.6	−1.3	−1.4	−1.3	−1.3	−1.4	−1.2	−1.5	−1.5	−1.5
Factor income	0.6	0.2	−0.8	−0.5	−0.8	−1.1	−0.9	−0.6	0.1	0.1	0.2
Resource balance	3.9	0.5	1.0	0.5	2.2	4.6	4.4	5.4	5.2	4.8	3.7
France											
Saving	21.3	20.4	22.5	22.4	22.1	20.6	19.3	19.8	19.7	19.7	20.1
Investment	21.6	19.4	19.6	21.0	20.4	19.6	19.0	20.0	20.1	19.8	19.6
Net lending	−0.4	1.1	2.9	1.4	1.6	1.0	0.3	−0.3	−0.4	−0.1	0.4
Current transfers	−0.6	−0.7	−0.9	−1.1	−1.1	−1.0	−1.1	−1.0	−1.0	−1.0	−1.0
Factor income	−0.3	−0.2	1.3	1.2	1.1	0.3	0.4	0.5	0.5	0.5	0.5
Resource balance	0.5	2.0	2.5	1.3	1.6	1.7	0.9	0.3	—	0.4	0.9
Italy											
Saving	21.2	20.1	20.3	19.7	19.6	19.4	18.1	18.1	18.3	18.9	20.4
Investment	22.7	19.4	19.7	20.2	19.7	20.0	19.6	19.6	19.6	19.8	20.3
Net lending	−1.5	0.7	0.7	−0.5	−0.1	−0.6	−1.5	−1.5	−1.3	−0.9	0.1
Current transfers	−0.1	−0.6	−0.5	−0.4	−0.5	−0.5	−0.6	−0.6	−0.6	−0.6	−0.6
Factor income	−1.6	−1.7	−0.9	−1.1	−0.9	−1.2	−1.5	−1.3	−1.2	−1.0	−0.7
Resource balance	0.2	2.9	2.1	1.0	1.4	1.1	0.6	0.4	0.5	0.7	1.3
Japan											
Saving	32.5	31.6	28.6	28.8	27.8	26.8	27.1	27.6	27.5	28.0	28.5
Investment	29.7	29.2	26.0	26.3	25.7	24.0	23.9	23.9	24.2	24.4	24.4
Net lending	2.8	2.4	2.5	2.5	2.1	2.8	3.1	3.7	3.4	3.6	4.1
Current transfers	−0.1	−0.2	−0.3	−0.2	−0.2	−0.1	−0.2	−0.2	−0.2	−0.2	−0.2
Factor income	0.5	1.0	1.3	1.3	1.7	1.6	1.6	1.8	1.9	2.2	2.5
Resource balance	2.3	1.6	1.5	1.5	0.6	1.3	1.7	2.0	1.7	1.7	1.9
United Kingdom											
Saving	17.4	15.6	15.1	15.0	15.0	15.0	14.8	14.8	14.9	15.1	15.8
Investment	19.4	16.8	17.8	17.5	17.3	16.7	16.5	17.0	17.3	17.5	18.3
Net lending	−2.0	−1.2	−2.7	−2.5	−2.3	−1.7	−1.7	−2.2	−2.3	−2.4	−2.5
Current transfers	−0.7	−0.8	−0.8	−1.0	−0.7	−0.8	−0.9	−0.9	−0.9	−0.9	−0.9
Factor income	—	0.3	−0.1	0.5	1.2	2.1	2.1	2.1	2.1	2.1	2.1
Resource balance	−1.4	−0.7	−1.8	−2.1	−2.8	−3.0	−2.9	−3.3	−3.5	−3.6	−3.6
Canada											
Saving	19.5	16.7	20.7	23.6	22.0	21.5	22.1	23.0	23.7	23.6	23.7
Investment	21.4	18.9	20.3	20.2	19.1	19.6	20.1	20.4	21.1	21.1	21.4
Net lending	−2.0	−2.3	0.4	3.4	2.9	2.0	2.0	2.6	2.6	2.5	2.4
Current transfers	−0.2	—	0.1	0.1	0.1	0.1	—	—	—	—	—
Factor income	−3.2	−3.6	−3.3	−2.4	−2.9	−2.5	−1.9	−1.7	−1.5	−1.4	−1.1
Resource balance	1.4	1.4	3.6	5.7	5.7	4.3	3.9	4.3	4.2	4.0	3.5

Table 43 *(continued)*

	Averages										Average
	1983–90	1991–98	1999	2000	2001	2002	2003	2004	2005	2006	2007–10
Newly industrialized Asian economies											
Saving	34.3	33.8	32.3	31.5	29.5	29.5	30.8	31.3	32.0	31.6	30.4
Investment	28.0	31.8	27.0	28.2	25.2	24.4	24.0	24.9	25.9	26.1	26.1
Net lending	6.2	2.0	5.3	3.3	4.3	5.1	6.8	6.4	6.1	5.5	4.3
Current transfers	0.2	−0.1	−0.2	−0.4	−0.5	−0.6	−0.7	−0.8	−0.8	−0.8	−0.7
Factor income	0.6	0.7	−0.1	0.3	0.6	0.8	1.1	1.2	1.0	1.0	0.9
Resource balance	5.5	1.4	5.6	3.5	4.2	5.0	6.4	6.0	5.9	5.3	4.1
Other emerging market and developing countries											
Saving	24.2	25.4	25.6	26.9	26.7	27.9	29.8	31.5	32.6	32.6	32.2
Investment	26.2	27.5	25.1	25.5	26.1	26.6	27.9	29.2	30.2	30.7	30.9
Net lending	−1.9	−2.2	0.4	1.3	0.6	1.3	1.9	2.3	2.4	1.9	1.3
Current transfers	0.7	1.2	1.2	1.3	1.5	1.8	2.0	2.1	1.9	1.6	1.4
Factor income	−2.3	−2.2	−2.1	−2.3	−2.2	−2.3	−2.0	−1.9	−1.4	−1.3	−1.0
Resource balance	−0.4	−1.1	1.4	2.3	1.3	1.9	1.9	2.2	2.0	1.6	0.9
Memorandum											
Acquisition of foreign assets	0.6	2.6	4.1	5.0	3.3	4.5	5.6	7.1	6.9	6.0	4.9
Change in reserves	—	1.3	0.8	1.4	1.9	3.0	4.7	6.0	5.4	4.9	3.8
Regional groups											
Africa											
Saving	18.5	16.6	16.5	19.3	18.5	18.4	20.0	20.6	21.3	21.6	21.5
Investment	21.6	20.1	20.7	19.0	19.6	20.2	20.4	21.0	21.6	22.1	22.0
Net lending	−3.1	−3.5	−4.2	0.3	−1.1	−1.8	−0.4	−0.4	−0.3	−0.5	−0.5
Current transfers	1.9	3.1	2.6	3.1	3.4	4.2	4.6	4.4	3.9	3.6	3.4
Factor income	−5.3	−4.5	−4.3	−5.1	−4.5	−4.9	−4.8	−4.6	−4.8	−4.5	−3.8
Resource balance	0.3	−2.0	−2.5	2.3	—	−1.1	−0.3	−0.2	0.6	0.3	−0.1
Memorandum											
Acquisition of foreign assets	0.6	0.7	3.2	4.2	4.6	3.7	3.8	3.8	4.2	3.8	2.9
Change in reserves	0.3	0.7	0.6	2.6	2.6	2.3	3.6	4.7	4.0	3.6	2.6
Central and eastern Europe											
Saving	26.3	20.2	18.6	18.9	18.7	18.8	18.6	19.1	19.7	20.6	22.3
Investment	27.4	22.9	23.6	24.7	21.8	22.8	23.2	23.8	24.1	24.8	26.2
Net lending	−1.1	−2.7	−4.9	−5.8	−3.2	−4.1	−4.6	−4.7	−4.3	−4.1	−3.8
Current transfers	1.7	1.8	1.9	2.0	2.0	1.9	1.7	1.7	1.8	2.0	1.9
Factor income	−2.7	−1.9	−1.6	−1.5	−1.7	−2.1	−1.9	−1.5	−0.9	−1.1	−1.2
Resource balance	−0.1	−2.6	−5.2	−6.3	−3.5	−3.9	−4.4	−4.9	−5.3	−5.0	−4.5
Memorandum											
Acquisition of foreign assets	1.8	2.5	3.0	2.9	1.6	3.1	1.8	2.1	1.6	1.2	1.1
Change in reserves	−0.2	1.7	1.8	0.7	−1.3	1.7	1.4	1.3	0.5	0.4	0.2
Commonwealth of Independent States[2]											
Saving	...	...	24.2	31.8	29.7	27.4	27.2	29.4	29.9	28.6	26.4
Investment	...	...	16.2	19.1	22.2	20.8	21.7	21.4	21.4	22.5	23.6
Net lending	...	...	8.0	12.8	7.5	6.6	5.6	8.0	8.5	6.0	2.7
Current transfers	...	...	0.8	0.8	0.7	0.9	0.9	0.8	0.6	0.5	0.4
Factor income	...	...	−3.7	−3.4	−2.1	−2.1	−3.3	−2.4	−2.0	−1.7	−1.3
Resource balance	...	...	11.0	15.4	8.9	7.7	7.9	9.7	9.9	7.2	3.6
Memorandum											
Acquisition of foreign assets	...	...	10.2	12.6	6.0	8.3	10.4	12.5	11.0	9.1	6.1
Change in reserves	...	...	0.9	4.7	2.8	2.5	5.8	6.9	6.9	5.9	2.9

Table 43 *(continued)*

	Averages		1999	2000	2001	2002	2003	2004	2005	2006	Average 2007–10
	1983–90	1991–98									
Developing Asia											
Saving	25.7	31.3	31.5	31.5	32.3	34.1	36.5	38.2	39.4	39.6	38.9
Investment	28.6	32.8	29.5	29.8	30.8	31.7	33.6	35.5	36.9	37.2	36.9
Net lending	−2.9	−1.6	2.1	1.7	1.4	2.5	2.9	2.7	2.5	2.3	2.1
Current transfers	0.9	1.3	1.4	1.5	1.6	1.9	2.2	2.4	2.0	1.6	1.4
Factor income	−1.4	−2.0	−1.6	−1.5	−1.7	−1.5	−0.6	−0.9	−0.4	−0.3	−0.4
Resource balance	−2.3	−0.8	2.2	1.7	1.5	2.0	1.4	1.3	0.9	1.0	1.0
Memorandum											
Acquisition of foreign assets	0.7	3.6	4.7	5.0	3.3	5.3	6.3	8.3	8.1	7.2	6.1
Change in reserves	0.2	1.8	1.4	0.9	2.7	4.7	6.0	8.2	7.1	6.5	5.4
Middle East											
Saving	17.5	22.9	25.2	29.4	26.4	25.0	27.3	32.0	34.9	33.8	31.9
Investment	23.0	25.6	23.0	22.6	23.6	25.5	25.4	25.4	24.7	25.1	24.9
Net lending	−5.4	−2.6	2.2	6.8	2.8	−0.5	1.9	6.7	10.1	8.7	7.0
Current transfers	−1.9	−2.3	−3.2	−2.2	−1.7	−1.3	−0.9	−0.7	−0.4	−0.6	−0.7
Factor income	−0.3	1.1	0.1	−2.9	−1.8	−4.5	−4.5	−3.5	−2.3	−1.4	0.2
Resource balance	−3.2	−1.5	5.3	12.0	6.3	5.3	7.4	10.9	12.8	10.7	7.4
Memorandum											
Acquisition of foreign assets	−1.8	−1.0	2.8	12.4	5.3	5.6	7.5	10.8	12.7	11.2	8.6
Change in reserves	−1.6	0.8	0.3	4.6	2.3	1.5	3.8	5.7	7.8	7.0	4.8
Western Hemisphere											
Saving	19.5	18.3	17.1	18.0	16.7	18.6	20.0	21.0	20.8	20.3	19.6
Investment	20.4	21.2	20.4	20.7	19.9	18.8	19.0	19.8	20.3	20.7	20.9
Net lending	−0.9	−2.8	−3.2	−2.7	−3.2	−0.2	0.9	1.2	0.5	−0.4	−1.2
Current transfers	0.9	1.1	1.3	1.3	1.5	1.7	2.1	2.0	1.9	1.8	1.8
Factor income	−4.5	−2.7	−2.9	−2.8	−3.1	−3.2	−3.4	−3.3	−2.7	−2.6	−2.4
Resource balance	2.7	−1.2	−1.6	−1.2	−1.6	1.2	2.2	2.4	1.3	0.4	−0.7
Memorandum											
Acquisition of foreign assets	0.7	1.8	1.3	0.6	1.8	1.2	3.1	2.7	2.1	1.5	1.3
Change in reserves	0.2	1.1	−0.7	−0.1	0.1	−0.2	2.0	1.3	0.9	0.5	0.4
Analytical groups											
By source of export earnings											
Fuel											
Saving	18.6	22.9	25.7	32.8	28.7	26.5	29.8	34.2	37.0	36.0	34.0
Investment	22.8	25.5	24.8	23.3	25.2	27.2	27.2	26.9	26.1	26.4	25.6
Net lending	−4.2	−2.7	0.9	9.5	3.6	−0.7	2.5	7.2	10.8	9.6	8.5
Current transfers	−2.1	−2.6	−3.0	−2.2	−1.7	−1.4	−1.0	−0.8	−0.5	−0.6	−0.5
Factor income	−1.3	−2.0	−2.3	−5.9	−4.3	−7.2	−6.8	−5.9	−5.0	−4.0	−2.3
Resource balance	−0.8	2.0	6.2	17.6	9.5	7.9	10.4	13.9	16.3	14.1	11.4
Memorandum											
Acquisition of foreign assets	−1.9	−0.8	2.6	12.9	7.4	6.2	8.8	11.0	13.6	11.6	9.3
Change in reserves	−1.0	0.1	−0.6	7.1	3.5	1.6	5.1	8.0	9.8	8.5	5.8
Nonfuel											
Saving	24.7	25.6	25.5	26.4	26.6	28.0	29.8	31.3	32.3	32.3	32.0
Investment	26.5	27.7	25.2	25.7	26.2	26.6	28.0	29.4	30.5	31.0	31.3
Net lending	−1.7	−2.1	0.4	0.7	0.4	1.4	1.9	2.0	1.8	1.4	0.8
Current transfers	1.0	1.5	1.5	1.6	1.7	2.0	2.2	2.3	2.0	1.8	1.6
Factor income	−2.4	−2.2	−2.1	−2.0	−2.0	−2.0	−1.6	−1.6	−1.1	−1.0	−0.9
Resource balance	−0.3	−1.3	1.0	1.1	0.7	1.4	1.2	1.3	0.9	0.6	0.1
Memorandum											
Acquisition of foreign assets	0.8	2.9	4.2	4.4	3.0	4.4	5.4	6.8	6.4	5.6	4.6
Change in reserves	0.1	1.4	1.0	0.9	1.8	3.2	4.6	5.9	5.1	4.6	3.7

Table 43 *(concluded)*

	Averages		1999	2000	2001	2002	2003	2004	2005	2006	Average 2007–10
	1983–90	1991–98									
By external financing source											
Net debtor countries											
Saving	20.0	20.0	19.5	20.2	19.7	20.5	21.1	21.5	21.7	21.9	22.2
Investment	23.3	23.6	21.1	21.8	21.1	20.9	21.0	22.1	22.5	23.0	23.4
Net lending	−3.1	−3.6	−1.6	−1.6	−1.5	−0.4	0.1	−0.5	−0.8	−1.1	−1.2
Current transfers	1.4	2.1	1.9	2.1	2.4	2.7	3.0	2.9	2.7	2.7	2.6
Factor income	−3.7	−3.7	−2.1	−2.4	−2.5	−2.6	−2.2	−2.4	−1.8	−1.8	−1.6
Resource balance	−0.9	−2.9	−1.5	−1.3	−1.4	−0.5	−0.7	−1.1	−1.7	−2.0	−2.2
Memorandum											
Acquisition of foreign assets	0.4	1.6	2.6	2.0	2.0	2.8	3.4	2.9	2.5	2.0	1.8
Change in reserves	—	1.1	0.9	0.6	0.7	1.8	2.5	2.1	1.4	1.2	1.2
Official financing											
Saving	16.2	18.0	17.4	18.1	18.1	20.4	20.9	20.7	21.6	22.0	22.0
Investment	22.4	24.7	17.6	19.2	19.1	18.8	19.3	21.5	22.1	23.1	23.5
Net lending	−6.3	−6.7	−0.2	−1.2	−1.0	1.6	1.6	−0.9	−0.6	−1.1	−1.4
Current transfers	2.1	2.6	2.9	3.1	3.6	4.6	5.0	4.5	4.3	4.2	3.9
Factor income	−5.4	−5.4	−2.0	−3.4	−3.6	−3.9	−3.2	−3.8	−2.0	−1.8	−1.7
Resource balance	−3.0	−4.1	−1.0	−0.9	−1.0	0.9	−0.2	−1.6	−2.9	−3.4	−3.7
Memorandum											
Acquisition of foreign assets	0.3	1.6	2.1	2.4	1.1	3.0	4.3	2.2	2.5	1.8	1.3
Change in reserves	−0.1	1.0	0.7	0.5	—	1.2	2.5	1.6	0.4	0.7	1.0
Net debtor countries by debt-servicing experience											
Countries with arrears and/or rescheduling during 1999–2003											
Saving	15.7	17.0	16.8	18.4	17.5	19.6	20.2	20.5	21.9	22.2	22.0
Investment	22.8	24.8	18.2	19.4	19.2	19.2	19.1	21.4	22.0	23.0	23.1
Net lending	−7.1	−7.8	−1.4	−1.0	−1.8	0.4	1.1	−0.9	−0.1	−0.7	−1.1
Current transfers	1.4	2.4	1.8	2.4	3.0	4.0	4.5	4.0	3.7	3.5	3.3
Factor income	−6.3	−6.3	−3.4	−5.7	−4.9	−5.0	−4.0	−4.7	−3.0	−2.9	−2.4
Resource balance	−2.2	−3.2	0.2	2.2	0.2	1.3	0.6	−0.2	−0.8	−1.4	−2.0
Memorandum											
Acquisition of foreign assets	−0.6	1.0	2.8	4.2	1.0	4.5	4.8	2.9	4.2	3.3	2.0
Change in reserves	0.1	0.8	0.8	1.5	0.2	1.2	2.3	2.2	1.4	1.5	1.5

Note: The estimates in this table are based on individual countries' national accounts and balance of payments statistics. For many countries, the estimates of national saving are built up from national accounts data on gross domestic investment and from balance-of-payments-based data on net foreign investment. The latter, which is equivalent to the current account balance, comprises three components: current transfers, net factor income, and the resource balance. The mixing of data sources, which is dictated by availability, implies that the estimates for national saving that are derived incorporate the statistical discrepancies. Furthermore, errors, omissions, and asymmetries in balance of payments statistics affect the estimates for net lending; at the global level, net lending, which in theory would be zero, equals the world current account discrepancy. Notwithstanding these statistical shortcomings, flow of funds estimates, such as those presented in this table, provide a useful framework for analyzing development in saving and investment, both over time and across regions and countries. Country group composites are weighted by GDP valued at purchasing power parities (PPPs) as a share of total world GDP.

[1]Calculated from the data of individual euro area countries.

[2]Mongolia, which is not a member of the Commonwealth of Independent States, is included in this group for reasons of geography and similarities in economic structure.

Table 44. Summary of World Medium-Term Baseline Scenario

	Eight-Year Averages		Four-Year Average					Four-Year Average
	1987–94	1995–2002	2003–06	2003	2004	2005	2006	2007–10
	Annual percent change unless otherwise noted							
World real GDP	**3.2**	**3.6**	**4.5**	**4.0**	**5.1**	**4.3**	**4.4**	**4.3**
Advanced economies	3.0	2.7	2.7	2.0	3.4	2.6	3.0	2.9
Other emerging market and developing countries	3.5	4.7	6.5	6.4	7.2	6.3	6.0	5.8
Memorandum								
Potential output								
Major advanced economies	2.7	2.6	2.5	2.6	2.6	2.5	2.5	2.5
World trade, volume[1]	**6.2**	**6.6**	**7.4**	**4.9**	**9.9**	**7.4**	**7.6**	**6.9**
Imports								
Advanced economies	6.2	6.5	6.2	3.6	8.5	6.5	6.3	5.9
Other emerging market and developing countries	5.3	7.2	11.8	8.9	15.5	12.0	11.0	9.6
Exports								
Advanced economies	6.3	6.0	5.9	2.8	8.1	5.9	6.8	6.2
Other emerging market and developing countries	6.2	8.2	11.0	10.7	13.8	9.9	9.7	8.8
Terms of trade								
Advanced economies	0.2	−0.1	0.1	0.8	−0.4	0.3	−0.1	0.0
Other emerging market and developing countries	−1.0	0.6	1.0	−0.5	3.3	2.2	−0.9	−0.5
World prices in U.S. dollars								
Manufactures	4.2	−1.8	7.3	13.4	8.8	6.2	1.3	1.4
Oil	1.5	5.8	15.1	15.8	30.7	23.2	−5.9	−3.0
Nonfuel primary commodities	2.5	−2.2	5.8	7.1	18.8	3.8	−5.1	−1.4
Consumer prices								
Advanced economies	3.8	1.9	1.9	1.8	2.0	2.0	1.9	2.1
Other emerging market and developing countries	65.4	12.8	5.5	6.0	5.7	5.5	4.6	3.9
Interest rates (in percent)								
Real six-month LIBOR[2]	3.4	3.3	0.5	−0.6	−0.3	1.0	2.1	2.4
World real long-term interest rate[3]	4.3	3.3	2.3	1.9	1.9	2.4	3.1	3.2
	Percent of GDP							
Balances on current account								
Advanced economies	−0.2	−0.3	−1.0	−0.8	−1.0	−1.1	−1.1	−1.1
Other emerging market and developing countries	−1.5	−0.5	2.6	2.1	2.9	3.2	2.4	1.4
Total external debt								
Other emerging market and developing countries	33.1	40.4	33.7	38.3	34.3	31.6	30.7	28.7
Debt service								
Other emerging market and developing countries	4.4	6.3	5.2	6.1	5.2	4.9	4.7	4.4

[1]Data refer to trade in goods and services.
[2]London interbank offered rate on U.S. dollar deposits less percent change in U.S. GDP deflator.
[3]GDP-weighted average of 10-year (or nearest maturity) government bond rates for the United States, Japan, Germany, France, Italy, the United Kingdom, and Canada.

Table 45. Other Emerging Market and Developing Countries—Medium-Term Baseline Scenario: Selected Economic Indicators

	Eight-Year Averages		Four-Year Average					Four-Year Average
	1987–94	1995–2002	2003–06	2003	2004	2005	2006	2007–10
	Annual percent change							
Other emerging market and developing countries								
Real GDP	3.5	4.7	6.5	6.4	7.2	6.3	6.0	5.8
Export volume[1]	6.2	8.2	11.0	10.7	13.8	9.9	9.7	8.8
Terms of trade[1]	−1.0	0.6	1.0	−0.5	3.3	2.2	−0.9	−0.5
Import volume[1]	5.3	7.2	11.8	8.9	15.5	12.0	11.0	9.6
Regional groups								
Africa								
Real GDP	1.7	3.6	5.0	4.6	5.1	5.0	5.4	4.9
Export volume[1]	4.9	5.4	6.8	5.6	6.3	7.2	8.1	5.5
Terms of trade[1]	−2.5	1.3	2.8	3.9	4.5	5.1	−2.2	−0.9
Import volume[1]	2.6	5.8	7.6	5.9	8.8	8.7	6.9	6.0
Central and eastern Europe								
Real GDP	−0.2	3.4	4.9	4.6	6.1	4.5	4.5	4.5
Export volume[1]	4.0	9.7	11.4	11.8	13.5	10.5	9.9	8.6
Terms of trade[1]	0.6	0.4	−0.7	−1.2	−0.7	−1.2	0.4	0.2
Import volume[1]	5.3	11.0	10.9	12.0	13.0	9.2	9.5	8.3
Commonwealth of Independent States[2]								
Real GDP	...	1.6	7.1	7.9	8.2	6.5	6.0	5.3
Export volume[1]	...	4.7	9.3	11.3	10.5	7.4	7.9	6.9
Terms of trade[1]	...	1.7	6.0	3.2	14.4	10.5	−3.4	−2.9
Import volume[1]	...	4.0	15.1	14.2	19.6	15.2	11.6	8.3
Developing Asia								
Real GDP	7.7	6.6	7.7	8.1	8.2	7.4	7.1	6.9
Export volume[1]	12.9	11.3	15.9	15.5	19.8	14.9	13.6	11.6
Terms of trade[1]	−0.1	−0.9	−1.1	−4.2	−0.2	−0.8	1.0	0.4
Import volume[1]	11.5	8.2	16.0	13.2	20.7	15.5	14.8	12.5
Middle East								
Real GDP	3.3	3.9	5.3	5.8	5.5	5.0	4.9	4.8
Export volume[1]	8.0	3.8	6.4	7.9	8.2	5.0	4.4	5.6
Terms of trade[1]	−3.2	5.9	4.5	1.6	11.5	9.9	−4.3	−2.3
Import volume[1]	0.7	7.6	6.0	1.7	8.1	8.0	6.2	6.5
Western Hemisphere								
Real GDP	2.8	2.2	3.9	2.2	5.7	4.1	3.7	3.4
Export volume[1]	6.7	7.3	5.8	3.2	9.7	4.6	5.6	5.3
Terms of trade[1]	−0.2	−0.8	1.6	3.7	3.6	1.0	−2.1	−1.2
Import volume[1]	9.9	4.4	7.2	1.0	12.1	8.9	7.1	5.7
Analytical groups								
Net debtor countries by debt-servicing experience								
Countries with arrears and/or rescheduling during 1999–2003								
Real GDP	3.6	3.2	5.9	5.8	6.3	5.8	5.8	5.6
Export volume[1]	6.3	7.3	6.2	4.7	6.1	7.1	6.9	5.6
Terms of trade[1]	−0.3	−0.8	1.1	1.8	2.0	2.1	−1.4	−0.5
Import volume[1]	4.4	3.9	8.6	7.8	9.2	10.0	7.6	6.1

Table 45 *(concluded)*

	1994	1998	2002	2003	2004	2005	2006	2010

Percent of exports of goods and services

	1994	1998	2002	2003	2004	2005	2006	2010
Other emerging market and developing countries								
Current account balance	−7.6	−7.9	4.2	6.1	7.9	8.3	6.4	2.6
Total external debt	177.8	172.1	126.0	112.6	92.7	83.1	80.4	68.8
Debt-service payments[3]	24.0	26.5	20.0	17.9	14.0	13.0	12.4	10.2
Interest payments	8.2	9.6	5.7	4.9	4.3	4.1	4.1	3.6
Amortization	15.9	16.9	14.3	13.0	9.7	8.9	8.3	6.6
Regional groups								
Africa								
Current account balance	−11.3	−16.2	−5.2	−0.9	0.4	2.3	1.4	−1.7
Total external debt	276.9	236.7	171.5	147.7	116.2	99.6	94.7	85.6
Debt-service payments[3]	24.4	22.9	15.3	14.3	11.7	8.9	9.2	7.8
Interest payments	10.2	8.7	4.9	4.3	3.1	2.7	2.9	2.6
Amortization	14.1	14.2	10.4	10.0	8.6	6.2	6.3	5.1
Central and eastern Europe								
Current account balance	4.2	−8.5	−8.5	−10.1	−10.7	−9.9	−8.8	−6.9
Total external debt	135.2	118.3	129.1	125.4	106.0	94.1	88.6	70.1
Debt-service payments[3]	19.1	24.2	26.3	24.7	21.8	19.1	18.7	13.8
Interest payments	6.4	10.1	8.8	8.3	6.6	6.2	5.9	4.5
Amortization	12.7	14.0	17.5	16.4	15.2	12.9	12.8	9.3
Commonwealth of Independent States								
Current account balance	2.4	−7.6	18.1	16.1	21.6	24.7	19.9	6.0
Total external debt	132.8	175.2	110.7	99.2	81.0	69.4	73.5	90.7
Debt-service payments[3]	8.3	23.4	18.0	12.9	10.0	13.2	10.6	15.5
Interest payments	4.9	13.3	5.2	4.3	5.9	5.1	5.4	6.9
Amortization	3.4	10.0	12.8	8.6	4.1	8.0	5.2	8.6
Developing Asia								
Current account balance	−5.0	9.2	9.2	9.0	8.5	6.8	5.9	3.8
Total external debt	139.3	129.3	84.7	73.2	63.3	60.6	59.1	49.6
Debt-service payments[3]	17.4	18.4	14.0	11.5	8.4	8.0	7.7	6.2
Interest payments	6.5	6.2	3.3	2.6	2.6	2.4	2.7	2.5
Amortization	10.9	12.3	10.7	8.9	5.8	5.6	5.0	3.7
Middle East								
Current account balance	−4.8	−16.0	10.5	17.5	26.4	32.4	29.4	24.1
Total external debt	146.8	178.2	107.2	94.9	75.3	64.1	64.0	57.0
Debt-service payments[3]	10.2	15.1	7.0	7.7	6.4	6.2	6.4	6.3
Interest payments	3.0	3.9	1.9	1.7	1.1	1.2	1.2	1.1
Amortization	7.2	11.1	5.1	6.0	5.4	5.0	5.2	5.1
Western Hemisphere								
Current account balance	−25.0	−31.0	−4.7	1.7	3.4	0.7	−2.4	−6.9
Total external debt	272.2	261.7	219.8	204.1	166.9	151.9	148.5	132.8
Debt-service payments[3]	57.2	52.1	42.1	41.0	31.1	28.4	28.1	22.7
Interest payments	16.8	17.1	12.3	10.6	9.0	9.0	9.0	7.5
Amortization	40.4	34.9	29.8	30.4	22.1	19.4	19.2	15.2
Analytical groups								
Net debtor countries by debt-servicing experience								
Countries with arrears and/or rescheduling during 1999–2003								
Current account balance	−19.3	−17.8	0.8	1.5	0.4	−0.8	−3.0	−5.7
Total external debt	378.6	358.2	282.5	256.6	217.3	197.2	189.8	163.1
Debt-service payments[3]	31.5	41.9	27.8	26.1	20.0	16.0	15.8	11.4
Interest payments	12.8	14.0	6.1	5.2	4.4	3.8	4.7	4.1
Amortization	18.7	27.9	21.7	20.9	15.5	12.2	11.1	7.2

[1]Data refer to trade in goods and services.
[2]Mongolia, which is not a member of the Commonwealth of Independent States, is included in this group for reasons of geography and similarities in economic structure.
[3]Interest payments on total debt plus amortization payments on long-term debt only. Projections incorporate the impact of exceptional financing items. Excludes service payments to the International Monetary Fund.

WORLD ECONOMIC OUTLOOK AND STAFF STUDIES FOR THE WORLD ECONOMIC OUTLOOK, SELECTED TOPICS, 1995–2005

I. Methodology—Aggregation, Modeling, and Forecasting

II. Historical Surveys

III. Economic Growth—Sources and Patterns

IV. Inflation and Deflation; Commodity Markets

V. Fiscal Policy

VI. Monetary Policy; Financial Markets; Flow of Funds

***Staff Studies for the
World Economic Outlook***

IX. External Payments, Trade, Capital Movements, and Foreign Debt

X. Regional Issues

XI. Country-Specific Analyses